CONTEMPORARY ENVIRONMENTAL ACCOUNTING

ISSUES, CONCEPTS AND PRACTICE

Stefan Schaltegger and Roger Burritt

Dr **Stefan Schaltegger** was appointed a full Professor of Management and Business Economics at the University of Lüneburg, Germany, in 1999. Between 1996 and 1998 he was an Assistant Professor of Economics at the Center of Economics and Management (WWZ) at the University of Basel, Switzerland, where in 1998 he became an Associate Professor of Business Administration. His research areas include corporate environmental accounting and environmental information management, sustainable finance, sustainable entrepreneurship, stakeholder management, environmental and spatial economics and the integration of environmental management and economics. Stefan is a member of a number of international editorial boards and committees associated with business and environment interrelationships and has presented papers and lectured widely throughout Europe. He also spent one year as Visiting Research Fellow at the University of Washington, Seattle, USA. Stefan can be reached at schaltegger@uni-lueneburg.de.

Roger Burritt, BA (Jt Hons.) (Lancaster, UK), M. Phil. (Oxford, UK), FCPA (Australia), CA (Australia), ACIB (London, UK), is a Senior Lecturer in the Department of Commerce at The Australian National University (ANU) in Canberra, Australia, where environmental and management accounting are his main areas of research and teaching. He is also the International Co-ordinator of the ANU's Asia Pacific Centre for Environmental Accountability (APCEA)—a networking group for people with an interest in environmental accounting and accountability. APCEA has branches in Argentina, Australia, China, Japan and New Zealand. Roger can be contacted at roger.burritt@anu.edu.au.

Contemporary Environmental Accounting

Issues, Concepts and Practice

Stefan Schaltegger and Roger Burritt

Greenleaf
PUBLISHING
2 0 0 0

© 2000 Greenleaf Publishing Limited

Published by Greenleaf Publishing Limited
Aizlewood's Mill
Nursery Street
Sheffield S3 8GG
UK

Typeset by Greenleaf Publishing.
Printed and bound, using acid-free paper from managed forests, by
Creative Print & Design (Wales), Ebbw Vale.

British Library Cataloguing in Publication Data:
    A catalogue record for this book is available from the British Library.

ISBN 1874719349 (hbk)
ISBN 1874719357 (pbk)

CONTENTS

ACKNOWLEDGEMENTS

This book is partially based on an earlier book, *Corporate Environmental Accounting*, which has been received very well in business. The co-authors of that first version, Kaspar Müller and Henriette Hindrichsen, have decided to concentrate on consulting. *Contemporary Environmental Accounting* is substantially revised and updated and contains various new chapters dealing with emerging issues of environmental accounting. We would nevertheless like to thank Kaspar and Henriette for their contribution to the earlier text.

We offer special thanks to Matthias Blom, Thomas Braun, Eric Ohlund, Ruedi Kubat and two anonymous reviewers for their valuable comments which helped to improve earlier drafts of the first edition. The second edition has profited substantially from comments by Frank Figge, for whose contribution we are grateful. This book is dedicated to our patient families in Europe (Vivian, Oliver, Gregory and Carolyn) and Australia (Patricia and Christopher).

The manuscript of this book is literally global. It has been transferred numerous times between Europe (Stefan) and Australia (Roger) and back by e-mail. This has allowed us to enjoy various positive and negative effects of computer technology. In this respect we are thankful to the computer assistants who fought against electronic viruses and bugs, repaired files and helped us to concentrate on writing.

Stefan Schaltegger and Roger Burritt, May 2000

PREFACE

This book is written primarily for students, professional accountants, managers and all who are interested in how environmental issues influence accounting. No prior knowledge of environmental accounting is necessary to understand the important questions examined. Nevertheless, academic accountants will also find this book provides a useful introduction into the issues at stake.

The main goal of this book is to discuss and illustrate contemporary conceptual approaches to environmental accounting. In addition, readers will be made aware of major controversial topics.

Many of the concepts discussed have been applied in companies in various countries in Europe, in the USA, and Australia. However, this book does not present a simple collection of examples from progressive-minded companies. To increase the usefulness of this book for courses in environmental accounting, each chapter concludes with questions for review. Relevant accounting standards and examples given to enhance understanding are shown mainly in special boxes in order not to detract from the flow of the text.

FOREWORD

John Elkington

Chairman, SustainAbility Ltd;
Chairman, Environmental and Social Accounting Committee, UK Association of
Chartered Certified Accountants (ACCA);
Member, EU Consultative Forum on Sustainable Development

Accountants have always seemed the most unlikely of revolutionaries, but—whether they like it or not—many have become increasingly involved in the environmental and sustainability revolutions.

Sometimes they have been asked to put a financial value on the past and potential future environmental liabilities facing a company or industry. Some have been asked to assess the present and potential future value of emerging market opportunities for particular technologies, products or value chains. Others have been pulled in to consider the implications of the wave of environmental and financial disclosure that swept through the business world in the 1990s.

Almost always, however, accountants have found themselves seriously—and sometimes dangerously—out of their depth. A key reason has been that, like economists, they found that their professional tools too often failed to a get a proper grip on the new problems and opportunities.

At the same time, as the environmental and sustainable development movements have moved into the political and commercial mainstreams, campaigners, consultants and corporate managers have increasingly encountered—and often collided with—various varieties of financial professional.

As the stakes rose, so insurers, lenders, bankers and even financial analysts began to get involved. As a result, corporate accountants, investment relations specialists and chief financial officers (CFOs) have also found themselves having to get their brains around concepts such as eco-efficiency, ecological accounting, environmental shareholder value, life-cycle assessment and the triple bottom line.

Too often, environmental professionals find that they cannot speak to these financial people in terms that are either intelligible or effective. To start with, the confusion and misunderstandings that flowed from this lack of a common language were often funny. Increasingly, however, they are emerging as a major barrier to real-world progress both in business and in markets.

This is why I so enthusiastically welcome *Contemporary Environmental Accounting*. In this key resource, Stefan Schaltegger and Roger Burritt provide not only early elements of a lingua franca but also a clear, professional set of briefings on an extraordinary range of issues, from contingent environmental liabilities and tradable emission allowances to eco-asset sheets and stakeholder involvement.

Many readers will probably be tempted to turn straight to the discussion of the extent to which corporate environmental management and performance affect shareholder value, in Chapter 8. But the book as a whole will handsomely repay study both by business people and by the growing range of individuals, organisations and institutions who companies are coming to consider as stakeholders. I suspect that this will soon be among the best-thumbed books in my own collection.

FOREWORD

Susan McLaughlin

US Environmental Protection Agency, Environmental Accounting Project

The economics principle 'the tragedy of the commons'—that individuals will overuse or abuse resources that belong to a group and for which they are not held responsible—is the basis for environmental regulation.

Regulations are intended to push responsibility for damage to the environment and to the public's wellbeing on to the polluting entities. Economic theory also assumes that individuals (and organisations) make rational decisions based on freely flowing information and thorough analyses of that information. If that were the case, regulated entities would translate promulgated regulations into incentives for organisational change, whether it be to reduce pollution and avoid the costs of regulatory fines, to achieve efficiencies, to maintain or grow market share or for other competitive reasons.

Unfortunately, in reality, economic theory rarely plays out so nicely. More typically, regulations are not optimally 'internalised' because within the regulated entities there is a disconnection between those who have the responsibility for complying with the regulations and those who are responsible for the production, design and delivery of the products. As discussed in this book, most organisations' information systems hide the costs of regulation, wasted materials and energy and of damage to the environment from those within the company who have the greatest ability to identify alternative ways of doing business.

This breakdown in information flows is the basis for the US Environmental Protection Agency's Environmental Accounting Project, a collaborative programme between industry, government and academia which is concerned with helping firms better track the costs and benefits associated with their environmental performance. Environmental accounting presents an opportunity for firms to address regulations in a cost-efficient fashion, to avoid exposure to future regulations and even to prove to the public that additional regulations are not always necessary. It is in the public's and firms' best interest that industry voluntarily seek opportunities for cleaner production and avoid the pressure for additional governmental controls.

Owing to the widespread perception of accounting as a historically-based, reactive discipline, it comes as a surprise to many that accounting can play such a key strategic role. Accounting is at the centre of how an organisation views, analyses and manages its finances and assets—including materials, energy and other natural resource assets. Although accounting for external reporting purposes may necessarily be historically focused, when environmental managerial accounting systems are appropriately adjusted they can play an important role in supporting forward-thinking decision-making. Accounting systems can provide up-to-the-moment operational data (in cost and physical units) that can help a firm reduce and avoid wasteful and environmentally damaging practices before they are transformed into significant major expenses in the form of purchases for pollution control devices, fines for exceeding regulatory limits, bad press for endangering the community and clean-up costs.

Better information flows are essential for supporting companies' total quality management, eco-efficiency, sustainable development and environmental reporting initiatives. This book contains extensive discussions of the possibilities for boosting such initiatives through environmental accounting. Readers will come away with a much better understanding of the myriad of issues and opportunities that lie in improving the flow of financial and ecological information in firms.

FOREWORD

Patrick Ponting

National President, CPA Australia

CPA Australia urges all companies to become accountable for environmental, social and economic costs and to factor these into their financial reports. This method of accounting, called triple-bottom-line reporting, links in with the objectives of sustainable development. Companies aiming for sustainability must perform not against a single, financial, bottom line but against the triple bottom line. Schaltegger and Burritt's book is an important and timely contribution to the ongoing quest for new forms of corporate disclosure which integrate financial, environmental and social reporting.

FOREWORD

Claude Martin

Director General, World Wide Fund for Nature

Sustainable society, sustainable economy, sustainable development. The term *sustainability* has filtered down, within the space of a decade, from a few think-tanks and government agencies to the municipal and corporate sectors of just about every country of the world. But what do we mean when we talk about sustainability? The World Wide Fund for Nature (WWF) defines sustainable development as 'improving the quality of human life while living within the carrying capacity of supporting ecosystems'.

Living within the capacity of supporting ecosystems is a vital concept which is sometimes forgotten in discussions about sustainability. All of humanity is utterly dependent on the Earth's ecosystems for the maintenance of basic life-support functions, such as the recycling of water, oxygen and carbon, the regulation of global temperature, rainfall and other climatic processes, forming soil, cycling elemental plant nutrients such as nitrogen and phosphorus, breaking down pollutants, controlling pests, pollinating crops and providing food, materials and fuel for much of the world's population.

A study by Robert Costanza and colleagues three years ago attempted to evaluate the Earth's ecological services to humanity in monetary terms, although, of course, we pay absolutely nothing for these services. One may choose to argue with the values they assigned to some of the ecosystems evaluated, but their findings were nonetheless staggering. The total value of the world's ecological services was estimated to be in the range of US\$16–54 trillion per year, with an average of US\$33 trillion per year. This figure is similar to global gross domestic product (GDP). In other words, the total productivity of nature is as valuable as the sum of all human economic activities.

The most important environmental issue that humans face today is how to live within the Earth's means: we are exceeding the carrying capacity of many life-supporting ecosystems. This does not mean the world is about to end, but it means the world is getting poorer. To use a financial metaphor, consider the Earth's ecosystems as natural capital, which produce an annual return or income. As long as our demands on the Earth's ecosystems for food, meat, wood, water and so forth do not exceed the annual ecological return, we can maintain the capital. That is another way of saying we are sustainable. But if we consume more than the Earth can produce, we deplete the Earth's natural capital. Each year humanity will become poorer, although this will not show up in conventional economic accounts.

Hence we need to revise our economic accounting systems to incorporate these vital ecological functions. But how can we continue to improve the quality of life and find gainful employment for the world's growing population without exceeding the Earth's ecological limits? The answer is that we must dematerialise economic activities and de-couple economic growth and resource consumption. Consider Paul and Anne Ehrlich's IPAT (impact–population–affluence–technology) equation:

$$impact = population \times affluence \times technology$$

For example, for carbon dioxide (CO_2) emissions:

$$CO_2 \text{ emissions} = population \times GDP \text{ per capita} \times CO_2 \text{ emission per unit GDP}$$

How can we reduce our impact on the Earth? We cannot reduce the first factor, population, at least not in the short term, and we need to increase the second, economic activity, in many parts of the world. So our best option is to reduce the last factor of the IPAT equation, the technological impact and resource intensity. This means increasing our eco-efficiency. The World Business Council for Sustainable Development defines eco-efficiency as:

> the delivery of competitively priced goods and services that satisfy human needs and bring quality of life, while progressively reducing ecological impacts and resource intensity throughout the life-cycle, to a level at least in line with the Earth's estimated carrying capacity.

There's that crucial phrase again: we must live within the Earth's capacity. Schaltegger and Burritt can be credited with highlighting in their text the importance for management of the link between value added and environmental impact added as a general definition of eco-efficiency.

This book makes a valuable contribution to the corporate sector's gradual adoption of environmental accounting systems which will allow us to measure how heavily we tread on the planet and thus learn to live within the capacity of its ecosystems.

FOREWORD

Stig Enevoldsen

Chairman, International Accounting Standards Committee;
Partner, Deloitte & Touche, Copenhagen

Reporting from companies has traditionally focused on financial reporting: in other words, hard-core financial data appearing in financial statements with supplementary financial disclosures in notes, as is already well defined in accounting standards and supplementary requirements from regulators and others. Over the years there has been an increasing tendency for financial statements to converge towards a more universal accounting language, something that has partly been achieved with IOSCO's recent recommendation that IASC's core standards be used to help companies list their shares in several countries. Company reporting is used to predict future performance, and, as enterprises are becoming increasingly large and exert greater influence on all aspects of life around the globe, future reporting will need to include other issues, such as environmental information. Accounting for environmental issues and environmental information is important in furthering sustainable development and improving eco-efficiency.

It is therefore important that environmental accounting and environmental reporting are researched and developed to improve the usefulness of the information supplied to investors. And it is important that guidelines of a global nature are developed and included in future financial reporting. This book addresses how to develop accounting systems and an accounting model with such aims in mind. It is important to deal with these issues in order to provide input for better accounting for the many types of intangible asset and liability we are facing in this stage of our society's development.

The annual report, or equivalent information provided on a real-time basis via the Internet, should be the vehicle for providing total company reporting covering all aspects of an enterprise's activities.

FOREWORD

Andy Oliver

Vice-President, Health, Safety and Environment, Shell International

Companies are economic entities with a responsibility to provide a return on shareholders' investment. Increasingly, companies are being asked not just 'How much money have you made?' but 'How did you make it?' There is a growing call for companies to move from the confines of financial responsibility to shareholders to accepting a broader accountability to stakeholders for environmental and social performance. This call is not coming just from pressure groups and company law reviews; it is also coming from within as an increasing number of companies seek to respond to society's heightened expectations of corporate behaviour. In many cases this is being driven by the desire of managers and staff for the company they work for to reflect their personal values.

Such developments are not in conflict. Improving corporate performance on this broad front is smart business and symptomatic of a well-run company most likely to deliver sustainable shareholder value. The business case is robust with benefits being achieved by:

☐ Reducing costs: in the short term by becoming more eco-efficient (doing more with less) and in the long term working to ensure nothing is wasted

☐ Creating options: anticipating new markets, driven by customers who are more environmentally and socially conscious, and evolving business portfolios and supply chains to match

☐ Reducing risk: managing the wider risks through a better understanding of what represents responsible behaviour

☐ Gaining customers: enhancing the brand by providing services and products built on sustainability thinking that is in tune with customer expectations—and we believe this leads to loyalty and market share

How to account for these actions and benefits is a matter of growing importance as an aid for informed decision-making. Companies are increasingly trying to put a value on environmental impacts. For example, we have started to include the value of carbon in our investment decisions for new projects that will produce emissions over 100,000 tonnes a year of carbon dioxide. An internal trading system is also being piloted, as well as developing some projects that may meet the Clean Development Mechanism requirements when these are agreed.

This is just one part of our intent to set all of our decision-making within the context of sustainable development by integrating economic, environmental and social considerations and balancing short-term priorities with long-term needs.

The development of key performance indicators for sustainable development will provide the logical framework for setting targets and driving continuous improvement across operations and for developing standards of reporting and verification.

Contemporary Environmental Reporting provides an important link between environmental and financial performance and paves the way for the more difficult task of accounting for social/ethical conduct.

Chapter 1
PURPOSE AND STRUCTURE

Corporate managers make decisions and act in the present, usually guided by their experience and the information available to them about the past. The aim of their present decisions and actions is to achieve objectives that are established for the future of their organisations. Such objectives are usually complex, but for commercial corporations the pursuit of financial gain for shareholders is a high priority. As the future is uncertain, managers need access to all the relevant information they can obtain about alternative courses of action available to them (Chambers 1957: 3). In this decision-making context, information provides purpose-oriented knowledge for users: that is, knowledge about how a desired future state might be achieved. Uninformed action is not considered to be a particularly successful way to make decisions in the long run. To generate information, managers have to measure and record data in the same terms as their specific goals. Therefore, the steps in managing information, after having determined a set of objectives and goals, are to collect, classify, analyse and communicate data that relate to the desired goals. Provision of such information in financial terms is traditionally the central topic of accounting. Conventional financial accounting provides the most important information management system for any company because it links all company activities with performance and expresses these in the form of a single unit of account—money—which can be used as a basis for comparing available alternatives. Accounting information to assist with decision-making is a fundamental idea behind contemporary corporate environmental accounting.

A second conceptual strand woven through this text relates to accountability. Accounting information not only assists decision-makers with the efficient allocation of scarce resources but also enables management and governing bodies to discharge their accountability to people with a right to know how organisations have used resources entrusted to them. This second strand is important because, as Ijiri (1983: 75) comments, an accountability-based framework considers relationships between the producer and user of information, not just the needs of a decision-maker. Organisations can be held accountable to external or internal parties. External parties include shareholders, the public, regulators, suppliers and consumers. Internal parties are predominantly represented by different levels of management and employees.

At the conceptual level, this book presents and discusses an integrated framework of environmental accounting. It examines the interrelationships between accounting, the environment and the management of information for decision-making and accountability purposes. In doing so, it proposes an extension of the scope of conventional accounting to include the practical environmental and economic implications of the concepts of corporate 'sustainability' and 'eco-efficiency'. During the past 25 years environmental issues have grown to become a major concern for company managers. Yet, although notions of 'eco-efficiency' and 'sustainable development' have entered discussions in boardrooms throughout the world, practical execution of these ideas still remains at an early stage of development.

Contemporary Environmental Accounting uses a micro-based approach to examine environmental accounting as it is, or could be, practised within companies. National environmental systems of accounting and reporting are not considered in detail, although some references to micro–macro links are made. The text does not explicitly deal with other related issues such as information technology (IT); the history and management of information systems (i.e. computer systems); data acquisition; database management; software issues (for a brief introduction, see Rikhardsson 1999a); the application of information management to specific industries; links between information management, leadership and corporate culture; management of information for media purposes; or market research.

The book is organised in four parts:

☐ Part 1: Introduction and framework

☐ Part 2: Environmental issues in conventional accounting

☐ Part 3: Ecological accounting

☐ Part 4: Integration

A number of discussion questions are provided for review at the end of each chapter. We will now discuss each part in greater detail.

Part 1 (Chapters 2–4) provides an introduction to environmental accounting and the management of relevant environmental information. It introduces the basic framework for contemporary corporate environmental accounting.

In Chapter 2 we explain the main drivers of recent growth in demand for new accounting systems that integrate environmental aspects of corporate activity.

In Chapter 3 we discuss the notions of environmental information as purpose-oriented knowledge and as a means of accountability. As the purposes of information management are to support decision-making to help managers achieve specific goals and to provide stakeholders with corporate environmental information that they have an ethical or legal right to know, concepts of sustainable development and eco-efficiency are introduced because they underlie decision-support and accountability relationships.

The overall framework of the book is then presented in Chapter 4. This chapter is the conceptual centrepiece of the book. Its ideas permeate the remainder of the text. Environmental accounting is concerned with effectiveness, efficiency and equity issues. Effectiveness can be considered in the context of policies designed to achieve sustainable development. Eco-efficiency ensures that ecological and economic matters are integrated

Part 1
INTRODUCTION AND FRAMEWORK
2   The emergence of environmental accounting management
3   The purpose of managing environmental information
4   The environmental accounting framework

Part 2
ENVIRONMENTAL ISSUES IN CONVENTIONAL ACCOUNTING
5   Overview, criticism and advantages of conventional accounting
6   Environmental management accounting
7   Environmental issues in financial accounting and reporting
8   Environmental shareholder value and environmental issues in other accounting systems

Part 3
ECOLOGICAL ACCOUNTING
9   Overview and emergence of life-cycle assessment and ecological accounting
10 The efficiency of approaches to environmental information management
11 Internal ecological accounting
12 External ecological accounting and reporting of environmental impacts

Part 4
INTEGRATION
13 Integration with eco-efficiency indicators
14 Integrating eco-efficiency-oriented information management into the corporate environmental management system
15 Summary

Figure 1.1 **Structure of the book**

in the environmental accounting framework. Finally, equity issues are brought to the fore through the concept of accountability.

☐ **Sustainable development** is development that meets the needs of the present without compromising the ability of future generations to meet their own needs (UNCED 1987: 87).

☐ **Eco-efficiency** expresses the efficiency with which ecological resources are used to meet established economic goals (Schaltegger and Sturm 1992a, 1992c; OECD 1998b: 7). Efficiency is the achievement of specific output goals with the minimum level of inputs.

☐ In an **accountability**-based framework, the objective of accounting is to provide a fair system of information flow between the accountor and the accountee (Ijiri 1983: 75).

The basic structure of environmental accounting, as explained in this book (see Fig. 1.1), reflects two aspects of measurement. The influence of environmental issues on an organisation's financial performance and the environmental impacts of corporate activities themselves have to be examined.

Measurement of the links between environmental and financial performance requires a discussion of environmental issues in both management accounting and financial accounting as these two systems provide the foundation for economic information about corporations. In addition, the influence of environmental management on corporate financial performance is assessed through the concept of shareholder value because this is an important measure of economic success. Both of these links provide measures of corporate eco-efficiency.

The main information management concepts related to the second aspect, the measurement of environmental impacts, are internal and external ecological accounting and life-cycle assessment. Ecological accounting, as developed in this book, is viewed as the application of the principles and methods of conventional accounting to the collection, classification, analysis and communication of environmental impacts measured in biophysical terms. Ecological accounting provides a major foundation for physical information systems relating to sustainable development. Life-cycle assessment is product-focused and measures environmental impacts in physical terms over the entire life of any given product.

Finally, a link is made between environmental management systems and environmental accounting. Accountability relationships between a corporation and its stakeholders form the focal point of this link. Central to accountability relationships is the development of communication media to make corporate environmental accounting transparent to outside parties. Environmental reporting and independent environmental assurance services hold the key to the development of successful accountability interrelationships.

Parts 2–4 of this book examine aspects of environmental accounting related to eco-efficiency, sustainable development and, finally, accountability.

In Part 2 (Chapters 5–8) we consider the implications of incorporating environmental issues in conventional accounting systems: that is, the implications for management, financial and other accounting systems. The term 'environmental accounting information' is used to refer to information about the environment expressed in financial terms.

In Chapter 5 we provide an overview of the benefits and costs of pursuing or neglecting corporate environmental protection and examine criticism and advantages of conventional accounting.

In Chapter 6 environmental issues in management accounting are discussed in considerable depth. Management accounting measures and reports financial and other types of information that assist managers in fulfilling the goals set for their organisation or organisational unit (Horngren *et al.* 2000: 2). Management accounting information systems are assumed to provide information about formulation of overall strategies and long-range plans; internal resource allocation; cost control of operations and activities; and performance measurement and evaluation of people. Consequently, this chapter examines the financial aspects of environmental impacts on management accounting information systems, including investment appraisal. After a review of the conventional management accounting approach to incorporating financial aspects of environmental impacts, a method of activity-based costing using material and energy flows is proposed.

The development of financial accounting standards related to environmental issues, including environmental assets and liabilities, is reviewed in Chapter 7 within the context of financial reporting.

In Chapter 8 we examine other environmental accounting systems and investigate links between environmental management and shareholder value. This analysis provides a systematic framework as well as indications about how corporate environmental protection should be characterised to enhance the value of a company.

Part 3 (Chapters 9–12) deals with ecological accounting systems, where the environmental impacts of the company on the natural environment are identified and measured, and where data are expressed in physical units (Chapter 9). The term 'ecological accounting systems' is used to refer to information about the environment expressed in biophysical terms. Part 3 explores the notion that goals need to be established about the ecological impacts of an organisation's activities and that accounting information is required in order to establish whether the set goals are achieved. The main emphasis is on provision of a set of accounting information that will allow measurement of the effectiveness of an organisation in achieving its goals for ecological impacts.

In addition, in Part 3, a measure of 'environmental impact added' (EIA) is introduced as an important component of the assessment of eco-efficiency. EIA is seen to be the denominator in an eco-efficiency ratio. Methods of environmental information management have to provide relevant and accurate information on environmental impacts for the least possible cost. Thus, corporate attempts to achieve sustainable development and eco-efficiency can be improved by increasing the relevance and reliability of environmental information provided and/or by reducing the costs of collecting, analysing and communicating this information.

Life-cycle assessment (LCA) was the first, and is still the most frequently used, approach to environmental information management. By using a graphical model, we analyse the efficacy and efficiency of LCA. Based on theoretical argument and supported by examples used within the context of LCAs, analysis shows that information created with the current approach to LCA is of poor quality and, in fact, of little value for decision-making and accountability purposes. The relevance of data quality and site-specific information for environmental management are seen to be important, even though managers are mostly unaware of these issues. The structure of ecological accounting corresponds to that of conventional accounting and a distinction is made between internal, external and other ecological accounting systems (Chapters 10–12). A set of core principles for ecological accounting is identified.

Given the relevance of site-specific information, internal ecological accounting is discussed in detail in Chapter 11. The main concerns of internal ecological accounting are related to the classification, recording, assessment and allocation of environmental impacts for a company and its various production sites (Sections 11.3–11.5). Investments in pollution prevention, designed to reduce environmental impacts, and the creation of environmental indicators are also addressed in this chapter (Sections 11.5 and 11.6), followed by a discussion of whether discounting projected environmental impacts might be a useful approach to measure the net present value of expected future environmental impact added (Section 11.7 and 11.8).

In Chapter 12 we examine external ecological accounting—the gathering of information and reporting to external stakeholders about environmental impacts as part of a company's accountability process. The main thrust of Chapter 12 is on environmental reporting to these stakeholders in a way that is equitable to the producers and users of information. Analysis of the current practice of reporting environmental impacts shows that much of the quantitative information in today's corporate environmental reports is quite meaningless. Hence some basic rules are introduced to help improve the information value in external ecological accounting and the reporting of corporate environmental impacts (Sections 12.3 and 12.4).

Part 4 (Chapters 13–15) begins with a discussion of how economic and environmental information can be integrated to help organisations effectively achieve their ecological and economic goals, while operating in an eco-efficient manner as shown by eco-efficiency indicators (Chapter 13). The purpose of eco-efficiency indicators is to operationalise eco-efficiency at the corporate level. Chapter 13 concludes with a section on benchmarking (Section 13.4).

In Chapter 14 the link between environmental accounting and environmental management systems is established. This chapter includes discussion about the concept of eco-control in the context of environmental accounting and shows how the resulting figures can be used for improved strategic decision-making and accountability. It also demonstrates how the management of eco-efficiency-oriented information can become part of the corporate environmental management system and considers specific issues related to redesign of existing accounting and reporting systems.

The book concludes with a summary and outlook for the future of environmental accounting (Chapter 15).

Questions

1. Explain how the notions of effectiveness, efficiency and equity are related to decision-making, sustainable development and accountability.

2. What is the difference between an accountor and an accountee? Is it important for the needs of both to be taken into account when designing an accounting system? Provide reasons for your view.

3. Environmental accounting systems have been proposed for sovereign nations as well as for companies. Consider how a macro (national) and a micro (company) view of environmental accounting might differ.

4. Why is a distinction made between conventional accounting and ecological accounting?

Part 1
INTRODUCTION AND FRAMEWORK
2 The emergence of environmental accounting management
3 The purpose of managing environmental information
4 The environmental accounting framework

Part 2
ENVIRONMENTAL ISSUES IN CONVENTIONAL ACCOUNTING
5 Overview, criticism and advantages of conventional accounting
6 Environmental management accounting
7 Environmental issues in financial accounting and reporting
8 Environmental shareholder value and environmental issues in other accounting systems

Part 3
ECOLOGICAL ACCOUNTING
9 Overview and emergence of life-cycle assessment and ecological accounting
10 The efficiency of approaches to environmental information management
11 Internal ecological accounting
12 External ecological accounting and reporting of environmental impacts

Part 4
INTEGRATION
13 Integration with eco-efficiency indicators
14 Integrating eco-efficiency-oriented information management into the corporate environmental management system
15 Summary

Chapter 2

THE EMERGENCE OF
ENVIRONMENTAL ACCOUNTING

Chapter 2 provides an introduction to the topic of environmental accounting. Environmental accounting is a branch of accounting that deals with

☐ Activities, methods and systems

☐ Recording, analysis and reporting

☐ Environmentally induced financial impacts and ecological impacts of a defined economic system

(see Chapter 4, Section 4.1.3). In the context of developed countries in particular, this chapter explains the main reason why environmental accounting has become a major issue for corporate management.

Section 2.1 examines why different accounting systems emerge. The development of environmental accounting is seen to result from stakeholder pressures (Section 2.2), and changing cost relations (Section 2.3). In addition, Section 2.4 shows that in most companies the collection of environmental data is poorly co-ordinated and lacks focus.

2.1 Reasons for emergence

Today, a large number of companies in developed countries collect, use and distribute information related to the natural environment. This reflects a fundamental change compared with a decade ago (e.g. see Gray *et al.* 1996: 81). Why have environmental matters become an important business issue?

Two main explanations can be given for management concern over environmental matters and for the development of environmental management information systems:

☐ Increasing **pressure from stakeholders** concerned about the impact of corporate activities on the environment has motivated (or pushed) managers to engage with environmental issues (Dyllick 1989). Environmental information systems facilitate this engagement by connecting responsible parties with environmental impacts (Ditz *et al.* 1995: 39).

☐ The **costs** of environmental impacts have risen substantially, so that environmental information has increasingly become economically relevant information for decision-making and accountability. In contrast, the costs of information management per unit of information have substantially decreased in recent decades. As a result, the relationship between environment related costs and the costs of environmental information management have changed.

In addition to these two reasons, reduction of trade barriers and increasing globalisation of the economy have led to additional competition between companies. The resulting, more intensive, pressure to produce and supply goods and services in the most efficient manner also encourages management to satisfy stakeholder demands as efficiently as possible. This provides an additional incentive for companies to improve data management about their eco-efficiency and accountability for environmental impacts.

2.2 Stakeholder pressure

At the beginning of the 20th century, dense, dark smoke and contaminated water were regarded as necessary evils of industrial economic activity. Today, society demands a higher-quality environment and is seeking that quality through policies on sustainable development, eco-efficiency and wider disclosure of information leading to improved company accountability. In many cases, environmental degradation associated with company activities is continuing (WWI 1995; Beder 1996) despite the progress made by part of the business community with regard to environmental performance since the rise of environmentalism in the late 1960s and early 1970s (*Economist* 1997b). As scientific findings illustrate (e.g. about the ozone layer and climate change), human impact on the natural environment today is not only local or regional but also poses a threat to the global ecosphere (see e.g. WWI 1995). Ongoing environmental degradation and the economic and social problems associated with it mean that increasing importance is being attached to information about environmental issues. Other types of information such as social accounting are also growing in importance (see e.g. Shell 1997); however, they will not specifically be examined in this book.

The stakeholders of a company are any individuals or groups having an interest in the company because they can affect and/or be affected by the company's activities (Freeman 1984: 41). The term 'stakeholder' indicates that these groups or individuals obtain some form of benefit and/or are exposed to some form of risk from the corporation's activities—financial, social or environmental. Stakeholders can be divided into internal and external groups, the two being separated by the boundaries of the company. Stakeholders include, for example, managers and employees within the company (internal stakeholders) and government regulatory agencies, shareholders, environmental pressure groups, suppliers, customers, local communities and the general public as external stakeholders (see Fig. 2.1).

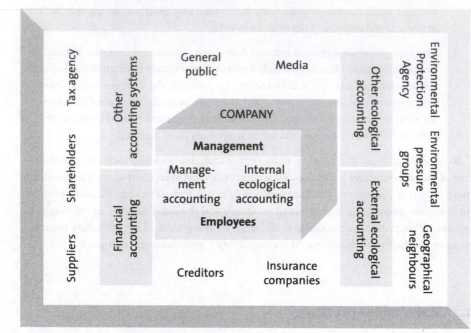

Figure 2.1 **Accounting systems and stakeholders**

Companies need material and intellectual resources (e.g. information and services) in order to perform, and these will be supplied by individuals and groups as long as relations are perceived to be favourable and fair. To verify that this is the case, stakeholders require information that must continually be collected, organised and reported. The stakeholder concept helps to explain:

☐ Why today's organisations have to consider a multitude of different interests if they wish to become successful in economic terms

☐ The need for new forms of stakeholder engagement if environmental improvement and greater accountability are to be achieved (Dyllick 1989; SustainAbility/UNEP 1996a, 1996b)

☐ How different accounting systems have evolved and will continue to evolve in the future

Accounting provides the most important corporate system of information collection and analysis. This is reflected in the notion of being held 'accountable', which means that someone has the duty to give an explanation for how resources have been used. The process of 'being held to account' determines, reflects, strengthens and solidifies the power relationship between the accountee and accountor (Maunders and Burritt 1991). Accounting systems are designed in such a way as to make management and employees accountable for their activities, through improved transparency about an organisation's activities, thereby promoting the engagement of stakeholders even where trust in the accountor may be lacking (SustainAbility/UNEP 1996a). In some instances improved transparency is encouraged through environmental compliance audits that are driven by, and also shape, environmental regulations (Power 1997: 60). As the penalties for undesirable environmental impacts have grown, so has the demand for environmental assurance and verification services. Voluntary self-assessments and self-informing environmental management systems have also recently been added to the range of assurance options available to improve accountability relationships (UNEP 1998; IISD 1998).

Environmental protection agencies and politicians play an important part in the process of turning environmental issues into business issues. They create an expanding volume of environmental law and supporting regulations designed to encourage environmentally benign behaviour by company managers. Furthermore, a range of economic instruments, using market-based approaches working through the price mechanism, are increasingly being seen as an effective means of addressing environmental problems (Panaiotov 1998). In society at large, awareness of environmental issues has been rising dramatically for the past 20 years and although most public opinion polls show that other topics (e.g. unemployment, crime and drugs) head the list of major public concerns environmental issues remain a high priority for consumers (see e.g. Meffert and Bruhn 1996; ABS 1999). The increase in number of environmental pressure group members has also reflected this for more than two decades (Cairncross 1991; Libby 1999; McKenzie 1998: 29; Tilt 1994). A statistical overview of the recent development in membership of selected environmental protection organisations in the USA is provided by Cairncross (1991). International and business organisations are increasingly having to deal with environmental issues, as shown by the growing number of international environmental agreements and public statements by business leaders (see e.g. ICC 1991; Schmidheiny 1992; Shell 1998).

These and other stakeholder activities have a major impact on business and have made a growing number of firms realise that it can pay to become a 'green' leader and that it can hurt financially to be an environmental laggard (Box 2.1). By improving a company's environmental performance many benefits may be obtained. Some improvements will have direct financial impacts such as decreasing liabilities and costs, whereas others will

Box 2.1 **Costs of chemical waste disposal in the USA**

Sources: Wheeler and Sillanpää 1997: 82; Whelan 1993

THE LOVE CANAL DISASTER IN NEW YORK STATE HAD A PARTICULARLY SOBERING impact on the US public and the chemical industry. Chemical wastes were dumped in a canal between 1942 and 1953 and covered. Later, the area was excavated and redeveloped and by 1976 residents were complaining about seepage of wastes and about health problems. The media took over and by 1980 a State emergency, and a federal emergency declared by President Carter, were linked to mob outrage. Permanent relocation of 700 residents cost US$30 million in compensation. A tax on the chemical industry was used to source a 'Superfund' created to clean up toxic waste sites. Between 1980 and 1995 approximately US$30 billion was committed to cleaning up Superfund sites.

lead to more intangible benefits such as better employee morale, an improved corporate image, the anticipation of future legislation and direct involvement in the development of future markets for environmentally benign products. However, not every kind of environmental management will be economically successful. Some means of environmental protection cause high costs whereas others lead to cost savings.

There are many ways to present a greener corporate image to the outside world. Nevertheless, positive benefits usually last for only a short time if there is no action to back up the words. Whereas most managers are concerned mainly with the increasing level of financial costs and liabilities related to environmental impacts (the words 'financial' and 'economic' are used interchangeably in this book) a growing part of the business community is seriously engaged in finding and implementing more sustainable environmental management practices. In order to find ways to reduce costs, or improve income, along with a higher level of environmental protection, companies need suitable management information systems.

A strong tendency to internalise external costs and environmental impacts, a main focus of environmental accounting, now characterises the political landscape of developed countries (OECD 1994a). However, with most companies, so far this has not led to the comprehensive reflection of environmental impacts within management information systems (Ditz *et al.* 1995; Gray 1993; Schaltegger 1996a).

This ongoing process of 'give and take' between corporate management and its stakeholders leads to the parallel development of different accounting systems because different stakeholders require different accounting information. Not every stakeholder receives exactly the quantity and quality of information requested. The accounting systems and practices, and the information provided, are a result of the actual distribution of power between the relevant stakeholder groups and management. The relative power of a stakeholder group is reflected in the process of lobbying for and setting accounting standards as well as in the accounting standards themselves. In addition, the question of who receives what information is also an important consideration given the role accounting systems play in the political context of corporate activities as well as in society. A group with relatively better and more adequate information will always have an advantage in lobbying processes (see Tilt 1994).

Because of ongoing environmental degradation and the problems associated with it, growing importance is attached to the provision of environmentally related information for stakeholders. Accounting, as one of the most pervasive and frequently used information-gathering systems, needs to adapt to this new situation if useful information is to be provided. Creation of new accounting practices dealing specifically with environmental problems is one possible way of responding (Gray 1993). To achieve new accounting practice, conventional financial accounting systems, with a focus on monetary aspects of activity, can be supplemented by ecological accounting systems which collect information about a company's impact on the natural environment. Such supplementary systems can be used for communication with (and accountability to) internal and external stakeholders. Excellent companies do not just ask what information stakeholders require, they engage stakeholders in a dialogue. It could be argued that, by increasing the transparency of a company's financial and ecological impacts, management will lose its power or will have to change its environmental behaviour at some economic cost to keep power. However, modern management theory argues that increased transparency will increase a company's market power because society is better informed and a competitive advantage can be gained (Porter 1980). In this way, management conforms to the demands of society, supports improved accountability and creates more positive feedback for (and from) its stakeholders. Stakeholders will thus be engaged directly in the accountability process. The most important stakeholder groups that influence environmental accounting will be mentioned throughout this book.

In contrast to external stakeholders, internal stakeholders traditionally derive much of their corporate financial information from management accounting, which is shown within the boundaries of the company in the box in the centre of Figure 2.1 (page 32). Usually, the information collected by the management accounting system will be subject to compromises introduced for external accounting purposes. Kaplan (1984: 409) was one of the first to recognise the dysfunctional impact of external financial reporting practices on management accounting, an impact caused by the short-term focus of financial accounting measures and the scope for managers to manipulate results. Though it is acknowledged that dysfunctional behaviour is not always present, the internal data collected should cover a much wider field than the financial requirements of external stakeholders alone. Management accounting is designed to facilitate internal decision-making and accountability and therefore provide necessary data mainly to inform management.

The second internal accounting system shown in Figure 2.1 is internal ecological accounting, so named because it is designed to fulfil the needs of managers to be informed about the ecological impacts of company activities.

Both internal accounting systems should be a prerequisite for external accounting, regardless of whether information is of a financial or an ecological nature. Internal and external stakeholders require the same kind of information, but internal stakeholders require a greater amount and degree of detail.

Internal and external stakeholders, when considered together, will be interested in the financial impacts of environmental activities as well as the physical impact a firm has on the natural environment. The first view could be called an 'outside-in' view (looking at which aspects from the outside have an impact on the organisation), whereas the other is an 'inside-out' view (looking at what impacts the organisation has on the natural environment). Ideally, both kinds of impacts should be integrated in the same accounting system. However, this would only be possible in practice if all environmental impacts were internalised. External stakeholders are divided into two groups. The first group (shown to the left in Fig. 2.1) is primarily interested in the financial outcome of environmental impacts from a company's activities (e.g. reduced profits because of fines imposed, or increased revenues promoted by a clean, green image), and the second group (shown to the right in Fig. 2.1) is predominantly interested in the ecological impacts of a company on the natural environment. External accounting systems provide the communication interface between management and external stakeholders.

Conventional financial and 'other' conventional accounting systems are shown to the left of Figure 2.1, with the main addressees being shareholders, suppliers and tax agencies. External ecological and 'other' ecological accounting systems are on the right in Figure

2.1, with their main addressees, namely environmental protection agencies, environmental pressure groups and geographical neighbours. It must, however, be stressed that this distinction between addressee groups is not necessarily very clear in reality. Shareholders, for example ethical investors, are most certainly interested in the environmental impact of a firm (Cummings and Burritt 1999) and may also be members of environmental pressure groups.

Changed stakeholder attitudes provide a necessary but not sufficient condition for the emergence of environmental accounting. The next section shows how the relative costs and benefits of providing environmental accounting information have changed over time and how these cost changes complement the increased demand from stakeholders who feel that they have a right to know (see OECD 1998a) how environmental factors influence their organisation.

2.3 Changing cost relations

Most companies employ accounting systems that were designed before anyone could anticipate the present-day importance of environmental costs and impacts. Until the 1990s environmental compliance costs and environmental impacts caused by company activities were either not significant or not easy or cost-effective for most manufacturing firms to monitor. At the same time, the costs of measurement and recording were relatively high.

In the past decade, this relationship has been reversed through development and enforcement of the widely accepted 'polluter-pays principle'. Today environmental compliance costs are large and are still increasing for many firms, whereas information systems for tracking those costs have become relatively inexpensive. Government regulatory agencies and the accounting profession have encouraged the tracking of compliance costs.

The relevance of internal company environmental costs are illustrated by the capital and operating pollution abatement and control expenses of US manufacturers which nearly doubled between the mid-1970s and mid-1990s (see Ditz et al. 1995; Eurostat 1994; OTA 1994; also, for a discussion of expected future developments, see Colby et al. 1995). In the German chemical industry the compliance and pollution control costs more than doubled in the same period (Fichter 1995). Fines for environmental non-compliance are also much higher than they have ever been before. Well-known examples of firms with high fines for environmental spills are Exxon and Occidental Chemical. Exxon faced a bill of as much as US$16.5 billion in addition to the US$1.1 billion paid in the State of Alaska and federal criminal penalties and the US$2 billion clean-up costs following the major oil spill in Prince William Sound in Alaska (Economist 1994b: 62). Occidental Petroleum agreed to pay US$120 million to the State of New York as compensation for the contamination of the Love Canal, which was detected at the end of the 1970s (NZZ 1994c: 19; Box 2.1 on page 33). In the USA, industry spends about 30% more than does the government on pollution abatement and control (Economist 1995: 62)

In other words, the opportunity cost of neglecting environmental issues has been substantially rising (see also Chapter 6). For most organisations, the reason why they are now introducing environmental accounting is the logical consequence of changed relative costs and benefits rather than of green idealism. Although there is encouragement for organisations to be mindful of the 'triple bottom line'—social, economic and environmental impacts (Elkington 1998; 1999: 18)—the financial bottom line still permeates business thinking and is at present the main driver for business actions (Ditz *et al.* 1995: 6).

Figure 2.2 summarises why, during the past decade, it has become increasingly sensible in economic terms to introduce systems for managing environmental information. Frey and Kirchgässner (1994: 365) put forward a similar argument for the collection of any form of information.

The marginal costs of collecting and analysing environmental data, C^{EA} (equal to the marginal costs of environmental information management) decrease with increasing marginal costs of negative impacts on the natural environment, C^{EI}. During the past decade these costs have also decreased as a result of the creation of advanced information systems and skills (compare the dashed line, C^{EI}_{new}, corresponding to costs with use of current technology, with the solid line C^{EA}_{old}, corresponding to equivalent costs a decade ago). The same has happened to the marginal costs of reducing environmental impacts

Figure 2.2 **Marginal cost curves for environmental information systems and environmentally induced financial impacts**

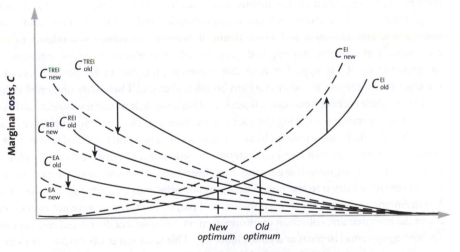

C = Marginal costs	C^{REI} = Marginal costs of reducing environmental impacts (prevention technologies, etc.)
C^{EI} = Marginal costs of environmental impacts (fees, fines, loss of reputation, etc.)	
C^{EA} = Marginal costs of environmental management (collection of information, organisation, etc.)	C^{TREI} = $C^{REI} + C^{EA}$. Subscripts 'old' and 'new' indicate the cost curves of a decade ago and those at present, respectively.

(C^{REI}); in this case, decreases in costs are a result of advanced pollution prevention and abatement technologies. Thus, the total marginal costs of pollution prevention, C^{TREI}, including environmental information management (the term 'pollution prevention' is used interchangeably with the term 'environmental protection' in this book), have been decreasing (compare curves $C^{\text{TREI}}_{\text{old}}$ and $C^{\text{TREI}}_{\text{new}}$).

The marginal costs of the environmental damage caused by the company, C^{EI}, on the other hand, increase with growing environmental impacts. Because of stricter regulations (and resulting fines and fees) the marginal costs of environmental impacts have been increasing over the past decade (compare the curves $C^{\text{EI}}_{\text{old}}$ and $C^{\text{EI}}_{\text{new}}$).

Hence, the optimal point for the environmental policy of a company has been sliding to the left on the 'environmental impacts' axis. This means that from an economic perspective over the past ten years it has become economical for many more companies to introduce environmental management and environmental information management systems.

2.4 Poorly co-ordinated collection of environmental data

The fact that more companies collect environmental data now than they did a decade ago does not say anything about how well they manage such data. In practice, most companies have poorly co-ordinated environmental data collection (Bennett and James 1996; Gray 1993). Despite their economic relevance, opportunities and threats, the costs and revenues, assets and liabilities and other financial impacts on companies related to the environment are usually not explicitly considered in corporate financial information systems (see e.g. Gray 1993, but note that a growing number of accounting software packages are beginning to incorporate environmental costs). These environmental influences nevertheless change economic figures, and because their monetary impact has been rising in many industries during the past decade (see e.g. Ditz et al. 1995; Fichter et al. 1997) they should be incorporated in accounting and finance practices. Today, especially, rigorous cost management requires thorough consideration of environmentally induced costs. However, even though arguments have been made for systematic use of environmental cost information to encourage best-practice behaviour (Burritt 1998), a survey of North American companies showed that several parties interviewed were not concerned about the unsystematic collection of information on environmentally related costs in cost accounting systems (Bennett and James 1996: 24). This situation exists despite very strict regulations (such as the US Comprehensive Environmental Response, Compensation, and Liability Act [CERCLA 1980], often referred to as the 'Superfund' Act) that have forced companies to bear the cost of billions of US dollars for environmental clean-ups and liabilities in recent years (Dirks 1991; Newell et al. 1990; Rabinowitz and Murphy 1992; Vaughan 1994). The clean-up costs for the Superfund sites alone are estimated to exceed US$500 billion in the next 40–50 years (EIU/AIU 1993).

Related to this, accurate recording and analysis of current and expected environmental impacts and of the use of environmental resources are prerequisites not only for the improvement of corporate environmental performance but also for the estimation of possible future market opportunities and costs brought about by new regulations (e.g. a ban on chlorofluorocarbons [CFCs]) and taxes (e.g. a tax on carbon dioxide [CO_2] emissions). One not entirely convincing explanation for the poor co-ordination of collection activities, related to the management of environmental information, is the wide range of addressees. In practice, the collection of environmental data serves various purposes and information requirements of different stakeholders.

Another reason may be that environmental information has not previously been given high priority by top management. Different departments and employees, however, had to collect environmental data to meet regulations and answer various requests by in-company and external stakeholders. As a consequence, information has been created at various places throughout the company and sometimes the same data have been collected twice or even more often. Evidence suggests that a commitment from top management is essential to success in protecting a company from environmental risk, including the risk of non-compliance with regulations because of administrative oversight (Hunt and Auster 1990: 12).

A third reason for the lack of co-ordination may be that the activities of managing corporate environmental data are often not oriented towards a clearly defined, overarching objective. Strategic planning for environmental outcomes becomes meaningless in this context, unless goals are well specified. The enhancement of eco-efficiency, discussed in the next chapter, can serve as a major, if not the major, purpose for environmental information management.

A fourth explanation for the present mostly rudimentary management of environmental information may be the high fixed costs of establishing information management systems. Production and distribution of environmental information, as with any kind of information, is often characterised by economies of scale. One unit of information can be transmitted at extremely low costs once the information management system is established. However, it makes sense to change and enlarge an existing system, and to bear the additional fixed costs, only if the added value of a new information management system is higher than its costs (Boockholdt 1999: 155).

Typically, when environmental information management commences, various employees throughout the company will make small adaptations to existing systems. Such development may continue until top management realises that the benefits of current information-gathering, minus the sum of the costs of these small adaptations, are smaller in the long run than the benefits minus the costs of a more fundamental restructuring of information management—through a new integrated environmental accounting system. This argument is in line with the theory of 'path dependency' (Goodstein 1995). Individuals and organisations continue to make relatively small short-term investments in a given path or (e.g. computer) system if the costs of changing to a more efficient path are perceived as being very high. In some cases, where the situation is characterised by a relatively short time-horizon, a decision-maker will continue to invest in the existing path even if the path-switching costs are lower than the net long-term gains in efficiency from changing the path.

As indicated by the Superfund Act example, and as will be illustrated in greater detail in Chapter 7, access to and use of environmental information has become ever more crucial to assure the economic success of a company (Judge and Douglas 1998), thereby increasing the potential benefits of additional environmental information.

In summary, this chapter has argued that the reduction of corporate environmental impacts on the environment is becoming increasingly related to economic feasibility as the costs of information management per unit of information generated, and of pollution prevention, are decreasing and the costs from harming the natural environment are increasing. However, many companies have not yet realised this situation because they have poorly developed environmental management systems. This book, therefore, explores approaches that encourage the successful management of environmental information and environmental impacts within a corporate environmental accounting framework.

Chapter 3 discusses the fundamental environmental accounting framework and the main issues associated with the set of different environmental accounting systems to be explored in depth in later chapters.

Questions

1. Why has the importance of environmental accounting to business grown in the past ten years?

2. What is an external stakeholder? Provide an example of a situation where pressure from external stakeholders has pushed managers to engage with environmental issues.

3. What mechanisms are available to help provide stakeholders with an assurance that a company complies with environmental regulations?

4. If fines for non-compliance are much higher than ever before, how might increased transparency, brought about by environmental accounting disclosures, still act as a competitive advantage to a company?

5. What are the reasons for most companies having a poorly co-ordinated collection of environmental data? How are these reasons related to the distinction made between fixed and variable costs of information management systems?

6. **Stakeholders' views.** Broken Hill Proprietary Co. Ltd (BHP). BHP is an Australian-based global mineral resources company. A tailings dam constructed at the Ok Tedi copper and gold mine in Papua New Guinea collapsed leading to over 700 million tonnes of tailings and waste rock being delivered directly into the Ok Tedi and Fly River systems over the past 15 years. Groups that relied on these rivers have lost their livelihood (e.g. fish stocks were destroyed). In 1994, these groups decided to bring an action against BHP in the Melbourne courts in Australia. An out-of-court settlement, so far costing over A$500 million

dollars, was reached with BHP in 1996 (BHP 1997: 2). In 1999, the Chief Executive Officer of BHP commented that, with the benefit of a new report and hindsight, BHP should never have become involved with the mining venture. The World Wide Fund for Nature has called for the giant Ok Tedi mine in Papua New Guinea to be closed immediately (*Australian* 1999: 7).

   a Identify the stakeholders involved in the Ok Tedi mining disaster.

   b Consider whether each stakeholder group, including management, is concerned about efficient decision-making, accountability of the organisation or both.

7. **Costs of information: increasing environmental expenditures.** Most major corporations are spending in the tens of millions of dollars annually on environmental costs, with the larger ones spending in the hundreds of millions and some spending more than US$1 billion per year (Epstein 1996: xxv).

   a What factors might have led to increases in environmental expenditures for organisations in environmentally sensitive industries (e.g. chemicals)?

   b Are there any offsetting factors that might lead to a reduction in the cost of obtaining information about environmental impacts?

8. **Shell's statement of business principles** (Shell 1998: 24): Principle 6, on health, safety and the environment (HSE).

   > Consistent with their commitment to contribute to sustainable development, Shell companies have a systematic approach to health, safety and environmental management in order to achieve continuous performance improvement . . . Shell companies manage these matters as any other critical business activity, set targets for improvement, and measure, appraise and report performance:
   >
   > • Every Shell company has adopted this policy and procedures.
   >
   > • Over 90 companies have HSE management systems in place. The target is for all Shell companies to have such systems installed by the end of 1999.
   >
   > • Independent auditors will check adoption of the HSE policy and procedures.

   a Why might Shell disclose its business principles to the public?

   b Identify the main concepts included by Shell in the above statement of business principles. Design a principle for your own organisation, or an organisation of your choice, that incorporates all of these concepts.

9. **Environmental compliance: a market opportunity.** Table 2.1 shows estimates of the size of the market for environmental technologies and services needed to comply with environmental standards. In 1996 the OECD, using a fairly narrow definition of the industry, estimated that the global compliance market would be about US$300 billion by the year 2000 (OECD 1996b).

   a List the trends observable in the figures contained in Table 2.1.

   b Explain the factors that have encouraged these trends.

Region	1992	2000	2010
North America	100	147	240
Latin America	2	4	15
Europe	65	98	167
Asia–Pacific	85	63	149
Rest of the world	0	7	0
Total	**252**	**319**	**571**

Table 2.1 **Size of the global environment compliance market (in US$ billions)**

Source: OECD 1996b: 117; based on figures provided by ECOTEC Research and Consulting, UK

10. Why is involvement of top management important to the success of a corporate environmental management and accounting system?

Chapter 3

THE PURPOSE OF MANAGING ENVIRONMENTAL INFORMATION

3.1 Environmental information as purpose-oriented knowledge

Good decisions are based on knowledge about the topic being considered. One way to improve decisions is to collect and analyse data. However, not all data necessarily improve the knowledge base that decision-makers require. Only data that are related to a desired goal and are highly likely to improve decision quality (i.e. purpose-oriented knowledge) are valuable. Such basic considerations are easy to express and seem logical in general terms. However, in practice, the management (i.e. the creation and analysis) of purpose-oriented knowledge faces many problems, as explained below.

3.1.1 Signals, data and information

Information can be understood in many different ways (see e.g. Biethahn *et al.* 1994: 2; Brockhaus 1992: 8f.; Keeney and Raiffa 1976). There is, however, no intention of filling the following pages with various definitions of information. A sample of different definitions can be seen in McNurlin and Sprague 1989 (p. 199f.) or Losee 1997. In order to clarify the topic for discussion in this text the basic and widely shared pragmatic viewpoint of Wittmann (1959, 1982), Chambers (1966), who saw information processing as the purposive and abstractive collection, arrangement, aggregation and transformation of singular signs (p. 162), and Schneider (1981) is assumed: that is, information is purpose-oriented data. Knowledge management is the name of a relatively new concept in which an enterprise consciously and comprehensively gathers, organises, shares and analyses its knowledge to further its aims. More specifically, to be purpose-oriented and beneficial, collection of information must create value. Thus, the collection, analysis and communication of data are only beneficial if their purpose is to create specific values: that is, to achieve desired states and goals (Keeney 1996).

According to Sterling (1970: 445) and Brockhaus (1992), information is to be distinguished from signals, signs, symbols, news, data and notifications (Fig. 3.1).

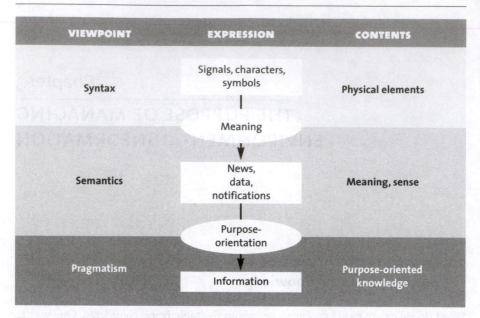

Figure 3.1 **Information as purpose-oriented knowledge**

Source: Brockhaus 1992: 9

In semiotics and linguistics, three basic points of view are distinguished (Brockhaus 1992; Sterling 1970): syntactics, semantics and pragmatics. The three are linked in the following way. Signals, characters and symbols are abstract elements (a syntactic perspective) which have to be given a real-world meaning (a semantic point of view) to turn into news, data or notifications. Finally, an orientation towards a specific purpose is needed to create information (a pragmatic approach).

A syntactical analysis concentrates on mathematical–statistical links. By themselves syntactical elements have no empirical content. Statements that are based on syntactic rules can be considered true or false by logical reasoning alone. For example, $2 + 2 = 4$ can be determined to be true by reference to mathematical rules.

A semantic analysis concentrates on the meaning that is created by combining signals, signs or characters. Therefore, news, data and notifications are the result of sequences of signals, signs or characters. A semantic relationship links the logical relationships, or links between signs, to the real world (Margenau 1996).

Whether news is understood depends on whether the sender and the receiver understand the signals in the same way (see e.g. McNurlin and Sprague 1989). Pragmatism, the third perspective, analyses and describes the commonly used pool of characters and signals and thus considers possibilities of interpretation of signals by people.

This text does not deal directly with the syntactic and semantic viewpoints, although it is concerned with particular environmental signs and signals. In fact, as Chambers (1966: 177) acknowledges in the context of communication of information, semantic, syntactic and pragmatic considerations are interwoven. However, the operational functioning of computer systems, data processing and related topics (see e.g. Dickson and Wetherbe 1985; Heinrich 1996; Vesely 1990) are not the focal point. This book does not discuss knowledge management in the sense of developing learning organisations or organisational culture. Instead, the interest is in how accounting concepts and their real-world measures affect people's behaviour. Hence, contemporary corporate environmental accounting must have a pragmatic orientation. Consequently, this book focuses on the third level of theory development, that is the characteristics and type of quantitative data and data management systems geared to specific management purposes.

According to Schneider (1981) and Chambers (1966), information is data that a decision-maker needs to explain future states of interest and to pursue a certain purpose. Information should provide a realistic picture of events about a company and its socioeconomic and natural environment (Riebel 1992: 251). Information is, simply, data focused towards a specific objective. Only the orientation of data towards a specific purpose creates information and thus a specific value for the recipients (see also Keeney 1996). Signals have an information content by virtue of their potential for helping recipients make selections between alternatives (Cherry 1961: 169).

From this pragmatic-laden focus, on purposive information acquisition and processing, a chosen course of action emerges as various alternatives are eliminated, 'but at all points, the evaluations of actions in terms of the actor's ends determine the outcome of the process' (Chambers 1966: 54). The critical test for any accounting system is whether it produces desirable, purpose-oriented behaviour from the people who receive the information provided.

Based on these fundamental, often neglected, aspects of decision-making, this book discusses the purpose-oriented accounting and management of environmental information.

3.2 Necessary objective

Financial accounting, designed to satisfy the information requirements of external stakeholders of firms (see Section 4.1.2), is used in almost all business organisations whether small, medium or large in size. Financial accounting, as the most frequently available conventional information management approach used by any company, is directed towards the purpose of maximising company profitability, subject to liquidity and solvency considerations (see e.g. Wilkinson 1989: 21f.). All other goals considered by various financial accounting systems such as high sales revenues, large contribution margins and increasing economic value added are derived from this overarching goal.

To link the collection and analysis of environmental data to the management of purpose-oriented knowledge, an overarching objective or operational goal has to be assumed. The two main environmental objectives that have often been proposed for the management of companies are 'sustainable development' and 'eco-efficiency'. To bring environmental information management in line with such objectives, these notions, however, need to be clarified.

3.3 **Sustainable development**

The need to strive for sustainable development has been proposed as a desirable policy for the world economy as well as for nations and companies (UNCED 1987). Furthermore, the principle of sustainability has been accepted by a growing cluster of international bodies, nations and companies in the developed world. In this context, the notions of sustainability, sustainable growth, sustainable development and sustainable society can be distinguished:

☐ **Sustainability.** The concept of sustainability comes from forest engineering and requires that the harvest of trees should not exceed the growth of new trees. The general interpretation of sustainability is that society should not use more natural resources than the natural environment can regenerate (for other definitions of sustainability, see e.g. Gray *et al.* 1996: 61; Bebbington, 1997). The underlying notion is one of generating a sustainable productive yield through forest management.

☐ **Qualitative (sustainable) growth.** Qualitative growth is considered to relate to every sustainable increase of welfare per capita, and welfare of society as a whole, which is achieved by a decreasing or constant use of natural resources as well as a decreasing or constant amount of pollution (BfK 1985: 15; see also Frey 1997: 159f.; Mishan 1980; Rose 1995).

☐ **Sustainable development.** Sustainable development (see e.g. UNCED 1987: 43, the so-called 'Brundtland Commission' of the UN World Commission on Environment and Development [WCED] ; SustainAbility 1993; WWF 1992, 1993) is defined as development that meets the needs of the present generation without compromising the ability of future generations to meet their own needs. It contains two key concepts:

    – The concept of 'needs', in particular the essential needs of the world's poor and future generations of humans, to which overriding priority should be given (Welford and Gouldson 1993).

    – The idea of limitations imposed by the state of technology and by social organisation on the environment's ability to meet present and future needs.

☐ **Sustainable society.** A society is sustainable if it is structured and behaves in such a way that it can exist for an indefinite number of generations (Meadows *et al.* 1992: 250). Karr (1993: 299) states: 'A sustainable society depends on a life-support system with integrity. Such a system is characterised by stability, realisation of inherent potential, capacity for self-repair, and minimal need for external support.' From this perspective, production as well as consumption must be sustainable.

The notion of sustainability is usually divided into two main sub-themes—weak and strong sustainability. Weak sustainability is associated with the idea that a community can use up its natural resources and degrade the natural environment as long as it is able to compensate for the loss with human (skills, knowledge and technology) and human-made (buildings, machinery, equipment) capital. From this perspective, in the extreme, natural and human-made capital can be considered equivalent because investment in either form of capital can generate the same income streams.

Weak sustainability has been an aid to business because it provides one justification for the continued use of non-renewable resources if human-made capital can be substituted. However, Gray raises the alarming prospect that, if environmental costs were deducted from a company's profit to obtain some idea of corporate environmental value added, there is a strong 'probability . . . that no Western company has made a "sustainable" profit for a very long time, if at all' (1992: 419-20).

Businesses adopting a weakly sustainable view of environmental issues need also to be aware of arguments put forward from a strong sustainability perspective. Strong sustainability argues for conservation of non-renewable natural resources (e.g. biodiversity) on the grounds of non-substitutability, irreversibility, equity and diversity (Beder 1996: 159-60). In practice, there are large uncertainties about the possibility of substitution between natural and human-made capital. Uncertainties exist at the technical level and, even where consensus exists about technology itself (e.g. the uneconomic nature of most fission reactors), differences in attitude about risks for future generations (e.g. waste disposal and risk management techniques) means that there can be no right or wrong view (Common 1995: 45-46). For seekers of strong sustainability, the concern is that environmental accounting is irredeemably contaminated by its hidden (ideological) assumptions and is 'open to capture' by those with 'a vested interest in down-playing ecological impact' (Maunders and Burritt 1991: 12, 17). As a minimum, strong sustainability reminds managers that they have to be aware of a broader set of perspectives about the relative importance of business in society. Both weak and strong forms of sustainability require that consideration be given by business to the need for accountability to various stakeholders.

The definitions of sustainable growth and sustainable development do not entirely match the biological approach based on the capacity of the Earth or specific ecosystems to sustain life (see e.g. Allenby and Fullerton 1992; Daly 1992). However, if a company is seen as a social system, its survival is also a result of its economic performance. Sustainable development forces environmental groups, business and government to recognise that environmental factors may have a long-term detrimental impact on economic performance and have not been given enough consideration in the past. Sustainable growth and sustainable development describe processes helping movement towards the desirable situation of sustainability and a sustainable society. Nevertheless, the term 'development' leaves more possibilities for interpretation than the term 'growth', as it specifically recognises social actors and does not exclude a 'sustainable decrease' of economic productivity. Equating development with economic growth is a fairly recent phenomenon (Sachs 1992). The concepts of sustainable development and sustainable society include sociopolitical aspects, whereas sustainability has been derived from a concept in natural science. However, as discussion of the emerging concept of sustainability illustrates, natural scientists concerned about ecology, and economists concerned about scarce and non-renewable resources, have come together to recognise that the world is a closed system and that drastic change within that system is progressively seen as wrong by government, the community and business (Maunders and Burritt 1991: 9).

In conclusion, the overarching goal of ecological accounting is to provide a first step in measuring, making transparent and thereby making accountable the movement of stakeholders in sustainable development towards a sustainable society. Business interpretation of this process is being made in the context of social, economic and ecological 'bottom lines'. According to the World Business Council on Sustainable Development (WBCSD), sustainable development involves the simultaneous pursuit of economic prosperity, environmental quality and social equity (Elkington 1999: 18). Elkington (1999) argues that companies aiming for sustainability should accept the need to perform not against a single, financial bottom line but against the triple bottom line.

Sustainable development is gradually becoming integrated into government policies that form a backdrop for business activities. In Europe, with the Amsterdam Treaty coming into force in the European Union (EU), with effect from 1 May 1999, the concept of sustainable development has been introduced in a number of key places including the new stated objective of the EU to achieve balanced and sustainable development. Furthermore, some countries (e.g. Canada) have institutionalised the role of an independent commissioner of the environment and sustainable development, a role that mandates the need for federal government institutions to improve environmental accountability (OAGC 1997: 11). The United Nations has its Commission on Sustainable Development (UNCSD) and the USA its President's Council on Sustainable Development (PCSD 1996). As Björn Stigson (1999: 1), President of the WBCSD, acknowledges, the business community is only just beginning to address the challenge of sustainable development through the notions of 'sustainability through the market', 'eco-efficiency' and 'corporate social responsibility'.

This short discussion of sustainable development and related concepts shows that environmentally induced economic issues are not explicitly covered (e.g. costs of fines imposed because of spills). Although proponents of ecologically sustainable development are more mindful of energy use, ecological preservation and waste minimisation than are users of conventional growth strategies (Shrivastava 1995: 941), sustainable development is still a very general objective which remains in the process of being operationalised. To direct the management of environmental information in a company requires more concise and measurable objectives and benchmarks. However, it does draw attention to the need for companies to consider a range of stakeholder perspectives in relation to any activities undertaken and to focus on an objective and the extent to which that objective is being achieved.

Bebbington and Thomson (1996: i) discovered, from a series of interviews with environmental managers and accountants, that the need to pursue sustainable development is not in doubt. At the operational level there is a need to address social concerns of eco-justice as well as environmental concerns through eco-efficiency. As the study of eco-justice remains in its infancy it is not considered in this book. Instead, attention is directed to the concept of eco-efficiency where considerable attention has already been given to metrics and reporting issues.

3.4 Corporate eco-efficiency

The concept of eco-efficiency was first introduced and discussed in academic literature (Schaltegger and Sturm 1990). However, the term 'eco-efficiency' did not become widely used until the Business Council for Sustainable Development (BCSD, since 1995 called the World Business Council for Sustainable Development [WBCSD]) and Schmidheiny published *Changing Course* at the United Nations Conference on Environment and Development (UNCED) summit in Rio in 1992 (Schmidheiny 1992; see also BCSD 1993). Eco-efficiency can be analysed at a global, regional or corporate level. For an application and measurement of eco-efficiency at a macro-economic level see Schaltegger *et al.* 1996 and for a national policy orientation see PCSD 1996. Hereafter, the focus is on corporate eco-efficiency. In practice, the term has been given different meanings and, as a result, has little precision. Therefore, it is very important to clarify the dimensions of eco-efficiency being discussed here.

First, however, the Organisation for Economic Co-operation and Development (OECD 1998b) and WBCSD (1999) notions of eco-efficiency are considered. The basic idea of economic–ecological efficiency was taken up by the BCSD which defined the term as follows:

> Eco-efficiency is reached by the delivery of competitively-priced goods and services that satisfy human needs and bring quality of life, while progressively reducing ecological impacts and resource intensity throughout the life-cycle, to a level at least in line with the Earth's estimated carrying capacity (1993: 9).

The OECD states that eco-efficiency:

> expresses the efficiency with which ecological resources are used to meet human needs. It can be considered as a ratio of an output divided by an input: the output being the value of products or services produced by a firm, a sector or the economy as a whole, and the input being the sum of environmental pressures generated by the firm, sector or economy (1998: 7).

The OECD is less concerned with guidelines for measuring eco-efficiency than the potential for improving eco-efficiency in an economy and the policies that might achieve this.

Based on the WBCSD's rather general notion of eco-efficiency, the WBCSD, through its Working Group on Eco-efficiency Metrics and Reporting (WBCSD 1999), has set about identifying a specific set of principles and 'core' and 'supplemental' indicators of eco-efficiency. The WBCSD recognises that there are numerous ways of calculating the ecological and economic dimensions of eco-efficiency and that these will depend on the individual needs of companies and their shareholders (WBCSD 1999: 11).

It can be seen from these approaches that, in general, efficiency measures the relation between outputs from and inputs to a process. The higher the output for a given input, or the lower the input for a given output, the more efficient is an activity, product or company. As the purpose of economic behaviour is to manage scarcity in the best possible manner, emphasis is placed on the need for managers to seek efficient outcomes.

Efficiency is a multi-dimensional concept because the units in which input and output are measured can vary. If inputs and outputs are measured in financial terms, efficiency is commonly referred to as profitability or financial efficiency. Typical measures of profitability include contribution margin percentage, return on sales, economic value added and return to equity on assets employed. Economic efficiency (or financial efficiency) indicates whether, and for how long, social activities can be sustained in economic terms.

If inputs and outputs are measured in technological terms, emphasis is usually placed on physical measures such as kilograms. Technological efficiency is also called productivity. Measures of productivity include output per hour and output per employee.

The difference between the best possible efficiency ratio (the ratio of outputs to inputs) and the efficiency ratio actually achieved is described as X-efficiency (Leibenstein 1966). The concept of X-efficiency is useful because it suggests that in practice organisations do not appear to be cost minimisers (using latest technology); rather they are more inclined to imitate their rivals in various policies and to follow industry norms and targets. To the extent that this occurs these organisations are technically inefficient. X-efficiency measures the extent of this technical inefficiency. Efficiency, because it is expressed as a ratio between a measure of output and a measure of input, is not bound to a financial or technological dimension: different dimensions can be combined by calculating cross-efficiency figures such as shareholder value created per employee.

As efficiency in general is the ratio between output and input, ecological efficiency can be interpreted as the relationship between a measure of output and a measure of environmental impact:

$$\text{ecological efficiency} \quad = \quad \frac{\text{output}}{\text{environmental impact added}} \qquad [3.1]$$

Environmental impact added is a measure of all environmental influences that are assessed according to their relative environmental impact. To measure ecological efficiency, tools of environmental information management are needed (see Chapter 14).

Two types of ecological efficiency measure can be distinguished: ecological product efficiency and ecological function efficiency. Ecologically efficient management of a company is characterised by a high ratio between products sold, or functions accomplished, and the associated environmental impact added.

Ecological product efficiency is a measure of the ratio between provision of a unit of product and the environmental impact created over the whole, or a part, of the product's life-cycle. Company managers tend to illustrate environmental improvements by communicating their total product efficiency or part thereof (e.g. the number of cars produced per unit of energy consumed). Ecological product efficiency can be improved by implementing pollution prevention techniques or by introducing end-of-pipe devices, reduced use of inputs per unit or through substitution of resources. Although, in principle, improvement of product efficiency is desirable, some products will never be as ecologically efficient as others in providing a certain service. For example, a car will always be less ecologically efficient than a bicycle.

The second formula for ecological efficiency, expressed in terms of ecological function efficiency, takes a broader view, by measuring how much environmental impact is associated with the provision of a specific function in each period of time. A function could, for instance, be defined as the painting of one square metre of sheet metal or the transport of a person over a certain distance. The alternative that causes the least environmental impact in fulfilling the specific function has the best ecological function efficiency. Ecological function efficiency is, therefore, defined as the ratio between provision of a function and the associated environmental impact added.

Ecological function efficiency can be improved by substituting products that have a low efficiency with highly efficient products (e.g. a bicycle instead of a car), by reducing the amount used to fulfil the function (e.g. car pools lead to a decreased demand for cars), by prolonging the life-span of products (e.g. longer corrosion guarantees on cars) and by improving product efficiency.

Environmental interest groups often prefer to measure the environmental record of a product according to its overall function efficiency (e.g. the ecological function efficiency of a car in transporting a person over a specific distance compared with the efficiency of a bicycle, public transport, etc.).

Both measures of ecological efficiency are useful, and their adequacy depends on the purpose of the investigation. The two ecological efficiency ratios can be applied to different levels of aggregation, such as a unit of product, a strategic business unit or total sales of a firm. In this context it is important to consider the total output and the absolute environmental impact: a large number of ecologically efficient products can be more harmful than a small number of ecologically inefficient items.

The cross-efficiency between the economic and the ecological dimension—economic–ecological efficiency—is the ratio between the change in value and change in environmental impact added. Economic–ecological efficiency is often referred to as eco-efficiency. Eco-efficiency does not cover all aspects of sustainable development, such as socio-cultural, political and technological aspects. In calculating the economic value added as well as environmental impact added, distributional issues are not assessed (e.g. whether products and services were oriented towards satisfying basic needs or whether participation of the workforce, or neighbourhoods, in decision-making and policies was practised). The prefix 'eco' refers to ecological and economic efficiency. It is sometimes called E^2 efficiency. In this book, eco-efficiency is represented as follows:

$$\text{eco-efficiency} \quad = \quad \frac{\text{value added}}{\text{environmental impact added}} \qquad [3.2]$$

As indicated above, there is no single measure of economic or ecological efficiency. The chosen measures will depend on the best information required for the purpose of the analysis. For instance the ratio of contribution margin per tonne of waste may be a measure of the eco-efficiency of the waste caused by a product, whereas the company's operating profit per tonne of waste may be a useful waste-related eco-efficiency indicator for the company.

Hence, eco-efficiency is a flexible and relevant approach. Eco-efficiency provides a means of measuring the combined economic and ecological performance of the management of an organisation for a specified period of time (Box 3.1). Over a period of time, trends in eco-efficiency can be distinguished.

IN 1995 LANDIS & GYR, TODAY PART OF SIEMENS CORPORATION, headquartered in Zug, Switzerland, employed some 16,000 people worldwide. In business year 1995 they generated a net profit of CHF110 million on sales of CHF2,889 million.

The concept of eco-efficiency means obtaining economic benefits from ecological improvements. In other words: one wants to increase added value yet consume as few resources as possible in order to minimise pollution of the soil, water and air.

Energy efficiency is a branch of eco-efficiency and involves generating the same value yet using less electricity, gas or oil. Figures for the period 1993–95 for Landis & Gyr are shown in the table below.

YEAR	TOTAL ENERGY CONSUMPTION*	TOTAL WASTE NOT RECYCLED*
1993	0.58	3.5
1994	0.58	3.2
1995	0.52	3.8

* Expressed in megajoules per Swiss franc of added value.

Box 3.1   **Eco-efficiency at Landis & Gyr Corporation**

Source: Landis & Gyr 1995: 3, 18

In the next section, a comparison is made between eco-efficiency and sustainable development.

3.5 The relation between sustainable development and eco-efficiency

The main relationship between sustainable development and eco-efficiency is illustrated in Figure 3.2. The concept of an 'eco-efficiency portfolio' can be applied at the level of a product, firm or nation, but here our concern is with the eco-efficiency of individual companies. For a more detailed discussion of the notion of an eco-efficiency portfolio, see Ilinitch and Schaltegger 1995.

In Figure 3.2 economic performance is measured on the vertical axis, and environmental performance is measured on the horizontal axis. If a third dimension of 'weak' sustainable development were to be included, where a trade-off between natural and human-made capital is assumed, a third measure, for 'social performance', would be necessary. The current situation, concentrating on economic and environmental performance, is defined as point 0, in the middle of Figure 3.2. Movements above (to the right of) the dashed diagonal 'eco-efficiency' line indicate that the ratio between economic and environmental performance has improved, as has economic–ecological efficiency.

However, sustainable development is characterised by movements towards the upper right quadrant of the diagram as well as an improvement in the social dimension (represented by arrow A plus a movement to better social performance in the third dimension [not illustrated]). 'Strong' ecologically sustainable development does not allow

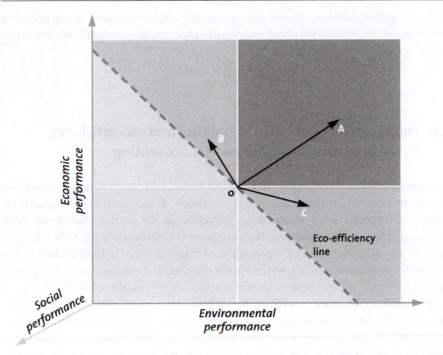

Figure 3.2 **Development and differentiation of eco-efficiency**

an increase in environmental impacts (i.e. movements to the left of the vertical line through point o, as illustrated by arrow B). The same argument applies to 'strong' economically sustainable development, which must be above the horizontal line through point o. Weak sustainability allows development above the eco-efficiency line.

In summary, if only the two dimensions of sustainable development (environmental and economic performance without social performance) are considered, the development of eco-efficiency can distinguish between, for example, a strong sustainable improvement in eco-efficiency (arrow A) and weak sustainable improvement of eco-efficiency (arrows B and C).

To focus on a strong sustainable improvement of corporate eco-efficiency can be seen as a mutually beneficial 'no-regrets strategy' for corporate environmental protection because measures taken result in an improvement in economic and environmental performance. Weak improvements in eco-efficiency imply either an improving economic situation that is traded off against lower environmental performance, or an improving environmental performance that is traded off against a lower economic level of performance.

A strong sustainable improvement in eco-efficiency is generally termed a 'win–win' situation for economic and environmental performance (see Walley and Whitehead 1994) and is promoted by government and business and accepted by non-governmental organisations (NGOs) involved in partnerships with government or industry. Yet the integration of environmental issues into business thinking goes beyond a focus on 'win–win' outcomes and, as explained in the next section, includes a set of strategies that may improve eco-efficiency without necessarily enhancing sustainability (see Reinhardt 1999).

3.6 Enhancing corporate sustainability and eco-efficiency as the purpose of environmental accounting

Previous discussion of sustainable development and eco-efficiency concepts shows that eco-efficiency is less broadly defined than sustainable development because it neglects aspects of corporate social performance. Nevertheless, for several reasons this book focuses only on the measurement and improvement of eco-efficiency. First, the measurement of eco-efficiency-oriented information can be regarded as fundamental to the measurement and movement towards strong sustainable development by companies. Second, although sustainable development is slowly being incorporated in the thinking of governments, overall progress at the corporate board level is negligible. In contrast to the idea of sustainable development, eco-efficiency has been supported very prominently as being a suitable goal for top management to adopt (see e.g. OECD 1998b; Schmidheiny 1992). It has already been included in the policies of many companies (see e.g. Roche 1995) and industry associations (see e.g. ICC 1991) and is being considered by companies involved in eco-efficiency pilot schemes (OECD 1999: Appendix E).

The notion of eco-efficiency, which combines economic as well as ecological aspects of environmental issues, provides some (although, at this point of the text, still crude) indications as to how it might be operationalised. Measures of the economic dimension include shareholder value, free cash flow, contribution margin, net profit and value added.

Possible measures for the ecological dimension and for eco-efficiency are discussed later in this book (Chapter 11 and Section 13.4). Basic measures of eco-efficiency can be combined in a number of different ways and can be disaggregated to serve the various information requirements of stakeholders, actors and addressees. In summary, to focus on eco-efficiency is not to reject the goal of sustainable development but represents instead a first pragmatic step towards 'strong' sustainable development.

Early attempts are being made to measure the social performance of business activities in a quantitative way (see e.g. GRI 1999; the first two sustainability reports of Global Reporting Initiative [GRI] were published in September 1999 by Bristol-Myers Squibb Company [USA] [www.bms.com/ehs] and Eastern Group [UK]; McPhail and Davy 1998). Eco-efficiency figures could, in due course, be combined with these to provide a full set of sustainable development indicators.

If environmental protection and improvement in corporate economic performance is a corporate goal, it makes sense to enable managers to achieve this by directing them towards the management of environmental information for the purpose of enhancing corporate eco-efficiency. Management of eco-efficiency-oriented information can, therefore, be defined as a sub-area of corporate management that deals with activities, methods and systems designed to classify, record, analyse and report on the environmentally induced financial and ecological impacts of a specified economic system (e.g. a firm, factory or product).

The value of environmental information management can be measured by any increase in eco-efficiency, and managers can be held accountable for their results by comparing actual and expected eco-efficiency for any period of time.

3.7 Further goals of environmental accounting

Corporate environmental accounting is not restricted to consideration of eco-efficiency issues. As mentioned before, efficiency is only one goal that managers pursue for their organisations. Other goals include effectiveness and equity. In terms of sustainable development, effectiveness relates to the extent to which goals or targets for strong sustainability are achieved. However, in terms of eco-efficiency, where a trade-off between economic and ecological capital is considered acceptable, effectiveness is related to whether either weak or strong sustainability is achieved. Add to this the possibility of achieving equitable social outcomes and the full complexity of environmental accounting possibilities soon becomes apparent.

The next section deals with basic information requirements to operationalise corporate eco-efficiency.

3.8 Information requirements to operationalise corporate sustainability and eco-efficiency

Based on the numerator (value added) and denominator (environmental impact added) of the eco-efficiency ratio (see equation [3.2] on page 51), two main groups of environmental information are relevant to any measure of corporate eco-efficiency: financial impacts, caused by environmental factors (called hereafter environmentally induced financial impacts), and environmental impacts of a firm.

To be made operational, these two groups of environmental data have to be guided by several requirements. If the purpose of managing environmental information in a company is to create information that can be used to enhance corporate eco-efficiency, data collection, analysis and communication have to be designed to take into account the following criteria:

☐ Cause of environmental impact

☐ Activity

☐ Responsibility

☐ Addressee interests

Management of environmental data will improve eco-efficiency only if it provides additional knowledge about the causes of environmental problems. Common examples of environmental problems include the depletion of the ozone layer, the greenhouse effect, acidification of air and therefore rain, nitrification of soil and therefore groundwater, photochemical smog, land degradation and the extinction of species. Environmental problems are caused by emissions (e.g. carbon dioxide [CO_2], nitrous oxides [NO_x]) and direct human interventions (e.g. hunting). These causes, in turn, are the consequence of specific company activities.

Therefore, operationalisation is only possible if information is related to the main activities that influence corporate eco-efficiency. Such activities include the operation of production processes and the purchase, disposal and design of products.

In addition, environmental data have to be linked to responsibilities: that is, to the responsible persons and specified positions of those who can influence these activities. This requires that any information be tailored to the specific job and working environment in question as well as the capabilities of the employee responsible.

Finally, eco-efficiency-oriented information has to be customised to the interests of the addressees as new information systems cause costs for the providers as well as for the users of information. This means that the collection, analysis and communication of data should be directed to the requirements of important stakeholders in the best way possible. One consequence of this requirement is that it must be feasible to choose different levels of aggregation of eco-efficiency-oriented information (Box 3.2). As a general guide, highly aggregated information can be seen as being important to top management and shareholders, whereas lower-level management and employees require more disaggregated information.

The process of meeting all these requirements is not without cost. As environmental information will become relevant in a company only if the expected costs of its creation are lower than the potential benefits, the costs of managing eco-efficiency-oriented knowledge have to be kept as low as possible.

One way of reducing expected costs is to adapt existing information management practices and structures instead of building up entirely new systems. Adaptation of

Box 3.2 **Nature of information**

❝ A [divisional] manager's area of control is only a subdivision of the firm as a whole. Logically, therefore, the costs used in the review of a manager's performance should be a subdivision of those used to review the performance of the firm as a whole. The costs are not *different*; they represent simply a lower or a higher level of aggregation ❞ (Wells 1978: 23; emphasis original).

❝ A management control system is ordinarily built around a financial core, since money is the only common denominator for the heterogeneous elements of inputs and outputs. Operational control data are often non-monetary. They may be expressed in terms of man-hours, number of items, pounds of waste and so on. . . Data in an operational control system are in real time and relate to individual events, whereas data in a management control system are either prospective or retrospective and summarise many separate events ❞ (Anthony 1965: 78).

existing systems is one possible approach for incorporating environmental accounting recognised by Gray *et al.* (1993: 4). Incremental change to existing accounting systems is likely to be a low-cost option, and favoured by managers, provided that the relevance and reliability of information is improved. Other possibilities include the need to introduce new accounting and information systems as appropriate, or to supplement existing systems with relevant information—an approach commonly used in macro-environmental accounting (see Bartelmus and van Tongeren 1994).

Questions

1. Distinguish between syntactics, semantics and pragmatics. Are these perspectives independent of each other or are they interwoven?

2. What is the critical test for any accounting system? Does this test rely on syntactic, semantic or pragmatic perspectives?

3. Define the two main environmental objectives proposed for management of companies: sustainable development and eco-efficiency. Are these objectives related?

4. Is sustainable development a useful, practical perspective for business to adopt? If yes, how is it useful? Explain your view, giving reasons.

5. The efficiency ratio measures the relation between outputs from and inputs to a process. According to the WBCSD, a company wanting to become eco-efficient should strive to:

   ☐ Reduce the material intensity of its goods and services
   ☐ Reduce the energy intensity of its goods and services
   ☐ Reduce the dispersion of any toxic materials
   ☐ Enhance the recyclability of its materials
   ☐ Maximise the sustainable use of renewable resources
   ☐ Extend the durability of its products
   ☐ Increase the service intensity of its goods and services

   Suggest measures that could be used to indicate improved efficiency in each of these areas.

6. How do ecological product efficiency and ecological function efficiency differ? How are they measured? Are measures of these two types of ecological efficiency linked?

7. Is a 'win–win' situation the only practical way to move business towards sustainability?

8. What are the characteristics of data required to generate knowledge about corporate eco-efficiency?

Chapter 4

THE ENVIRONMENTAL
ACCOUNTING FRAMEWORK

4.1 The structural framework

4.1.1 Two categories of environmental accounting

This chapter examines the environmental accounting framework taking into consideration that the different, sometimes conflicting, goals of important stakeholders may be linked with two main groups of company-related environmental information:

☐ Environmentally induced financial impacts

☐ Physical environmental impacts

It is not a surprise that many different perceptions of and examples relating to 'environmental accounting' exist (Schaltegger and Stinson 1994; EPA 1995). According to the generally applicable 'Tinbergen rule' in economics and public policy, a tool is less efficient and effective once it is required to pursue different goals that are not absolutely complementary (Tinbergen 1956). It is possible that none of the goals would be achieved in an effective or efficient manner. The implication is that different tools are needed to deal with non-complementary issues. With respect to accounting, this is one reason why separate accounting systems may be needed to address different sets of issues of concern to stakeholders. Every accounting system can be designed to provide specific information for different groups of stakeholders.

Table 4.1 illustrates the most important stakeholder groups and related accounting categories and systems. Examples of various stakeholders are shown in the left-hand column. The main body of the table is divided into two different categories of accounting:

☐ Conventional accounting

☐ Ecological accounting

The areas shaded in light and dark grey in Table 4.1 illustrate that these accounting categories deal with environmental issues and therefore are part of environmental accounting. It can be seen that environmental accounting covers issues in conventional accounting (environmentally differentiated conventional accounting) as well as in ecological accounting.

Stakeholders (examples)	Conventional accounting			Ecological accounting		
	Management	*Financial*	*Other*	*Internal*	*External*	*Other*
Management	● ●	◐ ◐	◐ ◐	◐	◐	◐
Shareholders		● ◐			◐	
Tax agency		◐	● ◐			◐
Creditors		● ◐			◐	
Ecological rating agencies		◐ ●			●	
Environmental Protection Agency	◐	◐	◐	◐	●	◐
etc.	•••	•••	•••	•••	•••	•••

▮ Environmentally differentiated accounting (in monetary units)

▯ Ecological accounting (in physical units)

▮ + ▯ Environmental accounting (environmentally differentiated accounting + ecological accounting)

● (Historically) most important accounting system for communication, analysis, etc. with respective stakeholder

◐ Additional accounting system for communication, analysis, etc. with respective stakeholder

Table 4.1 **The framework of environmental accounting: accounting systems and measures**

Figure 4.1 illustrates the link between eco-efficiency (as a major condition for sustainability) and accountability as the major goals of environmental accounting and the accounting concepts that will be discussed in this book.

To measure eco-efficiency and the environmental dimensions of sustainability, two types of information are necessary: economic and environmental. Economic performance is illustrated in the upper branch of Figure 4.1 and environmental performance is shown in the lower branch. Different accounting systems have been developed relating to the specific type of economic or ecological information required and the particular target audience.

Sections 4.1.2 and 4.1.3 provide a short overview of the two branches of accounting: environmentally differentiated conventional accounting and ecological accounting, respectively.

4.1.2 Environmentally differentiated conventional accounting

The dark grey shaded areas in the conventional accounting category of Table 4.1 are the environmentally differentiated conventional accounting systems. Being part of conventional accounting, they measure the environmentally induced impacts on the company in

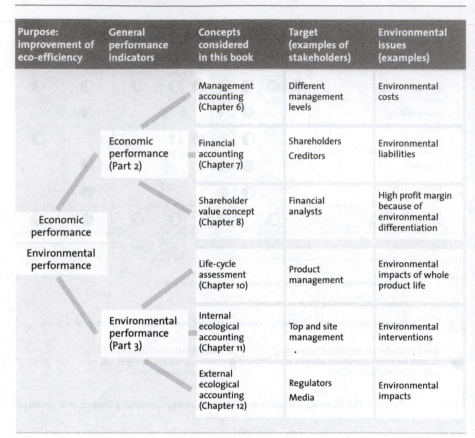

Purpose: improvement of eco-efficiency	General performance indicators	Concepts considered in this book	Target (examples of stakeholders)	Environmental issues (examples)
		Management accounting (Chapter 6)	Different management levels	Environmental costs
	Economic performance (Part 2)	Financial accounting (Chapter 7)	Shareholders Creditors	Environmental liabilities
Economic performance		Shareholder value concept (Chapter 8)	Financial analysts	High profit margin because of environmental differentiation
Environmental performance		Life-cycle assessment (Chapter 10)	Product management	Environmental impacts of whole product life
	Environmental performance (Part 3)	Internal ecological accounting (Chapter 11)	Top and site management	Environmental interventions
		External ecological accounting (Chapter 12)	Regulators Media	Environmental impacts

Figure 4.1 **Eco-efficiency, accountability and environmental accounting approaches**

monetary terms. The remainder of the conventional accounting category, which does not deal with environmental issues, is shown unshaded. Conventional accounting is further divided into three accounting systems:

☐ Management accounting

☐ Financial accounting

☐ Other accounting

4.1.2.1 Management accounting

Management accounting (also called managerial accounting or cost accounting) is the central tool and basis for most internal management decisions and is not usually directly available to external stakeholders (see Table 4.1). A management accounting system deals with questions such as:

☐ What are environmental costs and how should they be tracked and traced?

☐ How should environmentally induced costs be treated—should they be allocated to products or 'counted as overhead costs'?

☐ What are the environmental responsibilities of a management accountant?

4.1.2.2 Financial accounting

In addition to management accounting, financial accounting is typically designed to satisfy the information requirements of external stakeholders of firms with respect to financial impacts. Issues in financial accounting include:

☐ Should environmentally induced outlays be capitalised or expensed?

☐ What standards and guidelines exist concerning disclosure of (contingent) environmental liabilities, and what recommendations do they provide on how to treat these liabilities in accounting?

☐ What are environmental assets and how might they be measured?

☐ How should emission trading certificates be treated?

4.1.2.3 Other accounting

'Other conventional accounting systems' is a term used to cover several additional, specific accounting systems such as tax accounting and bank regulatory accounting. Tax accounting is mandatory for all regular businesses, as the government tax agencies require tax 'reports', and bank regulatory agencies, for example, have special accounting and reporting requirements. Each of these conventional accounting systems considers different aspects of how environmental issues influence organisations (see also Schaltegger and Stinson 1994). Tax accounting considers such issues as:

☐ The effect of subsidies on pollution abatement devices, possibilities and impacts

☐ How the costs for the remediation of landfills can be deducted from taxes

☐ The effects of accelerated depreciation on cleaner production technologies and the consequences of various environmental taxes (e.g. taxes on carbon dioxide [CO_2] emissions, sulphur emissions and on discharges of volatile organic compounds [VOCs])

Environmental issues related to other accounting systems include the question of insuring against contingent liabilities, and raising mortgages and bank credit.

4.1.3 Ecological accounting

As pointed out above, various internal and external stakeholders are interested in environmental issues. Therefore, to be useful, conventional accounting needs to incorporate the financial impacts of environmental issues and should also be extended to include a category of ecological accounting systems (shaded light grey in Table 4.1). A distinction between ecological and conventional accounting categories is necessary because:

○ From a material point of view, the focus of ecological accounting is very different from that of conventional accounting. The focus of ecological accounting is on environmental impacts whereas the focus of traditional accounting is on financial impacts.

○ Environmental and financial information are often derived from different sources.

○ Environmental information is often required for different purposes and by different stakeholders than is financial information.

○ Environmental information has different measures of quality and quantity (e.g. kilograms) from financial information.

The category of ecological accounting, which is shaded light grey in Table 4.1, measures the ecological impact a company has on the environment. Its measurements (unlike those of environmentally differentiated conventional accounting) are in physical terms (e.g. kilograms or joules). Ecological accounting can also be divided into three systems, corresponding to the structure of conventional accounting systems:

○ Internal ecological accounting

○ External ecological accounting

○ Other ecological accounting

4.1.3.1 Internal accounting

Internal ecological accounting systems are designed to collect information, expressed in terms of physical units, about ecological systems for internal use by management. Such information complements conventional management accounting systems. Methods of measuring the impact of a company's products and processes on the natural environment are a necessary foundation for good management decisions. Various ways of examining pollution discharges and damage to ecological capital have been developed over the past decade. Whether sophisticated or not, internal ecological accounting is a necessary precondition for any environmental management system.

4.1.3.2 External accounting

The counterpart of conventional financial accounting is external ecological accounting. Under external ecological accounting, data for external stakeholders interested in environmental issues—namely, for the general public, the media, shareholders, environmental funds, non-governmental organisations (NGOs) and pressure groups—are collected and disclosed. Over the past ten years hundreds of firms have published separate external environmental reports thereby providing a public stocktaking of their environmental impacts. Many of these reports are produced annually and contain extensive data on discharges of pollutants.

4.1.3.3 Other accounting

Other ecological accounting systems, which also measure data in physical units, provide a means for regulators to control compliance with regulations. Also, these accounting systems are necessary for computation of environmental taxes such as a CO_2 emission tax or a VOC discharge tax. Without information about discharge levels, environmental tax rates could not be multiplied by the volume of releases of pollutants to derive a figure for total taxes due. Apart from tax agencies and environmental protection agencies, which are primarily interested in specific information on discharges of specific pollutants, an increasing number of stakeholders such as banks and insurance companies require reliable information on the ecological impacts of companies as part of the risk assessment processes.

4.1.3.4 Summary

Table 4.1 shows how the information collected by these various environmental accounting systems has different values for different stakeholders. The most important accounting system for each stakeholder, historically, is marked by a solid black circle; additional systems designed for communication or analysis are indicated with a circle shaded half white and half black. Ecological accounting systems are relatively new and have only recently become important information tools for many stakeholders. Entries in Table 4.1 for ecological accounting systems therefore contain relatively few solid black circles. One exception is for government agencies in charge of environmental protection.

As environmentally differentiated conventional accounting systems and ecological accounting systems process information triggered by environmental issues, they constitute—when taken together—a company's environmental accounting system. The definition of environmental accounting used throughout this book is shown in Box 4.1. For other definitions and descriptions of environmental accounting, see Gray 1993: 6.

The fact that conventional and ecological accounting are recognised as two different accounting categories is no obstacle to their integration, as information from both accounting categories can be combined through separate analysis for use by managers and external stakeholders (see Part 4 of this book, on integration).

4.1.4 Towards the integration of economic and environmental information

This introductory discussion shows two developments converging on each other (Fig. 4.2). On the one hand, financially oriented stakeholders have begun to realise that some environmental information is relevant to their economic decisions. They have, therefore, started to adapt their main information management systems to include relevant environ-

Box 4.1 **Definition of environmental accounting**

ENVIRONMENTAL ACCOUNTING IS A SUBSET OF ACCOUNTING THAT DEALS WITH:
- ☐ Activities, methods and systems
- ☐ Recording, analysis and reporting
- ☐ Environmentally induced financial impacts and ecological impacts of a defined economic system (e.g. a firm, plant, region, nation, etc.)

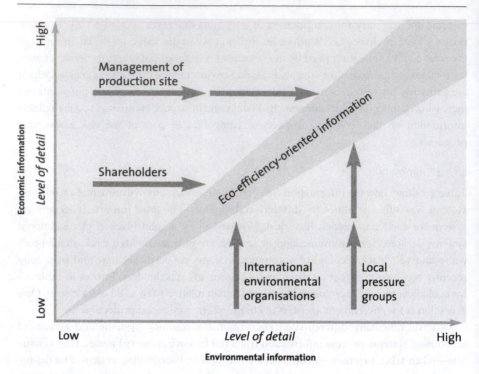

Figure 4.2 **Growing interest in eco-efficiency-oriented information**

mental issues. On the other hand, environmentally focused stakeholders have started to realise that some financial aspects of environmental issues (e.g. the cost of environmental protection) have a bearing on ecological issues. They are thus increasingly finding it necessary to deal with financial issues. As the interests of these previously often conflicting groups are converging, the integration of economic and environmental information and thus the management of eco-efficiency-oriented information is attracting more attention (see Fig. 4.2).

Depending on their specific interests, stakeholders focus on greater or lesser detailed economic and environmental information. Shareholders, for example, are traditionally mostly interested in aggregated financial information representing shareholder value or wealth. Shareholders have now started to consider general environmental information such as the financial relevance of environmental liabilities or the total amount of emissions that might be taxed in the near future (see e.g. Müller *et al.* 1994). International pressure groups such as Greenpeace are showing increasing interest in general economic aspects of companies such as the profitability of takeover candidates who are environmental laggards or the financial impacts of different pollution prevention approaches (see Greenpeace 1994; Leggett 1996).

A similar development can also be seen with the management of production sites and local pressure groups (given their local focus, local pressure groups are often referred to as 'NIMBYs' [NIMBY is an abbreviation of 'not in my back yard']), with the main difference being that these stakeholders use more disaggregated information (e.g. the costs and environmental impacts of specific production processes). As indicated by the expanding shaded area in the upper right-hand corner of Figure 4.2, the total number of possible eco-efficiency indicators grows with increasing specification of information.

In Part 2 of this book we examine the movement of company environmental accounting systems from the left to the middle and then to the right-hand side of Figure 4.2, through the consideration of environmental issues in the main financial information management systems and their influence on a company's economic performance. Following discussion of the management of environmentally induced economic information, Part 3 analyses the development of environmental information management systems and their economic consequences (movement from the bottom to the middle of Fig. 4.2).

4.2 Stakeholders influencing the agenda of environmental accounting

Because of the growing importance of environmental matters, issues of environmental accounting have attracted increasing attention in recent years. Many different interest groups are trying to influence environmental accounting methods and reporting practices. Therefore, emerging systems of environmental accounting have resulted from different group goals and perspectives as well as reflecting the relative power of critical stakeholders. Each group requires information to help with its decision-making or to provide a means of accountability where the group has a 'right to know' about corporate activities and impacts on the environment.

Table 4.2 gives an overview of important stakeholder groups influencing different systems of environmental accounting. Specifications and characteristics of published standards, regulations, guidelines and recommendations are discussed later in relevant chapters (especially Chapter 7) and sections.

Different environmental accounting systems are developed to provide information for important stakeholders and to help companies improve their environmental performance and thereby make progress on the path toward sustainable development.

Despite the lack of support from deep ecologists seeking 'strong' sustainability, quantitative measurement of impacts and the calculation of numbers that can be compared is, in the opinion of many business leaders and a large part of the scientific community, the only practical way to measure progress in the process of moving towards sustainable development and eco-efficiency (see Part 3 of this book). The comparison and aggregation of environmental impacts of various products, processes, firms, regions and nations is imperative, because the total amount of damage is what really matters from an environmental perspective. Nevertheless, quantitative accounting systems need to be supported by more qualitative assessments because not all environmental impacts can (or should) be counted. Supplementation of quantitative environmental accounting with qualitative measures will become inevitable as business and the various stakeholder groups

Stakeholder group	Type of accounting affected	Specifications for accounting	Characteristics
Regulatory bodies			
US Securities and Exchange Commission	Financial (Part 2, Chapter 5)	Very specific	Legally binding for firms listed on a US stock exchange
Department of Ecology (Washington, DC)	Management (Part 2, Chapter 4)	Very specific	Guideline accompanying a regulation
European Union (Eco-management and Audit Scheme and Eco-label)	Site, product or ecological (Parts 3 and 4)	General	Voluntary
Professional accounting and financial analysts' associations			
European Federation of Financial Analysts' Societies	Financial, external, ecological (Parts 2 and 3)	Specific	Statement and demand of financial analysts
UK Association of Chartered Certified Accountants	Financial (Part 2)	Specific	Environmental reporting awards
Australian Society of Certified Practising Accountants	Management (Part 2)	General	Environmental management
Fédération des Experts Comptables Européens	Financial (Part 2)	Specific	Framework for environmental reporting, guidelines for external ecological accounting and reporting
Society of Management Accountants of Canada	Management (Part 2)	Specific	Writing environmental reports
Canadian Institute of Chartered Accountants	Conventional (Part 2)	Specific and general	Statement of professional accountants
Accounting standardisation organisations			
International Accounting Standards Committee	Financial (Part 2, Chapter 5)	Specific	Topic has not been dealt with so far
US Financial Accounting Standards Board	Financial (Part 2, Chapter 5)	Very specific	Strong influence of US Securities and Exchange Commission
Other standardisation organisations			
British Standards Institution	Management, ecological (Parts 2–4)	General	Focus on environmental management systems
International Organization for Standardization	Management, ecological (Parts 2–4)	General	Focus on environmental management systems
Industry			
International Chamber of Commerce	General environmental (Part 1)	Very general	Starting point for environmental management
Minerals industry	Ecological (Part 3)	Specific	Voluntary code of environmental management
Chemical industry	General ecological (Part 3)	Very general	Starting point for environmental management, Responsible Care and voluntary codes of conduct

Table 4.2 **Principal stakeholder groups that have published standards, regulations, guidelines or recommendations affecting environmental accounting** *(continued opposite)*

Green organisations			
Coalition of Environmentally Responsible Economies/Global Reporting Initiative	External ecological (Part 3, Chapter 12)	Very general	Addresses environmental interests of potential investors; voluntary
SustainAbility	Environmental reporting (Part 3, Chapter 12)	Specific	Provides pro forma categories for assessing environmental reports
World Wide Fund for Nature	External ecological (Part 3, Chapter 9)	Specific	Addresses green stakeholders
Scientific Certification Systems	Product and external ecological (Part 3)	Specific	Addresses green customers

Other international organisations			
United Nations Environment Programme	General environmental (Part 1)	Specific intentions	Addresses corporations in UN countries
United Nations Centre for Trade and Development	External ecological (Part 3, Chapter 12)	General	Environmental performance indicators
United Nations Intergovernmental Working Group of Experts on International Standards of Accounting and Reporting	Financial, external ecological (Parts 2 and 3)	Specific	Guidelines for financial and ecological reporting
Tellus Institute	Management (Part 2)	Specific	Full-cost accounting; total-cost accounting; 'green' metrics
World Bank	Internal ecological (Part 3)	Specific to different sectors (e.g. mining)	Environmental assessment for scenario planning
World Resources Institute	Management, external ecological, (Parts 2 and 3)	General	Corporate environmental performance; environmental costs
World Business Council for Sustainable Development	Goal, management, ecological (Parts 1–3)	General	Eco-efficiency; shareholder value; environmental metrics
Organisation for Economic Co-operation and Development	Ecological (Part 3)	Very general	Addresses multinationals in OECD countries; eco-efficiency

Table 4.2 *(continued)*

progress towards a sustainable society (for the concept of sustainable society, see e.g. Karr 1993; and Part 3, Section 7.2).

Possible reasons for the development of environmental accounting include the need to measure environmentally induced financial impacts or the ecological damage done and the need to provide a means of developing closer relationships between organisations and society, by transferring the power of knowledge to society and increasing the transparency of organisations.

Type of accounting	Information collection and aggregation	Audit or Verification	Disclosure	Use of information
Management	Environmental costs are collected in a voluntary way to assist managers with decision-making and accountability.	Cost collection is for management purposes and may be verified by internal auditor.	External disclosure is voluntary.	Internal evaluation of profitability and communication
Financial	Company must estimate environmental liabilities and/or environmental assets.	External auditor considers impact of environmental liabilities for client, recognition, measurement and disclosure of natural capital.	Disclosure of certain environmental liabilities and assets is required in some countries.	Shareholder communication through financial reporting
Other (e.g. tax)	Company must determine amount of environmental taxes.	Tax authority can audit company to verify tax obligations.	Various environmental tax obligations must be disclosed and paid.	Evaluation of tax burden and communication with tax authority
Internal ecological	Emission and output monitoring	There are usually no assurance service requirements because collection of information is voluntary.	Typically carried out for internal purposes	Evaluation by managers
External ecological	Ecological impacts are classified and recorded.	Verifiers can verify records and accuracy of monitoring.	Records of monitoring must be disclosed to public in an aggregate or industry-based format.	Public and shareholder communication through voluntary ecological reporting
Other ecological	The basis for direct environmental taxes, emission allowances can be determined for regulatory bodies.	Regulator can verify records and monitoring accuracy.	Records of monitoring must be disclosed to appropriate regulator.	Communication with regulators through compliance audits and verification reports

Table 4.3 **Examples characterising environmental accounting systems**

Today's companies have to consider different, often conflicting, stakeholder interests. With increasing frequency, economically successful organisations in developed countries have to adapt themselves to new needs and demands and new external as well as internal stakeholders. Stakeholder groups and interests are in a constant state of flux. Table 4.3 illustrates some of the goals and characteristics of environmental accounting systems with examples of information collection and aggregation, audits and assurance services, disclosure requirements and the uses of information collected.

The need for additional environmental information is changing the structure and behaviour of organisations as they become more transparent. Requests for information by external stakeholders make internal organisational change (e.g. structures and responsibilities) necessary, because the required data have to be collected inside the organisation. However, it is important to note that information from environmental accounting on its own is insufficient for environmental management, and it has to be embedded into the larger context of environmental management. Only this ensures that the information gathered in the environmental accounting system is used efficiently, effectively and purposefully to improve the environmental performance of the company.

Questions

1. What is environmental accounting?

2. What are the main characteristics of the conventional accounting and ecological accounting categories? Why is the distinction necessary?

3. Explain the two major types of measure used in conventional accounting and ecological accounting. When consideration is given to environmental issues in accounting, what are the two main groups of information that stakeholders may be interested in? Provide examples.

4. What is the difference between management accounting and the other two types of conventional accounting—financial accounting and other accounting systems?

5. What is the difference between internal ecological accounting and the other two types of ecological accounting—external ecological accounting and other ecological accounting?

6. Provide one example of a question addressed by each of the three 'environmentally differentiated conventional accounting' systems. What distinguishes each of these examples from the questions addressed in 'conventional accounting' systems?

7. Link the following environmental transactions and events with the relevant environmental accounting system:

   ☐ A tax on emissions of carbon dioxide

   ☐ Capital expenditure on a water-recycling plant

☐ A 'per container' charge on the profits of managers who do not return empty chemical containers to a central storage area

☐ A tailings dam at a company mine is destroyed by an earthquake.

☐ Emissions of salt from a factory into a local river have increased.

☐ Managers plan to conserve biodiversity in the immediate surroundings of their factory site.

8. What is a stakeholder? Why are some stakeholders interested in comparing measures of corporate economic and ecological performance? Provide an example in which shareholders are the stakeholder group.

9. Do stakeholders influence environmental accounting systems? Do environmental accounting systems influence stakeholders? Provide an example to illustrate your argument.

Part 1

INTRODUCTION AND FRAMEWORK

2   The emergence of environmental accounting management
3   The purpose of managing environmental information
4   The environmental accounting framework

Part 2

ENVIRONMENTAL ISSUES IN CONVENTIONAL ACCOUNTING

5   Overview, criticism and advantages of conventional accounting
6   Environmental management accounting
7   Environmental issues in financial accounting and reporting
8   Environmental shareholder value and environmental issues in other accounting systems

Part 3

ECOLOGICAL ACCOUNTING

9   Overview and emergence of life-cycle assessment and ecological accounting
10 The efficiency of approaches to environmental information management
11 Internal ecological accounting
12 External ecological accounting and reporting of environmental impacts

Part 4

INTEGRATION

13 Integration with eco-efficiency indicators
14 Integrating eco-efficiency-oriented information management into the corporate environmental management system
15 Summary

Part 2

ENVIRONMENTAL ISSUES IN CONVENTIONAL ACCOUNTING

THE OVERALL INTENTION OF PART 2 IS TO DISCUSS ENVIRONMENTAL ISSUES IN the context of three main conventional accounting systems: management accounting, financial accounting and other accounting systems (e.g. tax). Conventional accounting information has been heavily criticised on the grounds that it helps contribute to environmental problems by providing distorted numbers as a basis for management and investment decisions. Details of these environmentally based criticisms directed at conventional accounting are summarised in Section 5.1. In spite of these criticisms, conventional accounting does possess some uncontested advantages. These are examined in Section 5.2.

Chapter 6 discusses environmental issues in management accounting. Today, every company faces environmentally induced financial impacts which are usually addressed through accounting. However, data on the economic effects of environmental issues have to date often been very poorly compiled by companies (see e.g. Bennett and James 1996; Williams and Phillips 1994), although, from a financial perspective, environmentally induced economic effects have, for management, been increasing in importance (see e.g. AAFEU 1994; Ditz *et al.* 1995; Fichter *et al.* 1997). This raises the question of why management has not put more emphasis on economic aspects of environmental issues. Based on a model related to the one used to explain the emergence of environmental information management (Section 2.3, Fig. 2.2), the introductory text of Chapter 6 discusses the monetary benefits from corporate environmental action and explains why this topic has not been given the attention it deserves. It also demonstrates the costs and opportunity costs of this neglect. Calculation of the opportunity cost of neglected environmental protection is undertaken later, through an example in Section 6.5.3. To support decision-making about environmental protection, financial impacts should be explicitly included, as separate items, in management and financial accounting. Section 6.1 provides details of the current approaches to environmental cost accounting, the main environmental issues of concern and the way they can be treated in management accounting. The main issues relate to tracking and tracing (Section 6.3) and allocation (Section 6.4) of environmental costs, and the incorporation of environmental considerations in investment appraisal (Section 6.5). Following specific examples, Chapter 6, on environmental management accounting, concludes with a discussion of the balanced scorecard as a more recent management information tool that is strongly linked to strategic management decision-making and future company development (Section 6.6).

Chapter 7 examines environmental issues in financial accounting. First, we present a discussion of the role of the main stakeholders that influence financial accounting (Section 7.1). Accounting standards are one of the main outputs from lobbying by stakeholder groups; hence a brief review of the underlying assumptions and conventions behind international standards of financial accounting and reporting is provided. With reference to this, and using international accounting standards as the basis for analysis, the subsequent sections examine major environmental issues in financial accounting. One important question is whether environmentally induced financial outlays should be capitalised or expensed (Section 7.2); another concerns whether and how the expenses (Section 7.3) and financial impacts on company assets (Section 7.4) should be treated and disclosed. In addition, there is discussion of the treatment of environmentally induced liabilities (liabilities induced by corporate environmental impacts), contingent liabilities (Section 7.5) and the special case of tradable emission allowances (Section 7.6). Finally, the influence of environmental issues on information reported in management's discussion and analysis (Section 7.7) is outlined.

Accounting figures show the economic impact of past environmental issues. To improve economic–environmental efficiency (termed eco-efficiency), any action has to be judged through its effects on a company's economic and environmental performance. Following a discussion of management accounting and financial reporting and their links with environmental issues, Chapter 8 specifically considers the kind of environmental management that is compatible with increases in shareholder value (SHV)—a means for assessing current and expected economic performance. The chapter opens by briefly considering the politics of accounting standard-setting, the dangers from introducing too many standards and the possible negative consequences for the quality of reported information of having too many standards (Section 8.1). Section 8.1 argues that a certain (low) number of accounting standards should not be exceeded because of the problems this creates; in particular, it argues that the value of information for the users of financial reports decreases as the number of standards increases beyond a specific point. The fact that there are now too many accounting standards distorts the information value of these standards for shareholders and is a possible explanation of why investors increasingly assess the value of companies on the basis of cash-flow data that are less influenced by financial accounting standards. The basic shareholder value method, its advantages and associated problems are then reviewed (Section 8.2). Finally, this leads to a discussion of how environmental management influences shareholder value (Section 8.3) and what kind of environmental management will help increase shareholder value (Section 8.4).

Chapter 5

OVERVIEW, CRITICISM AND ADVANTAGES OF CONVENTIONAL ACCOUNTING

5.1 Criticism and advantages of conventional accounting

5.1.1 Basis of criticism

Accounting systems are one of the most important management tools for every company. The function of accounting is to provide relevant, reliable and accurate information to guide the decisions of managers, investors and other stakeholders. Yet reality is so complex that this function often cannot be achieved at a reasonable cost. Hence, accounting systems are based on conventions about how to reflect something—a transaction, an internal transformation or an external event. In particular, the convention of using money and monetary calculation is among the greatest simplifiers of complex affairs (Chambers 1999: 122).

Although some conventions are necessary in order to manage complex reality, those used in conventional accounting have been heavily criticised. Some of the most extreme criticisms go so far as to maintain that all the conventions and the information collected by today's accounting systems mirror only what business and political leaders currently consider to be important for the economy and society, from their own perspective.

Conventions reflect the distribution of power between different stakeholders such as shareholders, managers, future generations and others (see Section 7.1). Since power relations between stakeholders are constantly changing, accounting systems, too, are generally under constant pressure to change, expand or adapt to provide the information that the most powerful stakeholders wish to be reported. As society changes, new information and new stakeholders also become important. This puts accounting systems under additional pressure to change. Consequently, pressure grows for economic activities to be reflected through other, more appropriate, conventions. Growing concern over company environmental impacts has generated criticisms of accounting conventions that are in general use. An environmental twist to conventional accounting provides the hallmark of a new aspect of stakeholder concern and involvement. The following sections point out the main criticisms made by stakeholders concerned about environmental aspects of company activities and also draw attention to other related criticisms of conventional accounting.

The last main section of this chapter concludes that in spite of criticisms aimed at conventional accounting the system has shown itself to be resilient and to provide a number of uncontested advantages that any future accounting system can build on.

5.1.2 Environmental criticism of conventional accounting

Historically, the first complex accounting systems evolved in the Renaissance period in the sixteenth century. One of the most extreme criticisms directed at accounting points to the influence of this historical period. The belief that humans are distinct from nature and, indeed, able to manage nature in a rational manner is still reflected in contemporary accounting practice. Although not immediately evident, this belief has led to some weaknesses in conventional accounting. In particular, the fundamental outlook of conventional accounting, with its focus on the accounting rather than on the ecological entity, has been criticised (see Maunders and Burritt 1991: 11; Wainman 1991).

The significance attached to events happening within an entity and the convention of ignoring events that take place outside an accounting entity lead to major problems when one tries to account for environmental damage. From a legal point of view, corporate environmental impacts often occur outside the transactional boundaries of a company, so that these environmental impacts are often treated as 'externalities' (Section 6.1.4). As they fall outside a company's legal boundary they have to be addressed by a company only in limited circumstances. Today, in general, accounting systems do not reflect environmental impacts caused directly or indirectly by a company. This situation will remain the same as long as organisations are treated as 'semi-closed systems with hard (legally based) accounting boundaries' (Maunders and Burritt 1991: 16). For example, if adverse environmental impacts occur because of the particular types of material used in production this is not directly shown in the company's accounts. Nevertheless, in some cases, customers may be able to sue the company or 'punish' it indirectly by not buying the company's products because of their adverse environmental impacts.

In other cases product or other potential liabilities will lead to internalisation of the costs of environmental impacts. Society also has other means for internalising environmental costs; for example through environmental taxes and regulation of pollution control devices. Yet it might take several years before some environmental impacts, for instance those flowing from products sold in the past, are recognised and the associated liabilities become material for a company, its suppliers or clients (see Box 5.1).

Conventional accounting systems do not provide information on how much the environment is harmed, no matter how high the social costs and no matter whether the damage is irreversible or whether carrying capacity is exceeded. If management relies only on conventional accounting information it will very often not even recognise that the environment has been harmed because:

☐ Natural and environmental resources are not included in balance sheets.

IN THE FOLLOWING TWO CASES ENVIRONMENTAL COSTS HAVE NOT BEEN reflected in the accounting systems of those who caused them, although many years later the negative financial consequences are internalised in the accounting systems of others (see also Section 3.1). The bulk of the consequences (financial and health effects) has not been paid for by the companies that caused the costs.

☐ In the 1960s the asbestos industry sold products that caused tremendous health damage in the 1980s and 1990s. Today, asbestos as a product has mostly been phased out, and insurance companies (which did not caused the damage) are having to foot the financial bill. The financial liabilities for pollution, illnesses such as asbestosis, clean-up liabilities and related claims have to be borne by the insurance industry (i.e. by today's premium payers). The claims are estimated to be US$2 trillion alone in the USA, of which US$11 billion is covered by reserves and provisions.

☐ The reinsurance industry faces a similar problem. It argues that it faces huge cash out-flows because of more frequent and severe storms that might be significantly correlated with the global warming effect. However, the insurance industry has never earned premiums to cover these costs.

Box 5.1 **Postponed internalisation of environmental externalities**
Source: Knight 1994: 48ff.

☐ Depreciation of natural capital is not internalised.

☐ Environmental damages are not considered, unless reflected in fines, penalties, licences and enforced clean-up costs.

Therefore, it has been argued that adverse effects on the environment can be seen—to a certain extent—as resulting from current accounting practices (see Maunders and Burritt 1991). Regardless of the accounting system in place, it will never be possible to reflect all environmental effects. At the time when the product is first developed or a new activity is initiated, it is impossible to estimate accurately every possible future risk.

Given that accounting has a dominant function in information systems, partly because it quantifies and simplifies a complex reality and partly because it can be used by businesses to downplay ecological impacts, adverse ecological impacts arise as a result of the use of conventional accounting information (Maunders and Burritt 1991: 12). Impacts of current accounting practices can be divided into two categories:

☐ **Direct effects on the environment.** As accounting information is used for decision-making both by internal and by external stakeholders, comprehensive information, as correct and as complete as possible, becomes crucial. Decision-making and evaluation of activities that have an environmental impact must rely on accounting information that often conforms to generally accepted accounting standards that are based on the conventions of financial accounting. Exclusion of externalities in these forms of accounting results in misleading accounting information being used by managers for financial and strategic decision-making. In short, internal costs appear too low because some costs are passed on to external parties and are not included in decision-making. As a result, managers favour products and processes with the lowest internal costs—not the ones with the lowest total costs to society, as represented by internal and external costs combined.

☐ **Indirect effects on the environment.** Indirect effects of conventional account-ing on the environment are connected with the mental framework unconsciously used when viewing the world. Conventional accounting, for example, although measuring income and financial wealth, does not question their distribution. Instead it accepts existing interpersonal, interregional and intergenerational distribution regardless of their moral or ethical flaws. For example, conventional accounting systems do not show who received the money spent by a company (interpersonal distribution), nor do they show the region in which company suppliers are situated (interregional distribution) or whether money is spent with the needs of future generations in mind (intergenerational distribution).

A further criticism points out the inherent discrepancy between conventional account-ing systems and natural ecosystems. For accounting, no upper limit to financial resources exists—the word 'enough' is never translated into numbers—whereas the natural environ-ment has such a limit reflected in the notion of 'carrying capacity'. From a macro-economic perspective this argument has been used as a criticism of the concept of gross national product (GNP) as a measure of wealth and the related constant striving for higher GNP (Gray 1992; Lutz and Munasinghe 1991). Environmental damage is not considered in this quest for higher monetary income and wealth, because no value is put on most ('priceless') environmental goods. The same critics also see it as undesirable to give environmental goods an artificial price (Hines 1991). Nature reacts according to com-pletely different laws than those assumed under the rules set down for conventional accounting systems; it is based on the interconnectedness and interaction of all substances and beings. Accounting systems, on the other hand, divide, separate and count everything independently. They use special accounts for every accounting item and finally aggregate many different items together in a standardised format such as a balance sheet, an income statement or a cash flow statement in ways that just do not add up even though the figures are relied on by managers and stakeholders (Chambers 1966).

The interdependence of time is also ignored in most conventional accounting systems. For example, outlays that are expected to produce future ecological benefits (e.g. pollution abatement expenditures) reflect negatively on current economic performance if the expenditures are considered to be expenses.

These procedures are not only seen to contribute to the problems alluded to above but also cause problems for financial analyses of companies, products, investments and production processes (Chapter 7).

Maunders and Burritt summarise their criticism of conventional accounting in the following way: 'By providing the only quantified analysis available, it is not decision support which is provided [by conventional accounting], but rather conditioning' (1991: 13). Conditioning that facilitates further exploitation and plundering of ecological systems is neither sustainable nor acceptable for the business of the future. Likewise, accounting systems that facilitate that conditioning must be changed.

5.1.3 Other criticism of conventional accounting

Criticism of conventional accounting is not limited to environmental argumentation. For several decades there has been a passionate discussion about the shortcomings of conventional accounting. Shortcomings are underlined by the long and continuing debate about how to calculate the relevant income figure, how income figures need to be adjusted for capital maintenance and what the correct earnings per share might be. Such discussion is dealt with extensively in the literature and is therefore not repeated here. See, for example, Chambers 1966, Johnson and Kaplan 1987a or Rappaport 1986 and 1998. One criticism has for instance resulted in the development of the concept of the 'shareholder value' which is based on free cash flows. The shareholder value concept still uses the financial information collected. However, the fundamental idea is that the value of a company should not be based on a multiple of its earnings but on its financially quantified strategic value. Free cash flows concentrate strictly on real cash inflows and outflows as a consequence of a company's strategy which leads to investment activities and future returns.

In former times management was dedicated to maintaining liquidity. When it was recognised that liquidity today does not necessarily lead to liquidity tomorrow, new indicators were created. The result is countless books on accounting, and many different accounting standards and conventions. For further discussion see Rappaport 1986 and 1998.

Some particular aspects of the general criticisms of conventional accounting are brought into focus through discussion of environmental accounting. First, conventional accounting has become too complex in its dealing with a complex world. Simon's theory of bounded rationality recognised that one mind cannot grasp more than a limited number of objects or phenomena at a given time, especially when solving a problem or making a choice (Simon 1957: 218). Conventional accounting should address the need for making a choice between serviceable and useless information requirements, thereby restoring a simplified focus on 'a common mode of calculation for prudent administration, the economical conduct of affairs, the pursuit of gain and the avoidance of financial disaster' (Chambers 1999: 123). Such simplification would facilitate the integration of relevant financial and biophysical data in decision-making rather than trying to add a complex veneer of biophysical data to an already overly complex set of financial data.

Second, output from double-entry book-keeping represents that borrowing should be shown as a debt on the liabilities side of a balance sheet and at the same time as cash on the assets side. It can be argued that this procedure enables companies and individuals to live beyond their means or, in other words, at the expense of the natural environment and future generations. A company that wishes to expand despite having an insufficient operating cash inflow can finance its debt as long as contracted debt ratios and rules are met. However, these additional financial resources lead to an increase in activity and sales and thus (in most cases) to an additional use of natural resources and to higher emissions. Consequently, fewer resources would have been used if debt financing had not been allowed. However, it is important to recognise that one of the main functions of debt financing is to bridge time differences between savers and investors and thus to contribute materially to the wealth accumulated by many nations and individuals.

Feminist criticism takes a slightly different view (see e.g. Cooper 1992a, 1992b; Gallhofer 1992). Accounting is seen to be a predominantly masculine (not necessarily male) discipline, used to control and suppress others. Conventional accounting lacks the strengths of the feminine way of dealing with life, such as non-competitiveness and giving (Cooper 1992a, 1992b). The masculine way of thinking, which stresses the utility-maximising goal of the unified, rational and self-centred being, has been blamed for the environmental destruction we witness today (Cooper 1992a: 27). One solution has been to propose the creation of a feminine libidinal economy, where feminine qualities, for example plurality, caring and harmony, flourish. Cooper summarises the feminine perspective in the following way (1992a: 37):

> we could perhaps imagine an accounting which is multiple, no debits or credits; which allows for many differences, these could not be added, therefore there would be no totals; it would not be concerned with profits, and even less afraid of loss; it would be concerned with gifts, what was given; it would contain no phallocentric economic terms; and it would not be competitive.

With the exception of Chambers, most points of critique detract from the actual function and use made of accounting. To overcome the environmental problems companies and society face today, practical concepts for actual improvement are necessary. In order to build a system of environmental accounting that addresses the need for simplicity, decision-relevant information, accountability and equity between masculine and feminine views, between minorities and majorities and between present and future generations, this book focuses on concepts that build on the strengths of accounting.

Nevertheless, the critique and shortcomings of conventional accounting systems and the information produced can motivate stakeholders to a variety of reactions.

5.1.4 Stakeholder reactions

In principle, three possible reactions exist whenever stakeholders do not agree with the present situation (Hirschman 1970):

☐ **Resignation and loyalty.** Stakeholders can accept (or ignore) the deficiencies of conventional accounting and 'indulge in the sweet side of life'. With this reaction, no improvements are possible as no energy is expended on changing the current situation.

☐ **Voice.** As already discussed, academics, professional accountants and managers have drawn attention to the weaknesses of conventional accounting for many years. Even at annual company meetings shareholders have raised environmental issues having an impact on business. Many suggestions have led to changes in existing practices and systems and have contributed to a gradual improvement in accounting practice. 'Voice' requires initiatives of important stakeholders and the readiness of all involved parties to contribute in a constructive way towards solving existing problems—something also championed by the feminist perspective.

☐ **Exit.** Investors and creditors can withdraw their financial resources whenever they do not appreciate a company's accounting practices. In practice, this would lead to a reduction in demand for the shares of a company and a reduction in its share price. Investors that are concerned to make 'ethical investments' will effectively withdraw their funds from companies that do not come up to expectation. With ethical investment, exit is caused by company activities that do not comply with the environmental expectations of the shareholder. Ethical investment is a small, but rapidly growing, sector of the global investment market (Cummings and Burritt 1999; Knörzer 1995; Schaltegger and Figge 1999). In addition, there are in existence different models and groups that represent an escape to a separate social and/or economic system (colony model) with different conventions of accounting. One way to exit the existing economic system is, for example, to live in a remote area. Another way is to establish 'colony currency and accounting models'. These models often work with negative interest rates to prevent people from striving for growth and to give incentives not to hoard money but to put it into circulation. For example, the *Wirtschaftsring* (economic circle) system in Europe is based on a special currency (called WIR). This currency is used only between traders and retailers. It has a different interest structure from market rates. Loans are credited with only very low interest rates. Mortgages can be raised with substantially lower than market interest rates. Other exponents of this colony model propose charging interest for debits (e.g. the Taler Community focus on a separate closed system of payments; see also e.g. Binswanger 1991; Binswanger and von Flotow 1994; Kircher 1994; Lauener 1994).

As we move into a new millennium it is becoming clear that many environmental problems are too severe to be neglected and too global in nature to allow a successful escape. Hence, loyalty and resignation to existing accounting systems are unlikely to be acceptable. Changes to existing systems, either incrementally or radically, will depend on the exercise of voice. It has been argued above that, in practice, incremental change is more likely to be feasible than radical change because:

☐ There are high costs associated with radical change to accounting systems.

☐ Many critiques of existing systems do not specify their preferred alternatives to those existing systems.

Finally, 'exit', encouraged by the discriminatory use of regulatory systems by government to favour 'good' performers, and through growing stakeholder awareness of the need to avoid environmental problems, might also provide an incentive for a 'green' change to conventional accounting systems. In practice, such change, whether caused by voice, exit or a combination of both, will build on existing strengths of conventional accounting systems and try to eliminate their weaknesses rather than destroy all conventional accounting systems and replacing them with *de novo* systems.

5.1.5   Uncontested advantages of conventional accounting

Given these relevant criticisms of conventional accounting, it must nevertheless be acknowledged that existing accounting systems offer certain uncontested advantages for all stakeholders:

☐ Over time, accounting systems provide systematic sets of financial information about a company to stakeholders. Internal and external stakeholders need information systems that reduce the complexity of the world to help them make decisions in conditions of bounded rationality. In this connection, quantification can be seen as a widely accepted way to add precision to reasoning about the world but, more importantly, quantification permits a basis for comparing alternative courses of action. Of course, quantification cannot deal with issues of morality, beauty and love, but it is a powerful instrument when a society seeks to examine alternatives available to overcome poverty, fiscal deficits or environmental degradation. The accepted rules of today's conventional accounting systems are used by businesses throughout the industrialised world.

☐ Conventional accounting systems purport to represent to outsiders an organisation's financial position at a stated date and changes in its financial position over a specified period of time, given a set of transactions, physical transformations and external events. In particular, conventional accrual accounting systems recognise, measure, disclose and facilitate management of assets and liabilities. The challenge for environmental accounting is to incorporate into the accounting process and associated statements the financial aspects of company activities that have an impact on the environment.

☐ The accountancy profession is represented throughout the world and any changes in accounting practice have the potential to produce a flow-on effect to all countries. Accounting can therefore be regarded as one of the most international 'languages' spoken by many different stakeholders worldwide. This is reflected in the growing economic importance of the accountancy profession. The importance and influence of the accountancy profession is reflected by its size. For example, in 1994 the 'big six' accountancy firms employed more than 400,000 people and achieved a turnover of approximately US$30 billion.

The message is that existing accounting systems need to be substantially improved rather than completely eliminated. Similarly, the business form and business activities remain to be worked with, to be improved, rather than entirely destroyed because they have an impact on the environment.

Conventional accounting systems reflect the human trait of accumulating fortune, wealth and power measurable in monetary terms. No accountant would suggest that changes to conventional accounting systems are sufficient to solve the enormous environmental problems of today and the future. Nonetheless, accounting is a necessary and important part of a pragmatic approach to the recognition and resolution of environmental problems by business. Of course, necessary incremental changes in accounting practices will redefine and enforce new power relationships between stakeholders in an organisation.

Among the main benefits to be derived from adjusting conventional accounting for environmental issues are:

☐ The provision of base information for considering the actual and potential economic consequences of environmental issues

☐ Provision of information that can facilitate adaptation by business in the face of imposition of new environmental regulations, and new economic instruments designed to influence environmental outcomes

☐ Facilitation of a management philosophy designed to make transparent and encourage economically advantageous measures of environmental protection

☐ Improved responsiveness to environmental issues raised by stakeholders

Given these strengths, criticisms and potentialities of accounting, the following questions remain:

☐ How can conventional accounting systems be changed so that they effectively reflect environmentally induced financial impacts (Part 2)?

☐ How can conventional accounting systems be extended so that they consider, in an effective and efficient way, impacts of company activities on the natural environment (Part 3)?

The first of these questions is dealt with in the following chapters of Part 2. First, an overview of conventional accounting systems is provided. Then, ways that environmental issues influence conventional management, financial and other accounting systems are illustrated.

5.2 Accounting for environmentally induced financial impacts

Business managers and other stakeholders look to conventional accounting to help provide relevant information about the growing economic consequences of environmental opportunities and environmental costs, such as those related to measures to prevent pollution (see also Chapter 2).

Only with relevant information can managers, shareholders and creditors consider the actual and potential economic consequences of environmental issues, adapt to the economic effects of new environmental regulations and have a mutually fruitful discussion with stakeholders about how best to implement pollution prevention (e.g. to reduce greenhouse gas emissions) and how to address opportunities linked with rising demand for clean products and processes (e.g. how electricity companies should respond to imposition of a government policy and signals for the future that by a set date 2% of electricity supply must be sourced from renewable sources).

Conventional accounting that incorporates environmentally induced financial information is called environmentally differentiated conventional accounting (see also Part 1, Chapter 4). It brings together environmental issues in management accounting, financial accounting and in other accounting systems (see Fig. 5.1).

Ideally, all impacts, including those borne by society and the natural environment, would be included in conventional accounting systems. In practice, as only a few externalities are internalised, either voluntarily or through direct and indirect regulation, strategic management decisions may be based on incomplete information that, from a societal perspective, may be economically misleading (e.g. when external costs are internalised following a lag in policy).

However, it would be even more misleading if management internalised externalities in its conventional accounting when they were not part of the actual economic effects on a business. Conventional accounting is an information system designed to measure the past economic performance of a company (i.e. the economic profitability, liquidity and solvency—in short, a cluster of financial circumstances of relevance to stakeholders). Mixing external and internal financial transactions (i.e. external and internal costs) in the accounts of a business would distort the actual figures so that they would lose their relevance for economic decision-making and accountability purposes. Some external events do have an impact on business. For example, inflation reduces the purchasing power of a company's capital over time and so adjustments need to be made to the capital base to reflect this situation. However, conventional accounting has not been very adept at addressing the impact of these external events in the accounts. Indeed, the accountancy profession's performance with inflation accounting has been inconsistent and slow, in spite of considerable 'voice' being expressed over a 70-year period, even though the usefulness of 'real' (inflation-adjusted) economic figures for analysis is unchallenged.

Environmental management accounting deals with environmentally induced costs, revenues and, where appropriate, asset values (e.g. for defining a controllable capital base in an investment centre). Environmentally induced costs will be examined in detail in

Figure 5.1 **Environmentally differentiated conventional accounting**

Environmentally differentiated conventional accounting

Environmentally induced financial impacts

| Environmental issues in management accounting | Environmental issues in financial accounting | Environmental issues in other accounting systems |

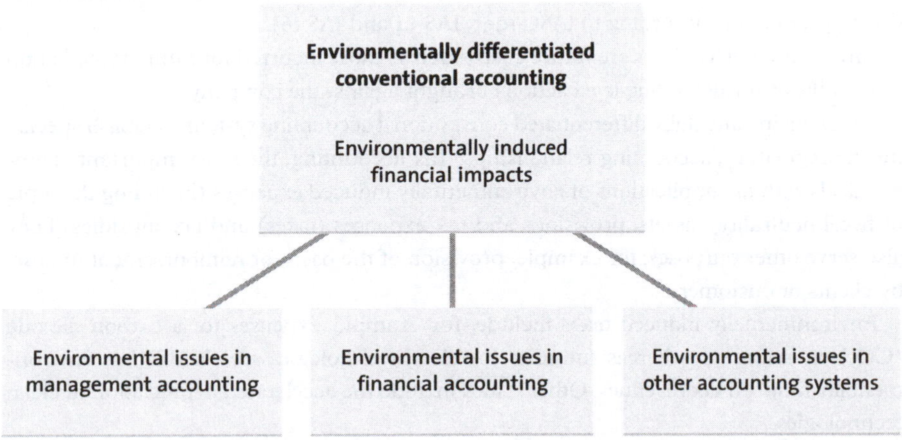

Section 6.1. Environmentally induced costs can be increased or reduced through efforts to achieve environmental protection. Typical financial costs related to environmental issues include: increased costs of environmentally benign raw materials; regulatory costs such as fines, fees and clean-up costs; and the increased production of waste. On the other hand, savings might be achieved through the better use of resources, a decrease in waste and fewer fines and licence fees.

Environmentally induced benefits or revenues can be divided into direct and indirect benefits or revenues. Direct revenues, for example, include the gains from sales of 'recyclables' (recyclable items), increased sales volumes of consumer products and higher prices of the products sold, sales of environmentally benign technology and even gains from trading in pollution credits (e.g. sale of sulphur dioxide credits, related to air quality, or sale of salt credits, related to water quality). Indirect effects are intangible and can, for example, include an enhanced image, increased customer and employee satisfaction, the transfer of know-how (intellectual capital) and the development of new markets for environmentally benign products.

Environmentally induced assets are not frequently recognised as important in management accounting but, in practice, expenditure on assets forms a critical part of investment appraisal systems, and asset bases can also be treated as part of the financial responsibility of divisional managers in larger companies. To the extent that asset bases could include natural capital, environmental management accounting needs to take assets into account.

Environmental financial accounting deals with revenues and expenses (shown in a periodic income statement, also called a profit-and-loss account) and with assets and liabilities (shown in a dated balance sheet).

Under the historical cost convention, costs are classified as expenses if they have provided a benefit that has now expired. Unexpired costs that can give future benefits are defined as assets, whereas property rights of creditors are classified as liabilities. Liabilities that can only be estimated are commonly called 'provisions'. If their occurrence is uncertain, liabilities are disclosed as 'contingent liabilities' (also called 'potential liabilities').

Environmentally induced expenses include, for instance, fines for illegal waste disposal, or clean-up costs required to restore land. For example, a scrubber can be recognised as an environmentally induced asset if it secures future economic benefits (through continued production, according to IASC 1995, IAS 14 and IAS 16).

Environmental liabilities are future costs, such as those incurred for future remediation of landfills or for defending legal actions brought against the company.

Other environmentally differentiated conventional accounting systems establish special, mostly regulatory, accounting relationships. Tax accounting, the most important example, deals with tax implications of environmentally induced expenses (including the topic of fiscal neutrality), assets, provisions and tax expenses (taxes) and tax subsidies. They also serve other purposes: for example, provision of the basis for reimbursement of costs by clients or customers.

Environmentally induced taxes include, for example, expenses for a carbon dioxide (CO_2) emission tax, whereas subsidies for clean technologies are classified as environmentally induced tax revenues. Other issues include the accelerated depreciation of clean technologies.

Information collected through environmental management accounting systems is often communicated to external stakeholders through financial accounting. Likewise, other environmental accounting systems derive most of their information from management accounting systems. Consequently, the next chapter examines environmental management accounting.

Questions

1. Chambers (1999) argues that money and monetary calculation are among the greatest simplifiers of complex affairs. What advantages does the use of a money measure of activity have for decision-makers?

2. According to Rubenstein (1994: 3):

> For the first time in accounting's sleepy history, there is a growing recognition among accountants and nonaccountants alike that accounting, the value-free, balanced system of double entries, may be sending dangerously incomplete signals to business, to consumers, to regulators, and to bankers.

   How does environmental accounting attempt to address the issue raised by Rubenstein that conventional accounting communicates incomplete signals?

3. Discuss the following issues relating to criticism of conventional accounting.
   - ☐ Conventional accounting uses the accrual convention. What is the accrual convention? What is the main benefit of accrual accounting? How might accrual accounting help with the management of environmental issues?
   - ☐ Explain the three main environmental criticisms of the conventions behind conventional accounting.
   - ☐ How might externalities be internalised?
   - ☐ Comment on the view that conventional accounting practices can have an adverse effect on the environment.
   - ☐ Is it true that conventional accounting knows the concept of more but that it does not know the concept of enough? Explain.
   - ☐ Can accounting conventions be changed to recognise the concept of enough?

4. What is the concept of 'bounded rationality'? How might the concept be used to help distinguish between the provision of serviceable and unserviceable accounting information in environmental accounting?

5. Reactions of stakeholders who do not feel that accounting provides serviceable information include: resignation and loyalty; voice; and exit.
   - ☐ Why are exit and voice of particular importance as strategies to support the development of environmental accounting?

☐ From a business perspective, is incremental or radical change to conventional accounting systems, because of environmentally induced effects, most likely to be feasible? Give reasons for your answer. Would your answer be different if you were an environmentalist concerned about global warming or a regulatory agency responsible for encouraging sustainable development?

6. Conventional accounting systems are said to have some 'uncontested advantages' over the absence of accounting systems. What are these 'uncontested advantages'?

7. Conventional accounting provides information about a 'cluster of financial circumstances' that are of concern to all stakeholders. What are these circumstances?

8. Is there a 'cluster of physical ecological circumstances' that can be identified as relevant to all stakeholders? List and relate them to the respective stakeholders.

Chapter 6

ENVIRONMENTAL
MANAGEMENT ACCOUNTING

This chapter will discuss environmentally induced financial impacts on a company's management accounting system. Management accounting 'is the identification, measurement, accumulation, analysis, preparation, interpretation, and communication of information that assists executives in fulfilling organisational objectives' (Horngren and Foster 1987: 2). Management accounting 'measures and reports financial and nonfinancial information that helps managers make decisions to fulfil the goals of an organisation. Management accounting focuses on internal reporting' (Horngren *et al.* 2000: 2). Synonyms for management accounting are 'managerial accounting' and 'cost management' (Garrison and Noreen 2000; Hansen and Mowen 2000).

The International Federation of Accountants (IFAC 1998: paragraph 1) defines environmental management accounting as follows:

> Environmental Management Accounting—the management of environmental and economic performance through the development and implementation of appropriate environment-related accounting systems and practices. While this may include reporting and auditing in some companies, environmental management accounting typically involves life-cycle costing, full-cost accounting, benefits assessment, and strategic planning for environmental management.

From these definitions it can be seen that IFAC, following definitions of management accounting such as that of Horngren *et al.*, makes no analytical distinction between financial and non-financial aspects of environmental management accounting. Bennett and James (1998a), in line with IFAC terminology, call these two aspects 'environment-related management accounting'. However, in this book, environmental management accounting is defined in a narrower sense to include only the environmentally induced financial aspects of accounting that help managers to make decisions and be accountable for the outcome of their decisions. Information about non-financial environmental impacts for decision-making and accountability are distinguished separately in an accounting system that is here called 'internal ecological accounting'. Internal ecological accounting is examined in Chapter 11. Environmental management accounting and internal ecological accounting are brought together in discussions about eco-efficiency.

Management accounting is one of the most important information tools used by managers. First, it supports strategic and operational planning, defined as the delineation of goals, prediction of potential results under various scenarios and implementation of ways of achieving goals. For example, given the broad objective of moving towards an ecologically sustainable business, a number of scenarios are possible (e.g. environmental crises intensify or ease). An appropriate goal might be to improve corporate eco-efficiency. This could be implemented through the introduction of a system that enables measures of economic and environmental progress towards eco-efficiency.

Second, management accounting provides the main basis for decisions about how to attain desired, or target, goals. If a goal is to reduce waste from raw material usage by 10% in a year, it is the management accounting system that provides information about targets, actual waste from raw material usage and a comparison of the two.

Third, management accounting facilitates feedback about results and acts as a control device. When a gap has been calculated between a goal and the actual level of achievement, a management accounting system provides reports about this gap to people responsible for the gap. With such information people responsible for the gap can take action to try to ensure that goals and actual performance are closer together in the next planning and control cycle (see e.g. Garrison and Noreen 2000: 5; Hansen and Mowen 2000: 268; Horngren et al. 2000: 4; Raiborn et al. 1996). These people are held accountable for their actions.

Through its essential function, management accounting provides relevant information to facilitate the most economic way of managing a company. As environmental issues begin to exercise increasing influence on corporate economic performance and, therefore, on corporate eco-efficiency, they need to be institutionalised in management accounting systems.

Ideally, management accounting provides the foundation for all other accounting systems (e.g. financial accounting), financial management (e.g. the shareholder value concept) and communication with external stakeholders (e.g. financial reporting). For this reason, it is logical for management accounting to be examined first, followed by financial accounting and a discussion of the shareholder value concept.

The basic need for environmental issues to be incorporated in conventional management accounting is to ensure that there is an accounting for the financial impacts of environmentally induced activities, such as environmental protection and investment in cleaner production processes. Management accounting information is used mainly to facilitate decision-making by and accountability of different types of company managers and support staff responsible for products, sites and divisions. Contrary to the regulated foundations of conventional financial and 'other' accounting (Chapter 8), management accounting is largely a voluntary activity and is not undertaken to satisfy the requirements of external stakeholders. Only on the basis of relevant and reliable information management will managers and employees be able to: assess the actual and potential economic consequences of environmental issues, adapt technical and financial performance to new environmental regulations and conduct a mutually beneficial discussion of how to implement best practice in pollution prevention.

Only when rules have to be established for cost reimbursement from customers can a required form of management accounting be institutionalised. For example, in the USA, cost accounting standards have been introduced for cost reimbursement when a private organisation provides unique services to government organisations on a cost reimbursement basis. Hence, there is a need to recognise that 'other' conventional accounting systems exist and are linked to management accounting.

In an ideal world, all impacts, including those borne by society and the natural environment, would be included in a management accounting system. In practice, business managers are not appointed with the specific task of voluntarily incorporating the cost of negative externalities in the financial management plans of their organisations. As only a small part of externalities are internalised, strategic decisions taken by managers will be based on incomplete information and this will be misleading and could lead to a misallocation of resources to activities that have been undercosted from a perspective based on social cost (Kreuze and Newell 1994).

However, the difficulty is that it would be even more misleading for stakeholders if management internalised externalities in its accounting if they were not part of the actual financial effects of a business. A mixture of external and internal financial impacts (i.e. external and internal costs) in the same accounts would distort the financial results so that stakeholders would no longer have the necessary information for making economic decisions about the accounting entity.

The first step for managers is to establish what environmentally induced (already internalised) financial impacts it actually incurs (Ditz *et al.* 1995). Hence, initially, management accounting considers only internally relevant financial effects that have an impact on the company as a separate legal entity. Whether a company then decides to internalise any further environmentally induced costs is a question related to its competitive strategy.

Management accounting is not a uniform accounting system as it has to serve various management levels and functions that require different data. The information gathered in management accounting can be divided into accounting for products and product lines, sites, divisions and for the whole company. Product, site, divisional and top managers typically require different information from an accounting system (Fig. 6.1).

Product managers, for example, are interested in environmental product liabilities, site managers in issues such as site-specific clean-up costs and divisional and top-level managers in aggregated information about environmentally induced financial impacts.

Conflict may exist between the wishes of these different types of manager to include financial impacts of environmental issues. For example, imposition of an environmental tax will lead to poorer financial results. If these results are used as the basis for evaluating a product manager's performance the imposition of such a tax will be resisted. In general, Stinson (1993) observes that product margins rarely rise at the same rate as imposed taxes, and as a result the performance of managers appears to worsen. In these circumstances, product managers have an incentive to fight a direct allocation of environmental taxes to 'dirty' products (Burritt 1998). However, the inclusion of environmental taxes within the general overhead cost category is not an acceptable solution to this problem from an eco-efficiency perspective. The true costs of the products would no longer be reflected by the accounting figures, leading to less than optimal management decisions (Kreuze and Newell 1994).

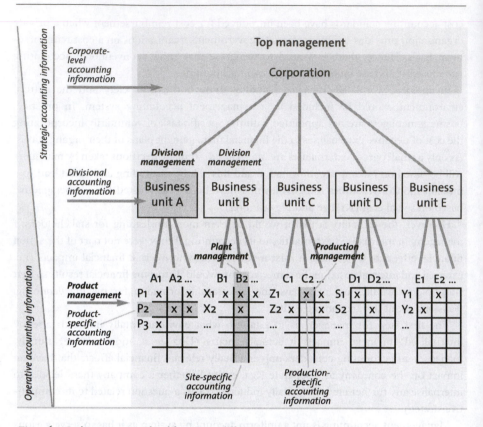

Figure 6.1 **Each management level focuses on different accounting information**

All levels of management accounting have the following concerns in common:

☐ The definition of environmental benefits, costs and opportunity costs

☐ Tracking and tracing of environmental costs

☐ Allocation of costs to products and activities

☐ Investment appraisal

These concerns are equally as relevant for management accounting and ecological accounting (Part 3) although their importance varies depending on the level of management involved (product, site, division or whole company). Each concern is addressed below.

6.1 Consideration of benefits and costs with regard to sustainable development and eco-efficiency

6.1.1 Cost and benefit links between sustainability dimensions

Sustainable development has three dimensions—economic, environmental and social. These three dimensions of sustainable development may interact to produce positive impacts (benefits) or negative impacts (costs), as shown in Figure 6.2. Hence, the following possible interrelationships may occur:

a   Economic activities can cause social impacts (e.g. social integration at the workplace; isolation of workers).

b   Social impacts can lead to economic benefits and costs (e.g. good working morale improves economic performance; health costs and loss of jobs reduce economic performance).

c   Social opportunities and problems can accompany environmental impacts (e.g. people develop an intrinsic motivation for nature conservation; deforestation occurs because of poverty).

d   Environmental issues can induce social benefits and costs (e.g. good environmental quality can cause migration; deforestation can cause migration).

e   Economic activities can have environmental impacts (e.g. as a result of the development of technology to improve water quality; increases in air pollution from factory waste).

Figure 6.2 **Relations between benefits and costs for the economy, society and the natural environment**

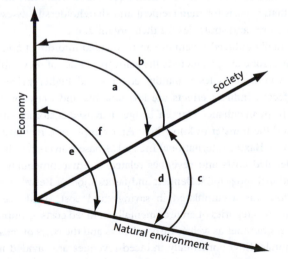

For definitions of a–f, see Section 6.1.1.

    f   Environmental impacts can result in economic impacts (e.g. natural attractiveness supports eco-tourism; toxic waste spills lead to clean-up costs).

In reality, environmental, economic and social dimensions are interrelated. Strong sustainable development is characterised by an improvement in all three dimensions (see also Part 1). However, this book focuses only on environmental issues from an environment–economy perspective. Arrows (e) and (f) in Figure 6.2 show eco-efficiency links.

The best way to improve eco-efficiency is to reduce harmful environmental impacts while at the same time keeping constant or increasing profitability (economically profitable environmental protection), for example by developing and selling more environmentally benign technologies—a proactive approach to environmental management. An alternative approach with the same result but a different focus is to try to increase profitability by using methods that also happen to reduce environmental impacts (environmentally beneficial economic activity)—a reactive approach to environmental management. The latter may be seen as a part of normal commercial activities whereas the search for measures of environmental protection that also increase revenues and/or reduce costs is usually seen as part of corporate environmental management. Both approaches are central to the management of eco-efficiency-oriented knowledge and require managers to integrate the environmentally induced benefits and costs of alternative business activities with normal commercial activities.

6.1.2 Environmentally induced benefits

Management accounting rarely includes classification, recording and analysis of environmentally induced benefits. Such benefits include environmentally induced additional revenues (e.g. revenues from sale of recyclables, the higher contribution margins from 'greener' products) and reduced costs (e.g. cost savings because less material is used). The relative size of these benefits and the amount of benefits compared with other investment projects provide a quantitative basis for management and shareholders to assess appropriate environmental measures and strategies for their organisation.

In general, environmentally induced revenues can be divided into direct and indirect categories. Direct revenues, for example, include the gains from sales of recyclables (new markets), an increased volume of sales (quantity effects) and higher prices for the products sold (price effects). Indirect effects are less tangible and may, for example, include benefits flowing from an enhanced 'green' image, increased customer satisfaction and employee morale, and the transfer of know-how. An example of direct and indirect classification is provided by Baxter International Inc., a US-based diversified healthcare company. It discloses detailed costs and revenues related to environmentally induced impacts (Baxter International 1994–1998; Bennett and James 1998b). Between 1990 and 1997 over US$100 million was accumulated in savings and cost avoidance. Baxter International distinguishes 11 categories of environmentally induced costs, grouping them into costs for proactive programmes as well as disposal costs and the costs of measures to remediate orphaned landfills. Environmentally induced revenues are divided into cost savings and income and into cost avoidance, including cost savings caused by a reduced amount of material inputs and packaging, avoided disposal costs and revenues from sale of recyclables (Table 6.1). The total of all net savings equals about 1.5% of Baxter International's income from continuing operations before taxes in 1997.

The calculation and disclosure of such figures is only possible with use of an advanced management accounting system. The result of being able to measure and disclose this information is twofold. First, the success of Baxter's advanced environmental strategy is measurable, targets can be established and actual performance can be compared with targets as part of environmental management. Second, the economic success of this approach can be communicated to internal and external stakeholders.

In practice, environmentally induced costs and cost savings are central to environmental management accounting. For that reason, and to simplify this chapter, there is a focus on 'costs'. However, expenses and assets will be discussed later (Section 7.2).

6.1.3 Environmentally induced costs

The term 'cost' is used in different contexts (and by different individuals) with different meanings. Even in economic literature and in accounting practice there are inconsistencies in the meaning given to the phrase 'environmental costs'. Economists tend to be concerned with costs as prices and for pricing, whereas accountants tend to focus on costs and costing for income determination and asset measurement purposes.

Table 6.1 **Environmental financial statement: disclosure of cost savings, income and cost avoidance arising from environmental protection activities (figures in US$ million)**

Source: Baxter 1997 at www.baxter.com/investors/citizenship/environmental/index.html

Source of cost reduction	Savings and income	Cost avoidance	Total financial benefit
Ozone-depleting substances cost reductions	1.4	0.3	1.7
Hazardous waste			
disposal cost reductions	−0.1	0.1	0.0
material cost reductions	−0.4	0.2	−0.2
Non-hazardous waste			
disposal cost reductions	0.0	0.2	0.2
material cost reduction	−0.1	3.0	2.9
Recycling income	4.1	0.5	4.6
Green Lights energy-conservation cost savings	−0.9	4.2	3.3
Packaging cost reductions	1.3	–	1.3
Total saving	**5.3**	**8.5**	**13.8**

From a 'deep green' (or ecocentric) perspective, the natural environment is seen to possess a value independent of humans. A deep green perspective implies that impacts on the environment must be considered irrespective of whether human society is affected. Ideally, accounting should, therefore, reflect all direct and indirect outcomes for the natural environment. From an all-embracing systems viewpoint, companies are subsystems of the economy, the economy is a subsystem of society and society is a subsystem of the natural environment (see Fig. 6.3). From this perspective, environmental accounting would include all costs that can possibly exist—social, economic and company-level costs. Every use of the environment could be seen as a 'consumption of goods and services' and could be expressed as an environmental cost. To attempt to do so, although, of course, an ideal situation, would in practice not be feasible. In this book the term 'environmental costs' is therefore used in a more selective sense.

The definition of environmental costs used here does not cover all costs for human beings and other species. Society faces costs that are not environmentally induced (e.g. because of social injustice). Environmental accounting, in the sense defined in Part 1 of this book, does not fully capture issues of social development and injustice although it is concerned with accountability of companies for the activities they undertake. The focus of environmental accounting used here is rather on environmentally induced economic costs, or those monetary and non-monetary impacts on the natural environment that somehow affect society through the economy.

Figure 6.3 **What are environmental costs?**

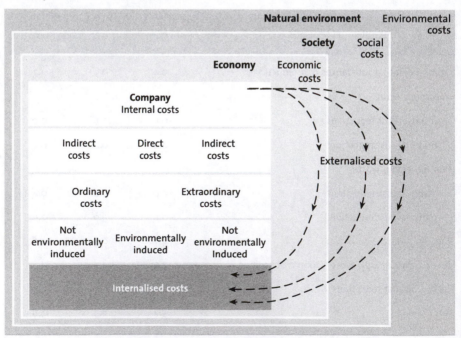

Some external costs affect society in a very direct way. This is the case, for instance, if the noise level near a road increases because of an increase in the volume of traffic. The costs of reducing these adverse effects (e.g. by building a soundproof wall) are usually borne by the government (i.e. taxpayers) even where outsourcing is used to construct new roads on behalf of government. If an anthropocentric approach is taken, the only part of environmental costs considered is the part that results in costs for human society now or in future. These are costs of degradation which have either a monetary or a non-monetary impact on the quality of life of at least one human being. In Figure 6.3 these costs are described as 'social costs' (sometimes also described as 'societal costs').

Negative external effects on the natural environment can also indirectly affect people. For example, a loss in biodiversity would result in few opportunities (options) for future generations to observe wildlife and they would also lose the satisfaction from knowing that species exist. Lost opportunities to gain psychic benefits from nature also induces economic costs. These so-called 'opportunity costs', or costs of foregone opportunities, which will be considered fully later in this book (see Section 6.1.6), are not shown directly in Figure 6.3 as they form a subset of 'economic costs'. Furthermore, economic costs are part of social costs. For example, as noted above, the extinction of species leads to social and economic costs because any reduction in the pool of genes results in a loss of potential benefits from those genes (e.g. for the potential development of pharmaceuticals through bio-prospecting). This is the case even if nobody (or hardly anybody) has ever viewed these species. Biologists compare the loss of a gene to the burning down of a library before anyone has had the opportunity to read the books (Arber 1992).

From a business perspective, the distinction between external and internal environmental costs is also crucial as external costs become economically relevant for a company only if and when they are internalised (Panayotou 1996). The distinction between these classes of cost is drawn below.

6.1.4 External costs

For the past two decades, the concept of 'external costs' has shaped discussion of environmental costs. External costs (also called 'negative externalities') are costs borne by people other than those who cause the costs and receive the concomitant benefits. Externalities can be divided into external costs and external benefits. People who gain from external benefits do not contribute to the costs of producing the benefit. The expression 'externality' usually designates external costs (see e.g. Baumol and Oates 1988; Frey *et al.* 1993; Pearce and Turner 1994). External costs are traditionally not reflected in the accounting systems of a company (Box 6.1).

Exceptions are the studies compiled by BSO and Origin (1993) and Ontario Hydro (see EPA 1998a). These two companies calculated and reported the annual external costs caused by their operations (Box 6.2). No contemporary information about full-cost accounting is available for these two companies, however, because BSO and Origin have merged to become Origin, and full-cost accounting is being downplayed in their accounts, and Ontario Hydro has withdrawn from full-cost accounting in the lead-up to its

" EXTERNAL IMPACTS MAY BE CAUSED BY DEGRADATION (POLLUTION, WASTE, ETC. and their effects on people and other living things) or by the consumption of natural resources, renewable or non-renewable. In many such cases, it is not possible to determine a price for that impact or the price may be distorted by, say, subsidies . . . External impacts may also be positive, for example, when an entity works on restoring the environment. Again, there may be currently no marketplace value or price recognition for such activities under normal accounting processes.

Conventional financial and management accounting, being transactions-oriented and entity-centred, cannot provide these types of information. Some entities are, however, developing approaches and methodologies to measure and report external costs. **"**

Box 6.1   **External impacts and their omission from conventional accounting**

Source: CICA 1997: Foreword

CFCS (CHLOROFLUOROCARBONS) CONTRIBUTE TO THE DEPLETION OF THE OZONE layer. Since stratospheric ozone shields the earth from ultraviolet radiation, depletion of the ozone layer allows increased levels of radiation to reach the earth's surface. Evidence exists to suggest that this depletion results in increases in skin cancer rates and damage to crops and fisheries. Thus, use of CFCs has an impact on the production function of farmers and fishers. Furthermore, with higher health costs and mortality, substantial technological costs are borne by society.

These costs are not shown in the traditional accounting systems of the CFC users. However, they reduce the overall efficiency of the world economy. They are partially reflected in the accounting systems of the farmers and fisheries (as decreases in revenues), hospitals (as increased turnover) and nations (as lower gross domestic product).

Box 6.2   **Accounting effects of externalities of CFCs**

privatisation (see EPA 1996a, 1998a: 310). However, their experimentation with full-cost accounting continues to be of interest, and further information is provided in Table 6.2.

There are two types of externality: technological (physical, such as pollution) and pecuniary (such as the impact of a company's input purchases on the prices other companies have to pay for these inputs). Technological externalities affecting the natural environment and society reduce the overall efficiency of an economy (for a distinction between pecuniary and technological externalities, see Baumol and Oates 1988: 29f.). However, externalities are sometimes 'picked up' in the accounting systems of other, uninvolved, companies if they alter their production costs. This can be illustrated by the example of CFC (chlorofluorocarbon) emissions (Box 6.2).

Stakeholders who have to bear these external costs and who find them reflected in their own accounts are likely to exert increasing pressure on politicians and companies to internalise external costs. In consequence, some environmental costs are internalised through governmental enforcement. Other external costs are internalised, in a voluntary way, for example, through negotiations with important stakeholders who bear external costs. The difficulty of internalising non-monetary externalities is that they somehow have to be assigned an induced price (e.g. through an environmental tax or liability) before they

Receptor	Pollutant	Unit value (Can$)	Monetised impact	
			Total*	Per kWh†
Mortality (statistical deaths)	SO_2, SO_4, O_3, NO_3	4,725,600	21.40	0.088
Morbidity (admissions)	SO_2, SO_4, O_3, NO_3, TSP	44,700	50.83	0.210
Cancer cases	Trace metals	408,397	9.53	0.039
Crops	O_3	n/a	8.32	0.034
Building materials	SO_2	n/a	5.70	0.024
Total			**95.78**	**0.395**

TSP = total suspended particulates; n/a = not available

* In Can$ millions, 1992   † In cents per kilowatt-hour of operation

Note: This table shows some preliminary estimates of average external costs caused by the generation of fossil fuel-based electricity in Ontario, calculated by using a 'damage-function' approach. The damage-function approach has been used by Ontario Hydro since 1974. It uses site-specific data and modelling techniques in combination with economic values in order to estimate the monetised value of external impacts and costs. The set of pollutants listed (including figures for mortality, morbidity and cancer cases) has a monetised impact of 0.395 ¢ per kilowatt-hour of electricity produced.

Table 6.2 **External costs of fossil fuel-based generation in Ontario, Canada, by Ontario Hydro**

Source: CICA 1997: 46

can be considered in conventional accounting. In spite of these difficulties, managers should anticipate a continuing movement towards internalisation of external costs through:

☐ The assignment of property rights over the environments in question

☐ Adjustment of prices and costs to cover the cost of pollution damage (a so-called 'Pigouvian' tax)

☐ Control of permitted quantities of polluting inputs, outputs or waste products

☐ Control of production processes through prescription of 'best available technology'

The pressure to internalise costs in these ways is increasing both through the gathering of scientific evidence and through the adoption of the precautionary principle by government.

6.1.5 Internal environmental costs of a company

Conventionally, internal company environmental costs (also called 'private environmental costs') have been defined as costs of corporate environmental protection (sewers, waste-water treatment plants; see also Fichter *et al.* 1997).

THE INTERNATIONAL ACCOUNTING STANDARDS COMMITTEE (IASC) DEFINES 'extraordinary' and 'ordinary' in International Accounting Standard (IAS) 8, section 6, as follows:

❝ Extraordinary items are income or expenses that arise from events or transactions that are clearly distinct from the ordinary activities of the enterprise and therefore are not expected to recur frequently or regularly. Ordinary activities are any activities which are undertaken by an enterprise as part of its business and such related activities in which the enterprise engages in furtherance of, incidental to, or arising from these activities. ❞

Box 6.3 **Ordinary and extraordinary costs**

These are costs of doing business and can be divided into ordinary and extraordinary costs (Box 6.3), into direct and indirect costs and into potential future costs (Fig. 6.4). Among the most obvious environmentally related costs are ordinary costs such as capital and operating costs for clean-up facilities. For example, environmental costs associated with the production of cars are ordinary costs for a car manufacturer (e.g. costs to treat the waste-water from production). An unexpected, exceptional accident, however, results in extraordinary costs (e.g. clean-up costs caused by the unexpected explosion at Esso's Longford gas plant in Melbourne, Australia).

Direct environmentally induced costs could be, for example, costs of scrubbers directly linked to the production of a specific type of car. Costs of joint clean-up facilities, such as a waste-water treatment plant, are indirect costs as they have to be specifically allocated to cost centres and cost objects. Potential future clean-up costs include costs of future remediation of landfills. Table 6.3 provides some examples of external and internal costs.

In contrast to the conventional perspective, environmental costs can be defined as the sum of all costs that are directly and indirectly related to material and energy use and their

Figure 6.4 **Two different perspectives of internal company environmental costs**

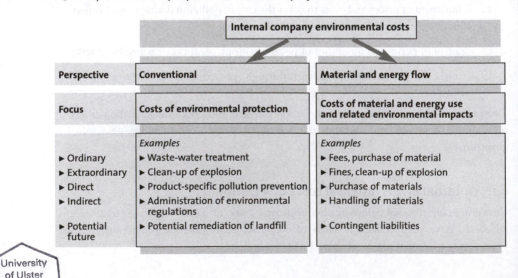

	Internal company environmental costs	
Perspective	**Conventional**	**Material and energy flow**
Focus	**Costs of environmental protection**	**Costs of material and energy use and related environmental impacts**
	Examples	*Examples*
► Ordinary	► Waste-water treatment	► Fees, purchase of material
► Extraordinary	► Clean-up of explosion	► Fines, clean-up of explosion
► Direct	► Product-specific pollution prevention	► Purchase of materials
► Indirect	► Administration of environmental regulations	► Handling of materials
► Potential future	► Potential remediation of landfill	► Contingent liabilities

External and internal environmental costs	

External environmental costs

- ▶ Depletion of natural resources
- ▶ Noise and aesthetic impacts
- ▶ Residual air and water emissions

- ▶ Long-term waste disposal
- ▶ Uncompensated health effects
- ▶ Change in local quality of life

Internal environmental costs

Direct or indirect

- ▶ Waste management
- ▶ Remediation costs or obligations
- ▶ Compliance costs
- ▶ Permit fees
- ▶ Environmental training
- ▶ Environmentally driven R&D
- ▶ Environmentally related maintenance
- ▶ Legal costs and fines
- ▶ Environmental assurance bonds
- ▶ Environmental certification/ labelling
- ▶ Natural resource inputs
- ▶ Record-keeping and reporting

Contingent or Intangible

- ▶ Uncertain future remediation or compensation costs
- ▶ Risk posed by future regulatory changes
- ▶ Product quality
- ▶ Employee health and satisfaction
- ▶ Environmental knowledge assets
- ▶ Sustainability of raw material inputs
- ▶ Risk of impaired assets
- ▶ Public/customer perception

Table 6.3 **Examples of external and internal environmental costs**

Source: Adapted from Whistler Centre for Business and the Arts. Environmental Accounting. Prepared by Berry and Failing 1996; IFAC 1998: section 29

resulting environmental impacts (see Fig. 6.4, see also Fichter *et al.* 1997). These environmentally induced costs include all costs that occur because material and energy flows are not reduced, such as, for example, fees (ordinary costs), fines (extraordinary costs), materials purchase (direct costs) or administrative costs that are caused by environmental regulations (indirect costs such as reporting costs) and contingent environmental liabilities (potential future costs). The conventional and the material and energy flow-based definitions of internal company environmental costs are reflected in conventional cost accounting (see Section 6.3).

Internal company costs can, moreover, be distinguished according to their measurability and their consideration in accounting (Fig. 6.5). Conventional ordinary and extraordinary direct costs are mostly quantified and are included in management accounting. Indirect ('hidden') costs, however, are often not explicitly recognised in management accounting but rather are considered to be part of general overhead costs. Less tangible costs include negative effects on the goodwill of a company.

Potential future (contingent) costs have to be estimated. They are sometimes included in accounts as provisions or charges on income. Large measurement problems can occur in the case of intangible costs (e.g. a loss of reputation) and in the case of external costs that are usually not directly reflected in accounts. Nevertheless, these costs can have an indirect effect on a company's level of economic success.

In the 1960s, the asbestos industry sold products that caused tremendous health damage in the 1980s and 1990s. Today, asbestos as a product has mostly been phased out and it is

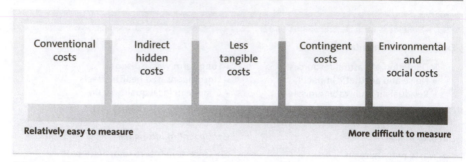

Figure 6.5 **The spectrum of measurability of environmental costs**

Source: Modified from EPA 1995: 14

insurance companies that often have to foot the financial bill. Financial liabilities for pollution, illnesses such as asbestosis, clean-up liabilities and related claims have all to be borne by the insurance industry and today's payers of insurance premiums (see Box 5.1 on page 78). Insurance claims have been estimated at US$2 trillion in the USA alone. Only US$11 billion of these are covered by reserves and provisions (Knight 1994: 48f.).

Typically, these costs have not been made transparent in the accounting systems of those responsible for them, although, years later, the negative financial consequences are being internalised.

6.1.6 Opportunity costs of pursuing or neglecting corporate environmental protection

Reflections on how much voluntary expenditure a company should make on environmental protection measures are dominated by discussion of relevant direct internal costs. Compulsory spending on environmental protection (e.g. spending forced by regulations) is not taken into account here as there is no legal choice but to incur such costs. A comparison of the direct and indirect costs of corporate environmental protection with other commercial investments is, without doubt, economically highly relevant. However, from an economic point of view, a comparison based on opportunity costs (Box 6.4) is even more important (see e.g. Hirshleifer 1980: 265; Wöhe 1990: 790). Economists consider that the economic cost of undertaking any activity has to be interpreted as the cost of the best alternative opportunity forgone. Opportunity costs are the costs that arise from the best unrealised opportunity whenever an alternative is chosen.

The reason for considering opportunity costs is that they show that no decision is without cost even if no direct internal or external costs arise. The opportunity cost of an investment in environmental protection is equal to the benefit of the most attractive alternative investment foregone (e.g. the return that could have been earned in the financial marketplace for the same level of risk). In turn, the environmentally relevant opportunity costs of non-environmental investments are the unrealised benefits of the most beneficial investment in pollution prevention. From this perspective, environmental costs include the costs of purchase and handling of material that becomes waste at a later stage in the production process.

OPPORTUNITY COSTS ARE THE COSTS THAT ARISE FROM UNREALISED opportunities whenever an alternative is chosen from a set of available alternatives. The opportunity cost of an investment in environmental protection equals the benefits of the most attractive alternative investment given up (e.g. in a production device or in the financial market). Opportunity costs of neglected environmental protection are the unrealised benefits of the most beneficial investment in pollution prevention. From this economic perspective, environmental costs are defined as the costs related to the best unrealised pollution prevention alternative. Like external environmental costs, opportunity costs are not recorded in management accounts in a regular, systematic way. Instead, they are provided to managers when a set of alternatives is being considered in a particular decision setting.

Box 6.4 **Opportunity costs**

As a result, the decision as to whether a company should voluntarily spend more money on pollution prevention should be based on the choice that has the lowest opportunity cost. Other things being equal, investment will take place until the net present value of all implemented projects, including environmental protection projects, is equal to zero. To arrive at the correct investment decisions requires knowledge of the benefits of voluntary corporate environmental protection. Yet many benefits of a company's environmental protection are, of course, not quantified, because they are intangible or external. Possible ways of including these benefits in investment appraisal will be discussed in Section 6.5.

Although the cost of environmental protection is both an internal cost and measurable within a conventional management accounting system, the possibility of reducing the opportunity cost of unrealised environmental protection is usually not considered by business. For example, omitted pollution prevention will cost business money if it could be undertaken with use of techniques that help profits rise. Opportunity costs of unrealised environmental protection are the forgone profits from environmental protection that cause internal costs for the company to be reflected in its accounts. The opportunity costs of unrealised environmental protection of a company are shown in Figure 6.6.

The horizontal axis in Figure 6.6 shows the environmental impacts of a cost centre's activities (e.g. a production process or site), of a cost object (e.g. a product or product group) or of a company. Costs are depicted on the vertical axis. In general, many internal costs of environmental impacts (C^{EI}) increase more than proportionally the higher the number of environmental interventions (e.g. fees, fines, liabilities and administrative costs to comply with regulations). Some fees or regulations become relevant when particular amounts of hazardous waste or materials are used. Special administrative activities become mandatory, and education costs can arise or grow more than proportionally when staff need special education because a certain minimal amount of waste is exceeded.

In contrast, the total costs of environmental protection (C^{REI}) falls with a higher incidence of environmental impacts because the fixed costs of environmental protection are spread out over many impacts because of a shared fixed element of cost. Hence, the optimal level of environmental impacts of a company is where the total costs ($C^{tot} = C^{EI} + C^{REI}$) are minimised, that is at Q_1, corresponding to total cost $C^{tot}(Q_1)$. This optimum

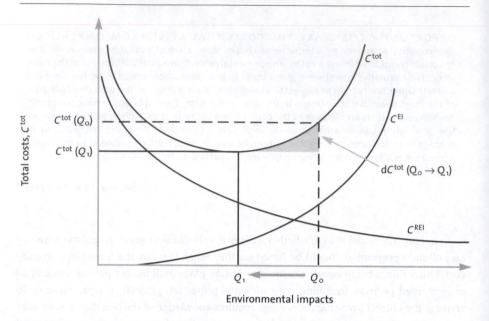

C^{REI} Costs of corporate environmental protection (costs of reducing environmental impacts)
C^{EI} The company's costs of environmental impacts
C^{tot} Total costs $(C^{EP} + C^{EI})$

Figure 6.6 **Opportunity cost of unrealised corporate environmental protection**

is where the sum of C^{REI} and C^{EI} is at a minimum and is not related to the crossover of C^{REI} and C^{EI} as Figure 6.6 shows total cost figures. It is, however, the same place as the point where the marginal costs of pollution prevention equal the marginal costs of environmental impacts (see Fig. 2.2 on page 57).

Unrealised environmental protection causes opportunity costs for a company whenever it exceeds Q_1 (e.g. at Q_0). These opportunity costs are shown by the difference between minimal total costs, $C^{tot}(Q_1)$, and actual costs, $C^{tot}(Q_0)$ of pollution—the area $dC^{tot}(Q_0 \rightarrow Q_1)$.

The question remains why a company would wish to take the opportunity cost of unrealised environmental protection into account. There are two main reasons. First, accounting systems have not adjusted. Second, in order to judge whether a company has incurred, an economic loss all investment opportunities have to be considered. The opportunity cost of unrealised environmental protection has to be compared with the net present value of the realised (or planned) alternative investments, as shown in Section 6.5. They are equal to the net present value of the most economic pollution prevention measure (the forgone alternative). The first aspect, the emerging importance of the opportunity costs of unrealised environmental protection, is illustrated in Figure 6.7.

Chapter 2 showed how the marginal costs of environmental impacts have been increasing for business in the past decade because of stricter regulations and stakeholder pressures. This has led to an upward shift of the total cost curve, so that the optimum point

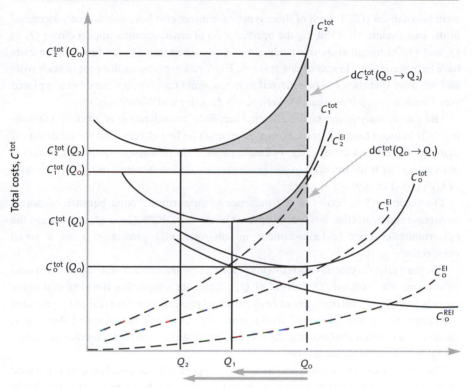

For definitions of variables, see Figure 6.6.

Figure 6.7 **Emergence of the opportunity cost of unrealised environmental protection**

in Figure 6.7 has been sliding to the left of the 'environmental impacts' axis. However, because environmental costs have been unimportant historically, the increase of environmentally induced costs has not been adequately reflected in conventional information systems (i.e. it has not been separately accounted for).

Figure 6.7 shows the development of opportunity costs of unrealised environmental protection based on the inclusion, in sequence, of indirect costs, intangible costs (e.g. loss of reputation) and newly internalised external costs.

Cost curves C_0^{EI} and C_0^{tot} illustrate the perceived cost situation if only the direct financial consequences of the environmental impacts of a company are considered. As discussed later, in many companies environmentally induced indirect costs such as administrative costs, required to comply with regulations, are often treated as overhead costs and are thus not explicitly considered in decision-making (i.e. in investment appraisal of pollution prevention technology). If these indirect and internal costs are included, the total cost curve shifts upwards to the left (C_1^{tot}). The cost curve would shift even further to the upper left if liabilities arising from formerly externalised costs (e.g. from dumping of toxic waste) were internalised (C_2^{tot}). Both of these types of indirect cost have substantially increased in the past decade, thus shifting the optimal level of environmental impacts from Q_0 to Q_1 and Q_2. Although economic analysis recognises their importance, few of these costs have been recognised in accounting systems. Exploration of the significance of such costs and the ways that they can be reflected in management accounting have been explored (see Ditz *et al.* 1995; IFAC 1998; Parker 1999; Schroeder and Winter 1998).

The above analysis shows the effects when little consideration is given to environmentally induced financial impacts on a company. The first effect is that the total costs of many profit and cost centres (e.g. polluting production processes, equipment) and cost objects (e.g. environmentally harmful products) are underestimated, as $C_0^{tot}(Q_0)$ instead of $C_2^{tot}(Q_2)$ (Fig. 6.7).

The second effect relates to the presence of opportunity costs because corporate environmental protection is not at its optimal level—area $dC^{tot}(Q_0 \rightarrow Q_2)$ represents the opportunity cost of underinvestment in environmental protection from a social perspective).

The third effect is that this leads to a lower level of environmental protection than would be economically optimal (Q_0 instead of Q_2). Evidence supporting the view that many economically beneficial measures of environmental protection are not realised is provided in a large survey in the US State of Washington (WSDOE 1992b, 1992c, 1993b). As a result, the less than optimal level of company eco-efficiency also means that eco-efficiency levels for the whole economy are too low.

This section can be summarised as follows: opportunity costs relating to unrealised environmental protection have been neglected for too long by many companies. Public pressure and increasing government legislation is making managers consider strategies for internalising these opportunity costs before they are 'forced' to do so. Once these costs are identified and recognised, as illustrated in Figure 6.7, managers will tend towards higher levels of environmental protection. Once the opportunity cost of unrealised environmental protection is recognised by managers, they will focus on ways to reduce these opportunity costs by lowering environmental impacts in a cost-efficient manner. In short, in anticipation of having opportunity costs of unrealised environmental protection forced on them, managers will implicitly adopt the concept of corporate efficiency where they look for a reduction in environmental impacts, while maintaining, or improving profitability. In Section 6.5.3 an example is provided showing how the opportunity costs of unrealised environmental protection can be calculated as part of an investment project. Of course, it should be noted that an environmental management accounting system does not record opportunity costs on a regular basis as these are not costs that are actually incurred by an organisation. Instead, they relate to anticipated costs as part of a decision to select one course of action rather than another.

One may ask two questions.

☐ Why do businesses need to know opportunity cost?

   Answer: at the time they make a decision they need to know the best alternative course of action to make sure that it is not as good as the alternative they are taking.

☐ When do they need to know opportunity cost?

Answer: at the time they make a decision, not after a decision is made because the opportunity cost (the cost of the best alternative not taken) may change at a later date.

Given the potential effects of neglecting the opportunity cost of unrealised corporate environmental protection, in particular the resulting corporate losses associated with being told what to do by regulatory bodies rather than choosing the best course of action in the ordinary course of business and the growing stakeholder concerns over environmental impacts, it is hardly surprising that some stakeholders have exerted their influence to try to ensure that environmental issues receive better consideration from companies in their management accounting systems.

6.1.7 External stakeholder influence on management accounting

Management accounting is designed for internal decision-making and accountability, which means, in principle, that managers cannot be forced to account for environmental impacts in a specific way. However, management accounting does not operate in a vacuum.

Financial reporting standards have been accused of exerting a strong influence on management accounting (Kaplan 1984), at the same time reducing the relevance of information provided by the management accounting system. When internal accounting systems influence external returns, for example by ignoring environmental impacts of company activities, investors need to be mindful of the need for improvement and may even try to influence internal changes. Although financial accounting standards are slowly changing (see Chapter 7), some additional environmentally oriented stakeholders, although having no effective power to tell managers how to organise their internal accounts, have substantially influenced management accounting practices so that environmental issues are now considered in greater depth. For example, in the USA, two of the most active stakeholders are the United States Environmental Protection Agency (EPA) and the Washington State Department of Ecology (WSDOE) (see WSDOE 1992a, 1993a; see also Spitzer 1992).

US EPA is a major player concerned with the 'greening' of management accounting practices (Box 6.5). It has issued guidelines on costing techniques and capital budgeting (EPA 1995c) to help educate managers on what environmental accounting is, what environmental accounting techniques are available to managers and how managers can carry out investment appraisals of alternative pollution prevention plans. In addition, US EPA provides information on techniques for determining the monetary value of potential environmental liabilities as well as on new approaches to environmental accounting, on case studies where environmental accounting has been successfully implemented and on software packages that can be used to promote environmental management accounting (Boyd 1998; Spitzer 1992; EPA 1995b).

WSDOE has established a regulation associated with the 1990 Hazardous Waste Reduction Act which requires companies either to carry out investment appraisals for

THE US EPA ENVIRONMENTAL ACCOUNTING PROJECT BEGAN IN 1992 in response to concerns from outside stakeholders. These stakeholders believed that pollution prevention (cleaner production) would not be adopted as the first choice of environmental management by industry until the environmental costs of non-prevention approaches and the financial benefits of pollution prevention could be seen by the managers who made business decisions. Adoption of environmental accounting techniques increases the visibility of environmental costs to company managers, thus improving the management of costs.

The mission of the project is to encourage and motivate business to understand the full spectrum of their environmental costs and integrate these costs into decision-making. The project offers educational materials, sponsors training, assists in organising conferences and maintains an international network of individuals from industry, accounting associations, not-for-profit organisations, academia, government and other groups who are involved in advancing environmental accounting.

For additional information about US EPA's Environmental Accounting Project, see www.epa.gov/opptintr/acctg.

Box 6.5   **US EPA and environmental accounting**

pollution prevention plans or, since 1997, to adopt an alternative environmental management system. A guideline for investment appraisal for pollution prevention has been published (WSDOE 1992a, 1993a).

The results of this regulation and its guidelines are quite impressive (see e.g. WSDOE 1992a, 1993a). Data collected for 1994, and adjusted for changing economic conditions, show a 34% reduction in hazardous waste generation compared with 1992. For 1997, the decrease is 44% compared with 1992. The initial target was a 50% reduction by 1995. Facilities are encouraged to establish reachable goals for reduction, recycling and treatment and to report their progress annually. Many economically favourable pollution prevention plans have been developed and implemented with use of these enforced investment appraisals.

The regulation had to force information about the economic consequences of pollution prevention plans on management. Obviously, information costs as well as lack of interest prevented management from seeking such information for itself earlier. One result of the legislation was that more pollution prevention activities were implemented as soon as financial information became available through the plans and as soon as the costs of information were made compulsory for management to bear. Most information costs related to the fixed costs of adapting existing cost accounting methods and computer programmes, and to education costs.

Referring to the discussion of Figure 2.2 in Section 2.4 (page 37), this result is not a surprise. According to this analysis, marginal costs of environmental impacts have grown unnoticed over many years as a result of the introduction of increasingly tighter regulations. As a result, the benefits of increased pollution prevention were not considered even though the marginal cost of obtaining information about cost-effective pollution prevention plans had fallen. Some pollution prevention measures may not have been economically beneficial to start with because of high information costs. However, as companies were forced by regulators to collect the information, management may have considered information costs to be sunk costs and thus may not have taken them into account when calculating the profitability of pollution prevention devices. In this context, being forced to collect information about pollution prevention plans as a requirement for continuing business operations can either improve or decrease a company's economic performance, depending on how high the information costs are compared with the (formerly unknown) economic benefits of pollution prevention. In this instance, the WSDOE has forced transparency and accountability in pollution prevention planning on managers through their capital budgeting procedures.

Other stakeholders are also beginning to bring pressure on managers to take environmental concerns into account. For example, recently the German Bundesumweltministerium (BMU) and Umweltbundesamt (UBA) have started to emphasise the importance of environmental cost accounting in companies (BMU/UBA 1996b). Likewise, professional accounting associations are now parading the advantages of environmental management accounting systems before their members (ASCPA 1999).

Moreover, introduction of new economic instruments, such as environmental taxes and tradable emission permits, would simplify management accounting by making future and external environmental costs of a firm an explicit part of decisions to trade in the market and by assigning them a monetary value. External financial costs would then be visible, internalised and would have to be considered in decision-making because ignorance about these costs would be removed by the introduction of 'official' or 'market-based' valuations and because the allocation of internal company environmental costs to cost centres and cost objects would be simplified. Thus, both the introduction of regulations and the establishment of market-based policy tools can help reduce the cost of obtaining information about corporate environmental impacts and their financial repercussions.

The next section presents an overview of the state of the art of different approaches to environmental management accounting.

6.2 Current methods of environmental cost accounting

6.2.1 Overview

Environmental cost accounting is described by IFAC (1998) as part of the core of environmental management accounting (see also Hummel and Männel 1993). The current methods of environmental cost accounting can be distinguished according to the definition used for 'environmental costs' (see Fig. 6.4 on page 100) and the cost accounting method proposed. Table 6.4 provides an overview of current methods of environmental cost accounting.

The particular cost analysis varies depending on the definition of the subject matter, as different costs are required for different purposes (Clark 1923). As discussed above, environmental costs can be viewed either as (1) costs of environmental protection or as (2) costs related to material and energy flows that could be reduced through an increased level of environmental protection. Opportunity costs of unrealised environmental protection occur if the net present value of pollution prevention measures is positive. Thus, view

(2) focuses on costs of unrealised pollution prevention. On the one hand, approaches dealing with the costs of environmental protection consider past and present costs, or future costs; whereas, on the other hand, approaches focusing on the costs of material and energy flows appear to be based only on past results (see Table 6.4).

To date, four methods have been used to deal with environmental costs. Some methods have been designed to produce separate calculations, not integrated into established company management accounting systems (Section 6.2.2). The other methods proposed include full-cost accounting (Section 6.2.2), direct costing (Section 6.2.3) and process costing (Section 6.2.4; for a general overview of cost accounting approaches, see

Table 6.4 **Overview of current methods of environmental costing**
Source: Modified from Fichter *et al.* 1997

	Costs of environmental protection		**Costs of material and energy flows**	
	Past and present costs	*Future (potential) costs*	*Past and present costs*	*Future (potential) costs*
Separate calculations	Emission reduction costs *(VDI 1979)*	Environmental budgeting *(Wagner and Janzen 1991)*		
Full-cost accounting	Full costs of environmental reduction *(Fleischmann and Paudke 1977; Popoff and Buzzelli 1993; Spitzer et al. 1993; Stölzle 1990; Haasis 1992; Wicke 1992; EPA 1993a, 1996a; CICA 1997)*	Consideration of the costs of environmental risks *(Neumann-Szyszka 1994; Harding 1998)*	Costs of remaining material *(Fischer and Blasius 1995; BMU/UBA 1996a)*	
Direct costing	Environmentally oriented direct costing *(Roth 1992; Kloock 1990, 1993, 1995)* Multi-stage direct costing *(Schreiner 1988, 1991)*	Costing of future environmental costs *(Freese and Kloock 1989; Roth 1992; Kloock 1993, 1995)*		
Process costing	Activity-based costing *(Ditz et al. 1995)*	Activity-based budgeting *(Borjesson 1997)*	Costing oriented towards material and energy flow *(Fichter et al. 1997; Kunert et al. 1995)* Activity-based costing oriented towards material flow *(Schaltegger 1996a; Schaltegger and Müller 1998)*	Activity-based budgeting oriented towards material and energy flow *(see Section 6.2.5, this volume)*

Coenenberg 1993; Freidank 1991; Garrison and Noreen 2000; Hansen and Mowen 2000; Horngren *et al.* 2000; Kosiol 1979; Parker 1999; Ulrich *et al.* 1989). In Section 6.2.5 a new approach considering future environmental costs—'material-flow-oriented and energy-flow-oriented activity-based budgeting'—will be discussed. Box 6.6 provides an overview of the main terms used to classify or categorise costs in different environmental cost accounting systems.

6.2.2 Separate environmental costing of pollution abatement and environmental full-cost accounting

The first authors to deal with environmental cost accounting were Fleischmann and Paudke (1977) and the Verein Deutscher Ingenieure (VDI 1979). Their approaches calculated the costs of end-of-pipe measures of pollution prevention incurred and reflected knowledge about environmental protection existing at that time. Environmental protection was seen only as a cause of additional costs to business. Whereas VDI proposed a separate procedure for calculating environmental costs, others attempted to integrate the measurement of pollution prevention costs into established management accounting systems either through full-cost accounting (CICA 1997; Fleischmann and Paudke 1977; Haasis 1992; Popoff and Buzzelli 1993; Stölzle 1990; Wicke 1992), direct costing (Kloock 1990, 1993, 1995; Roth 1992; Schreiner 1988, 1991) or, more recently, activity-based costing (Ditz *et al.* 1995). Environmental full-cost accounting and environmental activity-based costing have been applied in some companies, whereas no company-level examples of a practical application of direct costing to environmental costs are known (Fichter *et al.* 1997: 35), although direct (marginal) environmental costing is applied to electricity generation in the USA by economists by means of direct 'environmental adders' (or add-ons) at the industry level (Navrud and Pruckner 1997).

Full-cost accounting is the conventional method of cost accounting and traces direct costs and allocates indirect costs to a product, product line, process, service or activity (see e.g. White and Becker 1992). IFAC (1998: paragraphs 22 and 25) views full-cost accounting and environmental cost accounting as the same thing: 'the identification, evaluation, and allocation of conventional costs, environmental costs, and social costs to processes, products, activities or budgets'. A key element of this definition is the recognition that, to obtain full costs of an object, costs must be allocated to that object because they cannot be directly traced.

The term 'full-cost pricing' is also sometimes used as a synonym for 'full-cost accounting', but there are differences between the two as the provision of full-cost accounting information for decision-making does not require a company to adopt full-cost pricing (EPA 1996a, 1998a). Full-cost accounting is merely a necessary means to the introduction of full-cost pricing. Total cost accounting is another 'term sometimes [. . .] used as a synonym for "full-cost accounting" ' (EPA 1995a: 6). Not everyone uses the term 'full-cost accounting' in the same way. Some applications include only the internal costs of a company (i.e. those costs that affect the company's financial bottom line [White and Becker 1992]) whereas others (EPA 1996a, 1998a) include the full range of costs throughout the life-cycle of the product, from raw material extraction to product disposal. Some of

☐ **Activity-based costing (ABC) and activity-based accounting (process costing):** a product costing system 'that allocates [costs typically allocated to] overhead in proportion to the activities associated with a product or product family' (Gunn 1992: 104f., cited in Spitzer *et al.* 1993: 6); also referred to as 'enlightened cost accounting' (Todd 1992: 12f.). Activity-based costing focuses on costing activities and then allocating the cost of activities to products on the basis of the individual product's demand for those activities (Horvath and Mayer 1989, 1993; Parker 1999: 50).

☐ **Full-cost accounting:** a method of management cost accounting that allocates environmental costs (direct and indirect) to a product, product line, process, service or activity (White and Becker 1992). Not everyone uses the term 'full-cost accounting' in the same way. Some authors include only a company's private costs (i.e. those costs that affect the company's financial bottom line) (White and Becker 1992), whereas others include the full range of costs throughout the life-cycle of the product, from raw material extraction to product disposal, some of which do not show up directly or even indirectly in the firm's 'bottom line' (Spitzer *et al.* 1993: 5).

☐ **Full-cost pricing:** 'an economic concept of incorporating external environmental and social costs, as well as internal costs, in the prices of goods and services borne by consumers in the market place' (CICA 1997: 100).

☐ **Life-cycle costing:** A method in which all costs are identified with a product (process or activity) throughout its lifetime, from raw material acquisition to disposal (see also Spitzer *et al.* 1993: 6). Life-cycle costing may focus on internal costs, or it may attempt to consider internal and external costs.

☐ **Total-cost accounting:** 'a hybrid term sometimes used as a synonym for either of the definitions given to "full-cost accounting", or as a synonym for "total cost assessment"' (Spitzer *et al.* 1993: 6).

☐ **Total cost assessment:** long-term, comprehensive financial analysis of the full range of internal (i.e. private) costs and savings of an investment (White and Becker 1992; Spitzer *et al.* 1993: 7).

☐ **Internal costs:** the costs an entity incurs to prevent, mitigate or remediate its environmental impacts, or from failing to take such steps, or costs related to obtaining governmental or societal permission to carry on activities that may adversely affect the environment (CICA 1997: 100).

☐ **External costs:** costs incurred sooner or later by parties external to an entity resulting from impacts on the environment caused by that entity's operations, products and services (CICA 1997: 100).

☐ **Direct costing (or variable costing):** a method for costing inventory (stock) that attaches only variable manufacturing costs to each unit of inventory.

☐ **Absorption costing:** a method of costing inventory in which all variable manufacturing costs and all fixed manufacturing costs are included as costs capable of being inventoried for each unit of product.

Box 6.6 **Terms of environmental cost accounting**

these full costs do not show up directly or even indirectly in the 'bottom line' of the company (Spitzer *et al.* 1993: 5; EPA 1993a). Hence, the term 'full-cost accounting' can be misleading and has to be used with caution as it may or may not be seen to include environmental externalities (external costs). In this chapter, only internal company costs will be considered.

Different cost accounting approaches have, of course, various strengths and weaknesses, which are dealt with in depth elsewhere (see e.g. Burritt and Luckett 1982; Coenenberg 1993; Freidank 1991; Garrison and Noreen 2000; Hansen and Mowen 2000; Horngren *et al.* 2000; Kilger 1992, 1993; Kosiol 1979). Therefore, discussion of these approaches is kept rather brief (see also Fichter *et al.* 1997).

One of the advantages of calculating the costs of end-of-pipe devices separately is that it entails no change to the existing management accounting system (Fichter *et al.* 1997). For example, this costing approach is in line with requirements of the German federal law on protection against emissions (Bundesimmissionsschutzgesetz, BImSchG). It provides a direct comparison of the costs of various end-of-pipe technologies in different industries. However, as the approach also has its problems because it does not take into account integrated technologies (e.g. new, less waste-creating, production systems) or the costs incurred when environmental protection is neglected. In addition, the approach is reactive, as it focuses only on additional costs caused by environmental regulations. Although costs of end-of-pipe devices can be allocated to cost centres and cost objects, environmental protection is not integrated into management accounting and no clear indication is provided about how to treat such integrated technologies.

Traditionally, full-cost accounting is the dominant approach of cost accounting in general; for example, in Australia direct costing is not permitted for financial accounting purposes, thereby putting pressure on management accountants to ignore the approach. The advantages of applying full-cost accounting to environmentally induced costs includes the possibility of allocating these costs on the basis of the activities that cause the costs—their cost drivers. Central to cost allocation is the management process of establishing what the cost objects and cost centres are in an organisation and who is responsible (accountable) for them. As a result, environmental protection is seen as part of daily business, a spur to the search for potential savings, a market opportunity.

Among the flaws of the full-cost accounting approach are that environmental protection is generally regarded as a cost to business rather than an opportunity and the emphasis is mostly on end-of-pipe devices. Information on the pollution abatement costs of specific production processes and products is often not seen as being useful because end-of-pipe technologies largely cause fixed costs independent of the level of production so that the costs of end-of-pipe technology per product unit strongly fluctuate depending on capacity utilisation. Allocation of fixed costs to units of product is a much-frowned-upon procedure in management accounting. When environmental costs are treated as general overhead costs to be allocated, this will reduce the transparency of environmental costs so necessary for environmental cost management. It will also result in distorted costs for decision-making if no specific mechanism for the linking of environmental costs to products is defined. Viewing environmental protection as a cost-adding factor may, moreover, lead to a negative attitude towards pollution prevention. Furthermore, the opportunity costs incurred through the neglect of corporate environmental protection are not taken into account either. Hence, on grounds of faulty decision-making and poor accountability, full-cost accounting can be criticised if it does not try to identify costs that are specifically related to cost objects.

The main advantage of environmental direct costing is the emphasis placed on the possibility of tracing environmental costs to products based on economically plausible causal relationships (Burritt and Luckett 1982). Moreover, direct costing allows fixed and variable costs to be considered separately and, therefore, for a distinction to be made between information relevant to the short and the long run. Schreiner's (1988, 1991) multistage direct costing proposal suggests identification of environmental cost centres that can be used to pinpoint the localisation of potential savings from environmental protection. Schreiner also raises the issue that the costs of material and energy flows will have to be considered too. The practical problem with the direct costing approach is the necessity to separate environmental from other costs and the fact that no authors have provided clear criteria to help managers with this process. It thus remains unclear, for example, how the costs of integrated technologies should be tracked and traced. Apart from Schreiner's approach, the methods proposed do not take costs of neglected pollution prevention into account.

One of the main advantages of using activity-based costing to assess environmental costs—apart from the advantages that have been mentioned concerning environmental full-cost accounting—is the integration of environmental cost accounting into the strategic management process and its linking to management objectives and activities. However, as the experience gained in US companies shows (Ditz *et al.* 1995), the introduction of activity-based costing (process-based costing) can be quite expensive for most companies. In addition, as with all other approaches discussed so far, future environmental costs are not taken into account. However, an accounting system, such as activity-based costing, that encourages managers to try to trace environmental costs to products responsible for those costs is to be encouraged.

6.2.3 Environmental budgeting and the assessment of potential environmental costs

From the general definition of environmental costs as costs intended to protect the environment, some authors propose that potential or future costs (second column of Table 6.4) be assessed too. Wagner and Janzen (1991) designed a separate costing system along these lines. Integration of future costs of environmental protection using full-cost accounting has been discussed by Neumann-Szyska (1994). In principle, the assessment of future costs, especially when related to environmental issues, is very important indeed. Conventional accounting has been criticised for being far too oriented towards the past instead of towards present and future activities (see e.g. Johnson and Kaplan 1987a, 1987b). Also, direct costing, another popular conventional management accounting approach (see Horngren *et al.* 2000), is less decision-oriented than is activity-based costing because it concentrates on calculating the costs of specific business activities with use of volume as a cost driver rather than the richer set of cost drivers used in activity-based costing.

An important use of management accounting information is to assist planning for the future. Extending these approaches to include budgeting is, therefore, another advantage of the full-cost, direct-cost and activity-based approaches because the future consequences for the environment are required to be taken into account if managers use these methods. However, none of the approaches (Freese and Kloock 1989; Kloock 1993, 1995; Roth 1992;) has, at the time of writing, been implemented.

Apart from the pros and cons mentioned above, anyone attempting to undertake a consideration of future costs faces quite substantial problems when trying to estimate those costs. Estimation of the future costs of pollution prevention and environmental liabilities is particularly difficult as neither future technologies nor future demands of stakeholder groups are known. Furthermore, the explicit assumption in environmental budgeting that environmental protection is always related to a single case or project (Wagner and Janzen 1991: 124) does not always reflect reality. Parker (1999: 64), following an empirical survey of environmental costing in Australia, recommends change through adaptation of existing budgetary control systems, such adaptation to be governed by:

- [ ] The environmental management processes that are considered to be significant activities for the organisation involved

- [ ] The operational decision and control needs of the management team

- [ ] The degree of management's familiarity and comfort with environmental input–output statistics and costs

- [ ] The rate of change in accounting system innovation deemed appropriate to the organisation involved

Practice suggests that the need is to focus on key operational strategies with which managers may be familiar and comfortable—such as setting budgetary targets for land remediation projects, pollution control systems, waste management and recycling activities.

If management accounting can help to create purpose-oriented knowledge, the methods discussed so far need to be assessed within the context of the management objective of improving corporate eco-efficiency.

The methods listed in the first two columns in Table 6.4 focus on the costs of end-of-pipe environmental protection technologies and occasionally on integrated technologies (production processes 1 and 2 in Fig. 6.8). This perspective is based on the implicit rationale that increased environmental protection leads to higher costs—in this case, costs of end-of-pipe incineration of waste.

However, this perspective is irritating for managers wishing to enhance corporate eco-efficiency. The implied link between environmental and economic performance is in contrast to attempts to improve the company's economic record by improving the environmental record in a proactive way. This is why cost accounting methods that focus on the costs of environmental protection without highlighting the environmental gains are unlikely to create eco-efficiency-oriented knowledge. Information provided by these methods contradicts somewhat the management aim of enhancing corporate eco-efficiency.

6.2.4 Costs of material and energy flows

Recently, the traditional definition of environmental costs has been challenged (see Fichter *et al.* 1997). The next few sections will show that the focus of attention, accounting information and in-company incentives, change quite substantially if environmental costs

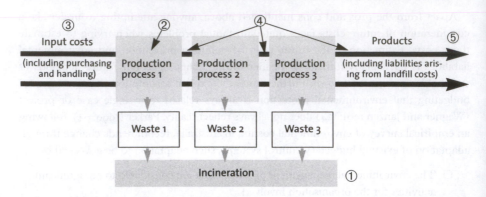

Figure 6.8 **Different definitions of environmental costs**

Source: Based on Fichter *et al.* 1997

are defined as all costs caused by material and energy flows that have an impact on the environment. Judged from this point of view, environmental costs are caused by any kind of material purchased and processed and the associated waste 'produced'.

Environmental costs are seen to include the costs of purchasing and handling materials that cause environmental impacts (costs number 4 in Fig. 6.8 show the material that has 'been bought only to become waste'). If waste were not produced, the material would not have had to be purchased. Purchasing and handling costs are therefore material-flow-related environmental costs. This also 'automatically' includes (i.e. without having to distinguish between normal production costs and costs of integrated environmental technologies) the costs of treating input materials by end-of-pipe (costs number 1 in Fig. 6.8) and integrated technologies (costs number 2 in Fig. 6.8) as well as the environmentally related internal company costs of the products sold (such as liabilities relating to products dumped in a landfill; costs number 2 in Fig. 6.8).

Thus, environmental costs can be lowered by reducing material flows as these cause environmental impacts. This way of thinking is in line with the plea of the Wuppertal Institute for Energy and the Environment to reduce material flows in order to tackle environmental problems (see Schmidt-Bleek 1994). As a result, environmental protection includes all activities that reduce material and energy flows. Furthermore, costs of scrubbers and effluent treatment plants are not regarded as costs of environmental protection but rather as environmental costs. The costs of environmental protection (i.e. reducing material flows) can then be regarded as the 'costs incurred to reduce environmental costs'. Opportunity costs of environmental protection occur if the difference between environmental costs and the costs of environmental protection is positive. Such a perspective fits in with a managerial objective of improving corporate eco-efficiency because the reduction of environmental costs is related to less, or less crucial, environmental impacts.

The first method, which focused on environmental costs as costs related to material and energy flows, applied the method of full-cost accounting (Fischer and Blasius 1995; BMU/UBA 1996b), whereas others have taken a process costing view (Fichter *et al.* 1997;

Kunert *et al.* 1995). Only slightly different is the approach whereby costs are allocated based on material flows to internal company activities such as, for example, various production activities (Schaltegger and Müller 1998).

One of the main advantages of full-cost accounting of material and energy flows is that any reduction of throughput and related environmental impacts is recognised as a reduction of environmental costs. This way of thinking spurs advanced corporate environmental management to renewed efforts (i.e. prevention instead of a mere abatement of pollution). The information provided is decision-oriented with a focus on improving corporate eco-efficiency. The search for potential cost savings by means of environmental protection is encouraged as the costs of neglected pollution prevention are calculated and made transparent within the company. In addition, it is much easier to distinguish between costs related to material and energy flows than between costs of integrated environmental technologies and normal production technologies. Integration of this method with cost accounting is facilitated if the identified material flows are related to cost centres, cost objects and associated activities.

One problem of this approach is that all material and energy flows of a particular company have to be known. Moreover, the implementation of a material-flow and energy-flow accounting system is expensive. This is partially because of the fact that the establishment of a satellite ecological accounting system is necessary (see Part 3) and this requires the introduction of a general account of all material flows, an allocation of related overhead costs to the material flows (e.g. the administrative costs to deal with permits related to material flows) and the definition of allocation keys. Allocation keys are bases used to link environment-driven costs to cost objects. A new kind of knowledge to promote ecological accounting (i.e. accounting for the amount of materials and energy used) is also required (on ecological accounting, see Chapter 4 and Part 3).

The following sections will discuss the process of accounting for materials-based and energy-based environmental costs. The main emphasis will be on environmental costs related to material flows as this approach is seen to provide the best example for understanding the information needed to improve corporate eco-efficiency. This discussion includes the costs of end-of-pipe technologies. The costs of pollution abatement are included with the environmental costs related to material flows. Pollution abatement measures are always taken to reduce the amount or change the composition of material and energy flows. When calculating the costs of managing specific material and energy flows, the pollution abatement measures involved have to be considered.

6.2.5 Material flow-oriented and energy flow-oriented activity-based budgeting

The overview of the existing approaches to environmental cost accounting (Table 6.4) shows that no cost accounting approaches considering potential future costs of material and energy flows have yet been proposed in the literature. This is surprising given the potential cost savings that can be discovered by taking a material flow-oriented and energy flow-oriented view of current production processes. It is to be expected that a future-oriented costing approach that considers the potential environmental costs related to material flows from investments, production processes and business operations would show even greater potential for cost savings compared with analysis based on past and current operations. The main reason why a proactive approach may uncover greater potential for cost savings is that measures to reduce material and energy flows are often much cheaper than measures for changing existing processes or installations. Thus, proactive environmental management may be best reflected through a material flow-oriented and energy flow-oriented activity-based budgeting approach.

The focus of this approach is budgeting for the potential future costs of all material and energy flows. For example, this includes budgeting for all materials that are expected to be purchased in the next period, the cost of logistics for these materials, the wages of the staff who deal with these materials and the expected costs of waste treatment.

Conceptually, this approach is the same as activity-based material-flow accounting but its figures represent expected future costs. Thus, this budgeting approach is based on assumptions made about the future material and energy flows calculated by means of trend extrapolations. However, given the prospective character of budgeting, this assumption can be altered to demonstrate what costs would be under different scenarios with growing or declining material and energy flows based on the expected sales and production systems in place.

The next section explores the identification (i.e. the tracking and tracing) of environmentally induced financial impacts on companies. Tracking and tracing is a precondition for correct tracing and allocation to cost objects (e.g. products) and cost centres (e.g. specific sites and production processes).

6.3 The tracking and tracing of environmental costs

6.3.1 Issues of tracking and tracing

Most companies employ accounting systems that were designed before anyone was able to anticipate the business costs associated with environmental impacts and regulatory compliance. Until recently, costs of environmental impacts and compliance were thought to be of marginal significance for many manufacturing companies. At the same time, the cost of tracking and tracing environmentally induced costs has been very high (see Haveman and Foecke 1998). Therefore, many companies simply included all environmental protection costs and many of the costs related to material flows in their general overhead costs, along with the president's salary, janitorial costs and other expenses that were not traced back to individual manufacturing processes and final products. A limited search of the Canadian Financial Database, which contained the annual reports from 1983 to 1989 of more than 500 public Canadian companies, revealed that very few companies separately disclosed environmentally related costs (Hawkshaw 1991: 24). This result is supported by the more recent surveys of Bennett and James (1996), Gray et al. (1998) and Parker (1999: 32).

In the past decade, this lack of attention to the need for separate identification of environmental costs has been reversed as new incentives, stricter environmental regulations and greater awareness of environmental issues by key stakeholders have changed management perceptions.

In many countries, capital investments and expenditure on environmental protection activities benefit from subsidies, tax exemptions and other advantages, whereas external costs of pollution are increasingly being internalised as polluters are being made to 'pay' for any environmental damage they cause. The most obvious way to internalise environmental costs is through the introduction of taxes, fines and fees. Such taxes, fines and fees have a very direct impact on management accounting. For example, customers may require a detailed calculation of a company's product prices once they have been increased because of new environmental taxes or charges. However, management accounting is usually not in a position to identify or disclose this information as the information system is often not designed to separate manufacturing costs from manufacturer's taxes, fees and fines. Management is also reluctant to disclose the contribution margins associated with important products.

As environmental costs grow in importance management accounting systems need to track charges, fines, fees and taxes because they have to be considered as part of the product costs. Because environmental costs related to material flows have become higher and continue to increase for many companies, and the costs of tracing environmentally related costs have become relatively lower compared with the costs of not tracing them at all (see Fig. 2.2 on page 37), the net benefits from tracking costs have grown. In consequence, the tracking and tracing of environmental costs have become more important to the process of correctly calculating the profitability of products, production sites and companies.

In spite of these needs and changed circumstances, many companies still do not attempt to calculate their environmentally induced costs. Most managers of such companies simply do not know whether the marginal costs of collecting environmental information and reducing environmental impacts are smaller than the marginal costs of environmentally induced fees, fines and image problems.

However, a growing body of examples has demonstrated that companies benefit financially from decisions made to trace, track and allocate environmentally induced costs, thereby improving the relevance of available information for decision-making (Box 6.7; see also White and Zinkl 1997).

The most important task of tracking and tracing is to determine which costs should be classified as 'environmental' compared with other costs. Generally, only those costs that are specifically related to environmental issues caused by material and energy flows and which are identifiable should be included, not those that relate to, or are part of, normal business activities.

The most important issues in tracking and tracing environmentally induced costs (and revenues) include:

☐ End-of-pipe technologies and integrated technologies (Section 6.3.2)

☐ Research and development (R&D) costs (Section 6.3.3)

☐ Costs of past and future production (Section 6.3.4)

KUNERT, A LEADING COMPANY IN THE TEXTILE INDUSTRY, HAS TRACED the environmentally induced financial costs for its production site at Mindelheim (Germany). Kunert reduced pollution by 20% and production costs by 1%–2%, equivalent to several million deutschmarks.

Source: Fritzler 1994: 20.

AMOCO OIL TRACED THE ENVIRONMENTAL OPERATING COSTS OF ITS Yorktown refinery in the USA and established that these comprised about 22% of non-feedstock operating costs. Further breakdown of these environmental costs indicated that the most obvious costs were not, in fact, the largest costs. Costs of waste treatment and disposal were dwarfed by the sum of environmental costs related to sulphur recovery, product specifications, administration, fines, fees and penalties, maintenance and depreciation. Identification of these different cost categories redirected management's attention to the activities that needed to be managed for cost-saving purposes.

Source: Ditz *et al.* 1995.

FOR PETROCHEMICAL COMPANIES OIL SPILLS CAN HAVE A DRAMATIC effect on company profitability through three types of environmental restoration costs—direct, indirect and repercussion costs. Direct costs include ship loss or repair, clean-up costs, legal costs and fines, civil and criminal damages and insurance premiums. Indirect costs can be linked eventually to the contaminating company and include clean-up costs incurred initially by government agencies, losses to local businesses, impact on staff recruitment and customer loyalty. Repercussion costs affect the organisation by extending costs to a wider group of organisations and include restrictions on future operations, increased industry-wide insurance premiums and loss of industry goodwill.

Source: Burritt and Gibson 1993

Box 6.7 **Environmentally induced costs are relevant**

☐ Life-cycle costing (Section 6.3.5)

☐ Environmentally induced assets and expenses (Section 6.3.6)

Revenues can be considered in a similar way to costs and therefore are not discussed separately.

6.3.2 Environmental technologies

Identification of internal environmental costs presents no problems if they are defined as costs of end-of-pipe technologies. End-of-pipe technologies are clean-up devices, which are mainly installed for cleaning purposes at the end of the core production process. Scrubbers and waste-water treatment plants are typical examples of end-of-pipe technologies. They can help to concentrate toxic substances and/or reduce toxic impacts. However, end-of-pipe technologies do not usually solve environmental problems at source, rather they 'catch emissions' before they are released uncontrolled into the natural environment. Another characteristic of technologies of this kind is that they shift emissions from one environmental medium to another (e.g. a scrubber shifts emissions from the air to the water and/or to the soil). End-of-pipe technologies have been encouraged in the past by regulatory authorities in order to control specific, identifiable sources of pollution. These regulatory authorities often specify the technology that must be used by a company in order to reduce pollution to an acceptable level.

Figure 6.9 shows a manufacturer with three production steps which all produce waste. The costs of 'environmental cost centres' that provide joint services to all or a number of production centres, such as incinerators and waste-water treatment plants, need to be identified separately from other overhead costs if they are to be controlled. In the example provided, the entire waste from production is treated in a jointly used incinerator on the production site. The costs of incinerating the waste from current production amount to $800. The remaining overhead costs for general administration and salaries of top management amount to $9,000. This example will be extended later in this chapter.

The identification and measurement of environmentally related costs is much more difficult with 'integrated technologies' (also called 'clean technologies'; e.g. the integration of coal-based electricity generation with gasification combined-cycle technology designed to improve the acceptability of coal-based power production). Integrated technologies are more efficient production technologies which reduce material and energy flows at the source, or before pollution occurs (e.g. a new device uses 50% less energy and creates 20%

Figure 6.9 **Tracking and tracing of environment-related costs**

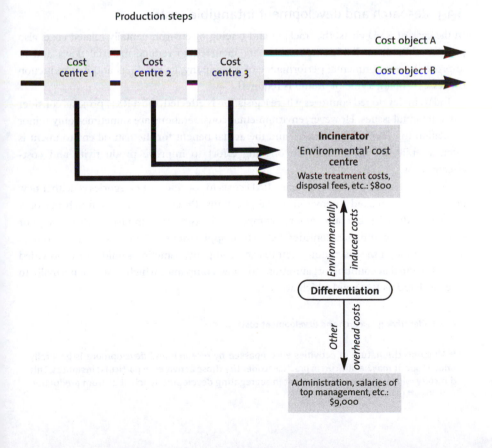

less toxic effluents than the old one). Environmental issues were already integrated when the technology was developed. Because of this integration of environmental protection into the production plant, the following question arises: What part of the production plant (the fixed asset) and of any associated maintenance expenditures are environmentally induced?

To answer this question in practice, a rule of thumb has to be developed (EPA 1995c). The main information needed is the cost difference in relation to the less favourable environmental solution. For example, 20% of the capital costs may be classified as environmental if the integrated technology has caused 20% extra costs compared with a comparable, non-integrated technology. In addition, if the integrated technology were to be installed two years earlier than could be justified solely on economic grounds, simply to comply with environmental regulations, the difference between depreciation costs of the old technology over two years and the depreciation of the new integrated technology may be considered as an environmentally induced cost.

However, costs should not be considered as environmentally induced if the integrated technology represents only present technological knowledge and if it has been installed for no other reason than the regular replacement of an old device—a purely commercial decision.

6.3.3 Research and development intangible costs

In the case of R&D costs, the tracking and tracing of environmentally related costs also presents difficulties. Which R&D costs are incurred to reduce material flows and to improve the environmental performance of a company, its products and its production processes? Again, a rule of thumb is required.

Today, in developed countries where legislation is effected, most R&D projects consider environmental issues. However, environmental considerations are sometimes only minor in relation to other considerations, and the actual benefit for the natural environment is often a 'spillover' from the main ongoing effort to improve productivity and cost-effectiveness.

The problem of tracking and tracing R&D costs to specific cost categories is neither new nor specifically related to environmental questions. Practices vary very much not only between industries but also among companies in the same industry (Box 6.8). For example, some companies consider the costs of applications as R&D costs whereas others do not. Although the discretion is left to each company, sometimes guidance is provided by professional accounting organisations to show companies which costs are normally to be considered as R&D and which are not.

Box 6.8 **Identifying research and development costs**

❝ Although the nature of activities encompassed by research and development is generally understood, it may be difficult in practice to identify those activities in particular instances. This difficulty will be particularly apparent in segregating development activities from production activities ❞ (AASB 1983: section 6).

Therefore, the general classification criterion needs to be interpreted on a case-by-case basis by management, to the effect that only those costs that are specifically related to environmental issues, and which are identifiable, should be included and not those that relate to or are part of normal business activities. This is a matter of management judgement.

6.3.4 The costs of past and future production

The tracking and tracing of costs incurred because of environmental considerations is further complicated by long-term effects which are more important when considering environmental rather than other issues.

Present costs can relate to past, present or future production activities. Examples of current costs of past production are today's clean-up, waste disposal and incineration costs. The current costs of future production include present capital costs (e.g. interest payments for environmental protection investments that will reduce material flows in the future; see e.g. Raftelis 1991). As part of accrual-based accounting, accurate matching of costs and revenues will reduce the amount of expenditure related to future benefits but charged in the present period. Instead, such future costs will be capitalised in an asset value.

Present production can be linked to past, present and future costs. Past costs of present production include, for example, the capital costs of past accounting periods that are written down through a depreciation charge. Future costs of current production are mainly liabilities and contingent liabilities.

A correct accrual-accounting-based tracking, tracing and recognition of (environmentally induced) costs requires that all (past, present and future) costs be treated in the accounting period in which they accrue and not necessarily when they have to be paid (see Table 6.5; on the accrual basis, see IASC 1995: 47, IAS F22). In other words: past, current and future costs of present production should be recognised and disclosed in the present accounting period. The situation is similar to the downward revaluation of assets—past costs of past production recognised in the present period should be counted as a loss in the present accounting period in accordance with the guidelines for re-valuing assets because of unexpected technological or market developments (see IASC 1995).

Table 6.5 **The recognition of costs when they accrue**

| | **TIME OF RECOGNITION OF COSTS** | | |
TIME OF PRODUCTION	Past	Present	Future
Past	✓		
Present		✓	
Future			✓

Taking future costs into consideration is problematical because their estimated amounts are mostly unknown, especially in the case of environmental issues such as contingent liabilities. One possibility is to insure against environmentally induced economic risks. In this way, the cost of an insurance premium facilitates recognition in the present. However, it is not possible to insure against a number of environmental risks. Comparisons with similar risks in the past or similar risks faced by other companies can be made in order to estimate probable liabilities. In the past decade, contingent environmental liabilities have become an important issue in financial accounting (see Chapter 7). The main problem is that disclosure of contingent liabilities might attract the attention of certain stakeholders and thus have unwelcome legal and economic consequences. However, greater transparency can also act as a defence for managers.

Unexpected current costs related to past and future production should be accounted for separately in the period in which they occur (or when they are realised) so as not to distort the calculation of current profitability from operations. Also, present costs resulting from past production should be identified as losses (extraordinary costs) to prevent the distortion of the correct calculation of operational profitability from present production.

Apart from considering past and future costs, the boundaries of accounting can also be extended to include the entire life-cycle of a product. The next section will examine life-cycle costing, a costing approach that is often promoted by environmentalists.

6.3.5 Life-cycle costing

The basic idea behind life-cycle costing is to identify, track and account for costs relating to the whole life-cycle of a product. Life-cycle costing (or 'cradle-to-grave' product costing) involves examining the costs of a product at R&D, design, production, marketing, distribution and disposal stages. Logistics behind value chains have provided an insight to the various stages in product life-cycles and this is why groups such as the Society of Logistics Engineers (SOLE) have developed life-cycle costing with the idea of taking all internal and external monetary costs of a product into account. Indeed, in some organisations the concept of 'cradle-to-cradle', where components of a product are recycled or re-used as an input to the next cycle of manufacturing, views the costing cycle as a closed-loop system.

All costs for the economic actors in a product life-cycle are identified with the product throughout its whole lifetime. The costs should preferably be measured in quantified terms, though, if this should not prove possible, qualitative judgements may be added (Spitzer *et al.* 1993: 6). Life-cycle costing encourages expansion of the accounting boundaries of the company to include suppliers and consumers as well as extending the time-horizon of accounting into the distant future. Thus, in principle, the focus on a narrow entity is discarded and a broader view adopted to allow inclusion of the whole life-cycle of a product. Yet, in practice, deriving monetary values for all life-cycle costs is somewhat unrealistic because of the 'infinite regress' problems associated with the need to define boundaries for any life-cycle. Hence, many organisations choose to focus on narrower aims, such as the US EPA Design for Environment programme, with its emphasis on environmental improvement and cost reduction at the design stage of any life-cycle.

The method of life-cycle costing should not be confused with the much more popular concept of life-cycle assessment (LCA), which focuses on the physical environmental impacts of a product life-cycle (see Chapter 10).

Although discussed in academic circles, life-cycle costing has not received much attention by the corporate sector to date. First, in a competitive market the price mechanism should already include the internalised environmental costs of suppliers if the products are priced correctly (through correct identification and allocation). In addition, because of uncertainty, external costs can be estimated only very roughly and so their information value may be very low.

Second, the concept of life-cycle costing suffers from major problems in practical applications. The collection of necessary information from economic actors outside the company (suppliers, customers and disposal costs) usually results in:

❑ Low-quality data

❑ Data of inconsistent quality

❑ High costs for data collection

To initiate life-cycle costing, management must define the boundaries of the life-cycle system under consideration. In doing so, management has considerable latitude in setting the boundaries of the system investigated. So far, no generally accepted criteria exist and this makes comparisons between alternatives difficult.

In most cases, the collection of information from outside a company results in poor-quality data. Unless a very powerful company can insist on obtaining and can verify the data from, for example, suppliers, employees in other companies have little incentive to concern themselves about the quality of information provided. For a supplier, some information might be of strategic importance or related to processes that are confidential or competitively sensitive. In addition, most companies have different information system configurations and these provide different details, classes and qualities of data. When ecological accounting is examined (Part 3), it will be seen that life-cycle assessment faces similar problems.

Despite its substantial deficiencies, the basic idea of systematically examining all the environmental costs of a product life-cycle can be useful as a general way of thinking to help in strategic management, especially for the early identification of contingent liabilities or of environmentally weak and strong points in an industry's value-added chain.

6.3.6 Environmentally induced assets and expenses

When tracking and tracing environmentally induced costs (e.g. to reduce material flows) a company is, sooner or later, faced with the question whether the costs should be defined as expenses or capitalised in asset values. In principle, and in accordance with accounting convention, an expense is defined as a cost that has provided a benefit that has now expired, whereas unexpired costs that can lead to future benefits are classified as assets (see also Section 7.2, Box 7.2).

The decision as to whether an environmentally induced cost item is identified as an asset or as an expense has a major impact on management decision-making. As illustrated in

Box 6.9, the distinction between assets and expenses is often not clear-cut in practice. To answer this question the following distinction between two types of environmental costs may be useful:

☐ The preventative costs of reducing the material and energy flows of a company

☐ The reactive costs of pollution abatement and those of environmental impacts caused by existing material flows (fines, fees and scrubbers)

The first covers costs incurred through the reduction of material and energy flows with the aim of conserving natural resources and reducing emissions or any kind of environmental damage.

The costs of pollution abatement (e.g. costs of purchasing and maintaining scrubbers) are incurred because some (excess) material and energy flows were not reduced. Expenditure for environmental impacts caused includes any extraordinary costs of non-compliance such as fines and the costs of litigation, as well as the ordinary operational costs related to unrealised environmental protection such as the fees paid for waste disposal and environmental taxes.

Generally, the costs of treating the environmental impacts of existing material and energy flows, as well as pollution caused, are the result of omissions or uncertainties and therefore tend to be treated as period expenses. On the other hand, any costs incurred in order to improve the future environmental record by reducing a company's material and energy flows tend to be recognised more easily as assets.

Unfortunately, standards, regulations and guidelines established for financial accounting and reporting have a major impact on how this issue is treated in management accounting (Kaplan 1984). As a result, less emphasis is placed on relevant data for decision-making and accountability and more emphasis is given to compliance with external accounting standards. If, for example, an outlay has to be counted as an asset in financial accounting, it will, for reasons of consistency, generally be treated in the same way in management accounting. The question whether to expense or to capitalise an environmentally induced outlay is therefore dealt with in greater depth in Chapter 7, on financial accounting.

Nevertheless, financial accounting guidelines leave management accountants with some discretion. Management should account for environmental costs in the most appropriate way for decision-making. Two contradictory effects are worth considering:

☐ Environmentally induced outlays that are recognised as assets increase the net assets and hence the net worth of a company. These assets will be depreciated

Box 6.9 **Asset or expense?**

A COMPANY HAS BEEN LEGALLY DUMPING HAZARDOUS WASTE ON A landfill for many years. Now, the contaminated site has to be cleaned up because of new legal requirements. Management decides to use the property in the future for other purposes. Are the clean-up costs incurred expenses or should they be capitalised and considered as assets because they enhance the future value of the property?

(the costs expire) over several accounting periods as they are used up. Thus, capitalisation spreads costs over several accounting periods. As a result, ratios of profitability to earnings per share will also be affected over a long period.

☐ If the outlay is regarded as an expense in an accounting period, profits, profitability and earnings per share will be affected for a short period only (the accounting period) although to a greater extent than if the outlay had been treated as an asset.

Once environmentally related financial impacts are tracked, traced and recognised, they are allocated to cost centres and cost objects.

6.4 Allocation of environmentally induced costs

6.4.1 The conventional approach

For many companies, where environmentally induced costs are significant, it makes sense to consider tracking and tracing such costs to help determine how much the company is affected financially by environmental issues. In addition, it is often argued that, to calculate accurate contribution margins, economic value added or profit margins, environmentally related costs should be allocated to products. Direct costs are taken to mean those costs that can be traced to cost objects, whereas indirect costs cannot be traced to cost objects; they can be allocated only by using a predetermined allocation base or key. Indirect costs are usually referred to as overhead costs. Where direct tracing of costs is not possible the main concern is to provide relevant information for those who need or can use it. In practice there is an inevitable grey zone where 'correct' information is not possible to obtain (e.g. how much of the chief executive officer's time is related to dealing with environmental issues?) and cost allocations have to be made. To help practitioners, US EPA (1995c: 12) suggests three approaches that can be considered when trying to link costs with cost objects (e.g. a product) in these circumstances:

☐ Allow the cost item to be treated as environmental for one purpose but not for another

☐ Treat part of the cost of an activity or item as environmental

☐ Treat costs as environmental for accounting purposes when managers agree that a cost is more than 50% environmental

The conventional approach to cost accounting is absorption cost accounting. Internal environmental costs are assumed by most organisations to be negligible (perhaps because historically they were negligible) and thus treated as general overhead costs to be divided between all cost objects by using a predetermined cost allocation base. Figure 6.10 provides an example. It illustrates a common situation where the costs of treating product B's toxic waste are included in general overhead costs which are then allocated to all products (both A and B) on the basis of an accepted cost allocation base.

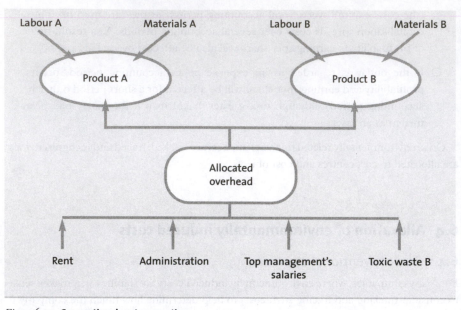

Figure 6.10 **Conventional cost accounting**
Source: Similar to Todd 1992

However, 'dirty' products cause additional emissions and require additional clean-up facilities relative to 'clean' products. An equal allocation of those costs, therefore, would subsidise relatively less environmentally benign products. Cleaner products, on the other hand, are 'punished' by this allocation rule as they have to cover costs they did not cause in the first place. In this case product A bears half the cost (assuming an equal allocation) of toxic waste caused by product B—a cost that can be traced to product B in its entirety. Product A is the cleaner product, but the cost allocation mechanism penalises it by making it look more expensive to produce than it really is.

A simple example in Table 6.6 provides another illustration of how equal allocation between products that have different environmental impacts can lead to sub-optimal management decisions. Two production processes are compared: process A is 'clean' and does not cause any environmentally induced costs for the company, whereas process B causes $50 of extra costs because it is environmentally harmful. If these costs are assigned to general overhead and allocated equally, both processes seem to create a profit of $75 (if $50 is allocated to overhead, $25 will implicitly be allocated to each process. This leads to a profit of $75 [$200 − $100 − $25]). In reality, however, process A has created a profit of $100, whereas process B has contributed only $50 to the company profit. This example illustrates how opportunity costs of unrealised environmental protection, as theoretically discussed in Section 6.5, can emerge. A profitable investment to improve the environmental record of process B may be considered unattractive, and the total costs may be underestimated as a consequence of distorted information.

	Process A ('Clean')	Process B ('Dirty')
Correct treatment of environmental costs		
Revenue ($)	200	200
Production costs ($)	100	100
Environmental costs ($)	0	50
Correct profit ($)	100	50
Environmental costs treated as overheads		
Revenue ($)	200	200
Production costs ($)	100	100
Environmental costs ($)	0	50
Overheads ($)	25	25
Book profit ($)	75	75
Error* (%)	−25	50

* ([Book profit − correct profit]/correct profit) × 100

Table 6.6 **An example of the effect of incorrect cost allocation**

Such inaccurate information may lead to a sub-optimal management decision whereby cost-based prices of products produced by the two processes are overstated or understated. Cross-subsidised 'dirty' products are sold too cheaply whereas environmentally benign products can be sold at too high a price. As a result, a market share can be lost in the most sustainable fields of activity and, at the same time, the company's position is enhanced in fields where environmental risk is underpriced and there is the possibility of a reduced or no commercial future.

Whenever possible, environmentally induced costs should, therefore, be directly tracked and traced to the respective cost centres and cost objects (especially products). Consequently, the costs of treating, for example, the toxic waste of product B in our example should directly and exclusively be traced to that very same product (Fig. 6.11) (see also Kreuze and Newell 1994).

As discussed at the beginning of this chapter, the focus of this section is on activity-based costing (ABC) and its link with material flows. ABC focuses on identifying the direct costs of activities and then allocating these activity costs to products. In this sense, ABC is similar to conventional cost accounting in that it relies on cost allocation to obtain cost information about products. Within this conventional framework, in order to operationalise the relevant factors affecting corporate eco-efficiency and accountability of divisional managers, the allocation of overhead costs should focus on identification of activities causing the environmental impacts of material flows and the person or group within the organisation responsible for such impacts. This is the main purpose of material flow-oriented activity-based costing, described in the next section.

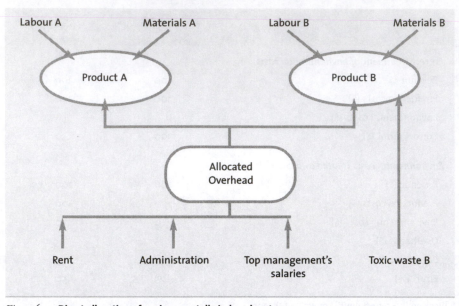

Figure 6.11 **Direct allocation of environmentally induced costs**
Source: Similar to Todd 1992

6.4.2 Material flow-oriented activity-based costing

Many terms and methods are used to describe and guide allocation procedures. In this book, an 'activity-based costing' approach is adopted. The term 'environmentally enlightened cost accounting' has also been used to refer to this costing process (Todd 1992: 12f.). Activity-based costing (ABC) represents a method of cost allocation that first traces costs to activities undertaken by cost centres in an organisation and, second, traces or allocates these costs to units of output or other cost objects (see e.g. Gunn 1992: 104f.; Hansen and Mowen 2000: 674; Spitzer 1992; Spitzer *et al.* 1994: 6; EPA 1995c). Cost centres and cost objects are defined on the basis of production and other organisational activities that are established in order to facilitate co-ordination and responsibility. Activity-based costs are calculated by adding the indirect joint fixed and the joint variable costs to the direct production costs of each product.

The main strength of ABC is that it enhances the understanding of the business processes and activities associated with each product. It reveals the activities where value is added and where it is destroyed and, as a result, facilitates activity-based management (Morrow 1992). In relation to the need to improve corporate eco-efficiency, costs are calculated on the basis of the material flows associated with activities. To simplify the following illustrative examples, energy flows are ignored, even though they can be treated in a similar way. In relation to a desire to improve accountability, ABC allows a clearer linkage to be drawn between responsibility centres and the environmental costs of those centres.

Not all environmental costs can be linked to cost centres. Although, where environmental costs are significant, it is inappropriate to continue to include all environmentally related costs under the heading of 'general overhead', some environmentally induced costs will remain part of general overhead. The type of costs that cannot be directly traced or allocated to units of output include, for example: costs for new insulation of head-office buildings; costs of past production that are clearly related to strategic management decisions of the whole company (e.g. environmental liability costs of products that have already been phased out).

Figure 6.12 (Schaltegger and Müller 1998) illustrates the main steps in material flow-oriented activity-based cost allocation. It shows a two-step allocation process: first, from joint environmental cost centres (e.g. an incinerator providing common environmental services) to the 'responsible' cost centres (e.g. production centres 1, 2 and 3); and, second, from the responsible cost centres to final cost objects (e.g. units of products C and D). After tracking and tracing, the costs of joint environmental cost centres, such as incinerators and sewerage plants, have to be allocated to the 'responsible' cost centres and cost objects.

Total input to production is 1,000 kg of material, 200 kg of which are treated as waste in the incinerator. Total incineration costs amount to $800. Given these figures, if we assume, for simplicity, that every unit of waste causes the same costs, the treatment of one kilogram of waste will cost $4 ($800/200 kg = $4/kg). This relationship we will call the cost allocation key (or base).

As a first allocation step, costs of the incinerator have to be allocated to the three cost centres (allocation 1) based on the cost allocation key: $400 to cost centre 1 ($4/kg × 100 kg of waste) and $200 to cost centres 2 and 3 ($4/kg × 50 kg each). The cost key reflects the amount of waste produced by each cost centre.

As a second step (allocation 2), cost-centre costs have to be allocated to the cost objects (e.g. products C and D). A second cost allocation key needs to be chosen for this allocation, one that reflects the separate costs of waste incineration that have been caused by each product within each cost centre (e.g. 100% for the 'dirty' product, product C, and 0% for the 'clean', or 'green', product, product D).

Figure 6.12 **Allocation of costs related to waste incineration**

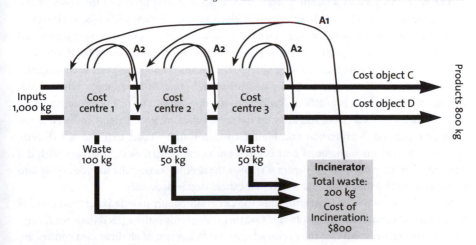

A1, A2: allocations 1 and 2, respectively

At present, even in some 'advanced' management accounting systems, many companies allocate the costs traceable to environmental cost (service) centres (e.g. an incinerator) first to production cost centres and, second, to products. However, additional environmentally induced costs, associated with the flow of raw materials and the waste emanating from production processes rather than a joint environmental cost centre (the incinerator in this case), are ignored. Yet some of these costs of waste could be saved and the profitability of products increased substantially if less waste were created in the first place. Waste uses manufacturing capacities, labour and increased administration. If no waste were produced, depreciation would be lower and the total salary bill would be reduced. Such greater efficiency in resource usage and productivity would lead to less waste and an improved financial bottom line. Furthermore, as illustrated above, improved resource productivity has the potential to reduce labour cost and thereby increase labour productivity.

The question to be answered concerns what activities (e.g. purchasing, production and incineration) are related to the generation of waste. For instance, in the example shown in Figure 6.12, 200 kg of the 1,000 kg input were purchased only to be emitted from the production process as waste, without creating any value. In this case, waste has caused a 25%—[(1,000 − 800)/800] × 100—increase in purchasing cost, higher costs of machinery depreciation and extra administration costs. Neglecting to track and trace these costs results in underestimation of the total costs of cost centres and cost objects (see Section 6.3) because such costs are assumed in the general corpus of 'period' costs, not being linked with environmental cost centres, production processes or products. Therefore, in conventional management accounting procedures, a third step whereby indirect costs are allocated to the cost centres and to cost objects is needed.

Figure 6.13 illustrates this third step of allocation on the basis of the above example illustrated in Figure 6.12. Recall that 1,000 kg of raw material inputs were purchased to create 800 kg of products. Of the 200 kg of waste, 100 kg are caused in step 1, and 50 each in steps 2 and 3.

The first and second allocation steps traced, tracked and allocated the costs of the environmental cost centre ($800 for incineration) to cost centres and objects. However, some environmentally induced costs have been excluded. The inputs that were purchased 'just to be thrown away', without creating any value, have an associated opportunity cost. As waste is not inevitable, or can be reduced, the inputs could have been used to create economic value. The value forgone, measured in terms of economic value added, contribution margin or profitability, represents the opportunity cost. Therefore, management should also track, label and account for these other environmentally induced costs, such as increased depreciation and higher costs for staff—costs that are not directly traceable to joint environmental cost centres but costs, nevertheless, that vary with the amount of production activity. Figure 6.13 takes these environmentally induced costs into consideration and illustrates that a third allocation step is necessary.

In the case presented it is assumed that the environmentally induced overhead costs of $9,000 are all variable, that the volume of waste in kilograms is the agreed basis for linking costs to cost centres and that the overhead costs per kilogram of all three cost centres are the same.

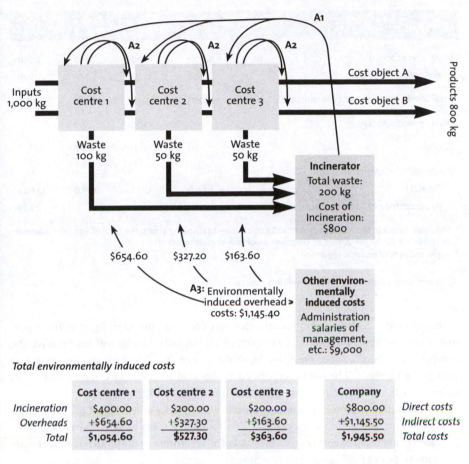

A1, A2 and A3: allocations 1, 2 and 3, respectively

Figure 6.13 **Allocation of environmentally induced indirect costs**

A total of 1,000 kg of material are processed in cost centre 1; 900 kg in cost centre 2; and 850 kg in cost centre 3 (see Table 6.7). If the total amount of processed material (e.g. 1,000 kg of 2,750 kg for cost centre 1) is taken as the allocation key, allocation rates for total environmentally induced overhead costs are: cost centre 1, 36.36%; cost centre 2, 32.73%; cost centre 3, 30.91%. Thus, the total overhead costs ($9,000) per cost centre are: cost centre 1, $3,273; cost centre 2, $2,946; cost centre 3, $2,782.

In this case the environmentally induced indirect (overhead) costs are calculated as follows. In cost centre 1, 100 kg of waste from the 1,000 kg processed is directly related to production in cost centre 1. Economically, however, the waste that later shows up in cost centres 2 and 3 causes additional costs in cost centre 1 because good input is spoilt. In total, 200 kg (100 kg + 50 kg + 50 kg) of the 1,000 kg of inputs purchased (20% of inputs) cause indirect costs in cost centre 1. Hence, in this case, the additional, environmentally induced indirect costs at cost centre 1 amount to $654.6 (20% [200 kg of 1,000 kg] of $3,273).

	Cost centre 1	Cost centre 2	Cost centre 3	Total
Kilograms processed	1,000	900	850	2,750
Percentage of total	36.36	32.73	30.91	100
Total overhead costs per cost centre* ($)	3,273	2,946	2,782	9,000
Waste processed (kg)	200	100	50	
Waste[†]	20	11.11	5.88	
Waste-induced overhead costs				
Total ($)	654.6	327.2	163.6	1,145.4
As percentage of total overhead costs				12.73

* Individual values in this row do not sum to $9,000 owing to rounding errors. The total of $9,000 is allocated in proportion to the percentage of kilograms processed at each cost centre.

† Expressed as % of material processed

Table 6.7 **Environmentally induced overhead costs**

In cost centre 2, 900 kg of material enter cost centre 2 (the 1,000 kg of initial inputs minus the 100 kg lost as waste at cost centre 1), but only 800 kg will finally leave the company as good products. Thus, 100 kg of the 900 kg (11.11%) of inputs that enter cost centre 2 cause waste. The total overhead costs allocated to cost centre 2 are $2,946. The indirect waste costs amount to $327.3 (11.11% [100 kg of 900 kg] of $2,946).

The costs in cost centre 3 amount to $163.6 (5.88% [50 kg of 850 kg] of $2,782).

In summary, as calculated, recognising environmental costs as activity-based costs to be traced or allocated to cost centres, the total of all environmentally induced indirect costs amounts to $1,145.3 ($654.6 + $327.3 + $163.6).

The total direct costs of the environmental cost centre (the incinerator) amount to $800 whereas the total of all indirect environmental costs amount to $1,145.5. The total of all environmentally induced costs is shown in Figure 6.13 for each cost centre as well as for the whole company. The cost total for cost centres to absorb has increased from the $800 cost of the incinerator to $1,945.5 because of the recognition of additional variable indirect environmental costs.

As the above example shows, the three-step allocation of environmentally induced indirect costs can provide motivation for management to reduce material flows thereby realising large efficiency gains as well as improving the company's environmental record (see also Burritt 1998). In other words, when environmentally induced indirect costs are allocated on the basis of material flows, information provided to cost-centre managers encourages them to improve the eco-efficiency of the company as well as to support environmentally benign methods of production.

An empirical example from the German metal industry is provided in Table 6.8. Other empirical studies demonstrate that savings of a factor of between 6 and 10 times are available for realisation and are highlighted if investment decisions for corporate environ-

CONVENTIONAL CALCULATION		COMPREHENSIVE CALCULATION	
Quantity	*Cost ($)*	*Quantity*	*Cost ($)*
Waste disposal		Waste disposal	
Fees	500,000	Fees	500,000
Disposal costs	300,000	Disposal costs	300,000
		First total	**800,000**
		Environmentally induced production costs	
		Logistics and transportation	150,000
		Additional personnel	250,000
		Additional depreciation	200,000
		Storage	100,000
		Total	*700,000*
		Second total	**1,500,000**
		Excess material input	
		Purchase	4,500,000
Comprehensive total	*8,000,000*	*Comprehensive total*	*6,000,000*

Table 6.8 **Example of the significance of the correct (comprehensive) calculation of environmentally induced costs: result of the method of conventional calculation compared with that of the comprehensive method of calculation**

Source: Wagner 1995

mental protection are based on information using comprehensive allocation rules (see e.g. Fischer *et al.* 1997; von Weizsäcker *et al.* 1997).

Up to this point, the volume of waste has been taken as the allocation key, or allocation base, for environmentally induced costs. However, as shown in the next section, this might not be the most appropriate figure in all cases.

6.4.3 Allocation keys

The choice of an appropriate allocation key (or base) is crucial in order to obtain comprehensive information for environmentally adjusted management accounting. The advantages and pitfalls of different allocation keys have already been extensively discussed in the accounting literature (see e.g. Burritt 1998; Young 1985). This section is therefore kept rather brief.

Allocation keys have been described as arbitrary and 'incorrigible' (Thomas 1974), because no theoretical justification can be provided for any particular key. Allocation keys are a matter of management and accounting judgement, based on knowledge of a particular business and the situation it faces. Under conventional accounting practices, it is important that any allocation key chosen is closely linked to actual environmentally related costs. In practice, the following four groups of allocation keys are widely discussed in relation to environmental issues:

O The volume of throughput (materials, emissions and waste treated)

O The toxicity of emissions and waste treated

O The environmental impact added (volume multiplied by the impact per unit of volume of the emissions treated)

O The induced costs associated with treating different kinds of throughput (materials and emissions treated)

One possibility is to allocate environmentally induced costs based on the volume of hazardous waste caused by each activity or cost object (e.g. volume treated per hour, waste per kilogram of output and emissions per working-hour of a machine). This key may be inappropriate in cases where the capital costs (interest plus depreciation of construction costs) as well as variable operating costs are not related to the total volume treated. Owing to higher safety and technological requirements, construction costs and variable costs often increase exponentially the higher the degree of toxicity of the waste treated. In many cases, these additional costs are caused by only a small percentage of the overall waste. Thus, the costs of a waste treatment or prevention facility are often not clearly related to the overall volume of waste treated but rather to the relative amount of cleaning required, depending on the type of waste.

Another possible key is to allocate environmental costs according to the potential adverse environmental impact that would have been added by the treated emissions. The environmental impact added is calculated by multiplying the volume of waste by the toxicity of the emissions. However, this allocation key may also be inappropriate as the costs of treatment are not always related to the environmental impact added.

Hence, following conventional practice, the choice of an allocation key has to be based on each specific situation. Allocation keys should be chosen on the basis of the specific costs caused by the different kinds of emissions treated. Sometimes a volume-related key best reflects the costs caused, whereas in other cases a key based on environmental impact is more appropriate. The appropriate allocation key depends on the variety and the kind of materials and emissions treated or prevented. Also, the time of occurrence may be relevant (past, current or future costs) because necessary data may for example not be available (e.g. the environmental impact created).

6.4.4 Conclusions

Companies have faced substantial increases in environmentally related costs over the past decade. As a result, there is more to be gained in financial terms from corporate environmental protection. However, many firms are still not aware of the potential savings they could achieve through the introduction of environmental protection measures. Four reasons account for this gap between potential and realised gains, as follows.

O Management often underestimates the actual amount of environmentally induced costs because most management accounting systems still do not isolate environmentally induced costs in the accounts. From a management perspective it makes sense to track and trace environmentally related costs to help determine how much the company is affected financially by environmental issues.

☐ The need for compliance with environmental protection regulations and measures is regarded as the sole cause of environmentally induced costs. This view has its origin in the fact that environmental costs are often thought of as the costs of installing and operating end-of pipe devices and other pollution abatement technologies. But there is a need for managers to expand the definition of environmental costs to include the costs of 'wasted' materials and energy. Associated with this expanded definition, which adds eco-efficiency issues to the need for compliance with standards, is the need for managers to consider environmental issues as a way of reducing overall costs, at the same time as reducing environmental impacts of corporate activity. Consequently, environmental protection includes all measures to reduce use of material and energy resources as well as end-of-pipe compliance technologies that lead to costs because of the need to treat 'excess' material (or waste).

☐ Environmentally related costs are considered to be general overhead costs. However, under conventional management accounting, in order to calculate product contribution margins more accurately, there is a need for environmentally related costs to be comprehensively tracked and allocated in the first place.

☐ Indirect costs of material and energy flows causing environmental impacts are neglected. In many cases, investment appraisal of environmental protection projects compares the direct (capital investment) and operating costs (labour and maintenance) of environmental protection with only the direct costs of waste and sewerage. Overhead cost savings, related to the environmental impacts of reduced material and energy flows, are often ignored altogether.

As a consequence, management accountants have four responsibilities with respect to environmentally induced costs. First, any environmentally induced costs have to be adequately defined, tracked and traced.

Second, only those costs that relate to the same production period should be treated as period costs (i.e. all past, current and future costs that relate to current production should be considered together).

Third, environmentally and economically responsible and accountable management needs to allocate environmentally induced costs to 'responsible' cost centres and cost objects. Indeed, as Burritt (1998) argues, companies seeking sustainable outcomes can give a corporate commitment to the introduction of an internal environmental cost allocation system designed to reduce environmental impacts by penalising poor environmental performance and risk-taking by 'responsible' cost centres. Activity-based costing helps to define the cost centres and objects related to production and management activities.

Fourth, there is no general rule for the ideal allocation key, but there are a number of reasons why allocation takes place, and these help determine the keys chosen (Zimmerman 1979). The suitability of an environmental cost allocation key depends on the variety and kinds of material flows and emissions prevented or treated. However, as far as possible, the allocation key should reflect the costs actually caused by an activity.

The implementation of these steps does not require a revolution in conventional management accounting but, from a business perspective, it is necessary. By inference, implementation of these steps implies the need for material flow-oriented and energy flow-oriented ecological accounting to be introduced. Such a change may meet with opposition, but it makes sense. This broader definition of environmental costs and changes in the way cost allocation is used to discourage activities with highly unfavourable environmental impacts can lead to a redistribution of power towards sustainable outcomes for any company. Without commitment, understanding and a desire for suitable change and learning, line managers with currently profitable products will tend to object to the introduction of allocation rules whenever they expect losses from those rules to affect their welfare. Also, in comparison, the 'internal company lobby' for cleaner activities, processes and products may be neither well established nor large enough to carry weight in decision-making. Environmental management accounting helps to recognise and address these issues (United Nations 1999).

Environmental impacts of company activities frequently have a long-term impact. Capital budgeting and associated investment appraisal techniques are specifically designed to take long-term financial aspects of investments into account. Clearly, it is important that long-term environmental outcomes are considered in long-term project appraisal. Therefore, the next section examines investment appraisal as a tool for managerial decision support and contemplates how environmental considerations should be addressed.

6.5 Consideration of environmentally induced financial effects in investment appraisal

6.5.1 General considerations

Investment appraisal (the financial measurement phase in capital budgeting) is one of the most important managerial activities. Other terms used in this context are 'economic feasibility analysis', 'total cost assessment' and, in an environment-specific sense, 'cost–benefit analysis' (Spitzer et al. 1993: 7). The basic notion behind investment appraisal is to provide financial information that facilitates a comparison between different investment alternatives. It is not the intention here to review the various methods of investment appraisal (see e.g. Götze and Bloech 1993; Horngren et al. 2000) but to discuss how environmental issues are best included in investment appraisal.

Gray (1993: 153) suggested there is no best way, because each method needs to take environmental considerations into account: 'Just as there is no single method of evaluating investment opportunities, there can be no single way of incorporating environmental considerations into investment decisions'. Nevertheless, the task of investment appraisal has been complicated by the increasing importance and uncertainty of environmentally induced future costs (Box 6.10; see also Epstein and Roy 1998). Although not discussed here, a similar argument holds true for financial investments (see e.g. Knörzer 1995; Schaltegger and Figge 1997, 1999). An outline of the shortcomings of methods such as the payback period, annuity method or the internal rate of return can be found in any textbook on corporate finance (see e.g. Brealey and Myers 1991).

The basic goal of investment appraisal is to calculate the net effect of the benefits and costs of different investment alternatives. Any determination of eco-efficiency is one necessary step towards sustainable development, which requires that environmentally induced costs and benefits be considered. This section will therefore focus on environmental costs including quantifiable economic benefits caused by cost savings. However, this is not meant to imply that environmentally related benefits such as higher sales or a better company image are not relevant.

Box 6.10 **Future consequences of investment in ozone-depleting chemicals**

BECAUSE OF SUBSTANTIAL UNCERTAINTY ABOUT FUTURE NET CASH flows, management is inclined to underestimate potential future outflows that are not certain. Ignorance about future trends has led many companies to phase out products that were warmly welcomed at the time of their introduction. For example, chlorofluorocarbons (CFCs) have been phased out as concern for the stratospheric ozone layer has mounted (Burritt 1995). CFCs were first manufactured in 1931 as safer substitutes for ammonia and sulphur dioxide, the toxic refrigerants then in use, because they were very low in toxicity, non-flammable, stable and extremely energy-efficient. Their use was heralded in the refrigeration industry and applications were soon found in thousands of products—automobile air conditioners, all home refrigerators and freezers, water coolers and fountains, aerosol sprays, asthma inhalers and cleaners for electronic circuit boards, among others.

The international Montreal Protocol Treaty was enacted in September 1987 and initially called for a 50% phase-down in CFC production in developed countries by 1998. In 1988 the US National Aeronautics and Space Administration (NASA) Ozone Trends Panel provided the first scientific consensus that CFCs were linked to ozone depletion. Since then, new science has prompted a more urgent response and the world's developed countries ended CFC production for sale by 1 January 1996.

There is, naturally, considerable resistance to phasing out a project once it has become apparent that investment assumptions made in the face of uncertainty have not been correct. Once investments have been made, a large financial incentive exists to delay any phasing out of the associated project. The production of ozone-depleting chemicals by DuPont serves as an example. The figures for the period 1986–96 are as follows (1986 = 100):

1986	1987	1988	1989	1990	1991	1992	1993	1994	1995	1996
100	117	119	112	66	51	43	35	33	29	25

The company has now ceased CFC production at all facilities around the world, except in Brazil, where the government has requested continued production to be allowable to developing countries under the Montreal Protocol.

First, delayed phasing-out extends the depreciation period, which increases the short-term profit potential. Second, the final companies in the business have no other competitors and benefit from exceptionally high profit margins (e.g. on DuPont and CFCs, see DuPont 1993). These advantages have to be weighed against a potential bad image, legal requirements and pressure from stakeholders.

The following approach to investment appraisal is related to total cost assessment, a method that has been advocated by the US EPA to evaluate capital investments. Total cost assessment attempts to describe a long-term, comprehensive financial analysis of the full range of internal (i.e. private) costs and savings of an investment (White and Becker 1992; Spitzer 1992: 7; Spitzer et al. 1994). The following steps towards inclusion of environmental considerations in investment appraisal can be identified:

☐ Expansion of the cost inventory

☐ A comprehensive allocation of costs

☐ Extension of the time-horizon and the use of long-term financial indicators (net present value and option value)

An expanded cost inventory considers four categories of costs:

☐ Direct costs (capital expenditures, operations, maintenance, expenses, revenues, waste disposal and energy)

☐ Indirect costs (administrative costs, regulatory compliance costs, training, monitoring, insurance, deterioration and depreciation)

☐ Potential liabilities (contingent liabilities, potential fees, fines and taxes)

☐ Less tangible costs (costs saved by not polluting and by having a better product image and better employee relationships)

The calculation of direct costs forms a necessary part of any method of investment appraisal. However, environmentally related costs are sometimes hidden in general overhead costs and therefore are not considered separately. In particular, indirect costs, potential liabilities and less tangible costs are often difficult or impossible to identify, measure and allocate. Nevertheless, these costs can very much affect the cost structure and thus the profitability of an investment. Hence, in many cases, it may actually be worthwhile to put some effort into identifying these costs.

It can be concluded that, depending on the definition used for environmental costs, as well as on the rules of allocation applied, environmentally related costs can substantially affect investment decisions and can determine which investments will be perceived as economically favourable. Many economically profitable investments, especially for environmental protection, would not be accepted if management were to rely on traditional allocation rules that consider only the direct costs of environmental cost centres (e.g. incinerator costs). As discussed above, three steps of a comprehensive allocation system can be distinguished:

☐ The allocation of costs of joint environmental cost centres (e.g. incinerators) to production cost centres and activities

☐ The allocation of costs of production cost centres to cost objects

☐ The allocation of environmentally induced indirect costs of excess material used to production cost centres and cost objects

A further step on the path to incorporate environmental considerations into investment appraisal is to extend the time-horizon and use long-term financial indicators. Environmental investments often have longer payback periods than other investments because the relevant benefits and losses often accrue many years in the future. However, this is not always true, as investment examples with very short payback periods in the Australian confectionery industry show (Box 6.11).

Use of payback, as illustrated in Box 6.11, emphasises the need for an investment to pay back within the shortest time possible. Once the payback time has been reached, future cash flows are ignored. Other investment appraisal techniques consider all cash flows associated with an investment. Hence, the use of financial indicators with a focus on long-term outcomes is essential, especially for assessing potentially high contingent liabilities and expected high future benefits beyond the payback period.

A second point is that managers need to be aware of possible long-term environmentally induced financial impacts. For example, new regulations that require the internalisation of previous external costs can be introduced at very short notice and so keeping an eye on potential environmental liabilities through long-term financial indicators is a necessary characteristic of good management. The USA 'Superfund' legislation—the Comprehensive Environmental Response, Compensation and Liability Act (CERCLA) of

---

Box 6.11 **Short payback of environmental investments at Cadbury Schweppes, February 1997**

Source: Environment Australia 1999

CADBURY SCHWEPPES PTY LTD'S PLANT IN RINGWOOD, VICTORIA, produces a range of confectionery products, including Easter eggs, chocolate bars and other chocolate-coated items. The plant currently produces more than 25,000 tonnes per annum of chocolate products, including the brand names Cherry Ripe, Crunchie Bar and Red Tulip. Cadbury Schweppes identified many opportunities for improvements based on the introduction of a few simple and innovative techniques to minimise waste. These cleaner production initiatives included:

☐ Recycling of solid waste

☐ Pipe insulation

☐ Chocolate moulding

☐ Caramel extrusion

The economic benefits of cleaner production initiatives are summarised in the table.

Initiative	Cost ($)	Savings ($ per annum)
Solid waste recycling	20,000	80,000
Pipe insulation	70,000	30,000*
Chocolate moulding	0	30,000
Caramel extrusion	330,000	185,000
Overall annual savings		780,000
Payback period		Less than 16 months

* Plus avoided capital expenditure

1980—provides a well-known example as it shows the enormous, unexpected financial impacts that may be caused by long-running environmental issues that suddenly catch the regulatory eye (see Section 7.5).

Calculation of long-term financial indicators will help managers to consider future environmentally induced financial impacts in advance. In particular, two long-term financial indicators have been discussed within the context of environmental accounting:

☐ Net present value (NPV)

☐ Option value

The NPV is calculated by using equation [6.1]:

$$\text{NPV} = \sum_{t=0}^{n} \frac{F_t}{(1 + r)^n} \qquad [6.1]$$

where

F_t is the net cash flow (cash inflow minus cash outflow) in time-period t

r is the discount rate (the opportunity cost of capital)

n is the number of periods

The opportunity cost of capital, or the costs of a non-realised alternate investment activity, is taken into account by discounting the net cash flows in each period. The sum of all discounted net cash flows determines the overall value of a project. Projects with a positive NPV should be accepted unless non-financial factors suggest otherwise. Likewise, projects with a negative NPV should be rejected.

When environmental considerations are taken into account, it could be argued that the concept of discounting is fundamentally unethical because a lower value is assigned to the needs of future generations, as represented by the discounting of future cash flows. This is in sharp contrast to the need to conserve assets for future generations because they have a high—rather than a discounted—future value. Economists argue that discounting is a necessary assumption for the discounted cash flow method to function, but, acknowledging its flaws, they propose the use of a lower social discount rate for environmentally related investments (e.g. Wicke 1998). Such environmental projects, designed to deal with problems that it is thought will become progressively more serious over time, then appear to be more attractive. Thus, with a lower discount rate, future costs appear to be more important and company investments need a longer time-horizon to pay off.

However, suggestions for the omission of discounting and the manipulation of the discount rate are problematic, as the calculated results do not reflect the actual economic situation. Many of the long-term environmental problems that give rise to these complaints against the NPV investment appraisal criterion relate to events which, if they were to occur, might be very far-reaching, or catastrophic, in their effects. Consequently, the problem could be seen as undervaluation of the absolute benefits to be derived from environmental services rather than any need to adjust the discount rate (Ahmad 1983). Any investment appraisal should indicate the full economic values of alternative investment opportunities. Other, non-economic, aspects might be considered separately but should not distort the economic analysis.

In addition to the above environmental cost–benefit considerations, the NPV method also has some problems from the point of view of economics (Box 6.12). First, it does not explicitly consider non-quantified and non-quantifiable effects. This is a weakness, especially for strategic management, where the potential for success has usually also to be evaluated with use of qualitative information. Second, as with any other method involving trying to evaluate future effects, much of the data used when calculating the NPV are uncertain. In other words: calculation of the opportunity cost of unrealised gains from environmental protection could conceivably be underestimated.

To a certain extent, decision-makers can address these problems by considering the use of option value. The net present value (NPV) rule—invest if the present value of expected cash flows is greater than the investment outlay or investment benchmark—implicitly assumes that a decision to invest is made immediately. It neglects the possibility of waiting to implement the decision until more information has come to light (the precautionary principle of sustainable development) and until some uncertainty about the future has been resolved. Real options valuation is a way of taking account of this possibility. Real options are flexible approaches allowing managers to postpone, expand or contract investment projects over time (see e.g. Loderer 1996; Mostowfi 1997).

An option represents a right, but not an obligation, to acquire expected future cash flows by paying the investment outlay and can thus also be defined as the right not to undertake a follow-on investment. The option value takes the NPV as well as the strategic value of investments into account (see Brealey and Myers 1991; Dixit and Pindyck 1993, 1995).

Strict application of the NPV method very often ignores the value of creating or exercising options or the costs of impeding future options, because the NPV method was conceived for the valuation of bonds that have constant, known future cash streams over a determinate future period. To choose a project with a positive NPV over one with a negative NPV might remove the possibility of a follow-on project with a positive NPV. For example, a follow-on project from the initial, positive-NPV, project may become too expensive or may lose feasibility because of environmental degradation arising from the

Box 6.12 **High clean-up costs in the distant future**

THE MANAGEMENT OF A COMPANY HAS TO DECIDE WHETHER TO INCUR clean-up costs of $100 million in 50 years as a result of an activity that increases its cash inflow today by $1 million.

According to the net present value (NPV) concept, management would be advised to choose the option that creates the cash inflow today, because the discounted value of the cash outflows in 50 years (discounted at a rate of 10%) is lower than the cash inflow of $1 million received today.

This means that, according to the NPV criterion, the company should use the natural resources now, cash in today and accept the postponed disposal costs. However, the damage of $100 million could be disastrous for future generations as well as for the company. The damage caused may reduce options available for future generations and prevent the company from making future investments. The effects on future business options should therefore be carefully considered too. One problem with this suggestion is that valuing the benefits of these options is not an easy task, given uncertainty and ignorance about the future.

POLLUTION PREVENTION EQUIPMENT WOULD ADD AN EXTRA $4 million to capital spending on a new factory costing $20 million. New equipment could prevent soil pollution that would have to be cleaned up in 10 years at estimated costs of $10 million.

The pollution prevention investment is not economical if the net present value (NPV) method is strictly applied. The discounted value of the clean-up costs is $3.9 million (with an assumed discount rate of 10%), which is lower than the prevention costs of $4 million. Therefore, the value of the company would be $0.1 million higher without the new equipment. However, in 10 years, soil contamination might completely prevent further operations. Thus, the NPV method might lead to a wrong decision from the viewpoint of long-run strategic management if the option of wishing to continue operations after 10 years is not considered as well.

Box 6.13 **Option value and net present value**

Source: Koechlin and Müller 1992

initial project (degradation that may not have occurred under the alternative, negative-NPV, project first proposed; Box 6.13).

Some investments create a special value within the context of other company invest-ments. Sometimes, an investment that appears uneconomic on its own might be crucial if, in fact, it creates an option that enables a company to undertake other profitable investments in the future. A negative NPV today only shows that the project in isolation from other company activities will not pay. However, the project could be very important within the context of any future projects a company may envisage. This effect is called the 'strategic value' of a project and can be expressed as a call option.

Because of emerging scientific evidence about environmental problems, new issues with large impacts on an industry come to the fore very quickly. Many crucial environmental projects (e.g. the launch of a 'green' product line or the introduction of an integrated environmental management programme within a company) are strategic in nature because of their long time-horizon as well as their effect on public perception (e.g. the signals they send out to the general public and to customers). The ability to be able to adapt quickly to new circumstances also clearly represents an option value. Information about ability to adapt is important for strategic management.

As with financial options in financial markets, the value of a strategic option increases with the variability of a project's cash flows (the risk of the project). With stricter legislation and increasing risk, investments to prevent environmental liabilities or to introduce 'green' product lines in order to create new markets have an option value. They entail the option to be more competitive in the future.

The strategic value of going further than merely complying with current regulations increases with the probability of future tightening of environmental laws. An option value can, therefore, be greater than the NPV of pollution prevention equipment (Dixit and Pindyck 1995; Koechlin and Müller 1992).

It has been shown above that using NPV as the main investment appraisal technique may lead to incorrect strategic decisions because the value of future options are ignored. Another issue is that cash flows in the distant future also tend to be underestimated if the option value is not also considered. Future free cash flows are addressed in the next section.

6.5.2 Total environmentally induced costs: an example

The following example shows how consideration of environmentally induced indirect costs of material and energy flows can substantially influence the result of an investment appraisal when compared with the allocation method most frequently employed. Calculations are based on the example used earlier (see Section 6.4.2 and Fig. 6.13 on page 133).

The total amount of environmentally induced costs is $1,945.40, $800 of which are direct costs of the environmental cost centre (i.e. the incinerator) and $1,145.50 are indirect environmental costs.

As shown in Table 6.9, when neglecting the indirect environmental costs related to raw material flow, a waste-reduction investment costing $1,700 to reduce a quarter of the waste is considered to be very unattractive (not profitable).

The direct cost savings are calculated at $200 per annum (a quarter of the direct incineration cost of $800). Assuming the waste-reduction investment is totally financed by credit (e.g. at an 8% interest rate), no change in financial risk structure and a depreciation period of five years, the sum of discounted net reductions of costs and the NPV would amount to $399 and −$1,301, respectively. The profitability index of the investment is negative (−76.51%) and, based on NPV or the index, the investment is therefore not worth accepting.

The result of the investment appraisal changes when the environmentally induced indirect costs of cost centre 3 ($163.60) are taken into account. The profitability index of the waste-prevention measure remains negative (−38%), as seen in Table 6.10. Nevertheless, only if we take into account the indirect costs of cost centre 3, as in Table 6.10, can we illustrate the underestimation of actual, total environmentally induced costs. Waste-reduction investments in cost centre 3 are attractive as they also stop costs related to

Table 6.9 **Investment neglecting environmentally induced indirect costs**

Costs and savings ($ per annum)	Year					
	0	1	2	3	4	5
Investment	1,700					
Operating costs		−100	−100	−100	−100	−100
Direct cost savings		200	200	200	200	200
Net reduction of costs		100	100	100	100	100
Discounted reduction of costs (discount rate of 8%)		93	86	79	74	68
Sum of discounted net reduction of costs	399					
Net present value	−1,301					
Profitability Index (%)	−76.53					

Costs and savings ($ per annum)	0	1	2	3	4	5
		Year				
Investment	1,700					
Operating costs		−100	−100	−100	−100	−100
Reduction of costs		364	364	364	364	364
Net reduction of costs		264	264	264	264	264
Discounted reduction of costs (discount rate of 8%)		244	226	210	194	180
Sum of discounted net reduction of costs	1,054					
Net present value	−646					
Profitability index (%)	−38.00					

Table 6.10 **Investment adjusted for one element of environmentally induced indirect costs**

material flows (i.e. waste) in earlier cost centres. By preventing 50 kg of waste in production step 3, costs can also be reduced in cost centre 2 (50 kg instead of 100 kg of processed waste) and cost centre 1 (150 kg instead of 200 kg of processed waste). Thus, the prevention of 50 kg of waste in cost centre 3 would reduce costs by $690.80 ($363.60 in cost centre 3 plus $163.60 [50% of indirect waste costs in cost centre 2] plus $163.60 in cost centre 1).

The total reduction of all environmentally induced direct and indirect costs of the waste-reduction investment amounts to more than a quarter of the total environmentally induced costs ([$1,945.50]/4 = $486.38). However, the sum of $690.80 could be an overestimation of the costs that can actually be reduced by the material-flow reduction (i.e. waste prevention) investment if some of the environmentally related indirect costs were fixed costs (e.g. cost of administration to comply with regulations) and if they did not decrease in line with the partial reduction in waste emitted.

For simplicity, a cost reduction of $600 per annum is assumed in Table 6.11. The sum of discounted net reductions of costs is now $1,996 and the NPV is $296. This results in an acceptable profitability index of 17.43%. In these circumstances, with cash flows defined correctly, the NPV criterion indicates that the correct decision is to accept the investment.

6.5.3 Opportunity cost of unrealised environmental protection: an example

As discussed at the beginning of this chapter, consideration of opportunity costs can show management whether it has neglected (or would neglect) potential gains in economic efficiency because of unrealised material-flow avoidance and pollution prevention.

Costs and savings ($ per annum)	0	Year				
		1	2	3	4	5
Investment	1,700					
Operating costs		−100	−100	−100	−100	−100
Reduction of costs		600	600	600	600	600
Net reduction of costs		500	500	500	500	500
Discounted reduction of costs (discount rate of 8%)		463	429	397	368	340
Sum of discounted net reduction of costs	1,996					
Net present value	296					
Profitability index (%)	17.41					

Table 6.11 **Investment considering all environmentally induced direct and indirect costs**

Opportunity costs of unrealised environmental protection occur if, for example, an omitted waste-prevention project would have reduced the total costs assigned to a cost centre or a cost object. In Figure 6.14 these opportunity costs are determined on the basis of the same theoretical example used throughout this chapter.

The function of perceived total costs, C^{tot}, in Figure 6.14 represents the perceived environmentally relevant costs without consideration of the environmentally induced indirect cost of the material flow. The perceived total costs are the sum of the costs of environmental impacts (C^{EI}) and the costs of environmental protection measures (C^{REI}). The company will, therefore, choose the optimal point on this curve, $C_0^{tot}(Q_0)$, at environmental impact Q_0. Sliding to the left on this curve, an additional investment in environmental protection which would reduce environmental impacts to Q_2 is perceived to have a negative NPV of $1,301, as in the example shown in Table 6.9.

However, taking the environmentally induced indirect costs into account, the actual total cost curve in Figure 6.14 is $C_0^{real\,tot}$. Opportunity costs of environmental protection can be a result of not recognising future environmental costs, insufficient differentiation of environmentally induced costs and inappropriate cost allocation. At environmental impact Q_0, the actual total costs, $C^{real\,tot}(Q_0)$, are not minimised so that opportunity costs of unrealised environmental protection occur for the company. Opportunity costs of unrealised environmental protection are determined by the difference between the minimal total costs, $C^{real\,tot}(Q_2)$, and the actual costs borne, $C^{real\,tot}(Q_0)$. These opportunity costs can be reduced by increased investment in environmental protection, thereby reducing the level of environmental impacts to Q_2. Once all environmentally relevant costs are included, the waste-prevention investment has a positive NPV of $296 (see Table 6.11) which is equal to the opportunity cost of environmental protection at point Q_0 compared with point Q_2.

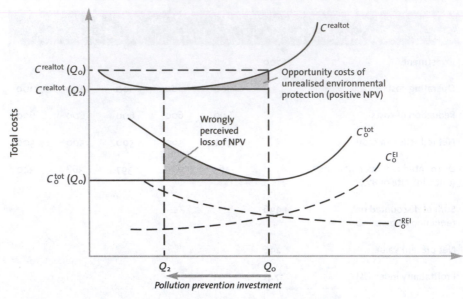

C^{REI} Costs of corporate environmental protection
C^{EI} The company's costs of environmental impacts
C^{tot} Perceived total costs ($C^{EP} + C^{EI}$)
$C^{realtot}$ Real costs

Figure 6.14   **Opportunity cost of unrealised environmental protection measures and the wrongly perceived loss of net present value**

6.5.4 The economic attractiveness of corporate environmental protection: an example

It may seem surprising that cost savings and positive NPVs related to the reduction of throughput have often not been realised. However, the collection and analysis of relevant information comes at a cost. In the past, costs of environmental accounting systems were considered to be higher than the benefits from being better informed. Establishment of an environmental information management system leads to fixed costs that can only be borne if sufficient economically relevant environmental information is provided. As discussed in Section 6.1, this is increasingly becoming the case.

There may be an additional economic reason why managers refrain from considering specific environmental projects even though these projects show a positive NPV—capital rationing. As management capacities and capital are scarce, managers cannot possibly invest in all alternative profitable projects at the same time. Only the most profitable investments are pursued. Selection of the most profitable investments requires a comparison to be made between them. In theory, the NPV of each marginal project decreases with every additional investment accepted, until the final project has only a very small NPV (for reasons of simplicity a static view is taken, neglecting synergetic effects between different investment opportunities). Internal capital rationing guides managers to accept only those projects with the highest absolute NPVs. In Figure 6.15 it is assumed that internal environmental projects (e.g. waste reduction) generally have a lower NPV than do non-environmental projects (e.g. investments in production machinery) with the difference reducing the higher the number of investments made (the curve of the environmental projects is lower than that of non-environmental projects).

On these assumptions, environmental projects become economically attractive once an NPV of NPV_0 is reached. When the highest NPV the company can reach is NPV_1 the optimal amount of environmental investments is P_1^E and of non-environmental investments P_1^{NE}.

To determine the economic priorities of investing, the opportunity costs, or the NPV, of different possible investment projects should be compared. Depending on whether investment appraisal is undertaken in advance or whether the calculations are made to assess the investment afterwards (ex post audit), the most profitable realised investment, or the most favourable planned alternative investment, will be used as a basis for comparison. In practice, management will often simplify the decision-making procedure by adopting a profitability benchmark (e.g. 15% in Table 6.12) for comparison.

Based on the earlier example, the forgone waste-reduction investment is compared in Table 6.12 with the realised investment on the basis of an assumed internal, corporate profitability benchmark of 15%.

The NPV of the realised investment now amounts to $255 (15% of the invested sum of $1,700), which is $41 lower than the forgone cost reduction (i.e. the opportunity cost) of unrealised environmental protection ($296). The difference determines the inefficiency

Figure 6.15 **Balancing the net present value of the alternative investment possibilities**

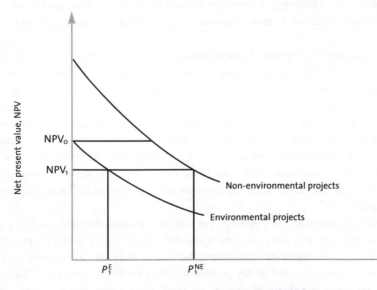

	Cost ($)
Forgone cost reduction of unrealised environmental protection (net present value)	296
Net present value of realised investment*	255
Forgone net present value	41
Forgone profitability index (%)	2.43

* A total of 15% of the invested sum ($1,700)

Table 6.12 **Opportunity costs of unrealised environmental protection**

of the decision or the forgone NPV. In our example, the waste-prevention investment would have had a 2.43% higher profitability index than the alternative project. In fact, corporate eco-efficiency could have been substantially improved by realising the waste-reduction investment (see also Sections 6.1 and 6.2).

6.5.5 Option value

Investments that lead to high sunk costs can determine a certain path for the company, at least for a few years. For example, if a pulp and paper manufacturer refrained from an investment in the prevention of toxic waste emissions it could steer the company towards very high path-changing costs in the future (for a discussion of the economic and environmental aspects of path dependency, see Goodstein 1995). History shows that environmental issues often emerge very quickly and that they can substantially alter the business environment, making it necessary to change from a less to a more eco-efficient path. This rapid pace of change is why environmental projects often tend to be of particular strategic relevance for many companies (e.g. BHP's Ok Tedi mining project; see Chapter 7).

The investment appraisal approach discussed so far does not explicitly consider all potential and strategically relevant aspects of an investment. Opportunity costs of unrealised environmental protection have been defined as the forgone benefits of environmental protection which lead to internal costs and are reflected in the accounts. However, an environmental investment can produce additional, intangible, difficult-to-measure and future, strategically relevant, benefits that exceed the benefits from reducing environmentally related internal company costs. For example, the omission of a waste-prevention investment could cause high costs in the future if toxic waste were to become an issue of high social relevance. In an extreme scenario, the survival of the organisation could be threatened.

One general way to consider such benefits is to take option values into account (see e.g. Dixit and Pindyck 1995). The price of an option is determined by the NPV of a project, the exercise price for any follow-on investment, the time to maturity (the date when the decision has to be made), the risk of the project and the risk-free interest rate. The last three factors influence the discount rate to be used. One major difficulty with the calculation of real option values is the need for management to determine the exercise price for the follow-on investment in advance when, usually, there is no observable market price for the underlying asset of real options, when real options are often shared with competitors and when frequently there may be several real options with the same underlying asset (Crasselt and Tomaszewski 1998).

In this context, methods of early diagnosis of company-relevant environmental issues can be of use (see e.g. Liebl 1996; Steger and Winter 1996). Not undertaking a project even with a negative NPV today might result in a follow-on project becoming either too expensive or not feasible (see Box 6.13). According to the theoretical analysis in Sections 2.3 and 6.1.6 and the illustration used throughout this chapter, potential company-relevant financial effects of environmental impacts have often been underestimated in the past. Consideration of real option value where it can be calculated and included in analysis may well influence the outcome of an investment decision. However, the problem remains that option value is very difficult to estimate.

6.6 The balanced scorecard

The success of managers can only be assessed in terms of progress made towards a given set of objectives (Kaplan 1995; Solomons 1965: 277). Hence, from period to period managers need to establish whether the goals established for their organisation, its business sub-units (e.g. divisions or departments) and for themselves have been achieved. Internal reports are drawn up to assist with this process. Information contained in internal reports can be used to identify whether performance is improving over time as well as whether performance is in line with strategic expectations. Reported information about performance also provides a basis for rewarding or penalising managers who are responsible for specified processes, activities or outcomes.

Conventional management accounting provides feedback about the present and past performance of managers and segments of a company (e.g. divisions). Some accounting tools also provide information about expected future developments for management decision-making and planning (e.g. NPV, real option value analysis and operations budgeting). However, in general, internal reporting about strategic performance is not well developed within conventional management accounting, although the notion of strategic management accounting has received attention in the 1990s (see e.g. Ratnatunga 1999; Smith 1995).

One tool of analysis that has been designed to provide information about performance at a strategic level has recently become popular under the name of the 'balanced scorecard' (Kaplan and Norton 1996). As the name implies, a balanced scorecard provides a selected set of performance measures that, when taken together, show whether a company, its sub-units and its individual managers have improved their (past) performance across a range of activities and outcomes (see also Bennett and James 1999 for a discussion of sustainable measures of performance).

Two important questions are raised by the idea of a balanced scorecard:

☐ Should relative (e.g. ratios) or absolute measures of performance be used?

☐ What types of performance can be measured and integrated?

Chambers (1966: 87) provides a good explanation of the reason why ratio scales, such as eco-efficiency measures, provide the most useful basis for performance measurement. He recognises that measurements can be classified into nominal, ordinal, interval and ratio scales. Nominal scales categorise data by definition (e.g. emissions of gas 1, carbon dioxide [CO_2], and gas 2, nitrous oxide [NO_x]), but with nominal measures there is no way to rank these two properties simultaneously, as they are independent of each other. Ordinal measures take a single property, say CO_2 emissions, and rank performance by position in a series; for example, company 1 has 10 sites emitting CO_2 gas whereas company 2 has 8 sites, and so on.

Interval scales provide a greater degree of measurement precision by using equidistant points on a scale to represent equal differences in the property being measured; for example, site 1 emitted 20,000 tons of CO_2 this month, 25,000 tons of CO_2 last month, and 30,000 tons the month before that. Provided that equal distances (e.g. an increment of 1 ton of emissions between 20,000–25,000 tons is the same as an increment of one ton between 25,000–30,000 tons) represent equal differences in the property being measured then interval scales will have a precise meaning.

Finally, ratio scales have the characteristic that, with the base value taken as zero, the ratio of any series of measurements in the scale remains constant for any change in the defined magnitude of the unit (Chambers 1966: 94). For example, the measurements of two weights bear the same relationship to one another whether those weights are expressed in ton or pounds, and the measurement of two financial magnitudes should bear the same relationship to one another, whether expressed in terms of sales revenue or assets at different points of time. The advantage of using a ratio scale is that for the purpose of classifying performance measurement every object can be classified uniquely by the number assigned to it on the scale.

One key consideration of the concept of the balanced scorecard is whether these different performance measures can be compared in any meaningful way. The balanced scorecard represents a management system that relates four basic modules to each other in order to support the implementation of the vision and strategy of the management (Fig. 6.16).

A balanced scorecard has a number of characteristics. It:

☐ Measures a set of key performance indicators (e.g. financial and environmental)

☐ Specifies goals and measures goal achievement in similar terms (e.g. in terms of environmental impacts and economic value added)

☐ Removes the focus on a single short-term measure of financial results such as return on capital employed, residual income or economic value added

☐ Provides physical as well as financial measures of performance

Furthermore, the balanced scorecard provides a strategic action process with the following four steps (Table 6.13):

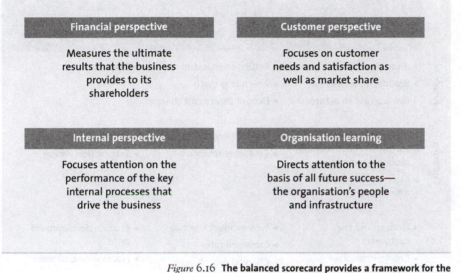

Figure 6.16 **The balanced scorecard provides a framework for the implementation of a strategy into operative measures**

Source: Kaplan and Norton 1996: 9

☐ Formulation and implementation of vision and strategy

☐ Communicating and linking

☐ Business planning

☐ Strategic feedback and learning

From an environmental perspective, one advantage of balanced scorecards is that they have an emphasis on long-term strategic performance as well as on short-run measures of performance. A balanced scorecard supplements traditional short-run financial performance measures with lead and lag criteria that measure performance from the perspective of long-term corporate strategy (Box 6.14). Conventional performance measurement systems emphasise lag indicators that monitor what has happened in the past within an organisation (Corrigan 1998: 30). An increasing focus on value-adding has shifted performance measurement principles towards lead reporting—the monitoring of what is happening now and possible links between lead indicators and potential future consequences for a company.

The need to use more than one measure of performance has long been recognised as being essential to achieving business success. Solomons (1965: 277ff.) identified seven areas of performance requiring measurement as a basis for maintaining control of divisionalised companies:

☐ Financial

☐ Productivity

☐ Marketing effectiveness

	Strategic objectives	Strategic measurements	
		Lag indicator	Lead indicator
Financial	▶ Improve returns ▶ Broaden revenue mix ▶ Reduce cost structure	▶ Return on investment ▶ Revenue growth ▶ Deposit service cost change	▶ Revenue mix
Customer	▶ Increase customer satisfaction with company products and people ▶ Increase satisfaction after the sale	▶ Share of segment ▶ Customer retention	▶ Depth of relation ▶ Satisfaction survey
Internal	▶ Understand the customers ▶ Create innovative products ▶ Cross-sell products ▶ Shift customers to cost-effective channels ▶ Minimise operational problems ▶ Create a responsive service	▶ New product revenue ▶ Cross-sell ratio ▶ Channel mix change ▶ Service error rate ▶ Request fulfilment time	▶ Product development cycle ▶ Hours with customers
Learning	▶ Develop strategic skills ▶ Provide strategic information ▶ Align personal goals	▶ Employee satisfaction ▶ Revenue per employee	▶ Strategic job coverage ratio ▶ Strategic information availability ratio ▶ Personal goals alignment (%)

Table 6.13 **The balanced scorecard as a strategic action process**

Source: Kaplan and Norton 1996: 10

☐ Product leadership

☐ Personnel development

☐ Employee attitudes

☐ Public responsibility

His aim was the development of an integrated set of measures designed to assess the many facets of business performance. Kaplan and Norton's balanced scorecard extends Solomons's analysis to include corporate strategy. For Kaplan and Norton, a balanced scorecard puts strategy and vision, not management control, at the centre of analysis. It

❝ THE BALANCED SCORECARD, A NEW MANAGEMENT SYSTEM DEVISED by Harvard Business School Professor Robert Kaplan and Renaissance Solutions President David Norton, was conceived with Information Age business dynamics in mind. It uses a broad range of 'leading and lagging' indicators—customer perspective, internal/business processes, learning and growth, AND financials—to evaluate whether a business is moving toward its strategic goals. Equally as important, The Balanced Scorecard is a communication system that bridges the gap between goals set at a high level, and the front-line workers whose performance is ultimately responsible for reaching them. The Balanced Scorecard lets executives express to thousands of employees how their individual efforts contribute to the business's success, and it lets employees tell executives what day-to-day realities affect their progress. ❞

Box 6.14 **What is a balanced scorecard?**

Source: www.gentia.com/balanced_scorecard/backgrounder.htm, on 16 June 1999

establishes goals but assumes that people will adopt whatever behaviour and actions are necessary to arrive at those goals rather than have their behaviour tightly controlled. Instead of tight control, with a balanced scorecard measures of performance are designed to pull people towards an overall corporate vision (Kaplan and Norton 1996).

A balanced scorecard is a useful tool for promoting awareness both of the financially induced and of the physical aspects of environmental management. It provides the opportunity to measure financial aspects of corporate environmental performance and, once a top management commitment has been made to integrate the environment into decision-making, planning and control, a balanced scorecard forces managers to decide about the relative weighting to apply to financial and environmental performance. Each company has to decide whether environmental performance should receive a high or a low weighting. Environmentally sensitive industries, such as mining, petroleum and chemicals, might be expected to include aspects of the environment in their 'balanced' performance measures. Kaplan refers to one petroleum company that ties 60% of its executives' bonuses to a weighted average of four financial indicators—return on capital, profitability, cash flow and operating cost. It bases the remaining 40% of bonuses on indicators of environmental responsibility, customer satisfaction, dealer satisfaction and employee satisfaction (Kaplan 1992).

At this point, no agreement exists on the appropriate set of environmentally induced financial measures and related environmental performance indicators to include in a balanced scorecard. It might be expected that similar industries would tend to use similar measures. However, in practice, diverse measures are being used by similar organisations. Recent attempts have been made to encourage a degree of standardisation in financial measurement of environmental performance. For example, the recommendations of the Sustainability Reporting Guidelines, an initiative of the Coalition for Environmentally Responsible Economies (CERES) (GRI 1999) are shown in Table 6.14.

The guidelines do provide two useful specific links between financial and other types of performance information. First, organisations are encouraged to report normalised data with use of appropriate normalising factors taken from the 'Profile of the reporting entity' (GRI 1999: 9). Second, in line with the argument above, reporting of information in ratio

QUANTITY	RECOMMENDATION
Statement of the chief executive officer	▶ Performance on benchmarks versus previous years and industry norms
Key indicators	▶ Indicators of economic aspects of operational performance
Profile of the reporting entity	▶ Net sales ▶ Debt : equity ratio ▶ Employee wages/salaries/benefits ▶ Total taxes ▶ Total assets ▶ Other (e.g. gross margin, value added, net profit)
Policies, organisation and management systems	▶ Management systems pertaining to social and environmental performance such as environmental accounting
Stakeholder relationships	▶ Use of information (e.g. performance benchmarks and indicators) by stakeholders
Management performance—pertaining to laws, conventions and other mandatory standards	▶ Magnitude of penalties for non-compliance with all applicable international declarations, conventions and treaties, and national, sub-national and local regulations associated with environmental issues ▶ Costs associated with environmental compliance: environmental operating costs (e.g. training, licensing, legal monitoring, permitting, waste management) and environmental capital costs (e.g. waste-water treatment plants, emissions control equipment) ▶ Environmental liabilities under applicable laws and regulations ▶ Site remediation costs under applicable laws and regulations
Operational performance	▶ None specified
Product performance	▶ None specified
Sustainability overview	▶ None specified

Table 6.14 **Sustainability reporting guidelines of the Coalition for Environmentally Responsible Economies (CERES)**

Source: GRI 1999

form (e.g. eco–efficiency indicators) is suggested as a useful, concise method to adopt. These foundations will assist transparency and accountability processes within organisations.

When implementing the balanced scorecard some rules may be helpful to secure its usefulness (Box 6.15).

Given a desire to integrate environmental strategy with other business strategies, it is important to translate environmental strategy into measures of performance that reflect a desire to reduce the use of materials and energy, to lower the proportion of waste (or residues) and to encourage environmentally benign process and product design. A balanced scorecard will facilitate this integrated approach to internal responsibility structures and accountability for management performance.

6.7 Summary

Rapid emergence of environmental issues has prevented many managers from being adequately informed about potential and actual environmentally induced costs and benefits. In addition, most management incentive systems have not been adapted to reflect this new situation. Given the growing importance of environmentally induced costs and

Box 6.15 **Seven rules for implementing a balanced scorecard support system**

Source: 'Automating the Balanced Scorecard: Maximising Corporate Performance through Successful Enterprise-Wide Deployment', www.gentia.com/products/rbsc_whitepaper.htm, on 25 October 1999

THE BALANCED SCORECARD MUST:

1. Provide linkage from the corporate vision to strategic objectives to key performance measures and show 'cause and effect': it must be more than a list of measures, from vision to strategy, to objectives, to measures, using drill-down and cause-and-effect diagrams.

2. Allow creation and linkage of organisation and personal scorecards: scorecards should be created and managed across business units, and individual scorecard portfolios should be built.

3. Support both quantitative and qualitative information: the numbers are important, but the commentaries add real meaning.

4. Encourage dynamic communication: it should be more than a reporting vehicle; it is a strategic feedback system. It must support feedback loops, dialogue, comments, personalised assessments and initiative management.

5. Be easy to set up and maintain: it should have standard implementation features with security and user access definitions and multiple language support.

6. Be enterprise-deployable: it should be deployable to all levels of the organisation and accessed by many users, across mixed platforms and information technology (IT) infrastructures (including the World Wide Web!).

7. Link through to tactical and operational business intelligence applications: it should exist in an integrated environment with linking feeder systems and drill-through to analytical applications specific to that organisation.

the decreasing marginal cost of providing information, it has been argued that the opportunity costs of unrealised environmental protection may be very significant for many companies. Furthermore, potential cost savings from unrealised pollution prevention has not occurred because environmental protection has previously been defined too narrowly in terms of end-of-pipe compliance-based technologies which merely cause additional costs for business.

A change in this perspective is long overdue. Environmental protection should focus on the reduction of material and energy flows and the related environmental impacts and economic advantages. Eco-efficiency provides a means of promoting this change in perspective. The argument that opportunity costs of unrealised environmental protection are relevant in practice has been supported empirically through a large survey of companies in Washington State (WSDOE 1992b, 1992c, 1993b). Acknowledgement, consideration and reduction of these opportunity costs of unrealised environmental protection is an imperative if corporate eco-efficiency is to be improved and the results communicated within the management structure in order to provide appropriate motivation and rewards for managers.

Accounting practices, especially environmental accounting practices, are extremely important in providing support for the new perspective because they strongly influence management actions. An appropriate accounting for environmentally induced costs and revenues enhances future profitability and reduces environmental impacts, first, because relevant costs and revenues are actually reflected in the accounting system, and, second, because only relevant information allows the most profitable management decisions to be taken.

Every level of management is interested in slightly different information. Product managers require different information from that required by site, division or top management. Management accounting should provide relevant information for all levels of management. In addition, data should be related to the activities that influence corporate eco-efficiency and internal accountability most directly.

It has been shown that many economically favourable investments are neglected if traditional rules of allocation and traditional methods of investment appraisal are applied without taking environmental issues into account. To improve corporate eco-efficiency the opportunity costs of environmental protection should be considered and compared with the opportunity costs of alternative investments. Also, strategic option value should be included in investment appraisal because in a growing number of companies environmental issues are, or are becoming, important for strategic management to be successful. How might such success be measured and reported internally? It has already been suggested (see Section 3.4) that a link between economic value added and environmental impact added would facilitate greater internal transparency about financially viable environmental strategies. In this chapter the power of using ratio analysis (e.g. through eco-efficiency) for measurement and internal reporting has been confirmed, and the growing interest in balanced scorecards that combine environmental and financial indicators has been noted. The question now is to consider whether there have been any parallel developments in external financial accounting.

Questions

1. 'Conventional management accounting systems provide the foundation for all other accounting systems.' What are the main differences and links between conventional management accounting and environmental management accounting?

2. Baxter International Inc. (USA) established the following environmental goals in 1997 for 2005: global targets to cut packaging, energy consumption, toxic emissions to the air and the generation of hazardous and non-hazardous wastes. Relevant estimates are provided in Table 6.15.

	Reduction goal* (%)	Base year	Savings†
Reduce air toxic emissions	80	1996	4
Reduce generation of hazardous and regulated waste	35	1996	3
Reduce generation of non-hazardous waste	35	1996	25
Improve energy efficiency	10	1996	13
Reduce packaging materials	20	1995	35

* Per unit of production
† Estimated annual savings and cost avoidance in 2005 were the goal to be achieved (in $ millions)

Table 6.15 **Sustainable development goals for 2005 at Baxter International Inc. (USA)**

   a What are the total estimated annual savings and cost avoidance for Baxter International from environmental improvements in 2005?

   b Are these savings driven by commercial or environmental management considerations? Discuss.

3. Use of the term 'economic cost' may be contrasted with use of the term 'accounting cost'. The term 'cost' is used in different contexts (and by different individuals) with different meanings. It is therefore useful to distinguish the accountant's use of the term from the economist's use.

   Accountants are concerned primarily with the proper recording and measuring of historical costs based on a uniform set of rules. They have developed a comprehensive system of recording and reporting data about costs, which is used by managers, investors, regulators and economists in carrying out their respective jobs. The data recorded in the books and records of a firm are referred to as 'accounting' or 'embedded' costs. Accountants have also developed various internal cost accounting rules concerning how costs should be allocated to various categories.

Economists, on the other hand, have developed a comprehensive set of theories concerning cost, which they use to describe, explain and predict the behaviour of firms and individuals (e.g. consumers). The field of economics thus provides the underlying theory of costs whereas accounting generally supplies most of the data that allow this theory to be applied in practice.

Whereas embedded costs—the accountant's measure of cost—are quite practical, readily available and fairly consistent from firm to firm, the economist's idea of cost is more useful in analysing the critical decisions made by management and government.

(Source: based heavily on text from Ben Johnson and Associates Inc. economic research and analysis; www.microeconomics.com/essays/cost_def/cost_def.htm)

    a What is the difference between an accountant's cost and an economist's cost?

    b How do financial accounting costs and management accounting costs differ?

    c Do accountants and economists have different views of environmental cost?

4. How do full-cost accounting and full-cost pricing differ? Are they related?

5. External and internal costs:

    a How do external and internal environmental costs differ? Provide three examples of an external, and four examples of an internal, environmental cost. In your examples of internal environmental costs include examples of one direct, one indirect, one contingent and one intangible environmental cost.

    b Are the following contingent costs internal or external: natural resource damages; personal injury damages; economic loss damages?

6. What are opportunity costs? Why are they important to managers? What is the opportunity cost of not investing in environmental protection? Provide an example to support your answer.

7. Compare and contrast the following two statements. Are they concerned with achieving eco-efficiency, eco-effectiveness or both?

    ☐ Businesses should sack the unproductive kilowatt-hours, tonnes and litres rather than their workforce. This would happen much faster if we taxed labour less and resource use correspondingly more.

    ☐ The purpose of management accounting information is not accuracy for its own sake but to influence managers towards an organisation's goals. By using cost allocation schemes to penalise poor environmental practices an organisation can encourage environmentally benign behaviour.

Chapter 7

ENVIRONMENTAL ISSUES
IN FINANCIAL ACCOUNTING
AND REPORTING

Environmental issues in financial accounting and reporting are examined in this chapter. The purpose of financial accounting is to generate financial information about a company in order to provide a basis for transparency and accountability relationships with stakeholders such as shareholders, creditors and non-governmental organisations. Financial reporting is used by managers to communicate the dated financial information to external parties. In particular, information reported reflects the financial position and changes in financial position of a company's dated cash-flow information and additional information considered beneficial for stakeholders to receive.

The main environmental topics in company financial accounting are the recognition, measurement and disclosure of environmentally related economic impacts on business (for the development of issues and practices in the USA, see Price Waterhouse 1991, 1992, 1993, 1994; for Europe, see Adams *et al.* 1998; Gray and Owen 1993; for a general survey of disclosure issues, see Mathews 1997).

Section 7.1 discusses the role and influence of standard-setters and regulators of financial accounting practices. The relevance of financial accounting standards can be demonstrated with the example of Daimler Ltd, a German automobile manufacturer. In 1993 Daimler sought to be listed on the New York Stock Exchange. Using German accounting standards, Daimler disclosed a profit of US$372 million; though based on use of US standards, the company had to disclose a loss of US$1.1 billion for the same year (*Economist* 1997a: 58, 59). Another example is provided by the Broken Hill Proprietary Company Ltd (BHP), an Australian resources company. Documents filed with the US Securities and Exchange Commission in 1994 showed that BHP expected to spend US$1.326 billion on 'restoration and rehabilitation' (Walker 1995: 11). However, the annual report distributed to Australian companies showed provisions for restoration and rehabilitation of US$695 million. A similar situation occurred several years earlier when BHP was publishing cash-flow statements in the USA, but not in Australia. The important message is that local financial accounting standards differ between jurisdictions and can substantially influence the economic results of a company. Hence attempts have been made to try to develop an internationally acceptable set of standards for financial reporting in order to help promote comparability between companies, for the same company over time and for the same transactions recorded in different countries (see White and Zinkl's 1997 comments on the need for movement towards standardised environmental metrics).

When examining sustainable development, corporate eco-efficiency and accountability, it is crucial to investigate how environmental issues are dealt with by financial reporting standards. The major question of whether and when environmentally induced financial outlays should be classified as assets or as expenses will be examined in Section 7.2. In this chapter we also cover the recognition, measurement and disclosure of: environmentally induced expenses (Section 7.3); environmentally induced financial impacts on assets (Section 7.4); environmental liabilities, contingent liabilities and environmentally related reserves, provisions and charges to income (Section 7.5); and tradable emission allowances (Section 7.6).

Section 7.7 addresses environmental issues in the management discussion and analysis (chief executive's review or director's review) section (MD&A section) of financial reports.

Environmental issues in financial accounting and reporting are concerned with revenues and expenses (as shown in the income statement, also called the profit and loss account) and with assets and liabilities (as shown in the balance sheet). Under conventional financial accounting practice costs are classified as expenses if they have created a benefit that has expired in the current reporting period. Unexpired costs that can lead to future benefits are defined as assets, whereas property rights of various creditors are classified as liabilities. Liabilities that can only be estimated are commonly called 'provisions'. If their occurrence is uncertain, liabilities are disclosed as 'contingent liabilities' (also called 'potential liabilities').

Environmentally induced expenses are, for instance, fines for illegal waste disposal or clean-up costs to restore land. According to the international accounting standards (IASs) of the International Accounting Standards Committee (IASC 1995, IASs 14 and 16) a scrubber can, for example, be recognised as an environmentally induced asset if it will lead to future economic benefits (i.e. if it facilitates the continuation of future production). Environmental liabilities are future costs such as those of future remediation of landfills or lawsuits.

7.1 Stakeholders' influence on financial accounting

The main stakeholders in management accounting are members of different management positions (e.g. top, product and site managers). Because they form an internal information system, management accounts are subject to almost no external regulation. Financial accounting and reporting, on the other hand, are strictly regulated and standardised. Investors (shareholders) and many other external stakeholders have an economic interest in receiving 'true and fair' information about the actual economic performance of a company. However, this wish to be given a true and fair view of a company's financial position and of changes in financial position is clouded by uncertainty about the actual value of a company and of its shares. Reduction of these uncertainties causes information costs to be incurred. One way of reducing these costs is for public, limited liability companies to publish financial reports to make their financial position transparent to their shareholders and other stakeholders. However, the relationship between stakeholders and management is characterised by information asymmetry. Managers have control of the information shareholders require. Furthermore, managers have every incentive to present economic results in the way that most favours themselves.

Hence, standard-setting bodies and regulatory agencies have been established to try to make sure that necessary information is supplied to stakeholders in an unbiased way. Financial reporting systems use standardised conventions about how to treat (recognise, measure and disclose) specific items. The result of introducing standards and conventions is that the information that is compiled and disclosed should lend support to stakeholder accountability and decision-making needs. Professional financial auditors review company accounting books and financial reports on the basis of these standards and associated guidance notes and interpretations, thereby maintaining credibility of the reported information and the public reporting process.

Financial accounting and reporting standards have, therefore, a big influence on what type of information is collected, analysed and considered for disclosure by management (for a discussion of the role of standards in facilitating communication, see Blankart and Knieps 1993). This is why it is so important for financially induced environmental issues to be adequately covered in financial accounting standards and conventions (see e.g. Achleitner 1995).

Figure 7.1 contrasts providers ('suppliers') of accounting frameworks and external users ('customers') of corporate financial reporting information. On the left-hand side, examples of prominent providers of regulations, standards, guidelines and recommendations for financial accounting are shown. Some of the main groups generating demand for financial report information are depicted on the right-hand side of Figure 7.1. They include shareholders, potential investors, financial analysts, banks, regulators, suppliers, the media and pressure groups.

Financial reporting should provide useful information to external stakeholders, either for decision-making purposes or to help fulfil accountability requirements. According to the IASC, 'The objective of financial statements is to provide information about the financial position, performance, and changes in the financial position of an enterprise that is useful to a wide range of users in making economic decisions' (1998a: IAS 1). These objectives are said to change with the economic, legal, political and social environment. It has also been argued that the content and quality of useful information depends on the specific context of the company (e.g. on the industry it is part of, such as agriculture). Although the IASC places its emphasis on decision-making, it is widely recognised that financial reporting is an important accountability mechanism that allows companies to demonstrate to their stakeholders how resources have been used. For example, the Australian Accounting Research Foundation (AARF), in its second statement of accounting concepts, defines the objective of general-purpose financial reporting as follows:

> Efficient allocation of scarce resources will be enhanced if those who make
> resource allocation decisions, such as those groups identified above, have the

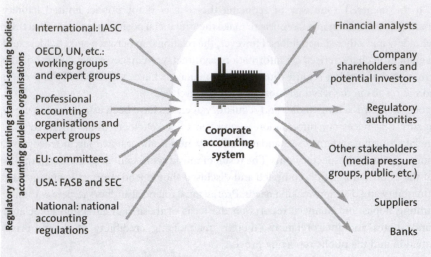

IASC International Accounting Standards Committee
OECD Organisation for Economic Co-operation and Development
FASB Financial Accounting Standards Board
SEC   Securities and Exchange Commission

Figure 7.1 **Different standard-setting bodies and stakeholders with a financial interest in a company**

appropriate financial information on which to base their decisions. General purpose financial reporting aims to provide this information. General purpose financial reporting also provides a mechanism to enable managements and governing bodies to discharge their accountability. Managements and governing bodies are accountable to those who provide resources to the entity for planning and controlling the operations of the entity. In a broader sense, because of the influence reporting entities exert on members of the community at both the microeconomic and macroeconomic levels, they are accountable to the public at large. General purpose financial reporting provides a means by which this responsibility can be discharged (AARF 1990: sections 13–14).

The standards and regulations supplied for companies to apply should serve as tools to help with stakeholder decision-making and to serve the public interest in providing even-handed information that facilitates an efficient functioning of capital and other markets.

Until recently, environmentally induced financial impacts were considered to be adequately covered under existing accounting and reporting standards and regulations. However, the increasing number of environmental issues has generated substantial financial consequences for companies. Therefore, various 'customers' of financial statements have started to influence standard-setting bodies and regulators to get them to alter existing, and to create new, reporting standards, regulations and guidelines.

Also, the most important regulators, standard-setters, professional organisations and other key groups with a stake in financial reporting have begun to acknowledge that existing standards may have to be augmented and that new guidelines should be provided. Three main groups ('providers') directly influence how the managing bodies of companies address environmental issues in financial reports:

☐ Regulatory bodies (e.g. the US Securities and Exchange Commission [SEC]): US SEC was founded in 1934 in response to the Wall Street crash. It supervises the US securities exchanges (Arthur Andersen 1994: 39). US SEC's mission is to administer federal securities laws and to issue rules and regulations to provide protection for investors and to ensure that the securities markets are fair and honest. This is accomplished primarily by promoting adequate and effective disclosure of information to the investing public.

☐ Standard-setting bodies such as the IASC or the US Financial Accounting Standards Board (FASB): the IASC was formed in 1973 to harmonise and improve financial reporting (*NZZ* 1995). It does this primarily by developing and publishing international accounting standards (IASs). These standards are developed through an international process that involves national standard-setting bodies, the preparers and users of financial statements, and accountants all over the world (IASC 1995: 7). The FASB was founded in 1973 (FASB 1994). Since then, FASB has been responsible for the US Generally Accepted Accounting Principles (GAAP). It is a private organisation without legal status. The US government can, however, influence the GAAP through SEC (Arthur Andersen 1994: 39).

☐ Other stakeholders (e.g. professional accounting organisations, international organisations; see e.g. CICA 1992).

Regulators have the strongest direct influence on the management of companies as they create legally enforceable requirements (Fig. 7.2). Nonetheless, regulators in different jurisdictions are strongly influenced by organisations which create financial reporting standards (standard-setting bodies). For example, in the USA, SEC is influenced by pronouncements made by the FASB, although SEC does not always accept such pronouncements.

In addition, other stakeholders, such as professional accounting bodies and financial analysts, or expert groups of international organisations (e.g. United Nations [UN], the Organisation for Economic Co-operation and Development [OECD], the Council of the European Economic Community [CEEC]; see e.g. CEEC 1994), publish guidelines and recommendations that influence standard-setters and regulatory bodies. Furthermore, environmental protection agencies also influence standard-setters. In the past few years some of these organisations have started to address the recognition, measurement and disclosure issues related to environmentally related financial impacts on companies. Most important for companies are the comprehensive national, supranational and international sets of reporting standards (Fig. 7.3).

National accounting standards differ from country to country. Hence an increasing number of multinational companies adopt international accounting standards. However, because of the significance of the US capital markets, US financial reporting standards exert a strong influence on other national as well as on supranational and international

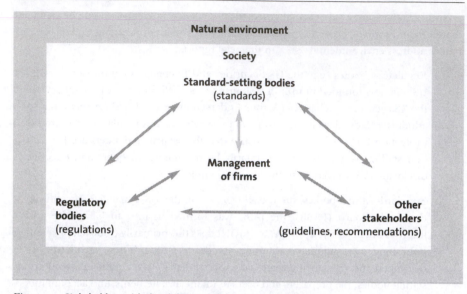

Figure 7.2 **Stakeholders with the ability to define guidelines, standards and regulations for financial accounting and reporting**

standards. In relation to financially induced environmental impacts, US regulations and standards are more advanced than are the international accounting standards (IASs). They might thus provide a benchmark for the direction that international standards are likely to take.

It can be expected that new standards will be issued which focus on environmental issues. However, given the problem that the presence of too many standards increases the costs of reporting and can lead to information overload, new standards should be issued only if they provide clear advantages for stakeholders. Much of the corporate information available to external stakeholders could be improved if existing standards were adapted and if the existing accounting principles were enforced more consistently by regulators.

Figure 7.3 **National, supranational and international accounting standards and regulations**

The IASC is the only global financial reporting standard-setting body. It has members from 143 professional accountancy organisations in 104 countries, representing over 2,000,000 accountants worldwide. It is therefore useful to take a look at the assumptions and conventions behind IASs (Fig. 7.4).

In order to meet the objectives of financial statements, reports are assumed to be prepared on the basis of two assumptions (IASC 1995: IAS 21 and following standards):

☐ Accrual

☐ Going concern

Under the accrual basis of accounting the financial effects of transactions or other events are recognised in the reporting periods in which they occur, to the extent that those financial effects can be recognised, irrespective of whether cash has been received or paid. Accrual accounting provides information about assets, liabilities, equity, revenues and expenses, and changes in them, that cannot be obtained by accounting only for cash receipts and payments. The assumption of a going concern implies that the company will continue in operation for the foreseeable future, specifically, for the next 12-month accounting period.

Figure 7.4 **Assumptions and qualitative characteristics of accounting information**

Source: Characteristics according to IASC 1995: 47-48

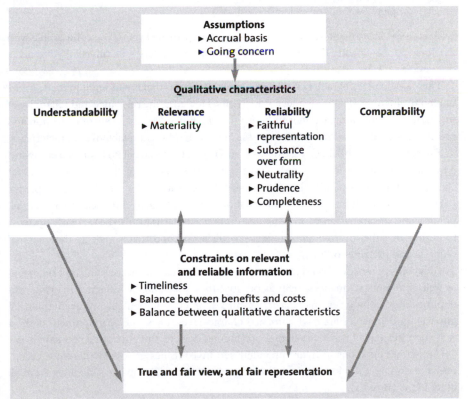

The information provided in financial reports should, moreover, meet specified qualitative characteristics (IASC 1995: IAS F25 and following standards) such as:

□ Understandability

□ Relevance

□ Reliability

□ Comparability

The disclosed information has to be understandable if studied with due diligence and must be relevant to the users of financial statements. Relevant information is determined by its materiality (prospective impact) for understanding the financial position of a company. The usefulness of financial information also depends on its reliability. According to the IASC, reliable information is characterised by being:

□ Faithfully represented

□ Correct in substance in contrast to just being formally correct

□ Neutral (free from bias)

□ Prepared with prudence (i.e. by adopting a certain degree of caution when making judgements)

□ Complete (without omissions)

To support investment decisions, the information provided should be comparable with the financial statements of other companies and with a series of financial statements disclosed over time.

These qualitative characteristics are the main attributes that are thought to make information useful to readers of financial statements. However, the relevance and reliability of financial reporting information is influenced by its timeliness, the costs of collection and possible trade-offs, which are often necessary between different qualitative characteristics.

Financial reports should give a true and fair view of the financial position of a company. The information provided, as well as the fair representation of financial position and changes in financial position, should be externally verifiable to be useful to the recipients.

However, the usefulness of given information varies with changes in the economic, legal, political and social environment. Thus, accounting standards have to be regularly updated to ensure that the information provided is still useful and that it reflects the changed requests and priorities of investors.

Today, environmental issues must be considered in financial accounting and reporting as well as in modern financial analysis because they substantially influence the risks and opportunities companies may face. Examples of environmentally induced financial impacts on companies are environmental charges, fees, fines, site abandonment costs, a reduction in value of heavily polluting production devices and environmental liabilities.

Companies operating in environmentally sensitive businesses should, therefore, recognise, measure and disclose environmentally related financial impacts separately from all other items (Box 7.1).

❝ [Recognition] involves the depiction of the item in words and by a monetary amount and the inclusion of that amount in the balance sheet or income statement totals. Items that satisfy the recognition criteria should be recognised in the balance sheet or income statement. The failure to recognise such items is not rectified by disclosure of the accounting policies used nor by notes nor explanatory material ❞ (IASC 1995: 63, IAS F82).

❝ Measurement is the process of determining the monetary amounts at which the elements of the financial statements are to be recognised and carried in the balance sheet and income statement. This involves the selection of the particular basis of measurement ❞ (IASC 1995: 63, IAS F99).

❝ [Disclosure] is appropriate when knowledge of the item is considered to be relevant to the evaluation of the financial position, performance and changes in financial position of an enterprise by the users of financial statements ❞ (IASC 1995: 64, IAS F88).

❝ Financial statements portray the financial effects of transactions and other events by grouping them into broad classes according to their economic characteristics. These broad classes are termed 'elements' of financial statements ❞ (IASC 1995: 54, IAS F47).

Box 7.1 **Definition of recognition, measurement, disclosure and elements**

Recognition is the formal recording of past or of probable future items (environmentally induced outlays) in the main body of the financial statements (Johnson 1993: 118), whereas measurement deals with the determination of the monetary amount of recognised outlays (Chambers 1966). Items that are relevant to the evaluation of the economic performance of a company are to be disclosed or incorporated into the balance sheet or the income statement.

US SEC is the first and so far only regulator that requires disclosure of all material effects of compliance with environmental regulations on required capital, expenditures, earnings and the competitive position of a company. Concern in the USA is about the impact of environmental compliance costs on the competitiveness of industry. If such costs are low, then their impact will be small. On the other hand, the imposition of environmental compliance costs (e.g. clean-up costs) will encourage companies to be proactive thereby avoiding future environmental costs by investing in cleaner processes and products. Whatever the merits of these arguments, in the USA disclosure of the material effects of compliance is required in the financial statement under 'Description of business' as well as under 'Legal proceedings' (SEC 101 and SEC S-K 103 [SEC 1993]).

The topics dealt with in financial statements are grouped into 'elements' (see the final quotation in Box 7.1) in order to enhance understandability and comparability. The elements related to measurement of the financial position in the balance sheet include assets, liabilities and equity; financial elements in the income statement comprise revenues and expenses.

Environmental issues do not influence all elements and procedures (recognition, measurement and disclosure) of financial accounting to the same extent. Consequently, the remaining sections of this chapter focus on some of the most important and most frequently discussed issues and procedures.

Issues \ Procedures	Tracking, tracing and recognition	Measurement and estimation	Disclosure and reporting
Capitalise or expense?	XX	X	
Environmentally related expenses	XX	X	X
Environmentally induced depreciation and devaluation of assets	X	XX	XX
Liabilities and contingent liabilities	X	XX	XX
Tradable pollution allowances	XX	X	X
Management discussion and analysis (MD&A)			XX

X = important   XX = very important

Table 7.1 **Issues in environmentally differentiated financial accounting and reporting**

The crosses in Table 7.1 indicate the main emphases within an environmental context:

O Classification of environmentally induced outlays as assets or as expenses (Section 7.2)

O Environmentally induced expenses (e.g. costs of remediation and pollution prevention, fees and fines) (Section 7.3)

O Environmentally related financial impacts on assets (e.g. impaired inventory and production devices) (Section 7.4)

O Environmental liabilities, contingent liabilities, reserves and provisions (Section 7.5)

O Tradable pollution permits or allowances (Section 7.6)

O The 'management discussion and analysis' section in financial reporting (Section 7.7)

One of the main areas of concern is the appropriate classification of environmentally induced outlays as assets or as expenses. The distinction is crucial in accounting, and financial accounting standards deal with this topic in detail.

The next section examines the issue of recognising environmentally induced costs as assets or as expenses.

7.2 Environmentally induced costs: assets or expenses?

The issue of whether environmental costs should be capitalised or expensed is one of the most controversial subjects for accountants as well as for financial analysts (Müller *et al.* 1994: 17; Fröschle 1993). In principle, under conventional financial accounting the difference between an expense and an asset is clear (Box 7.2). An expense is a cost that has led to a benefit and has now expired, whereas costs that have been incurred and can lead to future benefits (termed 'unexpired' costs) are classified as assets (Polimeni *et al.* 1986: 10). However, in practice, it is not easy to determine what the increased or decreased (economic) benefits of pollution prevention and emission reduction measures might be (see also Bragdon and Marlin 1972).

Environmental investments have been defined by the Canadian Institute of Chartered Accountants (CICA 1993) as those undertaken to:

☐ Prevent or mitigate environmental damage, or conserve resources

☐ Clean up past environmental damage

CICA identifies two approaches to the question of when to capitalise environmental costs (see CICA 1993; Holmark *et al.* 1995):

☐ The increased future benefits (IFB) approach: the disbursement has to result in an increase in expected future economic benefits from the asset.

☐ The additional cost of future benefits (ACOFB) approach: environmental costs can be capitalised if they are considered to be a cost of the expected future benefits from the asset, regardless of whether there is any increase in economic benefits.

Financial statements are prepared in order to report the financial performance of a company and should not be distorted with issues that are not material in financial terms. From a strict economic perspective, capitalisation of costs should be allowed only if these costs contribute to additional future economic benefits beyond those originally assessed (incremental future benefits, as in the IFB approach).

However, in special cases, the costs of clean-up or pollution prevention may qualify as assets if they are absolutely necessary for the company to stay in business, even though they do not affect expected future cash flows. In this case expenditure is securing the value of future assets, a value that would fall, perhaps to a 'forced-sale' value, if the expenditure were not made. Less clear is the treatment that should be given to other costs that may

Box 7.2 **Assets and expenses**

❝ An asset is a resource controlled by the enterprise as a result of past events and from which future economic benefits are expected to flow to the enterprise ❞ (IASC 1995: 54, IAS F49).

❝ Expenses are decreases in economic benefits during the accounting period in the form of outflows or depletion of assets or occurrences of liabilities that result in decreases in equity, other than those relating to distributions to equity participants ❞ (IASC 1995: 60, IAS F70).

enhance reputation but which are not directly attributable to a specific economic benefit or investment.

A further issue relates to a movement from end-of-pipe improvement to precautionary investment in environmental improvement. If a firm is using old-style end-of-pipe technology, it is likely to be much easier for the firm to isolate the costs of environmental compliance. This is because the costs can usually be more readily identified and fairly clearly attributed to environmental compliance purposes. Hence, identifying an asset value is relatively easy. However, the more that a firm adopts cleaner production approaches, the more difficult it becomes to identify its environmental compliance costs. If environmental management decisions are built into the whole production process, and produce both environmental improvements and cost savings, it is not easy to separate environmental management costs from expenditure designed to return a commercial profit (A'Hearn 1996).

From an environmental point of view, capitalisation in the accounts (and therefore the ACOFB approach) should be favoured if pollution prevention creates future environmental benefits. Furthermore, capitalisation facilitates amortisation over a number of years and therefore enhances long-term thinking (Williams and Phillips 1994).

Nevertheless, it could also be argued that most environmental protection activities are expenses because they reflect a repayment of debt to society and nature. From this perspective, the costs associated with environmental clean-up should be considered as ordinary expenses because they are necessitated by government environmental policy. The purpose of the cost is to use the land properly and protect the public rather than to create a more valuable commercial asset.

In this case, pollution is seen as an increase in the liabilities of a company (liabilities to nature). The costs of reducing liabilities should be expensed and not recognised as investments. Also, the payment of liabilities that were not recognised when they occurred should not be regarded as investments.

The ACOFB approach may be favoured if the rapid emergence of new environmental issues is considered to be unforeseeable and likely to cause unexpected future liabilities. In this case, prudent economic management would require those costs of environmental protection that impede possible future economic problems to be considered as assets.

The IASC has chosen the IFB approach (IASC 1995: IAS 16), whereas the Féderation des Expertes Comptables Européens (FEE) and the Emerging Issues Task Force (EITF) of the FASB have adopted the ACOFB approach. In the short run, such contradictory positions do little to enhance development of a 'global financial architecture' and the emergence of a truly global standard-setter within a global marketplace. In the long run, the FEE has decided to put its weight behind acceptance of IASC standards:

> In the long run IASs are the only option, if one does not want to have a separate set of European standards, and will help to achieve accounting harmonisation in Europe for listed companies and may in addition bring convergence in national standards (FEE 1999a).

This leaves the US GAAP as the other long-run alternative international base for standard-setting. Consideration is being given to assessing the acceptability of IASC

standards for securities listings by overseas companies in the USA, and detailed comparisons have recently been completed (FASB 1999).

IAS 16, section 14, allows the capitalisation of environmentally related costs for property,
plant and equipment if an increase of future economic benefits from other assets is
expected and if the costs are recoverable (Box 7.3). Capitalisation is possible if the costs
are necessary to comply with environmental requirements. However, it is not entirely clear
if to 'comply with environmental requirements' is limited to legal requirements or whether
voluntary activities to comply with social requirements might also qualify for capitalisation (the term 'legal obligation' could be clearer).

IASC has changed the perspective that it expressed in its earlier exposure draft. The
most important change is the omission of paragraph 24 of Exposure Draft E43, which
would have made explicitly clear that environmental clean-up costs and fines should be
expensed if they do not result in an improvement in the originally assessed standard of
safety or efficiency of the asset.

The FEE recommends that costs incurred to prevent future environmental impacts
should be capitalised (treated as an asset, providing expected future economic benefits)
whereas clean-up costs for past environmental damage should be expensed.

Also the EITF of the FASB has a consensus view that treatment costs of environmental
contamination should, in general, be expensed (see also GEFIU 1993). Nevertheless,
capitalisation is possible if one of the following three criteria is met (EITF 1990, issue 90-
8; for a more detailed discussion, see Williams and Phillips 1994: 329):

- The costs extend the life, increase the capacity or improve the safety or efficiency of property owned by the company.

- The costs mitigate or prevent environmental contamination that has yet to
  occur and that otherwise may result from future operations of activities. In
  addition, the costs improve the property compared with its condition when
  constructed or acquired, if later.

- The costs are incurred in preparing for a sale of property that is currently
  held for sale.

In summary, the IASC, the FASB EITF and the FEE all recommend expensing fines, fees
and costs of past environmental impacts. Capitalisation is allowed if a future economic
benefit is expected to result from present expenditure. Costs of voluntary activities to
comply with the requests of critical stakeholders in the company may not qualify for
capitalisation under IAS 16. The EITF and the FEE allow a capitalisation of costs that result
in the improvement of the safety or efficiency of the company property, even if no future
economic benefits are expected and no legal requirements exist. However, the EITF and
the FEE do not require capitalisation of those costs so that the decision whether to
capitalise or to expense is left to management. Arthur Andersen & Co. has criticised this
FASB EITF statement because it allows a free choice on whether to capitalise or to expense
(FASB EITF 1990: 21, discussion issue 90-8). This results in a lack of consistency in
conventional financial reporting.

Depending on the industry or its financial position, some companies may decide to
expense whereas others may capitalise environmental expenditure on voluntary pollution

❝ Property, plant and equipment may be acquired for safety or environmental reasons. The acquisition of such property, plant and equipment, while not directly increasing the future economic benefits of any particular existing item of property, plant and equipment, may be necessary in order for the enterprise to obtain the future economic benefit from its other assets. When this is the case, such acquisitions of property, plant and equipment qualify for recognition as assets, in that they enable future economic benefits from the related assets to be derived by the enterprise in excess of what it could derive if they had not been acquired. However, such assets are only recognised to the extent that the resulting carrying amount of such an asset and related assets does not exceed the total recoverable amount of that asset and its related assets. For example, a chemical manufacturer may have to install certain new chemical handling processes in order to comply with environmental requirements on the production and storage of dangerous chemicals; related plant enhancements are recognised as an asset to the extent they are recoverable because, without them, the enterprise is unable to manufacture and sell chemicals ❞ (IASC 1995: 261, IAS 16, section 14).

❝ [In] general, environmental contamination treatment costs should be charged to expense. Those costs may be capitalised if recoverable but only if any one of the following criteria is met:

1. The costs extend the life, increase the capacity, or improve the safety or efficiency of property owned by the company. For purposes of this criterion, the condition of that property after the costs are incurred must be improved as compared with the condition of that property when originally constructed or acquired, if later.

2. The costs mitigate or prevent environmental contamination that has yet to occur and that otherwise may result from future operations or activities. In addition, the costs improve the property compared with its condition when constructed or acquired, if later.

3. The costs are incurred in preparing for sale that property currently held for sale ❞ (1990, issue 90-8).

❝ Expenditure on repair or maintenance of property, plant and equipment is made to restore or maintain the future economic benefits that an enterprise can expect from the originally assessed standard of performance of the asset. As such, it is usually recognised as an expense when incurred. For instance, the cost of servicing or overhauling plant and equipment is usually an expense since it restores, rather than increases, the originally assessed standard of performance. Similarly, the costs of cleaning the environment and the payment of fines for breaches of environmental regulations resulting from the operation deferred as an item of property, plant and equipment. This is because they do not increase the future economic benefits arising from the related assets. The removal of contamination is also an expense except to the extent that the removal process results in an improvement in the originally assessed standard of safety or environmental efficiency of the asset ❞ (IASC 1992: 11, IAS E43, section 24, omitted in IAS 16).

Box 7.3 **Capitalise or expense?**

prevention. Management of other companies might seek to change the treatment at their own discretion. Although the method chosen has substantial implications, consistency in the treatment of environmental outlays is of critical importance to external stakeholders. Consistency reduces uncertainties about the contents of financial statements and adds quality to the disclosed information.

Although consistency is provided by use of international accounting standards, the divergent views of different accounting standards bodies serve to confuse stakeholders seeking comparable reported information over time and between companies. One possible way forward is to abandon the historical cost basis of conventional financial reporting. This may appear to be a radical step to take but, if assets were reported at market values instead of at accumulated cost, it has been suggested that clearer guidance would be provided for stakeholders (Chambers 1966). Expenditure on pollution clean-up would be treated as an expense and, if such expenditure led to an increase in the market value of an asset, the incremental gain in market value would be reported as a gain. If it produced a decline in the market value of an asset (e.g. property) a loss would be shown. In short, all environmental expenditure would be treated as a period cost, whereas asset values would be based on an independent calculation of market values.

The next section will examine the treatment of environmentally related expenditures that were recognised as expenses, and Section 7.4 discusses environmentally induced financial impacts on assets (e.g. depreciation or impairment).

7.3 Treatment of environmentally induced expenses

Environmental expenses are environmentally related costs that have provided a benefit that has now expired. Expenses are matched against revenues in the profit-and-loss account (income account). Despite the magnitude of environmental expenses in many industries (see e.g. Fichter *et al.* 1997), no financial accounting standard requires their separate recognition, although company law does lay down some disclosure rules (e.g. in Australia).

Environmental issues are clearly part of the risk structure of a company and, where important, they should be disclosed separately if environmentally induced financial risks are to be made transparent. Otherwise, investors will be unable to assess the level of risk of their investments. Separate classification of environmentally induced expenditures from other expenditures would allow investors and other financially interested stakeholders a fuller picture of economic performance as well as of the future opportunities and problems of any particular company. For example, in Australia this risk category has been formally recognised through introduction of s.299(1)(f) of the Company Law Review Act 1998 which stipulates that the directors' report for a financial year must 'if the entity's operations are subject to any particular and significant environmental regulation under a law of the Commonwealth or of a State or Territory—[provide] details of the entity's performance in relation to environmental regulation'. This provision is currently under review by the government.

Tax rules may also influence the treatment of environmental expenditures. In order to enhance 'green behaviour' some environmentally induced costs are subject to tax credits, tax deductions or tax exemptions. A tax credit reduces the tax liability of a company dollar for dollar. Tax deductions reduce corporate tax liability by screening income from taxation (Polimeni *et al.* 1986: 674). Tax exemptions exclude assets or income from being taxed. A tax credit for a certain amount is, therefore, more valuable to a company than a tax deduction or an exemption for the same amount.

Tax credits, deductions and exemptions are effective in most cases. However, sometimes they may act as disincentives. For example, a tax agency might allow certain environmentally induced expenditures to be deducted or regarded as tax credits. If these costs relate to increased asset values they might be classified as expenses in tax reports and as assets in financial reports. As another example, companies will increase their voluntary pollution prevention activities if the respective costs are tax-deductible. However, tax deductions and tax credits amount to externalisation of the costs because, in the end, it is society that pays by receiving smaller tax revenues.

Other costs, such as clean-up costs, are generally treated as ordinary expenses and therefore subtracted from income when calculating the taxable profit.

Certain expenditures are almost never tax-deductible. These include, for instance, legally imposed costs such as fines for breaching environmental laws and some clean-up costs.

Large fines and fees are a signal that a company is a laggard in implementing environmental policy. High insurance premiums may indicate that management has realised potential problems exist but that it is not yet ready to tackle the problems at their source. High premiums might also be interpreted to mean that implementing measures for risk reduction are less economical than taking out insurance. High environmentally induced operational expenditure may indicate that the economic costs of corporate environmental protection could be reduced by investments in more efficient pollution prevention technologies.

However, some first moves towards requiring separate disclosure are in sight (see also Müller et al. 1994: 17). US SEC has addressed the issue of the growing importance of financial impacts of environmental issues for companies. It asks for disclosure of environmental information that is economically material to the issue. This includes the effects on capital expenditures and earnings that compliance with federal, state and local environmental laws may impose.

The securities commissions of Ontario and Quebec (in Canada) require disclosure in the annual report of 'the financial or operational effect of environmental protection requirements on the capital expenditures, earnings and competitive position . . . for the current fiscal year and any expected impact on future years' (Moore 1991: 55; see also CICA 1993; Holmark et al. 1995: 75). This provides investors with information about the future environmental strategy of a company (CICA 1993).

The accounting advisory forum of the European Union recommends disclosure of the amount of environmental expenditures charged to the profit-and-loss account. Expenditures should be analysed in a manner appropriate to the nature and size of a business and/or the types of environmental issues relevant to the enterprise (AAFEU 1994).

Nonetheless, the mere differentiation of environmental expenditures from other expenditures does not provide all the necessary information for investors. At least one further distinction would be useful—between expenditures incurred to improve the environmental record of a company and expenditures incurred because of breaches of environmental law (e.g. fines). Furthermore, expenditures to improve a company's environmental record should be subdivided into outlays incurred for the repair, reduction and prevention of environmental damage. For investors, there is a substantial difference if, for example, one company spends $1 billion on clean-up work whereas another spends $1 billion on the prevention of pollution.

Environmental expenses are often recognised for the first time when they result in a cash outflow and not in the time-period when the expenses are expected to occur. Over the past decade this practice has changed as some companies have started to recognise contingent liabilities for potential fines and expected remediation costs for landfills. However, early recognition of such (potential) expenses requires collaboration with the environmental protection agency concerned. Recognition and disclosure of potential expenses will not be encouraged as long as some environmental agencies use disclosures about potential environmental expenses as evidence of a disregard for prevention activities.

Standards for financial reporting have been shown to influence management accounting, sometimes in an undesirable way (Kaplan 1984). To help address this issue, provision of a breakdown of environmental expenditures in financial reports would, therefore, help to provide an incentive for managers to separate these costs and, where possible, link them with specific company activities. In addition, the consistent treatment of environmental expenditures is a most important consideration for investors.

7.4 Treatment of environmentally induced financial impacts on assets

7.4.1 Assets as unexpired costs

Environmental issues can also have major financial impacts on the balance sheet (i.e. on assets and liabilities). However, it is not a simple matter of identifying the 'correct' figure for environmental impacts on assets and liabilities (Box 7.4).

So far, as with expenditures, no specific standards of financial accounting exist to clarify when environmentally induced financial assets must be recognised, measured and disclosed. Nonetheless, there are general accounting standards that discuss if and when an asset should be recognised (e.g. IASC 1995: 64, IAS F89).

Under conventional financial reporting standards, unexpired costs, expected to provide future benefits, are classified as assets. Ideally, it should be possible to obtain a reliable measure of these benefits. If the benefits cannot be reliably measured, assets should be disclosed in the notes, explanatory material or supplementary schedules (IASC 1995: 64, IAS F86).

The influence of environmental issues on assets is easiest to measure with:

☐ End-of-pipe and integrated technologies

☐ Obsolete inventories

Box 7.4 **Recognition of assets**

❝ An asset is recognised in the balance sheet when it is probable that the future economic benefits will flow to the enterprise and the asset has a cost or value that can be measured reliably **❞** (IASC 1995: 64, IAS F89).

End-of-pipe technologies specifically introduced to treat environmental impacts can be easily classified and recognised as environmental assets. This is more difficult in the case of pollution prevention technologies which, when introduced, are integrated into production technologies. Furthermore, environmental issues and regulations can substantially influence consumer tastes and market conditions and this can result in impaired or even obsolete inventories. These two issues are examined in the following sections.

7.4.2 End-of-pipe and integrated technologies

As a rule, according to the IASC, costs that do not lead to future economic benefits should be expensed in the period in which they are incurred (IASC 1995: 261). The FASB EITF, however, allows capitalisation if the costs mitigate or prevent contamination that is yet to occur and that may otherwise result from future operations or activities. In addition to this, the costs must improve the property compared with its condition when constructed or originally acquired. Nonetheless, no additional future economic benefit has to be expected for an asset to be recognised (EITF 1990: 2, issue 90-8).

End-of-pipe technologies definitely qualify as assets if they are necessary investments introduced to help obtain future economic benefits from other company assets. This is the situation whenever introduction of end-of-pipe technologies is required for legal compliance. Differentiation and also measurement is usually no problem with end-of-pipe technologies as they can easily be identified.

So far, however, no standard requiring a separate recognition, measurement or disclosure of end-of-pipe technologies exists. In addition to providing useful information to shareholders about expenditure on environmental protection, such a standard would create incentives for management to track, trace and link the outlays for end-of-pipe technologies with specific activities (see Section 6.3).

Integrated pollution prevention technologies are part of ordinary production assets. They are bought mainly for economic reasons. Therefore, these environmentally related assets are not separately identified as environmentally induced overhead costs, not even in companies lagging in their accounting practices. A correct classification as non-current financial assets is likely.

The environmentally related part of integrated technologies is often impossible to determine, leaving management a discretionary latitude when considering recognition. The installation of a new production process, for instance, may increase productivity, thus reducing costs per piece, and may simultaneously reduce energy and water consumption, thus reducing environmental impacts. In fact, most new production systems in the manufacturing and material intensive industry lead to increased productivity and reduced material and energy use. Environmental improvements are often a side-effect of technical and economic improvements.

Depending on the incentives given and management motivation, investments in such new production systems may be considered largely as environmental investments or largely as economic investments.

In the past, some companies felt pressed, for image reasons, to overstate the environmentally related part of their assets. Today, with increasing environmentally induced costs, firms are being confronted with a general shareholder concern that managers seek improvement in the economic efficiency of corporate environmental protection. Under such pressure, environmentally related assets tend to be underestimated. Integrated technologies should be recognised as normal capital investments (assets) because:

☐ The investments have mainly been made for economic reasons.

☐ A correct determination of the environmentally induced part of the integrated technology is difficult or impossible.

Such recognition implicitly allows for capitalisation of the environmental part of the investment. This provides an incentive for managers to favour integrated pollution prevention technologies instead of end-of-pipe technologies, as the latter often have to be expensed, thereby reducing short-run income.

Investments in integrated technologies should be mentioned in the management discussion and analysis (MD&A) section of a financial report. This allows specific reporting, of changes in environmental assets, by management. Any environmental improvements flowing from the introduction of environmental assets are reported in external ecological accounting (see the chapters in Part 3 of this book).

7.4.3 Impaired and obsolete inventories and other assets

New, tighter environmental regulations, or a change in consumer tastes, can reduce the financial value of product inventories. In some rare cases, inventories of semi-manufactured or final products can also increase in value or become obsolete. According to the IASC the exercise of prudence requires cautious valuations of assets such as inventories, although this notion tends to clash with the idea of reporting neutral, or unbiased, information.

Conventional financial reporting requires that a decrease in inventory value should be measured at its net realisable value if it cannot be sold at cost or higher:

> The cost of inventories may not be recoverable if those inventories are damaged, if they have become wholly or partially obsolete, or if their selling prices have declined . . . The practice of writing inventories down below cost to net realisable value is consistent with the view that assets should not be carried in excess of amounts expected to be realised from their sale or use (IASC 1995: IAS 2, section 89).

Furthermore, the loss of value should be recognised as an environmentally related loss. This allows (potential) investors to judge the economic consequences of omitted environmental strategies. Also, inventories of products that do not comply with new, tightened, regulations may fall in value. Such inventories should be recognised as a loss or be amortised faster than originally planned to reflect the real market value of the assets to shareholders.

In extreme cases, inventories or other assets (e.g. land) can turn into liabilities. For example, in the USA some creditors (banks) which held land as security against loans have become liable for clean-up costs that exceed the resale value of the land. As a result, in countries such as the USA a company should depreciate property (i.e. land) that is continuously being contaminated (see Rubenstein 1991). If the contamination happens through a single accident, the land should be re-valued. In contrast, the IASC has defined that 'land normally has an unlimited life and is therefore not depreciated' (IASC 1992: 629). The IASC, in other words, implicitly assumes that 'land' is equal to 'space'. Thus, its standard considers only the economic life of the space and disregards the 'ecological life' of the land. However, as the very high remediation costs in the USA demonstrate, land is much more than space. The contamination of land can substantially impair the economic life of a property. These internal costs should be reflected in financial statements either as an environmental impairment of assets or as an environmental liability.

There is already an exception that allows depreciation of land from which natural resources are being extracted. When natural resources are involved, land is amortised by means of a depletion expense. Depletion for GAAP is usually calculated using a units-of-production method, i.e. a certain rate per ton, barrel, cubic foot, or whatever. For tax purposes, depletion is calculated quite differently, normally as some percentage of revenue rather than cost.

The next section deals with environmental liabilities, which may be the main issue for many companies when dealing with environmental accounting and reporting.

7.5 Treatment of liabilities

7.5.1 Treatment in the past

In the past, environmental issues were not a high priority for management until they showed up as liabilities in the books of account. Yet some environmental liabilities have exceeded even the worst-case scenarios of management. Among the major disasters in the 1980s were those of Bhopal (Union Carbide), Schweizerhalle (Sandoz) and Prince William Sound (Exxon), all of which had substantial financial consequences for the companies involved (Box 7.5).

Furthermore, thousands of other companies have also been hit by major liabilities incurred through less spectacular spills and accidents (SDA 1994a).

However, in the USA, legislation has had a greater influence on environmental liabilities than some of these well-known accidents (Brüggemann 1994: 71f.). Notably, the Resource Conservation and Recovery Act of 1976 (RCRA) and the Comprehensive Environmental Response, Compensation, and Liability Act of 1980 (CERCLA, often referred to as the 'Superfund' Act), which enable the US Environmental Protection Agency (EPA) to enforce landfill remediation by companies, resulted in a major increase of corporate environmental liabilities (see e.g. Lobos 1992). Thus, environmental liabilities have become not only much more common but also much greater than ten years ago (Blacconiere and Northcutt 1997; Blacconiere and Patten 1994). A well-known example is Monsanto which in 1992 made a provision for liabilities to clean up waste sites which was almost 83% of its 1991 net income (McMurray 1992).

ON 24 MARCH 1989 THE GIANT OIL TANKER *EXXON VALDEZ* RAN aground in Prince William Sound on Alaska's west coast. Some 40 million litres of crude oil spilled into the sea, causing enormous damage to the marine flora and fauna.

On 13 July 1994 the jury of an Alaskan court ruled that the captain had been a reckless master, having a history of drinking, and that Exxon, which owned the tanker and the oil, had been equally reckless in allowing him to command the *Exxon Valdez*. The announcement of the court's decision in the first of four stages of the proceedings led to a 4% fall in Exxon's share price, wiping out approximately US$ 3.1 billion of its market capitalisation (in the short run). By then, the company had already spent US$2.5 billion on cleaning much of the 2,400 kilometres of beaches soiled by the spill, and a further US$1.1 billion to settle several claims under criminal law.

In the second phase of the proceedings, the compensation payments for the damages to the environment, fisheries and other affected industries were determined. Exxon has, for example, been sued for losses suffered by fishermen. The court decided that Exxon will have to pay altogether only US$268.8 million of the US$895 million originally demanded by the fishermen. However, this is still two times more than Exxon estimated the damage to be.

Third, the court has to decide about the fine. The 11,000 fishermen and other people (including a large group of indigenous people) living at Prince William Sound did demand a fine of US$15 billion. Having spent US$3.5 billion on clean-up, Exxon is confronted with a bill totalling US$16.5 billion: US$3.5 for clean-up, US$1.5 billion in compensation and the rest as punishment.

In a fourth stage, the court will deal with the claims of thousands of individuals and groups that do not belong to those of the third stage of the court case.

In early 1999 a US$5 billion punitive award was made against Exxon. Exxon has appealed against the award on the grounds that it is unjust and excessive.

Box 7.5 **Case study: *Exxon Valdez***

Sources: Aeschlimann 1994: 3; AP 1992a, 1994; SDA 1994b; *NZZ* 1994a, 1994b; *Economist* 1994b, 1994a; Vaughan 1994: 175; Exxon homepage on-line April 1999, www.exxon.com

The aim of CERCLA is to clean up abandoned waste sites (Superfund sites). The liability is regarded as joint and retrospective for all costs incurred in the clean-up. All parties involved can be held liable for the total costs of remediating the landfill. The liability exists even if the activity that caused the environmental problem was legal and the Superfund legislation did not exist at the time. US EPA can require any person or company involved to bear the total of all remedial costs, no matter how much of these the respective party has actually caused (joint and several environmental liability). This shows that environmental liabilities are one way of internalising external costs. Even banks that have given mortgages or managed closed properties can be held liable as mortgagees in possession (Ernst & Young 1992; Skellenger 1992). The cost of cleaning up Superfund sites is expected to exceed US$500 billion over the next 40–50 years (EIU/AIU 1993).

Less well known is that the Superfund amendments also require disclosure of environmental risks arising from company activities (see Dirks 1991; Newell *et al.* 1990; Rabinowitz and Murphy 1992). The International Federation of Accountants (IFAC) explains the four stages in risk assessment analysis (Box 7.6). The process of computation described is an important first step if it is later to have dollar values attached and be disclosed in financial reports.

The main questions regarding the treatment of the environmental liabilities of a company are:

❝ As corporations are increasingly responsible for the financial consequences of environmental contingencies, environmental risk assessments are a growing part of both financial and environmental management and are becoming more central to corporate governance at the board level. Management accountants can play a crucial role in estimating the potential cost of these contingent liabilities to the firm, the likelihood of their occurrence (risk factor), as well as their appropriate allocations. The process of risk assessment involves four stages of analysis:

1. Identifying hazards—The Royal Society in the UK defines hazard as a property or situation that in particular circumstances could lead to harm.

2. Estimating the probability of occurrence—Probability is defined as the frequency of occurrence of a defined hazard in a given period, usually presented as the mathematical expression of chance (such as 1 in 4 or a 25% probability).

3. Evaluating consequences—Consequences are the adverse effects or harm occurring as a result of realising a hazard in the short or long term (also known as the hazard effect).

4. Assessing risk—Risk is a combination of the probability or frequency of an occurrence of a hazard and the magnitude of the consequences of the occurrence and equals probability × occurrence. ❞

Box 7.6 **Environmental risks**

Source: IFAC 1998

☐ What are (contingent) environmental liabilities (Section 7.5.2)?

☐ Should they be recognised, and, if so, when (Section 7.5.3)?

☐ How can they be measured (Sections 7.6.4 and 7.6.5)?

☐ If and when should they be disclosed (Section 7.5.6)?

7.5.2 What are contingent environmental liabilities?

An environmental liability is an obligation to pay future expenditures to remedy environmental damage that has occurred because of past events or transactions, or to compensate a third party that has suffered from the damage. Liabilities have three essential characteristics (CICA 1993; see also AICPA 1994, 1995; IASC 1995: 54 [IAS F49b]):

☐ Liabilities 'embody a duty or responsibility to others that entails settlement by future transfer or use of assets, provision of services or other yielding of economic benefits, on a specified or determinable date, on occurrence of a specified event, or on demand.

☐ The duty or responsibility obligates the entity leaving it or . . . to avoid it.

☐ The transaction or event obligating the entity has already occurred.'

The essential characteristic of a liability is that the enterprise has a present obligation (Box 7.7). According to the IASC (1995 [IAS F60]):

> An obligation is a duty or responsibility to act or perform in a certain way. Obligations may be legally enforceable as a consequence of a binding contract

❝ A liability is a present obligation of the enterprise arising from past events, the settlement of which is expected to result in an outflow from the enterprise of resources embodying economic benefits. ❞

Box 7.7 **Liabilities**
Source: IASC 1995: 54 (IAS F49b)

or statutory requirement . . . Obligations also arise, however, from normal business practice, custom and a desire to maintain good business relations or act in an equitable manner.

Therefore, and under specific circumstances, voluntary pollution prevention and clean-up activities can also qualify as liabilities (see e.g. IFAC 1997).

Future financial consequences of environmental issues are often not certain because of the strong influence of frequently changing regulations and political decisions. The first uncertainty is related to the occurrence of liabilities whereas the second uncertainty concerns their amount:

☐ Will a liability become material (contingent liabilities)?

☐ How large will the liability be (measurement)?

Contingent liabilities (contingencies) are a common way of recognising uncertain outcomes (Box 7.8). A contingent environmental liability is an obligation to remedy environmental damage dependent on the occurrence or non-occurrence of one or more uncertain future events, or to compensate a third party that would suffer from such damage. Examples of (contingent) environmental liabilities that can emerge from corporate activities are:

☐ Soil contamination (e.g. from underground storage or spills)

☐ Groundwater contamination (e.g. from contaminated surface water or soil contamination)

☐ Surface water contamination (e.g. from point sources such as industrial processes)

☐ Air emissions (e.g. from fugitive emissions and transportation activities, as well as from sound, noise and light)

☐ Energy emissions (e.g. heat, radioactive or electromagnetic emissions, noise)

☐ Visual impact (e.g. because of buildings)

Box 7.8 **Contingent environmental liability**
Source: IASC 1995: 181 (IAS 10, 3)

❝ A contingency is a condition or situation, the ultimate outcome of which, gain or loss, will be confirmed only on the occurrence, or non-occurrence, of one or more uncertain future events. ❞

Liabilities and especially contingent liabilities are often associated with a large degree of uncertainty. For consistency and reliability purposes, liabilities must therefore possess certain characteristics in order to be recognised in the main body of a financial statement.

7.5.3 Recognition of environmental liabilities

So far, no specific standard has been issued purely for the recognition of environmental liabilities. Some authors argue that general accounting standards are already sufficient to accommodate environmental liabilities, if they are applied correctly (Hawkshaw 1991: 22f.).

The most important accounting standards specifying if and when to recognise (all) liabilities are IAS F91 and FAS 5 (Box 7.9). As a rule, environmental liabilities should be recognised in financial statements if they are material and if the liabilities or the events leading to the liabilities are probable and can be reliably measured (or reasonably estimated). The words 'probable' and 'reliably measured' (or 'reasonably estimated') are important for the interpretation of the main accounting standards:

> The word probable is used with its general meaning rather than in a specific accounting or technical sense, and refers to that which can reasonably be expected or believed on the basis of available evidence or logic but is neither certain nor proved (Adams 1992: 16).

Therefore, an environmental liability is probable if, for example:

☐ A legal obligation exists.

☐ The management wants to prevent, reduce or repair substantial environmental impacts (FEE 1993).

☐ A company in the US has been named by the US EPA as a 'potentially responsible party' to clean up a US Superfund site (Price Waterhouse 1992).

However, management has a considerable latitude in deciding when to recognise a liability even if it is likely to occur. First, interpretation is required about whether liabilities

Box 7.9 **Recognition of liabilities**

❝ A liability is recognised in the balance sheet when it is probable that an outflow of resources embodying economic benefits will result from the settlement of a present obligation and the amount at which the settlement will take place can be measured reliably ❞ (IASC 1995: 65 [IAS F91]).

❝ An estimated loss from a loss contingency . . . shall be accrued by a charge to income if both of the following conditions are met: (a) information available prior to assurance of the financial statements indicates that it is probable that an asset had been impaired or a liability incurred at the date of the financial statements. It is implicit in this condition that it must be probable that one or more future events will occur confirming the fact of the loss; and (b) the amount of loss can be reasonably estimated ❞ (FASB FAS 5, section 8; on pre-acquisition contingencies of purchased businesses, see FASB Statement 38).

are part of normal business risk, because liabilities must not be separately recognised if they are part of the normal business risk. Second, legal obligations can take many years to finalise and may be crucial for a company's survival. However, US SEC also states that management may not delay recognition of an environmental liability until only a single amount can be reasonably estimated (Holmark *et al.* 1995; Price Waterhouse 1992: 6).

Even more difficult than the definition of 'probability' is the formulation of criteria for when an environmental liability or contingent liability is 'reasonably estimable'. Thus, the main problem with environmental liabilities is the measurement, or estimation, of their amount.

7.5.4 Measurement of contingent environmental liabilities

A liability must be measured or reliably estimated in order to qualify for recognition in the main body of a financial statement. Key factors that can be considered when estimating environmental liabilities are:

- ☐ Current laws and regulations

- ☐ The extent of regulatory involvement

- ☐ The number and viability of the parties involved

- ☐ Prior legal, economic, political and scientific experience

- ☐ The complexity of the problem, existing technologies and available technological experience

(See also Holmark *et al.* 1995; Roberts 1994a; SEC 1993; Surma and Vondra 1992.)

Experience in estimating environmental liabilities has been gained especially in the US through implementation of provisions of the Superfund Act (CERCLA). The most important questions to be answered in the estimation process for clean-up costs are (see e.g. Barth and McNichols 1994; Holmark *et al.* 1995: 73; Price Waterhouse 1992: 15):

- ☐ What remedial action will be taken?

- ☐ What is the company's share of responsibility?

- ☐ What significant costs can be recovered from others?

- ☐ When will the remediation commence and how long will it take?

- ☐ If the planned remedial action does not work, what further actions are deemed necessary?

If a company has a probable and reasonably estimable contingent environmental liability, the best estimate should be recognised (FASB 1993 [FAS 5]; IASC 1995: 183 [IAS 10, 11]; Box 7.10). Among the factors for management to take into account in the evaluation of the contingency are the progress of the claim at the date on which the financial statements are authorised for issue, the opinions of legal experts or other advisers, the experience of the enterprise in similar cases and the experience of other enterprises in

> ❝ The estimation of the amount of a contingent loss to be recognised in the financial statements may be based on information that provides a range of amounts of loss which could result from the contingency. The best estimate of the loss within such a range is recognised. When no amount within the range is indicated as a better estimate than any other amount, at least the minimum amount in the range is recognised. Disclosure of any additional exposure to loss is made if there is a possibility of loss in excess of the amount recognised ❞ (IASC 1995: 183 [IAS 10, 11]).
>
> ❝ Among the factors taken into account by management in evaluation of the contingency are the progress of the claim at the date on which the financial statements are authorised for issue, the opinions of legal experts or other advisers, the experience of the enterprise in similar cases and the experience of other enterprises in similar situations ❞ (IASC 1995: 185 [IAS 10, 20]).
>
> ❝ An estimated loss from a loss contingency shall be accrued by a charge to income if it is probable that a liability has been incurred and the amount of the loss can be reasonably estimated ❞ (FASB 1993 [FAS 5]).

Box 7.10 **Measurement and estimation of contingent liabilities**

similar situations (IASC 1995: 185 [IAS 10, 20]). If there is no best estimate of the range of losses that could occur because of the contingency, its minimum amount at least should be recognised (IASC 1995: 183 [IAS 10, 8]).

For example, a company which has been informed by the environmental protection agency that its disposal site does not comply with legal regulations might still not know which remediation technique will be necessary, or what costs the company will face as a result. In such a case, at least the lowest costs of remediation should be recognised. An additional exposure to loss should be disclosed in a footnote and the management should mention that the amount cannot be estimated (Roberts 1994c: 4).

A special issue is whether counter-claims or claims against a third party should be offset against a liability. According to the IASC, an offset is allowed but not required (IAS 10, 13). Contrary to this, and in the interests of greater transparency and accountability, US SEC has decided that companies may not record or offset potential insurance reimbursements against the liabilities until received (SEC 1993: SAB 92). SEC recommends that the amount of the liability and the anticipated claim for insurance recovery be separately displayed as this most fairly presents the potential consequences of the contingent claim on the company's resources. The risks and uncertainties associated with the contingent liability are separate and distinct from those associated with the recovery claim (Napolitano 1995: 10; SEC 1993: SAB 92). A similar situation exists in the European Union under Article 7 of the Fourth Directive (Jones 1999: 159).

In addition, companies should refrain from discounting accrued liabilities to reflect the time value of money, unless the aggregate amount of the obligation and the amount and timing of cash payments are fixed or reliably determined. In addition, SEC stipulates that the discount rate used should not exceed the interest rate on risk-free monetary assets and should have provisions comparable to that of the environmental liability (Napolitano 1995: 10; SEC 1993: SAB 92).

Also, companies should not anticipate technological developments but base their estimates of future expenditures on existing technology—a notion of static efficiency

(Napolitano 1995: 10; SEC 1993: SAB 92; see also CICA 1995). The same is also true for the use of exchange rates, changes in which should not be anticipated by management.

Liabilities may be recognised even if they cannot be reliably measured. This is usually accomplished by making reserves, provisions or charges to income.

7.5.5 Environmental reserves, provisions and charges to income

Liabilities that can only be broadly estimated are often recognised as provisions (Box 7.11; IASC 1995: 51 [F64], 1998b; IFAC 1997). In principle, reserves for environmentally induced liabilities and contingent liabilities may be made according to the same rules as reserves for other liabilities. Reserves, charges to income or provisions for liabilities are intended to cover losses or debts that are clearly defined and that, at the balance date, are either likely to be incurred or certain to be incurred but uncertain as to the amount or as to the date on which they will arise (IASC 1993).

Provisions and contingent liabilities are contrasted in Financial Reporting Standard (FRS) 12 (ASB 1998: section 13) as follows:

> The FRS distinguishes between:
>
> - Provisions—which are recognised as liabilities because they are present obligations where it is probable that a transfer of economic benefits will be required to settle the obligations; and
>
> - Contingent liabilities—which are not recognised as liabilities because they are either: (i) possible obligations, as it has yet to be confirmed whether the entity has an obligation that could lead to a transfer of economic benefits; or (ii) present obligations that do not meet the recognition criteria in the FRS because it is not probable that a transfer of economic benefits will be required to settle the obligation, or a sufficiently reliable estimate of the amount of the obligation cannot be made.

Box 7.12 provides examples of recognition of an environmental provision, whereas Box 7.13 addresses provisions for clean-up of pollution.

The Canadian association for accounting standards, the Association Canadienne de Normalisation (ACN), has issued a special guideline for provisions for environmental liabilities due to contaminated landfills in its 'Canadian handbook' (ACN 1993: section 3060.39): 'When reasonably determinable, provisions should be made for future removal and site restoration costs, net of expected recoveries, in a rational and systematic manner by charges to income', and 'the accumulated provisions [should] be recorded as a liability'.

Box 7.11 **Provisions and liabilities**

❝ Some liabilities can be measured only by using a substantial degree of estimation. Some enterprises describe these liabilities as provisions. In some countries, such provisions are not regarded as liabilities because the concept of a liability is defined narrowly so as to include only amounts that can be established without the need to make estimates ❞ (IASC 1995: 51 [F64]).

Today, the IASC has defined liabilities in a broader sense (see Box 7.7; IASC 1995: 54 [F49]).

1. Contaminated land: legislation virtually certain to be enacted

An entity in the oil industry causes contamination but cleans up only when required to by law in any particular country. One country, in which it operates, has no legislation requiring clean-up, and the entity has been contaminating land in that country for several years. At balance date it is virtually certain that a draft law requiring clean-up of contaminated land will be enacted in the new year. In these circumstances a provision is recognised for the best estimate of the costs of the clean-up.

2. Contaminated land and constructive obligation

An entity in the oil industry causes contamination and operates in a country where there is no environmental legislation. However, the entity has a widely published environmental policy linked with a code of environmental management for the industry. In its policy the company undertakes to clean up all contamination that it causes. The company has a record of honouring the published policy. Here there is a constructive obligation because the conduct of the entity has created a valid expectation of those affected by it that the entity will clean up contamination. In these circumstances a provision is recognised for the best estimate of the costs of the clean-up.

Box 7.12 **Examples of recognition of a provision**

Source: based on ASB 1998

The initial reaction to the issue of a 'handbook' recommendation on site restoration was mixed. Critics argued that more time should be taken to develop a proper understanding of the problem and wondered whether it was practical to require entities to make provisions for environmental liabilities. However, the standard has been justified by the potential magnitude of the environmental liability costs incurred and by the need to achieve some consistency in practice (Hawkshaw 1991: 25; Moore 1991: 54). The Canadian standard has served as a guide for other national and international standards, as the examples of the newly issued regulations of US SEC and the FASB show (the FASB has also dealt with site restoration or exit costs of the nuclear and other industry groups; FASB 1994: 6). These new standards require companies to set up reserves to pay for future costs of environmental liabilities (Fenn 1995: 62f.).

Box 7.13 **Provisions for clean-up of pollution**

❝ The example of a site contamination can be useful. On the one hand, the contamination will normally affect the fair value of the site. On the other hand, if the site has to be repaired, the company will incur future clean-up costs.

In general, where the site contamination has to be repaired, because the company has a legal or contractual obligation or a commitment to repair it, and the amount of the future repair costs can be reasonably estimated, a provision for the estimated repair costs should be recognised, irrespective of the question of whether the fair value of the site exceeds its carrying amount.

As regards the question whether a value adjustment must be made due to impairment of the net carrying value of the site, it is recommended that a value adjustment should be made if the amount recoverable from the site has declined below its carrying amount and it is expected that this reduction in value will be permanent. The carrying amount of the site should however not be written down below its fair value ❞ (AAFEU 1995: 9-10).

The oil, gas and minerals industry as well as some public utilities often view site restoration costs as part of their operation costs. It has been argued that the oil and gas business is fundamentally different from a manufacturing facility because the latter does not have a finite production life (Adams 1992: 18). Nonetheless, if site restoration costs are material and probable they should be recognised and provided for by reserves or charges to income. The situation is typified by an Australian standard on 'Accounting for the extractive industries', as follows (ASRB 1989: section 40):

> Where there is an expectation that an area of interest will be restored:
>
> (a) The cost of restoration work necessitated by exploration, evaluation or development activities prior to commencement of production shall be provided for at the time of such activities and shall form part of the cost of the respective phase(s) of operations;
>
> (b) The cost of restoration work necessitated by any activities after the commencement of production shall be provided for during production and shall be treated as a cost of production; and
>
> (c) In determining the amount to be provided in any one financial period, the balance of the provision for restoration costs, after charging against it actual costs incurred to date, shall be reassessed in the light of expected further costs.

The commentary on restoration costs says furthermore (ASRB 1989: section 40, p. xv):

> It is frequently a condition of a permit to engage in extractive operations, that the area covered by the permit be restored after the cessation of operations. In any case, it may be policy of the company involved in the operations to carry out such restoration even if there is no legal obligation to do so. Restoration costs that it is expected will be incurred are provided for as part of the cost of the exploration, evaluation, development, construction or production phases that give rise to the need for restoration.

Accounting standards often do not provide entirely clear answers to the normative question of whether management should make provisions for contingent environmental liabilities and how large these provisions should be. Other obstacles also confront managers who are considering making environmentally related provisions. Taxes present one of the main obstacles. In many countries expenses are only tax-deductible when paid, because tax reporting requirements are very much focused on cash flows. Consequently, as provisions cannot be deducted from taxable income, there is little incentive for enterprises to record their (contingent) liabilities by charging them to income (Moore 1991: 55).

If liabilities do not have the characteristics required for recognition (e.g. if they cannot be reliably measured), and if they are unlikely to be considered as reserves, charges to income or provisions, they might nevertheless have to be disclosed.

7.5.6 Disclosure of contingent liabilities

Disclosure is the process of incorporating elements of financial accounting (assets, liabilities, equity, expenses and income) into the balance sheet, the income statement or separate sections and papers of disclosure such as notes to the accounts. Disclosure of restoration obligations is recommended in the United Kingdom, Australia and Canada and is expected by US SEC. All recognised items must be disclosed in the balance sheet.

Nevertheless, many environmental liabilities are difficult to estimate with any degree of certainty if they are associated with accidents or with the remediation of 'Superfund sites' (Li *et al.* 1997). Such items often possess the essential characteristics of an element (e.g. an expense) but fail to meet the criteria for recognition because, for example, their monetary amount cannot be determined (see Section 7.5.2 and Box 7.9). Thus, environmental liabilities disclosed in the balance sheet tend to be incomplete. To correct for this shortcoming, additional information can be disclosed in an off-balance-sheet statement.

As with standards for recognition, no standards have been developed solely to specify when to disclose environmental liabilities. However, it can be argued that general standards facilitate treatment of environmental liabilities, as long as these standards are applied correctly and are enforced by regulatory authorities.

The IASC, for example, requires disclosure of contingent losses even if they are not recognised unless the probability of a loss is remote (IASC 1995: IAS 10). Hence, non-recognised environmental liabilities relevant to an evaluation of the financial position of a company should be disclosed in the notes, explanatory material or supplementary schedules of the financial statement.

In the USA, liabilities (including environmental liabilities) have to be accrued for if they are material, probable and reasonably estimable (AAA/SEC 1995; FASB 1980: FAS 5; Rabinowitz and Murphy 1992; Roberts 1994a; Box 7.9). However, the occurrences of environmental liabilities associated with accidents or eventual remediation of landfills are often difficult to estimate with any degree of certainty (see e.g. IFAC 1997). Thus, they do not necessarily have to be recognised under the US GAAP (Abelson 1991; Roussey 1991). Nevertheless, in some cases US SEC has determined that disclosures of environmental liabilities were not made when they should have been made (Williams and Phillips 1994: 31; Zuber and Berry 1992).

US SEC has therefore described four possibilities for disclosing environmental liability information in financial statements (Holmark *et al.* 1995: 73f.), in the:

☐ Management discussion and analysis (MD&A)

☐ Notes to the financial statements

☐ Description of business

☐ Context of legal proceedings

SEC requires disclosure in the MD&A (SEC 1989: 22428) even if disclosures are made in other sections of the annual report (e.g. in the notes to the financial statement). The MD&A must include any known trends or any known demands, commitments, events or uncertainties that are reasonably likely to have a material impact on earnings and liquidity (SEC 1989). Disclosure is required whenever management is unable to determine if material effects on future results of operations or the financial condition are 'not reasonably likely' to occur (SEC 1989: interpretative release FRR 36).

A liability must be disclosed in the notes of the financial statement if it is probable that it has occurred, although no reasonable estimate can be made of the amount. Footnote disclosure of the contingent loss is appropriate if the likelihood of a loss is at least 'reasonably possible'. Only if the likelihood of loss is 'remote' is no disclosure necessary (Box 7.14).

Material effects on the required capital, expenditures, earnings and competitive position of the registered company related to compliance with environmental regulations are required to be disclosed in the description of business (SEC 1989: 101).

Legal proceedings that might have material effects on the company have to be briefly described (SEC 1989: S-K 103). The US EPA has agreed to supply corporate environmental information to the SEC. This particularly aims at companies that have been designated as potential responsible parties for the clean-up of Superfund sites but that have not recognised or disclosed any information about environmental liabilities in their annual report.

So far, no regulations for the disclosure of environmental liabilities have been published outside the USA. However, some initiatives may be mentioned. In the European Union, the Directive on Civil Liability for Damage Caused by Waste was introduced in 1993. This directive is similar to the Superfund law apart from not being retrospective. The financial implications for companies are, therefore, expected to be considerable.

The Intergovernmental Working Group of Experts on International Standards of Accounting and Reporting (ISAR) of the United Nations has issued the recommendation to include in the notes to financial statements environmentally induced liabilities, provisions and reserves as well as contingent liabilities with an estimate of the amount involved, unless the event is not likely to occur (United Nations 1991a: 98).

CICA (1993) recommends that:

☐ Environmental liabilities should be disclosed separately in financial statements.

☐ Environmental liabilities of individual materiality should be disclosed separately.

☐ A deferred charge should be disclosed in connection with the liability it relates to.

☐ The nature of any uncertainties of measurement should be explained.

Box 7.14 **Disclosure of contingent liabilities**

THE IASC 'REQUIRES THE DISCLOSURE OF CONTINGENT LOSSES THAT are not recognised unless the probability of loss is remote' (IASC 1995: 183 [IAS 10, 9]).

US SEC requires disclosure in the management discussion and analysis of any 'trend, commitment, event or uncertainty' that (SEC 1989, 22430):

☐ Is 'known'

☐ Cannot be determined to be 'not reasonably likely to occur' (this double negative is in the regulations)

☐ Is reasonably likely to have 'a material effect on the [company's] financial condition'

In Australia, in the 1990s, there was considerable concern about non-disclosure and inconsistent disclosure of restoration liability information by companies in the extractive industries. To address these issues, at a meeting of the Urgent Issues Group (UIG) of the Australian standards body (AARF) the following consensus recommendations were made (UIG 1995):

☐ Reporting entities in the extractive industries shall disclose separately the amount of restoration obligations recognised as a liability in their financial report.

☐ Reporting entities in the extractive industries shall disclose the accounting method adopted in determining the liability for restoration including:

  – Whether the total amount of restoration obligations is recognised at the time a disturbance occurs, is recognised on a gradual basis over the life of the facility as production occurs or is recognised on some other basis

  – Whether the amount of restoration obligations recognised includes the costs of reclamation, platform removal, plant closure, waste site closure, monitoring or other activities and, where material, the nature of those other activities

  – Whether restoration costs are estimated on the basis of current costs or estimates of future costs, current or anticipated legal requirements and current or anticipated technology

  – Whether the amounts of restoration costs have been determined on a discounted or undiscounted basis

  – Whether changes in estimates are dealt with on a prospective or a retrospective basis

☐ The financial report shall identify significant uncertainties, assumptions and judgements made in determining restoration obligations.

Specific uncertainties in calculating the liability, identified by the UIG, include assumptions relating to the nature and extent of the restoration that will be required, the environmental sensitivity of the location, changes in restoration technology and its impact on cost structures, relative inflation levels, the nature and extent of tax relief, if any, community expectations and future legislation.

Holmark et al. (1995: 75) proposed a general form for disclosing liabilities in a structured manner, as shown in Table 7.2. In fact, the formulation of new accounting standards defining the disclosure of environmental liabilities might not be necessary. However, true and fair reporting to external stakeholders requires a rigorous enforcement of existing standards as well as consistent reporting practices based on clear, generally accepted and established guidelines (see e.g. the United Nations Centre for Trade and Development [UNCTAD]'s 1998 report on environmental accounting and reporting practices). To ensure consistency in practice, management will often have to refer to precedents for guidance on whether and when to disclose environmental liabilities.

But, while the discussion about environmentally induced liabilities has attracted much attention, new topics of interest have recently been emerging. One of the most discussed market-based regulations is emissions trading. Emissions trading is an economic incentive-

Description	Amount of liability ($)	Prior provisions	Counter-claims	Notes
Liability 1				
Liability 2				
...				
Liability n				
Total				

Table 7.2 **Liability disclosure form**
Source: Holmark *et al.* 1995: 75

based alternative to command-and-control regulation that is estimated to have saved companies up to US$13 billion in compliance costs. In an emissions-trading programme, sources of a particular pollutant are given permits or allowances to release a specified volume of the pollutant. A government or trading agency issues only a limited number of permits consistent with the desired level of emissions. The owners of the permits may keep them and release the pollutants, reduce their emissions and sell the permits in the market or convey the permits to affiliated plants. The fact that the permits have value as an item to be sold or traded gives the owner an incentive to reduce emissions.

For many fields of application (i.e. stationary industrial emissions), emissions trading is regarded as the most efficient way to regulate pollution (see e.g. Ewer 1996; Frey 1993; Hahn 1984; Pekelney 1993; Stavins 1992; Tietenberg 1989). Tradable emission allowances are established in the USA and have been introduced on a smaller scale in other countries (e.g. Switzerland, Germany, the Netherlands, Australia and New Zealand). With this new regulatory instrument some testing accounting issues have emerged as well.

7.6 Treatment of tradable emission allowances

In all countries, companies are allowed to pollute the environment as long as they do not exceed legal emission standards. This right is usually implicit. However, the position changes if a system of emissions trading is introduced where the right to pollute is specifically certified by emission allowances (pollution permits). The total amount of pollution is strictly limited through the total number of pollution permits issued and the amount of pollution permitted, usually calculated by natural scientists based on the perceived carrying capacity of environmental media. An emission allowance is a certified right that allows a company to discharge a certain amount of pollution into the natural environment within a specified time limit. Thus, an emission allowance can be seen (a) as a (general) licence to pollute and (b) as a right to emit a specific level of pollutants in a specific period of time (e.g. a year). The right to emit a specified amount of pollution starts again every year (e.g. 100 tons of sulphur dioxide [SO_2] every year).

The idea of emissions trading is that it is not the individual source of emissions that is ultimately relevant for the environment but rather the absolute amount of emissions in a given region over a given period.

Pollution rights are mostly 'grandfathered' by the government or the environmental protection agency. Thus, the respective allowances are awarded to companies on the basis of their past emissions. Companies can sell their allowances or buy additional permits depending on whether their marginal costs of pollution prevention are lower or higher than the market price for the emission allowances. Companies facing high costs of pollution prevention are willing to pay a high price for emission allowances, whereas companies with low marginal costs of pollution prevention will attempt to improve their environmental record to a level below legal standards and then sell their unused rights. In this way, a market for the right to pollute is created.

Through emissions trading, the marginal cost of pollution abatement of all companies involved will tend towards equality over time. Ideally, for every company, as well as for the total economy, emissions trading results in the lowest possible costs of pollution prevention. However, this view that environmental degradation and despoilation can be checked through better pricing in a market created for trading pollution rights has been accused of reflecting the preferences of business rather than a mutually constitutive relationship between people and nature (Lehman 1996: 668). In short, the view expressed is that pollution should not be permitted. Instead, attempts to arrive at a sustainable solution to production need to focus on zero pollution as the ideal, rather than permitting polluters to continue with their practices through grandfathering of permits to degrade the environment.

As a minimum, it is suggested that pollution permits represent an end-of-pipe focus and are contrary to the current preferred emphasis on removing waste through preventative actions (Gibson 1996). In practice, emissions trading appears to have been accepted as a way of helping the international community reduce waste, for example through carbon dioxide (CO2) emissions trading, which is being considered as an international mechanism for reducing the impact of 'greenhouse gas' emissions on global warming.

Nevertheless, with the introduction of emission allowances as an economic instrument designed to reduce pollution over time, questions have emerged as to how emission allowances should be recognised, measured and disclosed in conventional financial accounting:

☐ Are emission allowances assets or expenses?

☐ How should emission allowances be recognised?

☐ How should the value of pollution permits be determined or measured?

☐ How should they be disclosed in financial statements?

Emission allowances fit the definitions of an asset as formulated by the IASC and the FASB: 'An asset is a resource controlled by the enterprise as a result of past events and from which future economic benefits are expected to flow to the enterprise' (IASC 1995: 54 [IAS F49]). Pollution permits are necessary for a company to receive future economic benefits as companies are not allowed to produce without such permits being granted. Pollution permits have a capital value because they can be bought and sold.

Some confusion might arise with the US Clean Air Act, as amended 1990, which regards emission allowances as 'limited authorisations' and not as 'property rights'. However, these authorisations are owned by the company, and holders are provided with substantial protection against expropriation. Emission allowances should, therefore, be recognised as assets. Nonetheless, the question remains of how emission allowances should be recognised in the financial statement. Three main options have been discussed within this context (Ewer *et al.* 1992; Wambsganss and Sanford 1996). Pollution permits could be classified as:

☐ **Inventory.** An inventory comprises assets: (a) held for sale in the ordinary course of business; (b) in the process of production for sale; or (c) in the form of materials or supplies to be consumed in the production process or in the rendering of services (IASC 1995: 84 [IAS 2, 4]).

☐ **Marketable securities.** Marketable securities are held with the intention of selling them in the short run, whereas investment securities are acquired and held for yield or capital growth purposes and are usually held to maturity (IASC 1995: 425 [IAS 30, 19]).

☐ **Intangible operating assets.** An asset is a resource controlled by the enterprise as a result of past events and from which future economic benefits are expected (IASC 1995: 47 [IAS 38]).

Tradable emission permits possess some of the characteristics of all three classifications, but do not exactly match any of the definitions.

Pollution permits are held for sale or consumption and could, therefore, be classified as inventory. For example, under the US Federal Energy Regulatory Commission (FERC) accounting requirements adopted for emission allowances created under the Clean Air Act amendments of 1990, purchased pollution allowances expected to be used to compensate for current pollution output are treated as inventory (Wambsganss and Sanford 1996). The cost of purchased allowances is considered to be a necessary cost of production. However, pollution allowances lack other characteristics of inventory: they are neither tangible nor necessarily held for current consumption.

If classified as marketable securities, tradable permits would have to be carried in two distinct portfolios—long-term and short-term. First, emission allowances not expected to be used during the current period are treated as non-current securities (a general licence for pollution). Second, pollution permits may be classified as current securities because they represent permission to pollute a predetermined amount within the current accounting period.

Tradable pollution permits could, in due course, also be treated as options (a right, but not an obligation to do something: i.e. to pollute) for they can be sold in the same way as options (Ewer *et al.* 1992: 71). As the market emerges, the certificates for future allowances would need to be treated as futures (Adams 1992: 3; Sandor and Walsh 1993).

Pollution permits possess some of the characteristics of intangible operating assets. For example, because pollution allowances have no physical form, they have the characteristics of intangible assets such as copyrights, franchises and licences. If pollution permits are recognised as intangible, they should be carried as non-current operating assets the same as any other licence (Ewer *et al.* 1992: 71).

Another issue relates to measurement of the value of pollution allowances. The main question is whether valuation based on historical cost, current cost or market exit price is most appropriate. The historical cost method values allowances according to the amount paid for them at the time of their acquisition. The current cost method assigns an amount of cash that would have to be paid if the same, or an equivalent, asset were acquired in the current accounting period (IASC 1995: 67 [F100]). Market exit price, or net realisable value, represents the exchange price between a willing seller and a willing buyer in the ordinary course of business. Valuation according to the net realisable (exit) value may provide a similar result to the current cost (entry price) method.

The historical cost method does not indicate market value. Initially, most permits are 'grandfathered' at no cost by environmental protection agencies and would not be recognised at all under conventional financial accounting treatment (Adams 1992: 3; Wambsganss and Sanford 1996: 646). As historical costs do not reflect market value or the contribution of emission allowances to the value of the company, management is provided with no incentive to realise pollution prevention at lower costs or to make a profit from selling unused permits, because no recognition is given, in the financial statements, to the allowances, to cost savings if pollution is reduced or to gains from trading pollution allowances.

From economic and environmental perspectives, a current market value must clearly be favoured over historical cost accounting. The current cost approach is not recognised in conventional financial accounting. Current cost equals the market entry value for acquiring the allowances. The market exit value reflects opportunity cost of assets held— the gain from using capital that is tied up in pollution allowances in the next best alternative (Edwards and Bell 1961). Clearly, these opportunity costs are relevant for management decisions. Only the use of a current market value allows the marginal costs of pollution prevention to be compared with the present marginal (opportunity) costs of keeping the permits. Under a current cost approach, if bought in the market, the cost of purchase would be expensed as the permits are sold. At the same time, adjustments would be made for increases or decreases in the market value of allowances between balance dates.

The argument that a market price is not given when the allowances are 'grandfathered' is not valid, for two reasons. Experience in the USA shows that pollution permits are usually already traded before allowances are granted. Evolution of the market in greenhouse gas emission credits is following this path. There are no national or international markets in emission credits, but trades are already taking place on a bilateral basis. Thus, it can be argued that a market price exists before the allowances have to be accounted for (Feder 1993; *NZZ* 1994c). A second consideration is that if a market is created for the first time and a price determined at the time of the first trade then any price variation between the opening trade and first balance date should be taken to the income account, in the same way that later exit price variations will be reflected in the accounts (Chambers 1966).

Another reason to apply the current market value approach is the fact that pollution permits are usually devalued over time by the environmental protection agency (the certified amount of pollutants that a permit holder may emit decreases over time). This reduction in value would not be considered under the conventional historical cost approach.

Useful disclosures include the monetary values of emission allowances along with the number of permits held. On its own, the monetary value does not tell readers of financial statements whether, for example, the market price of the permits has changed (price volatility and transparency) or whether more emission rights have been bought (a diverse balance of buyers and sellers). Both are necessary items of information for successful secondary and derivatives-based trading markets to emerge.

Obviously, many arguments can be found suggesting that emission allowances be treated in a variety of ways. Hence, a specific accounting standard to recognise, measure and disclose allowances in a consistent manner, separate from other items, is needed. As shown in the previous two sections, not all economically important environmental topics can be recognised in the financial statement in monetary terms. Management discussion and analysis (or a statement from the chairperson, review of the chief executive officer or statement from the director[s]) is, therefore, an important communications tool for disclosure about environmental issues in financial reports.

7.7 Management discussion and analysis

Every financial report provides a discussion and analysis of management's view of the company financial position and of changes in financial position. Discussion and analysis relate to a cluster of financial circumstances—liquidity, solvency, profitability and growth trends—and may also include forward-looking information. Disclosures are typified by regulation S-K in the USA where the management discussion and analysis (MD&A) examines information that is not, or not clearly, recognised as being represented by a monetary amount in the financial statements (Box 7.15). In an environmental context it is clear that most disclosures are, in fact, qualitative in substance and so disclosure in statements made by management, chief executive officers or the company chairperson are an important component in volume terms.

Formulation of the US MD&A requirements are 'intentionally general, reflecting the [Securities and Exchange] Commission's view that a flexible approach elicits more meaningful disclosure and avoids boilerplate discussions, which a more specific approach could foster' (SEC 1989: 1577); 'MD&A requires a discussion of liquidity, capital resources, results of operations, and other information necessary to an understanding of a [firm's] financial condition, changes in financial condition and results of operations' (SEC 1989: 1577). This perspective is also reflected by the explanation of what information is required and what 'optional forward-looking' is all about: 'Optional forward-looking disclosure involves anticipating a future trend or event or anticipating a less predictable impact of a known event, trend or uncertainty' (SEC 1989: 1579).

> ❝ MD&A requires a discussion of liquidity, capital resources, results of operations, and other information necessary to an understanding of a [firm's] financial condition, changes in financial condition and results of operations ❞ (SEC 1989: 1577).
>
> ❝ Required disclosure is based on currently known trends, events, and uncertainties that are reasonably expected to have material effects ❞ (SEC 1989: 1579).
>
> ❝ Optional forward-looking disclosure involves anticipating a future trend or event or anticipating a less predictable impact of a known event, trend or uncertainty ❞ (SEC 1989: 1579).
>
> ❝ Where a trend, demand, commitment, event or uncertainty is known, management must make two assessments:
>
> 1. Is the known trend, demand, commitment, event or uncertainty likely to come to fruition? If management determines that it is not reasonably likely to occur, no disclosure is required.
> 2. If management cannot make that determination, it must evaluate objectively the consequences of the known trend, demand, commitment, event or uncertainty, on the assumption that it will come to fruition. Disclosure is then required unless management determines that a material effect on the [firm's] financial condition or results of operations is not reasonably likely to occur ❞ (SEC 1989: 1580).

Box 7.15 **US management discussion and analysis (MD&A)**

In the MD&A, some companies provide an outline of their environmental policy (see Box 7.16), or a general statement of corporate commitment or comments about environmental processes and products (see also Jones 1999: 22).

In the UK the Hundred Group of Finance Directors (HGFD) believes that environmental policy should be addressed in the narrative section of an annual report and not be subjected to audit. But this view is changing as more verifiable information becomes available (HGFD 1992). In the past, it was usual to state simply that the environment was considered to be a very important issue. Today, many companies specify how they endeavour to cope with environmental problems.

Investors are interested in relevant qualitative and quantified information about how efficiently a company spends its resources on environmental matters (AP 1992b). They are looking for specific indicators of environmental performance linked with economic implications. A lack of focus in a company's environmental protection activities impedes effective decision-making and, as a result, is seen to lower the value of the company (Judge and Douglas 1998). Whereas financial analysts are, for example, less interested in past company achievements than in potential problems and opportunities or in programmes designed to meet future requirements, non-governmental organisations (NGOs) are more concerned about management stewardship over natural resources and clear transparency and accountability relationships.

Environmental issues (e.g. environmental liabilities) are among the most important factors that can drastically and unexpectedly influence the future economic performance of a company. Hence, SEC has emphasised the importance of the disclosure of environmental issues that might affect a company's financial condition (i.e. environmental

ISLAND TEL IS A TELECOMMUNICATIONS SUPPLIER ON PRINCE Edward Island (Canada):

❝ Island Tel is committed to the preservation of the environment in which it operates and, as a minimum, will ensure that all operations meet or exceed government requirements. The Company's environmental policy requires that reports identifying environmental concerns and incidents be provided to the Board of Directors each quarter. To date, no significant concerns or major incidents have been identified, and routine environmental issues have been dealt with appropriately.

Island Tel's Environmental Management System provides a programme of continuous improvement in awareness and procedure, regarding environmental issues and requires routine environmental audits of selected sites as well as specific regulated issues. The Environmental Management System is directed and supported by upper management and includes representation of all areas of the Company. ❞

Box 7.16 **Environmental policy of Island Tel in its management discussion and analysis**

Source: www.islandtel.pe.ca/, on 31 December 1999

liabilities) in the MD&A (SEC 1989: 1580). For potentially responsible parties a disclosure of the expected material effects of the clean-up of their sites is required (SEC 1989: 1580).

However, disclosure of most other environmentally induced issues is voluntary and subject to management discretion. Issues that might be considered in the MD&A include:

☐ The financial or operational effect of environmental protection measures on the capital expenditures, earnings and competitive position of the organisation for the current period and any expected impact on future periods (Moore 1991: 55, concerning SEC 101 and SEC S-K 103)

☐ The treatment of different environmentally induced financial impacts (e.g. if environmental costs are expensed or capitalised; see Müller *et al.* 1994: 19)

☐ Aggregate payments to be made in the longer run for future environmental expenditures (e.g. in the next five years; see CICA 1993)

☐ Environmental liabilities of individual materiality (CICA 1993)

☐ Contingent environmental liabilities that are either not probable (though the probability is not remote) or not reasonably estimable

☐ The scope and methods of consolidation

☐ The nature of any measurement uncertainties

A list of further recommendations on environmentally related issues that could be addressed in the MD&A has been made by ISAR (United Nations 1991a: 97f., 1991b). Apart from actual, expected and potential future financial consequences, ISAR also mentions ecological information that may not directly involve financial consequences. Such environmental topics may include information on:

☐ Environmental issues that are relevant to the organisation and the industry in which it operates

☐ The environmental impact of company operations

☐ The formal policy and programmes the company has adopted with regard to environmental protection

☐ Improvements made since the policy was first introduced

☐ Future targets and the quantification of these targets

Countries around the world are beginning to struggle with the exact qualitative disclosures required from their listed companies. For example, in Australia, s.299 of the 1998 Company Law Review Act only seeks a statement that relevant environmental laws have been complied with, and even this weak requirement is under threat of removal. Meanwhile, professional accountancy bodies and securities watchdogs have been trying to spell out more exactly the nature of disclosures implied by this section of the Act.

7.8 Summary

Financial accounting is a tool to collect the information required to be disclosed to external stakeholders (e.g. investors), whereas a financial report is the 'platform' for sharing this information. In the past, it was not economic for management to include many environmentally related issues in financial reporting.

However, this has changed with the increasing magnitude of environmental costs, especially growth in environmental liabilities and a move towards weak sustainability in government and business decision-making and accountability processes. Environmentally related issues are of increasing importance in the consideration of the financial position of many companies. Thus, to support the economic basis of decisions, companies with environmentally sensitive businesses should explicitly disclose environmentally induced financial impacts in their conventional financial reports. So far, throughout the world, only a few large companies have disclosed the particulars of environmentally induced financial impacts in a consistent manner. Recently, however, with increasing pressure from the international community, lower costs of information and improving measurement methods this situation has started to change.

Management still has a large element of discretion in deciding which environmental issues to recognise, how to measure these and what to disclose. Environmental management started during the 1990s to become an important issue in financial markets, hitherto a very conservative sector of the economy as far as environmental issues were concerned. The communication of accounting issues between those preparing financial statements and powerful external stakeholders is only at an early stage. As with other issues, the requirements of those stakeholders will drive companies to provide clear and understandable reports to help investors make informed decisions and to become more aware of the individual and systematic environmental risks associated with their investments as a basis for efficient portfolio analysis and selection.

The substantial environmentally related financial consequences for some companies requires a change in several of the current financial accounting and reporting practices. For some specific environmental questions, new standards and guidelines need to be developed, primarily in order to foster and ensure consistency in reporting (e.g. for the treatment of emission allowances).

Experience with accounting practices in the USA, where these issues have received considerable attention, suggests that more environmentally induced costs (e.g. liabilities) would be disclosed if clear international standards dealing with the main environmental topics were issued. Clear environmental accounting standards streamline the reporting process, improve comparability between companies at a point in time and over time and help reduce the costs of management. In addition, investors and other critical stakeholders such as NGOs and local communities, who may be guided by the search for sustainability, would be better informed. Only internationally accepted standards for financial accounting allow investors and other stakeholders to compare companies in a reliable way. (As will be shown later, the same argument applies to ecological reporting; see Part 3.) However, given the problem that too many standards increase the costs of reporting, new standards should be issued only if they bring a clear and demonstrable improvement to the present situation. Much of the externally available information could be improved if:

- ❍ Existing accounting principles were enforced more consistently by regulators and the accountancy profession

- ❍ Greater consideration were given to the need for measuring and disclosing market-oriented information about market-based activities of companies instead of the conventional focus on historical cost

- ❍ The drive for comparable information to support regional and global economic activities were to be couched in terms of integrated environmental and financial outcomes

As standardisation organisations tend to promote the creation of too many standards, it is particularly important for all readers of information in financial reports (e.g. shareholders and communities) that any new standards fill only otherwise uncovered gaps and support the fundamental notion of providing general-purpose reports about all entities, for all stakeholders.

However, the company's perspective must not be lost sight of in any move towards a more useful set of environmentally induced financial disclosures. In particular, companies will need reassurance that:

- ❍ Data collection and processing costs can be reduced.

- ❍ Internal and external auditing of the additional information will not be excessive.

- ❍ A level playing field for reporting will be encouraged so that no competitive disadvantages arise.

☐ Site remediation costs will actually become the responsibility of the party in control of a site at some future time thereby encouraging proactive recognition of the problem now.

☐ Existing discretion in environmentally induced financial reporting will be reduced through standardisation.

The next chapter will focus more specifically on shareholders as the stakeholder group by linking discussion about standardising financial accounting and reporting to the emergence of the shareholder value concept. This it achieves by analysing what motivates standardisation organisations and investors from a politico-economic perspective. Chapter 8 will also examine the influence of environmental issues and the type of corporate environmental management on shareholder value.

Questions

1. How do stakeholder groups relevant to environmental management accounting and environmentally induced financial accounting differ?

2. What reasons can you give in support of, and against, the development of separate financial accounting guidelines and standards that reflect the financial consequences of environmental issues?

3. Information disclosed in financial reports should have a number of characteristics (e.g. understandability, neutrality). What are these characteristics? Provide two examples of situations where there might be a conflict between these different characteristics.

4. Explain the difference between an asset and an expense in conventional financial accounting. Are pollution permits an asset? Comment on the view that letting companies hold pollution allowances as assets is contrary to the aim of reducing pollution.

5. Present a critical appraisal of the argument that only one international standard-setting institution is needed to establish financial reporting standards relating to environmental issues.

6. Tax-deductibility of clean-up costs—asset or liability?

> The IRS [US Inland Revenue Service] reversed its position on the accounting treatment of environmental clean-up costs in Revenue Ruling 94-38. Such costs arise when owners of real property are required to remove hazardous wastes from their land to maintain the environment and comply with environmental laws. However, whether these costs come under Sec. 162 or Sec. 263 in the Internal Revenue Code has long been subject to debate. Sec. 162 specifies that all ordinary and necessary repairs are tax deductible, while Sec. 263 states that capital expenditures such as permanent improvements that increase property value are

not deductible. In two earlier technical advice memoranda, the IRS ruled that clean-up costs were capital expenditures, and thus, not deductible. However, the agency reversed its position in Rev. Rul. 94-38, allowing taxpayers who comply with environmental laws to deduct these costs as expenses (Pritchard 1995).

Suggest reasons why the IRS might have difficulty in deciding whether clean-up costs are expenses or assets.

7. Distinguish between a liability and an environmental liability. Is there any difference, in principle, between the recognition criteria for normal and environmental liabilities in conventional financial accounting?

8. What are the advantages and disadvantages of permitting counter-claims for insurance claims to be offset in financial reports? Consider the views of management, shareholders and a non-governmental organisation such as Greenpeace.

9. If 'grandfathering' is accepted as the basis for allocating initial emission permits what is the likely impact on early action (action before trading schemes commence) being taken to reduce emissions? Consider your answer in the context of the emerging mechanism for greenhouse gas emissions trading.

10. Conventional financial accounting suggests that environmental permits should be measured by using the historical cost principle. One alternative is that current market prices should be used instead. Should exit prices that represent opportunity costs of capital tied up in permits, or current costs of replacing permits, be favoured instead of historical cost?

11. How important are environmental disclosures in the management discussion and analysis section of an annual report? Explain.

Chapter 8

ENVIRONMENTAL SHAREHOLDER VALUE AND ENVIRONMENTAL ISSUES IN OTHER ACCOUNTING SYSTEMS

The influence of environmental issues on financial performance has been a heavily discussed topic for many years (EIRIS 1989; Feldman *et al.* 1997; Gupta *et al.* 1996; Klassen and McLaughlin 1996; Li and McConomy 1999; McGuire 1981; Schaltegger and Figge 1997; Spicer 1978). In the previous chapter it was argued that consideration of environmental issues in existing accounting standards would be of benefit, both for the economy and for the environment, as it would improve transparency and accountability about the consequences of corporate activities for investors, management and other stakeholders. Greater transparency makes it easier to anticipate future economic and environmental impacts and directs attention to the need for improved allocation of scarce financial resources.

However, the possibility of introducing new financial reporting standards, or of changing existing standards, is fraught with difficulties. It requires careful management because such changes can, in themselves, increase uncertainty and encourage managers to reduce transparency by promoting a desire to increase secrecy about possible negative environmental impacts.

Analysis of the effect of an increasing number of financial reporting standards on transparency emphasises the importance of other information sources in addition to disclosures in financial reports. Information gleaned from these sources is particularly important to investors if they are to understand in a fair, full and timely manner the present and potential environmental costs (and revenues) that have an economically material significance (according to Commissioner of the US Securities and Exchange Commission [SEC] Richard Roberts, cited in Beets and Souther 1999: 130). This is one reason why it is considered that the economic influence of environmental management needs to be analysed from the shareholders' perspective by using a concept developed for the purpose—the shareholder value concept. Other explanations for the emergence of this concept include its focus on future issues and on a cash-based rather than accrual-based approach to share value, its relative simplicity and its intuitive logic. The concept of shareholder value is by no means new (see e.g. Studer 1992, 1996). It has, however, recently gained ground in theory and practice.

8.1 Standardisation of financial reporting and the value of information for investors

8.1.1 Growth of the number of financial reporting standards

As discussed in Section 7.1, accounting standardisation organisations and standards of financial reporting have been established to reduce uncertainty and to facilitate communication between management and external stakeholders, particularly investors. Information thus collected should support stakeholders in their decision-making and accountability processes. Professional financial auditors review corporate books of account and financial reports against these standards. Therefore, standards of financial accounting and reporting have a considerable influence on the kind of information that is classified, compiled, analysed and considered by management.

No doubt, compared with an unregulated and non-standardised situation, the improvement of comparability in accounting standards and auditing procedures and the inclusion of environmental issues in the standards and auditing procedures will increase the information value of published reports. An accounting standard is defined here as one numbered paragraph (or a set of contextually linked paragraphs) of an accounting standard system issued by a national or an international accounting standardisation organisation. Furthermore, the co-existence of and competition between several systems of standards (e.g. different sets of national accounting standards) can stimulate innovation so that the best sets of standards should prevail in practice.

Nevertheless, in most countries competition between different sets of standards is limited as regulators usually require the application of one specific set of standards. International accounting standards (IASs) are, apart from in the USA, the most important as they have an increasing influence on national standards in industrial countries and as they are adopted as national standards by most developing countries. In addition, for most sets of accounting standards, the number and especially the degree of detail of (non-environmental) accounting standards has increased considerably over the past decade (Fig. 8.1; see also *Accountancy* 1995; Tabakoff 1995).

Figure 8.1 shows, as an example, information about increases in the number of published international accounting standards over the period 1974–95. Changes to existing standards and new specifications for existing standards are not included.

One possible explanation for this development is the growing number of business and accounting issues to be considered as multinational activity increases. Although the number of business issues has increased and the globalisation of certain businesses is being promoted, many important new business issues, such as, for example, environmentally induced financial effects, have not been considered in any detail by the International Accounting Standards Committee (IASC; see Chapter 7). Instead, they have been examined and recommendations have been made by the United Nations (United Nations 1992c; UNCTAD 1998).

Politico-economic factors also lend support to this growth. Accounting standardisation organisations have an incentive to maximise the number of accounting standards and to encourage regulators to require their application. Income, job opportunities, the power of

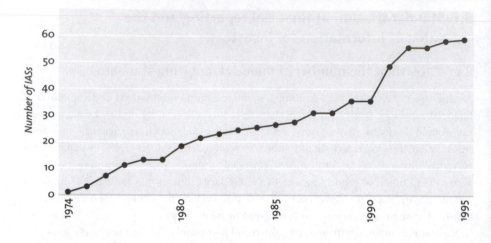

Figure 8.1 **Increase in the number of IASs between 1974 and 1995**

Source: Cairns 1995: 46f.

those setting accounting standards and the numbers of auditors and professional accountants are all positively related to the number of accounting standards. The accounting and auditing industry profits from the extension of accounting standards and regulations as economic rents are allocated to the accounting and auditing industry when companies are forced to comply with standards and thereby increase demand for the services of this industry. The accounting and auditing industry therefore has strong incentives to influence regulators to require an excessive amount of accounting and auditing services. In fact, as can be seen in Table 8.1, accounting services grew substantially between 1992 and 1996.

However, increasing the number of standards does not necessarily lead to better-informed investors (see e.g. Myddleton 1995: 92). Wygal *et al.* (1987) demonstrate the varied influence of different national accounting standards on reported net income for any given company.

As with all goods in general, the marginal benefit from additional accounting standards is likely to decline. The British Stock Exchange chief executive, Michael Lawrence, agreed within the context of accounting standards and regulations that 'there is a balance of regulation that is good for business—beyond that you get diminishing returns' (*Accountancy* 1995: 1). Introduction of some accounting standards without doubt improves the information value of financial reports because, for example, consistency should be ensured. Nevertheless, given the growing number of standards, the 'bottom-line effect' from the combination of various standards becomes less comprehensible to investors (Tribe 1994: 39). In the end, the overall implication is that the information contained in financial reports can be assessed only by highly specialised accounting professionals, thereby promoting growth in the accounting and auditing sector.

Executives of financial reporting panels acknowledge that the increased volume of complex accounting standards 'leads to errors in implementation and directs resources

Company	Growth in income (%)	Growth in number of employees (%)
Summit	74	70
Arthur Andersen	73	64
Deloitte Touche Tohmatsu	60	52
Price Waterhouse	50	56
RSM	48	56
Ernst & Young	46	39
Grant Thornton	44	46
Moores Rowland	39	37
Pannel Kerr Forster	35	39
Nexia	34	37
KPMG	31	25
HLB	28	28
Coopers & Lybrand	28	30
Horwath	28	35
BDO Binder	25	25
Average growth	*43*	*40*

Table 8.1 **Global growth of income and number of employees of the 15 largest accounting and auditing companies between 1992 and 1996 (excluding consultancy operations and mergers in 1997)**

Source: Roden 1996

away from money-making' (*Accountancy* 1995: 1). This increases the demand for accounting and auditing services (i.e. from large multinational accounting firms that have experts in every country and that can provide global support).

As a result of the reduction in transparency caused by the multiple effects of the increasing number of accounting standards, investors are less able to assess the economic value of accounting standards. Uncertainty grows even larger as financial accounting standards do not adequately cover important influences such as the environmental issues discussed in Chapters 6 and 7.

Moreover, tangential consideration of environmental issues in a few existing standards, or through the introduction of new standards, may increase investor uncertainty even more because investors have to assess which accounting standards consider environmental aspects and which do not.

The following two sections argue that excessive growth of financial accounting standards and the related loss of transparency and information value (net of costs) for investors provide incentives for the emergence of other models such as the shareholder value concept.

In this argument the number of accounting standards should not be confused with the number of accounting standard systems (e.g. IAS, US Generally Accepted Accounting

Principles [GAAP]). A large number of competing accounting standard systems may improve the quality of standards if the best standard system prevails, whereas growth in the number of accounting standards in any given accounting standard system may reduce transparency once a certain number of standards is reached. However, costs substantially increase for firms if they have to apply different regulated accounting standards in various countries (see e.g. *BAZ* 1997: 27).

The impact of excessive growth in financial accounting standards has also been acknowledged by Michael Sharpe, ex-chairman of the IASC, who stated that 'the myriad of different standards multinational companies have been forced to comply with over the years has cost them millions of dollars in administrative expenses, and this situation is in urgent need of attention' (quoted in Tabakoff 1995: 30).

8.1.2 Information value and cost of information

Investors can improve their knowledge about a company by consulting audited financial reports. By publishing financial data, such as the return on equity from past operations, and by complying with financial accounting standards, companies try to help investors in their assessment of potential investment value. Independent audit of financial reports against accounting standards guarantees a minimum quality of data (e.g. greater accuracy and reliability) and provides investors with information about the potential value of their investment.

Establishment of a corporate financial accounting system and audit procedures creates benefits and causes costs. Most costs of developing accounting standards are fixed and carried by professional accounting organisations. On the other hand, a company has to introduce and maintain accounting systems, hire an auditing firm and pay for its services and has to introduce its own internal audit group. The costs are fixed and variable (ongoing) elements. In turn, investors have access to the 'opinion' provided by an audit. An audit is an examination that is made in accordance with generally accepted auditing standards. A financial accounting audit investigates whether a financial report conforms to accounting standards and regulations. Its aim is to provide credibility to financial statements. This should reduce any uncertainty for investors about the true profitability of a company. At the same time, financial reporting information and its audit reduce uncertainty regarding the value of a shareholder's investment, thereby encouraging existing shareholders to be informed about their share value.

However, as argued in the previous section, the marginal value of financial accounting information decreases for the users of financial reports with the growing number and degree of detail in accounting standards. It can be expected that above a certain number of accounting standards the marginal improvement in financial information decreases and that it can eventually become negative. Beyond a certain number of accounting standards (given a constant quality of accounting standards) uncertainty increases because investors are no longer able to assess the quality of information received. Information is influenced by too many different accounting standards so that investors can no longer disentangle relevant from irrelevant influences on published accounting figures. A similar argument has been made by Bolton and Dewatripont (1995) about the capacity of company members to process information. Hence, as far as the value of information, V^{I}, is concerned, there will be an optimal number of accounting standards, $N(V^{I}_{max})$, influencing accounting information, recognition, measurement and disclosure (Fig. 8.2).

As a result, the relationship between the number of accounting standards, N, and the information value, V, for investors can be visualised as an inverted U-shaped function (Fig. 8.2). The information value function includes the benefits of information minus the costs for the investors to understand the information. However, it does not include the costs of companies to collect and report the information, although these costs reduce profits and are also borne indirectly by the investors. It can be assumed that the information value for investors is at least equal to their willingness to pay for financial information. Furthermore, in principle, the total costs, C, of establishing accounting standards, introducing and maintaining company accounting systems and hiring auditing services increase with the addition of every accounting standard (Fig. 8.2).

A large part of these costs is fixed as it is borne directly by the companies irrespective of how much investors invest. The costs of the independent auditing system are borne indirectly by the investors because audit costs reduce a company's profitability. Part of the auditing costs are borne by the state, as auditing costs reduce the taxable profit of a company and thus the tax-based income of the state through the tax shield generated.

From a social point of view, the optimum number of accounting standards ($N\star$) is where the difference between the information value and the cost of information, $V–C$, is at a maximum. From an investor's point of view, the optimum number of accounting standards is not where the maximum information value is created, $N(V^{I}_{max})$, but somewhere between $N\star$ and $N(V^{I}_{max})$, as only part of the company's total accounting and auditing costs are borne by the investors (this is where the marginal value equals the marginal costs of accounting standards).

Figure 8.2 **Number of accounting standards and the value and costs of information**

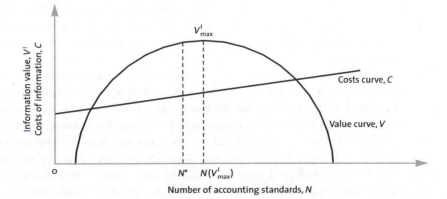

8.1.3 Regulation of financial accounting

In most developed countries the application of a certain set of accounting standards is legally required for joint-stock companies (Tabakoff 1995). Influencing regulators to require more standards as part of the compulsory accounting standard set could be considered as one means by which the accounting and auditing industry foster market growth and increase its size and income. Such regulations reflect a *quid pro quo* for corporate existence (mandated accountability) and create a demand for accounting and auditing services. The total demand for accounting and auditing services is higher than it would be without enforced accounting disclosure. As a result, the optimum number of standards is very likely to be exceeded: 'The volume of accounting regulation literature coming from various regulatory bodies [is] denting the competitiveness of UK companies' (*Accountancy* 1995: 1).

Referring to Olson's (1965) organisation theory of interest groups, the accounting and auditing industry, especially the small number of global players, can be expected to be better organised than the large number of investors. Global accounting and auditing firms with many specialised experts profit most from increasing specialisation and lack of transparency. This development has also supported an increase in the market share of the 'Big Six' in comparison with smaller accounting and auditing companies. In 1996 the Big Six were Arthur Andersen, KPMG, Ernst & Young, Coopers & Lybrand, Deloitte Touche Tohmatsu, and Price Waterhouse. The mergers of Price Waterhouse with Coopers & Lybrand and of Ernst & Young with KPMG support the argument that the size of 'global players' is an anti-competitive factor in the accounting and auditing market as the number of leaders is reduced.

In spite of their financial stake, most private investors are not affected by accounting regulations as much as they are by the auditing industry. In addition, most investors may not be completely aware of the effects of an excess number of accounting standards. As a result, the accounting and auditing industry has more influence in the political process which establishes mandatory accounting regulations than have investors.

If standard-setters, regulators and the accountancy industry are able to require more accounting standards than the social optimum, $N^\star$, the excess number of accounting standards, N^{excess} ($N^{\text{excess}} > N^\star$) will lower the potential net information value ($V^I - C$). Nevertheless, investors want to maintain their optimum level of information. It is, therefore, not a surprise that investors have an incentive to reduce their dependency on financial accounting information and to search for other sources for assessment of corporate share value.

Two conclusions in relation to the improvement of corporate eco-efficiency and accountability can be drawn from this analysis. First, neglect of environmental issues in financial accounting standards does not necessarily provide a justification for introduction of a myriad of new standards but instead leads to the need for including consideration of environmental issues in existing accounting standards. Second, environmental issues should be considered holistically across all standards in an accounting standard system (e.g. the IAS system) and not just in some of them. Third, if information value contained in financial reports decreases, for example, as a result of missing information or because only partial consideration has been given to environmental issues in the standard system, investors and financial analysts will try to replace some of the financial accounting information with more valuable information. A popular strategy for reducing such distortions is to provide financial information in terms of cash flow. One model based on cash flows, the shareholder value concept, has recently received considerable attention. To improve eco-efficiency and sustainable development, investors and management should, therefore, also consider analysing the financial effects of environmental interventions from the perspective of the shareholder value concept.

8.2 Approach, advantages and disadvantages of the shareholder value concept

In recent years the concept of shareholder value has become increasingly popular for valuation of companies and financial assets. With the growing importance of environmental costs, and with many companies earning money from environmental products and services, the question arises as to whether environmental management geared towards eco-efficiency is in conflict or in harmony with the philosophy of shareholder value. In the following sections an assessment of the shareholder value approach to environmental management is made. The impact of corporate environmental protection measures on the drivers of shareholder value will be analysed, and conflicting effects will be weighed against each other. It should be emphasised that analysis of corporate environmental protection based on shareholder value covers only one aspect of environmental management and that investigation of the effects of environmental management on shareholder value is only one element in a corporate shareholder value analysis.

The next section will briefly explain the fundamentals of shareholder value analysis. Starting with a discussion of value drivers, the types of corporate environmental protection measure that can increase shareholder value or at least limit the erosion of shareholder value are shown in Section 8.3. Conclusions are drawn about the features of an environmental protection system that are compatible with the shareholder value concept and therefore in line with improvement of corporate eco-efficiency. Finally consideration is given to how the different economic effects of environmental management can be weighed against each other.

8.2.1 The concept of shareholder value

The value of a company has traditionally and above all been determined mainly by examining its accounting data—mostly sales figures, earnings, profitability, liquidity and solvency based on book values—even though cash-flow methods for assessing company value have existed for a long time; note the recent tendency to value Internet stocks based on a multiple of their revenues rather than their earnings, because most Internet stocks have not reported any income to date. However, accounting information presents some serious problems (see Johnson and Kaplan 1987a): it relates to the past, and very much depends on the accounting standards applied, and so may be of little help in predicting the future business success of a given company.

This backward-looking approach is particularly questionable from an environmental point of view as new problems are constantly being revealed. Yet companies continue to establish valuations and strategies on the basis of past data. Future environmental changes that may affect the company do not find their way into the logic of such valuation methods until they are part of the company's past corporate history, when they can be used for predictive purposes. The fact that results reported by companies depend very much on particular accounting standards also presents a problem from an environmental point of view.

This is where the concept of shareholder value has advantages. Basically, shareholder value is a conventional investment calculation used to assess financial assets (particularly shares). In technical terms, shareholder value, V^{SH}, is the discounted net current value of a company's future free cash flow (Copeland *et al.* 1993: 72f.; Rappaport 1986):

$$V^{SH} = \sum_{n=1}^{} \frac{V_0^{FCF}}{(1+i)^n} - V^{BC} \qquad [8.1]$$

where

V^{SH} is shareholder value

V_n^{FCF} is the free cash flow in period n

V^{BC} is the market value of borrowed capital

i is the discount rate

The concept of shareholder value depends on expected free cash flow (V^{FCF}), as only this can be used to pay investors. Corporate value, V^C, is determined by discounting the expected free cash flow:

$$V^C = \sum_{n=1}^{\infty} \frac{V_n^{FCF}}{(1+i)^n} \qquad [8.2]$$

To arrive at the shareholder value, the value that is of benefit to shareholders (i.e. increased share prices plus dividends), borrowed capital has to be subtracted from corporate value. Unlike free cash flow, a simple income figure, for example, does not take into account the fact that part of a company's income has to be used for paying interest on borrowed capital, thereby reducing the amount that is available to pay shareholders.

8.2.2 Advantages of shareholder value-oriented analysis

Cash-flow figures reflect basic inflows and outflows of cash and thus cannot be manipulated as easily by accounting practices and standards as income based on accrual accounting figures (Copeland *et al.* 1993; Studer 1992: 306). Compared with figures used in financial accounting (e.g. income), shareholder value has a major advantage when it comes to environmental management: it is future-oriented and focused on long-term increases in company value. Like most environmental protection measures, shareholder value is concerned with investment now in order to derive future benefits.

Neither financial accounting systems nor the shareholder value approach explicitly embraces environmental objectives, but with their focus on economic variables both concepts have a strong, direct influence on business activities and thus an indirect influence on corporate environmental impact. However, the anticipatory nature of the shareholder value philosophy—particularly its orientation towards the future and its emphasis on sustainable value increases—has more in common with the principles behind eco-efficiency than those behind financial accounting, which is based on past transactions, events and standards, with use of historical costs rather than market values. This applies both to national (e.g. German commercial code HGB [*Handelsgesetzbuch*] or Swiss commercial law OR [*Obligationenrecht*]) and to international accounting standards (e.g. EU directives, IASs). One author recognised these problems several decades ago and sought to reconcile with cash-flow accounting those financial accounting standards based on cash and cash equivalents while gaining the benefit of accrual (asset-based and liability-based) accounting (Chambers 1966). Unfortunately, the accounting and finance professions have not fully advanced his system, and struggle on with historical cost accounting instead.

8.2.3 Disadvantages of shareholder value-oriented analysis

The philosophy behind the shareholder value concept is based on major problems. For example, the expectations of investors and management play a significant role in determining applicable discount rates and estimated future cash flows. If these expectations are poor predictors of the future (e.g. because of the neglect of future financial impacts resulting from existing environmental contamination), calculations will not correspond to the ideal shareholder value. Furthermore, values created in the distant future will often not be considered because, in practice, analysis of future trends is restricted to a period of five to ten years ahead, because of the reductionary effects of discounting cash flows. In these circumstances, there is a danger of inappropriate management and investment decisions being made. Thus, in terms of the inherent problems related to the shareholder value concept, the quality of the assessment of company value will depend more on the skills and expertise of the assessor than on the choice of assessment method (Studer 1992: 307).

Nevertheless, in modern business practice the concept of shareholder value has gained a great deal of support (see e.g. Volkart 1996). This may be because of an implicit acceptance of the idea that inaccurate expectations pose a lesser problem than reliance on the accrual-based record of past transactions and events, with its associated distortion of accounting information. This acceptance may be attributable to differences in transparency between the two approaches. Complete reliance on the accounting approach means that the effects of a large number of standards and practices have to be accepted en masse. The shareholder value approach is much more manageable, as only a few variables need to be considered (a forecast of free cash flow, discount rate including risk-free interest rate and a risk factor). As discussed in Section 8.1, the effects of accounting standards on the company result are impossible for almost anyone other than qualified accountants to analyse. For investors and company management, on the other hand, the assumptions on which shareholder value calculations are based are much more transparent.

In the following section, the type of corporate environmental management that helps to improve shareholder value is considered. Similar arguments may apply to environmental protection measures that reduce shareholder value. In such cases, it is a question of keeping the 'destruction' of shareholder value to a minimum.

8.3 How does environmental management influence shareholder value?

8.3.1 Focus on value drivers

To answer the question of how far a corporate environmental management system is in conflict or harmony with the shareholder value philosophy, more than a brief look at the underlying philosophy will be necessary.

One way to approach the issue is to discuss the conclusions that can be drawn about corporate environmental management from a shareholder value approach. This can be undertaken by considering the drivers of shareholder value.

With its strict emphasis on efficiency, the shareholder value concept is basically more conducive to economically efficient environmental protection, characterised by the fact that desired protection of the environment is achieved at minimum cost or with cost savings or additional profits. This is in line with the purpose of improving eco-efficiency.

According to Rappaport's thesis (1986), management measures can be assessed on the basis of 'value drivers' and management decisions related to investment, operational management and financing (Fig. 8.3). The value drivers behind changes in shareholder value include:

- ☐ Investments in fixed assets
- ☐ Investments in current assets
- ☐ Sales revenue growth
- ☐ Net operating margin and rate of tax on income
- ☐ Capital costs
- ☐ Duration of value increase

Value drivers are affected by environmental interventions to differing degrees, depending on the nature and size of the company. Environment-related investments include, for example, effluent treatment plants (fixed assets) as well as necessary working supplies such as chemicals used to neutralise acids (current assets).

Sales revenue growth and net operating margin may be affected, for example, by 'green' product lines. Duration of any increase in value is determined by asking how long a return

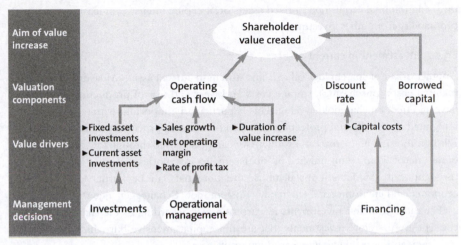

Figure 8.3 **Value drivers of shareholder value**

Source: Rappaport 1986

better than the market average can be achieved (Rappaport 1986). In contrast to these value drivers, capital costs do not affect the valuation of cash flows but do affect the discount rate. The weighted average cost of capital is calculated on the basis of interest rates on borrowed capital and dividends plus capital gains on equity. When determining capital costs, the risk incurred—including environmental risk—is implicitly taken into account through the level of interest rates and returns on equity (see Section 8.3.4).

8.3.2 Investment

Investment decisions are extremely important within the context of corporate environmental management, not only because they tie up a great deal of capital but also because they have a long-term structural influence on methods of production, on working procedures, on decision-making paths and on specialist skills. Also, investment decisions should reflect a company's assessment of the general environmental conditions expected to prevail in future.

8.3.2.1 Investment in fixed assets

Investments can increase shareholder value if they generate a return that is higher than the cost of capital. Therefore, capital-intensive investments in what are known as 'end-of-pipe' technologies (such as downstream air filters and effluent treatment plants) reduce shareholder value (see e.g. Gallhofer and Haslem 1997). This is because they require a large amount of capital (e.g. for the installation of an electrostatic filter) and also because they usually incur high operating costs (e.g. electricity consumption and special charges for disposing of filter dust) and do not usually generate any revenue.

As far as this value driver is concerned, the shareholder value concept directs attention towards environmental protection that is not capital intensive compared with today's level. When it comes to environmental investment, the focus should, therefore, be on measures involving minimal acquisition of fixed assets or, if capital intensive, at least on a par with profitability from other investments.

8.3.2.2 Investment in current assets

Another driver of shareholder value is investment in current assets. Measures that reduce material costs (purchasing), storage costs and wear and tear of production installations have an effect on shareholder value. This is particularly important within the context of integrated environmental protection technologies such as process optimisation (see e.g. Ellipson 1997). If an increase in productivity can be achieved through lower consumption of raw materials and semi-finished products, smaller inventories and consequently a lower throughput in production installations, the potential can be harnessed to increase economic and environmental efficiency (Epstein 1996; Schaltegger 1996a).

The most attractive investments in current assets according to the shareholder value concept are therefore investments that are not capital-intensive but which increase the efficiency and/or productivity of production processes.

8.3.3 Operational management

The effect of operational management on shareholder value is primarily determined by growth in sales revenue, the net operating margin and the rate of income tax. What is crucially important is the combined effect of these factors. For example, even with rising sales revenue and constant taxation, shareholder value can decrease if the sales growth is accompanied by deterioration in the profit margin. At the same time, declining sales revenue will not automatically result in a decline in the shareholder value of a company (Baumol 1959).

For sales revenue and profit margins to rise, the perceived benefit to customers must increase. Environmental factors may play a significant role here, particularly in consumer goods markets. Sales growth and net operating margin are determined through general development of the sector and through competitive position of a company within the sector (Porter 1989). Both factors may be affected in the short run and long run by environmental considerations.

Booming sectors usually mean rising sales and high profit margins for the companies operating within those sectors. Companies in stagnating sectors, on the other hand, usually have to contend with falling sales and shrinking profit margins because of tougher competition. Development of the sector can be related to the life-cycle of social demands and the life-cycle of products. The image of any industry is influenced by social demands and important events in the past. Sales from 'green' industries and of 'green' products are also influenced by the development of social demands, by an industry's image and by the environmental awareness of consumers. Environmental awareness has increased in many developed countries (for an example from Germany, see Meffert and Bruhn 1996).

Individual companies can further increase their shareholder value by improving their competitive position. According to Porter (1989), a distinction can be made between the price leadership and product differentiation strategies for improving competitive position relative to market rivals. Environmental factors can have a material impact on both strategies.

One way of achieving price leadership is to cut costs, thereby creating room for competitive pricing. With the growing internalisation of external environmental costs, and the trend towards matching overall costs to society with private company costs, the cost reduction goal of business is gradually coming into line with the ecological goal of reducing the burden placed by business on the environment. Therefore, it is safe to assume that, if external costs continue to be internalised in future, the price leadership strategy will become increasingly important in environmental management. This has already happened in recent years in the chemical industry, where substantial efficiency improvements have reduced current and future costs and environmental pollution. Costs have been cut through waste minimisation and energy and water savings, to name just a few general examples (for an example of how to calculate these savings, see Chapter 6). In very competitive markets it is possible to counter a deterioration in profit margins with a strategy of product differentiation, especially at a time of increased environmental awareness, when people are prepared to pay more for environmentally benign products. A strategy of 'green' differentiation is viable in certain markets.

Furthermore, sophisticated 'clean' technologies often benefit from tax concessions (through shorter write-off periods and subsidies; see e.g. Mooren *et al.* 1991). The additional income or reduced costs also help enhance profit margins unless treated as ex post windfall gains by companies.

Environmental factors may also have a substantial impact on company tax burdens. In this context, income taxes usually play only a secondary role because tax authorities do not actually discriminate between the earnings of environmentally 'friendly' and environment-polluting companies except through the provision of tax allowances for certain environmental activities.

Other taxes and levies such as trading capital taxes, energy taxes or nitrogen emission duties may be financially as well as ecologically relevant. For example, the installation of end-of-pipe filters may lead to an increase in fixed assets, as well as to higher repair, maintenance and disposal costs. The tax burden on capital employed may lead to a further environment-related reduction in shareholder value.

To calculate the effect on shareholder value of implementing or not implementing various environmental protection measures, a modern management accounting system as discussed in Chapter 6 and a related system of eco-control are essential.

8.3.4 Financing

Available financing methods and their associated costs can have a major impact on shareholder value. In the past, banks and insurance companies have seriously underestimated the importance of corporate environmental protection (*Economist* 1994c). In recent years, however, new environmental protection regulations and more stringent rules on liability, particularly in the USA, have led to an environment-related increase in the costs and risks associated with lending. Banks increasingly discriminate between environmentally benign and environmentally polluting companies. Financing conditions attached to government-subsidised loans and development programmes have further widened the gap. Some investors (e.g. ethical and environmental trusts) have also begun to take ecological aspects into account when deciding where to invest their funds.

The discounting rate for calculating shareholder value corresponds to the weighted average cost of capital, C^{cap}, and is made up of the weighted costs of borrowed capital (C^{BC}) and equity capital (C^{EC}):

$$C^{cap} = \left(\frac{C^{BC}}{C^{BC} + C^{EC}}\right)C^{BC} + \left(\frac{C^{EC}}{C^{BC} + C^{EC}}\right)C^{EC} \qquad [8.3]$$

The most obvious ways of reducing total borrowed and equity capital costs through environmentally benign behaviour and projects are to take advantage of lower interest rates on environmental loans and to be recognised by banks (creditors) for environmental fund and ethical fund investments. Any cost advantage attainable through good environmental management can be described as a 'green bonus', a signal that if returns are competitive a green company has a wider choice of fund sources than has a 'dirty' company.

Of far greater importance, however, is the impact of environmental risks on capital costs (see e.g. Vaughan 1994: 39f.). Potential environmental risks can result in a rise in the interest rate on borrowed capital and thus in a higher discount rate for calculating shareholder value. However, the environmental risk a company runs is also reflected in the costs of equity capital. When assessing the environmental risks of a company or sector, a distinction between systematic and unsystematic risks is useful.

Unsystematic risks can be 'diversified away' by investors and are thus, according to the capital asset pricing model (Lintner 1965; Sharpe 1964), not rewarded by the financial markets. This is because the combination of a large number of risks produces a broad spread of risks so that, with the aggregate selection of investments, what starts as a collection of high-risk securities eventually becomes a risk-free portfolio. The required profitability for the entire portfolio can be made equivalent to the profitability of a single risk-free security.

In fact, the costs of equity are by definition higher than the interest rate for risk-free investments, as in practice some risks, such as risk of recession, cannot be diversified away even in a large portfolio. This is because of systematic risks. Systematic risks occur whenever different companies are exposed to the same or similar risks. The probability that other companies will be affected increases if such a risk materialises for one company. The extent to which a company is affected by such systematic risks is measured by the so-called 'beta factor'.

An example of a systematic risk, from an economic the point of view, is that of volatile energy prices. This risk has a strongly systematic character because an increase in the price of a fuel (e.g. as a result of a CO_2 emission tax or an energy tax) is usually accompanied by price increases for other types of fuel. If a particular fuel storage installation were to blow up, this would be described as an unsystematic risk, because an accident of this kind will not affect all the other storage plants.

In the light of increased demand, the above example of a systematic effect applies even to renewable energy sources. Practically all companies need energy to produce their goods and services. Thus, increasing energy prices affect (practically) all companies in a market simultaneously. Such a risk cannot be completely diversified and will, therefore, lead to higher costs of equity, depending on the extent to which a company is affected by the systematic risk.

The fact that environment-related risks are highly systematic in nature is often overlooked (see e.g. Figge 1997). The only way of reducing the financial consequences of systematic risks in order to improve eco-efficiency is to reduce the risk itself. Within an operational context, this can be achieved through efficiency improvements. Once recognised, lenders and insurance companies will not offer credit and insurance contracts that face systematic environmentally induced financial risks.

The introduction of an energy tax (or other environmental taxes and levies) represents such a systematic financial risk. Diversification across the types of fuel used will thus have only a very limited effect. An effective and cost-efficient hedging of this risk through diversification is therefore not sensible in practice. Companies that operate in an energy-intensive way are thus particularly exposed to the risk of higher energy prices. The only way of dealing with this risk in order to increase shareholder value is to use less energy (i.e. become more energy-efficient) by following an eco-efficient path.

Given the growing costs associated with non-compliance, environmental taxes, changing consumer preferences and environmental liabilities, other financial stakeholders have also become interested in environmental issues. Banks and other creditors are interested in environmental impacts on the financial position of customers borrowing money.

Loss of some loans is part of the normal business risk faced by banks, but they have not, in the past, been exposed to the impact of environmentally induced risks. However, in the USA, within the context of the 'Superfund' legislation (the 1980 Comprehensive Environmental Response, Compensation and Liability Act [CERCLA]), some banks have been made liable even for the remediation costs created by customers who have become insolvent ('lender liability'). The financial consequences for lenders can be substantially larger than the amount of the credit given.

For the first six years after the enactment of the Superfund legislation, lenders were specifically exempted from bearing any clean-up costs. However, in 1986 a Maryland district court ruled that, if a company were to go into liquidation because of a contaminated site, lenders should be treated like owners (Hector 1992: 10f.) and could be sued for the costs of clean-up. As clean-up costs can be many times larger than credit given, perhaps even forcing the lending bank itself into bankruptcy, banks are therefore becoming increasingly cautious about lending money to possible polluters. Hence, small and medium-sized companies without the necessary resources to cover potentially large environmental liabilities face particular difficulties when trying to obtain loans.

In 1990 a panel of federal judges ruled that if a bank, or any other secured lender, is able to influence or control company management it ought also to be treated like an owner (Gray 1993: 185). As a result, some banks have introduced questionnaires to establish whether prospective liabilities exist. To protect themselves, banks have started to require environmental audits from firms before they assess the risk of certain sites. Of course, these costs are all passed on to customers, unless the company seeking the loan can demonstrate its 'green' credential through, for example, certified environmental management systems. A poor environmental record can create difficulties when trying to obtain

HECTOR (1992: 107) PROVIDES AN ILLUSTRATIVE EXAMPLE FOR lender liability:

" In 1980 the Bank of Montana-Butte lent $275,000 to a local company that coated telephone poles with PCP [pentachlorophenol] and other chemicals to protect them against rot and insects. The company collapsed in 1984, leaving behind a heavily contaminated site. Regulators and courts prosecuted previous owners of the land, including Atlantic Richfield. However, they also pursued 'The Bank of Montana-Butte'. The projected cost of the clean-up, $10 million to $15 million, was several times larger than the bank's total capital of $2.4 million. "

Box 8.1 **Lender liability**

a loan (see e.g. Hector 1992: 109; Box 8.1). In short, audits and legal costs significantly increase the price of lending to companies with poor environmental practices.

In April 1991 the US Environmental Protection Agency (EPA) issued regulations that clarify the right of any bank to conduct environmental audits and the circumstances under which it can foreclose on contaminated property or lend money to finance a clean-up without running the risk of being treated like the owner of the site in question.

Although the above examples apply to US sites (Box 8.1), the issue of lender liability has now started to attract attention everywhere. For example, the effects of a lender liability regulation as well as the possible consequences of its introduction in Europe were discussed in the financial sector (ACBE 1993). EU legislation on contaminated land, on civil liability caused by waste and the polluter-pays principle have changed the lending practices of banks quite considerably (Box 8.2). To date, environmentally induced credit risks are practically always connected to hazardous waste and the remediation of production sites. At present, the potential environmentally induced credit risk caused by other environmental impacts, such as emission of greenhouse gases, are expected to be low but to increase in the future (Mansley 1995).

Insurance companies are also taking environmental issues into account when considering insuring risks. They want to be informed about the environmental performance of their customers and about the possible financial consequences of spills, accidents and remedia-

Box 8.2 **Superfund legislation and lending practices in the USA**

IN AN EMPIRICAL STUDY OF US BANKS SIMON (1991: 16) ANALYSED the effects of the Superfund legislation on creditors' lending practices:

☐ 88.1% of the US banks studied had changed lending procedures since the introduction of the Superfund legislation in order to avoid environmental liability.

☐ 62.5% had rejected loan applications because of the possibility of environmental liability.

☐ 45.8% had discontinued loans to certain businesses because of fear of environmental liability.

☐ 16.7% had abandoned property rather than taking title because of environmental concerns.

☐ 13.5% had incurred clean-up costs on property held as collateral.

tion (Cochran and Wood 1975; Cohen *et al.* 1995; Schaltegger and Figge 1997). The Superfund legislation has also substantially influenced the insurance industry. According to Wheatley, 'The situation in the United States is so serious that it threatens the solvency of the whole insurance industry' (quoted in Gray 1993: 218).

The main concern for insurance companies (as for banks) is, of course, to obtain a current estimate of risks and opportunities. In many cases is not yet clear to what extent insurance companies face systematic environmental risk. However, environmental risks have started to become a substantial component of insurance premiums. Companies involved in the production and transport of chemicals and involved in waste disposal sites are especially likely to face higher insurance premiums.

One main problem for (re-)insurance companies is that the risk of natural disasters has increased since the premiums were calculated. For example, insurance premiums to cover damages caused by storms, floods and other natural disasters that are thought to be a consequence of the 'greenhouse effect' (or 'global warming') have never been calculated at today's level of risk assessment (Schweizer Rück 1995).

As insurance companies will at some point have to cover these previously unanticipated losses, today's clients will have to pay higher premiums than they might have expected to cover current and future costs. As a result, the external costs of past generations will have to be internalised and borne by current and future generations. This effect is likely to continue; it will tend to lead to high insurance premiums for today's generation and could very well result in under-insurance or no insurance. Management should therefore anticipate these trends by trying to insure environmental risks early through long-term contracts with fixed conditions.

New insurance instruments dealing with environmental risks have evolved in recent years because of increasing concern over environmental costs and liabilities as well as the inherent uncertainty associated with environmental issues (Figge 1997). Environmental insurance is a financial mechanism that reduces the exposure of a company to environmental risks in exchange for the payment of a premium. Environmental cover is divided into two categories:

☐ Pure risk transfer

☐ A programme combining risk management and risk transfer

The first category represents a physical transfer of risk from the client to the insurance company. Typically, third-party physical injuries, property damage and losses emanating from the insured site are covered.

Environmental insurance can be part of the business strategy of a company. However, it will never entirely replace prevention activities because an insurance company is interested in reducing uncertainties and its own risk. As the relationship between insurers and companies is generally characterised by 'moral hazard', thorough environmental audits are conducted before an insurance contract is signed. Annual monitoring is the norm before renewing a policy (EIU/AIU 1993: 86). Such activities do provide general support for improvements in corporate eco-efficiency.

Risk management and risk transfer coverage form the second category and constitute a company-funded risk-management programme designed to include clean-up and third-party liabilities. Such programmes are generally used by large corporations with heavy environmental exposures. Any valid claims up to the annual insured limit are paid in full by the insurance company and recovered from the fund. If the losses are higher than the accumulated capital, the insurance company will cover the additional costs over a predefined period (EIU/AIU 1993: 86). Such insurance tools help companies to hedge risks such as those emerging from the Superfund regulation.

Nevertheless, the re-insurance industry expects that major environmental risks, if shown to be systematic, might not be insurable in the future (see e.g. Münchner Rückversicherung 1995). Hence, these risks will have to be covered by the companies themselves (e.g. treated as capital damage resulting from natural catastrophes as a possible consequence of the greenhouse effect).

As a result, environmental issues will also increase uncertainties and risks for investors, creditors and other stakeholders (Figge 1995; Lascelles 1993). Company management is therefore increasingly being challenged to demonstrate financial viability in the face of environmental risks. A simple way to do so is by covering insurable risks and by informing stakeholders in an open and consistent way through adoption of a financial accounting and reporting system based on international standards. The link between financial reporting and shareholder value shows that information value for investors can be improved when financial reporting is co-ordinated with the shareholder value concept.

8.3.5 Duration of value increase

As a forward-looking concept, the shareholder value approach also takes into account future changes in prices, sales and costs. Here, it is assumed that the returns from an investment will, in the long run, converge on the cost of capital. After a certain time no further increase in shareholder value will be possible. Hence it is necessary to specify the period over which it will be possible to achieve a return higher than the capital cost.

Another way of increasing shareholder value is to increase the duration of the value gains. This factor is extremely important, particularly in an environmental context. New environmentally problematic products, which today enable a company to achieve above-average returns and thus enhance shareholder value, may tomorrow become a burden on shareholder value if for environmental reasons prices and sales fall earlier than expected. On the other hand, if the period during which the higher than average return is attainable can be prolonged (e.g. through environmental innovations that allow a price premium to be earned), shareholder value will be increased.

8.4 Consequences for environmental management

8.4.1 Consequences for operational management

If the concept of shareholder value is understood as an approach to achieving a lasting increase in a company's value, it is certainly compatible with economically efficient environmental management. Therefore, it is entirely consistent with the idea of eco-efficiency-oriented accounting systems. The final three sections are organised as follows: first, in this section certain conclusions regarding corporate environmental management are drawn; second, in Section 8.4.2 the different economic effects of environmental protection measures are assessed on a quantitative basis (see e.g. Müller and Wittke 1998; WBCSD 1997); and, finally, limits to shareholder-value-oriented environmental management are discussed in Section 8.4.3.

Progressive operational environmental management will increase shareholder value:

☐ The greater the 'authenticity' of costs (i.e. the greater the extent to which external costs are internalised [e.g. by levies])

☐ The better that future needs to internalise environmental risks can be anticipated (e.g. the future costs of cleaning up previous environmental contamination)

Obviously, the shareholder value approach does not take a positive view of every act of environmental management but only of measures enhancing enterprise value in the long run and thus of eco-efficiency-improving measures that (Schaltegger and Figge 1997):

☐ Are capital-extensive: using software rather than hardware (to give 'smarter', smaller, cheaper installations)

☐ Have low material consumption: reducing throughput (to give lower purchase, storage and depreciation costs)

☐ Are sales-boosting: increasing the benefit and attraction to customers (to achieve more desirable products and services for more customers)

☐ Widen margins: increasing the benefit to customers and reducing the costs of producing products and services (to achieve higher prices because of greater benefit and lower operating costs through improved operating efficiency)

☐ Safeguard the flow of finance: gaining the confidence of the capital market (to achieve lower and more unsystematic risks, and a 'green bonus')

☐ Enhance value over the long term: anticipating future costs and earnings potential

The consequence for information management is that data concerning the drivers of shareholder value and the above-mentioned characteristics are needed to assess how corporate environmental management can actually improve eco-efficiency (i.e. improve the value of the company through environmental protection measures).

8.4.2 General assessment of the different economic effects of environmental management

By incorporating the concept of shareholder value into the formulation of corporate environmental management it is possible to integrate into a single measure the relevant parameters on which an economic decision is based.

When assessing the cash inflow and cash outflow generated by alternative proposals, it is necessary to take account of the impact on different value drivers, that is, the impact on (Fig. 8.4):

☐ Expected additional cash outflow caused by the net investment

☐ Necessary additional net cash inflow from operational activity

☐ Expected additional risk

If, for example, management decisions are based solely on expected income, there is a risk of making an investment that may promise the highest return in absolute terms but may have only a low return relative to the required capital investment and thus may deliver only a poor return. Second, it is possible that an investment will involve not only a high return but also a high risk that may not be adequately compensated by the return.

Additional enterprise value is determined not so much by the absolute additional income but by the relative additional return after adjustment is made to take into account anticipated risk. In this way, the concept of shareholder value offers an ex ante valuation method for the implicit integration of the relevant parameters on which economic decisions are based.

To sum up, it may be said that a system of environmental management geared to increasing shareholder value provides a way in which the financial impact of environmental management can be assessed on the basis of the value drivers. At the same time, it provides a way of quantitatively assessing conflicting financial effects on an ex ante basis and weighing them against each other.

Figure 8.4 **Integrated financial evaluation of environmental management**
Source: Schaltegger and Figge 1997

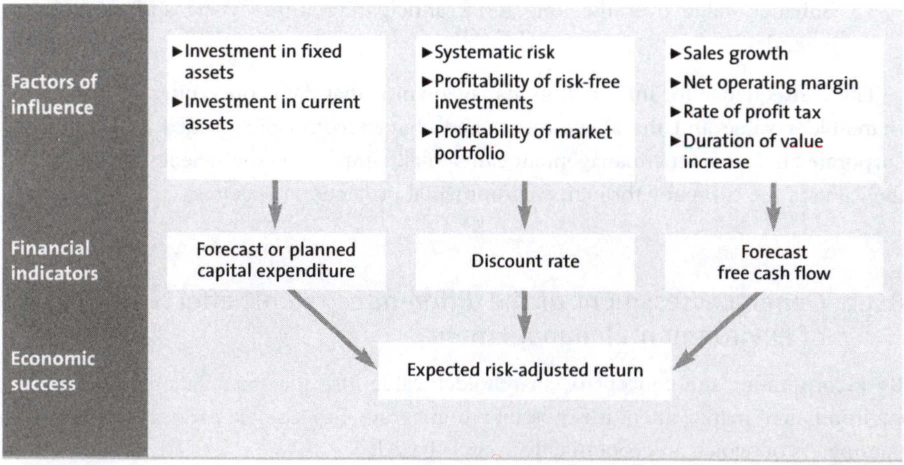

8.4.3 Limits to shareholder value-oriented environmental management

A system of environmental management that enhances shareholder value is essentially in harmony with a market-oriented environmental policy and the concept of eco-efficiency. However, it is constrained by what the legal, political and market circumstances will allow and by what other stakeholders demand.

Within the context of corporate environmental management, the concept of share-holder value faces certain economic and social hurdles. In addition to the fact that financial liquidity is not explicitly included in the calculation of shareholder value problems may also arise wherever and whenever a company is unable to avoid certain risks through diversification—because of its size, perhaps. As investors can diversify their investments, unsystematic environment-related risks are not considered in the calculation of the discount factor. Nevertheless, these risks can be relevant for management if they cannot be balanced internally and if they influence the economic success of the company or perceived environmental credibility of environmental management.

The shareholder value concept takes only market risks into account. However, companies are also exposed to the risks of a possible loss of social acceptance and of legitimacy (Cowe 1994; Gray *et al.* 1996). In this regard, the fact that the concept does not support any explicit analysis of the social aspects of corporate environmental protection and of corporate learning processes can be regarded as a significant shortcoming. In particular, the shareholder value approach stands in the way of the concept of sustainable development if it is used to argue for a redistribution of resources between social and ecological interests on the one hand and the interests of capital providers on the other.

If company management wishes to succeed in the marketplace and in society, it must safeguard its legitimacy. This may mean refraining from courses of action which, according to a purely arithmetic analysis, would lead to the biggest increase in shareholder value. Even from a strictly economic viewpoint, it is necessary therefore not only to consider the net present value of free cash flows but also to take into account any option value (see Brealey and Meyers 1991; Dixit and Pindyck 1993) of being able to remain in business.

8.5 Summary

As environmental issues are of growing relevance for groups whose interest is primarily financial, it is essential for investors, financial analysts and management to examine the impact a company's environmental management has on its enterprise value.

This chapter, therefore, has described the effect of different approaches to environmental management on the market value of a company. The shareholder value approach is used as the main method because this has been a particularly useful approach to business valuation. Provided the significant shortcomings described are kept in mind a shareholder value-oriented approach to environmental management can help guide company management decision-making and improved eco-efficiency. However, it will do nothing to improve accountability to other stakeholders and provides only a partial analysis of environmental management issues.

If the concept of shareholder value is understood as one method of assessing enterprise value to be compared with conventional financial accounting figures, it will bring corporate environmental management closer to the basic principles of eco-efficiency. An environmental management system compatible with shareholder value can reduce the potential for conflicts between the environmental objectives of a company and its financial objectives. The concept also provides a clear idea as to which types of environmental protection measure will provide a lasting increase in enterprise value and which should therefore be considered for implementation as a matter of priority.

It has been shown that environmental protection measures that enhance enterprise value are not capital-intensive and consume fewer materials. Furthermore, such measures increase sales revenue, raise margins, protect the flow of finance and increase the long-run value of a company. The shareholder value concept also enables an integral appraisal of the different economic effects of environmental management. At the same time, however, it is always necessary to consider company legitimacy, the option value of alternative courses of action and the fact that some environmental investments must be made to support these at the expense of shareholder value in the short run.

Questions

1. What is shareholder value? Given that there is a range of stakeholders interested in corporate environmental impacts, what arguments can be advanced for emphasising shareholders and 'value' attributable to them?

2. Is there a relationship between the number of accounting standards issued and demand for accounting and auditing services? Explain this relationship. Given this relationship, should environmental accounting standards be added to the set of existing standards?

3. 'Shareholder value is cash-oriented.' Do you agree with this statement? Give reasons.

4. Shareholder value, as a concept, faces a number of problems. List these problems. Can any of the problems be overcome?

5. Are systematic and unsystematic environmental risks related? Why, or why not? Are banks concerned about systematic environmental risks? Are insurance companies concerned about unsystematic environmental risks? Explain.

6. What set of eco-efficiency characteristics is the shareholder value approach concerned with identifying?

7. Can option values be used to promote corporate legitimacy?

Part 1

INTRODUCTION AND FRAMEWORK

2 The emergence of environmental accounting management
3 The purpose of managing environmental information
4 The environmental accounting framework

Part 2

ENVIRONMENTAL ISSUES IN CONVENTIONAL ACCOUNTING

5 Overview, criticism and advantages of conventional accounting
6 Environmental management accounting
7 Environmental issues in financial accounting and reporting
8 Environmental shareholder value and environmental issues in other accounting systems

Part 3

ECOLOGICAL ACCOUNTING

9 Overview and emergence of life-cycle assessment and ecological accounting
10 The efficiency of approaches to environmental information management
11 Internal ecological accounting
12 External ecological accounting and reporting of environmental impacts

Part 4

INTEGRATION

13 Integration with eco-efficiency indicators
14 Integrating eco-efficiency-oriented information management into the corporate environmental management system
15 Summary

Part 3

ECOLOGICAL ACCOUNTING

DETERMINATION OF ECO-EFFICIENCY FOR A COMPANY REQUIRES THE INFORMATION management system to incorporate the financial impacts of environmental issues and also to compute information about environmental impacts of corporate activities. Environmental information is defined as knowledge about the impact of corporate activities on the natural environment. Chapter 1 drew attention to the fact that ecological accounting deals with the lower branch of accounting in Figure 4.1 (page 60), insofar as it concerns a company's environmental performance.

Part 3 of this book describes the main contemporary developments in the emerging field of environmental information management and its concern with the measurement of corporate impacts on the environment. Systems for calculating and reporting environmental information are relatively new compared with financial information systems. From an economic perspective, different measures of environmental protection should be compared if the most effective method is to be derived. Hence, a company that is pursuing corporate eco-efficiency should check whether the environmental information management approach applied can provide accurate and relevant environmental information in a cost-efficient way.

In Chapter 9 the applicability of the conventions of financial accounting to ecological accounting are investigated.

Chapter 10 proposes a model to help assessment of the efficiency of environmental information management methods and applies this model through life-cycle assessment (LCA)—the first and in practice most frequently applied tool of environmental information management.

Further approaches that attempt to measure and communicate the impact of company activities on the natural environment include (internal) ecological accounting and (external) ecological reporting. Ecological accounting looks for quantified information as a way to provide a systematic assessment of environmental impacts. As with the LCA method, its measurements are restricted to physical terms (e.g. measurement of emission levels in kilograms of emissions, or energy consumption in joules of energy consumed). Despite the fact that some environmental assets and impacts can be assigned a monetary value, it is by no means feasible to measure all environmental impacts of a company in monetary units. Ecological accounting tends to be favoured by supporters of 'strong' sustainability (see Chapter 3) because it does not attempt to express the environment in monetary terms and therefore does not directly facilitate commercial exploitation by profit-based institutions (Owen 1994: 42).

Ecological accounting adapts the basic principles of management accounting to environmental information management. It deals with the activities, methods and systems of recording, analysing and reporting impacts of a defined economic system (the reporting entity) on the natural environment. Ecological accounting focuses on production sites, plants and companies. The non-financial accounting approaches presented are currently applied in a wide range of companies, including several international corporations (see e.g. Schaltegger and Sturm 1998).

Internal ecological accounting seeks to provide ecological information for internal management purposes (Chapter 11). It is an extension of traditional management accounting designed to satisfy a manager's need to be informed about a company's environmental impacts. State-of-the-art ecological accounting and the most recent developments in site-oriented internal corporate ecological accounting are examined in Chapter 11. Internal ecological accounting is a necessary precondition for any environmental management system including ecological investment appraisal and associated discussion of figures based on discounted future environmental impacts. In principle, internal ecological accounting and reporting is a prerequisite for external ecological accounting. Internal and external stakeholders may require the same kind of information, though the amount and degree of detail will vary.

As with conventional financial accounting and reporting, external ecological accounting and reporting also take into account the information requirements of external stakeholders (see Chapter 12). For many different reasons, external stakeholders are interested in the environmental performance of companies:

☐ Lenders, investors and insurers wish to ensure that environmental risks are being sensibly managed.

☐ Governments are concerned about compliance with regulations.

☐ The trust of local communities needs to be assured if future corporate plans are to be realised.

☐ Employees are responsible for internalising core corporate values and being held to account.

☐ Other pressure groups (e.g. non-governmental organisations [NGOs]) seek assurances about company learning as well as confirmation of environmentally benign activities.

In 1995 over 300 companies from various industries published extensive annual environmental reports with detailed data on their discharge of pollutants (Naimon 1995) and 71,670 reports from 21,490 facilities were made public by the US Toxic Release Inventory in 1997 (EPA 1997: 1-6). In principle, external accounting and reporting provides information of a more general and consolidated nature than does internal ecological accounting. Chapter 12 presents an overview of external ecological accounting and reporting.

Chapter 9

OVERVIEW AND EMERGENCE OF LIFE-CYCLE ASSESSMENT AND ECOLOGICAL ACCOUNTING

In the past, ecological accounting was sometimes seen as a tool used by a few relatively progressive companies who were able to overcome institutional barriers and constraints and secure necessary resources with which to experiment. However, this situation has changed faster than expected. Environmental laws and regulations already in force in the USA, in Europe and in some other countries have created a new area of substance 'accounting' as a basis for effluent-monitoring reports which many companies have to submit to regulators.

Although these laws and regulations can impose substantial costs on individual businesses (and, indirectly, on society), several studies (e.g. as summarised in Cairncross 1991) found that the benefits of these regulations to society and, indirectly, to its businesses are often even greater than the costs (see e.g. Stinson 1993). In the future, comprehensive ecological accounting and reporting might become mandatory.

In the USA the Toxic Release Inventory was established in 1989 and today requires the reporting of discharges of 651 substances by all companies with more than ten full-time equivalent employees. In Denmark, Chapter 5 of the Danish Environmental Protection Act, requiring public disclosure by companies of environmental impacts in so-called 'green accounts', was established in 1995 (see e.g. Reuters 1995a, 1995b; Rikhardsson 1999b). The UK is encouraging its top 350 listed companies to provide voluntary disclosures about their 'greenhouse gas' emissions (ENDS 1998b: 6), and this year (2000) Australia has introduced compulsory reporting of pollutant discharges (EIA 1999: 8).

Tax and environmental protection agencies are primarily interested in specific, regulated information on discharges of equally specific pollutants. Without information about discharged effluents or used resources, variable environmental tax rates could not be multiplied by the respective quantities to obtain tax-payable figures.

The increasing number of stakeholders who require environmental information also includes banks (e.g. when lending money) and insurance companies (e.g. when underwriting contracts).

Another reason for the emergence of ecological accounting, apart from stakeholder pressure (see Section 2.2), consists of changing cost relationships (Section 2.3). Over the past two decades the marginal internal costs of environmental impacts have been increasing significantly (because of fines, fees, taxes, employee leave and loss of consumer acceptance). In contrast, the marginal costs of accounting for environmental emissions, as well as the marginal costs of reduction, have declined over the same period. As a result, the relative value of information about environmental impacts has increased, but technological development has led to a decrease in the costs of reducing environmental impacts. In addition, improved information technologies have reduced the marginal costs of compiling information and of generating ecological accounts and reports.

Ecological accounting also delivers information for product-oriented and production-technology-oriented innovations. Therefore, today's ecological accounting is acknowledged to be important even when it is not explicitly requested by stakeholders.

In spite of these developments, the question of whether ecological accounting really is necessary is occasionally raised. Is conventional financial accounting more accurate than it used to be, and does it not already recognise some environmental impacts? Today's rising tide of corporate environmental reporting provides an unequivocal answer: measuring, reporting and managing corporate impacts on the environment is becoming a necessary component for successful business (see e.g. Naimon 1995). Consequently, management theory and education have also accepted the need for environmental information management.

Conventional financial accounting is far from being able to recognise all environmental costs, even if the boundaries and the time-frame of financial measures are extended. It is true that ecological accounting still lacks a consistent set of international standards, or a well of widespread expertise and experience (on the possibility of developing an 'epistemic' community of ecological accounting experts dealing with ozone depletion, see Burritt 1995). Nevertheless, this also applies, to some extent, to conventional financial accounting, as shown by the many discussions about the 'correct' mode of financial reporting (see Chapter 7).

Recent argument, based on the idea of ecologically sustainable development, suggests that, if the environmental impacts of companies require a separate accounting system or significant changes to existing accounting systems, so too do other issues such as the social impact of companies. This is theoretically correct. However, ecological accounting, broadly defined, has already been established in a great many companies and by far exceeds social accounting in practical importance.

Companies are only just beginning to reinvent their concern for social accounting and reporting issues (McPhail and Davy 1998; Shell 1998). A long period of development is anticipated before the social (a subset of the environmental) has developed a well-honed set of accounting and reporting tools. In the meantime, although social issues have a high magnitude of importance, if environmental and ecological systems fail or are severely damaged by corporate activities there may well be no society to worry about. In addition, several signs, such as the growing interest of regulators and financial markets, strongly indicate that it is becoming more attractive and necessary for companies to consider their impact on the natural environment.

The next chapter will deal with the efficiency of tools to manage environmental information. Some general reflections are illustrated by a model presented in Section 10.2. Then, the life-cycle assessment (LCA) approach, which is currently the most common environmental information management tool, will be analysed.

Questions

1. What is the main difference between environmental accounting and ecological accounting?

2. Why might 'deep green' environmentalists favour the presentation of corporate information in ecological accounts but reject disclosures in environmentally adjusted financial accounts?

3. Which environmental management concept encourages managers to favour the combined development of internal ecological accounting and management accounting. Explain.

4. Why should business worry about the environment? How might ecological accounting help reduce such worries? In your answer consider the views of three different stakeholders.

5. Should accountants establish themselves as a community of experts on ecological accounting and reporting issues?

6. Triple-bottom-line reporting, based on the notion of ecologically sustainable development, aims to report on financial, social and ecological positions and impacts. Is 'ecological' accounting and reporting more important than 'social' accounting? Consider the answer from the viewpoint of each of the following: (a) the accounting profession; (b) environmental managers; and (c) corporate executives. Make it clear how you are defining the 'environment' before further considering your answers.

Chapter 10

THE EFFICIENCY OF APPROACHES TO ENVIRONMENTAL INFORMATION MANAGEMENT

10.1 Environmental information as subject matter of measurement

Environmental 'protection and conservation' is one aim of recent moves to encourage ecologically sustainable development. Protection and conservation are considered necessary because the world has finite environmental resources. Also, the world has only limited financial resources available to address environmental issues, although these could be expanded at the possible cost of hyperinflation and economic ruin. Clearly, companies and governments should spend their limited environmental budgets efficiently if they are to obtain the highest possible benefit for the environment. Although the overall aim is effective management of social and economic interactions with ecological systems, an important goal is to recognise that, at present, use and destruction of natural resources form a part of the industrial process associated with capitalism, with communitarianism and all other institutional structures and processes available throughout the world. Such use and destruction require considerable introspection, especially when the long-term consequences of present actions are considered. In consequence, from an economic perspective, tools to assess environmental management efficiency need to be developed and used by all companies (i.e. the tools must promote economic efficiency and lead to ecologically sound decisions). In order to improve environmental performance and corporate eco-efficiency through environmental information management, a clear understanding of environmental information is needed.

The vast majority of corporate environmental impacts originate with activities that are attempting to create value for consumers. Economic activities cause environmental interventions, such as emissions and use of resources. Environmental interventions represent the exchange between the anthroposphere (the human world) and the environment, including resource extraction, emissions into the air, water or soil and aspects of land use (Udo de Haes 1995). An inventory (a list of items in a collection) of these environmental interventions can be recorded in tabular form (e.g. an emissions inventory, such as the main greenhouse gas emissions). Because almost every corporate activity has some influence on nature, it will never be possible to record all environmental interventions. Instead, a rule of thumb is needed to help companies record a relevant set of environmental interventions.

Transformation processes (dilution, dispersion, synergies and chain reactions) mean that not every environmental intervention causes the same environmental impact (e.g. contribution towards the generation of photochemical smog or land salinisation) or the same change in ambient environmental quality. Every environmental intervention causes an environmental impact, though not every emission release or economic activity necessarily leads to an environmental effect (e.g. photochemical smog in a region, or deforested land) and environmental damage (e.g. human lung diseases or unproductive land). Environmental effects are the consequences of environmental intervention in an environmental system whereas environmental damage is deterioration in the quality of the environment not directly attributable to depletion of resources or pollution (Heijungs *et al.* 1992: 92).

Nature has the ability to adapt, but only insofar as threshold levels, or the carrying capacity of an ecosystem, are not exceeded. The presumption is that scientists can accurately assess carrying capacity, but there is considerable uncertainty associated with scientific estimates. The degree of damage is influenced by factors such as persistency, mutagenic, carcinogenic or accumulation potential (for an introduction to eco-toxicity, see Ottoboni 1991).

Impact chains are also complicated by some of the inherent characteristics of environmental impacts, such as high uncertainty because of changing conditions, or qualitatively fuzzy information. In summary, because of the sheer complexity of nature there is often no agreement, even among natural scientists, about what exactly constitutes a specific case of environmental damage.

The various relations described so far are what some natural scientists attempt to assess. However, not all societies and people attach the same importance to environmental effects and environmental damage. Therefore, environmental impact added by human activity has to take into account sociopolitical and economic preferences. Sociopolitical and economic valuation attempts to take these preferences into account.

In view of these very complex interrelationships, the extent to which environmental information management might help clarify the link between economic value added and environmental impact added by corporate activity has to be examined. In order not to try to reinvent the wheel, it is desirable to identify and use conventional information management concepts (e.g. of accounting) that can be adopted by environmental management information systems.

When collecting and classifying environmental information, various objects can be the centre of attention. The main objects are:

☐ Products (a customer perspective)

☐ Geographic sites (a spatial perspective)

☐ Businesses (an industrial perspective)

None of these objects is automatically the right or wrong perspective to adopt. Instead, the appropriateness of an object depends on the purpose and task of the analysis on hand. Every object can have a broader or narrower focus. The narrowest focal point for all environmental information management—whether from a product, spatial (geographic site) or industrial (total business) perspective—is a single production step. Therefore, any compilation of environmental information activities will, as a rule, start with the investigation of single production steps.

The focus (i.e. the boundaries of the system considered) can be narrow or broad for each object:

☐ From a product perspective, it is possible to focus on one production step, all production steps in a specific plant, all production steps of that product within a company or a complete product life-cycle and also to incorporate transformation steps occurring outside company boundaries.

☐ A spatial (geographical) perspective may cover one production step, a production site, a local region, a nation or a supranational area.

☐ From an industrial perspective, a single production step, a business (e.g. a strategic business unit), a company, an industry or the world economy can be examined.

In one extreme scenario, all three dimensions merge: the environmental interventions of all geographical regions (the world) would equal those of all corporations, businesses and industries (the world economy) and of all product life-cycles (world output of products).

The subject matter of environmental information management is independent of the object, focus or system boundaries that are chosen. Management collects, analyses and communicates information on ecological properties. As environmental properties are manifold, different aspects are considered:

☐ Ecological assets (ecological capital goods) such as land, forests and biodiversity

☐ Use of ecological assets such as non-renewable material resources and energy carriers (e.g. mineral ores, oil) and renewable material resources and energy carriers (e.g. wood, water)

☐ Environmental interventions such as material emissions and any associated pollution (substances and substance combinations, e.g. carbon dioxide [CO_2], nitrogen oxides [NO_x], volatile organic compounds [VOCs]), and energy emissions (energy types such as heat, radiation, noise)

According to the nature of the topics, the subject matter of environmental information management can be broadly divided into:

☐ Assets (stocks) at a specific point of time, such as the stock of fish in a lake, or the amount of discovered gold reserves

☐ Flows in each period, such as emissions of air pollutants

The following section discusses a model to help assessment of the efficiency of methods used to manage information about environmental properties.

10.2 General considerations and model

The key tool for measuring how much environmental protection has been achieved with limited financial resources is eco-efficiency. Eco-efficiency is defined as the ratio between an economic measure and an environmental performance indicator; hence the efficiency of environmental management can be measured by the ratio of the net economic costs and benefits (numerator) of actions taken to the ecological benefits (denominator) emanating from the application of environmental management tools. The ecological benefit of an environmental management tool, such as eco-efficiency, is demonstrated by its ability to provide relevant, representative information and to support ecologically and economically beneficial decisions. In most cases, net ecological benefits cannot be measured in monetary units. Instead, as an approximation, ecological benefits, in the sense of actual and potential effects on the natural environment, can be measured in physical quantified units, even if the relative magnitude of ecological effects and their positive or negative impact remain somewhat uncertain.

To improve eco-efficiency, the tools of environmental management themselves have to be effective and efficient too: that is, they must be economically efficient and lead to ecologically sound decisions.

Figure 10.1 provides a model as a basis for discussion of the eco-efficiency of an approach to environmental information management. The first quadrant (quadrant I) of the figure, to the upper right-hand side, shows the marginal costs of pollution prevention and the marginal costs of environmental impacts (representing fees, administrative costs, etc.) that are borne by the company. Although measuring environmental performance instead of environmental impacts, this quadrant corresponds to Figure 2.2 (page 37), which was discussed in Section 2.3. Economically efficient environmental protection is characterised by a balance of the marginal costs of environmental protection and environmental impacts.

In the quadrant to the upper left-hand side (quadrant II), the marginal costs of an environmental management information tool are compared with the amount of environmental data created by an application of this tool. The more data generated, the flatter the slope of this relationship and the greater the potential for useful information to be produced at a given cost.

The function in the lower left-hand quadrant of Figure 10.1 (quadrant III) shows the extent to which data collected about the environment are transformed into information relevant to decision-makers who want to improve the environmental record and the eco-efficiency of their company. The function is horizontal if the data are absolutely meaningless in relation to the desired object, and gets steeper the more purpose-oriented knowledge that can be created out of relatively smaller amounts of environmental data.

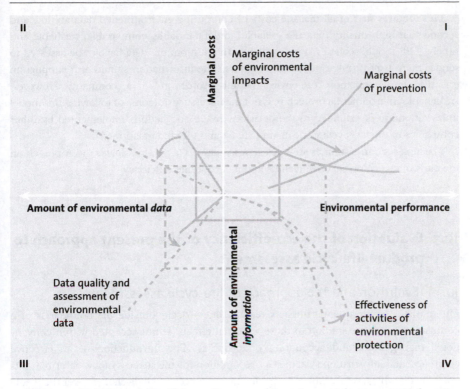

Figure 10.1 **Model to assess the efficiency of an approach to environmental management information**

The difficulty in creating this general, purpose-oriented knowledge is to capture all aspects of the causal chain between value added in economic terms and environmental impact added. The main factors influencing this functional relationship are data quality and the quality of environmental impact assessment.

Finally, in the lower right-hand quadrant (quadrant IV), the amount of environmental information generated is related to corporate environmental performance. This function is determined by the effectiveness of corporate environmental management. The link between environmental information management and effective environmental protection is that environmental information has to be related to the activities (e.g. production), places (e.g. cost centres) and objects (e.g. products) of a company. The closer that knowledge emanating from the processes represented in quadrant III (knowledge that is generally oriented towards the purpose of environmental protection) is to the actual situation, the closer a company will be to achieving its objective of reducing environmental impacts.

The goal of any efficient approach to environmental information management is to improve environmental performance by reducing costs of or increasing revenues to the company. In Figure 10.1 this would lead to a shift of the curves, as indicated by the dashed lines.

This requires first of all that the costs of computing environmental data are low and second that high-quality data (i.e. reliable, understandable, comparable, verifiable and timely [FEE 1999b: section 6]) are available. In addition, the data have to be assessed to render them useful (relevant) to stakeholders. The information should also support an effective implementation of environmental protection in a company. However, sustainable environmental protection is not the necessary outcome of following this model unless attention is extended to the decisions made and actions implemented by other companies in the life-cycle value chain (Shank and Govindarajan 1992).

The next section examines life-cycle assessment (LCA) and evaluates the approach on the basis of its ecological effectiveness and its economic efficiency.

10.3 Evaluation of the eco-efficiency of the present approach to product life-cycle assessment

10.3.1 Evolution and the approach of life-cycle assessment

Often, major environmental impacts (externalities) occur outside the boundaries of a company. Giving recognition to these 'external effects' is not accepted within conventional management and accounting philosophies. The introduction of an effective environmental information system is a precondition for the success of any reform in this area. This is why several authors have called for a survey of all discharges over the whole life-cycle of products (Fava *et al.* 1991, 1992; Lave *et al.* 1995; NCM 1995; Ream and French 1993; SustainAbility *et al.* 1992; SWMD 1995). Life-cycle assessment (LCA) is considered to be one of the most important environmental information management approaches (see e.g. Pidgeon and Brown 1994; Töpfer 1993). LCA takes a broad view of product life-cycles (see OECD 1998b) and largely corresponds to the philosophy of 'deep greens' (see e.g. Maunders and Burritt 1991).

LCA philosophy has been adopted by management accounting under the term 'life-cycle costing' (Section 6.3.5). LCA calculates environmental impacts in physical terms, whereas life-cycle costing attempts to measure the (financial) costs of a product during its lifetime in monetary terms.

A broad range of objects, such as infrastructure, processes or activities, can be examined on the basis of an LCA (for environmental impact assessment and projects in the context of biodiversity conservation, see e.g. Commonwealth of Australia 1999) but the most common application still focuses on products. Today, the main reasons for companies to implement LCA are eco-labelling norms and regulations (CEEC 1992) as well as the market credibility of some eco-labels (see e.g. SCS 1996). LCA and eco-labels are closely connected because, before permission for an eco-label can be awarded, an assessment of all relevant environmental impacts related to the particular product is needed. LCA provides a pragmatic basis for such an assessment of impacts.

The first eco-labelling schemes were devised in Germany (1978), Canada, Japan, Norway and Austria. In 1992 an eco-labelling regulation was passed in the European

Union (CEEC 1992). International eco-labels, for example for wood products (Forest Stewardship Council) and fish (Marine Stewardship Council), also have a presence. Within companies, LCA is mainly an issue for middle management (i.e. product and marketing managers). Nevertheless, divisional management and, in very rare cases, top management may be involved in the assessment of the life-cycle of important products that are of high public interest. For example Volvo's response to regulations adopted in Sweden require a strategic top management commitment because 'environmental product declarations' in Sweden extend across production, car operation, recycling and other environmental management issues (ENDS 1999a: 26; Box 10.1).

Holistic thinking is often considered a must for assessing all environmental interventions over the whole life-cycle of all company products (Gray 1992, 1993). LCA tries

Box 10.1 **Environmental product declarations in Sweden**

Source: Volvo, www.extras.volvocars.com/epd/epd1.htm

THERE IS AN INCREASING DEMAND ON THE MARKET FOR LCA-BASED, QUANTIFIED information about environmental performance of products and services—so-called type-III environmental declarations. Such information is needed in several marketplaces (e.g. in the raw material supply chain, within the framework of an environmental management system and for 'green' purchasing or procurement).

Swedish industry has initiated and established a type-III environmental declaration programme called the 'environmental product declaration' (EPD) system. It is based on ISO TR 14025—a document in the ISO 14000 standard series. The EPD system is a system for science-based and comparable environmental information open for all products and services to support continuous improvements based on a flexible in-company product-development process.

One of the most important properties of a certified environmental product declaration is that it provides comparability between declarations within a given product group or service type. To achieve this, the basic data must be calculated in the same way and with the same general rules. This applies, for instance, to different forms of assumptions as well as to the setting of system boundaries and the choice of calculation methods.

AN EXAMPLE: CERTIFICATION STATEMENT OF VOLVO CARS

Lloyds Register Quality Assurance Limited (LRQA) certifies that Volvo Car Corporation's EPD, reference S80 1999, dated October 1998, applying to gasoline engine versions for the North American market, is based on LCA techniques. The LCAs comply with the requirements in 'Bestämmelser för Certifierade Miljövarudeklarationer (MVD) Requirements for Certified Environmental Product Declarations'.

The EPD is balanced and complete. Data were collated accurately and properly. The design of the internal audit system, applicable to the EPD, is based on the requirements in ISO 14001 but internal audits have yet to be carried out.

It covered the following activities:

☐ Assessment of compliance with the standards identified above

☐ Review of the rationale for the selection, definition and determination of indicators and their link to LCA

☐ Verification of data parameters, based on a sample approach, to evaluate the accuracy and completeness of the data

☐ Validation of the EPD document for consistency, balance and completeness with regard to the definitions, determination methods and data presentations to capture all environmental interventions, or the environmental impact added, caused by a product, process or service during its total life-cycle, from 'cradle to grave'. Henn and Fava (1984: 548) use the term 'cradle to cradle' to describe the 'rebirth, or reincarnation, of the resources being used for a subsequent product's lifetime'. In addition to the environmental interventions ascertained by site-oriented information management systems, it is also necessary to consider data obtained from suppliers, their subcontractors and from customers and disposal companies. Consequently, internal company information has to be supplemented by data on the environmental impacts of the pre-life-cycle and post-life-cycle steps outside the corporate accounting entity—particularly information about environmental impacts of suppliers and post-use disposal or re-use. Figure 10.2 illustrates the environmental impact added life-cycle chain for a product during its lifetime.

The goal of LCA has been defined the following way:

> The life-cycle assessment is an objective process to evaluate the environmental burdens associated with a product, process, or activity by identifying and quantifying energy and materials used and wastes released into the environment, to assess the impact of the energy and materials used as well as the releases to the environment, and to evaluate and implement opportunities to affect environmental improvements. Assessment covers the entire life-cycle of the product, process, or activity, encompassing extraction and processing of raw material, manufacturing, transportation and distribution, use/re-use/maintenance, recycling, and final disposal (SETAC 1991: 1).

The first attempts at developing the LCA were made in the 1960s and 1970s, when studies calculated energy requirements or chemical inputs and outputs associated with various production processes, energy systems or packages (Basler and Hoffmann 1974;

Figure 10.2 **Environmental impact added (EIA) life-cycle**

Source: Schaltegger and Sturm 1994

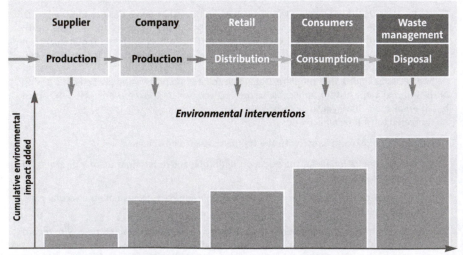

Transportation is not shown in this figure. Environmental interventions are, for example, emissions.

Henn and Fava 1984; Schalit and Wolfe 1978; for a recent discussion of input–output analysis, or eco-balancing as it used to be called, see Jasch 1999). Initially, LCA stood for product life-cycle analysis. Many other terms describing the idea of LCA were used as well: life-cycle systems analysis, eco-balancing, eco-profiles, resource and environmental profile analysis (REPA) and product life-cycle assessment. Today, the expression 'life-cycle assessment' is used for those approaches to product-oriented ecological accounting that aim to take all environmental interventions during the whole life-cycle of products, services or infrastructure into account. In contrast, the term 'life-cycle analysis' covers a broad range of methods with economic, social, political and ecological tasks (Henn and Fava 1984).

LCA has been a research topic for more than three decades now. Many regulators (e.g. the US Environmental Protection Agency [EPA], the German Umweltbundesamt [UBA], the European Union), national and international organisations (e.g. the Society of Environmental Toxicology and Chemistry [SETAC], the Nordic Council of Ministers) consider LCA in various ways. Even national and international standardisation organisations have started to consider LCA. The International Organization for Standardization [ISO], for example, has published a standard (ISO 14040) for the process of making an LCA. For example, Volvo's environmental product declaration was executed as a sampling exercise based on requirements in Swedish regulations (Miljövarudeklarationer [MVD]), the ISO 14040 series and ISO DIS 14031 (environmental performance evaluation). However, it has only recently considered contents, quality of information and assessment approaches (for discussion of the ISO 14040 f. standard, see ISO 1994b).

Recent interest in LCA reflects two things: a broad shift to a more sophisticated, holistic, system-oriented approach to reducing environmental impacts, and a shift in investment based on an acceptance by industry (at least in Europe, USA and, recently, Japan) that environmental concerns are not transitory and that significant changes to all stages of production, from resource availability to product disposal, are inevitable (Ryan 1996: 1).

The most active international research organisation is SETAC, which has published a wide range of papers and guidelines on LCA (see e.g. Consoli 1993; Fava *et al.* 1991). Traditionally, SETAC has examined questions of environmental chemistry and toxicology, but one section of the organisation specifically covers LCA. SETAC is divided into SETAC US and SETAC Europe. The LCA working groups of SETAC Europe address: (1) inventory; (2) screening (development of a rougher, faster and cheaper way to locate the most important impacts); (3) impact assessment; (4) case studies; (5) conceptually related programmes (e.g. product design programmes); and (6) education. Recommendations published under the aegis of SETAC are widely accepted as they often reflect the consensus of many LCA experts, although, historically, SETAC is strongly influenced by scientists from the Centre for Environmental Sciences of the University of Leiden, Netherlands (see e.g. Heijungs *et al.* 1992).

The structure of LCA is usually illustrated as a triangle (see Fig. 10.3), with inventory, impact assessment and improvement assessment shown laterally and goal definition and scoping in the middle (SETAC 1991).

Goal definition and scoping are activities that initiate an 'LCA, defining its purpose, boundaries and procedures. The scoping process links the goal of the LCA with the extent

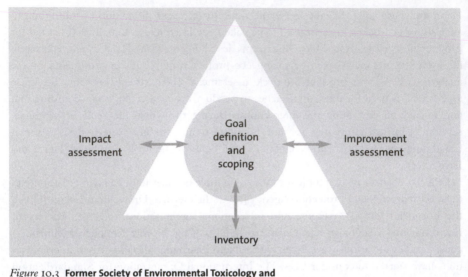

Figure 10.3 **Former Society of Environmental Toxicology and Chemistry (SETAC) framework of life-cycle assessment**

Source: SETAC 1991

or scope of the study, i.e. the definition of what will or will not be included' (Udo de Haes 1995). The life-cycle inventory is a technical, data-based process of quantifying energy and raw material requirements, air emissions, water-borne effluents, solid waste and other environmental releases throughout the life of a product, process or activity (see e.g. Batelle 1993; Harding 1998: 150; SETAC 1991; Udo de Haes 1995).

Impact assessment is a technical, quantitative and/or qualitative process of character-ising and assessing the effects of the resource requirements and the environmental weights to be attached to impacts identified in the inventory component. Ideally, the assessment should address ecological impacts, human health impacts and resource depletion as well as other effects such as habitat modification and noise pollution (see Batelle 1993; Harding 1998; SETAC 1991; Udo de Haes 1995). Improvement assessment is a systematic evalua-tion of the needs and opportunities to reduce the environmental burden associated with energy, use of raw materials and emission of waste throughout the whole life-cycle of a product, process or activity. This analysis may include quantitative and qualitative measures of improvement such as changes in product design, use of raw materials and industrial processing (see e.g. SETAC 1991).

Discussions about impact assessment have long dominated LCA research. In contrast, improvement assessment has only recently been thoroughly examined within the context of LCA (Klüppel 1998). This is unfortunate as improvement assessment is a core activity in actually managing and reducing environmental impacts. Currently, the focus is tending toward inventory analysis and data recording.

Although new illustrations have been chosen in various organisations (for the ISO presentation, see Fig. 10.4), the triangular presentation shown above is still a very popular way to summarise LCA as it symbolises the main steps of the present LCA approach. For example, the base of the triangle represents an inventory with its highly detailed

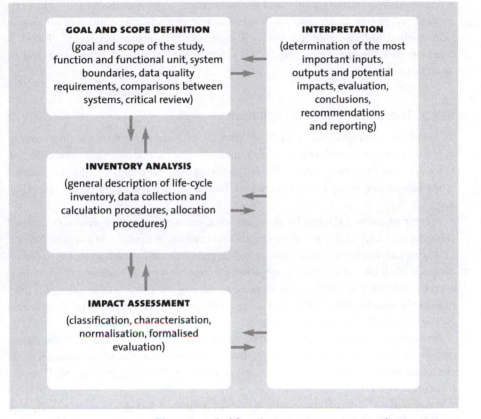

Figure 10.4 **The life-cycle assessment concept according to ISO 14040**

Source: ISO 1994b

information (Fig. 10.3). The narrowing of the triangle at its apex represents the fact that improvement assessment is based on less detailed information. However, in some cases, an improvement assessment can be directly employed on the basis of the inventory without assessing impacts. This is why the side representing 'improvement assessment' is shown as a subsequent phase of impact assessment and is also connected to the side labelled 'inventory'. Goal definition and scoping are located in the middle of the triangle because all stages of LCA must be viewed in light of the initial definitions of goals and boundaries.

In contrast to financial information concepts such as those presented in management accounting, the LCA approach is not designed to provide continual assessment but rather to carry out a single ecological investigation of a product (see also Carlton and Howell 1992). Today's LCA practice can be regarded as undertaking one-time, single-case comparative ecological calculations related to the environmental impacts of a product before it is approved, as well as comparative assessments between alternative products. In the remainder of this section the present approach to LCA is evaluated based on the model proposed in Section 10.2. First, the influence of the LCA method on costs of data collection is discussed. Second, data quality and the information content of the data used in LCAs are analysed. Finally, conclusions are drawn about the potential contribution of the present LCA method towards improvement of a company's environmental record. Issues in common with site-specific ecological accounting, such as impact assessment, will be discussed in Chapter 11.

10.3.2 The costs of data compilation

To complete a comprehensive LCA, all data concerning environmental interventions induced by a specific product in an environmental impact added chain has to be collected. However, with increasing 'distance' from the company, the collection of data becomes more difficult and costly to implement and the quality of information deteriorates (Fig. 10.5).

A comprehensive LCA can be extremely time-consuming and expensive to conduct (Graedel *et al.* 1995). Table 10.1 gives a simplified example of the costs of a comprehensive LCA where all data have been measured and directly collected at each step of the product life-cycle of a job lot of 500 t-shirts. It has to be stressed that one unquantified part of these costs has the characteristics of an investment as some of the information produced for this LCA can be used for future LCAs and act as a 'benefits transfer' for future production and product life-cycle assessment purposes.

An extensive product life-cycle analysis for the whole life of the product's components can obviously be undertaken only in isolated cases, for example, when mass products attract widespread notoriety as did Styrofoam cups, milk packaging and McDonald's hamburger containers (Box 10.2).

Compared with internal surveys, the quality of computed data decreases drastically with declining company influence on the rather distant life-cycle stages in the chain. In practice, it is insufficiently rewarding and far too inefficient for any one company to collect all the

Figure 10.5 **Comparison of the costs of compilation and quality of information in a life-cycle assessment**

Source: Schaltegger 1997a

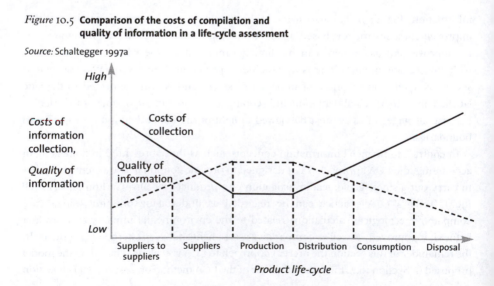

Quantity	Cost ($)
Consultant's fee	150,000
Costs of lost working time (data compilation)	300,000
Costs of measurement and analysis	150,000
Proportion of costs of software programme	5,000
Total (1 job lot of 500 t-shirts)	**605,000**

The steps of product life-cycle considered are: cultivation and production of cotton, transport, manufacturing, confectioning, dyeing, packaging and disposal.

Table 10.1 **Illustrative costs of undertaking a comprehensive life-cycle assessment for a job lot of t-shirts**

product-specific data from its suppliers and customers. The fact that the benefits of 'remote' data are small (low quality and low level of representativeness), and that the costs of collection are exorbitant, are reason enough for various companies to refrain from conducting LCAs after their first experience with this method. Many small and medium-sized companies that have to obtain their own data discontinue LCA. Among the companies still experimenting with LCA is Procter & Gamble Ltd. This company was among the first to carry out an LCA comparing disposable nappies with traditional towel diapers. For further company examples see Gray 1993: 171f.).

To overcome the problem of the high costs incurred when compiling information on distant parts of the life-cycle chain, several institutions have begun to publish data with average environmental interventions for the manufacturing and disposal of basic materials and products. These so-called background inventory data (also called basic inven-

Box 10.2 **Life-cycle assessment and milk packaging**

Source: ENDS 1994a

THE ALLIANCE FOR BEVERAGE CARTONS AND THE ENVIRONMENT, WHICH compared liquid paperboard with plastic milk packaging, funded an LCA. The study found that cartons perform better than do plastic bottles in terms of air emissions, consumption of energy and of non-renewable resources and disposal volume, but they 'lose out' in terms of water emissions. The study was criticised by scientists within the European Union for a number of methodological and data quality issues. These included the fact that the consultants undertaking the study had used industry-average data for the plastic bottle, but company-specific data for cartons. The EU group was critical of this practice because company-specific data tends to come from well-managed firms.

The value of LCAs is that they provide a useful cross-section of environmental information at a particular moment in a product's life. They cannot and indeed are not designed to award a permanent overall 'score' to a product. For practical reasons, the data collected are limited in scope and the results are only applicable for a short space of time, as technological developments, marketing, appreciation of environmental issues and legislation are constantly changing.

tory data or service data) mostly represent the average environmental interventions related to a particular material (e.g. the number of kilograms of CO_2 emitted to supply 1 kg of polyvinyl chloride [PVC]). The public availability of these data helps small and medium-sized businesses to carry out LCAs and ensures that most LCA applications are based on the same or similar data for inputs and waste of pre-production steps (i.e. resources, materials, semi-manufactured goods) and post-production steps (i.e. waste-water in publicly owned treatment plants). In fact, introduction of background inventory data means that the costs of carrying out an LCA have declined. This is why the use of background inventory data has become increasingly popular. However, the use of averages related to these databases can be misleading if there is a gap between the product being examined and the products within the database.

The best-known examples of 'background inventory databases' are those of packaging materials (see e.g. BUJF 1993; BUS 1984; BUWAL 1991; CCME 1995; Hrauda *et al.* 1993; UBA 1992), plastics (see e.g. PWMI 1992) and energy systems (generation of electric power, extraction and pre-combustion of coal; see e.g. ESU 1994; Fritsche *et al.* 1989). There is considerable work under way in Europe, the USA and Canada to establish common industry databases that are in accordance with the format of ISO standards and available through electronic means of delivery.

Table 10.2 provides an example of the costs of an LCA with use of basic inventory data as source material. Calculation of the costs of the LCA is based on the same job lot of t-shirts as in Table 10.1.

The cost differences between Table 10.1 and 10.2 are striking. Although a comprehensive LCA has some potential information investment benefits, the effect of these benefits have not proven to be substantial. Common databases allow staff to consult existing literature and assessments instead of having to measure data at all steps of the life-cycle. Quite often it is even not necessary any longer to read background papers, as the basic inventory data are already included in LCA software database programmes. With declining costs of information collection, the amount of data available has increased in the past few

Table 10.2 **Illustration of costs for a theoretically calculated life-cycle assessment of one job lot of t-shirts**

Quantity	Cost ($)
Consultant's fee	5,000
Costs of lost working time (data compilation)	3,500
Costs of measurement and analysis	0
Proportion of costs of software programme	3,500
Total (1 job lot of 500 t-shirts)	12,000

The steps of product life-cycle considered are: cultivation and production of cotton, transport, manufacturing, confectioning, dyeing, packaging and disposal.

years. This explains why, in practice, many of today's LCAs tend to rely on basic inventory data as well as specific company data. It is the presence of these basic inventories of data that facilitates government regulation of product environmental profiles. Hence there is an incentive for government to encourage development of common databases. The problem with this approach to LCA is that the quality of data becomes suspect.

The next section deals with the quality of data and the information value created under the present approach to LCA.

10.3.3 Data quality and information

The effect on data quality of using basic inventory data reduces the benefits of cost reduction from use of LCA. A first major drawback of LCA is the lack of representativeness, relevance and precision of data collected. This drawback is mostly connected with the use of background inventory data. As shown in Figure 10.5, errors, uncertainties and imprecision in inventory data increase (shown as a decrease in quality of data in Fig. 10.5) as distance from the information collector (the company) increases. With the collection and use of background inventory data, this situation is exacerbated. As the seminal work of Johnson and Kaplan (1987a, 1987b) in management accounting has shown, the relevance of information is no longer assured when data are outdated, widely aggregated and distorted through the use of unrepresentative 'averaging' instead of product-specific data. (The average in statistical terms may not even represent an actual observation from one of the LCAs in a database; for example, when the mean of the distribution of observations is used. If the mode is used then the problem is lessened somewhat because the mode represents the most frequently observed value.)

The industry average represented by background inventory data hides the highs and lows of especially good and bad manufacturers (e.g. assuming an industry average of 12 g of NO_x per kg of polyethylene produced, some manufacturers may cause emissions of less than 1 g whereas others may emit more than 15 g). One reason why practitioners and scientists might increasingly be inclined to overlook the small differences and changes that eventually lead to severe environmental degradation could well be their growing preoccupation with statistical aggregates that project much greater stability than actually exists: 'Using existing data entails selecting information which is relevant and appropriate to the defined issue or "problem", from a range of available sources which are commonly used in either existing studies or models of a similar topic' (Harding 1998: 87).

Compilation of statistics based on background inventory data that were centrally collected has to be undertaken by trying to abstract from sometimes minor (but crucial) differences in context and circumstances. Environmental interventions that, for example, differ in their place, or time of occurrence, are aggregated as though they represented similar kinds of figures, although their local and time-specific environmental impacts may be highly significant for many decisions.

Clearly, models of environmental interventions are restricted by assumptions made by environmental scientists. These are related to the values, assumptions and conditions under which the models have been developed and tested (Harding 1998: 88). Furthermore, the context and geographical region for each model will be different, but common databases trivialise the possible importance of these differences. They do, however, make data available at a lower cost.

The conclusion is that background inventory data reduce the costs of data compilation charged to individual users but result in a loss of the representativeness and accuracy of the information provided. To use such data divorced from specific company data and knowledge is risky behaviour. There are several options for companies to consider. Lewis (1996) summarises four of these as follows (Fig. 10.6):

- ☐ **Life-cycle review.** In this approach a flowchart is used to assess the basic components of a product life-cycle. It provides structure and system boundaries but lacks quantitative data.

- ☐ **Matrix approaches.** In this approach a matrix is drawn up with environmental concern as one dimension and life-cycle stage as the other. Each element is given a rating between 0 (highest impact on the environment) to 4 (lowest impact). The aim is to identify problem areas and design options that could improve a product's overall rating. This method is used by AT&T in the USA for discovering important gaps in matrix elements.

- ☐ **Streamlined LCA.** This is an LCA that does not necessarily collect data on all inputs and outputs at every stage of the life-cycle. There are a number of different approaches to streamlining; for example, a 'bottleneck LCA' concentrates on a particular issue that is known to be important in the life-cycle of a product, such as energy consumption during use. An alternative is to use

Figure 10.6 **Practical approaches to life-cycle assessment (LCA)**

Source: Lewis 1996

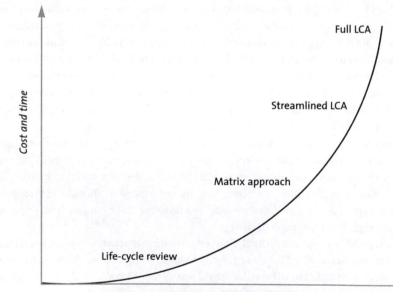

company data for important processes and to use industry averages for less important processes.

☐ **Comprehensive (full) LCAs.** These LCAs are quantitative and rely on measured, calculated and estimated data.

Table 10.3 demonstrates the uncertainty of basic inventory data with a typical example of the emissions of three pollutants accumulating through the production of polyethylene. Data published by the European plastics industry (PWMI 1992) are 5.2–27.2 times larger than those of the Swiss environmental protection agency (BUWAL 1991). The difference between the two data sources is between 429% and 2,627% of the Swiss data.

It has been acknowledged in the LCA community that the data are of disputable quality (Fava *et al.* 1992). As a result, the error caused by data uncertainty in an LCA can easily become larger than the differences in ecological impacts of products and services that LCA is designed to highlight.

First, LCA is of value for internal and external decision-makers only if the information has been verified in accordance with generally accepted, standardised, procedures. To date, such procedures have been standardised only for the environmental management of sites and companies.

Second, today's LCA practices suggest the consolidation (aggregation) of environmental interventions at various points of time and with different spatial impacts (Perriman 1995; Schaltegger 1997a). However, aggregated figures of local emissions do not provide any valuable information as they reveal nothing about potential or even actual environmental impacts. One kilogram of mercury emitted in one hour at one place may kill many people, but the same amount emitted over a year at a hundred places may not have any appreciable impact. The LCA inventory shows aggregated intervention data with local impacts at very different places. What environmental significance can be attributed to an LCA inventory total of 40 tons of total organic compounds (TOCs) in waste-water, made up of 20 tons discharged in Australia, 15 tons discharged in Germany and 5 tons discharged in the USA? The sum of these local interventions has little meaning. Only global interventions can be aggregated meaningfully on a global level (Müller *et al.* 1994).

Table 10.3 **Basic inventory data, from the European Centre for Plastics and the Environment, Plastics Waste Management Institute (PWMI) and the Swiss Bundesamt für Umwelt, Wald und Landschaft (BUWAL) on the emission of three pollutants in the production of polyethylene**

POLLUTANT	POLLUTION EMITTED*		DIFFERENCE	
	PWMI 1992	BUWAL 1991	Weight	Percentage[†]
Particles	3	0.11	2.89	2,627
NO_x	12	1.3	10.7	823
SO_2	9	1.7	7.3	429

NO_x = nitrogen oxides SO_2 = sulphur dioxide
* Grams of pollutant emitted for each kilogram of polyethylene produced
† Weight difference as a percentage of the BUWAL total

Third, the same is true for the current methods of impact assessment (see Section 11.4). The various product-related production, consumption and disposal activities in an environmental impact added chain occur at different times and are spread over different places. Hence, environmental interventions have different impacts on different habitats because they are characterised by distinct ecological absorption capacities.

Most concepts of impact assessment completely fail to consider local circumstances and habitats, although they do have a spatial dimension. The assessment approaches either rely on national environmental targets (sociopolitical methods) or economically and culturally inclined budgets (socioeconomic approaches), or they relate to the spatial dimension of specific environmental problems (classification and characterisation).

The conclusion is that, from an ecological perspective, the current LCA approach, which uses basic inventory data, is of little practical use as it does not provide information on actual (or potential) environmental impacts in the situation in which they occur. Instead, it provides information about hypothetical environmental impacts, which may be divorced from spatial and cultural contexts.

The next section discusses the incentives created by the present LCA approach for managers of corporate environmental protection.

10.3.4 Incentives for actors managing corporate environmental protection

The present LCA approach creates adverse incentives and effects for various actors involved. Data collectors who calculate and publish basic inventory data depend on the information provided by different companies in the industry being considered. From an economic perspective, background inventory data based on averages suppress the initiative to become an industry leader with above-industry performance. Similarly, advanced manufacturers are punished for being seen as members of a 'dirty industry' whereas laggards benefit as free-riders on the more advanced companies in the same industry. In short, the averaging effect does not stimulate innovation in environmental protection.

Moreover, the relation between a data collector and a supplier of data is characterised by information asymmetry. Thus, the only inherent incentive given by background inventory data is to encourage the industry to hand out biased, or at least favourable (and unchecked), inventory data. The suppliers of data have—without cheating—considerable discretionary latitude as to the data they specifically want to pass on. Possibilities include annual, monthly or hourly average data, calculated or measured data, the average data of several production processes or of the best production process and data derived under ideal production conditions. As a result, the quality of estimated and calculated data, as well as the quality of data received from different companies, varies substantially. Thus any derived industry average is an artificial figure without any real meaning.

Published data represent industry averages. Hence, users of background inventory data and purchasers of raw materials cannot distinguish between suppliers based on their environmental performance because such performance is not transparent. 'Dirty' suppliers of a 'clean' material often pollute more than 'clean' suppliers of a 'dirty' substitute material. In these circumstances, choice of a supplier is sometimes environmentally more important than the choice of an input such as a raw material or a semi-manufactured product (Pohl *et al.* 1996).

10.3.5 Conclusions regarding the efficiency of the present life-cycle assessment approach

At first sight, the demand for an assessment of all environmental impacts of the whole life-cycle of all of a company's products seems to make excellent sense. This is why the potential benefits of LCA have been extensively emphasised in academic as well as in professional literature (see e.g. Fava *et al.* 1991; Gray 1993). However, when the practicality of this approach is considered, LCA in its present state of development is an inefficient way of curbing environmental impacts—even if the process of conducting an LCA is seen to be more important than the arithmetic result of the LCA.

LCA can be useful if treated as a general tool for strategic management. However, if and when it is used as an information tool the present method of undertaking product LCA, and especially the use of background inventory data, has major flaws which drastically impair the effectiveness and efficiency of the approach:

☐ Ecologically, the information provided by the LCA may result in incorrect decisions, because, first, inventory data lack representativeness, relevance and precision, and, second, because the consolidation (aggregation) of environmental intervention data usually ignores spatial (locality) and time differences.

☐ Economically, the present LCA approach causes perverse incentives for stakeholders as well as high costs for a company to create a small benefit (see Lifset 1991: 76).

Today, product LCA is able to provide only a static image of 'hypothetical' environmental impacts of a limited number of products. Background inventory data reduce the costs of data collection accruing to individual users but result in an even higher loss in the representational quality, accuracy and relevance of information provided. In contrast, continuous environmental improvement requires equally continuous ecological accounting consisting of relevant and representative information.

The LCA community has responded to these criticisms by making a semantic distinction between a 'threshold approach' and an 'equivalency approach' (Udo de Haes 1995; White *et al.* 1995). The threshold approach considers only those life-cycle processes that 'lead to a surpassing of environmental thresholds' at the respective locations. The equivalency approach adheres to a 'general prevention principle', adding together all environmental interventions, no matter what impact they cause. However, neither this distinction nor these two approaches reduces the validity of the criticism that the aggregation of interventions with local impacts, which occur at different places, does not provide accurate or representative information.

Given this fundamental and unresolved criticism of LCA, it raises the question of whether the very idea of considering environmental impacts over the whole product life-cycle should be disregarded. Certainly, in some cases, overall eco-efficiency could be enhanced to a greater extent through better product design that reduces environmental impacts caused by customer use (e.g. washing machines that use less energy and water) than with investments to reduce environmental impacts of processes and from inputs used by the company conducting an LCA.

LCA aims to be a holistic approach that facilitates consideration of ecological effects and encourages optimisation. Ideally, all environmental impacts across the whole product life-cycle could be comprehensively recorded and assessed according to their potential environmental impacts. This would encourage a comprehensive assessment of product design and reduction of environmental interventions over the whole product life-cycle at the least possible cost. The benefits of an LCA would undoubtedly be high in such an ideal world.

The next section will examine possible strategies to improve present LCA approaches thereby leading to more effective and efficient environmental management.

10.3.6 Possible strategies to improve life-cycle assessment

How can an LCA, or the calculation of environmental impacts of products, be improved and fashioned into an ideal, comprehensive management tool? Basically, there are three possible paths to secure an improvement (see also Lewis 1996; Schaltegger 1997a):

1. More research and more data. One popular suggestion is that the usefulness of LCA for decision-making could be improved with additional research into provision of better background inventory data and better software tools.

2. Simpler and cheaper tools. Another approach is to develop and use simpler and cheaper tools, to focus on a limited number of relevant interventions and to carry out screening methods instead of building up detailed inventories.

3. Abandon the present LCA method and concentrate on site-specific tools and information. A third proposition is to concentrate on site-specific tools instead of LCA and to focus on a continuous recording of the accurate, actual and representative data of individual companies.

The following equation, published by SETAC (Fava *et al.* 1992: 32), shows that the basic assumption behind path 1 is that the quality of data and the quality of the LCA method are independent:

$$\text{quality of LCA information} = \text{quality of data} \times \text{quality of LCA method} \qquad [10.1]$$

According to this point of view, it makes sense to focus on the improvement of basic inventory data. It has been argued in this section, though, that data quality is above all the result of an application of the present LCA method. The quality of information provided by an LCA is, therefore, largely determined by the method used (as well as by other factors not discussed here):

$$\text{quality of LCA information} = \text{function of the quality of the method, and the}$$
$$\text{quality of data given the quality of the method}$$
$$[10.2]$$

From an economic perspective, the emphasis on current LCA development will without doubt fail because the organisational approach adopted is too centralised. The attempt to collect information on the various steps of a life-cycle (and therefore from many different economic actors) from one central place causes extremely high costs of data compilation. This is also reflected by the need for ever-larger capacity in computer systems to handle inventory data.

Today, background inventory data or material are centrally collected for each industry (so there are several central collectors). Consequently, to facilitate access for companies, the collection of background inventory data will ultimately be combined to include all materials, semi-manufactured products and industries.

To continue on this path, intensive co-operation between the actors involved in a product life-cycle will be necessary. However, such developments result in the establishment of cartels and are in stark contrast to liberal markets and economic theory in general, where companies seek to gain a competitive advantage for themselves from their actions (Ryan 1996). This view is gaining relevance within the context of regionalised and global efforts to deregulate and liberalise markets. Therefore, proponents of path 1 must expect increasing opposition in the future.

In addition, the incentives for the actual suppliers of information (i.e. the industry providing information to the central collector) are not good. Former economies in Eastern Europe have shown that central collection of information and central planning face enormous hurdles. The general case for a third party overriding the preferences of individual transactors and site-specific knowledge frequently results in ineffective and inefficient results.

Path 2 is promising and is based implicitly on the general 80:20 rule—that, for example, 80% of the problem can be recognised and solved at 20% of the costs whereas an additional improvement of 20% requires 80% additional resources. According to this rule, concentration on a limited number of environmental interventions can substantially reduce costs. However, for an LCA this approach neither improves the poor quality of the data (in terms of its accuracy, nearness to actual data, or representativeness) in the background inventory nor necessarily solves the problem that only environmental interventions with global impacts should be aggregated on a global level, and similarly at the regional and local levels. In addition, the question of what are generally relevant environmental interventions and who is to decide what they are for screening purposes still needs to be addressed and rests on judgement and expertise.

The next section will examine path 3, the concentration on site-specific information, and combine it with the LCA philosophy to develop a 'site-specific LCA' as one of a useful set of environmental management tools.

10.3.7 Site-specific life-cycle assessment

As mentioned above, the credibility of data to external stakeholders can only be guaranteed through external audit of site-specific information in accordance with international standards. The economic problem in general, as well as the problem of environmental protection, is:

how to secure the best use of resources known to any of the members of society, for ends whose relative importance only these individuals know. Or to put it briefly, it is a problem of the utilisation of knowledge which is not given to anyone in its totality (Hayek 1945: 520).

In economic terms, it is best to encourage actors to collect necessary data for decision-making individually rather than to promote a central collection of LCA data, including background inventory data. This means that, initially, every company should concentrate on accounting for those environmental interventions that can be measured fairly readily in quantitative terms: that is, the site-specific environmental interventions of each specific company. Unfortunately, this will increase the cost of data collection relative to the use of background inventory data (see Fig. 10.5; Tables 10.1 and 10.2). This will be more efficient than a centrally planned compilation of original (primary) data as it uses the established information channels of every organisation, avoids any fallacies of aggregation and supports the development of an empathy for, for example, environmental considerations of managers and employees involved with environmental management processes and company environmental performance. This decentralised collection of data leads to higher quality and accuracy of data as well as a better representation of the actual situation (a desired shift of the curve in quadrant III, Fig. 10.1). As specific company tools that are used will be compatible with established methods of accounting and management, this company-specific information can be better related to company-based financial information (represented by a desired shift of the curve as illustrated in quadrant IV, Fig. 10.1).

In order to collect product-specific information, incentives should be provided for the industry to maintain the specific product information that has already been recorded and audited separately for each manufacturing and warehousing unit. From an economic point of view, individual companies should be able to organise themselves to collect the necessary data. The objective of a site-specific LCA concept is to compile an LCA based on site-specific data about the life-cycle steps of a product (Fig. 10.7). All data have to be collected, recorded and audited at each site, for each company.

This is in contrast to an entirely centrally organised compilation of data. No background data would be necessary anymore. The data used for decision-making would be specific, representative, collected individually and usually would have a consistent, verified standard of quality. According to authors such as Porter (1990), who proposed the idea that strict environmental standards may foster competitiveness, product-oriented accounting can prevail only if industry is given clear standards to work with and a more active role so that it can voluntarily use its entrepreneurial powers to devise innovative solutions.

Incentives for individual companies to collect necessary high-quality data should therefore be guided by data quality and auditing standards. Such a central framework of standards to encourage decentralised action will be necessary to help stakeholders distinguish when they are reading high-quality data rather than low-quality data.

To encourage this development, governments will have to establish strong incentives for audited, site-specific ecological accounting as well as for companies to establish co-operation between suppliers, producers and customers (strategic environmental alliances) for the independent gathering of audited site-specific data for the various steps of a product life-cycle. Only standardised, site-specific data can be compared over time

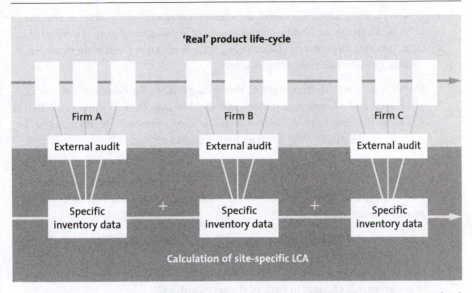

Figure 10.7 **Compilation of data for a site-specific life-cycle assessment (LCA)**

and between companies. Therefore, standardisation organisations and/or governments have to define clear standards of site-specific ecological accounting (see Section 12.3). The EU Eco-management and Audit Scheme (EMAS) and ISO 14000 series standards do not specifically examine data quality in ecological statements. However, use of site-specific life-cycle assessment does address this issue. Site-specific LCA data is verifiable and could also be useful to external stakeholders for accountability and cash-flow implication purposes. Hence, information collected inside the company could also be used for external purposes.

Today, background inventory data are also provided by each industry, but the difference is that the calculated background inventory data are not representative (they are only an unrepresentative industry average), the data are not audited and no managers really know what the source of the data is (there is no guarantee of consistent data quality).

If company-specific and site-specific ecological accounting is to be standardised and verified, relevant data could be passed on as product information from one company to the next and used for benchmarking of similar sites. Thus, introduction of corporate ecological accounting would facilitate product-oriented accounting for subsequent companies in the product life-cycle chain.

The next chapter will address internal ecological accounting.

Questions

1. Distinguish between environmental impact, environmental quality and environmental effect. How are these related to life-cycle assessment?

2. Products, geographic sites and businesses represent three objects for the collection, classification and communication of physical environmental information. Are these three objects related in any way? Why is it important for managers to distinguish between the three objects?

3. Stocks and flows are important in the management of a company's financial affairs and in the management of its ecological affairs (or of its impacts). What, if any, is the interrelationship between these two concepts in financial and environmental affairs? Why are they both important?

4. Tools of environmental management need to be eco-efficient. What is eco-efficiency? What is an eco-efficient tool? Provide a critical analysis of the view that conventional life-cycle assessment is not an eco-efficient tool of environmental management.

5. Explain each of the relationships outlined in the quadrants in Figure 10.1 (page 239). Detail the actions that would lead to a favourable change in direction in each of the four relationships described in the figure. What actions would lead to unfavourable changes in each of the relationships?

6. List the problems with life-cycle assessment. Explain which level of management is appropriate for addressing each of these problems.

7. What are the advantages and disadvantages of certified environmental product declarations? Assuming that you are the environmental manager of Global Autos, with companies operating in Sweden, Germany, the USA and Australia, would you provide environmental declarations in Sweden? Would you provide such declarations in the other countries? Give reasons for your answer.

8. Describe the environmental impact-added life-cycle chain. Select one particular industry and list the environmental interventions for each function in the chain. Rank the functions in terms of their expected total environmental impact added. How might a manager use this information to improve eco-efficiency? Consider the relationship between costs and quality of information in your answer.

9. Background inventory data represent average environmental interventions related to a particular material used in a particular industry. Who supplies such information? Why has background inventory data been the subject of considerable criticism? Is there an alternative to background inventory data that overcomes the criticisms made?

10. For a small eco-tourism company keen to use life-cycle assessment for competitive reasons, is a streamlined life-cycle assessment, life-cycle review, matrix approach or comprehensive approach the best tool to adopt? Consider the advantages and disadvantages of each tool before making your choice.

11. Scientific uncertainty about emissions data can be large. The precautionary principle suggests that decision-makers err on the side of caution when there is

scientific uncertainty. Examine the data in Table 10.3 (page 251). If only these two sets of data were available, which set would the precautionary principle suggest an environmental manager should use in decision-making?

12. What is the 'free-rider' problem? Why does it discourage innovation in environmental protection and the adoption of high environmental standards? Can anything be done to overcome the free-rider problem?

13. Is there a link between product-specific and site-specific life-cycle assessment? Which of these practical ways of drawing boundaries to the life-cycle assessment system will best help companies to consider ecological catchments and biodiversity in their eco-efficiency thinking?

Chapter 11

INTERNAL ECOLOGICAL ACCOUNTING

The expressions 'ecological accounting' and 'ecological statements' used here correspond to the terms used in financial accounting and subsume a variety of expressions such as 'green accounting', 'environmental accounting' and 'green or environmental reporting'. As in traditional accounting, the main tasks of ecological accounting consist of the classification, collection, recording, allocation, analysis and communication of data. There are, however, some major differences: environmental interventions are measured in physical units not in financial units and have to be assessed in physical terms as they usually have no market price. Most assessment methods convert physical units (e.g. kilograms of carbon dioxide [CO_2] emissions) into artificial units (e.g. ozone-depleting potential [ODP]) in order to express the environmental impact added by an activity (e.g. emissions of CO_2).

This chapter examines internal ecological accounting. This system of accounting is designed to provide information for decisions made by internal stakeholders, primarily managers. After a review of the historical development and basic procedures of ecological accounting (Section 11.1) the following aspects of internal ecological accounting are considered:

☐ Site-oriented accounting and associated procedures of ecological accounting, including definition of accounts, recording and aggregation of environmental interventions (Sections 11.2 and 11.3), assessment of environmental interventions (impact assessment) (Section 11.4) and allocation of environmental impact added (Section 11.5)

☐ Ecological indicators (Section 11.6)

☐ Ecological investment appraisal (Section 11.7)

☐ Net present environmental impact added (NPEIA) (Section 11.8)

The chapter concludes with a discussion of links between internal and external ecological accounting (Section 11.9).

In principle, the internal ecological accounting approach corresponds to the concept of conventional management accounting examined earlier (Chapter 5). Internal ecological accounting serves as:

☐ An analytical tool designed to detect ecological strengths and weaknesses

☐ A decision-support technique concerned with highlighting relative environmental quality

☐ A measurement tool that is an integral part of other environmental measures such as eco-efficiency

☐ A tool for direct and indirect control of environmental consequences

☐ An accountability tool providing a neutral and transparent base for internal and, indirectly, external communication

☐ A tool with a close and complementary fit to the set of tools being developed to help promote ecologically sustainable development

In most cases, internal ecological accounting is voluntary and not specifically undertaken to satisfy the demands of external stakeholders. Ideally, the internal ecological accounting system should—like the conventional management accounting system—lay the foundation for external and all other ecological accounting systems. It provides, therefore, the starting point for discussion of ecological accounting systems, including those designed for external purposes. This is the reason why the first academic approaches to ecological accounting focused on internal measures. Viewed from a historical and empirical angle, however, corporate internal ecological accounting started to develop and to be applied after powerful external stakeholders (e.g. environmental protection agencies and non-governmental organisations [NGOs]) were able to force or cajole companies into informing them about company emissions. With increasing environmental costs, new regulations and rising demand from stakeholders requiring information about a growing number of environmental interventions the need for an efficient internal environmental information system emerged.

In the past few years, many companies have come to recognise that the structure of conventional financial accounting systems might provide a useful starting point for the efficient organisation of environmental information systems (see e.g. GRI 1999; Schaltegger and Sturm 1998; WBCSD 1997). However, because the range of information needs has been so broad, many different approaches to internal ecological accounting have been developed. Therefore, this chapter focuses only on the most important perspectives and approaches adopted for the contemporary practice of internal ecological accounting.

Comprehensive internal ecological accounting provides useful information for all managers, regardless of their responsibilities and hierarchical level. Typically, different managers have different perspectives and place emphasis on differing aspects of information (see Fig. 6.1, page 92). Also, the degree of detail required by managers at different levels varies, with top management requiring more aggregate information than operations management. For example, a product manager has different information needs from those of a site or divisional manager. This is why an internal ecological accounting system needs to be able to distinguish between:

☐ Site-oriented or spatially oriented accounting

☐ Product-oriented accounting

☐ Business-, company- or industry-oriented accounting

Production managers have to take account of the contribution made by their own production activities. They will, for instance, want to know their share of the environmental interventions released by jointly used clean-up facilities. Sewage plants and incinerators usually treat the waste of several production processes and products. Therefore, emissions released by these facilities have to be allocated to the respective production processes and products. Production managers have to ask sewage plant managers to provide information on how much their production activities have contributed to the emissions of the sewage plant. They also have to obtain information, which may be critical for waste management, from the managers of jointly used incinerators (Laughlin and Varangu 1991).

Site managers want to be informed about the impacts of their plants whereas divisional managers need to know about the environmental interventions of all sites and products of the division for which they are responsible. Historically, ecological accounting began at either the plant or the company level. The first approach—called 'ecological book-keeping'—was put forward by Müller-Wenk in 1978. Site-specific ecological accounting sometimes also takes into account the ecological impact on a factory's natural surroundings, because the site manager may later be held accountable for restoration when ecological damage occurs.

Product managers are interested in product-specific information. Therefore, they need to know the share of environmental interventions caused by products at every step in production. As discussed in Section 10.3, if extended beyond production this perspective is usually described by the term 'life-cycle assessment' (LCA).

Divisional managers request information at the level of an organisation's strategic business units. Demand is for environmental information that is both strategic and aggregated, rather than operational and disaggregated and, depending on the analytical focus, also has a site or product orientation.

Neither top management nor divisional management is particularly concerned with detail. Instead, they need to acquire an overall picture by using consolidated information about the whole company or division, including all its sites and products. Although top management focuses on aggregate information, in some cases (e.g. for media statements or meetings with pressure groups) top and divisional managers require detailed information to be provided about operations.

For the purpose of analysis, managers will require the scope of accounting information to be adjusted to their specific goals and level. The process of specifying boundaries for the ecological accounting system will be strongly influenced by demands of key internal and external stakeholders as well as the expected cost–benefit ratio associated with collection and analysis of additional data. From an environmental perspective, for any project evaluation all management levels should consider the use of ecological investment appraisal. A specific method of appraisal—ecological investment appraisal—is outlined in Section 11.7.

No matter what the perspective or focus chosen, some activities are common to all internal ecological accounting systems:

☐ **Recording, tracking, tracing and allocation of environmental interventions.** The purpose of recording is to derive an inventory registering all environmental interventions in physical terms (e.g. kilograms or joules, or, more generally, in physical units). These environmental impacts are then tracked (directly by tracing, or indirectly through allocation) to the various stages of production, sites and products (environmental impact added [EIA] objects) that caused them in the first place.

☐ *Assessment.* An assessment is made of the relative severity of environmental interventions and calculation of environmental impact added (e.g. determination of whether interventions critical).

Impact assessment is a technical, quantitative and/or qualitative process for classifying, characterising and assessing the ecological effects of resources required and pollutants released. The following section examines these common internal ecological accounting activities in a site-specific context.

11.1 Basic procedures and their historical development

Initial approaches to 'ecological book-keeping' (Müller-Wenk 1978; Ullmann 1976) and 'corporate ecological accounting' (Schaltegger 1996a; Schaltegger and Sturm 1992a) describe information tools that take up the issue of production-site and company-level environmental interventions from engineering and accounting angles (Dierkes and Preston 1977). The main objective of these approaches, as well as of a modern management tool termed 'eco-control', is to support site managers in the continuous, systematic registration, allocation and assessment of non-financially measured ecological impacts emanating from production sites, plants and companies.

Today, several important environmental regulations encourage site-specific ecological accounting. These include requirements for the US Toxic Release Inventory (TRI) and the European Eco-management and Audit Scheme (EMAS). The influence of both systems on external accounting and reporting is discussed in Chapter 12 (on external ecological accounting) as they establish accounting links between companies and their external stakeholders.

Historically, ecological accounting began at plant and company level. In the English-speaking West, site-specific ecological accounting for new projects is often referred to as 'environmental impact assessment'. 'Environmental impact assessment' is also the general term for the assessment of environmental interventions, irrespective of whether the recorded interventions are related to a site, project, product, nation or other system. For a short introduction to environmental impact added as a preventative management tool, see Welford and Gouldson 1993 or Glasson *et al.* 1994.

'Environmental impact assessment' is a confusing term because, for example, in life-cycle assessment this denotes a general procedure for assessing environmental interventions. Interpreted in the regulatory sense, it usually describes a set of regulated procedures for computing environmental impacts caused by on-site activities. Site-specific ecological accounting considers these impacts on the natural surroundings of a factory. Here, environmental impact assessment 'is essentially a process that seeks to identify and predict the impacts of a new development [e.g. a new production site] on the environment, to mitigate them where possible and to monitor the actual impacts' (Fuller, cited in Gray 1993: 80). The framework of environmental impact assessment 'is specifically developed to minimise the potential environmental impact of new developments at the earliest possible stage—the design and development stage' (Welford and Gouldson 1993: 31). In this conventional application, environmental impact assessment can be defined as the formal and systematic collection and analysis of information relating to possible environmental effects of a new or significantly altered project. Even where not required by law, it is in any case good business practice to undertake an environmental impact assessment.

Site-specific ecological accounting has received increased attention in Europe because of the EU Directive on Environmental Assessment (85/337). As will be shown in Section 11.4, the term 'impact assessment' is also used as a basis for calculating the weights (relative importance) of environmental interventions.

The basic steps in ecological accounting are shown in Table 11.1. First, the ecological accounting function has to be included in a company's environmental policy. Second, the accounting framework has to be defined and relevant data compiled (Section 11.2).

To obtain an EIA statement, an inventory of environmental interventions has to be collected, recorded, aggregated and assessed according to their relative impacts. The impact assessment procedure has three steps: classification, characterisation and valuation (Section 11.4). In the next step, accountability for environmental impact added has to be identified in order to determine which production steps and products are 'responsible' for any environmental impacts caused (Section 11.5).

To secure effective and efficient continual improvement, it is necessary for ecological accounting to be integrated with conventional accounting and environmental management systems (Part 4). Given such an integrated system, the resulting economic–ecological information can be analysed to help determine the company's ecological strengths and weaknesses. The environmental management system provides feedback support as a basis for management control and implementation of required improvements.

11.2 Definition of accounts and recording

11.2.1 Subject matter and accounts

Ecological accounting favours quantified data as a basis for measuring the extent of environmental interventions (related to use of resources, material and energy emissions, or, as it is called in this book, environmental impact added) and ecological assets on hand at any particular point (e.g. land, forests and water reserves). In addition, critical qualitative information must also be taken into account.

STEP	OUTCOME
Stage 1: **Goal definition**	
1. Define goals	Goals are defined.
Stage 2: **Creation of accounting framework**	
2. Define accounts	Accounts are defined.
Stage 3: **Creation of an inventory**	
3. Record data	Data sheets are produced.
4. Aggregate data	An aggregated inventory is created.
Stage 4: **Assessment of impacts**	
5. Classify information	Impact categories are produced.
6. Characterise information	Indicators and eco-profile are produced.
7. Value information	Index and eco-balance are produced.
Stage 5: **Allocation of responsibility**	
8. Allocate accountability	Detailed site- and object-related information is produced.
Stage 6: **Performance improvement**	
9. Integrate information	An environmental management system is created.
10. Interpret results	Ecologically weak points are identified and the potential to reduce them is created.
11. Implement and control	The situation is improved.

Table 11.1 **Basic steps in ecological accounting and their outcomes**

The main subject matter of environmental information management can broadly be divided into management of information relating to:

☐ Assets (stocks) at a specific point of time

☐ Changes in assets (flows) in each specified period

This distinction provides the basis, in principle, for construction of an ecological asset ('eco-asset') sheet that lists all eco-assets at a specific point in time and of an EIA statement listing all flows (inputs and outputs) during a specific period of time.

11.2.2 The eco-asset sheet

Adaptation of a financial balance-sheet concept to ecological accounting has not been a simple process of development. Championed by the United Nations since 1993, various vague ideas and analogies have been put forward. One such analogy to financial capital is the view that 'environmental quality [is] a stock, a kind of capital that is "depreciated" by the addition of pollutants and "invested" in by abatement activities' (Solow 1992: 13).

Environmental quality is taken to represent the substance of an eco-asset in the same way that economic services represent the substance of a financial asset in conventional financial accounting.

In a figurative sense, this comparison is quite convincing. However, this balance-sheet analogy raises the question of whether there are environmental liabilities that correspond to environmental capital or eco-assets. Furthermore, it is by no means clear when environmental assets might become environmental liabilities, and vice versa. (For example, when is a stream so polluted that it is no longer an environmental asset but an environmental liability?)

From the point of view of accounting, a first attempt to consider the environment as a natural capital stock was made by subdividing the total 'capital' available into three categories (Gray 1993: 290f.):

☐ Critical natural capital requirements of the biosphere: elements essential for life

☐ Other (sustainable, substitutable or renewable) natural capital: elements of the biosphere that are renewable or for which reasonable substitutes can be found

☐ Artificial capital: elements created from the biosphere that are human-made (e.g. machines, buildings and roads)

Artificial capital has been expanded at the expense of the first two categories of natural capital. It is argued that to achieve sustainable development critical natural capital must not be diminished. Others have since extended this categorisation. For example, Jones (1996) categorised natural capital when exploring the issue of accounting for biodiversity. He devised six categories of criticality for natural inventories of biodiversity, where level 1 is seen as being the most important because an inventory at this 'full and complete' level is crucial if more detailed inventories (lower levels) are to be feasible:

Level 1: Categorisation by habitat type and natural capital status

Level 2: Inventory of listed and protected flora and fauna (i.e. critical natural capital) by species and by total population on all habitats

Level 3: Inventory of critical habitats of flora and fauna by species

Level 4: Inventory of critical habitats of flora and fauna by total population

Level 5: General inventory of flora and fauna by species

Level 6: General inventory of flora and fauna by population

Once a natural inventory is established, an organisation's non-critical habitats would be valued at either market value or at an amenity value, complemented by ecological grading to overcome any mismatch between economic and ecological valuations. Ecological grading would be conducted on a five-point scale where grade 1 represents a habitat with great ecological worth, and grade 5 a habitat with little ecological worth. The habitat categorisation, market valuations and ecological grading scheme would all complement and reinforce each other.

This approach has not been generally accepted by the business community, perhaps because the distinction between the three categories of capital is difficult and arbitrary. Also, the primary concern of business remains with the financial bottom line and businesses are aware that techniques for putting financial values on eco-assets are fraught with difficulty (see Burritt and Cummings 1999).

It does not seem possible or sensible to seek to apply balance-sheet concepts to ecological accounting in a consistent way. Attempts to compare ecological assets and ecological liabilities do not seem to provide any helpful information as all natural assets are ultimately only 'borrowed' from nature, although some people maintain that we keep such assets in trust (e.g. Barton 1999; Rubenstein 1991). Nevertheless, depending on the industry, companies own or influence considerable quantities of natural assets (e.g. mining companies, forest management companies, agri-business, chemical companies, government agencies and conservation companies). Therefore, ecological assets should be part of any ecological accounting if they are affected by company activities. For this purpose, a list of all eco-assets can be created showing eco-assets at a particular point in time—the end of an accounting period. However, there are distinct differences between such an eco-asset sheet and a balance sheet:

☐ An eco-asset sheet facilitates comparisons between accounting periods (longitudinal comparisons) but does not counterbalance assets with ecological liabilities and ecological equity.

☐ An eco-asset sheet does not reflect a balance between items.

☐ All eco-assets are from a single 'lender', namely nature.

☐ No concepts exist to aggregate eco-assets into a single unit of measurement and so categorisation of natural assets is of vital importance for management purposes.

Several eco-asset sheets, although tagged with various names, have been drawn up for nations at a macro-economic level. Some member countries of the Organisation for Economic Co-operation and Development (OECD) have tried to account for their physical resource endowments in this way (OECD 1994b). Norway has classified its total resources into material and environmental resources. Accounts have been developed for fish and forest reserves as well as for various minerals and energy resources (Alfsen *et al.* 1987; see also ABS 1997; OECD 1994b: 13). Recent reviews of these accounts indicate, however, that the successfulness of adjusted accounts has been uneven. France is the country with the most comprehensive system of accounting for resource endowments to date, and the objective is no less than to account for all interactions between the economy and the environment (INSEE 1986a, 1986b). So far, France's system has only partly been implemented. The Netherlands has adopted a system to determine where a loss of function takes place in relation to water, air and land. Until recently, environmental assessment has focused on problems related to natural resource destruction or depletion, and increasingly sophisticated scientific methods and technologies are used for monitoring and assessment (UNEP 1991: 35).

From a corporate point of view, eco-assets (e.g. forests or land) can be registered and described on an eco-asset sheet (Table 11.2). Natural assets are rarely accounted for at company level because only a few industries own or control substantial amounts of unsealed land or other natural resources. However, some companies have recorded fauna and flora situated on their sites and have actively started to create and manage biotopes on roofs and in open places (for examples of the eco-asset sheets of ten Swiss companies, see Buser and Schaltegger 1998; for comments on management of biodiversity for rehabilitation of mine sites, see Burritt 1997).

An eco-asset sheet is not an exact analogue for a financial balance sheet. It simply represents a 'photograph' of the natural assets of a company at a certain moment. All ecological assets that a company owns or controls on a given date are listed. An eco-asset sheet contains all ecological assets and also includes an inventory of various species inhabiting, for example, land and forests. Over-harvesting reduces natural capital values, whereas good maintenance and sustainable harvesting keeps or even improves eco-assets. Activities such as those leading to the extinction of species, land clearing and soil erosion represent a devaluation of ecological assets (reduction in the number of species and size of forests).

Table 11.2 provides a sample company eco-asset sheet. The list shows ecological values measured in a variety of physical units (kg, m², number of species, etc.). At present there is no one-dimensional method of comparing and aggregating ecological assets, but attempts are being made to standardise measurements of similar natural assets to facilitate comparisons and aggregation of data.

An eco-asset sheet is basically an inventory. Nonetheless, its construction often provides an eye-opener for management to help them recognise actual and potential ecological assets, potential corporate impacts on these assets and the need for careful management and preservation. The financial importance of an eco-asset sheet increases with the

Table 11.2 **Possible content of an eco-asset sheet**

Soil, ground
- ▶ m² sealed
- ▶ Quantity of soil
- ▶ Quality of soil (pH value, concentration of heavy metals, etc.)
- ▶ Resources (e.g. ores)
- ▶ Wetness/dryness
- ▶ . . .

Air quality
- ▶ Ambient air quality
- ▶ . . .

Fauna, flora, habitats
- ▶ Number of species
- ▶ Kind of species
- ▶ Kind of habitats
- ▶ Separation of habitats by roads, etc.
- ▶ . . .

Surface water
- ▶ m³ of water flow
- ▶ m of drainage
- ▶ Water quality (oxygen, pH value, etc.)
- ▶ Speed of water flow
- ▶ Height of water level
- ▶ . . .

Underground water
- ▶ Water level
- ▶ Quality (oxygen, toxins, etc.)
- ▶ . . .

Landscape
- ▶ Kind of vegetation
- ▶ Kind and size of constructions (e.g. chimney, electric power lines)
- ▶ . . .

probability, amount and current set of financial contingencies and liabilities identified (see also e.g. Bailey 1991; Haasis 1992; McMurray 1992: 17; Ross 1985; Surma and Vondra 1992) as well as with the increasing scarcity of natural resources and the marketability of eco-assets. Recently, some companies (e.g. Dow Chemicals) have started to create and express a financial value for ecological assets by, for example, establishing harvesting rights for rainforests. A parallel tendency exists at the macro level for analysis to move beyond the physical assessment of ecological assets toward financial representation of values of natural assets for land, forestry, fish and subsoil resources (ABS 1997).

An eco-asset sheet can be related to the land owned or controlled by a company. This is a useful tool for mining and waste-management companies or for forestry industries concerned about rehabilitation when non-renewable resources have been removed and about tracking biodiversity while managing renewable resources. In Norway, eco-asset sheets have been established for state-owned companies dealing with forest products as well as for the ministries of forestry and fishery (see Alfsen *et al.* 1987). Some ministries in Costa Rica have also established eco-asset sheets (see Repetto 1992).

Nevertheless, most companies are probably interested in a broader perspective, looking at the ecological assets they actually affect. In some cases, in order to move from an ecological asset balance on one eco-asset sheet to the balance on the following sheet a year later, calculation of the ratios between currently known, economically accessible eco-assets and the additional resources supplied to and used up annually by the company can be made. Observations over time show changes in the relative scarcity of the listed eco-assets. The use of natural resources represents a flow of materials and energy and is therefore recorded in an EIA statement. On a global scale, a recorded accumulated use of natural resources represents a decrease in ecological assets. For many companies, this aggregate level of information may not be a high priority, because it may appear that plenty of the resource (e.g. a particular species of fish) is available today. However, this might change in the future as individual companies compete for an ever-diminishing supply of natural capital.

Despite the tendency for companies to consider only their own use of and impact on supplies of natural resources, the eco-asset sheet is a very valuable tool for management wishing to obtain an overview of the 'stock of environmental values' on which it relies. Furthermore, it is a starting point for helping management recognise actual and potential financial assets and liabilities related to their stock of eco-assets. In the past, the importance of financial liabilities associated with eco-assets has often been severely underestimated (McMurray 1992: 17). Eco-asset sheets are therefore useful attention-directing tools for management.

Eco-asset sheets stocks will not be discussed further here because the management and measurement of pollution flows (waste-streams) is of greater practical relevance to a larger number of companies in most industries. However, it should be remembered that there is a need for eco-asset stocks and flows to be articulated if a comprehensive understanding of company impacts is to be obtained. In practice, at present most companies and their stakeholders concentrate on environmental flows. One reason for this focus is that company-specific environmental flows are the main cause of major environmental problems whereas many companies do not own or monopolise substantial amounts of the world's eco-assets. Also, environmental flows are easier to measure than are eco-asset stocks. The next section addresses the recording and measurement of these environmental flows.

11.2.3 The environmental impact added statement

The basic idea of the EIA statement corresponds to an income statement in traditional accounting. Flows of material and energy inputs and outputs into the natural environment are recorded and assessed for a specified accounting period. As illustrated in the following sections, ecological accounting deals mainly with flows of environmental interventions.

To account for environmental interventions one can record, track, trace and, if necessary, allocate these interventions to objects of concern to managers (e.g. products, production lines and divisions). The use of accounts to record and present financial flows is a widely accepted practice. In view of the need for practical ways to handle data, and because efficient procedures for recording material and energy flows have been established in conventional accounting, it is sensible and cost-efficient to use a similar procedure for ecological accounting. The main difference is that data on environmental interventions are recorded in physical (e.g. kg, m^3, l) rather than monetary terms. However, an input–output account takes only direct environmental interventions into account. These have to be assessed before their relative environmental impact can be appreciated. Indirect, antagonistic and synergetic impacts can be only partially recognised in the assessment and are not considered in an input–output account.

In the USA the main driving force for compiling corporate input–output accounts of environmental interventions is the TRI. Similar regulations (though mostly less systematic and comprehensive) exist in other countries (e.g. in Germany, the Netherlands and north-western Switzerland) or are being introduced (e.g. Australia).

First, detailed material and energy flow diagrams have to be prepared for all manufacturing processes. These can be obtained in a comprehensive manner only through detailed observation of actual production and by recording all material and energy flows. Such a record permits management to establish a general chart of accounts. Table 11.3 shows an example of a standardised input–output account.

On the left-hand side, all material and energy inputs into production (natural resources, semi-manufactured goods and raw materials) are listed with an identification number. On the right-hand side, all desirable and undesirable material and energy production outputs (desired output, emissions, waste) are presented along with their identification number. Identification numbers allow all inputs and outputs to be classified, grouped as necessary and tracked. For example, 107 and 201 relate to recyclates and downcyclates. Recyclates are recycled products. Downcyclates are products that have been recycled but have a lower material and economic value (the recycling is not perfect but quality decreases with the process: e.g. because of dirt in the material, ink in the paper or because the material is unstable).

The material inputs are divided into mineral resources, biomass, water, energy carriers and other materials. Energy carriers (e.g. oil) are registered as material resources. Energy, as such, is linked to some kind of material. To consider the energy content of a given

Group	Description	Group	Description
10	Material inputs	20	Material outputs
100	Mineral resources	200	Products
101	Biomass		*(Environmental impact added*
102	Water		*object)*
103	Fossil energy carriers	201	Recyclates and downcyclates
1030	Crude oil	203	Emissions
1031	Coal	2030	Landfill
1032	Gas	2031	Water emissions
104	Regenerative energy carriers	20310	Total organic compounds
105	Materials	20311	Sulphur
106	Recyclates and downcyclates	20312	Water
		20313	. . .
		2032	Air emissions
		20320	Carbon dioxide
		20321	Nitrogen oxides
		20322	Volatile organic compounds

Table 11.3 **Example of an input–output account**

material flow and the material flow as well would be a double-counting of basically the same thing from two different viewpoints. That is why electric power, electromagnetic (light, heat and ultraviolet radiation) and ionising radiation, as well as mechanical energy and noise, belong to the energy category of inputs and outputs that needs to be accounted for separately.

The record of energy sources should be separated from the registration of material flows to avoid double-counting and possible confusion. According to the law of the conservation of energy, the total of both mass and energy on the input and output side of the account has to be equal. The left-hand side and the right-hand side of an ecological account must balance, as the sum of mass and energy cannot be changed. If a large number of activities is to be listed, special sub-accounts can be opened in this 'aggregate' account (e.g. an account for the use of petroleum, or an account for CO_2 emissions). Depending on the purpose of the analysis, management will classify its ecological accounts by, for example, single production steps, buildings or areas.

Transfer of effluents and energies from one account to a subsequent account or to an aggregate account can be undertaken in the same way as in basic book-keeping except that transactions are entered as physical units of measurement (e.g. kilograms, joules). By using this procedure, one can aggregate the incoming and outgoing mass and energy flows and define them according to their specific source. The result equates with an income statement in conventional financial accounting. Aggregate material and energy flows can be registered at the end of an accounting period. For many activities, a journal can be used for continuous registration.

Table 11.4 shows an example of such a journal for registering resource and energy use as inputs into production processes and as environmental interventions (outputs). As a minimum, the following information should be recorded:

Date	Text	Preceding step	Following step	Input	Output	Quantity (kg)	Quality of data	Place (EIA centre)
1 Jan 00	Storage	Supplier X		Oil		100	Measured	Storehouse A
3 Jan 00	Burning	Natural env.		O_2		200	Measured	Process B
3 Jan 00	Burning		Natural env.		CO_2	200	Calculated	Process B
3 Jan 00	Burning		Natural env.		SO_2	95	Calculated	Process B
3 Jan 00	Burning		Natural env.		CO_2	5	Calculated	Process B
3 Jan 00	Discharge		Natural env.		CO_2	200	Calculated	Scrubber
3 Jan 00	Discharge		Natural env.		CO_2	5	Calculated	Scrubber
3 Jan 00	Discharge		Natural env.		SO_2	95	Calculated	Scrubber
⋮	⋮		⋮		⋮	⋮	⋮	⋮

EIA = environmental impact details added   env. = environment

Table 11.4 **Sample journal to register the use of resources and environmental interventions**

☐ The date

☐ A short description of the transaction

☐ A note stating where the flow came from and where it went to

☐ The input or output (ideally with its identification number from the chart of ecological flow accounts)

☐ The quantity

☐ The quality of the data used

☐ The place

Information about data quality is extremely important for interpretation of the results and any search for better alternatives (Wynn and Lee 1993). Possible categories of data quality are:

☐ Measured data

☐ Calculated data

☐ Estimated data

☐ Secondary data from suppliers

☐ Secondary data gleaned from literature (e.g. industry-average statistics)

The use of measured data is the ideal and usually is the best reflection of the specific situation. Nevertheless, it is helpful to note the analytical techniques used to obtain an idea of data reliability and how well one set of data can be compared with other data. Measured data also varies, even if the same technique of analysis is used. Differences in measured data can occur, for example, if a different measurement time-period is chosen, or if an annual rather than a monthly measure of average results is presented for comparison.

In economic terms, because of high marginal cost it makes no sense to aim for a full inventory of all mass and energy flows; in any case, this goal can rarely be achieved because of the presence of scientific uncertainty. Usually, data collection protocols (journals) will be developed over several years, digging deeper into flows each year and stopping only when the benefit from more detailed information matches the cost of its compilation.

In order to simplify the recording procedure, a list of effluents and environmental interventions accounted for can be established based on their perceived priority. Such a list can also provide guidance for managers looking for the dividing line between material and immaterial flows as, even in a small or medium-sized manufacturing company, a few hundred substances and energy flows might conceivably need to be examined. This type of data compilation undoubtedly requires a computerised management information system, but even with computerisation it is helpful to set priorities with regard to waste-streams. To obtain the necessary quality and detail of data is an arduous task that has to be very carefully executed.

So-called 'loss-track accounting' is a special case of ecological accounting for material and energy flows (Pojasek 1997, 1998; Pojasek and Cali 1991a, 1991b). The method of loss tracking computes losses of material or energy that are not part of the desired output. Manufacturing losses are considered to cause pollution (or waste) and lower the economic efficiency of production processes and products. The loss-tracking system is a computer-based tool that enables management to identify the location and circumstances of each process loss. It allows specific loss-reduction performance to be monitored through close observation of the actual manufacturing process. Typically, all measuring units (e.g. volume, container units, weight) are converted into pounds (or kilograms) of dry weight (Pojasek and Cali 1991a: 119f.).

11.3 Aggregation

After all environmental interventions have been recorded at the site where they actually occur, aggregation for control and accountability purposes can take place. Similar kinds of environmental intervention, recorded in terms of physical units, are aggregated in a departmental EIA account (Table 11.5). Interventions are aggregated for each site or cost centre (e.g. a sewage plant) where they occur.

The production site, time-period and place are identified in the account heading. Data from the journal (Table 11.4) are aggregated in the corresponding categories of inputs and outputs. To avoid confusion, each input and output is marked with an identification number. The second and third columns show the quality of data and the EIA responsibility centre before (preceding step for inputs) or after (following step for outputs) the 'East Valley' site. The column to the right shows quantities used (inputs) and quantities either released or transferred to another production or treatment step (outputs). This accounting system has been useful in practice because all relevant information is summarised and available.

Ident. no.	Quality of data		Tons per period
1	**Inputs**	**Preceding step**	
101	Propylene	Measured	Production site A	3,111.04
102	Sulphur	Calculated	Production site A	960.00
103	Copper	Calculated	Production site A	69.60
104	Sodium bicarbonate	Measured	Supplier Bart	2,000.00
105	Compressed CO_2	Measured	Supplier Neal	5.60
106	Ethane	Measured	Supplier Sela	20.00
107	Cooling water	Estimated	Pumping station	2,000,000.00
108	Water	Measured	Pumping station	96,000.00
10	**Total input**			**2,102,166.20**
2	**Outputs**	**Following step**	
201	Product A	Measured	Drying	869.09
210	**By-products**		
211	Waste-water, consisting of:		
212	Water	Estimated	Waste-water plant	89,760.00
213	TOC	Calculated	Waste-water plant	3,014.40
214	AOX	Calculated	Waste-water plant	0.56
215	Copper	Calculated	Waste-water plant	0.08
	Total by-products			**92,779.04**
220	**Recycled and downcycled by-products**		
221	Cooling water	Measured	Recycling	200,000.00
230	**Emissions**		
231	Air pollution from scrubber:		
2311	CO	Measured	Environment	2,002.40
2312	N_2O	Measured	Environment	101.60
2313	SO_2	Measured	Environment	78.40
2314	Particulates	Measured	Environment	7.20
2315	Copper	Measured	Environment	0.08
	Total emissions			**2,199.12**
232	**Disposal**			0.00
20	**Total output**			**2,598,013.40**
30	**Difference between input and output**			**495,847.20**

Production site   East Valley
Time-period   One month, from 1 January to 1 February 2000
Production quantity of period   869.09 tons

Note: Polluted air is cleaned in a multi-purpose scrubber and measured twice a day.

Ident. no. = identification number CO_2 = carbon dioxide   TOCs = total organic compounds
N_2O = nitrous oxide SO_2 = sulphur dioxide

Table 11.5 **Example of a departmental environmental impact added account of a production site**

Sometimes, a complete inventory provides enough information to see what the main environmental problems are and where they originate. In such a case, priorities for environmental protection and pollution prevention can be defined by using the inventory. However, in most cases the inventory provides an enormous amount of unassessed, detailed data that cannot be interpreted accurately by management. If this is the case, an impact assessment of the inventory data is clearly necessary.

11.4 Impact assessment

11.4.1 Goal and characteristics of impact assessment

If, as is often the case, the inventory table is burdened with an excessive amount of detail, and, if comparison of environmental interventions is ambiguous, decision-makers need a practical approach to assess the relative harm (i.e. impact) of different environmental interventions.

Impact assessment is a technical, quantitative and/or qualitative process for classifying, characterising and assessing the effects of resources required for production and any associated environmental loading. Ideally, such an assessment should address ecological impacts, human health impacts and resource depletion, as well as other effects such as habitat modification and noise pollution.

Ecological assessment of environmental interventions and, therefore, the reduction of numerous available physical measures to just a few units or even one unit of measurement, should occur only after aggregation has been carried out for each identified environmental interventions site. The advantage of this approach is that different assessment methods can be based on the same inventory data and then compared with each other. For this reason, ecological accounting is not restricted by today's level of knowledge about environmental harm caused by environmental interventions; it also allows new weights to be applied at a later time.

It would be desirable for an impact assessment to take into account direct, indirect, parallel and serial impacts as well as spatial, time, social, political and economic aspects. So far, however, the complexity of the material allows only some of these criteria to be included.

Today, many disciplines (e.g. natural sciences, engineering and economics), universities, research institutes, environmental consultants, environmental protection agencies (the USA, Canadian, Danish, Dutch, German and Swiss environmental protection agencies are among those most active in the area of ecological accounting) and working groups with activities that are international in scope (e.g. the Society of Environmental Toxicology and Chemistry [SETAC]) handle measures and criteria for environmental impact assessment and promote their own concepts. Over the past decade, impact assessment has emerged as a highly interdisciplinary field of research. In the recent past, new interest groups, especially professional accounting bodies, standardisation organisations (e.g. the International Organization for Standardization [ISO] and Deutsches Institut für Normung [DIN]) and regulatory bodies (e.g. the European Union Commission) have indirectly begun to influence this arena in a number of ways.

Some professional accounting associations worth mentioning here are:

☐ The American Institute of Certified Public Accountants (AICPA)

☐ The Association of Chartered Certified Accountants (ACCA, UK)

☐ The European Accounting Association (EAA)

☐ The Canadian Institute of Chartered Accountants (CICA)

☐ CPA Australia (CPAA)

☐ The Féderation des Experts Comptables Européens (FEE)

So far, there is no consensus among researchers or users, although much research has been completed. Moreover, the proponents of different assessment approaches are competing with each other to find the best approach. Competition is not merely at the scientific level, because several groups are also strongly lobbying regulators, environmental protection agencies, national and international organisations and other opinion leaders. This is particularly obvious, for example, in a brochure issued by the Swiss environmental protection agency, Bundesamt für Umwelt, Wald und Landschaft (BUWAL), establishing the concept of eco-scarcity (BUWAL 1991), as well as in publications by SETAC Europe supporting the assessment method developed by the Center of Environmental Studies, University of Leiden (CML) (explained later in this section).

As a result of the lack of an acknowledged ecological accounting standard-setting committee, recommendations and guidelines exist today, but there are no standards. The political nature of decision-making has to be recognised as a constraint on standard-setting, especially where ecological issues are complex and where numerous competing stakeholders are engaged in the sociopolitical process. The lack of standards acts as a threat to the implementation and achievement of sustainable outcomes, to transparent accountability relationships and to attempts to meet the challenge of sustainability. The issue is therefore considered in more detail in the next section.

11.4.2 Approaches to impact assessment

Figure 11.1 surveys the main approaches to impact assessment. Many different approaches to impact assessment have been published and numerous variations are available in practice (for an overview, see Schaltegger and Sturm 1994). Differences between the approaches are caused mainly by the fact that different researchers (sciences) ask different questions. In the past, the wide variety of assessment methods was perceived as a problem and a single, objective approach to assessment was judged to be most desirable. However, environmental impacts are in fact viewed in different ways (through different lenses) by different social groups so that recorded data need to be interpreted with use of different assessment concepts. When comparing various impact assessment methods, it is important to realise that different methods provide answers to different questions. Corporate ecological accounting and LCA, as a rule, use non-

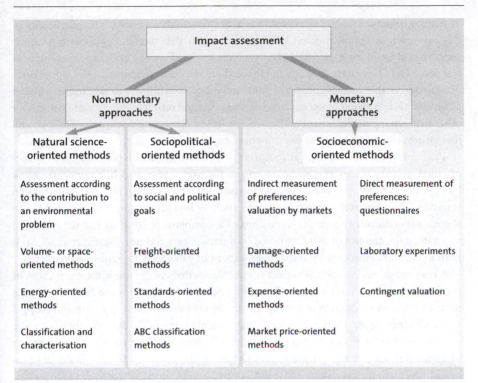

Figure 11.1 **Approaches to impact assessment**

monetary methods, whereas socioeconomic studies (e.g. on the external costs of traffic) commonly use monetary approaches.

11.4.2.1 Non-monetary approaches

A first group of assessment approaches covers non-monetary impact assessment concepts. These methods can be distinguished as being oriented towards natural science and sociopolitical concerns. The former can be subdivided into energy-oriented and volume-oriented methods that can be distinguished by their approaches to classification and characterisation.

Natural science-oriented approach

With the slogan 'megatons instead of nanograms' (Bierter 1994), scientists of the Wuppertal Institute in Germany proposed concentration on the measurement of volumes of material and natural resources which can be linked to the production of one unit of output (Schmidt-Bleek 1994). Emphasis should not be on measuring smaller and smaller quantities of toxins but rather on the larger material flows. They reason that every movement of material requires energy, has a negative environmental impact on the environment and that, above all, volumes of material flows should be reduced.

The Wuppertal approach is associated with such ideas as 'Factor 4' and 'Factor 10', which embody the notion that the amount of wealth that can be extracted from one unit of natural resources can be increased in practice fourfold or tenfold. The practicality of this approach is complemented by the observation that demand is moving towards services and away from activities that use high levels of energy and large quantities of resources (von Weizsäcker *et al.* 1997). Hence, there is a derived demand for new measures designed to enable management, investors and other stakeholders to determine whether a company is increasing or decreasing its energy, natural resource, hazardous chemical or other material inputs per unit of output, increasing or decreasing waste and emissions and increasing or decreasing its net use of natural capital.

The concept of an 'ecological footprint' (Wackernagel and Rees 1996) is a space-oriented approach. An ecological footprint measures how much natural space, or biologically productive space, is needed to sustain current consumption and production activities. The approach answers questions such as how much forest area is needed to absorb a specific amount of CO_2 emissions of a company, or what area of sea is needed to produce the amount of fish consumed by a person or a country (Sturm *et al.* 1999). It is an important consideration in the development of sinks for CO_2 emission reduction.

A majority of environmental impact studies shows that energy use is the main cause of most environmental interventions. Therefore, some scientists propose focusing on the measurement and reduction of energy use and energy losses (see e.g. Frank and Ruppel 1976; Grittner 1978; Odum 1996). Energy-oriented methods do not focus on the measurement of energy carriers (fuel, gas, electric power, etc.) but on the energy contents of material flows (see e.g. Grittner 1978; Odum 1996). The basis for this is the physical law of thermodynamics which has been applied to economic activities by Georgescu-Roegen (1971). The availability of energy is measured in terms of entropy. High entropy means that the availability of energy is low. The second law of thermodynamics says that 'In an *isolated system, spontaneous processes* occur in the direction of increasing entropy' (Atkins 1979; our emphasis). The target should, therefore, be to minimise the creation of entropy caused by economic activities. That is the target is to conserve energy embodied in resources in line with long-term thinking embodied in the principles of ecologically sustainable development and the practices suggested by the Wuppertal Institute (see e.g. Daly 1968; Georgescu-Roegen 1971; Rifkin 1985).

Odum (1996) has introduced the notion of 'emergy' (spelt with an 'm') as a resource-specific measure of energy use that represents energy of one kind (e.g. from coal, electricity or solar sources) previously required directly and indirectly to make a product or service. The emergy concept potentially has a wide application. There is a different kind of emergy for each kind of available energy. For example, solar emergy is measured in units of solar emjoules, coal emergy in units of coal emjoules and electrical emergy in units of electrical emjoules.

Overall, energy-oriented and volume-oriented assessment concepts have not been widely applied, perhaps because they do not recognise toxicity or parallel, indirect, serial, social, political and economic aspects. (Note, however, that this does not apply to Odum [1996], with his direct links to economics, information as an energy carrier and money measures.) It should be noted that energy-oriented methods require a great deal of scientific skill.

Classification and characterisation methods attempt to answer the question about what has been contributed to a specific environmental problem (e.g. the greenhouse effect, depletion of the ozone layer or acidification) by an activity, product or site. Classification and characterisation methods consider indirect impacts of the particular environmental problem but cannot take into account series of parallel direct and indirect impacts. The classification and characterisation concept of the CML in Leiden, the Netherlands, has attracted particular attention. A definition of an impact assessment with three main steps has been proposed (see e.g. Guinée and Heijungs 1993; Schaltegger and Kubat 1995; Udo de Haes 1995) and is summarised below.

Impact assessment is a quantitative and/or qualitative process to characterise and assess the effects of the environmental interventions identified in the inventory table. In principle, the impact assessment component consists of the following three steps: classification, characterisation and valuation.

☐ Classification is the first step within impact assessment, which identifies the impacts and which, as far as possible, attributes environmental interventions to a number of predefined impact categories (e.g. greenhouse effect). Environmental interventions contributing to more than one impact category are listed more than once.

☐ Characterisation is the second step in which a quantification (and eventually an analysis and aggregation) of the impacts within the given impact categories takes place. This step results in effect scores (environmental indicators or EIA indicators) of the EIA profile. An environmental indicator (also EIA indicator or effect score) is the aggregated contribution of environmental interventions to one impact category. The figure with the environmental indicators for all impact categories is called the environmental profile.

☐ Valuation is the third step, which weights the effect scores of the environmental profile against each other in a quantitative and/or qualitative way as a basis for drawing conclusions. The valuation step can result in an EIA index.

This structure of a general procedure for impact assessment is shown in Figure 11.2.

The result of classified inventory data is impact categories (e.g. the category 'greenhouse effect', or the category 'depletion of the ozone layer').

The characterisation of these grouped data leads to EIA indicators (also called effect scores when expressed as the aggregated contributions to one impact category) with a single number for each environmental problem being taken into account. For example, the contribution to the greenhouse effect is measured by the 'greenhouse warmth contribution' indicator; or depletion of the ozone layer is measured by the 'ozone depletion contribution' indicator. The 16 impact categories defined by CML, and associated characterisation factors, are listed in Heijungs *et al.* 1992.

Mathematically, these indicators are calculated by multiplying the physical quantity of environmental interventions released (e.g. CO_2, methane [CH_4]) that have been classified in the same impact category (e.g. greenhouse effect) with weighting factors (e.g. 1 for CO_2, 11 for CH_4) that assess the relative contribution to the particular environmental problem (e.g. the contribution to the greenhouse effect measured in CO_2 equivalents). As an example, Burritt (1995: 224) briefly discusses the mathematical calculation of one

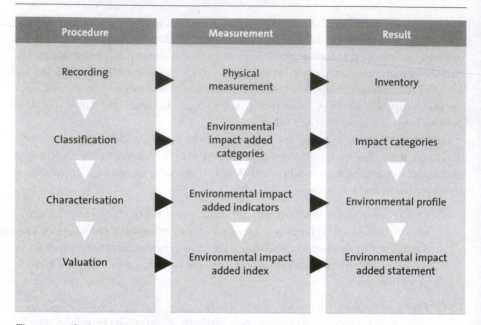

Procedure	Measurement	Result
Recording	Physical measurement	Inventory
Classification	Environmental impact added categories	Impact categories
Characterisation	Environmental impact added indicators	Environmental profile
Valuation	Environmental impact added index	Environmental impact added statement

Figure 11.2 **The impact assessment procedure**

environmental indicator, ozone depletion potential (ODP), for a set of ozone-depleting substances (ODSs, such as chlorofluorocarbons [CFCs] and hydrochlorofluorocarbons [HCFCs]) in order that they can be used to help in the control of ODS emissions. The figure that integrates several environmental indicators is called an environmental profile.

Sociopolitical-oriented approach
So far, no single approach to the (sociopolitical and economic) valuation of environmental profiles, for calculation of an EIA index, has prevailed. Previous valuation methods do not rely on classification and characterisation but refer only to an inventory of environmental interventions.

Sociopolitical-oriented impact assessment concepts represent the next group of assessment methods. These valuation methods attempt to weight environmental interventions according to politically determined targets. General environmental goals (such as maintaining atmospheric balance) are broken down into specific objectives (such as reducing gases that contribute to the greenhouse effect by $x\%$). These targets can, for example, be defined as environmental standards (e.g. ambient concentration values) by regulators and governments or as intervention loads (e.g. loads of emitted pollutants). Goals for carrying out an ABC analysis (not to be confused with activity-based costing), mainly for internal company purposes, can also be determined by management.

Standards-oriented and loads-oriented approaches were among the first impact assessment concepts ever developed (see e.g. BUS 1984). The logic behind these methods is that company management should orient themselves based on the priorities set by regulators or the government. The fundamental idea is to make explicit the relations between sociopolitical targets set for various environmental interventions (e.g. ambient standards or targets concerning total loads of pollutants). These targets represent the relative importance assigned to individual interventions.

Tables 11.6 and 11.7 provide examples of the concept of a standards-oriented approach to assessment. Standards are based on acceptable quality levels. Notice the importance of applying weights to ambient standards for emissions of specific pollutants (e.g. aluminium, mercury and iron) in order to balance their relative significance.

Standards issued as national environment protection measures (NEPM) by the National Environment Protection Council (NEPC) in Australia are illustrated in Table 11.6. These standards are mandatory. Standards form part of an integrated approach to pollution control at the federal level in Australia. NEPMs are not simply sets of ambient standards for different pollution media. They may consist of any combination of goals, standards, monitoring and reporting protocols and guidelines. NEPMs may relate to any one or more of the following:

☐ Ambient air quality

☐ Ambient marine, estuarine and fresh-water quality

☐ The protection of amenity in relation to noise (but only if differences in environmental requirements relating to noise would have an adverse effect on national markets for goods and services)

☐ General guidelines for the assessment of site contamination

☐ Environmental impacts associated with hazardous wastes

☐ The re-use and recycling of used materials

☐ Motor vehicle noise and emissions

In an NEPM a goal means the desired outcome, for example:

☐ Protection of human health

Table 11.6 **Ambient air quality standards in Australia for selected pollutants**

Source: NEPC 1997: 11

Pollutant	Averaging period	Maximum concentration*	Goal (10 years)[†]
Carbon monoxide	8 hours	9.00 ppm	1 day a year
Nitrogen dioxide	1 hour	0.125 ppm	1 day a year
	1 year	0.03 ppm	None
Lead	1 year	0.50 µg m^{-3}	None

* ppm = parts per million   1 µg = 10^{-6} g
† Maximum time for which emissions may exceed the maximum allowable concentration

Medium and pollutant	Ambient standard			Weighting factor
	mg m^{-3}	mg l^{-1}	mg mol^{-1}	
Air				
CO_2	579		13.701272	1
CO	8		0.189152	72
NO_x	0.03		0.000709	19,316
Water				
Aluminum		0.1	0.001803	7,599
Iron		1	0.018031	760
Mercury		0.001	0.000018	759,852
Landfill				
Aluminum		1	0.018031	760
Cadmium		0.01	0.000180	75,985
Tin		0.2	0.003606	3,799

Note: 1 mol of a substance is 6×10^{23} molecules or atoms of that substance (i.e. molecules in the case of carbon dioxide [CO_2], carbon monoxide [CO] and nitrogen oxides [NO_x], and atoms in the case of aluminium, iron, mercury, cadmium and tin).

Table 11.7 **Example of a standards-oriented assessment approach**

Source: Schaltegger and Sturm 1994

☐ Preservation of ecosystems

☐ Restoration of water quality to support aquaculture

A standard is a measure of environmental quality. It is a quantifiable characteristic of the environment against which environmental quality can be assessed—a surrogate for the actual environmental values that are to be protected. It may be:

☐ A simple numerical standard (e.g. pollutant concentration greater than 10 ppm [parts per million])

☐ Area-specific (e.g. the pH must be within 1 unit of the average background level)

☐ A complex numerical standard (e.g. species diversity index must be greater than 10)

A protocol is the procedure to be followed to determine whether a standard or goal is being met. Guidelines provide guidance on how standards or goals may be achieved (e.g. nutrient management strategies), or how specified environmental problems can be addressed (e.g. site contamination). Guidelines are not mandatory.

Standards and goals for ambient air quality relating to carbon monoxide, nitrogen dioxide and lead in Australia are shown in Table 11.6 (NEPC 1997: 11). The ambient standards of lead as a pollutant are listed in micrograms (μg; $1\,\mu$g $= 10^{-6}$ g, i.e. one millionth of a gram) per cubic metre (i.e. in μg m^{-3}).

A second illustration is taken from the regulations of the Swiss environmental protection agency, BUWAL (for more details, see Schaltegger and Sturm 1994). In the third numerical column of Table 11.7 milligrams of pollutant per mol (mg mol^{-1}) of environmental medium are used as a common unit of measurement (e.g. mg carbon dioxide per mol air or mg mercury per mol water). Bringing the different units of measurement to a common denominator of one mole (1 mol) of environmental medium facilitates a comparison between the relationship of standards for all environmental media (1 mol of a substance is 6×10^{23} molecules or atoms of that substance).

After converting the standards of each pollutant into the same units of measurement, the second step is to make the ambient standard of one pollutant (e.g. CO_2 as leading substance) equal to one. All other standards are given a weighting factor relative to the leading pollutant, CO_2 (e.g. the weight for carbon monoxide [CO] is calculated as 0.189152 mg mol^{-1} divided by 13.701272 mg mol^{-1}, which is equal to 72 [note, the weighting factor has no units as the units of mg mol^{-1} in the numerator of the sum cancel out the units of mg mol^{-1} in the denominator]). The result is a scale representing the relationships between the ambient standards of all pollutants. This permits a fairly comprehensive weighting method based primarily on emissions (Table 11.7).

Sociopolitical-oriented approaches have attracted much attention in the past. One way of anticipating the possibility of tighter or looser regulations is to look at the prevailing legal obligations and to follow ongoing environmental debate in public and legislative bodies. In this way, possible future liabilities can be anticipated. Although this is a less than optimal approach to environmental decision-making it does take financial aspects into account.

However, sociopolitical assessment approaches are also questioned because they accept the political (non-scientific) nature of concentration—or load-based—standards. In addition, they carry the odium of political expediency (and out-of-date regulations). They also reflect the weight given by regulators to different environmental media. The weighting scheme therefore varies between countries (Grimsted *et al.* 1994). Furthermore, standards-oriented assessment methods do not explicitly consider indirect, parallel or serial environmental impacts.

ABC analysis (not activity-based costing) has been implemented in some very advanced companies, notably in Germany (see e.g. Hallay 1992; Lehmann 1990; Lehmann and Clausen 1991). The principal assumption of ABC analysis is that a few interventions (A interventions) cause most of the impact (e.g. 20% of all activities or interventions cause 80% of all impacts) and that many aspects or interventions (C interventions) contribute very little to the impacts (B interventions may be regarded as intermediate between A and C interventions.

ABC analysis is restricted to a limited operational area because any management has considerable discretionary latitude as to the assessment procedure, and there is no proof of having applied a high or 'objective' standard. Furthermore, ABC methods do not explicitly consider indirect, parallel or serial environmental impacts. Nevertheless, this approach can be very valuable for internal purposes.

11.4.2.2 Socioeconomic (monetary) approaches

The group of monetary impact assessment concepts has evolved from socioeconomic research and can broadly be split into direct and indirect methods for measuring people's preferences for environmental quality (for an overview, see Hautau *et al.* 1987; Himelstein and Regan 1993; Johanson 1990; Pearman 1994; Pethig 1994; Schwab and Soguel 1995; Staehelin-Witt 1993). The second group of concepts is based on market valuation of environmental damage, or on expenses and market prices of goods and services for protection against environmental interventions. The first set of approaches attempts to measure people's preferences directly, by using laboratory experiments or contingent valuation methods. With a few exceptions (Burritt and Cummings 1999; Steen and Ryding 1994; Tellus 1992), monetary approaches have rarely been applied to impact assessment and ecological accounting at a corporate level. However, corporatised (commercial) organisations in the public sector have experimented with the monetised concept. For example, Australian Capital Territory Electricity and Water Corporation (ACTEW 1994) used contingent valuation and choice modelling to assess the amount participants were willing to pay for water-stream protection over the company's planning horizon to 2020, and as a basis for water pricing policy in a period when political activity over privatisation was beginning to emerge.

Damage-oriented impact assessment methods measure the monetary loss caused by environmental damage (e.g. loss of species), or the replacement value of environmental services (e.g. a forest). They are ex post economic measures that are mostly used to prove the severity of environmental interventions to politicians.

The expense-oriented assessment method provides an answer to the question of which direct costs and opportunity costs people would actually accept if they were to use or protect specific environmental assets (e.g. a lake or a species).

The market-price method asks what costs people would accept to repair (repair costs) or prevent (prevention costs) environmental damage or to protect themselves against environmental interventions (e.g. by buying noise protection devices). Burritt and Cummings (1999) explore the use made of expense-oriented and market-oriented assessment methods by a conservation company quoted on the Australian Stock Exchange. In 1998 the company used its economic valuation method to report non-current assets of Aus$93 million instead of a conventional financial accounting figure of Aus$12 million.

People can also be asked about their preference as to environmental quality. This can be tested directly in an artificial laboratory situation or through contingent valuation approaches which ask about activities or problems that occur in concrete situations (see e.g. Hautau *et al.* 1987; Schulz 1985).

The basic questions raised in socioeconomic assessment methods are summarised in Table 11.8. Monetary assessment methods do not explicitly take indirect, antagonistic or synergetic environmental impacts into account although they might theoretically be taken into account under the heading of citizens' 'willingness to pay' or 'willingness to accept'. Nonetheless, it must be assumed that time and spatial differences of environmental impacts are included in the valuations. All monetary assessment methods have to contend with the problem that derived monetary values cannot be linked to single environmental interventions. Compared with non-monetary concepts, results are not sufficiently dis-

Approach	Question
Expense	What costs do people accept to use or protect a specific environmental asset?
Willingness to pay	How much are people ready to pay for the reduction of a specific environmental problem?
Willingness to accept	How much has to be paid in order that people will be willing to accept a deterioration of environmental quality?
Prevention costs	How much money do people spend to protect themselves against environmental problems? How much are they ready to spend on preventative measures?
Damage costs	What are the (monetary) costs of environmental impacts for society?

Table 11.8 **Leading questions related to different monetary assessment approaches**

aggregated. However, it is possible to link monetary with non-monetary assessment approaches to derive financial values for environmental interventions. This can be achieved by determining monetary values for specific classes of environmental impacts (e.g. the greenhouse effect), thereby allowing the relative contribution of different interventions (e.g. CO_2, methane) to be traced back to the particular environmental problem in question. Hence, monetarisation of the impact of environmental interventions linked with specific environmental problems is possible (see Burritt and Cummings 1999; Schaltegger *et al.* 1996). However, the necessary level of scientific discussion is exceedingly rare in corporate practice.

11.4.2.3 Comparison of approaches to impact assessment

The distinction between scientific, sociopolitical and socioeconomic assessment concepts is based on differences between the questions pursued by these different disciplines. It is important to realise that no single assessment concept is generally superior to any other weighting method and that these assessment concepts are designed to provide different answers to different questions. Hence, the choice of an assessment method should depend on the aim of the analysis. A number of methods may need to be employed if answers are required to questions which span the three disciplines.

Figure 11.3 illustrates the whole continuum of methods, from objective, experimentally confirmed, scientific knowledge to sociopolitical and socioeconomic judgement about the environmental harm of environmental impacts based on intersubjective (feasible confirmation by more than one party) rather than objective confirmation. The figure compares different steps in ecological accounting (quantity and type of information) as well as the different groups of assessment methods. On the right-hand side of the figure is subjective information over which there is the possibility of disagreement between individuals and the need for intersubjective testing of data if those data are to be useful.

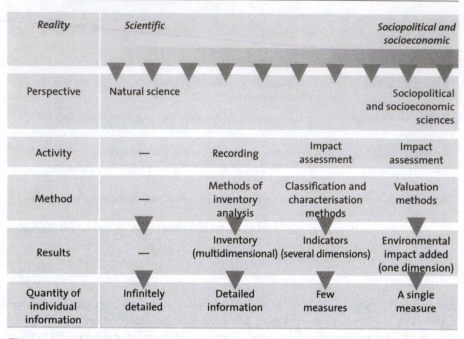

	Reality	Scientific			Sociopolitical and socioeconomic
Perspective	Natural science				Sociopolitical and socioeconomic sciences
Activity	—	Recording	Impact assessment		Impact assessment
Method	—	Methods of inventory analysis	Classification and characterisation methods		Valuation methods
Results	—	Inventory (multidimensional)	Indicators (several dimensions)		Environmental impact added (one dimension)
Quantity of individual information	Infinitely detailed	Detailed information	Few measures		A single measure

Figure 11.3 **Environmental impact added—between scientific reality and sociopolitical or socioeconomic reality**

At the other extreme, there really is no assessment method that can reflect reality in a completely objective manner, as natural scientists often assume (see the debate between Watts and Zimmerman [1978, 1990] and Christenson [1983]). As discussed in Section 11.2, a subjective judgement has to be made even when recording environmental impacts. For example, one can ask the following questions:

☐ Which environmental interventions are to be considered—all emissions of more than 1 g, 1 mg, 1 kg?

☐ What techniques of analysis are to be employed?

☐ Are the data measured, estimated, calculated or taken from literature?

☐ Are the measured data average or specific, annual or monthly?

The influence of intersubjectively testable social, political and economic approaches increases with every step nearer to the calculation of environmental impact added. Likewise, the number of measures falls and attendant simplification increases as environmental impact added is approached. At the same time, the basis for comparison is improved the nearer the measurement process is drawn to this goal. Classification and characterisation methods result in multi-dimensional environmental profiles (e.g. one value for the contribution to the 'greenhouse effect', one value for the contribution to photochemical smog) that are oriented towards the scientific method's view of reality which is hedged by a reductionist philosophy. The space-oriented ecological footprint approach focuses on how much natural regenerative capacity is needed to compensate for environmental impacts; the sociopolitical and socioeconomic assessment methods possess the potential to include social, political and economic judgements about environmental problems.

State of the art in impact assessment can be summarised as follows:

☐ There is no overall accepted standard for impact assessment. Many different concepts and research institutions are competing with each other and new developments are continually taking place. However, agreement may be reached that classification, characterisation and valuation are important steps in an impact assessment procedure (e.g. Udo de Haes 1995).

☐ Many of today's weighting models are designed for emissions. Also, the number of EIA units represents only one category of environmental impacts, namely those resulting from pollution. Extinction of species, the clearing of virgin forests and soil erosion affect ecological integrity (Burritt and Cummings 1999; Karr 1993) and represent a 'devaluation' of ecological assets (e.g. number of species, size of forests), whereas sink development (e.g. planting trees to absorb carbon dioxide) represents a 'revaluation' of ecological assets. With the partial exception of the ecological footprint and expense-oriented approaches, these ecological impacts are not included in the number of EIA units but may be represented in an eco-asset sheet. However, no generally accepted weighting scheme for ecological assets exists to date.

☐ Regulators and, to a certain extent, standardisation organisations such as ISO have partially entered the arena of impact assessment. Nevertheless, standards and regulations are not expected in the near future.

☐ Movement towards the integration of physical measures of ecological impact and financial measures of impact is discernible.

The following conclusions can be drawn for companies:

☐ No impact assessment concept is perfect. Nevertheless, the fact that some approaches have a sociopolitical or socioeconomic perspective should not be rejected as being non-scientific. Furthermore, any particular user of an assessment concept has to ensure that the methods employed are designed to answer questions that are relevant to them.

☐ Any choice of an impact assessment method should be guided by the following questions:
  – What information is of interest to the company (e.g. its contribution to specific environmental problems or its sociopolitical preferences)?
  – Which approaches may answer these questions best?
  – Which impact assessment approach is preferred by the communication partners (stakeholders)?
  – How is comparability going to be facilitated?

O Sensitivity analysis can be conducted by management to establish a robust, results-based information set, to make sure the information is useful for decision-making and to facilitate moves towards sustainability, greater transparency, comparability and accountability.

From a site-specific point of view, environmental impact added is calculated for devices and production steps at the point where environmental interventions are released (e.g. joint clean-up facilities such as sewage plants and incinerators) or for production sites as a whole. However, once the environmental impact added is calculated and shown in the departmental accounts of sites and joint clean-up facilities, managers might wish to know more about environmental impacts that are caused by production steps where no environmental interventions are directly released and about products and product groups. To achieve this, environmental impact added has to be allocated (relocated) from joint clean-up facilities to production centres and cost objects (e.g. specific products).

11.5 Allocation

11.5.1 Allocation based on material flows and activities

In conventional accounting the purpose of material flow-oriented activity-based costing (Section 6.4.2) is to calculate the total costs induced by material flows and cost objects (e.g. products and product groups). Activity-based costing is pursued in order to find out precisely where and through which activities a company earns or loses money. Internal ecological accounting establishes where and through which activities a company produces or reduces environmental interventions and impacts. It also aims to show which products and product groups contribute most to overall environmental impact added.

If one uses a description analogous to that of management accounting, one can see that internal ecological accounting distinguishes between:

O **Environmental impact added centres.** These are 'places' where material and energy are processed or where activity flows enter the natural environment. Each centre can be the responsibility of a designated member of the organisation. The person responsible for each centre is accountable for environmental impacts added within the organisation. Examples of EIA centres include production steps, sites, incinerators and sewage plants.

O **Environmental impact added objects.** These are analogous to cost objects in traditional cost accounting. They describe the products, product groups, departments or divisions that are seen to be responsible for the creation of both value added and environmental impact added. EIA objects should ideally correspond to a company's cost objects, because they are used as the basis for compiling value added that is then used to calculate eco-efficiency.

O **Environmental impact-added allocation rules and keys.** Allocation rules are general procedures used to link environmental interventions with appropriate objects in order to provide information for decision-making. Environmental impact added allocation keys describe the relation between an EIA object and environmental interventions that have occurred. As with cost allocation rules, EIA allocations are based on management judgement rather than on any conceptually correct mechanism.

☐ **Environmental impact added drivers.** These are factors that lead to environmental impacts. Examples of EIA drivers are CO_2 emissions that are associated with the greenhouse effect or emissions of volatile organic compounds (VOCs) that cause photochemical smog.

Allocation is not usually a critical issue when the boundaries of an accounting system are defined according to spatial (geographical) criteria (e.g. for a catchment when water-based environmental interventions can occur) or if emphasis is on the entire company (when allocation to segments is not required). For this reason, allocation of environmental interventions is more likely to be an issue for middle and lower management levels (product and production managers) than for higher management levels (top and divisional management). However, if any disputes arise then appeal mechanisms will involve higher levels of management. In addition, allocation is not of concern when constructing eco-asset sheets. Spatial accounting considers only the environmental interventions or assets related to a given region.

When narrower system boundaries are considered (e.g. for each production step or for each product), the situation changes. In developed countries, clean-up facilities such as sewage plants and incinerators act as EIA centres from which most point-source emissions are released into the natural environment. But these facilities do not directly cause environmental interventions.

EIA-centre accounting provides information about where 'overhead environmental interventions' of jointly used clean-up facilities (e.g. an incinerator) are actually created, or where they actually occur. Likewise, EIA-object accounting addresses the question of which products, processes or activities cause the environmental interventions that have been traced or allocated to EIA centres, as well as where responsibility and accountability for these impacts resides. The same questions are addressed in management accounting when costs are allocated to cost centres and cost objects. Linking environmental impact added to all centres and objects requires that both direct and indirect environmental impact added are taken into account.

EIA-object accounting is primarily a tool for internal management use. It focuses on products and product groups that correspond to specific environmental interventions. By estimating each object's environmental impact added, this accounting method sets out to determine, for example, how much pollution can be linked with each product or product group.

To estimate the environmental interventions that it is fair to link with an object for decision-making or motivation purposes, 'joint' environmental interventions from multi-purpose clean-up facilities, such as scrubbers and sewage plants, have to be allocated to the objects 'responsible'. In order to achieve this, allocation rules and keys have to be defined. Only when the environmental impact added of the centres and objects have been calculated can priorities for pollution prevention be formulated (e.g. reduction of greenhouse gases at production step B). Furthermore, for operational managers to improve the environmental record of the area they are responsible for, representative EIA drivers (e.g. electricity consumption at production step B drives the contribution to the greenhouse effect) have to be determined. If it is felt that cost savings will result from the improved environmental record then allocation rules adopted by senior management can be skewed against a particular centre in order to encourage lower-level managers to be proactive in reducing environmental impacts (Burritt 1998).

11.5.2 Allocation of indirect environmental impact added

Tracing and allocation of environmental interventions to centres makes it possible to determine how much the different EIA centres and objects have contributed to environmental impact added by common clean-up facilities. Similar allocation procedures to those used in cost accounting are called for. Utmost care must be taken not to count waste flows twice when they are processed by on-site treatment, storage and disposal units (Pojasek and Cali 1991a: 123). In conventional cost accounting, calculation of the gross margin of a product unit requires the tracing and allocation of all related costs. Similarly, in EIA object accounting, in order to calculate the environmental impact added caused by a specific product, it is necessary to link all environmental interventions to the responsible EIA object, either through direct tracing or through the use of indirect allocation rules.

The procedure for allocating environmental impact added to centres and objects is illustrated below by means of the same basic example that was used for environmental cost accounting in Section 6.2. The term 'environmental impact added (EIA) units' is used in order to generalise and simplify the example.

EIA objects A and B are manufactured in three production steps (EIA centres 1–3 in Fig. 11.4). Waste caused by the production processes (a total of 200 kg) is treated in an

Figure 11.4 **Tracing environmental impacts to environmental impact added (EIA) centres and objects**

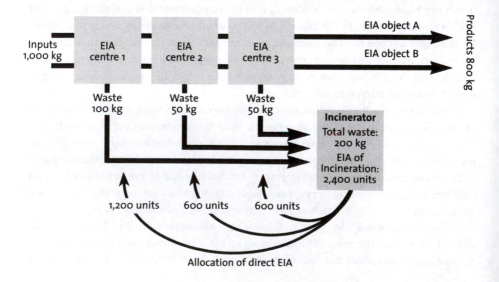

Allocation of direct EIA

incinerator. Pollution, toxic waste and waste-water generated by the incinerator amount to 2,400 units of environmental impact added. For simplicity's sake, it is assumed that all production steps cause the same kind of waste but in different amounts. In this case, direct environmental impact added by the incinerator can be traced to the EIA centres according to the amount of waste transferred from each EIA centre to the incinerator (centre 1: 1,200 EIA units, centres 2 and 3: 600 EIA units each).

At present, these are the only environmental impacts environmental managers and process engineers take into account when arriving at their decisions. This is the best treatment to use in most cases where the incidence of indirect environmental interventions is very low. However, when indirect interventions are material, management should consider whether allocation of impacts to responsible centres is desirable. Potential categories of indirect environmental impacts linked to the flow of material, which is treated in the incinerator, may be caused by transportation, handling, logistics and administration. The question to be answered concerns what indirect activities (e.g. logistics, transport and administration) are linked to the waste. These kinds of environmental impacts are particularly relevant in the case of transport-intensive businesses or wherever substantial administrative activity (e.g. at head office) uses a significant amount of electricity. Table 11.9 provides an example of how indirect environmental impact added can be determined (e.g. how to link transport impacts with EIA centres).

Only that part of the total indirect environmental impact added of each EIA centre that is related to the waste treated in the incinerator should be allocated to the EIA centres (e.g.

Table 11.9 **Material flow-related indirect environmental impact added (EIA)**

| | EIA centre | | | |
	1	2	3	Total
Material processed				
Weight (kg)	1,000	900	850	2,750
Weight as percentage of total weight*	36.36	32.73	30.91	100
Total units of indirect EIA	109	98	93	300
Waste processed				
Weight (kg)	200	100	50	350
Weight as percentage of total weight‡	20	11.11	5.88	
Units of waste-induced indirect EIA**	21.8	10.9	5.6	38.3
Units of direct EIA				2,400
Total indirectly induced EIA as a percentage of direct EIA				1.6

* Weight as a percentage of the total weight processed in all three centres (2,750 kg)
‡ Weight of waste processed at the specified centre as a percentage of the total weight of material processed at that centre (numerical row 1)
** The proportion of waste processed at the specified centre (numerical row 5, divided by 100) multiplied by the total number of units of indirect EIA in that centre (numerical row 3)

109 EIA units to centre 1, 98 units to centre 2, and 93 units to centre 3 [300 units in total]). For instance, 20% of the material processed in EIA centre 1 is waste. Thus, one-fifth of the total indirect environmental impact added of an EIA centre is to be allocated to the respective centre (20% of 109 EIA units = 21.8 EIA units). Based on the material-flow procedure, the sum of the direct and indirect environmental impact added can be determined (Fig. 11.5).

However, in the example in Table 11.9, the indirect environmental impact added amounts to 1.6 % of direct EIA. Considering the relatively small amount of indirect environmental impact added, in most cases it will not make sense to have a separate identification of indirect environmental impact added in internal ecological accounts. However, where companies face substantial administrative burdens, because of laws regulating the handling of toxic materials, separate allocation of environmental impacts to EIA centres may help to draw the attention of managers to these impacts.

Figure 11.5 **Total environmental impact added and environmental impact added per environmental impact added (EIA) centre**

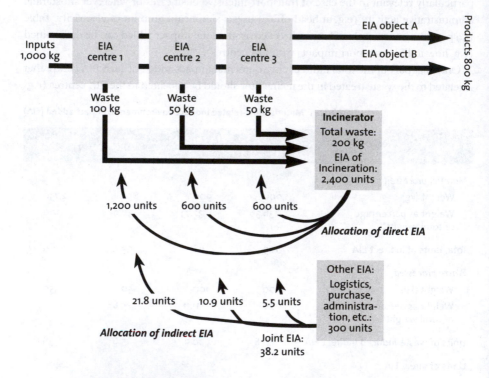

	EIA centre 1	EIA centre 2	EIA centre 3	Company
Direct	$1,200.00	$600.00	$600.00	$2,400.00
Indirect	+$21.80	+$10.90	+$5.50	+$38.20
Total	**$1,221.80**	**$610.90**	**$605.50**	**$2,438.20**

As a result of exploring this allocation procedure, management can identify situations where it is worthwhile allocating environmental impact added to the EIA centres and objects, and which products and product groups within those centres are linked with the generation of corporate environmental impact added. This analysis facilitates a more focused investigation of the potential for reducing environmental impacts and for improving corporate eco-efficiency.

A special application of EIA object accounting is used to compare results based on a standard calculation of environmental impact added. An increasing number of institutions have published basic inventory data (based on average industrial environmental interventions) related to the manufacture of core materials and products such as steel, aluminium, glass, paper, packaging materials and energy systems (see e.g. BUWAL 1991; ESU 1994; Fritsche *et al.* 1989). These data and associated practices, or alternatively data and practices of the best companies, can be used to establish EIA benchmarks for manufactured goods (Schaltegger 1994a). Calculation of actual environmental interventions, for example for the production of a specific product, can then be compared with such a benchmark, that is, the best or 'average' equivalent production process for that product (see e.g. Dyllick and Schneidewind 1995). As the availability of data increases, comparisons with similar cleanest-production-process benchmarks will become more common.

In the above example, it is assumed that the 'mass' of waste acts as a suitable allocation key. However, this is not always the case. As with conventional management accounting, choice of allocation rules and keys substantially influences the information contained in ecological accounts and the decisions based on such information. The greater the complexity of allocation rules and keys, the greater the possibility that distortions will occur. If, on the one hand, management wishes to be proactive in attempts to cut waste to improve its environmental record, then use of allocation rules and keys should be encouraged (Burritt 1998). If, on the other hand, management can see little gain to be made from waste reduction that is indirect to EIA objects, then it would be advisable not to become involved with the allocation process. Therefore, the method of analysis chosen and the system boundaries adopted for EIA centres and objects should ensure that internal ecological accounting provides information of the highest relevance to the specific management situation. As shown in Chapter 10, this means that site-oriented and company-oriented accounting tends to provide more relevant information than does product-oriented accounting.

11.5.3 Allocation rules and keys

The importance of the chosen allocation rule is particularly evident if material flows and EIA calculations are then linked to costs. Figure 11.6 further illustrates a typical allocation problem in ecological accounting. Production waste from product A is burnt in a large incinerator. Hot waste-water from this process is used to heat plant P before being discharged as sewage. Assuming that a common additive indicator for environmental impact added is available (i.e. 1 sewage emission unit = 1 air emission unit), the total environmental impact added by the incinerator is 93 EIA units (60 air emission units plus 33 sewage emission units).

A total of 33 sewage emission units in the form of hot waste-water leave the incinerator: 3 of these units are lost from a leaking pipe before they can be used; the remaining 30 of these units are used to heat plant P and are then discharged as sewage. Installation of a new heating system for production plant P would result in emissions of 40 EIA units, compared with the 33 EIA units currently emitted.

Focusing on the incinerated waste from one specific product, the question arises of how much and what types of emission are generated by this product. The allocation problem is common in product-oriented ecological accounting and life-cycle assessment. In the above example, burning the waste from product A leads to air emissions of 60 EIA units.

A variety of practical allocation rules for environmental impact added are available. These are examined below in relation to the example provided in Figure 11.6:

☐ **Full charge** (or producer pays). All environmental interventions are charged directly to the incinerator (EIA centre) and are allocated in full to the production department and then to the product being produced (product A being treated as the EIA object). The environmental impact of product A would be (60 + 3 + 30) EIA units = 93 EIA units. In this case the total of 93 EIA units is allocated as 93 EIA units to product A and 0 EIA units to plant P.

☐ **Transfer charge** (or user pays). As the incinerator 'produces' heating water for plant P, the end-user is responsible for all emissions. In this case the total 93 EIA units is allocated as 0 EIA units to product A and 93 EIA units to plant P.

☐ **Equal allocation based on number of parties.** As two parties are involved in the example, the indirect environmental impact added has to be allocated proportionately to both production centres and from these to products produced by these centres. Given an equal allocation in this case, pollution added by the incinerator is 50% of 93 EIA units = 46.5 EIA units. The 46.5 EIA units of the incinerator are charged to the production area responsible for product A. Environmental impact added by production plant P would also be 46.5 EIA

Figure 11.6 **Allocation of environmental interventions**

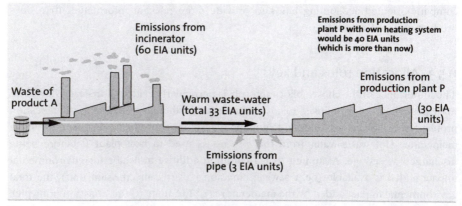

EIA = environmental impact added

units. If another party were involved, the total EIA would be divided by three. In this case the total 93 EIA units is allocated as 46.5 EIA units to product A and 46.5 EIA units to plant P.

☐ **Substitution bonus** (or opportunity charge). The environmental impact added by the incinerator is reduced by the EIA that would be caused if plant P had its own water heating (40 EIA units), but the leakage is a result of transport to plant P which would be unnecessary if plant P were to have its own heating system. Pollution added by the incinerator (and, through deduction, by product A) is, therefore, calculated as (93 − 40 + 3) EIA units = 56 EIA units, and only the pollution actually released (3 EIA units) is charged to plant P. Thus the total is 86 EIA units, allocated as 56 EIA units to product A and 30 EIA units to plant P.

☐ **Differential bonus.** Because the decision not to install a heating system by plant P reduces only those pollutants that would arise from that particular heating installation (e.g. sulphur dioxide [SO_2]), the incinerator may not be relieved of all of its emissions, but only by the pollutants actually saved (e.g. SO_2 but not nitrogen oxides [NO_x]). The environmental impact added by the incinerator would thus be smaller than 93 (the 60 EIA units arising from air emissions plus the pollution that would not be typical of a new heating system for plant P [this will consist of a proportion, but not all, of the 3 EIA units currently leaking from the pipe plus a proportion, but not all, of the 30 EIA units of waste-water]). The EIA of plant P would be smaller than 33, that is, a proportion, but not all, of the 3 EIA units leaked waste-water plus a proportion, but not all, of the 30 EIA units hot waste-water used by the current heating system.

☐ **Cascade-use bonus.** The waste-water from the incinerator that is forwarded to plant P is treated as a raw material. No waste-water emissions from the incinerator are charged to product A. The incinerator, and therefore the product, is assigned responsibility for all air emissions from the incinerator (60 EIA units). Production plant P is charged for its own waste-water emissions plus the emissions from the waste-water pipeline (33 EIA units = [3 + 30] EIA units). The total is now 93 EIA units, allocated as 60 EIA units to product A and 33 EIA units to plant P.

Although all allocation rules focus on different aspects of the allocation issue, it is essential to be aware of the incentives created by each rule for the different parties affected. The manager of the incinerator should have an incentive to promote further use of waste-water recycling, and managers in the plant producing product A and of production plant P should be encouraged to find and implement ways to use their waste-water.

To encourage a transaction, impacts of allocation schemes on responsibility for environmental impacts need to be considered. 'Full charge' and 'transfer charge' create incentives that will encourage only one party. Full charge encourages production at plant P, whereas transfer charge encourages the production department that produces product A.

'Equal allocation' can be inequitable and creates somewhat perverse incentives. For example, someone using or recycling 10% of the waste-water of the incinerator is 'punished' by being allocated 50% of the total pollution, which increases their recorded environmental impact. With the 'substitution' and 'difference' rules, the calculated incremental environmental impact added, based on an opportunity charge, may exceed actual total releases.

Considering the incentives created for all parties involved, the 'cascade-use bonus' allocation rule seems to be the most useful. It is essentially a producer-pays system with transfer charges for waste that can be used as inputs at a later stage of production. The possibility exists that the (two) parties negotiate an agreed transfer charge such that both areas benefit from any gains made (e.g. plant P would gain 7 EIA units by not installing a new heating system {[40 − 30 + 3] EIA units} and this could be split, say, 4 to the plant producing product A and 3 to plant P, with both parties benefiting from the action) (see Solomons 1965). Alternatively, it could be that central management decides to become involved in the allocation process and records common environmental interventions in a central account but traces only direct environmental impacts to centres.

Allocation rules provide a general procedure and a systematic approach for linking environmental impacts with EIA centres. For example, the cascade-bonus allocation rule accepts that pollution generated by the incinerator should be allocated to all products burned in the incinerator. As a rule, because several products are usually burned in an incinerator at the same time, if allocation is to occur, agreement has to be reached on the basis for deciding how much of the environmental interventions should be allocated to each product, products A, B and C, say. To carry this allocation process through, concrete allocation keys are needed. Allocation bases have to be defined specifically for each situation. Possible allocation keys for product A, linked to the example shown in Figure 11.6, include:

☐ Capacity used by the incinerator (such as burning time). If waste from product A burns in the incinerator for 10 minutes and uses the incinerator at full burning capacity during this time, the pollution that the incinerator releases in ten minutes should be allocated to product A. Here, allocation is based on a measure of input to the incinerator.

☐ Total weight or volume of waste from product A. If waste from product A weighs 100 kg, which is 1% of the total volume burned in the incinerator in a given period, 1% of the pollution of the incinerator should be allocated to product A. Here, allocation is based on a measure of input to the incinerator.

☐ Weight or volume of key pollutants, such as heavy metals, generated by product A when it is burned. If the main driver of total environmental impact added from incineration is the discharge of heavy metals, and if the burning of product A in this incinerator causes 0.5% of the total release of heavy metals by the incinerator, product A is allocated 0.5% of all emissions from the incinerator. Here, allocation is based on a measure of output from the incinerator.

☐ The activity that causes environmental interventions. Environmental impact added by joint clean-up facilities is allocated in proportion to those activities associated with the material flow induced by a product or a product family. Here, allocation is based on a measure of the process. If the activities linked with storage are related to 10% of the environmental impact, 10% of EIA is allocated to storage.

Allocation keys are based on physical measures. The allocation key chosen should be indicative of the cause of environmental impact added, even when this cause is not directly discernible. It must make practical sense to the parties involved. Thus, activities such as machine hours will often be chosen for waste produced by incineration. However, for reasons of simplicity or because of a lack of data, capacity utilisation, weight or volume will serve well in some cases.

Once environmental impact added is calculated for the centres and objects, and once it is related to the environmental impact activities, management has a more transparent basis for assessing the contribution made by individual centres to different environmental problems and for taking action to curb environmental interventions while improving environmental performance (Martins *et al.* 1995). Developing and implementing improvement strategies will, in most cases, require a set of pragmatic operational environmental indicators linked directly to corporate activities.

11.5.4 Operational environmental indicators

Environmental impact added (EIA) indicators are of interest mainly to upper-level management for strategic management issues. For operational environmental management striving to improve corporate environmental performance, EIA indicators will, as a rule, be too general. Thus, operational environmental control parameters need to be defined (see e.g. Azzone and Manzini 1994; Azzone *et al.* 1996; Böhm and Halfmann 1994; BMU/UBA 1997; Clausen *et al.* 1992; Dietachmair 1996; Dyllick and Schneidewind 1995; Eckel *et al* 1992; Goldmann and Schellens 1995; Günther 1993; Kottmann *et al.* 1999; Loew 1996; Loew and Hjálmarsdòttir 1996; Loew and Kottmann 1996; Peemöller *et al.* 1996; Seidel *et al.* 1989, 1994; Spiller 1996; Wiethoff 1996; Young and Rikhardsson 1996).

Currently, the majority of publications dealing with environmental indicators discuss various possible ratios between inputs of material and energy (e.g. the use of electricity) and outputs (e.g. CO_2 emissions per unit of product). However, as shown in Figure 11.7, a variety of other environmental indicators related to infrastructure, environmental management systems, education and training and the state of the environment are possible. However, many of these publications lack an in-depth discussion of an overarching goal or a definition of what these indicators should ultimately help measure and achieve.

Given the vast number of possible combinations, it does not make sense simply to establish a general list of specific indicators. Moreover, in order to arrive at operational environmental control parameters on the basis of EIA indicators, there will, first of all, have to be an analysis of the causes of environmental impact added. Questions raised by this analysis include:

☐ Which factors (activities, substances, energies and materials) are mainly responsible for environmental impact added?

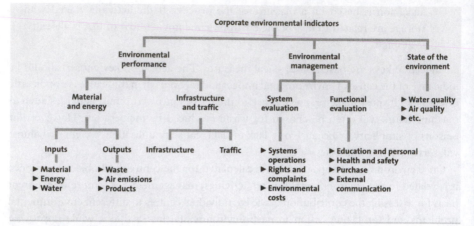

Figure 11.7 **Systematisation of environmental indicators**

Source: Similar to BMU and UBA 1997: 5

☐ Which EIA centres cause the main environmental impact added?

☐ Which factors identified as the main causes of environmental impacts can be controlled?

If, for instance, an impact assessment shows that the main part of the environmental impact added concerns winter smog (the environmental field of action) and is caused by SO_2 emissions, the search for the cause leads to identification of an EIA centre (e.g. an energy plant), an EIA driver (e.g. fuel) and/or to an EIA object (e.g. product group A). Knowledge of this information is used, for instance, to define a central indicator for operational control of a specific product group (e.g. 'consumption of fuel, EIA product A'). The selection of suitable indicators should be determined separately for every company, department and product—in the same way that financial indicators are deduced in management accounting. Indicators for operational environmental control ought to be directly associated with classifications in the standard chart of accounts. They should, furthermore, have a direct relationship to those activities that are the responsibility of, and can be controlled by, specific employees.

Certain large companies might be interested in building up a system of activity-related and responsibility-related control indicators. Such a system can be structured, for example, according to the functional areas in the value chain listed in Table 11.10 (for examples of such a structure, see Günther 1993; Horngren *et al.* 2000).

Apart from performance-related environmental control indicators, many other kinds of indicator, related to infrastructure, education, personnel and health and safety, are possible and may support corporate environmental management (see e.g. Dietachmair 1996; Günther 1993; Kottmann *et al.* 1999; Loew and Hjálmarsdòttir 1996; Seidel *et al.* 1989, 1994). These indicators are not discussed here as they do not directly focus on improving corporate eco-efficiency. The integration of environmental and economic indicators and a discussion of eco-efficiency-oriented indicators will be examined in Chapter 13.

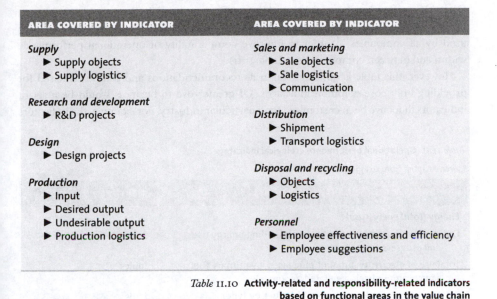

AREA COVERED BY INDICATOR	AREA COVERED BY INDICATOR
Supply ▶ Supply objects ▶ Supply logistics	*Sales and marketing* ▶ Sale objects ▶ Sale logistics ▶ Communication
Research and development ▶ R&D projects	*Distribution* ▶ Shipment ▶ Transport logistics
Design ▶ Design projects	*Disposal and recycling* ▶ Objects ▶ Logistics
Production ▶ Input ▶ Desired output ▶ Undesirable output ▶ Production logistics	*Personnel* ▶ Employee effectiveness and efficiency ▶ Employee suggestions

Table 11.10 **Activity-related and responsibility-related indicators based on functional areas in the value chain**

Whatever the set of operational environmental control indicators chosen, measurement problems have always to be kept in mind. Furthermore, movement in an indicator should always reflect an actual reduction or increase in environmental impact added. In addition, each indicator must relate to activities that can be influenced by the responsible, accountable actors whose environmental performance is being measured.

Contrary to general EIA indicators (or indexes), specific operational control indicators have the advantage that they are, as a rule, easily communicated and therefore particularly suitable for control by operating managers and executives. These specific ecological indicators are considered further in the next section.

11.6 Ecological indicators

Ecological indicators are quantifiable measures used to gauge, record and effectively communicate ecological conditions in physical terms. Ecological indicators, designed to help internal control of corporate impacts on the environment, vary from company to company depending on a number of characteristics such as the industry, management style and philosophy, tightness of regulation, technology, size and structure. This said, it is popular to try identify a number of common (generic) environmental impacts that need to be kept under control by all companies. These impacts relate to different environmental media (e.g. impacts on air, water and land) and require different ecological indicators (e.g. related to materials use, energy use, water use, emissions to air, discharges to water and the number, volume and nature of accidental or non-routine releases to air, land or water). Organisations with an international presence, such as the

Global Reporting Initiative of the Coalition of Environmentally Responsible Economies (CERES; White and Zinkl 1998), provide guidance about a set of indicators that could be used by all companies in order to improve comparability of operational performance within and between companies (see Table 11.11).

However, this table is quite general in its recommendations and can be criticised for providing only core common indicators. Of greater use to business would be a set of indicators that have been customised for a particular industry. For example, the indicators

Table 11.11 **Operational performance ecological indicators**

Source: Adapted from GRI 1999

ENVIRONMENTAL MEDIA (SUB-CATEGORY)	MEASURE
Energy (total energy use)	
Objectives, programmes and targets regarding energy use and progress toward same	Joules
Total use of electricity (amount purchased, by primary fuel source; amount self-generated by source)	Joules
Total fuel use (vehicle and non-vehicle fuel, by type)	Joules
Other energy use (e.g. district heat)	Joules
Materials (total use of materials excluding fuel)	
Objectives, programmes and targets regarding materials use and progress toward same	Tonnes*
Objectives, programmes and targets regarding procurement and use of virgin and reclaimed materials and progress toward same	Tonnes*
Water (total use of water)	
Objectives, programmes and targets regarding water use and progress toward same	Litres
Land	
Habitat improvements and sinks	Unspecified
Damages caused by enterprise operations	Unspecified
Non-product output (waste prior to treatment, off-site recycling and disposal, including outline of objectives, programmes and targets)	
Non-product output returned to process or market or not hazardous)	Material type** Management type†
Non-product output to land	Material type** Management type†
Non-product output to air	Emissions to air, by type
Non-product output to water	Discharges to water, by type

* Metric tons, equal to 1,000 kg or 2,205 lb　** Hazardous or non-hazardous　† Recycled, re-used or remanufactured

INDICATOR	MEASURE
Recycling	▸ Pole return rate (%) ▸ Percentage chemicals recycled ▸ Percentage batteries recycled by type
Waste management	▸ Amount of solid waste generated per employee ▸ Amount of solid waste generated per unit of output
Releases and emissions	▸ Percentage lead in solder ▸ Percentage change in boiler emissions
Compliance attention-directing	▸ Number of regulatory inspections
Internal accountability	▸ Pesticide use for clearing right of way ▸ Recycling rate in different divisions

Table 11.12 **Possible ecological indicators for the telecommunications industry**

shown in Table 11.12 might be useful to the telecommunications industry, but may not be of concern to a steelworks.

Identification of key customised ecological indicators will increase the information value for managers by permitting production-unit, site-based, divisional, product-based and company-based targets to be established. Furthermore, a common metric allows comparisons to be made between segments (e.g. sites) of a large organisation. Actual performance can be compared at a point in time (e.g. 1999, site X, pole return rate expected = 28%; 1999, site X, actual pole return rate = 25%). In addition, comparisons can be made over time (e.g. 1998, site X, pole return rate = 20%; 1999, site X, pole return rate = 25%). These indicators reflect a higher pole return rate between 1998 and 1999 for site X, but a worse-than-expected result—something for which the manager of site X can be held accountable.

Following a number of costly incidents (e.g. BHP's multimillion-dollar compensation payments because of the tailings disaster at the Ok Tedi gold and copper mine (see Chapter 2, Question 6, page 40) the minerals extraction industry has recently become enthusiastic about identifying environmental impacts. By way of example, take WMC Ltd (previously known as Western Mining Corporation Ltd), a large Australian mining company. The company has a chequered environmental record. According to the Minerals Policy Institute (MPI 1998) two environmental incidents should be of prime concern to top management:

☐ The chemical contamination of groundwater around its gold and copper mines in Western Australia

☐ Its campaign with other mining companies against reforming Filipino mining legislation in the wake of a major tailings dam disaster.

In fact, since 1995 WMC has publicly disclosed the successes and failures of its environmental performance, but of greater importance is the encouragement being given to managers and workers to improve the environmental performance of areas for which they are responsible and over which they have control. To this end a series of site reports have been prepared for internal use—a series that in 1998 was also made public (WMC 1998) as shown in Table 11.13, which reveals the 1998 site report for Agnew Gold Operation in Western Australia. Targets for site environmental indicators were disclosed along with appropriate measures of performance (Table 11.14). Also, relevant data on the site show the absolute and relative environmental performance measures for each environmental medium over a five-year period (Table 11.15).

Examination of data from other sites shows that each site is different in a number of ways, although there are core elements that can be compared with use of standard measures. Site data reflect the operational details of environmental performance such as progress toward environmental targets, towards managing significant aspects and impacts and towards the implementation of environmental objectives.

For large companies the management gains from recording a detailed set of environmental indicators are easy to see. Information about each environmental impact object (site, product line, division) becomes transparent and, once transparent, its importance

Table 11.13 **Environmental performance areas for WMC Ltd's Agnew Gold Operation, according to its three-year Environmental Improvement Plan to:**
  ▶ **Further develop the environmental management system**
  ▶ **Develop an aspects and impacts register**
  ▶ **Reduce resource use and emissions per unit of activity**
  ▶ **Integrate environmental objectives into the site business plan**

Source: WMC 1998

MEDIUM	ENVIRONMENTAL PERFORMANCE
Water	In the last 18 months, there has been a 0.6% reduction in kilolitres of water per tonne of ore milled.
Energy	In the last 18 months, there has been a 2.2% reduction in energy used per tonne of ore milled as a result of replacing some old and inefficient equipment.
CO_2 and SO_2	In the last 18 months, an 8% reduction in CO_2 and a 55% reduction in SO_2 emissions per tonne of ore milled was primarily a result of replacing diesel fuel with natural gas-generated power.
Rehabilitation	Little rehabilitation has occurred in the last few years at Agnew, as all mining is underground and most waste rock is used underground as backfill; there are no active waste rock dumps on-site; approximately 200 old drill holes were capped.
Minimisation of waste	Each week an average of 8 m³ of domestic rubbish and 12 m³ of industrial rubbish is sent to landfill.

CO_2 = carbon dioxide SO_2 = sulphur dioxide   tonne = metric ton, equal to 1,000 kg or 2,205 lb

Parameter	Base year* value	Target**	Target reduction (% per annum)
Water	1.16[†]	1.06[†]	3
Energy	255[‡]	232[‡]	3
CO_2	36[‡‡]	32[‡‡]	3

* Base year = 1998   ** Target date = December 2001   † Kilolitres used per tonne ore milled
‡ Megajoules used per tonne ore milled   ‡‡ Kilograms emitted per tonne ore milled
tonne = metric ton, equal to 1,000 kg or 2,205 lb

Table 11.14 **WMC Ltd's targets for environmental indicators for the Agnew Gold Operation**

is easier to assess and control. Whether site, product and segmental detail is of use to small companies having only one site, a small number of products or a single production department, or to a company not involved in an industry with sensitive environmental issues, is an important question for chief executive officers to consider. A number of benefits exist for small companies that develop environmental indicator information for internal use within their companies. These companies will have:

☐ A basis for planning ecological improvements that might also be financially (and competitively) advantageous

☐ Greater awareness of physical environmental obligations (and potential liabilities)

☐ A catalyst for the development and setting of environmental objectives

☐ A means by which employees may become systematically involved in efforts to reduce consumption of natural resources

Table 11.15 **Absolute and relative environmental performance of WMC Ltd's Agnew Gold Operation site**

Site data	1994–95*	1995–96*	1996–97*	1997–98*	1998**
Industrial water use					
Per tonne of ore milled (kl)	1.125	1.270	1.041	0.992	1.162
Total (megalitres)	1,187	1,287	1,154	1,140	1,324
Industrial energy use					
Per tonne of ore milled (MJ)	327[†]	306	253	242	255
Total (terajoules)	928[†]	310	281	278	290
Carbon dioxide emissions					
Per tonne of ore milled (kg)	51[†]	46	38	34	36
Total (tonnes)	145,099[†]	46,635	41,888	38,852	40,517

* July–June   ** Revised annual period, January to June   † Includes Leinster mine in 1994–95
kl = kilolitres   MJ = megajoules   kg = kilograms   tonne = metric ton, equal to 1,000 kg or 2,205 lb

- ☐ A system that facilitates management by exception for time-constrained management, with emphasis being placed only on a small set of key indicators

- ☐ A system that encourages long-term thinking

A number of questions need to be considered when setting out to develop a relevant set of ecological indicators:

- ☐ Are data sets available to support the indicator, or is a new data-gathering system needed?

- ☐ Are the data reliable and will they be available to enable comparability in future periods?

- ☐ Do technical staff accept that an indicator is an appropriate measure of environmental quality?

- ☐ Does the ecological indicator help managers with decision-making and accountability?

- ☐ What should be the correct level of data disaggregation? Small companies will require a higher level of aggregation for operational purposes than will larger, decentralised companies.

- ☐ How can different indicators be compared? Can they be aggregated into a single ecological indicator?

Varied approaches are available for companies seeking guidance on indicator development (see e.g. Kottmann *et al.* 1999). For example, the Global Reporting Initiative (GRI) has a set of general operational indicators (GRI 1999). The World Business Council for Sustainable Development (WBCSD) promotes the measurement of eco-efficiency performance through a set of core uniform indicators (WBCSD 1997; see Table 11.16) and a set of supplemental indicators that can be made specific to each business (EEEIW 1999; Table 11.16).

Core indicators and supplemental indicators when combined can be used to reflect the eco-efficiency profile of a particular company. Likewise, ISO 14031 (ISO 1999b), the new draft international standard on environmental performance evaluation, has its own approach. It provides a three-way classification of indicators into:

- ☐ Environmental condition

- ☐ Operational performance

- ☐ Management performance

In a similar way to that promoted by the WBCSD, the ISO standard provides a list of possible indicators that users may choose to reflect their own needs. Both of these approaches try to balance the rigidity of a common set of indicators with the flexibility of specific sectoral, industry or specific company indicators.

In practice, sets of common and sectoral indicators are available for any company seeking to develop its own approach, but many of these sets of indicators have been based

Product creation ecological impact	Ecological profile
Core indicators	
Consumption of	
Energy	150,000 gigajoules
Materials	100,500 tonnes
Water*	160,000 cubic metres
Emission of	
Greenhouse gases	6,000 tonnes CO_2 equivalent
Ozone-depleting substances	15 tonnes CFC 11 equivalent
Acidification compounds	200 tonnes proton equivalent
Volatile organic compounds	160 tonnes
Supplemental indicators	
Nutrification compounds	–
Persistent organic pollutants	Natural gas consumed = 1,200 gigajoules
Priority heavy metals	–
Chemical and biological oxygen demand in water effluents	Electricity consumed = 35,000 gigajoules
Land use	–

* Net consumption   Giga = 10^9 CO_2 = carbon dioxide   CFC = chlorofluorocarbon

Table 11.16 **Core and supplemental indicators in a corporate environmental profile: company Y**

Source: Based on Lehni 1999

on limited project work, and their general applicability is still uncertain. In addition, specific sets of indicators need to be developed by each company, but templates for ecologically sensitive industries (e.g. chemicals) can be accessed without having to 'reinvent the wheel'. In summary, a number of practical issues face each company when developing a set of ecological performance indicators:

☐ Simplicity is to be preferred to complexity (use a few key measures that are easy to comprehend).

☐ Flexibility is to be preferred to rigidity (there is no master set of indicators that suits all companies; develop a set that is applicable to your business and permit change in the set of indicators and over time as experience dictates is necessary).

☐ Be aware that quantifiable physical performance indicators will be most useful if they can be related to other sets of indicators that are used to assess company performance (e.g. profitability, liquidity and solvency, or value added).

☐ If concern is with production processes, then core elements of the value chain will need to be identified and their own indicators identified; however, if concern is with the product being produced, life-cycle assessment will be a necessary analytical component.

The WBCSD explains key aspects of indicator identification and classification through three components—categories, aspects and indicators (Lehni 1999). Categories are the broad areas of environmental impact (e.g. resulting from the production or use of a product). Aspects are general types of information relating to a particular category (e.g. production of a product leads to material consumption and non-product output). Indicators are measures of individual aspects (e.g. tonnes of material consumed or tonnes of carbon dioxide emitted). When a responsibility and control infrastructure has been developed, and when ecological indicators have been identified, measured, classified, recorded and reported internally, the foundation for well-informed, integrated decision-making and transparent internal accountability in the search for sustainable business practices will be in place.

Ecological indicators provide one main tool to assist company moves towards eco-efficiency. An additional tool to help achieve ecological efficiency at the operational level is to assess the ecological effects of investments. Consequently, the next section will examine the fundamentals of ecological investment appraisal.

11.7 Ecological investment appraisal

Ecological investment appraisal sets out to determine whether the environmental impacts of a specific project can be reduced and, if so, by how much. Methods of ecological investment appraisal have been employed for many years for calculating the net ecological impact of investments in pollution prevention and site restoration. Some investments, such as clean-up facilities or pollution prevention devices, are undertaken exclusively for ecological purposes, others are normal commercial investments but with ecological considerations forming an integral part of the proposal. However, concern here is with ensuring that environmental measures are effective, efficient and equitable.

Two values, namely the environmental impact added that is caused by production, operation, maintenance and disposal, and the environmental impact reduced by technology, have to be accounted for when evaluating end-of-pipe technologies such as sewage plants, scrubbers and incinerators. To determine the net environmental effect, the environmental impact added that is expected to be reduced by new or improved technology can be subtracted from the measure of environmental impact added created by the project.

When assessing the environmental consequences of investments intended to prevent pollution, environmental effects and reductions are, in practice, rarely discounted. This is in stark contrast to financial investment appraisal where, in most countries (Japan being one exception), it is normal practice to discount future nominal cash flows in order to obtain discounted cash flows that are then used as a guide to decision-making.

The typical argument against discounting investments that prevent pollution is that discounting would be contrary to the actual purpose of environmental protection, namely, to reduce future environmental impacts not simply to improve the present situation. Discounting would reduce the value of future benefits, especially as many costs that are expected to be incurred far in the future (e.g. of rehabilitating mine sites, garage sites or factory sites) and that will be saved if an environmental investment takes place will be reduced if discounting is used. However, as will be argued in Section 11.8, this perspective presents some problems. Two main measures for use in ecological investment appraisal are the:

☐ Ecological payback period (EPP)

☐ Ecological advantage ratio (EAR)

The EPP measures how long it takes to reduce the environmental impacts caused by an investment. It calculates the relation between environmental impacts that are caused by introducing the technology, and the annual reductions in impacts that result from it. This key calculation is of special interest for pollution prevention devices. As no discounting is used, the ecological payback method does not suffer from the inherent weaknesses of the conventional financial payback method. Instead, it is used to complement discounted cash flow approaches (e.g. net present value [NPV]).

$$\text{EPP} \quad = \quad \frac{\text{EIA caused by the initial investment}}{\text{annual reduction of EIA through the investment}} \qquad [11.1]$$

The investment is beneficial in ecological terms if its life-span is longer than the EPP.

Theoretically, all environmental impacts should be taken into account over the life-cycle of an investment. In practice, the EPP method is calculated usually only for selected key substances affected by the investment (e.g. for CO_2 or water or for energy; see e.g. Fritsche *et al.* 1989: 233f.; Suter and Hofstetter 1989). Of course, as with financial payback, ecological benefits are not specified beyond the break-even period using the EPP, and if these benefits are significant they will not be accounted for.

The EAR method has also been used for some time, especially for appraisal of pollution prevention devices (see e.g. ASVS 1990: 24), and it addresses this problem with the EPP. The EAR measures whether environmental impact added (EIA) has been reduced by an investment and, if so, by how much over the life of the investment. Thus, the absolute value of the gross reduction of environmental impact added (200 units, say) is divided by the environmental impact added caused by the pollution prevention investment (100 units, say):

$$\text{EAR} \quad = \quad \frac{\text{EIA reduced over the total investment period}}{\text{EIA caused by the investment}} \qquad [11.2]$$

Investments are efficient in ecological terms if the ratio on the right-hand side of equation [11.2] is greater than 1 (in the above example, EAR = 200 units/100 units = 2) and are inefficient if it is less than 1 (for ecological efficiency, see Section 3.4). The larger the ratio, the better the investment from an ecological point of view. As mentioned above, expected future environmental impacts and reductions are not discounted.

Seen from a global point of view, end-of-pipe technologies often prove to be surprisingly ineffective in ecological terms (with an EAR less than 1). This means that the overall reduction in environmental impact added they achieve is smaller than the environmental impact added that they cause. Despite this, such investments continue to be made, frequently encouraged by 'command-and-control' regulatory mechanisms. However, such end-of-pipe investments can still make sense when environmental impacts caused by production and disposal of products occur in one place and ecological impacts are reduced in another. For instance, in Figure 11.8, environmental impact added is reduced by an amount c by a scrubber installed on site C. Yet, in aggregate, increased use of electric power, which is generated at site A, as well as the additional filter dust disposed of at site D, cause an increase in environmental impact added that is greater than the reduction achieved on site C ($c < a + d$; see Fig. 11.8).

Another issue from an ecological perspective is that it may make sense in some cases for a company to reduce environmental impacts in order to prevent regulated threshold levels from being exceeded in certain highly polluted areas, even if more environmental impact added is caused in cleaner regions. This is a generic problem when 'offset' is used as a means to reduce pollution (see Burritt and Lehman 1995). This basic idea lies behind the public policy tool of netting (see e.g. Tietenberg 1992).

Figure 11.8 illustrates the reduction of environmental impact added in a 'hot spot' (highly polluted area) so that the ambient air quality falls beneath the threshold level (i.e. beneath the ambient air quality standard). Increased pollution on production and disposal sites (sites A and D) is greater than the reduction in environmental impact added on site C, but is encouraged by regulations that require compliance with an ambient standard at site C. Thus situations occur where environmental clean-up activities are ineffective from an overall viewpoint (with an EAR less than 1), but are considered effective given the goal of reducing environmental impacts in 'hot spots', or in the context of specific compliance

Figure 11.8 **Regulatory clean-up measure reflected by a negative ecological advantage ratio: effective or ineffective?**

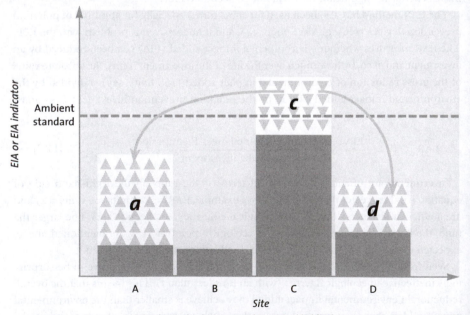

Note: a, c and *d* = change in environmental impact added (EIA) at sites A, C and D, respectively

with standards laid down because of concentrations of pollution in certain industrial regions. In the case of ineffective abatement measures, however, it is desirable for companies to find ecologically effective pollution prevention measures rather than be driven by regulation into undesirable ecological investments.

Capital investments in integrated technologies and measures to reduce throughput are only just beginning to arouse interest. For example, movement to combined electricity generation technologies in the UK has led to a reduction in 'greenhouse gas' emissions during the 1990s which effectively helped the country meet its Kyoto greenhouse gas emissions reduction target without any further action. In general, however, integrated technologies and measures to reduce throughput have received less attention than might be expected. Cost accounting reinforces this situation as it often neglects the actual costs of throughput (see Section 6.2).

As discussed earlier, in relation to environmental cost accounting, integrated measures of pollution prevention that reduce material flows often cut costs by more than the amount expected. In most cases, these approaches represent a proactive approach to environmental management and are more environmentally effective. Likewise, they encourage efficiency because they require fewer material inputs than do end-of-pipe solutions to environmental problems.

In principle, the ecological advantage ratio and ecological payback can adopt the same basic approach outlined above. However, with integrated technologies, problems of tracking and tracing the share of environmental impacts caused by environmental technology being integrated with a commercial production device may be difficult and arbitrary.

Being proactive is, then, discouraged by conventional cost accounting techniques that have to fall back on rules of thumb for arbitrarily assigning ecological impacts from projects to commercial and environmental drivers. In practice, fewer cost accounting problems occur when measures that are designed to support good ecological outcomes by reducing throughput are introduced separately. It is simpler to trace effects in these circumstances. However, whether integrated technologies or end-of-pipe technologies are used, assessment of all projects that prevent or reduce material and energy flows needs information about these material and energy flows. Whether commercial or environmental reasons drive the process is of less significance.

The next section explores the issue of whether future environmental impacts should be addressed by using discounting and whether a net present value of future environmental impact added may provide useful information.

11.8 Net present future environmental impact added

If the concept of discounting future cash flows makes sense financially in order to assess the value of a company, then company executives may well ask whether discounting future environmental impacts may provide useful information, for example, for investment appraisal. To achieve this, the expected future environmental impact added would have to be forecast. This is possible for many investment projects. However, discounting future environmental impact added is commonly opposed. Maunders and Burritt (1991: 23) suggested that a radical modification of the net present value approach, in which prices are based on 'existence values' could provide the way ahead. In this section an alternative radical approach is explored, based on net present environmental impact added (NPEIA).

It could be argued that the basic idea of environmental protection is to protect future values (or values for future generations) and that discounting these values would represent a reduction in values ascribed to the future. Supporters of this perspective feel that the discounting of future environmental impacts (in comparison with today's impacts) reflects a subordination of future environmental quality and would therefore be contrary to the very notion of environmental protection. According to this argument, the sum of future environmental impacts added are equal to the sum of all, non-discounted, environmental impacts by any company with a portfolio of projects and an infinite life. From a long-term perspective, future environmental impact added would be infinitely large. Two conclusions seem possible based on this analysis.

First, the conventional conclusion is that the calculation of an aggregate future environmental impact added does not make sense—it has no meaning, except for any specific project bound in time (e.g. 40 years) and space (e.g. site E in country Z).

The second conclusion could be to accept the discounting of future environmental impact added: that is, to accept the discounting of future environmental interventions. This second perspective would be acceptable only if the discounting of future environmental impact added were to provide valuable information for decision-makers. Discounting has been accused of being counterproductive to sound environmental management and policy (see e.g. Pearce and Turner 1994). No doubt, discounting the value of environmental services (such as good air quality, or old-growth forests) seems to contradict the basic philosophy of environmental conservation. An important motivation for protecting the natural environment is to pass on environmental services to future generations. The value of present production activities is, therefore, strictly linked to the future. However, this argument is less convincing if the perspective is changed slightly by asking whether protection of an environmental good now (present value) is preferred to a delay in protection (future value).

From a purely environmental perspective, discounting of future values is desirable if the focus is placed on environmental impacts instead of on environmental services because there is a natural temptation to suggest that present protection against environmental impacts is preferred to future protection, hence the future should be discounted in some way. The question to be answered is whether it makes sense to delay the release of, for example, CO_2 emissions or any other impact on the environment. Does it matter whether a given amount of pollutants is emitted today or in 100 years' time?

As mentioned above, it makes more sense to reduce environmental impacts today than to delay them. However, several reasons can be suggested for delaying the reduction of environmental impacts if the choice is simply to delay or not delay:

☐ First, the availability of better scientific evidence in the future may improve knowledge about the effects of specific substances emitted. This argument is analogous to that of an archaeologist who seeks to discover the lessons of prehistory captured in the layers of a site that will need to be irreversibly destroyed if the information is to be discovered and recorded. If the archaeologist waits before engaging in the process of creative destruction of a site, scientific techniques for interpreting any evidence and artefacts might improve and more valuable knowledge might be gained than otherwise would have been the case.

☐ Second, the development of new technologies may enable future management to reduce or prevent emissions that at present cannot be further reduced in an economical way. Greater knowledge about the effects of environmental interventions can lead to both a higher (e.g. as with CFCs) or a lower (e.g. as with SO_2) assessment of their harmfulness.

☐ Third, the possibility of delaying environmental impacts may be worthwhile as by spreading emissions over time particularly harmful burdens (hot spots) or threshold levels may be avoided.

The possibility of delaying pollution can be viewed as an example of a 'real option' (for a discussion of real options, see Dixit and Pindyck 1995).

As a result, in some circumstances it may very well make sense to discount environmental impacts even from a purely ecological perspective. However, as with the discounting of cash flows, sometimes the technique is not merited because of other pressing factors, for example potentially ruinous financial crises that must be solved urgently if the company is to survive. If the EAR is greater than 1, from an ecological perspective it would be desirable for the company to survive. Here, the analogy is with an archaeologist facing an urgent situation, for example a 'rescue dig' in order to recover any information from the layers uncovered on a site before that site is destroyed (e.g. by natural forces or by redevelopment of the site). In these circumstances there is a present imperative to rescue any information before the site is destroyed. Likewise, some ecological issues are seen as crises and, although in the fullness of time they might not turn out to be as critical as anticipated, there is a chance they could be disastrous and so a precautionary approach suggests that environmental impacts be curtailed now rather than in the future (e.g. in the case of the production and use of halons).

To use another analogy with the concept of net present value, a long-term indicator taking into account future environmental impacts may support long-term thinking. The corresponding adequate measure could be termed 'net present environmental impact added (NPEIA):

$$\text{NPEIA} \quad = \quad \sum_{n=1}^{N} \text{EIA}_n \quad \cdot \quad \frac{1}{(1+i)^n} \qquad [11.3]$$

where:

NPEIA is the discounted aggregate future environmental impact added

EIA_n is the environmental impact added in period n

i is the discount rate

N is the total number of periods

The concept of NPEIA relies on the measurement of expected future environmental impact added. However, there is still the question of what discount factor should be chosen. Given the fact that today's environmental services have no price and that many environmental impacts are rarely given a price, the treatment of environmental impacts proposed here—analogous to the treatment given to economic services—may be considered an improvement.

From a pragmatic perspective, use of the same discount rate as applied to the economic assessment of a company and its investments may be the easiest weight to use. The argument that environmental services are often not replicable and thus should have a higher value does not require a change in the discount rate if it is accepted that the option to delay environmental impacts has a positive value. At the same time, it must be recognised that, in practice, financial management of a company involves more than a simple consideration of a set of discounted cash flows. This is an economic ideal based on neoclassical economic theory with all its restrictive assumptions. In practice, executives are concerned from day to day about a cluster of financial circumstances—profitability, liquidity, solvency and changes in these, as well as their asset, liability and equity base. Management of some of these will require a short-run response for survival, whatever the net present value indicates about future values.

Likewise, EPP, EAR and NPEIA are one set of potentially useful measures for assessing ecological investments. Exigencies that may prevail in the short run, and resulting ecological impacts, may result in very high EPP, EAR or NPEIA figures indicating the overriding importance of reducing ecological impacts to encourage survival, even at a high economic cost.

Use of NPEIA for ecological investment appraisal will change some results when compared with the investment appraisal approaches discussed in Section 11.7. The NPEIA approach is likely to encourage comparison of a wider set of pollution prevention and reduction measures. However, it is not necessarily needed to support decisions about how much environmental protection should be pursued by a company. Regulatory and ethical issues also have a bearing on this question. Nevertheless, the NPEIA indicator has more in common conceptually with net present value and can thus be directly compared with this economic indicator in investment appraisal.

11.9 From internal to external ecological accounting

Chapter 11 has revealed the structure and principles of internal ecological accounting. Internal ecological accounting provides information to different internal stakeholders such as to product, production, site, divisional and top managers. It has also shown that the balance-sheet concept cannot be applied consistently to ecological accounting. However, eco-asset sheets may be a helpful device for companies that cause direct impacts on ecological assets (e.g. mining and logging). Today's ecological accounting approaches focus mainly on emissions (or flows), such as the discharge of toxins and pollutants. Costs related to these environmental interventions have been increasing over the past few decades, whereas the costs of information technologies have decreased. Therefore, a systematic and cost-efficient system for the continuous accounting for environmental impact added is needed and can be justified. As the current product life-cycle assessment approach has often proven to be both ineffective and inefficient, managers should focus, initially, on site-specific accounting, which distinguishes EIA objects, centres and drivers.

For improved comparisons over time and between entities, some standardisation in ecological accounting indicators is clearly necessary. For effective communication to external stakeholders, internal ecological accounting information has to be prepared in a transparent manner and in line with generally accepted standards. This is why in Chapter 12 the basic conventions of accounting, as defined by the International Accounting Standards Committee (IASC), are examined and basic assumptions behind accounting and conventions of ecological accounting are explored.

For external ecological accounting, companies can refer to these conventions to help increase the reliability, comparability and transparency of their environmental reports.

Questions

1. Internal ecological accounting provides information for a number of internal environmental impact added objects. What are these objects? Does internal ecological accounting information differ depending on the object chosen (e.g. site, product) or is the same information needed by all managers?

2. Are there any circumstances when top management will be interested in detailed ecological accounting information? Explain.

3. How does an EIA statement add value for internal management?

4. What is an eco-asset sheet? Does the value of eco-assets balance with those of eco-liabilities and eco-equity?

5. What is critical natural capital? Provide examples. For a company, who determines whether natural capital is a 'critical' ecological resource? Is there a difference between 'other' natural capital and artificial capital? Are they substitutes for each other?

6. Why is it that techniques for putting financial values on eco-assets are fraught with difficulty?

7. Compare environmental stocks and flows with financial stocks and flows. When tracking and recording these stocks and flows, what are the similarities and differences in processes used?

8. List the main categories of data quality. Do environmental indicators use all, some or none of these categories. Provide an example to support your view based on one environmental medium (e.g. water quality, air quality).

CONTEMPORARY ENVIRONMENTAL ACCOUNTING

9. Distinguish between the main approaches to impact assessment. Explain the three steps that lead to construction of an EIA index. Can environmental impact added ever be negative?

10. Construct an environmental profile for a company of your choice. How might the profile be of use to management?

11. The field of 'ontology' studies different views of reality. Why are different ontological viewpoints important when determining the volume of information that needs to be produced by an ecological accounting system for managers?

12. Name and explain two allocation rules and two allocation keys. Why are allocation rules and keys important to lower-level management? If you were a site manager in a chemical company, with a single incinerator for all sites located on your site and under your control, which rule and key would you favour? Give your reasons.

13. Can the environmental impacts of one EIA centre be linked to the environmental impacts of another EIA centre? Provide an example to confirm your view? Do any control or responsibility problems arise? If there are any problems, how might they be resolved?

14. Distinguish between direct and indirect environmental impacts of a division. Provide an example to illustrate the difference. Why is the difference important to a site manager?

15. 'Environment regulations require investments in end-of-pipe technology to clean up pollutants': Explain whether you agree with this statement. Does this mean that a company should not undertake an economic appraisal of whether 'end-of-pipe' investments are worthwhile? Give reasons for your view.

16. What is the main difference between core and supplemental ecological indicators? Provide an example of each. Would it be useful to have all production site managers to report to top management on a common set of ecological indicators? Explain.

17. Examine the suggestion that small and medium-sized companies do not need information from a core set of ecological indicators related to their business.

18. Net present value and net present environmental impact added have a number of similarities and differences. List and explain these. Consider the arguments for and against discounting future environmental impacts.

Chapter 12

EXTERNAL ECOLOGICAL
ACCOUNTING AND REPORTING
OF ENVIRONMENTAL IMPACTS

12.1 Stakeholders, regulations and incentives

This chapter explores the notion of reporting ecological accounting information about companies to external groups. First, the main regulatory developments encouraging, and sometimes requiring, companies to report to external parties about their environmental impacts will be examined (Sections 12.1.1–12.1.5). Given that the relationship between management and external stakeholders is characterised by information asymmetry, it will be seen that external reporting requirements can lead to the provision of low-quality information about ecological impacts (often referred to as a problem of adverse selection; see Akerlof 1970) (Section 12.1). In short, managers have information that external parties would like to be made aware of prior to making decisions about their relationship with a company. However, disclosure of certain types of information (e.g. negative corporate impacts on the environment) may not be in the best interests of managers because their security and rewards might be threatened by external parties that hold managers accountable for their actions. Managers respond by making selected, favourable disclosures. External parties then have to introduce incentives to encourage managers to tell the full story in a transparent way. This general incentive and information problem is often discussed under the heading of 'principal agent relationships' (see e.g. Eisenhardt 1989).

There is no question that ecological reporting exerts a major actual and potential influence on a variety of important stakeholders (Chynoweth 1994; Konar and Cohen 1995; Saporito 1993). Hence, environmental information has become part of marketing and public relations for many companies. However, dubious claims and an improper use of information by some companies in the past have diminished or destroyed these reputational gains and, at the same time, reduced the incentives for other companies to improve their own environmental record. To obtain gains from marketing, and from improving reputation or credibility, environmental leaders have to be clearly distinguishable from companies that concentrate on mere 'window-dressing' or 'cosmetic' accounting. Environmental information will be reliable and comparable between companies if and only if widely accepted international standards of ecological accounting are established and adhered to (Schaltegger 1997b).

Analogous to financial accounting, introduction of basic standards for ecological accounting is needed in order to secure disclosure of a minimum standard of information quality. As discussed in Section 12.1 the introduction of standards of accounting and reporting may improve the value of information for external stakeholders. Led by the Féderation des Expertes Comptables Européens (FEE; see Adams *et al.* 1999) and the Intergovernmental Working Group of Experts on International Standards of Accounting and Reporting (ISAR) of the United Nations, some professional accounting organisations have begun to take up this issue and to develop draft guidelines. These are discussed further below.

Section 12.2 will consider the basic assumptions and main qualitative characteristics of ecological accounting and compare these with the principles used in conventional financial accounting. Aspects relating to the possible consolidation of environmental impacts in ecological reporting will be examined in Section 12.3.

12.1.1 Regulators as important stakeholders

Some stakeholders care little about a company's financial position and are primarily interested in its ecological impacts. Environmental pressure groups, geographical neighbours (local communities) and environmental protection agencies (as regulators) are typical of this group of stakeholders. Irrespective of the attitude management has towards environmental protection, requests from these groups always have to be taken seriously if the groups can exert a substantial positive or negative influence on a company's operations or success. Historically, the most important stakeholders with an interest in receiving ecological statements are regulatory bodies, particularly environmental protection agencies (Ilinitch *et al.* 1998). Because they have legal enforcement powers, they can compel companies to produce and deliver the information they require. They can also make companies responsible retrospectively for environmental impacts (e.g. Superfund clean-up sites in the USA; CERCLA 1980). An agency needs information concerning environmental interventions to check how well the regulations are being met, to assess the severity of environmental problems particularly at the aggregate level and to use that information as a basis for designing environmental policies that will achieve established environmental goals.

Environmental protection agencies have typically applied 'command-and-control' policies to regulate measures of environmental protection within their geographical areas. However, in the past decade they have moved to adopt a mix of regulatory instruments in order to help ensure that goals relating to environmental interventions are met. Command-and-control instruments are now supplemented by economic instruments, codes of practice and other forms of responsive regulation based on market mechanisms and ethical persuasion (see e.g. Ayres and Braithwaite 1992; Tietenberg 1992). Braithwaite *et al.* (1987) developed an enforcement taxonomy for 96 Australian government agencies involved in regulation. Two major dimensions were found to underlie the typology—the first related to the degree of emphasis on enforcement or punishment, and the second was linked to the extent to which a command-and-control approach was emphasised rather than the co-operative development of self-regulatory practices.

Ayres and Braithwaite (1992: 21) concluded that:

> Increasingly within both the scholarly and regulatory communities there is a feeling that the regulatory agencies that do best at achieving their goals are those that strike some sort of sophisticated balance between the two models [of regulation]. The crucial question has become: When to punish; when to persuade?

Managers concerned with external ecological accounting need to ponder the comments on design of regulatory systems made by Gunningham and Grabosky (1998) if they are to appreciate the importance of information disclosure in avoiding tight command-and-control regulatory regimes. Gunningham and Grabosky outline the following five principles of regulatory design:

☐ Prefer policy mixes incorporating a broader range of instruments and institutions.

☐ Start with the least interventionist measure that works.

☐ Ascend a dynamic instrument pyramid to the extent necessary to achieve policy goals.

☐ Empower participants who are in the best position to act as surrogate regulators.

☐ Maximise opportunities for win–win outcomes.

Given these principles, they argue that

☐ Regulatory policy mixes should consist of multiple complementary instruments tailored to specific policy goals (e.g. reductions in 'greenhouse gas' emissions).

☐ Highly interventionist prescriptive instruments tend to be less efficient, less effective and less politically acceptable than low interventionist (self-regulatory) solutions.

☐ In terms of efficiency, highly coercive strategies tend to involve substantial administrative and enforcement costs, whereas highly prescriptive strategies are associated with reduced flexibility and hence greater compliance costs.

In terms of efficiency, less coercive and less prescriptive policies are favoured (Blamey and Sutton 1999).

Usually, technical standards are defined for production technologies in order to regulate the discharge of pollutants. In this context, depending on particular national laws, companies have to demonstrate that they comply with established standards. This is also the case when applying for subsidies to introduce relatively environmentally benign technologies (e.g. the generation of electricity by wind farms).

However, market-based regulations such as environmental taxes or emissions trading require companies to monitor, record and report their releases. Some kind of ecological accounting is necessary to ensure communication (education) between the regulatory agency and the company. In practice, the necessary information is often collected, prepared and communicated several times over (in parallel) by various company employees. Systematic corporate ecological accounting can, therefore, decrease the costs of measurement, data keeping, reporting and co-ordination as well as promote a grounding in corporate self-regulation.

The difference between ecological accounting and conventional business accounting systems resides mainly in the measurement and nature of the subject matter: ecological accounting systems measure environmental impacts in physical rather than financial units. Corporate effects on ecological assets (such as forests and lakes) that are owned, controlled or influenced are rarely reported. The main focus is on information about the total level of emissions and on increases and decreases in emissions.

As outlined in Chapter 2 Section 2, the users of specially designed ecological reports are often attentive readers of externally published ecological statements. One of the main demands made by stakeholders interested in ecological outcomes is for environmental impact information to be disclosed. However, their specific and detailed information requirements cannot be met through general public reports, in part because of the 'commercial in-confidence' nature of activities reported.

As suggested above, through economic instruments environmental regulations can be used to change prices or to focus directly on the quantity of pollutants discharged in order to help achieve desirable outcomes. This section, however, analyses other regulatory ecological accounting systems that are designed to classify, calculate, analyse and report information about discharges of pollutants to environmental protection agencies.

No attempt is made to examine the accounting policies and rules of different national environmental protection agencies because of the differences that exist between them. Instead, focus is placed on the most prominent regulations that have imposed specific regulatory ecological accounting systems on companies, including:

☐ The Toxic Release Inventory (TRI) and similar regulations in member countries of the Organisation for Economic Co-operation and Development (OECD) countries creating pollution release and transfer registers (PRTRs), in accordance with Chapter 19 of Agenda 21, which calls on governments to implement and improve databases about chemicals, including inventories of emissions (Section 12.1.2; see also Stockwell *et al.* 1993)

☐ The US 33/50 programme (Section 12.1.3)

☐ The US emissions trading programmes (Section 12.1.4)

☐ Other regulatory incentives (Section 12.1.5)

12.1.2 The US Toxic Release Inventory

The US Toxic Release Inventory (TRI) is an excellent example of a national regulatory ecological accounting system (Khanna *et al.* 1998). The US Congress created the TRI in 1986 as part of the Emergency Planning and Community Right-to-Know Act (EPCRA). TRI data were first published in 1988; as a rule, the information disclosed is a year old by the time it is actually reported. At an aggregate level, TRI data define a macroeconomic ecological account of toxic releases. Section 313 of EPCRA, called the 'Toxic Release Inventory', is a requirement for specified industries to report releases of over 650 chemicals and chemical categories (termed 'Section 313 chemicals') to air, land (landfills and surface piles) and water (including underground injection wells) as well as the locations and quantities of chemicals stored on-site, and off-site transfers of waste for treatment or disposal at a separate facility (*CMR* 1994a, 1994b). TRI establishes an ecological accounting relationship for this list of substances (*CMR* 1994b; Arora and Cason 1995).

In 1990, US Congress also began to force plants to start recording the recycling of chemicals and pollution prevention activities (Begley 1994; Hess 1994). In 1994, the US Environmental Protection Agency (EPA) received around 80,000 submissions for each TRI-listed chemical from 23,000 facilities (*Nation's Business* 1994: Aif., 1994c). Every company has publicly to disclose the number and quantity of the releases for each site. This information is publicly accessible to all interested stakeholders and is also used by eco-rating organisations. Organisations that use TRI data include the Investor Responsibility Research Centre (IRRC) and the Council on Economic Priorities (CEP; see e.g. Ilinitch and Schaltegger 1995).

Nearly three-quarters of the TRI pollution releases came from public joint-stock companies. Statistically, it is highly significant that shareholders of companies with large amounts of toxic releases experienced abnormally negative returns in response to the first release of the TRI information (Hamilton 1995: 98f.). This suggests that published TRI information may influence investors and that environmental issues may profoundly influence the financial performance of companies.

So far, interpretation of TRI data is difficult as the absolute numbers do not say anything about the corporate eco-efficiency because sales revenue, economic returns and value added of the reporting companies are not mentioned. Thus, in TRI reports larger companies almost inevitably have higher emissions than do smaller companies. However, larger companies are not necessarily more environmentally harmful just because of their size. This is why more recent reports based on TRI data often publish ratios such as TRI releases per US$1,000 of sales revenue (see e.g. Arora and Cason 1995). However, these economic–ecological figures do not consider the spatial and time aspects of such releases. However, time-series and spatial information are available on-line to users of TRI data (see also Hess 1994: 8f.). For example, Magnesium Corporation of America, in Utah, is listed as the company with the highest total environmental releases in the USA. Time-series data are provided in Table 12.1.

Clearly, the total volume of reported releases has declined over the ten-year period, but there are limitations in the TRI data which affect interpretation. Although the TRI is the most comprehensive national source of information about toxic chemical releases in the USA, it has critical limitations:

- The TRI does not cover all toxic chemicals that have the potential to affect human health or the environment adversely.

- The TRI does not require reporting from many major sources of pollution releases, only a limited number of chemicals are covered.

Year	Air releases	Water releases	Land releases	Under-ground injection	Total environmental releases	Total off-site transfer	Total production-related waste
1988	109,748,910	0	1,180	0	109,750,090	0	n/a
1989	119,060,170	0	200	0	119,060,370	55	n/a
1990	95,049,131	0	220	0	95,049,351	260	n/a
1991	64,936,955	0	250	0	64,937,205	1,390	112,943,105
1992	76,908,063	0	0	0	76,908,063	250	117,492,861
1993	73,300,250	0	0	0	73,300,250	2,800,000	126,651,000
1994	55,776,250	0	0	0	55,776,250	2,400,000	105,530,700
1995	64,339,080	0	0	0	64,339,080	0	118,053,700
1996	65,311,364	0	0	0	65,311,364	0	297,126,000
1997	62,335,864	0	0	0	62,335,864	0	284,600,300

n/a: Data are not available because total production-related waste was not reported until 1991.

Table 12.1 **Toxic releases (as listed in the Toxic Release Inventory [TRI]) in the state of Utah by the Magnesium Corporation of America: environmental releases, transfers and production-related waste (in pounds weight)**

Source: EPA 1999

☐ The TRI does not require companies to report the quantities of toxic chemicals used or the amounts that remain in products.

☐ The TRI does not provide information about the exposures people may experience as a consequence of chemical use, or their impact.

☐ As companies are responsible for the accuracy of TRI data they submit to US EPA, and as little or no enforcement has taken place to date challenging inaccurate reporting by facilities, the extent of material errors in (and the reliability of) reported data is unknown.

☐ Chemical releases and waste generation are usually estimated not measured. EPCRA does not require any specific monitoring of emissions, and the estimation of releases (with use of emissions factors developed for various production processes or by means of process modelling) is generally cheaper than measuring releases.

☐ Because the TRI does not require reporting on the quantities of toxic chemicals used there is no way for the public to know whether the TRI release and off-site transfer data reported are reliable. If chemical use data were reported, it would be possible, with use of ecological accounting, to conduct a mass-balance evaluation of a plant. Chemical input to a process would be compared with chemical output (including amounts of chemicals consumed in a process, incorporated into a product, released to the environment or transferred off-site).

If facility data did not balance, that would indicate the reported releases or waste generation were inaccurate (see Epstein *et al.* 1995).

Nevertheless, the TRI system is a substantial step towards external ecological accounting and reporting of environmental interventions. It certainly indicates a good performance record as far as reduction of emissions is concerned. In 1993 regulated industries in the USA released a total of 2.81 billion pounds of emissions into the environment, compared with 3.21 billion pounds in 1992 (Hanson 1995: 4f.). By 1997 this had diminished to a total of 2.11 billion pounds of emissions. Overall industrial releases also decreased between 1991 and 1992 by a full 6.5%. By 1997 total emissions were 63% lower than they were in 1988 when the government began to publish TRI data (Arora and Cason 1995; Hess 1994, see also www.scorecard.org).

With the addition of 286 further chemicals to the list of 320 substances for which US manufacturers and users have to file annual TRI reports, the reported amount released did, of course, increase. A rule that the US EPA issued in the summer of 1995 was intended to create a consolidated environmental database programme to reduce the reporting costs of the industry (*Environment Today* 1994; Hess 1995: 24). In fact, costs of reporting are not easy to interpret. In 1995 the Chemical Manufacturers' Association alleged that US EPA's idea for requiring chemical use reports could potentially double their TRI reporting burden, with a large chemical manufacturer predicting a cost of US$1.5 million in the first year and US$800,000 each year thereafter (EPA 1995d: 7). However, other chemical companies reported expected costs of US$64,000 initially and US$24,000 per annum afterwards, for a less complex chemical facility. This range is large and can make or break a proposal from a commercial business perspective. Although the issue is sensitive for business, in practice the pattern seems to be an initial over-inflated estimation of average cost, followed by lower actual reporting costs. In addition, it is quite possible that offsetting financial benefits will accrue to the reporting company as the information can be used internally to help reduce operating costs (e.g. to pinpoint key areas requiring cleaner production) and to promote a philosophy of eco-efficiency.

In European countries and Canada pollution registers aim to fulfil tasks similar to that of the TRI in the USA (*Chemical Engineering* 1993; Hosbach *et al.* 1995). They are different from specific project-based systems in place in Norway, France, north-west Switzerland and Costa Rica (e.g. Alfsen *et al.* 1987; BAK 1992–1999; Repetto 1992). Emission inventories (EIs) were established in the Netherlands in 1990, followed by a Chemical Release Inventory (CRI) in the United Kingdom in 1991 (*CW* 1994). The Canadian National Pollutant Release Inventory (NPRI) was introduced in 1993, whereas in the European Union (EU) the Polluting Emissions Register (PER) has been under discussion since 1995. Denmark has introduced probably the most advanced regulation in Europe requiring ecological accounting and reporting. At the other end of the spectrum, countries with smaller total emissions such as Australia are still in the process of introducing a national pollutant inventory. There has been sufficient experience with pollutant release inventories in the 1990s to appreciate and try to rectify major problems. For example, the 1991 UK CRI received criticism from the non-governmental organisation (NGO) Friends of the Earth (Taylor 1995) and a call for the following improvements:

☐ Reporting should be against a standard list of chemicals.

☐ The scope of the inventory should be increased to include sectors and facilities that are not controlled by integrated pollution control (e.g. mining operations, sewage treatment, gas drilling and distribution).

☐ Plans should be drawn up for chemical release reduction programmes with stated targets.

☐ Geographical identification should be provided of site locations.

☐ The emitting company and its parent company should be identified.

☐ There should be materials accounting, including output in products.

☐ Reporting and validation procedures should be improved.

New environmental protection agencies can learn from earlier mistakes and attempt to benchmark their inventories against best-practice reporting systems. In the UK, the main compiler of registers of emissions, effluents and wastes is the Environment Agency, established under the Environment Act 1995. Under the previous name of Her Majesty's Inspectorate of Pollution the UK's first CRI was published in 1994. In 1999, following the introduction of an Environment Agency, the CRI was renamed the Pollution Inventory (PI) and a wider range of pollutants and industries were included. The 1998 inventory covered the emissions of 150 chemicals from over 2,000 of the largest industrial processes in England and Wales. Emissions are reported by type, industrial sector and local authority. Improvement programmes have led to significant overall reductions in emissions from sites which the Agency regulated between 1990 (figures based on best available estimates) and 1998. There was:

☐ A 59% reduction in lead emissions (a reduction from 475 tons to 194 tons)

☐ A 48% reduction in particulates (123,000 tons to 64,000 tons)

☐ A 58% reduction in sulphur dioxide, which contributes to acid rain (2,870,000 tons to 1,216,000 tons)

☐ A 61% reduction in benzene (4,600 tonnes to 1,800 tons)

☐ A 66% reduction in PM10s, which are small particulates with diameters of less than 10 micrometres (1 micrometre [1 μm] = 1 millionth of a metre [10^{-6} m]) (100,000 tonnes to 34,000 tons)

Over the next few years the PI is being expanded to become a comprehensive inventory of pollutants in local authorities by including:

☐ Information on emissions from other processes regulated by the Agency such as landfill sites and sewage treatment works

☐ Detailed information on annual emission limits and other controls set by the Agency for each pollutant and on whether they have been exceeded

☐ Details on whether companies have been prosecuted, or subject to any other enforcement action, by the Environment Agency

☐ More information on the health impacts of individual pollutants (Hutchings 1999)

The PI will be used by the UK government and the Agency to meet national and international environmental reporting commitments. The Commission of the European Communities is finalising details of the EU-wide PER as required under the EU Integrated Pollution Prevention and Control (IPPC) Directive, and the UK Environment Agency suggests that the Commission might use the PI as a model for this work.

The proposed PER of the EU is planned to be based on an approach similar to that of the UK PI and US TRI. As with the TRI, no reporting will be necessary below minimum emission levels. The main reason to consider the establishment of PER is to improve the transparency and availability of information for citizens (Hosbach *et al.* 1995). The EU's planned inventory of polluting emissions will name major polluters (as is the case in the UK) but will cover only a very limited number of substances emitted. The EU executive intends to publish the first PER in 2001 on the basis of emissions data to be collected in 2000 (ÖB 1995; Wicks 1998). The register is being set up as a result of the EU's 1996 directive on IPPC, which requires the Commission to publish an 'inventory of the principal emissions and sources responsible' every three years on the basis of data supplied by member states. Of the 15 EU member countries, only France, the UK, the Netherlands, Germany, Austria and Finland have emissions inventories.

The OECD is reworking its guidelines for national PRTRs based on worldwide experience with national pollutant registers (OECD 1995; OECD 1996a). In 1998 the OECD agreed to review its PRTR *Guidance Manual* for governments and identify areas where supplemental policy and technical guidance might be needed to better share methodologies for estimating pollutant releases, verifying the data, standardising reports and comparing PRTR data across borders, as well as using PRTRs to indicate cleaner technology and technology transfer opportunities (OECD 1999).

12.1.3 The US 33/50 programme

During the administrations of presidents Reagan and Bush, US EPA was faced with restrictions on its financial and administrative resources. As a consequence, EPA had to find new approaches to environmental regulation. This is when the so-called '33/50 programme' was introduced. With the 33/50 programme, companies that voluntarily signed a legally binding agreement to cut emissions of the 17 most widely used, most toxic chemicals in the USA by 33% from 1988 to 1992, and then by 50% in 1995, were marked by the US EPA as environmentally responsible. These 17 substances are also covered by the TRI (Hess 1994). Industry went beyond the interim goal, as TRI releases and transfers of these chemicals decreased by 46% by 1992 (Arora and Cason 1995).

The 33/50 programme proved to be very successful as the relationship between regulators and company management changed from a command-and-control policy toward a partnership between two co-operating parties each with a voluntary moral obligation to perform. It has now established the Partners for the Environment programme which includes efforts such as the 33/50 programme, WasteWi$e, Climate Wise, Green Lights, Energy Star, Water Alliances for Voluntary Efficiency, the Pesticide Environmental Stewardship programme, Indoor Air, Indoor Radon, Design for the Environment, the Environmental Leadership programme, CSI and Project XL. Partners are achieving measurable environmental results often more quickly and with lower costs than would have been the case with command-and-control regulatory approaches. The US EPA views these partnership efforts as key to the future success of environmental protection.

As a result of these new relationships, ecological accounting and reporting systems are needed. These regulatory ecological accounting systems need to be characterised by clear, mutually accepted accounting rules, so that a measurement of performance of each programme becomes possible. The US EPA instigated its Environmental Accounting Project in 1992 and, at a Stakeholder's Action Agenda meeting the following year, promotion of a number of economic incentives was suggested, including introduction of:

☐ Voluntary partnership programmes (e.g. Green Lights, 33/50, WasteWi$e, Design for the Environment)

☐ Standardised environmental reporting of, for example, environmental cost information

☐ 'Safe harbours' for disclosure of environmentally liability estimates

☐ Loans, investment tax credits and depreciation policies that could enhance the returns from environmental projects (Heigl 1989)

☐ Awards or recognition for performance meeting or exceeding regulations

☐ Pollution prevention planning regulations with environmental accounting components

☐ Market-based environmental solutions such as pollution credits and emissions trading that require sound environmental cost information

Because of its growing significance, the last of these, emissions trading, is examined briefly in the next section.

In the event, US EPA did not pursue any of these activities and its Environmental Accounting Project has focused on encouraging and motivating business to understand the full spectrum of their environmental costs and to integrate these costs into decision-making.

12.1.4 Emissions trading

One of the most sophisticated regulations to reduce corporate environmental impacts is emissions trading (see e.g. Dobes 1998; Hahn 1984; OECD 1994a; Tietenberg 1992; United Nations 1997). The basic idea behind emissions trading is that companies may release emissions only to the extent that they own emissions certificates granting them the right to pollute. The emissions certificates are allocated to parties at the beginning of any period and can be traded. The total level of environmental interventions is limited because only a defined number of tradable emissions allowances are available.

The rationale behind emissions trading is that companies with high emissions of pollutants will try to reduce their emissions to avoid buying additional allowances. They will also sell any surplus emissions allowances to those companies that have not been able to reduce their emissions to acceptable levels and who need to buy extra allowances to remain in business. These companies tend to have high marginal abatement and/or prevention costs and it is cheaper for them to buy emissions certificates than to invest in pollution prevention.

Different concepts and terms have been used in connection with emissions trading, such as 'bubbles', 'offsets', 'netting' and 'banking' (see e.g. API 1990; Beder 1996; Frey *et al.* 1993; Hahn 1984; Hahn and Stavins 1991; Tietenberg 1980, 1989, 1992).

'Emission bubbles' are defined geographical areas within which a specified total volume of discharges must not be exceeded. Regulators do not determine which companies have to reduce emissions. They leave it to individual companies to reduce emissions where it is most cost-efficient. Those that do not reduce emissions have to pay the market price for emissions allowances; those that do reduce emissions get a cost advantage over other companies because they can sell their emission allowances at market price (see e.g. Byrd and Zwirlein 1994). Implicit in this concept is the idea that the regulator seeks continual improvement from companies and, over time, reduces the total level of emissions permitted thereby increasing the market demand and price of allowances. Therefore, the bubble concept provides some flexibility in satisfying regulatory standards that apply to a defined level of emissions in a specific region.

'Offsets' are employed if a company wants to expand its production or to relocate in an area where regulatory standards are not met. In this case, a company has to adhere to the strictest standards and compensate for its new emissions by buying tradable permits from other sources in this area (i.e. in effect by paying others to reduce their emissions). Offsets have also assumed importance under the Kyoto Protocol (United Nations 1997) whereby countries are permitted to encourage the development of carbon sinks (e.g. planting trees to sequester, or trap, carbon) as an offset to emissions of carbon dioxide (CO_2) from other sources. It is expected that companies will be encouraged to develop such offsets (e.g. planting trees in overseas countries; or establishing wind farms to offset factory pollution) when national and international carbon credit emissions trading schemes are formally introduced.

Although it is likely to be a number of years (2008–12 is, at present, the first commitment period for governments to achieve set targets for the reduction of 'greenhouse gas' emissions) before a formalised broad-based emissions trading market is established, bilateral trades are already occurring (e.g. in the case of BP Amoco; see ENDS 1999b). The Kyoto Protocol has been designed to accommodate a cap and trade emissions trading system. Such a system sets a quantity target and allows the market to determine the price or marginal cost of abatement. The aim is to achieve a particular environmental outcome, not a price outcome as, for example, a carbon tax would try to achieve. Based on US experience, characteristics of these trading schemes necessary for success include:

☐ A fixed emissions cap as the backbone, with a performance standard to allow flexibility in compliance alternatives

☐ Full banking and trading of allowances to allow firms significant flexibility in compliance investment and decision-making

☐ A high-quality monitoring system to allow effective monitoring of compliance as well as to facilitate banking and trading

☐ A publicly open allowance-tracking system to help create a transparent and self-enforcing compliance system

☐ Automatic high penalties for non-compliance, to help achieve a high compliance rate with low transaction costs

Ecological accounting performs a key monitoring and tracking function for these schemes. Studies by the US Government Accounting Office have concluded that the allowance trading approach has achieved strict environmental goals at dramatically lower costs than have traditional forms of regulation. These benefits appear to derive primarily from the flexibility and innovation caused by the emissions cap approach itself, though banking and trading have added to cost reductions. For example, under the Acid Rain programme, contained in Title IV of the Clean Air Act Amendments of 1990, the combination of high-quality monitoring, a public allowance-tracking system and high penalties resulted in 100% compliance without the need for enforcement action in 1995 or 1996 (ELI 1997).

'Netting' is probably the most common form of tradable permit. Here, the 'trade' takes place within a facility, and existing sources can be exempted from new source requirements (operating allowances and permits to enlarge production) as long as no significant increases occur within the facility as a whole.

Emission banking enables companies to 'save' the reduced emissions for future use (OECD 1994a: 88). Emissions trading—even when the scope is company internal (see e.g. www.bpamoco.com)—places a price on environmental interventions. Thus, every kilogram of emissions released directly increases costs, whereas reductions of emissions are potential sales (i.e. income opportunities). Thus, emissions trading internalises environmental interventions into conventional corporate accounting even though the main goal of regulators is a reduction of environmental interventions.

Regulators depend on being correctly informed about company releases in order to check whether the values of certificates match actual releases. To reiterate, comprehensive emissions trading requires a precise monitoring system (Stevenson 1992) and an ecological accounting system with clear rules and standards to ensure consistent and correct reporting of emissions of regulated substances.

To complement these, in order to detect the most cost-efficient opportunities for prevention, managers need an internal ecological accounting system that informs them about where (environmental impact added [EIA] centres) and what discharges (EIA drivers) are caused by which cost objects (a particular process or site). In addition, managers need to be informed about marginal prevention and abatement costs in order to decide whether to buy or to sell pollution rights (Staehelin-Witt and Spillmann 1992; Tietenberg 1992).

Therefore, internal ecological accounting needs to be co-ordinated with management accounting. Given the attraction to regulators of using emissions trading mechanisms, because they are self-enforcing for companies, through the use of economic incentives but backed up by the threat of command and control (e.g. a carbon tax) if unsuccessful (Ayres and Braithwaite 1992), companies need to consider implementation of the elements seen by regulators as necessary for success, including ecological accounting.

Tradable permits have been introduced in several countries, notably the USA, Canada, Australia, Germany and Switzerland. Environmental interventions controlled through such programmes are mainly air emissions with the aim of reducing problems such as photochemical smog, the depletion of the ozone layer, river salinity and acid rain (NSW EPA 1995; OECD 1994a: 87). Empirical studies show that emissions trading can help to achieve environmental goals in a more cost-efficient way (e.g. Burtraw and Mansur 1999; CEC 1999; for a company internal example, see www.bpamoco.com).

When introducing emissions trading, companies have to show emissions allowances in their conventional accounts (see Section 7.6) and build up an efficient ecological accounting system to take full economic advantage of the new freedoms provided by this approach to regulation. In Europe, emissions trading is applied in some cases in Germany and the Netherlands. It was applied in the two cantons of Basel, Switzerland; however, the system in Basel is no longer operative as the federal government reduced the gap between the federal standards and the stricter regional standards and thus reduced the trading range to zero. In Basel, permits to pollute could only be sold by a company if it was able to prove that it was more than 20% below regional emissions standards (see e.g. Staehelin-Witt and Spillmann 1992). Even with this system of tradable emissions allowances, ecological accounting is needed to measure, report and prove that emissions have actually been reduced (Schaltegger and Thomas 1996).

12.1.5 Other regulations and standards requiring external ecological accounting

Chapter 40 of Agenda 21 (United Nations 1992e) calls for the development of indicators for sustainable development. In particular, it requests countries at the national level and international governmental organisations and NGOs to develop and identify such indicators (paragraph 40.6). Taking up this challenge, the United Nations Commission on Sustainable Development (UNCSD) has, over the past few years, derived a set of 134 sustainability indicators for countries to adopt in pilot projects, which are to be completed by 2000.

Indicators are classified within a driving-force–state–response (DSR) framework:

☐ Driving-force indicators focus on human activities, processes and patterns that have an impact on sustainable development.

☐ State indicators measure the 'state' of sustainable development.

☐ Response indicators are concerned with policy options and other responses to changes in the state of sustainable development.

Specific environmental indicators have been developed in accordance with environmental issues identified in Agenda 21. Examples of indicators for environmentally sound management of hazardous wastes are shown in Table 12.2.

The use of the DSR framework does not mean that it is possible at this stage to identify any causal relationships among driving-force, state and response indicators. Instead it is seen as a way of categorising indicators to fit the needs of producers and users. The recording of indicators and their changes over time in ecological accounting systems is critical if patterns and relationships are to be determined from time-series data in order to reduce environmental interventions. To demonstrate success, the United Nations Environmental Programme (UNEP) records success stories of communities, countries, industries and companies that implement these indicators as voluntary initiatives (see Box 12.1).

The UNCSD indicators are based on the following principles. They are:

☐ Primarily national in scale or scope (countries may also wish to use indicators at State and provincial levels)

☐ Relevant to the main objective of assessing progress towards sustainable development

☐ Understandable, that is, they are clear, simple and unambiguous

☐ Realisable within the capacities of national governments, given their logistical, time, technical and other constraints

Table 12.2 **Examples of indicators for environmentally sound management of:**
(a) solid wastes and sewage-related issues; (b) hazardous wastes

Source: UNCSD 1992

Type of indicator	Description
(a)	
▶ Driving-force	▶ Rate of generation of industrial and municipal solid waste
▶ State	▶ Amount of household waste disposed per capita
▶ Response	▶ Expenditure on waste management
	▶ Degree of waste recycling and re-use
	▶ Degree of municipal waste disposal
(b)	
▶ Driving-force	▶ Rate of generation of hazardous wastes
	▶ Amounts of imports and exports of hazardous wastes
▶ State	▶ Area of land contaminated by hazardous wastes
▶ Response	▶ Expenditure on treatment of hazardous waste

DESCRIPTION

Australians are high per capita generators of waste and the Australian government at all levels is committed to halving waste between 1990 and 2000. The National Kerbside Taskforce project is a partnership among Commonwealth, State and local governments and major industry sectors to establish viable, voluntary plans and programmes to reduce post-consumer waste significantly, as one central part of broader national waste-reduction strategies.

RESULTS

Significant success has been achieved in reducing waste levels: when kerbside recovery was still organised on a State-by-State basis, recovery levels were rather low (3%–6% of volume). Through the partnership initiative, all major cities now have comprehensive kerbside recycling systems. The participation rate is high and the recovery rate has increased to as much as 15%–25%.

Industries produce voluntary waste-reduction targets; participation rates average about 60%–70%. Owing to long-term buy-back contracts, prices of recovered materials stabilised, increasing the sustainability.

LESSONS LEARNED

The programme has expanded greatly without the need for changes in legislation or other regulatory measures.

Box 12.1 **Kerbside waste recycling in Australia**

Source: 'Success Story: The Australian National Kerbside Taskforce', www.un.org/esa/sustdev/success/ccpp1.htm

☐ Conceptually well-founded

☐ Limited in number, remaining open-ended and adaptable to future developments

☐ Broad in coverage of Agenda 21 and all aspects of sustainable development

☐ Representative of an international consensus, to the extent possible

☐ Dependent on data that are readily available or available at a reasonable cost–benefit ratio, that are adequately documented, that are of known quality and that are updated at regular intervals

Other principles also have a bearing on the way regulators approach initiatives with industry and businesses. The Bellagio principles (IISD 1996) are one such set of principles (Box 12.2). These principles serve as guidelines for the whole of the assessment process including the choice and design of indicators, their interpretation and communication of the result. They should be applied as a complete set. They are intended for use in starting and improving assessment activities of community groups, NGOs, corporations, national governments and international institutions.

Of particular importance is attention given to the provision of institutional capacity for data collection, maintenance and documentation through ecological and environmental accounting, but only as support for a voluntary regulatory initiative encouraged by international, rather than national, organisations.

Another environmental regulation that establishes a regulated ecological accounting relationship is the EU Eco-management and Audit Scheme (EMAS). In fact, EMAS is not an accounting standard but a standard for an environmental management system (see Part

GUIDING VISION AND GOALS

Assessment of progress toward sustainable development should:

☐ Be guided by a clear vision of sustainable development and goals that define that vision

HOLISTIC PERSPECTIVE

Assessment of progress toward sustainable development should:

☐ Include a review of the whole system as well as of its parts

☐ Consider the wellbeing of social, ecological and economic subsystems: it should consider their state as well as the direction and rate of change of that state and it should consider their component parts and the interaction between those parts

☐ Consider positive and negative consequences of human activity in a way that reflects the costs and benefits for human and ecological systems, in monetary and non-monetary terms

ESSENTIAL ELEMENTS

Assessment of progress toward sustainable development should:

☐ Consider equity and disparity within the current population and between present and future generations, dealing with such concerns as resource use, over-consumption and poverty, human rights and access to services, as appropriate

☐ Consider the ecological conditions on which life depends

☐ Consider economic development and other, non-market, activities that contribute to human and/or social wellbeing

ADEQUATE SCOPE

Assessment of progress toward sustainable development should:

☐ Adopt a time-horizon long enough to capture both human and ecosystem time-scales thus responding to needs of future generations as well as those issues current to short-term decision-making

☐ Define the space of study large enough to include not only local but also long-distance impacts on people and ecosystems

☐ Build on historic and current conditions to anticipate future conditions: where we want to go, where we could go

PRACTICAL FOCUS

Assessment of progress toward sustainable development should be based on:

☐ An explicit set of categories or an organising framework that links vision and goals to indicators and assessment criteria

☐ A limited number of key issues for analysis

☐ A limited number of indicators or indicator combinations to provide a clearer signal of progress

☐ A standardising measurement wherever possible to permit comparison

☐ A comparison of indicator values to targets, reference values, ranges, thresholds or direction of trends, as appropriate

Box 12.2   **The Bellagio principles of sustainable development indicators** *(continued opposite)*

Source: IISD 1996

OPENNESS

Assessment of progress toward sustainable development should:

☐ Make the methods and data that are used accessible to all

☐ Make explicit all judgements, assumptions and uncertainties in data and interpretations

EFFECTIVE COMMUNICATION

Assessment of progress toward sustainable development should:

☐ Be designed to address the needs of the audience and set of users

☐ Draw on indicators and other tools that are stimulating and serve to engage decision-makers

☐ Aim, from the outset, for simplicity in structure and use of clear and plain language

BROAD PARTICIPATION

Assessment of progress toward sustainable development should:

☐ Obtain broad representation of key grass-roots, professional, technical and social groups—including youth, women and indigenous people—to ensure recognition of diverse and changing values

☐ Ensure the participation of decision-makers to secure a firm link to adopted policies and resulting action

ONGOING ASSESSMENT

Assessment of progress toward sustainable development should:

☐ Develop a capacity for repeated measurement to determine trends

☐ Be iterative, adaptive and responsive to change and uncertainty because systems are complex and change frequently

☐ Adjust goals, frameworks and indicators as new insights are gained

☐ Promote development of collective learning and feedback to decision-making

INSTITUTIONAL CAPACITY

Continuity of assessing progress toward sustainable development should be assured by:

☐ Clearly assigning responsibility and providing ongoing support in the decision-making process

☐ Providing institutional capacity for data collection, maintenance and documentation

☐ Supporting development of local assessment capacity

Box 12.2 *(continued)*

4 of this book). Nevertheless, the EMAS regulation substantially supports the emergence of ecological accounting as it also requires ecological accounting and public reporting of site-specific environmental interventions of companies that voluntarily join the system (COM 1993; Schaltegger and Sturm 1995). In 1999, EMAS was extended from being a voluntary initiative for manufacturing to cover financial institutions, the public sector and agriculture.

Contrary to the ecological accounting relations defined by TRI 33/50 and emissions trading programmes, EMAS does not clarify how many and which environmental interventions have to be accounted for. However, the accuracy of reported data has to be verified by an independent, certified verifier. The verifier also checks the reliability of the data and information in the environmental statement that is used to communicate information about environmental performance to stakeholders and the public.

Other extensions to EMAS that occurred in 1999 are its added concern to involve small and medium-sized enterprises, at the same time ensuring compliance with the requirements of EMAS by increased verification frequency and strengthened supervision of the work performed by verifiers. EMAS therefore provides new opportunities for the accountancy and verification professions in relation to both consultancy and compliance (CEC 1998; Hibbit 1994: 97f.).

As will be discussed in Part 4, private standardisation organisations (i.e. the British Standards Institution [BSI] and the International Organization for Standardization [ISO]) have also defined similar standards of environmental management systems (British Standard [BS] 7750, ISO 14001 [ISO 1994a]) which require some kind of ecological accounting system. Indeed, EMAS has been amended to allow integration with ISO 14001 as a base building block for the eventual full implementation of EMAS.

The next section will examine the contemporary effects of these regulations, calling for external reporting of environmental impacts.

12.2 Effects of current regulations that require the reporting of environmental impacts

12.2.1 Information costs and stakeholder involvement

Based on the general considerations outlined in Section 10.2 (see also Fig. 10.1, page 239) and the model presented there, the effects of regulations that require the reporting of environmental impacts on corporate costs and on data and information quality are discussed below (Schaltegger 1997b).

The rationale behind regulations such as the US TRI, the European EMAS and the Dutch and Danish regulations on 'green accounting' and reporting is the expectation that stakeholders will be better informed about environmental impacts given lower costs of information compilation and analysis (*International Environment Reporter* 1995; *Business and the Environment* 1995b; Bebbington and Rikhardsson 1999; *IER* 1995). This will spur the involvement of stakeholders such as environmental pressure groups, media and neighbours (see e.g. COM 1992, 1993). Furthermore, this would allow financially oriented groups such as banks, insurance companies and investors to obtain a better assessment of any environmentally induced financial credit risks related to their insurance contracts and investments. As a result of stimulating stakeholder involvement, ecological accounting information could become an external motivator for management to increase its efforts toward corporate environmental protection.

These expected links are supported by some empirical evidence, as seen below. Environmental pressure groups are not the only groups interested in corporate environmental performance—investors, banks, insurance companies and customers have increasingly started to be concerned (Müller *et al.* 1994; Porter and van der Linde 1995: 127; Schmidheiny and Zorraquín 1996). Clearly, the reporting of environmental impacts has encouraged and facilitated the involvement of stakeholders.

Although it is not feasible to measure information costs for each group of company stakeholders, there is no doubt that regulations encouraging monitoring and reporting of ecological information have reduced the costs of information collection and compilation for the recipients of environmental data (*Business and the Environment* 1995a; Hamilton 1995).

The fact that shareholders of companies that release large amounts of toxic substances experienced high negative returns in response to the first publication of TRI information (Hamilton 1995: 98f.) shows that information on environmental impacts has a bearing on the financial performance of shareholders' investments and influences shareholder evaluations.

The reason why financial markets react becomes clear once the effects on management of improved information and disclosures of environmental information are considered. Public reporting forces companies to track their environmental impacts. This, in turn, provides management with information about contingent liabilities. Management is then encouraged to identify a larger set of options for pollution prevention (*Business and the Environment* 1995a: 6). Porter and van der Linde (1995: 132) support this line of argument. They hold the view that managers often have incomplete information and limited time and attention at their disposal. Not all profitable opportunities for environmentally benign products and processes are known. As a result, incentives to report environmental performance encourage the compilation of information about pollution prevention opportunities and thus reduce the personal costs of information to managers (although not necessarily to the company).

For EMAS, the Danish regulation on green accounting and for other recent forays into ecological accounting and reporting similar outcomes can be expected to those associated with publication of the US TRI—lower cost and greater participation. However, because these regulations have existed for only a short time, any overall assessment of their effect on stakeholder involvement remains problematic. Nevertheless, it remains an open question as to whether reduced information costs (freedom of information) for stakeholders and increased stakeholder awareness have actually resulted in greater intolerance and penalisation of environmental laggards, except for a number of high-profile large companies.

12.2.2 Information quality

Whether the quality of information disclosed by companies is high or low has to be assessed by its readers. Some general criteria can be used for assessing the quality of information revealed in ecological statements. First, information is of no use if is not understood by the recipients. Second, the information needs to address relevant environmental problems of interest to users of ecological statements (e.g. environmental liabilities incurred, environmental projects undertaken by a company). However, even understandable and relevant information may be of only limited value if it is unreliable. For the information to be regarded as reliable, the recording methods must be known and verifiable, the presentation must be free from bias and uncertainties must be taken into account and disclosed. In addition, and of great importance, the value of information is influenced by its comparability both over time (consistency) and between companies (see White and Zinkl 1999: 124).

Most ecological reporting is characterised by information asymmetry between the providers (the accountors) and the recipients (the accountees) of ecological statements (Ijiri 1983; Schaltegger 1997b). In general, employees and supervisors have first-hand information about actual environmental impacts of a given production process and are better informed than are management or external stakeholders. In most cases, recipients of information know little about specific processes and are unable to judge the quality of information provided. In addition, users of ecological statements are uncertain about the quality of information provided (i.e. in comparison with other companies). This is reinforced if many different kinds of information (e.g. emissions of individual pollutants, aggregated figures and product-specific figures) are disclosed in ecological reports.

Without countervailing institutions, information asymmetry may lead to adverse selection within the information-recording process. The result—a 'market for lemons' (Akerlof 1970) in which demand from users who are unable to distinguish good-quality information from poor-quality information—will, by default, encourage sellers of poor-quality information to flood the market and the sellers of good-quality information to exit. Countervailing institutions help reverse this situation, improve the quality of disclosures and increase transparency and thereby improve corporate accountability.

It may be assumed that EMAS, TRI and other ecological reporting initiatives will have beneficial effects spurring external stakeholders to become involved and promoting the uptake of internal 'ecologisation' processes in corporations. However, involvement and increased demand from stakeholders do not guarantee per se that the signals provided in ecological accounting statements are of value to external stakeholders. External stakeholders do not give any indication about how to measure, collect, analyse and disclose information on corporate environmental impacts.

In general, management has an incentive to produce ecological statements at the lowest possible cost. The provision of high-quality information is expensive and provides a strong incentive for adverse selection, that is, for the provision of ecological statements with poor-quality information (for a similar argument involving second-hand cars where the buyers are unable to assess the quality, see Akerlof 1970).

Adverse selection does not have to be a problem if management has special, internal or intrinsic reasons for receiving high-quality information. However, neither EMAS, TRI nor other regulations on 'green accounting' provides clear requirements concerning the procedures applying to the compilation of information and in most cases the quality of the information cannot be assessed by the recipients of these ecological statements. Little direction is provided about the measurement, collection, analysis and disclosure of information about corporate environmental impacts. Thus, given the existing incentives associated with provision of ecological statements, it should be expected that poor-quality information will tend to drive out good-quality information (a Gresham's law of information quality; Ojala 1998). Unless an institutionalised incentive system is introduced that promotes the sharing of information ecological accounting projects will fail.

12.2.3 Current information quality problems in ecological accounting

Public disclosure of information about company environmental impacts has to be based on some form of ecological accounting system. Currently, a major problem of ecological accounting is that the quality of information disclosed in ecological statements is uncertain and varied.

As noted in Section 12.1.2 this situation is true even for disclosures in special ecological statements intended only for regulatory agencies—such as the US TRI. When the TRI was established, some companies had problems with compiling the information required. Some companies reported zero emissions to US EPA whereas others reported too many because they counted their emissions twice (e.g. related to production and consumption). Given that since 1988 the number of TRI reports has increased significantly, quality of information is an important issue. In 1994 approximately 23,000 facilities reported their chemical releases and EPA received about 80,000 submissions for each TRI-listed chemical (*CMR* 1994b).

The main reasons for low-quality information in ecological statements include:

☐ Different and varying sources of information

☐ Uncertainty about the accuracy and representativeness of the published information

☐ Consolidation (aggregation) of environmental interventions with different spatial impacts and the significance of compiled and reported information

To compute accurately all of a company's actual environmental impacts and to compile credible, high-quality, representative, targeted and actual data can be very time-consuming and expensive. Thus, not all information on environmental impacts relies on measurement. In many cases, pollution data are calculated or estimated. In other cases, information is gleaned from the literature. This use of different sources of information may result in inconsistent and low-quality data.

Even with measured data, some uncertainty about the accuracy and representativeness of information remains. Even different choices of measurement technique can lead to significant differences in reported information. Furthermore, differences in reported data occur if different measuring time-horizons are chosen or if an annual average instead of a monthly average is presented. In addition, average reported figures may hide the highs and lows of especially good and bad events (e.g. hours, days, weeks, months).

Today's corporate ecological statements show consolidated data related to local environmental interventions across a range of very different sites. However, aggregated amounts of local emissions are not useful information because they do not reveal anything about actual or potential environmental impacts (also see Section 10.3). Therefore, the aggregate sum of those local interventions holds little meaning for stakeholders because, mathematically, they do not have a common aggregate measure representing their significance. Only global interventions can be sensibly aggregated on a global level (Müller *et al.* 1994).

12.2.4 Information quality and the improvement of corporate eco-efficiency, accountability and sustainable outcomes

Ecological statements can create value (i.e. purpose-oriented knowledge) for stakeholders only if the published information provides reliable, understandable, comparable, timely and verifiable information (FEE 1999b; Schaltegger *et al.* 1996) about corporate ecological impacts and actions taken that lead to reduced impacts.

In some cases, stakeholders will be better informed through an increase in environmental reporting. However, in most cases the given quality of information in ecological statements remains uncertain. As a result, stakeholders are unable either to make better-informed decisions or to discriminate effectively between environmental leaders and environmental laggards because existing regulations for ecological accounting neglect the issues of information quality and adverse selection. Regulations, because of the data aggregation problems outlined above, support neither better cross-comparisons nor better longitudinal studies of corporate environmental performance. Any improvement in corporate eco-efficiency and any moves towards improved accountability and sustainable outcomes cannot be measured or controlled on the basis of existing low-quality data and information.

In the long run, recipients of ecological statements will appreciate that published information is of low quality and low value and that there is a critical need to support structural changes that will raise the standard of disclosure. In the immediate future, poor and confusing information could very well reduce the demand for ecological statements and may lead to a reduction in stakeholder involvement, even if the costs of information remain low. However, reduced demand for ecological information should not be confused with a low potential value from ecological accounting disclosures but rather should be seen as a structural problem reducing the actual usefulness of ecological statements in the short term (Schaltegger 1997b).

One way to improve information quality is to establish market-based environmental rating organisations (Burritt 1999b). A number of the traditional rating organisations (e.g. Moodys, Lloyds Register) now try to assess corporate environmental risk. Each rating agency has a different scheme for risk assessment because each agency relies on market sales of its credit ratings and each tries to obtain a competitive advantage through its predictive models of environmental (and other business) risks. However, they face similar information problems as other recipients of environmental information. Furthermore, they face mostly financing problems too (Figge 1995). Thus a promising approach may be to establish countervailing institutional rules (e.g. to verify ecological statements independently according to generally accepted standards of ecological accounting). So far, such verification procedures have been standardised for environmental management systems, but as far as the quality of published environmental information is concerned attempts to standardise verification procedures are specific to the country, programme or environmental media concerned (Burritt 1999c; see also White and Zinkl 1999).

The development and adverse effects of an excess number of financial accounting standards has been critically analysed in Chapter 8 Section 1. However, unlike financial reporting, standards for reporting on environmental impacts remain ad hoc in nature.

Thus, given an inverted U-shaped relation between information content and the number of standards (Fig 8.2, page 209), the development of a limited set of well-designed standards for ecological accounting and reporting, that can be independently verified, would very much increase the usefulness of environmental reporting (Beets and Souther 1999; Deegan and Rankin 1999: 336).

As a result, commonly accepted standards for ecological accounting are needed to improve the quality of information and to stimulate further the involvement and identification of external stakeholders with corporate environmental management. This by far extends the current guidelines of environmental reporting (see e.g. CEFIC 1993; Chaddick *et al.* 1993). The compilation of data requires a well-specified ecological accounting system, and clear rules have to be established about how to measure and report on the regulated emissions. Only then can consistency over time and comparability between companies be ensured.

US EPA is mindful of these suggestions in actions recently taken to standardise pollution profile disclosures on the Internet. Beets and Souther (1999: 130) observe that, early in 1998, US EPA began requiring additional Internet disclosures of companies in five large industries: oil, steel, metals, automobiles and paper. The affected companies must report the number of plant inspections in the previous two years, non-compliance ratings, dates and amounts of penalties imposed, the number of spills, pounds of material spilled and any resulting injuries or deaths, a hazard rating for each factory based on the toxicity of the chemicals released, the ratio of pollution releases to production, the racial and income profiles of those living within three miles of each plant and information from the TRI (but no eco-efficiency data are required).

Standards of ecological accounting would have to define accounting practices as well as the basic assumptions and qualitative characteristics of the disclosed information, in a similar way to the standards set by the International Accounting Standards Committee (IASC) in conventional financial accounting. Only environmental information that has had independent verification according to these ecological accounting standards would allow stakeholders to make sensible cross-company and time-series comparisons between the environmental impacts of different companies.

The following section provides some indication of how such standards of ecological accounting might be formulated and recent progress towards such formulation.

12.3 Conventions of ecological accounting

12.3.1 Standardisation of ecological accounting

Standardisation is feasible only if it is possible for a generally accepted method of external ecological accounting to be developed. With standardisation, application is likely to be more widespread, and greater comparability between product and company ecological data can be achieved. With wider application and greater comparability ecological accounting data will be more likely to influence the decisions of stakeholders and their level of satisfaction with management accountability. Section 8.1 indicated that standardisation of ecological accounting should not, however, be overstated because this would reduce the information value of ecological statements.

In conventional financial accounting, preparation of financial statements is based on a set of fundamental qualitative assumptions about accounting data. These conventions are assumed rather than recorded with each financial statement issued, because it is assumed that they are generally accepted. They provide the infrastructure for accounting records. These attributes provide a systemic framework for recording information, thereby adding value for users from the disclosures made in financial statements (IASC 1993: 61, 1995). This is why the next two sections examine these conventional assumptions (Section 12.3.2) and qualitative characteristics (Section 12.3.3) in the context of their applicability to ecological accounting (Maunders and Burritt 1991; Schaltegger 1997b; Schaltegger *et al.* 1996).

Ideally, external financial as well as external ecological information should be based on internal accounting information. However, for efficiency reasons (usually related to the fact that external financial reporting is required by regulation and internal reporting is added on to regulated requirements) the structure and contents of internal accounting follows financial accounting conventions. Therefore, an understanding of the development of external ecological accounting conventions is crucial for assessing the practical effectiveness of ecological accounting as a whole.

12.3.2 Underlying assumptions of ecological accounting

As discussed in Section 7.2 according to the IASC the two most important assumptions behind conventional financial accounting are 'accrual' and the 'going-concern' basis of accounts. Under the accrual basis of accounting, effects of transactions are recognised in the period in which they occur (and not when cash is received or paid). Transactions and changes to assets, liabilities and equity are recorded and reported in the corresponding financial statements. The purpose of the accrual accounting convention is to inform users of financial statements about past transactions related to a period and of the present position of future obligations (liabilities) and resources (assets). Possible future influences of past transactions are thus reflected in the present dated set of accounts (in the balance sheet and income statement).

Adoption of the assumption of accruals in ecological accounting means that potential future environmental impacts (reductions in ecological assets) following upon a corporate activity should not be recorded when the physical impact is actually going to take place but rather should be recognised at the time the activity is created. The accrual basis ensures that users of ecological statements are informed about past impacts on the environment and about future impacts on eco-assets that will arise from these past activities. Hence, ecological accounting statements provide the type of information about past transactions, physical transformations and events that is most useful for integrated ecological decision-making—that is, information about eco-assets and changes in eco-assets.

The going-concern assumption implies that a company, as a separate legal entity, will continue in operation for the indefinite future. The expectation that a company is a going concern implies that the organisation has 'neither the intention nor the need to liquidate or curtail materially the scale of its operations' (IASC 1994: 41) other than in the normal course of business (Chambers 1966). In cases where a substantial decrease of operations is required (e.g. by creditors pressing for payment) financial reports should be prepared and disclosed on a 'gone-concern' or forced-sale basis.

Application of the going-concern approach in ecological accounting under conditions of sustainability means that ecological statements should normally be prepared on the assumption that an enterprise will continue in operation for the foreseeable future, with neither the intention nor the necessity of materially increasing or reducing the scale of its environmental impacts. If such an intention or necessity exists, consideration has to be given as to whether ecological statements should be prepared on a different basis and, if so, the basis used would need to be disclosed. A possible interpretation of this could be that a company has to prepare its ecological statements on a different basis whenever an increase in its environmental impacts might substantially change its influence on the environmental quality of an ecosystem.

What might this 'different basis' for the preparation of ecological statements be when necessity dictates a necessary increase or reduction in environmental impacts? On the positive side, continual reductions in environmental impacts are the *sine qua non* of strong eco-efficiency and sustainable development. As such, they are to be encouraged. In other words, there is no tension between sustainability and strong eco-efficiency because the latter assumes that a going concern will be reducing its environmental impacts over time rather than striving to maintain an optimal level of ecological impacts. Hence, going concern would be better thought of as incorporating a downward trend in ecological impacts with an ideal of zero environmental interventions. With scarce physical resources in existence, a company that seeks to sustain its environmental impacts at a certain level per unit of output will not remain a going concern in a financial sense once competitors perceive the opportunity to reduce environmental impacts and costs.

For users of ecological statements, both assumptions—accrual and going concern—are equally important. They imply that the potential environmental impacts taking place in the future are of importance and that they should be reducing over time whereas eco-assets should be built up.

From a preventative point of view, stakeholders interested in a company's ecological impacts wish to be informed about potential impacts (potential reductions in eco-assets) not only when the interventions actually occur but also when they are threatened to occur. The accrual convention adjusts eco-asset balances up or down depending on actual and expected impacts or preservation activities. For example, consider the case of a mining company that has control of 100 kg of eco-assets that are all going to be removed and converted into tailings (waste) and products in equal amounts over five years. Accrual ecological accounting would show the amount of eco-assets as 80 kg after one year, with 20 kg being the change in eco-assets during the first year. A note would indicate that all the irreplaceable eco-assets will be removed in four years time. This is an extreme case because the eco-assets cannot, by definition, be sustained.

A more typical case would be where, for example, the eco-asset is 100 litres of potable water in a closed-loop industrial process. The company emits toxins into the water at a rate that slowly reduces water potability until, after 10 years, the accumulated effects make the water unacceptable for human consumption. At that point the eco-asset moves from being a going concern to a gone concern and no more potable water services can be obtained. Ecological accounting would need to reveal that the quality of water was declining steadily over time. It would also predict that if the rate of decline continued the eco-asset would lose its potability by a certain date. This type of information can be used for predictive purposes (when the potable services are expected to be destroyed), for descriptive purposes (how the potability services are being affected) and for policy-making (e.g. eco-taxes will be imposed to ensure that rates of toxin emissions will be reduced to a level that maintains the potability of the 100 litres of water).

The importance attached not only to current environmental interventions but also to future interventions becomes clear. In practice, ecological accounting measures environmental interventions when they actually take place. It can be argued that the time-interference (when the release of toxins occurs) is critical to sustainability of the natural environment (e.g. the water quality). Nevertheless, to account for emissions when they are released one must take into consideration the time-lag between the activity occurring and its reported effects. From the point of view of management incentives, this perspective creates a problem because feedback (reporting of the environmental interventions) is not clearly and directly linked to the cause (the activity). Instead, a lag occurs.

The going-concern convention can be used in ecological accounting to effect continual improvement and eco-efficiency.

Encouragement of these aspects of sound environmental management and performance does not diminish the importance of also reporting expected (or target) impacts of current corporate activities so important to a proactive management style symptomatic of environmental leaders rather than laggards. The analogous situation in conventional financial reporting would be disclosure of planned as well as actual results. Hence, accrual and going concern do provide a feasible way forward as standard conventions for ecological accounting (see Box 12.3).

12.3.3 Qualitative characteristics of ecological accounting

Chapter 7 addressed the qualitative characteristics of financial statements. Therefore, this section will consider only the application of these principles to ecological accounting.

In ecological accounting, qualitative characteristics are the attributes that make the information provided in ecological statements of value to users. Interpreted according to IASC (1994: 42): 'Qualitative characteristics are the attributes that make the information provided in financial statements useful to users'. The idea and contents of the qualitative characteristics which have been defined by the IASC (1994: 42f.) for financial statements can also be considered for application to ecological accounting. In this case, the four main qualitative characteristics for ecological statements are:

☐ Understandability

☐ Relevance

☐ Reliability

☐ Comparability

THE ACCRUAL BASIS OF ACCOUNTING

The practical application of the accrual basis of accounting requires that the results or impacts of activities should be disclosed in the period in which those activities occur. In financial reporting, for example, use of the accrual basis is driven by recognition of the (IISD 1996) 'critical event' (as occurring at the point-of-sale). There may, however, be variations on this central theme, including recognition of revenue and profit on a percentage-of-completion basis in the case of long-term contracts.

Relevant and credible sustainability reporting requires an accrual approach based on the point of production or timing of impact. Sustainability reporting needs to address the accrual (or matching) concept to ensure that production activities, emissions and waste and societal impacts are appropriately related from an activity perspective.

THE GOING-CONCERN ASSUMPTION

An enterprise that is categorised as being 'a going concern' is generally expected to continue operations for the foreseeable future (note that the 'foreseeable future' in financial reporting terms is rarely longer than 18 months after the balance-sheet date). This principle is adopted in financial reporting with the result that assets are conventionally carried at current or historical cost rather than at liquidation values. A fully developed approach to sustainability reporting will have to pay close attention to the broader implications of the going-concern concept.

As longer-term environmental impacts and prospective environmental legislation can be very important for financial statements, it seems appropriate that sustainability reporting standards should include a requirement that, when potential environmental liabilities are significant, the environmental element of the broader sustainability report should provide a clear indication of whether the enterprise is capable of funding necessary remediation and/or clean-up procedures. On a related point it can also be argued that, although environmental liability provisions do serve to inhibit the ability of an enterprise to make distributions to its shareholders, this does not at the same time guarantee the availability of cash resources to fund a necessary remediation process. In the event of a corporate failure this may throw the cost burden onto the public purse.

At a policy level there may be strong arguments for requiring enterprises operating in environmentally sensitive industries to ensure adequate provision of financial resources. In part this may be handled through the conventional insurance framework, but for known long-term liabilities some form of 'environmental bonding' could serve to insure society should the organisation in question fail as a financial going concern.

Box 12.3 **Accrual and going-concern conventions**

Source: GRI 1999

The contents and form of the following discussion of the qualitative characteristics of ecological accounting are based on, and interpreted, according to IASC (1994). Given the moves being made by many countries to harmonise their standards with IASC pronouncements, this seems a constructive way to approach a discussion of the analogous qualitative characteristics of ecological accounting information.

12.3.3.1 Understandability

The benefits of ecological statements (reports) have to exceed the costs. Therefore, the benefit is determined by its usefulness for decisions, its ability to help to allocate resources efficiently and also by the resulting improved accountability relationships with stakeholders and improved competitive advantage. Hence, ecological accounting standards and statements are issued only if they are seen to be beneficial and important to companies and their critical stakeholders. For companies, the costs of ecological statements arise from compilation, processing, analysis, education, verifying, reporting, increased pressure of stakeholders and any loss in competitive advantage, but the direct company costs and opportunity costs of compilation, analysis and interpretation are indirectly borne by stakeholders.

To increase net benefits, the information in ecological statements should be readily understandable to users, who are assumed to have a reasonable knowledge of environmental assessment and the corresponding industry. Not only should environmental interventions be disclosed but also this information should be benchmarked against top performing companies (for a discussion of recent benchmarking initiatives, see Young and Welford 1999). This can be achieved by benchmarking all others against the best performer within the relevant industry (as happens in Japan), against a set of top performers (such as the top decile [top 10%] of performers), by providing unequivocal definitions interpreting scientific wording where necessary and by using recommended metrics and formats for comparison.

12.3.3.2 Relevance

Ecological information disclosed must be relevant to the users of ecological statements if its publication is to be justified. The information prepared should help people integrate ecologically oriented factors into their decisions by helping to evaluate past, present and future events, or by confirming or correcting past evaluations (confirmative value related to accountability) (interpreted according to IASC 1994: 42). The confirmative value is descriptive in its orientation. At the same time the predictive value of information in ecological statements is enhanced if unusual, abnormal or infrequent environmental impacts are separately identified and disclosed. It also implies that, for example, the environmental impacts of accidents or unanticipated contingencies that increased or reduced production in an abnormal way, and of reduced emissions because of unusual events such as strikes, should also be disclosed.

The relevance of information is also affected by its character and materiality (prospective impact). In some cases, the character of information alone is sufficient to determine its relevance. For example, the emergence of a new environmental problem that is thought of by society as potentially serious may affect the assessment of risks and opportunities facing a company irrespective of the information that science and management have previously thought to be relevant. For example, if the greenhouse effect is regarded as serious, information concerning CO_2 emissions by business is also relevant.

Information is material if its omission or misstatement might conceivably adversely affect the decisions of users or affect the discharge of accountability by the management or governing body of an entity.

In some cases, both nature and materiality are important. Take, for example, the case of the installation of a new scrubber. The nature of the ecological statement would be that the new scrubber reduces the environmental impact caused by the company, whereas its materiality would focus on the potential environmental impact (e.g. with regard to a specific threshold level) once the scrubber is operational.

12.3.3.3 Reliability

To be useful, information has also to be reliable and to provide a valid, consistent description of environmental issues (e.g. air or water emissions expressed in technical terms). For ecological data, this implies that information has a certain quality and that ecological impact has been correctly assessed. Because this is very difficult to judge, at least the methods by which the data have been determined must be presented as well as the reasons why data are disclosed in the way they are.

Some information may be relevant but so unreliable that its recognition and disclosure may be potentially misleading. For example, if the validity and amount of an environmental impact is disputed, it may be inappropriate for an enterprise to recognise and disclose the maximum environmental damage, although it may be appropriate to disclose the amount and circumstances of the potential maximum environmental damage. Qualitative judgement is not usually sufficient for a rational or clear assessment of environmental impact added but, where no other means are available, it should be clearly stated. In this way, the information helps to represent faithfully the environmental impacts it either purports to represent or could reasonably be expected to represent.

Faithful representation also implies that environmental impacts are accounted for and presented in accordance with their substance and ecological reality and not merely with their legal form (reporting substance rather than form). The substance of an enterprise's environmental impact is not always consistent with its legal form. For example, an enterprise may dump waste legally in one country even if it is forbidden to do so in another place. Or a company may dispose of an asset in such a way that the documentation purports to pass legal ownership to another party. Nevertheless, an agreement may exist that ensures that the enterprise continues to dump its hazardous waste on the property in question. In such circumstances, the reporting of a sale would not faithfully represent the transaction entered into.

To be reliable, information contained and methods used in ecological statements have to be neutral, that is, free from bias. If, for example, a company emits benzene, which technically is a volatile organic compound (VOC), it should state this separately and not cover this substance under an account for VOCs, which generally are made up of less toxic substances than benzene. A second example, provided by the Global Reporting Initiative (GRI), relates to a furniture manufacturer that discloses purchases of wood but does not provide ecological information about the sources of the wood (e.g. renewable managed forests). Omission of information about the controversial issue of the source of wood supplies may bias the judgements and opinions of user groups.

Those preparing ecological statements have to accept the uncertainties that inevitably surround many events and circumstances. Such uncertainties are recognised by the disclosure of the nature and extent of the events and circumstances and by the exercise of prudence in the preparation of the ecological statements. 'Prudence' is the acceptance of a degree of caution in the exercise of judgement needed when making required estimates under conditions of uncertainty. In conventional financial reporting prudence is now largely frowned on because it tends to clash with the principle of freedom from bias or faithful representation, where assets or income are neither overstated nor understated and where liabilities or expenses are not understated or overstated. Prudence is also taken to mean that unrealised gains should not be reported whereas unrealised losses that have already occurred should be disclosed, again exhibiting a bias in reporting.

However, in ecological accounting, if a prudent approach is used it means that the precautionary principle should be adopted (i.e. if scientific evidence is unavailable or unconfirmed then it is best to err on the side of preservation of the environment). Hence, reliability of ecological statements is affected when the precautionary principle is used.

Use of the precautionary principle could temper the disclosure of unreliable data. For example, if a company is undertaking a new development and is unsure whether biodiversity will be seriously affected, the possibility of incurring costs, or of not being able to progress with the development, should be disclosed rather than merely disclosing the expected economic benefits of development without recognising a possible ecological constraint on expected outcomes.

Ecological liabilities (the obligations of a company) and costs (e.g. environmental interventions and their impacts) should not be understated, and ecological achievements (e.g. reduction of emissions) should not be overstated. Furthermore, under the precautionary principle, unrealised clean-ups of landfills should not be reported, but unrealised (future) environmental impacts that have already been triggered should be disclosed (e.g. waste caused that is currently stored in order to be dumped in the future). It should be noted that there remains some conflict here with the notion of faithful representation, because to be 'free from bias' ecological impacts should be neither understated nor overstated but should faithfully represent the situation. Use of the precautionary principle can be criticised on these grounds; however, its use in sustainable development is a type of affirmative action to be used in a transitional period by compensating for general ignorance of ecological impacts in the past. The main concern is not to overcompensate for such impacts in the future.

To be reliable, any information contained in ecological statements has to be as complete as possible within the limits of materiality and cost. An omission can cause information to be false or misleading and thus to be unreliable and deficient in terms of its reliability.

12.3.3.4 Comparability

Users have to be able to compare an enterprise's ecological statements over time in order to identify changes in the ecological position and changes in performance (longitudinal comparison). Furthermore, users should also be able to compare ecological statements from different enterprises in order to evaluate their relative environmental positions, performance and changes in environmental position (cross-company comparisons). Hence, consistency is required in the measurement and display of ecological interventions and eco-assets over time as well as for different enterprises.

Consistency has been recognised as an important qualitative characteristic for the preparation of financial statements (IASC 1994: 45). It is assumed that accounting policies are consistent from one period to another, thus stressing the uniformity in methods used during a period and when comparing periods over time. The purpose of this convention is to ensure comparability of accounting information over time. For ecological accounting, the consistency assumption means that a specific item has to be treated with use of the same methods, no matter which period in which it occurs or where (spatially) it occurs.

Information in ecological statements should be comparable over time. This is certainly essential for comparison's sake.

Use of the consistency convention when addressing ecological problems has been the subject of criticism (Gray 1994; Maunders and Burritt 1991: 11f.). It has been stated that the character of nature is non-linear (e.g. the release of 1 kg of sulphur dioxide [SO_2] will have completely different impacts depending on threshold levels or on its time of occurrence) and that the limited absorption capacities (threshold levels) of ecosystems differ vastly between seasons and regions. For environmental protection, time differences in releases and in impact levels are crucial (e.g. an additional 1 kg of SO_2 emitted in Eastern Europe will usually have a more severe environmental impact than one emitted in northern Norway). Therefore, it has been suggested that the consistency assumption leads to incorrect reporting and hence to incorrect decisions about the ecological impacts. For example, company A has emitted 100 kg of nitrates into a river system each year for the past 20 years with no observed or observable adverse effects. The consistency convention implies that if another 100 kg of nitrates are emitted next year there will also be no adverse effects. However, this final emission release may reduce the quality of water (e.g. through eutrophication) below an acceptable threshold because of cumulative effects. In other words, a report this year of no adverse effects and unchanged behaviour next year cannot be taken to lead to the same ecological result.

The main point about consistency is that consistency of practices over time will facilitate intertemporal comparisons between statements (whether financial or ecological). The issue raised by Maunders and Burritt (1991) is that the requirement for consistency may conflict with reality, as illustrated above. Clearly, it is not appropriate to permit inconsistent rules or practices when deriving ecological statements that report environmental interventions. For, example, quantities of emissions need to be additive if they are to show total emissions produced in a period, and a consistent measurement technique is needed if eco-asset balances are to be meaningful statements of ecological position at a given time.

No doubt, the assumption of linearity is not valid for ecosystems and, therefore, site-specific methods for assessing emissions and other ecological interventions are vital to ecological accounting. Consistency does not mean that an item (e.g. an emission of 1 tonne of SO_2) will have to be treated in a fixed and rigid way no matter when and where it occurs, but it *will* be recorded as an emission of 1 tonne of SO_2. Consistency requires application of the same methods to all places where company sites are located. Consistency allows methods to be applied that distinguish different cases in a consistent manner. The methods used should be consistent over time despite any adaptations for spatial and temporal differences.

The basic assumption of consistency means that a specific item is treated in the same way by using the same clearly defined methods over time. These methods may very well take into account temporal and spatial differences. In other words, the methods of assessing an environmental intervention should be used in a consistent manner, but they should also consider spatial and temporal differences.

Because users wish to compare the environmental position, performance and changes in the position of an enterprise over some length of time, it is important that ecological statements show the corresponding information for the preceding periods; that is, no information should be omitted without substantial reasons or without an explicit statement. Without the convention of the consistency-in-reporting method, users of ecological statements could not rely on the information provided. Users should always be informed of the accounting policies employed in the preparation of ecological statements, any changes in these policies and the effects of such changes.

Consistency should not, however, be confused with uniformity or allowed to become an impediment to the introduction of improved accounting methods and standards (e.g. in order to internalise negative external effects).

12.3.3.5 Summary

In summary, these guiding principles lead to a number of practical interpretations when drawing up ecological statements for disclosure:

☐ Use should be made of the best scientific information, methods and advice, and information should be presented in an accurate, balanced and accessible way.

☐ The methods of recording information and analysing data should be disclosed.

☐ Data and information should be presented without bias.

☐ Reported information should be disclosed in ways that ensure transparency and open access.

☐ Information should be presented in a comparative form.

☐ Wherever possible, environmental information should be disclosed in ways that reveal the context of place and time.

☐ Principles of ecologically sustainable development, such as the precautionary principle, need to be considered when drawing up ecological statements.

These qualitative characteristics are the main attributes that make information useful to readers of ecological statements. Nevertheless, they do exhibit some constraints.

12.3.4 Constraints on relevant and reliable information

Application of the main qualitative characteristics and of appropriate accounting standards should usually result in ecological statements that convey what is generally understood as a true and fair view of ecological position and changes in ecological position over time (interpreted according to IASC 1994: 46). However, the quality of reported ecological information is impaired by three main constraints (interpreted according to IASC 1994: 46):

☐ Timeliness

☐ Balance between benefits and costs of ecological accounting

☐ Trade-off between qualitative characteristics

First, timeliness rejects any undue delay in reporting information to ensure that it does not lose relevance. Nevertheless, time constraints should not be used as a subsequent excuse for omissions in measuring or recording or for providing low-quality data.

Second, the costs of computing more and better information about environmental impacts should not exceed the benefits to be derived from information about the natural environment. Ecological as well as economic–ecological efficiency are measures used to help decide whether the ratio of benefits to costs is greater than unity.

Last, in practice, a balance between different qualitative characteristics is often necessary. Occasionally, different qualitative aspects have to be traded off against each other in ecological accounting and reporting (as in all accounting systems). For example, management may need to balance the relative merits of timely reporting with the provision of reliable information. In achieving a balance between relevance and reliability, the overriding consideration is how best to satisfy the ecological decision-making needs of users. Ecological impacts with a high degree of uncertainty could be stated qualitatively or be accounted for in a transitory account. In the context of ecological statements, it must be recognised that some principles are not independent of other principles and, in these circumstances, either a managerial judgement has to be made as to whether one principle should dominate in a particular situation (e.g. prudence or freedom from bias; consistency or relevance), or whether a tighter, independent set of principles should be derived for the compilation of ecological statements.

12.4 Consolidation

12.4.1 Methods and scope

External ecological accounting can be oriented towards products, sites, businesses or companies (at the corporate and/or group level). Many environmental reports focus on all levels. These levels represent the accounting entity for which the reports are being drawn up (e.g. the site or the group). Group reports (company-oriented) are published mainly by multinational companies and therefore contain data that have to be aggregated from different enterprises based in different countries. This raises questions concerning the consolidation of ecological data.

The topic of consolidation is another well-known area in conventional financial accounting. Two main issues can be distinguished:

☐ The method of consolidation: how can data from different companies in different countries be aggregated?

☐ The scope of consolidation: what is the appropriate scope of consolidation?

Sections 12.4.2 and 12.4.3 discuss the principles of consolidation in financial accounting. On this basis, methods for consolidation in ecological accounting will be considered in Section 12.4.4.

12.4.2 Methods of consolidation

Multinational companies use specific procedures for consolidation. These procedures are defined by the main financial accounting standard-setting organisations. In practice, three methods of consolidation are used. The method applied depends on the share one company controls of another.

All major financial accounting standards (e.g. the international accounting standards [IASs] of the IASC; the US generally accepted accounting principles [GAAPs]; EU directives) impose the following consolidation rules:

O Full consolidation

O The equity method

O The proportionate method

Full consolidation is used by a parent company that controls the majority of the voting rights of a subsidiary (50% or more of the voting rights). Assuming the parent company has complete control over the group of companies and that there is economic unity in the group, the parent company integrates the subsidiary's income account and the balance sheet into group balance sheet and income accounts. Minority interests are reported only for the minority's share of equity and income:

> Control is presumed to exist if the parent owns, directly or indirectly through
> subsidiaries, more than one half of the voting power of an enterprise unless, in
> exceptional circumstances, it can be demonstrated that such ownership does not
> constitute control (IASC 1995: IAS 27, section 12).

The equity method is applied to associates; that is, for holdings between 20% and 49%. According to the IASC (1995: IAS 28, section 3), 'an associate is an enterprise in which the investor has significant influence and which is neither a subsidiary nor a joint venture of the investor'. It is assumed that a parent company has a significant influence on its associate: 'Significant influence is the power to participate in the financial and operating policy decisions of the investee but is not control over these policies' (IASC 1995: IAS 28, section 3). The equity method considers only the actual share of equities and no other financial figures such as debt, sales, assets or liabilities. As equity-consolidated investments are valued on an annual basis, the changing value of such investments is reflected in group accounts (Zenhäusern and Bertschinger 1993). Therefore, the equity method does not permit the real size, the economic debt : equity ratio (in comparison with the accounting debt : equity ratio) or the risk of a group to be assessed. For this reason, many financial analysts require additional information concerning total sales and liabilities.

The proportionate method is applied to investments of between 1% and 19% of the share capital in a company as well as to joint ventures, on the basis of the percentage held. According to the proportionate method, operational investments (but not financial investments) are reflected in the group accounts of the parent company and the purchase price based on costs incurred. In most cases, the value accounted for remains unchanged and therefore does not increase or decrease under this approach.

Consolidation procedures (i.e. for full consolidation) require elimination of inter-company transactions (e.g. between two subsidiaries, one of which supplies goods to the other). For example, a parent company has three subsidiaries: A (with sales of 200), B (sales of 75) and C (sales of 50). Companies B and C exclusively supply company A. Thus, total group sales amount to 200 and not 325. The aim of this elimination is to avoid including the same accounting figures twice. For ecological accounting this means that the transfer of waste between a parent company and its subsidiaries or between subsidiaries must not be double-counted.

In environmental reports, the methods of consolidating ecological data are rarely disclosed. Hence, external stakeholders cannot judge the methods used to consolidate data concerning environmental interventions of group subsidiaries. As no standards exist, it is not clear whether subsidiaries have applied similar consolidation principles.

In practice, many companies consolidate ecological data by using a method similar to that of full consolidation; however, they disregard minority interests and sometimes even investments up to 49.9%. Hence, the consolidation practices for ecological accounting can be assumed to differ in most cases from those of financial accounting. For example, WMC Ltd (formerly Western Mining Corporation Ltd), in its 1998 environmental progress report, developed a consistent set of reporting measures applicable to each site and to the company as a whole (e.g. newly disturbed land in hectares and newly rehabilitated land in hectares). The following comments put readers on guard about the lack of comparability behind aggregated data—something the company admits will be addressed in later reports:

> Aggregate company-wide data are shown below. Detailed individual site data, *for our main operations only*, are given in the site reports contained in the pocket at the back of this report . . . Much of the supporting data in this report, including consumption and emission numbers, are not directly measurable, but are determined from the best data and estimates available (WMC 1998: 27; emphasis added).

WMC acknowledges that associate company Alcoa World Alumina and Chemicals (40% owned) is not included in the aggregated company-based report, neither is subsidiary Mondo Minerals Oy (50% owned), but no consolidation principles are mentioned. In these circumstances, the disclosed group emissions do not necessarily reflect the actual environmental impact of the group. This fact has to be carefully taken into account when calculating and interpreting eco-integrated figures such as sales per ton of CO_2 emitted, or total industrial energy used by operations.

12.4.3 Scope and subject matter of consolidation

In financial accounting, the scope of a consolidation indicates which companies are integrated and which companies are not integrated into the consolidated group figures. Consolidation of ecological interventions has an additional element of value to stakeholders because externalities for one site or company can be included within a set of group accounts thereby internalising activities. For example, if an associate company recycled waste for the main production company, elements of the life-cycle are included that would not be included if, say, outsourcing occurred. Consolidated accounts would reflect the benefit of recycling within the group ecological accounts rather than disposal of waste to an unknown fate. An interpretation of group figures without knowing the scope of consolidation is actually quite useless. For a meaningful analysis, the methods of consolidation have to be known and all subsidiaries have to apply the same accounting policies in similar circumstances (IASC 1995: IAS 27, section 21).

To obtain reliable information about the total group environmental impact added, only environmental interventions within the same geographical range of impact should be aggregated. For instance, if a company operates on a global scale, only environmental interventions with a global impact should be aggregated (e.g. CO_2 related to the greenhouse effect).

On a group level, aggregation of environmental interventions that have local impacts is meaningless. However, local environmental interventions must be disclosed separately from the aggregated environmental impacts recorded in external ecological group statements, and in any case they should be aggregated and assessed at a plant level.

12.4.4 Conclusions regarding consolidation in ecological accounting

If preparing consolidated ecological statements, statements of the parent and its subsidiaries are combined on a line-by-line basis by adding items of environmental interventions. Consolidated environmental interventions have to be in the same geographical range of impact (interpreted according to IAS 27, section 26). At least the following three main principles should be taken into account when consolidating environmental data for external ecological reporting:

☐ All subsidiaries should apply the same consolidation methods. Thus, top management and chief accountants should each issue clear consolidation guidelines for ecological accounting.

☐ In external ecological accounting, consolidation policies should be disclosed. Meaningful interpretation of ecological statements for a group of companies is not possible without disclosure of the consolidation method used.

☐ To avoid distortions when calculating key eco-integrated numbers, the same consolidation principles should be used in ecological and financial accounting. International standards of financial accounting already exist. Thus, if there are no substantial reasons to do otherwise, the same principles should be applied to external ecological accounting as to financial accounting.

With regard to the last point, according to the standards used in practice, full consolidation should be applied to subsidiaries controlled by the parent company (50% or more of the voting rights). For stakes of 20%–49%, the equity method is used, whereas smaller holdings, of 19% and below, should be treated by using the proportionately correct consolidation method.

If a subsidiary is consolidated according to the equity method, additional economic information should be provided (such as total sales, total debt, total profit or loss and total assets).

This additional information allows the correct calculation of eco-integrated key figures, such as profits per tonne of CO_2 emitted, that assist in eco-efficiency and shareholder value calculations (also see Chapter 13).

12.5 Summary

Environmental information has become a formal part of external communication for many companies. However, improper use may diminish reputational gains and therefore reduce incentives to improve a company's environmental record. To increase reputational gains and company credibility, environmental leaders have to distinguish themselves from companies merely 'window-dressing' to make ecological interventions look better than they really are.

Readers will trust ecological data and will be able to make comparisons between companies if and only if widely accepted international standards of ecological accounting are established. Introduction of uniform standards would provide certainty in reporting requirements, enhanced understanding of company performance and consistency, transparency and comparability within and between companies, at a point in time and over time.

A minimum amount of standardisation is necessary for reported data to be relevant for the readers of corporate ecological statements. Although it is encouraging to see the recent surge in calls made and schemes outlined for standardisation in ecological reporting (e.g. FEE 1999b; GRI 1999; White and Zinkl 1999), there is a clear need for one organisation to drive the process to completion if a plethora of additional attempts to 'reinvent the standardisation wheel' is to be avoided. Australia provides one case in point where resources appear to be misdirected as the country sets about establishing its own set of national guidelines for public environmental reporting.

External ecological accounting implies the need to apply accounting principles and structures to classify, compile, analyse and disclose environmental impact added. From an economic as well as from an ecological perspective, it makes sense to investigate whether the accounting principles as formulated by the IASC (taken as a representative of conventional international financial accounting standards) are also suited for use in ecological accounting. It has been confirmed that, subject to how to deal with trade-offs, problems with timeliness and a basic cost–benefit criterion, application of the basic assumptions and conventions of financial accounting to external ecological accounting may provide a useful framework.

Common assumptions and conventions would be the basis for any form of standardised external ecological accounting. Independent verification is possible only if clear and measurable standards have been defined. In this sphere, considerable work remains to be done by accounting standardisation organisations. Standards and independent verifications reduce information costs and increase the usefulness of the information provided by ecological accounting for external stakeholders.

Questions

1. What are the pressures on managers to report biased ecological impact information to stakeholders? How might these be alleviated?

2. Regulation can no longer be viewed simply in terms of 'command and control' over companies. Discuss two alternatives to direct regulation and explain, by using the notion of an enforcement pyramid, whether there is any link between these alternatives and 'command-and-control' methods.

3. By using the five principles of regulatory design outlined in this chapter, consider how ecological reporting to external stakeholders provides a fundamental foundation for regulation of relationships between companies and stakeholders.

4. Are conventional financial accounting and external ecological accounting complements to each other or substitutes for each other? Discuss.

5. What are the features of the US Toxic Release Inventory that other ecological reporting systems should consider adopting? Are there any problems with the TRI reporting system? If so, how can these be overcome?

6. How many chemicals should be reported on in toxic release and national pollutant inventories and polluting emissions registers? What criteria have affected your choice?

7. Why is monitoring and information disclosure critical for the success of emissions banking and trading?

8. Do the principles behind the indicators put forward by the UN Commission on Sustainable Development have any connection with the principles behind corporate external ecological reporting? Are there any important differences between the two sets of principles? Explain.

9. What are information quality and environmental quality? Are they related? Why is low-quality information said to drive out high-quality information?

10. How might low-quality information in ecological statements be improved? In your answer, name two specific institutional mechanisms.

11. What assumptions underlie ecological accounting? Consider whether one assumption behind ecological accounting and reporting is more important than the other assumptions.

12. How do the notions of 'going concern' and 'gone concern' affect ecological statements?

13. Do the needs for and uses of internal and consolidated ecological accounting differ? If so, how? Are the two related?

Part 1

INTRODUCTION AND FRAMEWORK

2 The emergence of environmental accounting management
3 The purpose of managing environmental information
4 The environmental accounting framework

Part 2

ENVIRONMENTAL ISSUES IN CONVENTIONAL ACCOUNTING

5 Overview, criticism and advantages of conventional accounting
6 Environmental management accounting
7 Environmental issues in financial accounting and reporting
8 Environmental shareholder value and environmental issues in other accounting systems

Part 3

ECOLOGICAL ACCOUNTING

9 Overview and emergence of life-cycle assessment and ecological accounting
10 The efficiency of approaches to environmental information management
11 Internal ecological accounting
12 External ecological accounting and reporting of environmental impacts

Part 4

INTEGRATION

13 Integration with eco-efficiency indicators
14 Integrating eco-efficiency-oriented information management into the corporate environmental management system
15 Summary

Part 4
INTEGRATION

PART 4 WILL BRING TOGETHER THE INTEGRATION OF ECOLOGICAL AND ECONOMIC information systems. Integration of ecological and conventional accounting provides the basis for defining and measuring indicators of corporate eco-efficiency. The purpose here is not to explore general indicators for corporate environmental management, rather it is to discuss the development of corporate eco-efficiency indicators. Eco-efficiency is defined as a ratio between economic and environmental performance. To be made operational, an eco-efficiency indicator has to be subdivided and linked to a company's responsibility and accountability structure as well as to specific company activities (Chapter 13).

Contrary to the expectations of many practitioners when discussing environmental indicators, it is not the intention in this part to provide long lists of general indicators that could easily be adopted for use in any given company. There is already a sufficient number of such lists without any further lists being added (see e.g. Kottmann *et al.* 1999; Loew and Hjálmarsdòttir 1996; Seidel *et al.* 1998). In practice, although it may work to devise a list for fairly general indicators, for specific operational indicators the list would be unmanageably long because of the large set of specific environmental indicators that are possible (e.g. for different kind of emissions) and the many possible ways of combining these environmental indicators with relevant economic indicators. Therefore, the focus will be on a discussion of how to integrate indicators to determine eco-efficiency in a relevant and useful manner for decision-making and accountability purposes. In addition, there will be discussion of the need to integrate information management with corporate environmental management in order for eco-efficiency to be improved.

Chapter 14 will discuss how economic and environmental information management can be linked with a corporate environmental management system. This is applied by using the concept of integrated ecological and economic control, called hereafter eco-control. Eco-control is the application of control to financial and environmental management and therefore works systematically to integrate information from management and conventional financial accounting with information from internal and external ecological accounting.

Chapter 15 concludes Part 4 and the book with a summary.

Chapter 13

INTEGRATION WITH ECO-EFFICIENCY INDICATORS

13.1 Convergence of economic and environmental interests

Ideally, from an economic perspective all environmental interventions should be expressed in the same monetary units of measurement and should be included in management and financial accounting and reporting systems. However, as already shown, conventional accounting is inadequate because it has not been able to measure all environmental interventions with use of a common metric: money. Insufficient internalisation of environmental impacts is not a 'fault' of conventional accounting because external events (e.g. pollution of downstream stakeholders) are simply not taken into account unless:

☐ The regulatory 'mix' of instruments sets about to design such an outcome (e.g. economic incentives are used to achieve environmental policies).

☐ Regulatory instruments (e.g. economic incentives) provide a measure of money or money's worth that can be included in management and financial accounts.

As illustrated in Table 4.1 (page 60) and Figure 4.2 (page 64), groups with a predominant economic interest in a company (e.g. shareholders) have always been interested in financial information and have hardly ever been interested in environmental information unless it has affected their cash flows in a material way. However, as discussed in Part 2, for many companies environmental issues have grown in economic importance—so much so, in fact, that economic groups have gradually become more interested in gaining access to corporate environmental information. Similarly, environmental groups that were interested exclusively in environmental impacts in the past have now realised the important function of economic information in encouraging attempts by corporations to achieve their environmental goals. Many environmental groups are therefore increasingly keen to take economic information about companies into consideration. An illustration of this development is the increasing concern shown by Greenpeace in the role of environmental issues in financial markets (see e.g. Leggett 1996).

As a result of this development, society's focus is moving towards eco-efficiency as the main tool to help integration of economic and environmental issues and information.

Integration of ecological accounting and conventional accounting is therefore an important consideration for management who are concerned to save money and/or reduce corporate impacts on the environment and is necessary for measurement of corporate eco-efficiency. This situation has also been recognised by, for example, Gray *et al.* (1993: 120), who mention that accounting for energy has to include energy costs as well as quantitative energy units: 'Accounting only in [energy] units, while it may be better environmentally, rarely produces the hard cash motivators for control and does not necessarily lead to minimising energy costs.'

13.2 Integration of information management systems

As economic and environmental groups are increasingly becoming interested in each other's priority areas economic information is sometimes derived from ecological information systems and environmental information from financial information systems. Management and financial accounting can, for example, serve as sources of information to help identify material flows and to calculate the amount of specific emissions. Also, ecological accounting can serve as a valuable input for management accounting and financial reporting. For instance, managers cannot predict environmentally induced contingent liabilities if they have no idea about actual and expected environmental impacts. Other examples include situations where toxic releases or hazardous waste sites lead to higher costs, where taxes are levied for releases of carbon dioxide (CO_2), as is the case in some Scandinavian countries (see e.g. OECD 1994a) or where licence costs are based on the level of pollution loads emitted, as with load-based licensing operating in New South Wales, Australia (Protection of the Environment Operations [General] Regulation 1998, clause 17[3]).

Given the growing probability that government will promote internalisation of external effects, financial investors are also becoming more interested in ecological accounting figures. Furthermore, internal ecological accounting is an enabling device designed to help management calculate the most cost-effective environmental protection measures (on the need for enabling accounting systems, see Cuganesan *et al.* 1997).

However, these links do not establish explicit eco-efficiency information. Eco-efficiency (defined as economic–ecological efficiency) is the ratio between value added and environmental impact added (EIA; equation [3.2], page 51), or between an economic performance indicator and an ecological performance indicator (see also Section 3.4). Therefore, any improvement in corporate eco-efficiency requires explicit integration of economic information (the flow of financial funds such as income, expense, revenues and costs, which is linked to changes in stocks of funds [assets, liabilities and equities]) from conventional accounting with environmental information (environmental interventions such as emissions and resource use, which is linked with changes in eco-asset balances) derived from ecological accounting.

Companies can follow the eco-efficiency path (EP) procedure (also called the eco-rational path method [EPM]; see Schaltegger and Sturm 1992a) as a way of integrating economic and environmental information in their organisations (Fig. 13.1). The EP procedure is a simple, practical procedure for integrating two dimensions: an economic dimension (on the left-hand side of Fig 13.1) and an ecological dimension (on the right-hand side of Fig. 13.1). The integration process distinguishes three steps on the eco-efficiency path: accounting, judgement and decision.

Modules 1 and 3 relate to step 1: accounting. In module 1, the monetary inputs, outputs and outcomes of conventional accounting are computed. Module 3 represents the recording of ecological effects in units of environmental impact added calculated through ecological accounting.

Modules 2 and 4 relate to step 2: judgement. In module 2, an economic performance indicator representing a measure of economic efficiency is calculated. Such measures include: net present value (NPV), return on capital employed (ROCE), economic value added (EVA) or contribution margin (CM). These key numbers are supplied by any well-functioning management-control systems. Module 4 involves the calculation of ecological efficiency, as the measure of environmental impact added per product, product group or other functional unit. Modules 2 and 4 involve judgement in the provision of data for isolated, ecological or economic efficiency measures and estimates. One aim is to ensure that these measures are intersubjectively testable in order that they may be confirmed as being correct by a verification process.

Figure 13.1 **The eco-efficiency path procedure**

Source: Adapted from Schaltegger and Sturm 1992a: 206

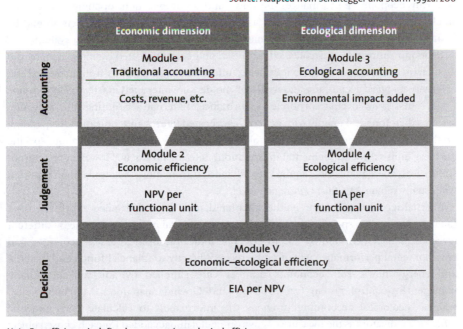

Note: Eco-efficiency is defined as economic–ecological efficiency.
EIA = environmental impact added   NPV = net present value

Step 3 is the final step: provision of integrated information for decision-making. Module 5 integrates steps 1 and 2 (modules 1–4) by combining the economic and ecological efficiency measures and by calculating environmental impact added per chosen unit of economic performance (e.g. environmental impact added per dollar contribution margin of a product, or environmental impact per unit of net present value [NPV]). In module 5 a measure is chosen by management to help business put environmental aspects of sustainable development into practice. The measure is linked to a company's responsibility structure, through responsibility centres (e.g. strategic business units, products or sites). Integration of economic and ecological performance indicators provides a systematic way for environmental issues to be integrated with internal and external stakeholders' decision-making and accountability processes.

In order to establish the basic eco-efficiency path to follow, financial and ecological accounting systems have to be integrated at the conceptual level (for large firms, a computer model is needed). Basic relationships are illustrated in Figure 13.2. The two major dimensions of corporate eco-efficiency are depicted: environmental performance on the left-hand side, and economic performance on the right-hand side.

Environmental performance, measured as corporate environmental impact added, can in principle be assessed from a natural science perspective or from a sociopolitical perspective (see Section 11.4). No matter which perspective is chosen, corporate material and energy flows have to be recorded. For purposes of environmental, economic and eco-efficiency comparisons, EIA drivers, centres and objects can be assumed not to change.

Economic performance can be measured from manager (Chapter 6) and from investor (Chapters 7 and 8) perspectives. Regardless of the perspective chosen for assessing company economic performance, the flow (and, by implication, opening and closing stocks) of financial funds must be measured. Cost centres and cost objects should be defined and applied consistently to management and ecological accounting systems.

Economic information is collected, analysed and communicated by management and financial accounting, whereas environmental information is managed through internal and external ecological accounting. External stakeholders are interested mostly in 'bottom-line figures' that show overall corporate performance. External accounting and reporting systems therefore deal mainly with general, aggregated figures and indicators. Depending on the results disclosed, external stakeholders may want to gain knowledge about specific business units (through segmental information), sites or products. However, apart from some cases where regulators require more detailed information, the information reported will usually remain at a fairly aggregate level.

Internal accounting systems, on the other hand, provide more detailed information and the basis for various specific economic and environmental indicators for use by different levels of management and by employees. The indicators used to assess economic and environmental performance will often be related directly to financial funds and material and energy flows. Key economic numbers are supplied by any well-functioning management-control system (see Anthony and Govindarajan 1998; Merchant 1998), whereas ecological accounting provides the information to calculate environmental efficiency indicators as the measure of environmental impact added for each chosen object (e.g. unit of product, product group or division).

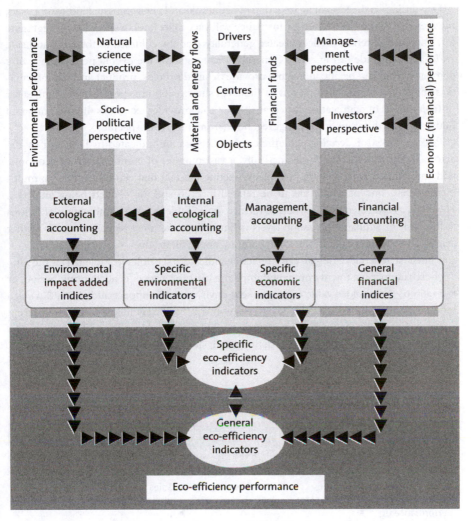

Figure 13.2 **Management of information to improve corporate eco-efficiency**

13.3 Developing eco-efficiency indicators

To measure corporate eco-efficiency, the set of economic and ecological information available has to be transformed into eco-efficiency information. In other words, economic numbers (measured in monetary terms) and environmental figures (measured in ecological terms) as indicators of efficiency have to be integrated. The integration of economic (numerator) with ecological (denominator) performance indicators provides a combined measure, a ratio for measuring economic–ecological efficiency (eco-efficiency), thereby allowing environmental issues to be incorporated with economic factors in decision-making and accountability processes.

Depending on the level of aggregation of economic and environmental indicators used, the measure for eco-efficiency performance will vary in its level of specificity—aggregate information will tend to reflect greater generality (see the columns to the left-hand side and right-hand side in Fig. 13.2). General indicators show the overall performance of a company, whereas specific indicators provide detailed process, product and site information about operations. The first row in Table 13.1 shows economic performance figures for different levels of aggregation, whereas the last row provides examples of environmental figures for the different levels of aggregation (from general to specific).

Possible links for deriving eco-efficiency indicators are indicated in Table 13.1 by the arrows in the middle row. Mathematically, a vast number of combinations of economic and environmental figures are possible, reflecting the fact that eco-efficiency is a multi-dimensional concept which has to be related to each specific context being analysed. However, as indicated by the width of the arrows in Table 13.1, the combination of figures at the same or similar aggregation levels will usually make most sense in practice (wider arrows show a higher plausibility that combinations will produce useful indicators).

The most general, aggregate eco-efficiency indicator (see link 1 in Table 13.1) is the ratio of short-run income to environmental impact added for a specific accounting period, or the ratio of shareholder value to net present environmental impact added (NPEIA) as a long-term indicator. As the NPEIA (see Section 11.8) is closely linked to the net present value and residual income as a measure of shareholder value, it can be used as the equivalent environmental figure for defining long-term eco-efficiency indicators.

Table 13.1 **Systematic collection of eco-efficiency information (examples of absolute figures)**

	Overall corporate eco-efficiency	General eco-efficiency indicators	Specific eco-efficiency indicators	
			Output	*Input*
Purpose: improvement of economic performance figures (numerator)	▶ Income ▶ Shareholder ▶ . ⋮	▶ Net revenue ▶ . ⋮	▶ Sales revenue of product X ▶ . ⋮	▶ Labour costs ▶ . ⋮
Possible links to eco-efficiency indicators	①	②	③	④
Purpose: improvement of environmental performance figures (denominator)	▶ Environmental impact added ▶ NPEIA ▶ . ⋮	▶ Contribution to global warming ▶ . ⋮	▶ CO_2 emissions ⋮	▶ Consumption of oil ▶ . ⋮

EIA = environmental impact added   NPEIA = net present environmental impact added

Arrows show possible links for deriving eco-efficiency indicators, the width of the arrows suggesting the plausibility that the given combination will produce a useful indicator (wider arrows indicate greater plausibility; narrow arrows indicate less plausibility).

Other fairly general indicators (see link 2) combine economic performance figures such as net revenue and free cash flow with environmental performance figures such as the contribution to global warming, ozone depletion potential and the contribution to photochemical smog. Free cash flow, and a product's net revenue, can be directly influenced by the financial consequences of specific environmental problems that affect a specific cost object.

Examples of specific eco-efficiency indicators include indicators based on material-flow outputs such as revenue per kilogram of CO_2 emitted (link 3), and input-related indicators such as the costs incurred per litre of oil consumed (link 4). To communicate with different levels of management and employees, it may nevertheless be valuable to use indicators combining different levels of aggregated economic and environmental figures. Given emerging knowledge about the links between financial consequences of environmental problems and different energy and material inputs, many stakeholders will become interested in such 'cross-level' indicators. Investors, for example, may want to calculate indicators such as the shareholder value per unit of contribution to global warming (the 'greenhouse effect') (link 5), the shareholder value per unit of CO_2 emitted (link 6) or the shareholder value per kilogram of oil consumed (link 7). Such indicators may enable investors to assess the relative financial susceptibility of a company to the possible internalisation of external greenhouse-effect costs, or rising oil prices caused by an energy tax related to the greenhouse effect.

Apart from taking into account the level of aggregation, a definition of useful eco-efficiency indicators requires that they be focused on the stakeholder's area of interest. As Figure 13.3 illustrates, different stakeholders to whom a company is accountable are interested in different kinds of information as well as in different levels of detail. Investors, for instance, are traditionally interested in the broad financial aspects of a company and only in environmental information that has a bearing on future financial positions and changes in position (i.e. in aggregated, company-wide financial information and in the kinds of environmental information that are economically relevant). Global pressure groups such as Greenpeace concentrate their attention on corporate accountability for environmental impacts, that is, on aggregated information on environmental impacts and the kind of economic information that, in environmental terms, is most relevant to their campaigns. Consumers and product managers tend to focus on specific, product-related information.

As mentioned earlier (Section 4.1.4; Figure 4.2, page 64), the focus is increasingly shifting towards integration of economic and environmental data and on taking into account more detailed information. Some differences in the degree of detail taken into account by different stakeholder groups will, of course, remain. However, leading companies have started to address more detailed aspects of eco-efficiency-oriented information. The result of this analysis is that any eco-efficiency indicators should address the aspects the respective stakeholders are truly interested in.

Of critical importance is that eco-efficiency indicators must be unambiguously defined in such a way that the economic and environmental dimensions measured reflect and are focused on the activities of concern to specific stakeholders (Table 13.2). For instance, for any communication with shareholders that adopts a long-term view, a long-term economic

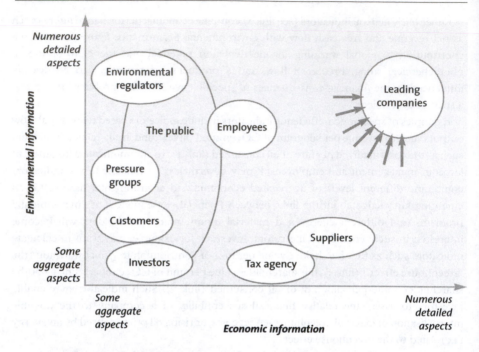

Figure 13.3 **Stakeholders' traditional interest in different kinds of information and different degrees of detail: company-related information**

Table 13.2 **Examples of eco-efficiency indicators**

Stakeholder group	Examples of eco-efficiency indicator	Focus
Shareholders	SHV ÷ NPEIA	Assessment of financial investment
Government, top management	VA ÷ EIA	Assessment of impacts on society as a whole
Government, top management	(corporate taxes) ÷ EIA	Assessment of impacts relevant for the government and the tax agency
Top management	Income ÷ EIA	Assessment of annual performance
Site management	ROCE ÷ EIA	Assessment of site
Project management	NPV ÷ NPEIA	Assessment of capital investment project
Divisional management	CM ÷ EIA	Assessment of product group
Product management	CM ÷ EIA	Assessment of product

CM = contribution margin   EIA = environmental impact added
NPEIA = net present environmental impact added   NPV = net present value
ROCE = return on capital employed   SHV = shareholder value   VA = value added

indicator such as the shareholder value (SHV) must be related to a long-term indicator of environmental impact such as the NPEIA. For short-term analysis, a combination of return on equity with environmental impact added may be useful. Or, if the impacts of a company on society as a whole are the object of attention, a necessary eco-efficiency measure would be value added (VA) per unit of environmental impact added (EIA).

By definition, internal and external stakeholders have different views and are interested in different indicators. Divisional management may, for example, need to focus on the economic and environmental impacts of strategic business units or sites. Middle and lower levels of management focus on product groups, product units, sites and production steps. As indicators are used to guide management control and strategic planning activities, indicators must be defined with care and must take the specific circumstances of a company into account.

For most actors, economic, environmental and eco-efficiency indicators start to make sense only if they are related to objects within their own sphere of control—that is, objects these actors intend to influence, actually can influence, have an incentive to influence and for which they receive rewards for influencing. Thus, depending on the main interest of a stakeholder, an eco-efficiency indicator has to be related to standards for comparison that are controllable and relevant at the level of concern (e.g. the division, site, process or activity). Possible denominators for comparison are dollars invested (for investors), product units (for product management) and machine hours (for engineers controlling a production process). Table 13.3 provides some examples of denominators for eco-efficiency indicators.

To be useful for decision-making and accountability purposes, each denominator should be linked to the specific sphere of influence of each stakeholder. Investors, for instance, are traditionally interested in the shareholder value created per share as this allows them to assess the additional value from their financial investment. Taking an eco-efficiency view, investors will monitor the ratio of SHV to NPEIA for each share and the ration of SHV to the amount they paid for each share.

Furthermore, to support eco-integrated investment decision-making, project-related financial and environmental information is necessary. Examples of indicators for pollution prevention measures include net costs or revenues per kilogram of reduced throughput,

Table 13.3 **Examples of stakeholders and possible denominators for eco-efficiency calculations**

Stakeholder	Possible denominator
Investors	Per dollar invested
Sales managers	Per dollar of sales
Product managers	Per product unit
Engineers	Per machine hour
Employees	Per hour of labour Per unit produced

costs of scrubbers per cubic metre of polluted air and costs of sewage plant per hectolitre of sewage caused (1 hectolitre = 100 litres). Establishment of eco-efficiency indicators provides one major practical aspect of eco-control. A second aspect relates to the benchmarks, targets or level of predictions that must be made if some comparison is to be made between expected and actual eco-efficiency. The next section examines benchmarking of eco-efficiency indicators as an important element in attempts by company management to 'close the loop' through an integrated eco-control system based on following the eco-efficiency path.

13.4 Benchmarking

It is simply not enough for management to consider, accept, understand and implement steps and modules along their eco-efficiency path if they wish to gain value for their stakeholders. As with all management control, eco-control requires complete and systematic accounting and reporting if it is to improve performance and if it is to produce the rewards that flow from improved performance. Once it is agreed that environmental impacts need to be anticipated and reduced (e.g. CO_2 emissions at plant X), once a specific measure of financial performance has been identified (e.g. cost per unit of output) and once a way of bringing these two measures together has been communicated, negotiated and accepted, other aspects of the eco-control process have to be addressed.

Prime among these other aspects is the setting of targets or benchmarks for improvement in eco-efficiency indicators. Benchmarks provide the standard against which actual performance is judged. Performance against benchmarks is used by internal and external stakeholders as a basis for future action and for further continual improvement.

A common procedure in financial and management accounting is to examine performance over a number of previous periods (years), to consider the success, or otherwise, of observed trends and to make a plan for the future based on past performance. Trend analysis is used as a basis for management policy and future plans and actions. Essentially, this approach to planning and control relies on measures of past performance and assessment of whether performance was acceptable after the event. Benchmarking, or comparison with other companies or similar processes or activities along a complex of performance indicators, plays a vital part in the planning and control process (White and Zinkl 1997).

A second approach to performance assessment is simply to compare relative performance at a particular point of time (rather than over time) with other companies or similar processes or activities along a complex of performance indicators. Once again, benchmarking is needed, but a time dimension is not important to the assessment.

Both the above-described approaches to performance assessment depend on the availability of a benchmark, target or standard for comparison. For all companies, processes or activities examined, comparisons will be informative only if the accounting information systems yield figures that are complete through time and (for financial information) expressed in up-to-date monetary amounts (Chambers 1970). In order to make comparisons, assurance is needed that figures have been derived in similar ways. However, because internal information for benchmarking is likely to be more reliable than external benchmark information, such assurances are often not easy to obtain.

Five main types of benchmarked information may be available (Bartolomeo 1998):

☐ Internal benchmarking

☐ Best-in-class benchmarking

☐ Competitive benchmarking

☐ Sector benchmarking

☐ Eco-rating

In internal benchmarking the company, its sites, processes, products and divisions form the objects of benchmarking. Eco-efficiency is a focal point of this form of benchmarking. Company managers are the main audience for internal benchmark information, and questionnaires and environmental audits provide the main source of information. The Global Environmental Management Initiative (GEMI) is one internal management benchmarking system that is based on principles of the International Chamber of Commerce's (ICC's) Business Charter for Sustainable Development. The ISO 14000 series also provides benchmark information, as does the EU Eco-management and Audit Scheme (EMAS) for site comparisons.

Best-in-class benchmarking refers to the performance of a select group of companies. Generally, best environmental management practices (e.g. the practices followed by the top decile of performers) are the focus of attention for comparisons and target-setting by company managers and industry associations. Joint benchmarking projects and available literature provide the information on these benchmarks. However, regulators are beginning to consider best-in-class benchmarking as a way to drive continual improvement in company environmental performance. For example, in 1999 the Japanese government introduced the 'top runners approach' in which the highest standard in any given industry becomes the minimum standard for the whole industry in terms of energy efficiency and reductions of greenhouse gas emissions (JEA 1998).

Competitive benchmarking of environmental performance is used by company managers to establish best practice by referring to procedures followed by immediate rivals in an industry or competitors with a generic function to be benchmarked (e.g. purchasing practices). A wider source of information—literature, trade journals, reports by consultants, environmental reports and statements—has to be used because of the confidentiality of some competitor information. Eco-efficiency comparisons are of particular importance in this form of benchmarking.

Sector benchmarking is more specific and closely allied to industry association membership and activities. Industry associations obtain benchmark information to help educate their membership about key issues as a basis for lobbying government on behalf of industry and in order to monitor compliance with environmental codes of practice (or management). Industry associations obtain information from members through questionnaires (and expect full support) and from environmental reports and statements.

Eco-rating is used by finance companies (banks and insurance companies), rating agencies, by ethical investors (with 'green' funds as part or all of their portfolio), by environmental groups and by non-governmental organisations (NGOs). For example it is used by the US Investor Responsibility Research Center [IRRC], which calculates a compliance index, and by the US Council on Economic Priorities [CEP], which provides an emissions index (toxic chemicals per unit of turnover) (see Figge 1995).

Opportunities for benchmarking environment-related performance measurement have been undertaken by a wide range of organisations in recent years (James and Bennett 1998: iii). These include:

☐ A study of the implementation of environmental performance indicators in 12 Norwegian and Swedish companies

☐ The International Organization for Standardization (ISO)'s draft guidelines on environmental performance evaluation

☐ A study of standardised performance indicators by the World Resources Institute (WRI; based in Washington, DC)

☐ Various practical guidance reports by organisations such as Business and the Environment (based in Arlington, MA)

☐ Two reports produced jointly by the United Nations Environment Programme (UNEP) and SustainAbility on environmental reports and the indicators used within them

☐ An initiative by five Swiss banks to develop standardised disclosure of environmental data

☐ The creation of new standards and guidelines on environmental reporting in Germany and Australia.

When the Global Reporting Initiative (GRI) of the Coalition of Environmentally Responsible Economies (CERES) and the eco-efficiency metrics project of the World Business Council for Sustainable Development (WBCSD 1999) are included, the list and potential confusion for business seems almost endless.

Other possible problems associated with the benchmarking of eco-efficiency indicators include:

☐ It may not be possible to obtain information about ecological interventions and economic performance of competitors because of confidentiality and/or concern over losing competitive advantage.

☐ Benchmarking the economic dimension of eco-efficiency is likely to be easier than benchmarking the ecological dimension because company financial reporting has a long history, standardisation has been much discussed and transparency has been improved over time.

☐ Benchmarking of environmental management performance can be used to divert attention away from physical environmental performance and associated indicators of eco-efficiency. What is of particular importance is that management be assessed on its effectiveness in achieving eco-efficiency benchmarks once established. This is related to the need to have well-defined responsibilities, effective communication of the eco-efficiency objective and leadership rather than laggard behaviour on environmental issues.

☐ Many companies still refuse to acknowledge that their effects lead to any environmental interventions, and they do not even consider the notion of eco-efficiency (cost savings always come as a surprise to them [BRT 1998: 41]) let alone the importance of benchmarking.

This range of problems means that the use of eco-efficiency indicators has limitations, as outlined in the next section.

13.5 Limits and important criteria

Suitable indicators can provide relevant time-series and cross-sectional (comparisons at a point in time) information about the current state of eco-efficiency and indicate potential for its improvement. However, at present, the use of eco-efficiency indicators is limited, for a number of reasons.

First, eco-efficiency indicators can support decisions and improve accountability relationships only if the figures they are based on are reliable (requiring information quality) and if they are calculated in the same way (requiring consistency in the accounting approach). As no generally accepted standards of ecological accounting exist, application is limited mostly to internal comparisons between strategic business units, production sites and other internal responsibility centres as well as to internal comparisons made over time.

Second, even if the data quality were perfect, eco-efficiency indicators would have to be used with some care. Indicators and figures can be imprecise, they can be either too narrow or too broad for a particular decision and therefore may provide an inadequate representation of the situation. Hence, any definition of indicators needs to be compiled with great care. Furthermore, in most cases eco-efficiency figures cannot take all aspects of a decision into account and, as they are necessary but not sufficient information for decision-making and accountability purposes, they must be complemented by other quantitative and qualitative information and considerations.

In addition, the fact that it is theoretically possible to devise an almost infinite number of indicators may encourage the 'production' of more figures and indicators than actually make sense (for comments on restricting the set of indicators, see CICA 1994: 87). The manager's task is therefore to establish a useful, small, set of indicators which can be overseen. As the ideal number and type of indicators result from clearly defined objectives, management should consider the following criteria when devising the set of indicators relevant for their company:

☐ The purpose for undertaking measurement must always be kept in mind when eco-efficiency indicators are defined.

☐ The level of imprecision of indicators that are based on estimates, rather than reported after environmental interventions have actually occurred, should be stated.

☐ Economic and environmental figures combined in an eco-efficiency indicator should be characterised by use of the same time-horizon and the same scope.

☐ Improvement in the figures reported by an indicator should also lead to an improvement in corporate eco-efficiency.

☐ Each indicator must provide relevant information for the stakeholder group and it must relate to activities that are controllable by the actors whose performance it attempts to measure and who are going to be held accountable for actual performance.

☐ The method that is used for computing eco-efficiency indicators should be disclosed, otherwise the figures may be misinterpreted by stakeholders.

An example of the final criteria listed above relates to an indicator designed to show cost per unit of output of compliance with regulations. Cost calculations will make assumptions about whether full-cost accounting is to be used, about which elements of cost are to be included (capitalised or expensed) and about how to discover and link regulations applying to different parts of a product's life-cycle. Another example concerns performance represented by percentage compliance with regulations. This is likewise subject to misinterpretation because the level of established standards varies across jurisdictions, calculations can be based on readings made by a regulatory agency or those made by the company and compliance may not be at the same aggregated level throughout a company.

It is not necessarily an obvious or easy task to meet the above-listed criteria, as examples published in a number of environmental reports demonstrate. Problematic indicators would be, for example, the number of pencil leads or ink cartridges per square metre of office space in a bank or an insurance company. Important questions in this context are: what is the plausible link between pencil leads and office space? What is the relevance of this indicator for the environmental and economic performance (eco-efficiency) of the company? Does it make sense to influence this indicator? Who can use and reasonably influence this indicator?

If indicators are not focused on the relevant aspects of corporate environmental performance they cannot generate knowledge about actual environmental impacts or corporate eco-efficiency. In the above example, both the indicators—number of ink cartridges or pencil leads per square metre of office space—can be improved by increasing the amount of space used (at the same time increasing the environmental impact of another indicator—space used). As these indicators are not clearly purpose-oriented they cannot effectively support an improvement in environmental performance or corporate eco-efficiency.

It must not be overlooked that the 'major' reason for defining environmental indicators is to reduce corporate environmental impacts, based on absolute and relative results.

Furthermore, the purpose of formulating eco-efficiency indicators is to integrate financial and ecological measures of business activity in order to improve the eco-efficiency of an organisation. If effectiveness is being assessed by the extent to which ecologically sustainable development is being achieved, eco-efficiency indicators will also need to reflect impacts of corporate activity on human society.

The 'political' reason for integrating and assessing economic and ecological effects is to address and include the needs of different corporate stakeholders. Depending on the need for information and the goals of stakeholders, different sets of economic and environmental performance measures will be chosen. The Organisation for Economic Co-operation and Development (OECD), the United Nations and WBCSD (Mcnaghten *et al.* 1997: 148f.; OECD 1998) are currently developing specific environmental indicators to communicate with company stakeholders such as customers, the community (neighbours), government, NGOs, the financial community and employees. However, this (necessary) stakeholder orientation for indicators should not distract from the purpose of defining indicators, namely to improve corporate eco-efficiency as a contribution towards ecologically sustainable economic development.

By converting environmental impact added into dollars, or by using monetary weights such as environmental taxes, direct subtraction of environmental costs from economic performance indicators (e.g. net revenue) is possible. However, such calculations do need to be identified separately in company accounting systems so that stakeholders can then use the resulting indicators as they see fit. It is a dictum for most businesses that short-run and long-run survival depend on income and cash flow; it is equally as simple and important for business management to recognise that without the environment and without ecological biodiversity there is no society, without society there is no economy and without an economy there is no opportunity for win–win business situations. Eco-efficiency indicators provide a necessary tool for helping business and its stakeholders appraise progress along the eco-efficiency path towards participatory, education-based and information-guided sustainable development.

13.6 Summary and implications

Measurement of eco-efficiency requires the definition of indicators that combine economic and environmental figures. Basic information can be obtained from management and financial accounting as well as from the internal and external ecological accounting systems described in this book. Given the expanding possibilities for data processing, an almost infinite number of ways for combining economic and environmental data is possible and practicable. However, businesses should beware of overloading themselves and their stakeholders with data. Useful indicators have to be purpose-oriented and focused on the interests and activities of specific stakeholders. In addition, the time-horizon and the eco-efficiency object (e.g. a strategic business unit or a product unit) must be the same if plausible, interpretable eco-efficiency indicators are to be generated by accounting systems.

Eco-efficiency indicators can provide useful information, over time and between companies, about the current state and potential for improvement. Indicators can support decisions and help support accountability relationships (internal and external) only if the figures are calculated consistently (e.g. for the same time-periods). As no generally accepted standards for ecological accounting exist today, perhaps the range of application should be limited to internal use by managers, especially for comparisons between individual sites or divisions of a company over time, until a standard is agreed.

Eco-efficiency data and indicators provide a simple basis for action. Action is based partly on what the competition is doing within the competitive framework established by stakeholders. For example, government environmental and industry policies provide support to enable management to adopt eco-efficiency as a goal. Government has the ability to establish supportive initiatives that reward businesses for energy, material and water savings, to encourage extended producer responsibility and accountability for all life-cycle effects, to foster a supportive environment for research, development and eco-innovation and to reduce perceived critical environmental problems such as greenhouse gas emissions. However, external stakeholders enable rather than drive eco-efficiency. Management drives eco-efficiency in any business. Once eco-efficiency is an accepted goal, competitive benchmarks are used to set eco-efficiency targets as an integral part of a company's strategic planning process. Derivation and disclosure of regular and systematic corporate eco-efficiency information requires management information systems (financial and ecological) to be developed and integrated with corporate environmental management systems, an issue toward which the next chapter now turns.

Questions

1. What is eco-efficiency? How is it measured? Why is it measured? Where is it reported?

2. List the main stakeholder groups in a company. Consider whether and why each stakeholder group might be interested in corporate eco-efficiency indicators. What level of information is each group most interested in for decision-making and accountability purposes? Explain.

3. What is an environmental intervention? How are environmental interventions and eco-efficiency related?

4. 'Eco-efficiency provides a measure of "win–win"—an action is undertaken if it saves money and environmental interventions are reduced.' Is eco-efficiency too concerned about saving money rather than helping to preserve the environment?

5. What are the three steps that can be taken along a corporate eco-efficiency path? How are the five modules related to development of a measure of eco-efficiency?

6. Why is the distinction between general and specific indicators of eco-efficiency important for accounting in (a) ecological and (b) financial terms?

7. Benchmarking of eco-efficiency indicators faces a number of practical problems. What are these? Can they be overcome? Why is internal benchmarking more common than external benchmarking?

8. The objective . . . is not to develop one single approach to measuring and reporting eco-efficiency. Rather it is to establish a general, voluntary framework that is flexible enough to be widely used, broadly accepted and easily interpreted by the full range of businesses. This is based on a recognition that the specifics of defining, measuring and communicating eco-efficiency will necessarily vary from one business to another, and that comparisons between different business must be approached with great care (WBCSD 1999: 2).

   Can there be one generally accepted set of eco-efficiency indicators for assessing business performance? Give reasons for your view.

9. 'Eco-efficiency provides necessary but not sufficient indicators of environmental performance.' What is environmental performance? Provide an example of another type of information that is important when assessing a company's environmental performance.

10. How are the limits on using eco-efficiency indicators related to accounting?

Chapter 14

INTEGRATING ECO-EFFICIENCY-ORIENTED INFORMATION MANAGEMENT INTO THE CORPORATE ENVIRONMENTAL MANAGEMENT SYSTEM

This chapter provides an understanding of the role of eco-efficiency information management in corporate environmental management. This chapter will present a very brief overview of the most important regulations and standards relating to corporate environmental management. These include EU regulations on the Eco-management and Audit Scheme (EMAS) and eco-labels as well as British Standard (BS) 7750 of the British Standards Institution (BSI) and the International Standard ISO 14001 of the International Organization for Standardization (ISO). For a large number of companies, eco-control has become the most important and comprehensive environmental management system in the past few years. Because of a range of regulations, and most of all because of the introduction of new standards for corporate environmental management, ecological accounting has become a core element of environmental management systems (see e.g. Orwat 1996; Schaltegger 1994a). This chapter will therefore conclude by examining the role of eco-efficiency information management as part of a management eco-control process.

14.1 Standards of corporate environmental management

For the past ten years various stakeholders defining standards of good environmental management practice have influenced corporate strategies for environmental management and environmental information management. The growing importance of environmental management is reflected by a number of important regulations and standards in force or being prepared, all with the aim of harmonising environmental management practices and procedures. Standardisation and its application to company systems are the most important aspects of effective environmental management. Standards can be technical, related to performance or be process-based and they provide the foundation for continual improvement in relation to established benchmarks.

Among the most significant standards in recent times are BS 7750 (BSI 1992), the EU directive on EMAS (COM 1993) and standard ISO 14001 (or ISO 14004 for companies not seeking certification) of ISO (1994a, 1999a). ISO 14001, which is now being adopted widely, is a process standard. ISO is currently developing a family of 'environmental management' standards that address management systems and the environmental aspects of products in the areas of life-cycle assessment (LCA) (ISO 14040), labelling (ISO 14020) and environmental performance evaluation (ISO 14030; see also ISO 1994c). These are not discussed here. Not specifically discussed here either is the EU regulation on the voluntary eco-labelling of products (see CEEC 1992).

Standard-setting organisations such as the BSI, ISO, as well as other national standard-isation organisations have formulated standards against which corporate management systems can be audited. These standardisation organisations are private institutions financed by industry. Their markets (i.e. sales) depend on the price of auditing and certification services as well as on the reputation of the organisation for ensuring that the material audited is of a high quality. The quality of these auditing services is, in turn, checked by regulators, who verify corporate environmental audits.

BS 7750, released as a draft standard in 1992 (and released as an actual standard in 1994), was the first standard for corporate environmental management systems. It has substantially influenced ISO 14001, which was published as a draft version in 1994 and as a final document in 1996 (Hillary 1995: 294; Sheldon 1996; Tibor and Feldman 1997). Although ISO 14001 encompasses the general elements of BS 7750, it allows greater flexibility in application.

A major motivation for companies to establish environmental management systems comes from the European Commission's (COM) introduction of the voluntary EMAS for production sites and companies (COM 1993). The term 'audit' could be misleading, because EMAS covers much more than a traditional legal compliance audit. EMAS enables companies to have their sites audited according to criteria for 'good environmental management practices' (Pariser and Neidermeyer 1991) and, if they fulfil the requirements of the directive, to use (restrictively) a label that confirms that a specific site has an environmental management system in place and that it has successfully completed an external environmental audit. The label can only be used on a letterhead or on environ-mental and financial reports and is not attached to products.

As shown in Figure 14.1, an important part of EMAS focuses on the process of ensuring that an environmental management system is in place and functioning (Altham and Guerin 1999; Fichter 1995; Hillary 1993; Würth 1993).

To comply with the provisions of EMAS, a company must have implemented an environmental management system that helps to:

☐ Formulate an environmental policy and goals for corporate environmental protection

☐ Secure efficient environmental accounting (or information management)

☐ Evaluate environmental performance (and support decision-making)

☐ Plan and steer company activities

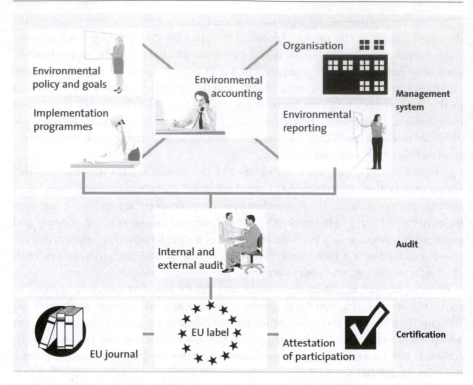

Figure 14.1 **Core components of the EU Eco-management and Audit Scheme**

☐ Implement the respective plans

☐ Build up an effective and efficient organisation

☐ Communicate with internal and external stakeholders (environmental reporting)

In addition, the existence and functioning of the corporate environmental management system has to be verified by external auditors.

Companies that comply with these requirements are free to display an EMAS logo on their letterhead, something that it was hoped would become a mark of environmental excellence. It was expected that market pressure, especially in inter-corporate business relationships, would encourage companies to participate in EMAS (see e.g. Fouhy 1995: 49; Heuvels 1993). However, as an economic analysis of the incentives provided by EMAS (Karl 1992, 1993) and early experience show, this reason for participation may have been overestimated in the past (see e.g. Janke 1995; Lindlar 1995; Sietz 1996). In addition, competition continues between EMAS and ISO 14001 as alternative environmental management standards. Frequent reports on the relative take-up of these rival schemes continue (see e.g. ENDS 1998a). Emphasis on membership and cost is critical; for example, ISO reveals 'More than 80% of 500 companies surveyed on their experiences with implementation of [ISO] environmental management systems (EMSs) found them to be cost-effective, with over 60% quoting payback periods on their investment of less than 12 months' (ISO 1999a). However, gradual signs of mutual dependency between standards organisations are being recognised with the launch of the Standards Actions in the Global Market Forum in November 1999, bringing together all parties with a stake in environmental standardisation.

The economic effects of EMAS have been analysed by the independent working group of entrepreneurs (Arbeitsgemeinschaft Selbständiger Unternehmer [ASU]) for Germany. Based on a survey and questionnaire with almost 800 companies they found that the costs of implementing an EMAS-conforming environmental management system was around US$100,000 on average. One-third of companies reduced costs by up to US$80,000 per year, and one-third by up to US$320,000 per year; the remaining companies did not report any cost reductions. For the nearly 800 companies surveyed, the average payback period on investments in the environmental management system and on environmental protection measures was only 1.5 years (ASU 1999).

Figure 14.2 shows the idea behind ISO 14001. The main requirements for the environmental management system are similar to those of EMAS. The company must establish:

☐ An environmental policy

☐ An environmental accounting or monitoring system

☐ Implementation plans

Figure 14.2 **Core parts of ISO 14001**

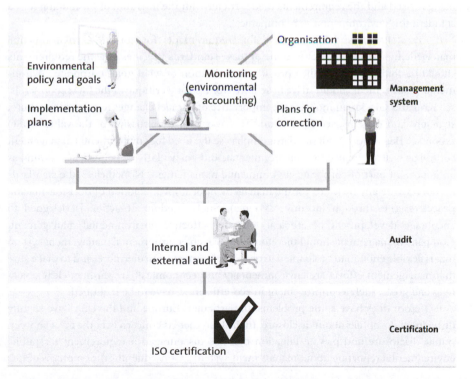

☐ Plans for correction

☐ An effective and efficient organisation

As with EMAS's 1998 changes that extended the scheme to non-industrial companies, external revision of the ISO corporate environmental management system is necessary. One defect requiring attention is that, in contrast to the EMAS, ISO 14001 does not require companies to adopt external ecological reporting.

Also, EMAS (until 1998) and ISO were both site-oriented. However, ISO 14001 does not exclude the application of its standard to products. Just as with quality standard ISO 9000, strong pressure was expected to be exerted on companies to have their production sites certified. First tendencies show that in some business-to-business relationships the fulfilment of an environmental management standard is becoming a requirement for suppliers (see e.g. Fichter 1995). Differences between the standards are small—apart from the fact that ISO 14001 does not require a public disclosure of environmental impacts.

Politics and market pressure will determine which standard will prevail in the years to come. However, ISO is a clear favourite. First, ISO 14001 is an international standard also applied widely (e.g. in the USA, Japan, South-East Asia and Switzerland) whereas EMAS covers only member countries in the European Union (EU). Second, ISO and its national standardisation organisations are private organisations that have already established commercial relationships with companies (e.g. with ISO 9000). Last, a thorough study and comparison of the two standards shows that ISO 14001 will cause a smaller administrative workload for the companies involved. These points may be reasons why EMAS is currently being revised and the requirements made stricter with the intention of positioning it as a standard for 'environmental star companies'.

BS 7750, EMAS and ISO 14001 define requirements for corporate environmental management systems. However, none of these standards specifies how the requirements should be fulfilled, nor do they provide an indication of what goals corporate environmental management should strive to achieve (for a strong critique of the ISO 14000 series, see Krut and Gleckman 1998; for the importance of parallel changes to corporate culture, structure and systems, see Epstein and Roy 1997; for a discussion of the value of ISO 14000, see Begley 1997). All standards emphasise the need for environmental management control as well as the need for environmental, and particularly ecological, accounting as an important part of corporate environmental management. Nonetheless, the standards do not provide any methods for the management or implementation of decision-making processes, (i.e. through incentive systems). Such freedom of action is designed to encourage development of efficient tools for effective environmental management. Company management should therefore establish an environmental management system that is flexible enough to be adapted to new developments. Furthermore, and to make sure that management efforts are environmentally and economically rewarding, clear objectives and goals, such as improvement in eco-efficiency, have to be identified.

ISO 14001 does have some problems. In particular, Europe and the USA have slightly different philosophies about disclosure. In the USA there is concern over the links between public disclosure and private litigation that has discouraged a requirement for public environmental reporting about management systems. Consequently, the emphasis of ISO

14001 on compliance with processes rather than improved environmental performance makes it more appealing to some companies, but at the expense of credibility, feedback to stakeholders and external accountability. EMAS also appears to be stronger than ISO 14001 not only because it requires public disclosure but also because disclosures are specified—activities, environmental issues raised, pollution emissions (including emissions reductions and targets for continual improvement), waste generation and comments about overall environmental performance—and must be verified by an independent verifier. However, ISO 14001 is an internationally recognised standard that can be applied by all companies—small, medium-sized and large—and does identify a small set of core issues to be addressed. In this sense, it is a good starting point for any company wishing to institute an environmental management system.

The next section will provide a brief overview of the most important methods of corporate environmental management. After this, in Section 14.4, integration of environmental accounting into the management eco-control process will be discussed as it has risen to become one of the most important environmental management concepts being applied to practice (see e.g. Günther and Wagner 1993; Hallay and Pfriem 1992; Hopfenbeck and Jasch 1993; Janzen 1996; Schaltegger and Sturm 1992b, 1992c, 1995, 1996; Schulz and Schulz 1994).

14.2 Methods of corporate environmental management

This is not the place to discuss specific environmental management tools in depth but rather to show the link between the main tools of corporate environmental management with environmental accounting and environmental management systems. Figure 14.3 indicates that contemporary methods of corporate environmental management are not particularly new and that they rely on well-known traditional management tools.

Environmental accounting, auditing and reporting, eco-control and total quality environmental management (TQEM) are all based on traditional accounting notions of auditing, reporting, control and total quality management (TQM) (Dobyns and Crawford-Mason 1991; Greenberg and Unger 1991; Petrauskas 1992). LCA and costing is a special case of ecological accounting and simply corresponds to calculation (costing). It represents a single-time ecological calculation (ecological costing) with its scope extended to cover the entire life-cycle of a product.

Whichever standard of environmental management is adopted—BS 7750, EMAS, the EU regulation for a product eco-label or ISO 14001—they all address some of the following key functions of 'good environmental management':

☐ Goal-setting

☐ Information management

☐ Support for decision-making, organisation or planning of environmental management programmes

CONVENTIONAL MANAGEMENT TOOLS		ENVIRONMENTAL MANAGEMENT
Calculation, costing	▶▶▶▶▶	Life-cycle assessment
Accounting	▶▶▶▶▶	Environmental accounting
Auditing	▶▶▶▶▶	Environmental auditing
Reporting	▶▶▶▶▶	Environmental reporting
Total quality management	▶▶▶▶▶	Total quality environmental management
Control	▶▶▶▶▶	Eco-control

Figure 14.3 **Methods of environmental management derived from methods of conventional economic management**

Source: Schaltegger 1994a

☐ Steering, implementation and control

☐ Communication

☐ Internal and external auditing and/or review

Figure 14.4 provides an overview of various well-known environmental management methods and shows which tools support the key functions of environmental management as defined by EMAS and ISO 14001 (see also UNEP 1995). Other tools of environmental management such as environmental business re-engineering are not explicitly shown as they are usually derivatives of the previously mentioned set of tools. These tools support different corporate environmental management functions, and are discussed briefly below.

14.2.1 Life-cycle assessment

The main focus of LCA is on data management (single calculations) and assessment (see Section 10.3). LCA also addresses some aspects of goal-setting (strategy and planning) and decision support. However, other functions of corporate environmental management, such as steering and communication, are not supported or are only partially supported by LCA.

14.2.2 Environmental accounting and reporting

Traditionally, accounting is the main corporate information management tool (see e.g. DTTI/IISD/SustainAbility 1993). All management activities rely on or are at least influenced by accounting information. Environmental accounting, as shown especially in Chapter 4, is the application of established tools of accounting (i.e. tools of information management, analysis and communication) to environmental management. However, environmental accounting is a management tool and must be comprehensively incorpo-

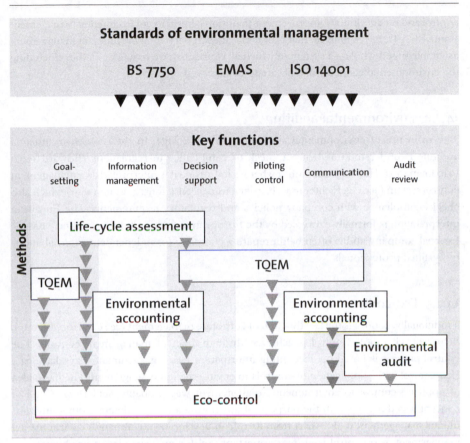

BS = British Standard   EMAS = EU Eco-management and Audit Scheme   ISO = standard of the International Organization for Standardization   TQEM = total quality environmental management

Figure 14.4 **Functions and tools of corporate environmental management**

Source: Schaltegger 1996a

rated into the environmental management process. Only then can environmental information be integrated into goal-setting, steering, implementation and communication.

14.2.3 Total quality environmental management

TQEM is the application of the principles of TQM (Deming 1982, 1993; Walton 1986) to environmental management. In this connection the term 'quality' is expanded to include environmental quality. TQEM is based on statistical tools to achieve quality control, namely, various charts for data analysis, steering and internal communication (PCEQ 1991). In addition, TQEM is based on a statistical and engineering philosophy and supports goal-setting with an emphasis on the continuous improvement of quality. In its original form TQEM, does not integrate measures of economic performance with measures of quality or, rather, environmental quality. Apart from an emphasis on statistical quality control and on continuous improvement (a notion central to environmental management standards), TQEM is holistic, that is, it looks at each part of environmental management as an integrated whole—a system in which all elements have to work together (including the environmental element) if goals are to be achieved.

14.2.4 Environmental auditing

The main use of environmental auditing is as a checklist. In the USA environmental auditing is understood as being a check of compliance to regulations (Edward 1992; Friedman 1992; Hall and Case 1992) whereas in Europe it is interpreted as a management control system (see e.g. Fichter 1995; Paasikivi 1994; UNEP 1995: 4; Vinten 1991) which also checks compliance with company policies and regulatory requirements. The European interpretation is formally expressed by the European regulation for the voluntary EMAS. Internal company audits often help prepare a company for independent external audits by certified professionals.

14.2.5 Eco-control

Traditionally, control is the key function of corporate management (see e.g. Horvath 1990; Schierenbeck 1996). Control is achieved through a set of management controls. The control process is based on accounting information (see e.g. Neumann-Szyszka 1994). Eco-control is the application of controls to environmental management. The basic idea of applying control to environmental management was probably Seidel's (1988). The concept was designed with the purpose of integrating and co-ordinating other environmental management tools. Apart from its role in developing a company's environmental management, eco-control is also an important tool for management of production-site environmental performance in accordance with EMAS, ISO 14001 or BS 7750 (see e.g. Fichter 1995). Eco-control ensures that environmental issues are dealt with through a continuous, company-wide process, by focusing on incentives for making congruent decisions (decisions where individual and company goals are the same)—that is, through use of internal taxes to achieve the desired behaviour (see also Burritt 1998).

14.2.6 Summary

Figure 14.4 shows that environmental accounting and reporting, LCA, TQEM and environmental auditing are tools that are particularly strong in supporting specific functions of environmental management. It is also clear that every environmental management method aimed at supporting real improvement in performance will have to rely on some kind of environmental accounting. Environmental accounting supports information management, that is, compilation, analysis and decisions based on environmentally induced financial and environmental impact added (EIA) data.

However, information is not a substitute for action but is necessary for informed action. To improve a company's environmental record in an effective and efficient way, the environmental information that has been collected and analysed must be channelled into an environmental management feedback process. In conventional financial management, accounting information is used as the main input for control and decision-making. Eco-control, by analogy, is the systematic process and anchor for corporate environmental management.

The next section will examine eco-control in further detail as it is the only approach that relies on environmental accounting and was designed as a co-ordination and integration device for other tools of corporate environmental management.

14.3 Management eco-control

14.3.1 Perspectives on eco-control

Management eco-control is the application of financial and strategic control methods to environmental management. The concept of eco-control has also been applied to the state, to public administration and public policy (see Schaltegger *et al.* 1996). It provides a decision support system for management (Schneidewind *et al.* 1997; Vedsø 1993). Eco-control is among the most popular corporate environmental management approaches in continental Europe but is largely unknown in the English-speaking West. Several concepts of eco-control have been developed in the German-speaking parts of Europe (Austria, Germany and Switzerland) and successfully applied by an increasing number of multi-national, medium-sized and small companies.

Originally, eco-control was designed for the manufacturing industry (see e.g. Hallay and Pfriem 1992; Schaltegger and Sturm 1998; Schulz 1991; Seidel 1988). Recently, it has also been applied to service industries (e.g. banking; see Knörzer 1995) and to the management of fauna and flora (Buser and Schaltegger 1998).

As financial and strategic control are defined in a number of different ways, it is no surprise that a number of versions of eco-control have been published. Three main approaches to eco-control can be distinguished (Schaltegger and Kempke 1996):

❑ Financially oriented eco-control methods attempt to compute, analyse, steer and communicate environmentally induced financial impacts (see e.g. Fischer 1993; Kloock 1990a; Schreiner 1988; Wagner and Janzen 1991). These methods rely on environmentally differentiated conventional accounting. Money is used as the unit of measurement (one-dimensional).

❑ Ecologically oriented eco-control methods are based on satellite systems of ecological accounting that are an extension of existing accounting and control systems. Their purpose is to steer corporate impacts on the natural environment (see e.g. Hallay and Pfriem 1992; Lehmann and Clausen 1991; Schulz 1989; Seidel 1988). The units of measurement used are couched in physical terms (one-dimensional).

❑ Economically–ecologically integrated concepts of eco-control integrate the two approaches mentioned above (Günther 1993; Schaltegger and Sturm 1992b,

1998). They take into account the evaluation and steering of financial and ecological impacts of corporate activities. Measurement is two-dimensional: in terms of monetary units per unit of environmental impact added.

All three eco-control perspectives can be used for strategic as well as for operations management.

The financial consequences of corporate environmental protection are usually an important constraint on companies. Nevertheless, the potential cost savings from trying to avoid behaviour that leads to imposition of environmental taxes or liabilities can often only be detected, and the eco-efficiency can only be calculated once environmental interventions have already been analysed. Therefore, a control of environmentally induced financial flows is necessary but not sufficient for comprehensive environmental management.

Also, mere control of environmental impacts that a company causes is insufficient for effective and efficient environmental protection. Sustainable corporate environmental management will be successful only if it enhances rather than reduces a company's competitiveness and only if expenditure can guarantee satisfactory environmental protection.

In conclusion, integrated economic and environmental information appears to be necessary for effective and efficient control-based environmental management. The following section will deal with integrated eco-control.

14.3.2 The process and concept of integrated eco-control

Integrated eco-control is a permanent, institutionalised, internal management process based on environmental accounting and reporting. The concept of eco-control, corresponding to financial and strategic control, is concerned with the environmental and financial impacts of a company. Eco-control can be divided into five procedures (Figure 14.5):

1. Goal and policy formulation

2. Information management (environmental accounting and reporting)

3. Decision support

4. Steering and implementation

5. Internal and external communication

All environmental management systems, including EMAS and ISO 14001, require an environmental policy as well as clear and measurable annual environmental protection goals. With a focus on the aim of improving corporate eco-efficiency, economic and ecological aspects of operational goals should both be considered.

Information management is the core of any environmental management system. In practice, it is often the case that only what is measured is managed. The establishment of an environmental accounting system is one way of increasing the efficiency of information management.

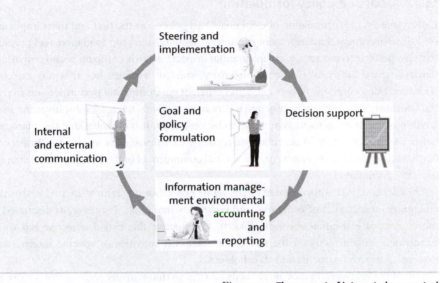

Figure 14.5 **The concept of integrated eco-control**

Source: Schaltegger and Sturm 1998

Managers frequently suffer from excessively detailed information that hampers efficient selection and use of relevant data. Any information concerning environmental interventions has therefore to be assessed according to its relevance. Furthermore, integration of economic and environmental aspects is necessary. Effective environmental management requires incentive systems to steer (or 'pilot') and implement corporate plans in the most efficient manner. Internal communications play a central role in efficient implementation. However, communications with external stakeholders are also supported by internal processes and this increases the gains from sound internal environmental management.

Although it is important to establish a clear structure and plan for all procedures, steps do not necessarily have to be completed in sequence. Nevertheless, the five procedures are presented in logical order in the next five sections.

Specific 'guiding' instruments are needed in order to implement the eco-control process. The process provides management with a detailed analysis of the place, cause, extent and timing of environmental impacts. In addition, the total corporate environmental impact caused should be kept in mind when dealing with individual problems. This will avoid ineffective and inefficient developments (e.g. spending more and more on scrubbers to reduce smaller and smaller amounts of sulphur dioxide [SO_2] instead of reducing far worse environmental impacts from nitrogen oxides [NO_x]).

The importance of each eco-control procedure depends on the environmental issues faced by the company and on their effect on commercial success factors. However, companies should consider carefully whether they have given enough thought to every procedure. Too often, environmental management tools are introduced without any clear understanding of the corporate environmental strategy being followed.

14.2.3 Goal and policy formulation

Unfortunately, the formulation of clear goals and policies as the first and most important step of environmental management is often neglected. Many top managers feel pressure to do something to reduce the environmental impacts of their companies and embark on 'environmental activism' that contains many isolated activities but that has no clear direction. For a company to be a good and efficient environmental performer and to reap the benefits of being an environmental leader in its markets, the reason for investing in an environmental management system has to be very clear. It is essential that top managers define the purpose of environmental management activities and are involved in the process of goal-setting in order to ensure organisational commitment to the environmental strategy once it is formulated.

On a general level, improvement of corporate eco-efficiency is an attractive goal as this encourages integration of economic and environmental goals. However, as discussed in the context of eco-efficiency indicators, to be effective this broad objective has to be subdivided, with a focus on the needs, interests and activities of specific internal and external company segments and stakeholders.

One of the first steps in moving towards a situation that is under eco-control is to assess and rank exposure to and importance of different environmental issues for overall company performance. Depending on this initial analysis, the operational goals of eco-control and the perspective taken will differ. Analysis should be conducted from the point of view of a company stakeholder; that is, one must ask which aspects of eco-efficiency, and thus which eco-efficiency indicators, are relevant for the different stakeholder groups. The potential degree of exposure to different environmental issues should guide the company in its implementation of eco-control. Here, environmental science must play its role by providing management with an idea of what, from a scientific point of view, the most dominant environmental issues are and how they apply to the company. Knowledge of main issues is important because sooner or later such issues are likely to influence company success, whether through new legislation, through public or consumer perception and behaviour or otherwise.

Table 14.1 shows an exposure portfolio. The expected exposure of the company to different environmental problems (e.g. the greenhouse effect or the depletion of the ozone layer) is shown across the table. The importance assigned to these environmental issues by various stakeholders is depicted down the table. Those stakeholders that are most important economically for the company are shown in bold. For most companies, governmental stakeholders such as environmental protection agencies, customers, non-governmental organisations (NGOs) and investors are among the most powerful and are usually treated as the most important stakeholders where environmental issues are concerned.

The relative importance that different stakeholders assign to environmental problems can be measured by surveys or be discussed in company working groups guided by learning-circle kits that highlight the main issues as a basis for discussion. In contrast, company exposure to different environmental problems is revealed by environmental audit and ecological accounting (SustainAbility/UNEP 1996b). The relative economic importance of different stakeholders depends on the amount and exchangeability of

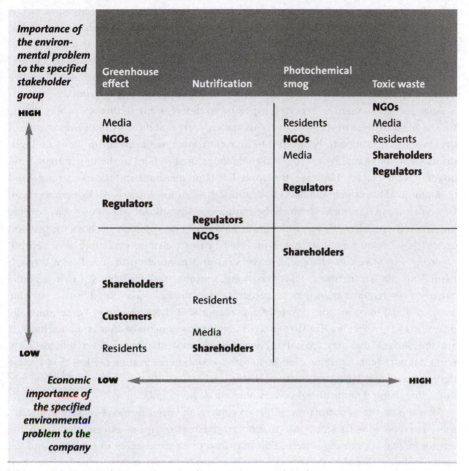

Table 14.1 **Key environmental issues and environmental exposure of an example**

Source: Schaltegger and Sturm 1998

resources provided as well as the possibility of substituting one specific stakeholder group for another. Companies tend to negotiate with stakeholders in sequence, because of limited or 'bounded' rationality (Cyert and March 1963; Simon 1957) unless there is a critical incident when instant communication with all stakeholders is needed.

In the example shown in Table 14.1 stakeholders who are concerned about the environment—shareholders, customers, NGOs and environmental regulators—are seen to have the strongest influence on the economic success of the company. However, only shareholders (who feel the economic consequences of toxic waste) and environmental regulators (who are interested in legal compliance with regulations concerning photo-chemical smog and toxic waste) are deeply concerned about the environmental problems to which the company is strongly exposed.

In the beginning, this first procedure is mainly a task for top management to tackle. However, in order to cover the whole range of corporate activities, it is recommended that representatives of different departments are involved from the beginning. In a second step, lower down the organisational hierarchy, line and staff managers who investigate and formulate opinions on topics of special importance in their field of competence should be involved in the formulation of the strategy by contributing to working groups.

Analysis of a company's expected exposure to different environmental problems, the weight given to these problems by various stakeholders and the economic importance of the stakeholder groups to be taken into account enable management to focus on high-priority environmental issues (the stakeholders printed in bold in the upper right-hand quadrant of the table). However, the upper left-hand quadrant and the lower right-hand quadrant in Table 14.1 should also be scrutinised, albeit less intensively, by management. Issues of low public priority to which the company is a significant contributor may become important if a problem triggers a change in stakeholder perceptions. In short, the position of stakeholders on any issue noted in Table 14.1 can change over time and, second, company exposure can change as its process and production mixes change through natural adaptation, mergers, takeovers, joint ventures and franchises. Environmental management requires managers to recognise that the risks associated with corporate environmental impacts and stakeholder perception of those risks can be substantially different. Hence there is a need to manage scientific assessments of environmental hazards and the 'outrage' that may accompany an environmental intervention, even if in technical terms it is not a high-risk issue (Sandman 1986). People perceive things as less risky if these things are controllable not uncontrollable, voluntary not involuntary, familiar not unfamiliar, natural not artificial and chronic not acute (Sandman 1986).

After this first eco-control procedure is complete, and priorities have become apparent, more detailed eco-efficiency information is gathered by using information from the environmental accounting system. This may lead to a reassessment of priorities and the revision of operational goals.

14.3.4 Information management (environmental accounting and reporting)

The recording of information about environmental interventions and environmentally induced financial information is necessary in order to build a basis for decisions rooted in an eco-efficiency criterion. Therefore, efficient environmental management requires well-designed systems of environmentally differentiated accounting and ecological accounting.

Recording begins after having established an environmental accounting system for the company. Identification of potential sources of data is the first step in compiling data in the environmental accounts. Special attention must be paid to existing sources of environmentally relevant data, such as management accounting for materials and the amount of energy used, site permits for some pollutants, production statistics or the technical specifications of production machines.

From an economic perspective, because of the costs of data collection, it does not make sense to aim to provide a comprehensive inventory of all mass and energy flows—quite apart from the fact that this goal cannot be achieved anyway because of scientific limitations on data measurement and availability. Usually, the process of data compilation will need to be spread over several years, digging deeper each year until at the margin the benefit obtained from more detailed data is equal to the cost of obtaining those data.

Management accounting and ecological accounting employ similar terminology and methods, which ensures that managers and staff compiling data and users, being able to understand the approach easily, have a gentle learning curve. Management accounting benefits from having an inventory of environmental data in which environmentally induced costs, such as energy costs, pollution abatement costs or the costs of material flows, can be traced or allocated to appropriate cost centres and cost objects.

Although a focus on selected 'relevant environmental interventions' does not provide the same breadth of information for pollution prevention strategies as a wider focus on interventions, as fewer resources need to be devoted to the compilation of data on selected interventions, it can still offer a sound basis for improvement of corporate eco-efficiency through eco-control.

Contrary to common belief, measurement of economic performance has also gone through a rapid phase of redevelopment in recent years, with increases in shareholder value being promoted as the benchmark for economic success (see Chapter 8). Management should therefore be aware of the effects of corporate environmental management on a company's shareholder value.

14.4.5 Decision support

The goal of the third procedure for achieving eco-control is to provide decision-makers with a logical and transparent method for taking environmentally and economically sound decisions in accordance with the data obtained from the second procedure (Figure 14.6).

The reason for collecting information on corporate environmental impacts as well as on environmentally induced financial impacts is the calculation of eco-efficiency. Further measures, such as EIA indicators for specific environmental problems (e.g. the greenhouse effect), are necessary to improve analysis of the different facets of environmental impacts and to identify alternatives for their cost-efficient prevention and reduction.

One effective way to visualise eco-efficiency is through an eco-efficiency portfolio (see Ilinitch and Schaltegger 1995; Schaltegger and Sturm 1994). At a conceptual level, this matrix-oriented tool can help companies evaluate environmental and economic impacts of specific products, strategic business units and industry mix (for diversified companies). Additionally, this tool supports strategic decisions involving divestiture, acquisition, product development and marketing, communication with external stakeholders and negotiation with environmental compliance groups and regulators.

Portfolio approaches have been used for several decades to help diversified companies analyse their business mix (for the Boston Consulting Group matrix, see Hedley 1977; Hill and Jones 1992; Hofer and Schendel 1978; for other matrices, see Hill and Jones 1992; Pearce and Robinson 1991). Although the dimensions of the models and corresponding matrices vary, each dimension addresses only the economic aspects of the corporate portfolio. Although most managers would agree that environmental decisions affect

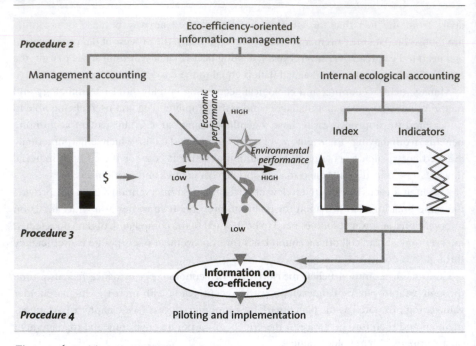

Figure 14.6 **Decision-support system**

Source: Schaltegger and Sturm 1998

economic success, the environmental dimension has only recently been explicitly incorporated into strategic portfolio analysis.

Figure 14.7 illustrates the eco-efficiency portfolio matrix previously introduced in Section 3.4. The eco-efficiency portfolio involves quantifying the environmental impact added of business activities and comparing it with the business's economic performance. The vertical axis measures economic performance, and the horizontal axis shows the environmental impact added. This general approach is applicable to any company or product group and can be employed with as many or as few details as are relevant to a manager. Terminology used is similar to that used in the Boston Consulting Group matrix (see Hedley 1977: 10). However, the matrix combines different dimensions so that the conclusions cannot be interpreted in exactly the same way.

The optimum position on the eco-efficiency matrix is the 'green star' with its high economic impact and low environmental harm. An example of this sort of product might be a high-market-share, recyclable white paper produced by an energy-efficient mill that uses a non-chlorine bleaching process. Non-plastic-coated paper and greeting cards made from recycled paper tend to be products with high contribution margins for which the demand is relatively large yet which also have a relatively low environmental impact if produced in this way.

The opposite matrix cell, the 'dirty dog' position, is to be avoided, although it may actually result from a combination of management decisions, the history of the company, imposition of tighter standards, increased industrial risk and newly emerging environ-

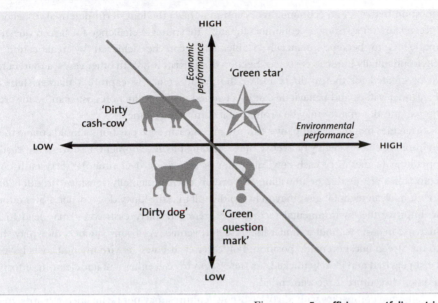

Figure 14.7 **Eco-efficiency portfolio matrix**

Source: Schaltegger and Sturm 1995, 1998

mental issues. An example of a 'dirty dog' product might be bleached pulp produced by a smaller, older, energy-intensive mill that uses a chlorine-based bleaching process. Such mills cannot achieve the economies of scale needed to gain high market shares in their commodity markets. From an integrated ecological–economic perspective many products manufactured with such generic methods cause environmental harm without producing significant economic benefits.

Many intermediate positions exist between these two extremes. 'Dirty cash-cows' tend to possess high market shares in mature or declining 'dirty' industries. An example of a 'dirty cash-cow' might be plastic-coated, white paper from a relatively large and efficient pulp mill that uses chlorine bleaching technologies and which benefits from the paper industry lobbying for low emission standards or high pollution quotas. Such businesses can, in the short run, be highly profitable for companies and the communities in which they operate, so that there is an economic incentive to continue production. This position is very weak and risky in the long run, however, because of the increasing possibility that a potential loss of reputation, as well as liability for a potential environmental disaster, could turn into actual costs for the company. Increasingly, stakeholders and 'watchdog groups' search for ways to establish financial and also criminal penalties for such actions.

A counterpoint to the 'dirty cash-cow' might be the 'green question mark'. A 'green question mark' is in a weak position because of its low financial contribution, even though it is an environmentally attractive business. Examples of this position are high-priced, biodegradable paper products. Such products may have experienced either a limited success or failure in their markets, depending on their cost structure, their technology and their ability to convince a growing number of consumers that paying premium prices for environmentally sound products is worthwhile. Products that may be categorised as 'green question marks' in an economic recession may have the long-term potential to become 'green stars' in a stronger economic climate. The strategic challenge for 'green question marks' is to become financially viable. This can be achieved by reallocation of environmentally induced costs (see Section 6.3; Burritt 1998). In other cases, a market has to be created for the products and/or the producer has to capture a market share. If consumer values and behaviour can be changed, or if production costs can be lowered, 'green question marks' may be profitable at some future time.

Strategies that move companies toward 'green cash-cow' positions should enable them to improve eco-efficiency or even achieve sustainable development. Likewise, the cost of operating in the 'dirty cash-cow' quadrant is increasing over time. If 'dirty cash-cow' companies are unable or unwilling to develop environmentally sensitive products and invest in clean technologies, they may rapidly fall into the 'dirty dog' corner. Later efforts to improve the environmental record of entrenched 'dirty cash-cows' may lead to an increase in costs without a similar increase in revenues. As a consequence, they may shift to the 'green question mark' position. For 'dirty cash-cows', environmental costs have to be supervised and closely tracked. As they begin to rise, either a major clean-up effort or a quick divestiture is recommended.

Although companies with 'dirty cash-cow' cultures may not be inclined towards green solutions, a conflict or trade-off between environmental and financial goals is not inevitable. Proactive, innovative pollution and risk prevention strategies and the intro-duction of environmentally benign inputs may improve the company's environmental position. Such actions may also increase the contribution margin and net present value through lower input and production costs or through increasing sales and therefore may even move 'dirty dogs' into the 'green star' quadrant.

Depending on the purpose of analysis, a three-dimensional eco-efficiency portfolio matrix with one ecological and two economic performance indicators (e.g. market growth and profitability) can be drawn. The advantage of a three-dimensional portfolio matrix is that more measures can be integrated and illustrated. However, the portfolios and their interpretation become quite complicated.

The eco-efficiency portfolio matrix has been used to evaluate strategic options on at least three levels: corporate, business and product (see e.g. Ilinitch and Schaltegger 1995). Table 14.2 shows the interaction between the three strategic levels, their stakeholder groups and the types of decision associated with each.

The interpretation of eco-efficiency portfolios is as delicate as the discussion of portfolio matrices suggests. The most obvious strategic alternatives for management in the context of static and/or dynamic eco-efficiency portfolio analysis seem to be:

☐ Eliminate 'dirty dogs'.

☐ Invest in 'green stars' to keep them profitable and green.

☐ Invest in the 'greening' of 'dirty dogs' and shifting them into a 'green star' category if possible, or eliminate them.

☐ Invest in order to improve the 'economic health' of 'green question marks', thereby shifting them to green cash-cow positions, if possible, or eliminating them.

	INTERNAL		EXTERNAL	
	Stakeholder group	Focus	Stakeholder group	Focus
Corporate strategy level	Top management, strategic planning management, environmental management, government, public and investor relations, financial management, legal management	Corporate strategy and policy, environmental record and image of company environmental compliance	Green investment, fund management, investors, watchdog groups, government and regulatory agencies	Selection of shares, bonds, etc., firms to blame, environmental compliance
Business strategy level	Division SBU management, competitor analysis management, marketing management, purchasing department	Relative position and strengths of company, potential assets and liabilities	Competitors, industry analysts, investment bankers, industry consultants, purchasing groups	Relative position and strengths of competitor, cost-effective pollution prevention, contingent liabilities
Product strategy level	Product management, marketing management, patenting and licensing management, manufacturing management	Sales arguments, potential assets, comparison of technologies, evaluation of environmental impacts and compliance, communication with agencies	Consumers, marketing consultants, green labelling groups, regulatory agencies, lawyers, manufacturers	Purchase, consumption, communications, environmental harm, compliance, product liability suits, purchase, liabilities

SBU = strategic business unit

Table 14.2 **Strategic dimensions of eco-integrated portfolio matrices**

Source: Ilinitch and Schaltegger 1995

These general conclusions are delicate as the analysis and practical application of the Boston Consulting Group matrix shows (for further discussion of the pros and cons of a portfolio matrix approach, see Hill and Jones 1992: 273f.; Jauch and Glueck 1988: 269f.). Nevertheless, such portfolios are mainly a way to visualise and integrate information from ecological and conventional accounting for strategic purposes. In practice, management also appreciates another use of eco-integrated accounting information: namely, for investment appraisal.

At the corporate strategy level, companies are concerned with their portfolio of businesses and with the issues that affect the company as a whole. Much has been written about the economic impact of a company's portfolio of businesses in terms of risk diversification, managerial complexity and economic profitability (see e.g. Hill and Jones 1992; Schendel and Hofer 1978). Understanding the relationship between environmental actions and economic results is increasingly important at the level of corporate strategy, because environmental choices affect the reputation of a company as well as its bottom line. The discussion in Part 2 of this book as well as environmental rankings that have appeared in the popular and business press vividly illustrate this point (see e.g. Banks and Ballard 1997; Crawford 1992; HUI 1994, 1996; Rice 1993; Speich 1992; Vaughan and Mickle 1993; Weir and Yamin 1993). Strategic options at the corporate strategy level include choosing which new businesses to enter, evaluating potential candidates for acquisition and divestiture, allocating scarce or constrained resources among business units, monitoring and enhancing a company's reputation and evaluating its ability to obtain good financing conditions compared with its competitors.

At the business strategy level, options include evaluating the potential impact of new, complementary and substitute products on the reputation and performance of the strategic business unit (SBU) and assessing the strategic position of a business unit in relation to its industry competitors. Additional possibilities include the acquisition of patents and production capacity, new plant locations and product mix decisions.

At the product strategy level, options include investment in technological innovations, the exploration of new uses for products, product marketing decisions, relaunches, environmental upgrades and the discontinuation of certain products.

Internal stakeholders such as top management, divisional managers or product managers may have access to the most accurate and specific data available. However, interested external groups such as investors, consumers and quite often regulatory agencies, too, must base their decisions on information available to the public, which tends to be more general and less reliable. Nevertheless, actions by external stakeholders are a function of the economic and ecological information available about a company, its businesses and products. Also, companies must assess their position in relation to that of their competitors by using externally available data. Therefore, it is important for corporate managers to consider both internal and external data in their analyses.

An important consideration when comparing companies or products with use of the eco-efficiency matrix is the industrial environment within which the company or product exists. It is idealistic to assume that 'dirty' industries can be eliminated from the industrial landscape, at least in the foreseeable future, even though ecological modernisation of industry has this as an aim. In practice, advanced companies in 'dirty' industries should be identified and encouraged on the basis of any improvement they can achieve and their relative position within their industry rather than in comparison with standards applying to all other companies (the best-of-the-class approach). This basic consideration is commonly used today for the assessment of different companies and industries by eco-efficiency funds (see e.g. Cummings and Burritt 1999; Schaltegger and Figge 1999). Similarly, businesses that score significantly below their competitors in relatively 'green' industries should be more carefully scrutinised by regulators and other stakeholders and encouraged to improve their records.

Eco-integrated matrices allow management to undertake both a static and a dynamic analysis by comparing the position of products, SBUs or companies over a certain period of time. All movements towards 'green star' positions represent sustainable growth of economic performance along with a reduction or maintenance of environmental impacts.

Economically or environmentally proactive strategies lead to better ecological and/or economic performance through innovation. Environmentally and economically reactive strategies, on the other hand, are characterised by being second-best imitations performed with a time-lag. The result of poorly enforced or defensive strategies can be no movement at all in the eco-efficiency matrix. As general recommendations are always dangerous, it is very important to analyse all opportunities available to convert 'dirty dogs' into 'green stars'.

In practice, the following different approaches to improve the 'greenness' of products, business units and companies can be observed:

☐ **The repair approach.** By focusing on a specific product, the environmental intervention that causes most EIA units is investigated; for example, a scrubber is added to the production step that releases an environmental intervention.

☐ **The exchange approach.** Inputs that cause hazardous environmental interventions are, for instance, replaced by other, less harmful inputs (e.g. the replacement of halons by hydrochlorofluorocarbons [HCFCs]).

☐ **The quick strategic approach.** For example, the product with the highest environmental impact added per dollar yield is eliminated.

☐ **The functional approach.** Management tries, for instance, to find entirely new and 'greener' ways to fulfil a certain function (e.g. to meet the wishes of buyers), by, for example, replacing a product by a service.

It is clear that in many cases only a functional approach will lead to an overall improvement in the economic and ecological results. However, sunk costs related to investments in production processes often limit this strategy. The functional approach is therefore often a long-term strategic choice rather than an operational option. Furthermore, as discussed next, any decision taken on the basis of information processed and created has to be implemented effectively if it is actually going to lead to an improvement in corporate eco-efficiency.

14.3.6 Steering and implementation

Many environmental management tools fail to consider the importance of the implementation process. It is therefore crucial to design the organisation for environmental management carefully. Being a large and complex matter in itself, this issue can only be touched on here (for a more detailed overview, see Birke *et al.* 1997; Pfriem 1991; Winter 1997). An important consideration is that environmental protection should not be delegated to a separate supporting team composed of specialised staff. If corporate environmental management aims to be effective, responsibilities have to remain with line managers, even though they have staff supporting their decision-making. New organisational forms provide additional reinforcement for this view. For example, network-form organisations are designed with line managers as the entrepreneurs, strategists and decision-makers, with middle managers as horizontal integrators building competences across the company and with top management to challenge the status quo rather than to allocate resources (Hope and Fraser 1997).

Eco-control addresses different levels within the organisation and combines the very different tasks of shop-floor environmental data compilation and strategic environmental management. By using the language of managers, it helps lower the barriers to implementation. In addition, it bridges the gaps between different users of environmental management information.

Based on a divisional form of organisation, information must be collected by production managers and passed on to middle management controllers. The controllers have to consolidate data and prepare those data for the top management so that top management can make strategic decisions. Line managers need access to the data they require to meet their responsibilities, be it for the marketing of a product, the appraisal of a new investment in production equipment or the control of operational or even strategic performance at a site.

Implementation is crucial to eco-control. More and more companies have developed sophisticated systems of performance evaluation to remunerate their employees. One way of ensuring the successful integration of eco-control is to link the remuneration package of managers to defined eco-efficiency targets. As with eco-efficiency indicators in general, the range of possible performance indicators is, in principle, unlimited. However, just as with payments linked to financial performance, incentive structures must be chosen with great care and linked to the measures that are under a manager's control and that are linked to activities for which a manager is accountable. Nothing creates more frustration than targets that cannot be achieved because of factors beyond the control of the manager or employee being evaluated.

Eco-efficiency performance indicators always have an economic and an environmental dimension. Conventionally, upper-management performance indicators have a strategic dimension (e.g. 10% annual reduction of company contribution to the greenhouse effect per dollar of shareholder value). For lower management levels these performance indicators must be more detailed and divided into economic and environmental indicators (e.g. based on the assumption that coal usage is the main contribution to the greenhouse effect, the environmental performance indicator can be defined as coal usage per unit of product manufactured). Another aspect of implementation is that it is important for people whose performance is being measured to be involved in the definition of the indicator.

If a decision-support system shows that a company's environmental problems are linked to only a few clearly defined substances, an internal tax system can be established. Internal 'taxation' works in the same way as external taxation through the macroeconomic fiscal system, by adding costs to the most harmful substances and undesirable practices. As an internal system, the taxes can be revenue-neutral for a company but can create a strong incentive for the various levels of management (e.g. product managers and divisional managers) to find environmentally benign and therefore internally 'untaxed' solutions for their products across the whole life-cycle. Implementation tools should also take careful account of the corporate culture, existing management tools and the importance of environmental accounting and internal reporting in order to maintain accountability linkages.

14.3.7 Internal and external communication

Internal and external communication are of major and growing importance for the successful management of a company and thus form an integral part of the eco-control process. Internally, the link between environmental strategy and corporate success has to be explained, and progress towards established targets or benchmarks needs to be documented (Walleck *et al.* 1991; Watson 1993). Managers should be familiar with the environmental issues in their area of responsibility and how the company is dealing, or plans to deal, with them. Managers should also have a clear idea of how they can use the information derived for eco-control to help improve corporate competitiveness.

The main focus of this text is on site-related, division-related and company-related information management. Thus, environmental accounting and eco-control place the emphasis of environmental management on company processes. These do not include environmental impact over the life-cycle of a company's products. However, this may produce insufficient relevant information for companies that have negligible emissions from their sites but produce highly scrutinised products with environmental problems. In such cases, an LCA of products based on site-specific information as discussed in Section 10.3.7 is to be recommended. If this approach is not applied, management should use screening and early detection methods (for an overview, see Liebl 1996; Steger and Winter 1996). Furthermore, consumer perceptions and buying patterns are also important. This implies that market-oriented information about consumer behaviour is important (see e.g. Meffert and Bruhn 1996; Monhemius 1993). Moreover, the role of eco-marketing and the communication of environmental issues in consumer markets will also have to be considered.

At both the site and company level, the increasing importance of external communication about environmental issues is apparent because of the fast-growing number of environmental reports. Although many of these reports still read very much like public relations brochures, more and more of them are exhibiting a clear environmental strategy and report in some detail about company targets, progress towards these targets and the actions and environmental management tools used to reach them. Although there are as yet no clear generally accepted standards for environmental accounting and reporting (see Chapter 12), stakeholder interest is growing in these reports. The contents of the report should reflect a company's specific situation and should address the information needed by each stakeholder group. A balance between local, site-oriented reporting and consolidated figures for the whole company has to be achieved. Site-specific data will be important to people living in the neighbourhood of plants and factories, local authorities with responsibilities for planning and zoning and employees working on a specific site. If necessary, detailed site-specific data can be computed and disclosed. Such data should be assessed in accordance with their relevance for the specific plant or factory environment. Consolidated, company-wide data are more relevant for shareholders, customers and top management who are trying to position the company relative to their competition. For multinational companies, only environmental interventions that have a global impact should be consolidated. Environmental interventions with local impacts do not have to be aggregated but need to be shown separately for different sites.

14.3.8 On achieving eco-control

If the concept of eco-control is to be widely adopted by companies of all sizes in all industries throughout the world in their attempts to improve environmental management practice and environmental performance, three practical issues need to be addressed relating to the conversion of existing accounting and reporting systems to environmental accounting:

☐ First, a contemporary assessment of the characteristics of the current accounting and reporting system needs to be undertaken.

☐ Second, support needs to be given to the operators and users of existing accounting and reporting systems during the transition towards a revised system of environmental accounting and reporting.

☐ Last, the existing accounting and reporting systems need to be redesigned and, once redesigned, need to be implemented.

Maunders and Burritt (1991: 16) refer to these issues as being part of the process of 'de-conditioning' and 'reconditioning' in relation to values and beliefs as well as to the learning of new skills by information producers and users. Accountants have a natural advantage when it comes to the redesign of accounting and reporting systems. They are the gatekeepers of existing external and internal accounting systems that serve management decision-making, planning and control functions including external communication. Their expertise in audit and independent verification provide credibility to the product of their labour and, as noted in the previous two sections, the implementation and communication principles 'albeit focused on a different vector of objectives' (Maunders and Burritt 1991: 17) are unlikely to be radically different from those that accountants currently practise.

Any systematic move towards the introduction of a new accounting and reporting system that is based on the importance of economic outcomes and also embodies the philosophy that 'green' is good (while recognising that there are limits to 'greenness', just as there are limits to financial gain in a period—would companies really want to operate with zero wages, free material inputs and all costs being borne by others?) will have to address a number of questions in order to implement some of the suggestions made in this book. These questions relate to examination of the current accounting and reporting system, support services for stakeholders during the transition to environmental accounting and redesign and implementation for eco-control (Box 14.1).

14.4 Summary

No serviceable environmental management is possible without environmental accounting. Environmentally differentiated and ecological accounting provide necessary information for decision-making, steering, implementation and communication (reporting). However, the mere compilation and analysis of data will not improve a company's environmental track record. The value of environmental accounting and the economic and ecological information it provides depends on how well accounting information is incorporated into environmental management.

**CONTEMPORARY ASSESSMENT OF THE CHARACTERISTICS
OF THE CURRENT ACCOUNTING AND REPORTING SYSTEM**

1. **How has the existing accounting and reporting system developed?**
   a Why are reports required—to enable integrated decision-making, for accountability purposes or as a guide to government policy-making?
   b Are reports tied to financial benefits?
   c Who is reporting at present (organisation names, sectors, types)? Are they large, medium-sized or small? Are they allies, partners, industry associations or multinationals with domestic connections?
   d Who is supposed to be reporting?
   e When are reports expected?
   f Are reports being submitted speedily?

2. **To whom are organisations reporting (which stakeholders)?**
   a Is accounting information reported to external parties (e.g. regulators, the financial community, media, local communities, non-governmental organisations, customers)?
   b Is the information reported internally (e.g. to employees)?
   c Is feedback from any of the stakeholders being received about the contents of reports? If yes, is any of this feedback critical? Has feedback helped improve performance and/or credibility?

3. **What is the typical content of an accounting report?**
   a Have the contents been analysed?
   b Has attention been paid to the length of the report?
   c Are forecast and actual figures included? Is there a comparison between forecast and actual figures included?
   d Are base data included?
   e Is benchmark information included?
   f Are there exception reports for managers?
   g How much and what type of information (e.g. qualitative versus quantitative) is disclosed to the public?
   h Are there any 'commercial-in-confidence' issues?

4. **Are reports being made annually?**
   a How many reports are being made and from which sites, divisions, product centres?
   b When are reports received?
   c Are any new reports expected in the immediate future?
   d How are reports submitted—as hard copy, in electronic form and/or on-line?

5. **Is the reported information used by stakeholders—internal and external?**
   a How is it used?
   b Is the information linked to established goals?

6. **What types of support (internal and external) are being given to reporters by the company?**

Box 14.1 **Questions relating to implementing environmental accounting and eco-control** *(continued over)*

PROVISION OF SUPPORT SERVICES TO STAKEHOLDERS DURING TRANSITION FROM THE CURRENT ACCOUNTING AND REPORTING SYSTEM

1. What support services can be offered to help participants with problems in drawing up or understanding their reports?
   a What staff, services, tools (to provide support direct to stakeholders and to help industry advisers and associations with the transition phase), manuals and documentation can be offered as help?
   b What constraints are there on the introduction of the new system—lack of participant time or expertise or lack of financial resources—and how will support be offered to overcome these problems?

2. What reactive advice can be provided to stakeholders?
   a Has assistance been provided to understand the technical aspects of the report?
   b Has an industry association or a mentor made an examination of draft reports prior to publication?
   c Has verbal advice and/or feedback been received on draft reports?
   d Have written comments been received on the draft reports?

3. What proactive advice can be provided to stakeholders?
   a Have problems been anticipated (e.g. has the interdisciplinary nature of reported information been addressed)?
   b Has any support that will be offered to overcome these problems been clarified?
   c Has a meeting of the chief executive officer, environmental staff, technical accounting staff and industry advisers been held to explain changes?

4. Has consideration been given to how best to provide information about the materiality of data reported?

5. What accuracy levels are expected?

6. What level of comprehensiveness is expected?

7. What information has been provided to help stakeholders?
   a Are the contents of manuals understood internally?
   b Are there any technical problems with the environmental and accounting calculations?
   c In what format are the reports presented?
   d Is there a help-line for external readers?

REDESIGNING AND IMPLEMENTATION OF THE ACCOUNTING AND REPORTING SYSTEM TO FACILITATE ECO-CONTROL

1. What can be learned from eco-control accounting and reporting mechanisms in other countries or in other companies (see review in this book)?

2. What are the incentives (e.g. cost allocations) that are going to be used to encourage rapid take-up of the new accounting and reporting system?

3. What is the potential for synergies and linkages with other accounting and reporting requirements?

Box 14.1 (continued)

4. Why should environmental accounting and reporting be carried out?
- a Will there be improvements in accountability?
- b Will the report maintain credibility (social acceptance)?
- c Will the report build eco-efficiency capacities?
- d Will reporting encourage training and familiarisation with problems?
- e Does the report show the relative position of the company as a good or bad performer, as a leader or a laggard?

5. Which centres should report?
- a Should there be reports for sensitive and less-sensitive sites?
- b Should there be reports to deal with individual products and product lines?
- c Should there be responsibility-based reports?

6. To whom should centres report?
- a Who are seen as being the critical stakeholders?
- b Is reported information to be made available to all critical stakeholders?

7. What is the ideal content of a report?
- a Is there reconfirmation of support from top management—are there links between reported information and an organisation's environmental policy, strategies and management systems?
- b What is the accuracy—what should the threshold for materiality be for reporting?
- c What financial information is reported?
- d Should the cost of compliance be reported?
- e Are capital and operating costs of actions reported and, if so, are they reported separately?
- f Are measures of financial effectiveness reported (absolute and normalised)?
- g Are measures of financial efficiency reported (absolute and normalised)?
- h What minimum information is required in order to meet specified goals?
- i What minimum information should be reported to the public?
- j Are other reporting systems complemented by the report?
- k Should the requirements of reporting be differentiated based on size or industry type?

8. What level of assurance should be offered to stakeholders for the redesigned accounting and reporting system prior to implementation?
- a What environmental management tools should be developed and integrated?
- b Have any new accounting and reporting tools (e.g. an on-line reporting system, a hot-line) been tested?
- c What development and testing of pro forma accounting system and reports have been undertaken (form and content)?
- d Have workshops and training programmes been provided on the new accounting and reporting system?

Box 14.1 *(continued)*

So far, the most comprehensive approach to environmental management is the eco-control procedural framework. This facilitates the integration of all important corporate environmental management tools. Environmental accounting supports information management and decision-making; tools of TQEM and environmental auditing help managers to improve implementation, steering and control; and external ecological accounting forms a critical part of the stakeholder communication and accountability process. Eco-control is designed to co-ordinate all tools supporting environmental management. Eco-control places the focus of environmental management squarely on in-house processes. It does not attempt to include environmental impacts over the life-cycle of a company's products. Instead, this management concept can be adjusted to the specific production site and company. A chemical company handling thousands of toxic substances will need to employ a more sophisticated concept of eco-control and will need to pursue different goals from, for example, a furniture manufacturer or a service company. It has been shown for many small, medium-sized and large companies that eco-control has enabled companies to manage and improve their eco-efficiency, their environmental performance and the environmentally induced financial impacts of a company and its production sites (see Schaltegger and Sturm 1998).

More and more companies are claiming that achieving sustainable development is one of their main goals. There is broad agreement that sustainable development has three dimensions—economic, environmental and social. Today, implementation of tools to help movement towards sustainable development are becoming increasingly important for those companies wishing to assure their long-term success. Tools for assessing a company's social performance are still in a very early stage of development. There is far less consensus over social aspects of sustainability than with the other two dimensions—economic and environmental—and it is these other two dimensions that have formed the main thrust of this chapter on eco-control. However, eco-control by its very nature is concerned with influence and power relationships as well as with economic and environmental issues. Although the social dimension is not taken into account, eco-control as a notion is rapidly growing into a core management tool available to all companies and is going through similar stages of development to those followed by financial control. The next step is to integrate developments in management control with eco-control as a foundation for sustainable development.

Questions

1. Standards can be technical, performance-based or process-based. Distinguish between these three categories and identify the category that applies to standards for environmental management systems.

2. What are the main similarities and differences between BS 7750, EMAS and ISO 14001? Is one of these systems to be preferred over the other two?

3. What are the main functions of good environmental management? Which environmental management tools are related to each of these functions? Are there any environmental management tools common to all functions?

4. Eco-control has been explained with use of three different approaches. What is eco-control? Explain the difference between the three approaches. Is there a link between the integrated approach and eco-efficiency? Explain.

5. Eco-control has five procedural steps. Think of an important corporate environmental intervention (e.g. emission of waste-water). With reference to this corporate environmental intervention, explain each procedure and consider the effect of each procedure on environmental management.

6. 'Information management is the core of any environmental management system.' Do you agree with this statement? How important is accounting information in an environmental management system? Outline three of the main characteristics of environmental accounting that provide necessary support for sound environmental management.

7. Portfolios are constructed to reduce risk for a given level of economic return. In this context, why would a company be interested in constructing an eco-efficiency portfolio?

8. Is there any notion of a trade-off between risk and return involved in an eco-efficiency portfolio matrix? How are 'green stars' and 'dirty dogs' related? In your answer cite examples from an industry with which you are familiar.

9. Implementation plays a critical part in environmental management. Why might environmental management fail at the implementation stage? Can these reasons for failure be corrected or avoided?

10. Redesign and implementation of accounting and reporting systems to incorporate environmental and ecological considerations faces a number of practical considerations. List and rank four of these considerations. Is implementation of environmental and ecological accounting likely to be more difficult for small or for large companies? Explain.

Chapter 15

SUMMARY

The world has a 200-year industrial legacy which has helped to improve the standard of living and provide access to goods and services and to cheap energy for many of the world's population (but not for those as yet untouched by industrialisation but who aspire to industrialised levels of affluence and environmental amenity). As time passes, the world seems a smaller place from any individual company's perspective and there is recognition that natural resources and environmental media (e.g. supplies of air and water) are not infinite. There is also recognition that the world cannot continue to absorb ever-increasing quantities of waste from industrialised living processes. Unless nature's resources are used more effectively and efficiently and are more equitably spread among the world's population an environmental crisis will occur, given the increase in global human population. Companies have to come to terms with this scenario.

Individuals have their own preferences and thus care about environmental and economic values. Values should therefore be the driving force behind decision-making in corporate management. For the past two decades environmental issues have become ever more influential on corporate economic values, and protection of the environment has become an important goal for many individuals, for some companies and for society. Through increased stakeholder pressure and changed cost relations, increasingly, companies have started to address problems of natural resource use and waste levels through the gathering, tracking and disclosure of environmental information. However, the compilation of data is often very badly co-ordinated and lacking in focus. Indeed, it is often unclear what specific value the collection, tracking and reporting of data is intended to create.

Management of information is not just about the handling of large amounts of data but rather about the creation of purpose-oriented knowledge, designed to achieve measurable goals and to enhance value (i.e. to meet desired states). Knowledge creation means restricting data computation and focusing on the recording, analysis and communication of information about specific goals. This book has shown how information systems and environmental information management can be oriented towards the goal of improving corporate eco-efficiency within a framework that recognises the desirability of long-term sustainable development by all companies, for all people, and that recognises the need for improved transparency and accountability for natural resource usage and waste-streams emanating from corporate activities.

To improve company eco-efficiency management must be informed about relevant environmentally induced financial impacts on the company as well as about environmental impacts added by corporate activities. Accounting is the central economic information management system for most companies. It forms the basis for integrated planning. It forms a core element in most integrated corporate control systems. Therefore, this book has examined environmental information issues in the context of management accounting, conventional financial accounting and reporting. In addition, environmental issues have been discussed in the context of the forward-looking shareholder value concept.

In management accounting, identification, tracing, measurement and allocation of costs to environmental cost centres can uncover hidden sources of loss that can, once their significance is identified, be reduced. Cost allocation can be used to improve the behaviour-influencing capacity of information, resulting in an improved environmental record leading to better environmental performance and an increase in company profitability at the same time.

Environmental issues have also started to shape financial accounting and reporting. The main goal when considering environmental issues in accounting standard-setting must be to improve the usefulness of information supplied to investors, regulators and other stakeholders. This does not, by itself, provide justification for the introduction of a large number of new financial accounting standards dealing with environmental issues. An excess of accounting standards will only confuse readers, waste resources on accounting and generate uncertainty about the 'bottom-line effects' on company performance, both financial and environmental. Furthermore, an excess of standards means that the overall implications for quality of information contained in financial reports can be assessed only by highly specialised accounting professionals rather by non-specialised readers.

This constraint on understandability imposed by having an excess of standards is one possible explanation for the emergence of the shareholder value concept in environmental accounting: standards have lost their perceived relevance and an alternative has replaced them. Other possible explanations are related to conditioning advantages provided by the approach—that is, a focus on the concept on the value of equity at a time when capital markets are coming to dominate the world economy, the long-term perspective and an orientation towards the future. Because the shareholder value concept is becoming a popular approach for investors when assessing company and share value, managers that are concerned about corporate survival in the long term should give serious consideration to environmentally induced influences on shareholder value. This can be achieved by evaluating the influence of environmental management on 'drivers' of shareholder value identified in this book.

Nevertheless, as long as external effects do not continue to be internalised, conventional financially oriented information management systems will not provide sufficient information for those stakeholders that are trying to gain direct, unadulterated knowledge about effects of corporate activities on the natural environment. Even from a purely economic perspective, information about corporate environmental impact is relevant: first, because such information is needed in order to be able to assess its economic consequences and, second, because environmental information can serve as a lead indicator for possible and probable future economic impacts on a company. If management relies only on financial information in its management systems, it might not even recognise that the environment has been harmed and that potential economic problems, which can threaten a company's future, may have been caused.

In addition, economic information systems do not provide information on how much the environment is harmed, no matter how high the external costs, whether the damage created is irreversible or whether the carrying capacity of certain environmental media (e.g. land, water courses) is exceeded.

This is an important reason why, in developed countries, ecological accounting has become part of today's regular business practice for leading businesses, although this is often not recognised as such. The reason for the rapid emergence of corporate ecological accounting is the economic importance of environmental issues for business and the fact that environmental impacts are not internalised in the market system and therefore are not recognised in conventional accounting. Consequently, new information management tools have emerged to help with the assessment of environmental impact added, thereby filling the gap created.

To assess the efficiency and effectiveness of an approach to environmental information (e.g. such that it provides relevant, reliable and accurate information) a model for assessing its usefulness has been proposed. The model has then been applied to life-cycle assessment—the first, and currently best-known, ecological management information system. Because of inherent problems with data quality and lack of data, which are impossible to overcome in an economical way, it is recommended that companies should not use background (industry-average) inventory data to carry out product life-cycle assessments. Instead, in order to increase the overall value of information, management should primarily concentrate on site-specific, business-specific and firm-specific ecological accounting where representative and more accurate data can be used to support decision-making that, in fact, can result in reduced corporate environmental impacts.

Most of this book has, therefore, focused on companies and their sites as cost objects and environmental impact added centres. Their periodic costs and periodic environmental impact added can be calculated as a basis for planning, action and control. However, it should not be overlooked that products and environmental issues related to products are also a very important part of business. Based on the ideas and methods discussed here, for example, the philosophy of improving the quality of data used in life-cycle assessment and emphasis on site-specific information, strategic management and product marketing would be able to anticipate potential major environmental problems with their products and product lines and mixes.

Internal ecological accounting can be structured with use of similar procedures to those of conventional management accounting and will benefit from knowledge and experience of existing accounting procedures and systems. Ecological accounts can be systematically structured and recorded in line with conventional charts of accounts. This process lends further support to computerised recording, aggregation and impact assessment systems, thereby increasing the efficiency of data handling. To increase the value of information, ecological accountants must continually keep track of data quality and use data to address the main questions raised by applied impact assessment models. Only a clear understanding of the basic intention of these assessment models can lend support to a relevant and valuable interpretation of environmental indicators. Net present environmental impact added has been suggested as one possible long-term future-oriented indicator that could be considered as the major focus of value-based analysis.

One reason why companies are taking the need for ecological accounting seriously is increased stakeholder and regulatory pressure. In developed countries, environmental regulators concerned with specific environmental or ecological problems have established quite specific, well-defined ecological accounting and reporting requirements for communication with company management. Many regulatory accounting systems are compulsory and have developed in an ad hoc way as part of constructive government–business interrelationships. Other schemes are voluntary, and self-regulating, being encouraged by industry associations concerned with retaining decision-making power in the hands of their corporate members. Where compulsory requirements exist, most firms have not yet linked the various strands of regulatory accounting systems. The result is inefficiency because of the need for parallel compilation of the same data by different employees communicating with different regulatory bodies. In order to reduce costs of compilation and reporting, ecological accounting needs to be carried out as economically as possible by linking internal and external ecological accounting systems. Then an optimal degree of synergy can be established. Well-designed external and internal ecological accounting systems can substantially reduce costs and difficulties with environmental regulations and possible reporting overloads.

External ecological accounting can begin with existing regulated environmental reporting activities. Once a systematic and efficient ecological accounting system has been established for reporting to regulatory agencies, it can be enlarged with little effort and cost. Extensions would include other, non-regulated, environmental interventions and calculation of overall corporate environmental impact added.

External ecological accounting and reporting is currently flourishing as a complement to financial accounting and reporting. Nevertheless, external ecological accounting is still an 'open house' for the various methods and perspectives being introduced. Therefore, conventions are needed to back up external ecological accounting and to improve the quality of information for readers of ecological statements.

Despite many problems, conventional accounting has provided certain advantages for business and society, otherwise it would not have survived and become the central corporate information management system for more than 100 years. The relative success of conventional financial accounting, as an approach for communication with external stakeholders, is largely based on its underlying conventions that have been designed to reduce information costs and guarantee a certain standard of information quality. Both information quality and conventions have received heavy criticism but, to date, they have not been deposed. Therefore, not surprisingly, initial suggestions for a set of underlying assumptions and conventions for external ecological accounting have been drawn from conventions related to financial accounting and reporting.

Despite many encouraging developments in the field of environmental information management the need for integration between environmental accounting and environmental management must constantly be kept in mind. Merely enlarging conventional accounting through a supplementary ecological accounting system will not help to integrate environmental problems in decision-making processes, will not bring the importance of environmental issues into focus and will not actually lead to continuous improvement in corporate environmental performance. As the Commission of the European Communities (CEC 1999: 6) admits, the focus on sustainable development, largely addressing environmental issues since the summit in Rio de Janeiro in 1992, has been an ambitious vision that has produced 'rather limited practical progress'. The message for companies is that serious environmental problems remain and that management will have to become part of the solution. Like it or not, ecological and financial issues will be integrated, and establishment of internal and external ecological accounting systems will become a priority, not just for the leaders, the large multinationals that have expertise to throw at these problems, but also for small and medium-sized businesses.

This book has attempted to show that the management of environmentally induced economic (financial) information and information about corporate environmental interventions can be integrated on the basis of a simple set of eco-efficiency indicators. In principle, although an infinite number of indicators is mathematically possible, to be useful the indicators should meet some corporate economic and ecological plausibility criteria. Furthermore, management of eco-efficiency-oriented information has to be co-ordinated with the corporate environmental management system. Any corporate accounting information system is justifiable only on the basis that it lends support to corporate management activities. One way towards integration was illustrated through the example of eco-control.

A key paradox for management seeking to anticipate the importance of environmental opportunities and constraints for their company is that if they establish eco-efficiency-oriented information they not only create more information and knowledge for their own and their stakeholders' benefit but they also generate more knowledge about their own lack of knowledge. Socrates's statement that 'I know that I do not know anything' illustrates that the gaining of more information and knowledge also raises new questions—sometimes raising more questions than answers. In practical terms this means that the management of eco-efficiency-oriented information has now stepped beyond the threshold of quick and simple answers. However, exploration of additional approaches and procedures has to be taken further before eco-efficiency-oriented information management can become an integrated and integral standard in daily business for the majority of companies—something that this book attempts to justify and encourage as an important practical step on the long road toward 'strong' sustainability.

BIBLIOGRAPHY

AAA/SEC (American Accounting Association/US Securities and Exchange Commission [Liaison Committee]) (1995) 'Mountaintop Issues: From the Perspective of the SEC', *Accounting Horizons* 9.1 (March 1995): 79-86.

AAFEU (Accounting Advisory Forum of the European Union) (1994) 'Environmental Issues in Financial Reporting' (Working Document of the Accounting Advisory Forum, July 1994): 6.

AAFEU (Accounting Advisory Forum of the European Union) (1995) 'Environmental Issues in Financial Accounting' (document XV/6004/94 cl. rev. 4).

AARF (Australian Accounting Research Foundation) (1990) 'Objective of General Purpose Financial Reporting: Statement of Accounting Concepts 2' (Melbourne: AARF).

Abelson, R. (1991) 'Messy Accounting', *Forbes*, 14 October 1991: 172, 174.

ABS (Australian Bureau of Statistics) (1997) *Natural Resources in National Balance Sheets: Year Book Australia 1997* (publication 1301.0; Canberra: ABS).

ABS (Australian Bureau of Statistics) (1999) 'Environmental Issues: People's Views and Practices' (March, catalogue no. 4602.0; Canberra: ABS): 56.

ACBE (Advisory Committee on Business and the Environment) (1993) 'Report of the Financial Sector Working Group' (London: ACBE).

Accountancy (1995) 'Ball Back in the Auditors' Court', *Accountancy* 2: 1.

Achleitner, A. (1995) *Die Normierung der Rechnungslegung* (Zürich: Treuhand-Kammer).

ACN (Association Canadienne de Normalisation) (1993) 'L'ISO choisit le Canada pour jouer un rôle clé dans le domaine de l'environnement', *Environment Information* 2.1.

ACTEW (Australian Capital Territory Electricity & Water Corporation) (1994) *ACT Future Water Supply Strategy: Our Water, Our Future* (Canberra: ACTEW).

Adams, J. (1992) *Accounting for Environmental Costs: A Discussion of the Issues Facing Today's Businesses* (Norwalk, CT: Financial Accounting Standards Board).

Adams, C., W. Hill and C.B. Roberts (1998) 'Corporate Social Reporting Practices in Western Europe: Legitimating Corporate Behaviour?', *British Accounting Review* 30.1: 1-21.

Adams, R., M. Houldin and S. Slomp (1999) 'Towards a Generally Accepted Framework for Environmental Reporting', in M. Bennett and P. James (eds.), *Sustainable Measures: Evaluation and Reporting of Environmental and Social Performance* (Sheffield, UK: Greenleaf Publishing): 314-29.

Aeschlimann, J. (1994) 'Exxon Guilty: Now the Demands for Billions Emerge', *Basler Zeitung* 137 (15 June 1994): 3.

A'Hearn, T. (1996) 'Environmental Management and Industry Competitiveness' (paper presented at the Environmental Management and International Competitiveness conference, Commonwealth of Australia, Canberra).

Ahmad, Y.J. (1983) *Environmental Decision-Making. I. An Introduction to the Application of Cost–Benefit Analysis* (London: Hodder & Stoughton).

AICPA (American Institute of Certified Public Accountants) (1994) 'Disclosure of Certain Significant Risks and Uncertainties: Proposed Statement of Position' (New York: AICPA, revised draft).

AICPA (American Institute of Certified Public Accountants) (1995) 'Environmental Remediation Liabilities: Proposed Statement of Position' (New York: Environmental Accounting Task Force, Accounting Standards Division, AICPA, exposure draft).

Akerlof, G.A. (1970) 'The Market for "Lemons": Quality Uncertainty and the Market Mechanism', *Quantitative Journal of Economics* 84.4: 488-500.

Alfsen, K., T. Bye and L. Lorentsen (1987) *Natural Resource Accounting and Analysis: The Norwegian Experience* (Oslo: Statistisk Sentralbyrå).

Allenby, B., and A. Fullerton (1992) 'Design for the Environment: A New Strategy for Environmental Management', *Pollution Prevention Review*, Winter 1992: 51-61.

Altham, W.J., and T.F. Guerin (1999) 'Where does ISO 14001 fit into the environmental regulatory framework?', *Australian Journal of Environmental Management* 6: 86-98.

Anthony, R.N. (1965) *Planning and Control Systems: A Framework for Analysis* (Boston, MA: Harvard University Press).

Anthony, R.N., and V. Govindarajan (1998) *Management Control Systems* (Boston, MA: Irwin McGraw–Hill).

AP (Associated Press) (1992a) 'Some investors turn to "clean, green" companies', *The Seattle Times*, 21 April 1992: C3.

AP (Associate Press) (1992b) 'Transcripts show chaotic Exxon spill response: First concern was appearances; Dumping toxic waste also discussed', *The Seattle Times*, 18 November 1992: 1, 12.

AP (Associate Press) (1994) 'Exxon zahlt 20 Millionen Dollar Entschädigung', *Basler Zeitung* 173: 10.

API (American Petroleum Institute) (1990) *The Use of Economic Incentive Mechanisms in Environmental Management* (Washington, DC: API).

Arber, W. (1992) 'Why the Earth's Genetic Biodiversity Cannot Be a Matter of Indifference', in D. Koechlin and K. Müller (eds.), *Green Business Opportunities: The Profit Potential* (London: Pitman): 21-32.

Arora, S., and T. Cason (1995) 'An Experiment in Voluntary Environmental Regulation: Participation in EPA's 33/50 Program', *Journal of Environmental Economics and Management* 28: 271-86.

Arthur Andersen (1994) *Transparente Rechnungslegung und Berichterstattung von Banken* (Zürich: Arthur Andersen/Schweizerische Vereinigung für Finanzanalyse und Vermögensverwaltung).

ASB (Australian Accounting Standards Board) (1983) 'Accounting for Research and Development Costs: Statement of Accounting Standards AAS 13' (Melbourne: ASB, Australian Accounting Research Foundation).

ASB (UK Accounting Standards Board) (1998) 'Provisions, Contingent Liabilities and Contingent Assets' (financial reporting standard 12; Milton Keynes, UK: UK ASB, September 1998).

ASCPA (Australian Society of Certified Practising Accountants) (1999) 'Business Management Guidelines: Environmental Management Series' (Melbourne: ASCPA in conjunction with the Society of Management Accountants of Canada, March 1999).

ASRB (Accounting Standards Review Board) (1989) 'Accounting for the Extractive Industries' (accounting standard ASRB 1022; Melbourne,, ASRB, October 1989).

ASU (Arbeitsgemeinschaft Selbständiger Unternehmer) (ed.) (1999) *Öko-Audit in der mittelständischen Praxis* (Bonn: ASU).

ASVS (Arbeitsgemeinschaft Schweizerische Vereinigung für Sonnenenergie) (1990) *Solar 91: Für eine energieunabhängigere Schweiz* (Bern: Eigenverlag).

Atkins, P.W. (1979) *Physical Chemistry* (Oxford, UK: Oxford University Press),

Australian (1999) 'BHP Urged to Shut Down Mine', *The Australian*, 28 August 1999: 7.

Ayres, I., and J. Braithwaite (1992) *Responsive Regulation: Transcending the Deregulation Debate* (New York: Oxford University Press).

Azzone, G., and R. Manzini (1994) 'Measuring Strategic Environmental Performance', *Business Strategy and the Environment* 3.1 (Spring 1994): 1-14.

Azzone, G., R. Manzini, R. Welford and C. Young (1996) 'Defining Environmental Performance Indicators: An Integrated Framework', *Business Strategy and the Environment* 5.2 (June 1996): 69-80.

Bailey, P. (1991) 'Full Cost Accounting for Life-Cycle Costs: A Guide for Engineers and Financial Analysts', *Environmental Finance* (Spring 1991): 13-29.

BAK (Konjunkturforschung Basel AG) (1992–1999) *Wirtschaft und Umwelt* (Basel: BAK).

Banks, G., and C. Ballard (1997) *The Ok Tedi Settlement: Issues, Outcomes and Implications* (Canberra: National Centre for Development Studies and Resource Management in Asia–Pacific, Australian National University).

Bartelmus, P., and J. van Tongeren (1994) 'Environmental Accounting: An Operational Perspective' (working paper 1; New York: Department for Economic and Social Information and Policy Analysis, United Nations).

Barth, M., and M. McNichols (1994) 'Estimation and Market Valuation of Environmental Liabilities Relating to Superfund Sites', *Journal of Accounting Research* 32 (Supplement): 177-209.

Bartolomeo, M. (1998) *About the Usefulness of Environmental Performance Evaluation* (Turin: Fondazione Eni Enrico Mattei).

Bartolomeo, M., M. Bennett, J. Bouma, P. Heydkamp, P. James, and T. Wolters (2000) 'Environmental Management Accounting in Europe: Current Practice and Future Potential', *European Accounting* 1: 31-52.

Barton, A.D. (1999) 'A Trusteeship Theory of Accounting for Natural Capital Assets', *Abacus* 35.2: 207-22.

Basler and Hoffmann (1974) *Studie Umwelt und Volkswirtschaft: Vergleich der Umweltbelastungen von Behältern aus PVC, Glas, Blech und Karton* (Bern: Eidgenössisches Amt für Umweltschutz).

Batelle (1993) *Life-Cycle Assessment: Public Data Sources for the LCA Practitioner* (Washington, DC: US Environmental Protection Agency).

Baumol, W.J. (1959) *Business Behavior, Value and Growth* (New York: Macmillan).

Baumol, W., and W. Oates (1988) *The Theory of Environmental Policy* (Cambridge, UK: Cambridge University Press, 2nd edn).

Baxter International (various years) *Environmental Performance Report* (New York: Baxter International Inc.).

BAZ (Basler Zeitung) (1997) 'Standards erschweren "kreative" Buchführung', *Basler Zeitung* 279 (29–30 November 1997): 27.

BCSD (Business Council for Sustainable Development) (1993) 'Getting Eco-efficient: How can business contribute to sustainable development?' (Proceedings of the First Antwerp Eco-Efficiency Workshop, Antwerp, November 1993, Organised in Association with the Industry and Environment Office of the United Nations Environment Programme and the Commission of the European Communities, Directorate-General XI).

Bebbington, J. (1997) 'Engagement, Education and Sustainability: A Review Essay on Environmental Accounting', *Accounting, Auditing and Accountability Journal* 10.3: 365-81.

Bebbington, J., and P. Rikhardsson (1999) 'Compulsory Environmental Reporting in Denmark: An Evaluation', *Social and Environmental Accounting* 19.2: 2-4.

Bebbington, J., and I. Thomson (1996) 'Business Conceptions of Sustainability and the Implications for Accountancy' (research report 48; London: Chartered Association of Certified Accountants, Certified Accountants Educational Trust).

Beder, S. (1996) *The Nature of Sustainable Development* (Newham, Australia: Scribe Publishers, 2nd edn).

Beets, S.D., and C.C. Souther (1999) 'Corporate Environmental Reports: The Need for Standards and an Environmental Assurance Service', *Accounting Horizons* 13.2: 129-45.

Begley, R. (1994) 'TRI releases fall and "wastes" rise: Industry disputes expanding list', *Chemical Week* 154.16 (27 April 1994): 9.

Begley, R. (1997) 'Value of ISO 14000 management systems put to the test', *Environmental Science and Technology/News* 31.8.

Bennett, M., and P. James (1996) 'Environment-Related Management Accounting in North America', in C. Tuppen (ed.), *Environmental Accounting in Industry: A Practical Review* (London: British Telecom): 15-71.

Bennett, M., and P. James (1998a) 'The Green Bottom Line', in M. Bennett and P. James (eds.), *The Green Bottom Line. Environmental Accounting for Management: Current Practice and Future Trends* (Sheffield, UK: Greenleaf Publishing): 30-60.

Bennett, M., and P. James (1998b) 'Making Environmental Management Count: Baxter International's Environmental Financial Statement', in M. Bennett and P. James (eds.), *The Green Bottom Line. Environmental Accounting for Management: Current Practice and Future Trends* (Sheffield, UK: Greenleaf Publishing): 294-309.

Bennett, M., and P. James (eds.), (1999) *Sustainable Measures: Evaluation and Reporting of Environmental and Social Performance* (Sheffield, UK: Greenleaf Publishing).

Berry, T., and L. Failing (1996) *Environmental Accounting* (Vancouver: Whistler Centre for Business and the Arts).

BfK (Bundesamt für Konjunkturfragen) (1985) *Qualitatives Wachstum: Bericht der Expertenkommission des Eidgenössischen Volkswirtschaftsdepartements* (Bern: BfK).

BHP (Broken Hill Proprietary Company Ltd) (1997) 'Environmental Report' (Melbourne: BHP).

Bierter, W. (1994) 'ÖkoEffizienz: Megatonnen statt Nannogramme', *Basler Zeitung*, 30 July 1994: 15.

Biethahn, J., H. Mucksch and W. Ruf (1994) *Ganzheitliches Informationsmanagement. I. Grundlagen* (Munich: Oldenbourg, 3rd edn).

Binswanger, H.C. (1991) *Geld und Natur: Das wirtschaftliche Wachstum im Spannungsfeld zwischen Ökonomie und Ökologie* (Stuttgart: Haupt).

Binswanger, H.C., and P. von Flotow (eds.) (1994) *Geld und Wachstum: Zur Philosophie und Praxis des Geldes* (Stuttgart: Wirbrecht).

Birke, M., C. Burschel and M. Schwarz (1997) *Handbuch Umweltschutz und Organisation* (Munich: Oldenbourg).

Blacconiere, W.G., and W.D. Northcutt (1997) 'Environmental Information and Market Reactions to Environmental Legislation', *Journal of Accounting, Auditing and Finance* 12.2: 149-78.

Blacconiere, W.G., and D.M. Patten (1994) 'Environmental Disclosures, Regulatory Costs, and Changes in Firm Value', *Journal of Accounting and Economics* 18: 357-77.

Blamey, R., and T. Sutton (1999) 'Social Marketing and Regulatory Compliance' (Paper presented at the Fifth Annual Innovations in Social Marketing Conference, Montreal, Canada, 18–20 July 1999).

Blankart, C.B., and G. Knieps (1993) 'State and Standards', *Public Choice* 1: 39-52.

BMU/UBA (Bundesumweltministerium and Umweltbundesamt) (1996a) *Leitfaden betrieblicher Umwelt-kennzahlen* (Bonn: Vahlen).

BMU/UBA (Bundesumweltministerium and Umweltbundesamt) (eds.) (1996b) *Handbuch Umwelt-kostenrechnung* (Munich: Vahlen).

BMU/UBA (Bundesumweltministerium and Umweltbundesamt) (eds.) (1997) *Betriebliche Umwelt-kennzahlen: Leitfaden* (Munich: Deutsch).

Böhm, M., and M. Halfmann (1994) 'Kennzahlen und Kennzahlensysteme für ein ökologie-orientiertes Controlling', *UmweltWirtschaftsForum* 8 (December 1994): 9-14.

Bolton, P., and M. Dewatripont (1995) 'The Time and Budget Constraints of the Firm', *European Economic Review* 39: 691-99.

Boockholdt, J.L. (1999) *Accounting Information Systems* (Boston, MA: Irwin McGraw-Hill, 5th edn).

Borjesson, S. (1997) 'A Case Study on Activity-Based Budgeting', *Journal of Cost Management* 10.4 (Winter 1997): 7.

Bouma, J., and T. Wolters (eds.) (1999) *Developing Eco-Management Accounting: An International Perspective* (Zoetermeer, Netherlands: Economisch Instituut voor het Midden en Kleinbedrijf).

Boyd, J. (1998) 'Searching for the Profit in Pollution Prevention: Case Studies in the Corporate Evaluation of Environmental Opportunities' (publication 742-R-98-005; Washington, DC: US Environmental Protection Agency, Office of Pollution Prevention and Toxics, April 1998).

Bragdon, J., and J. Marlin (1972) 'Is Pollution Profitable?', *Risk Management* 19.4.

Braithwaite, J., J. Walker and P. Grabosky (1987) 'An Enforcement Taxonomy of Regulatory Agencies', *Law and Policy* 9.3: 323-51.

Brealey, R., and S. Myers (1991) *Principles of Corporate Finance: Application of Option Pricing Theory* (New York: McGraw–Hill).

Brockhaus, R. (1992) *Informationsmanagement als ganzheitliche informationsorientierte Gestaltung von Unternehmen: Organisatorische, personelle und technologische Aspekte* (Göttingen, Germany: University of Göttingen).

BRT (Business Roundtable) (1998) 'A Benchmarking Study of Pollution Prevention Planning Best Practices, Issues and Implications for Public Policy' (Washington, DC: Business Roundtable, August 1998).

Brüggemann, A. (1994) 'Umwelthaftung des Darlehensgebers', *Schweizerische Zeitschrift für Wirtschaft* 2/94: 71-82.

BSI (British Standards Institution) (1992) *Specification for Environmental Management Systems* (BS 7750; London: BSI).

BSO/Origin (1993) *Annual Report 1992* (Utrecht: BSO/Origin).

Buhr, N. (1998) 'Environmental Performance, Legislation and Annual Report Disclosure: The Case of Acid Rain and Falconbridge', *Accounting, Auditing and Accountability Journal* 11.2: 163-90.

BUJF (Bundesministerium für Umwelt, Jugend und Familie) (1993) *Ökobilanzen von Packstoffen in Theorie und Praxis: Eine Iststandserhebung* (Vienna: Institut für ökologische Wirtschaftsforschung).

Burritt, R.L. (1995) 'Accountants, Accountability and the "Ozone Regime"', *Accounting Forum* 19.2/3: 219-43.

Burritt, R.L. (1997) 'Environmental Disclosures in Annual Reports of Australian Gold and Copper Mining Companies with Activities in Papua New Guinea and/or Indonesia' (working paper 1997/13, Resource Management in Asia–Pacific Working Paper Series; Canberra: Research School of Pacific and Asian Studies, Australian National University).

Burritt, R.L. (1998) 'Corporate Environmental Performance Indicators. Cost Allocation: Boon or Bane?', in M. Bennett and P. James (eds.), *The Green Bottom Line. Environmental Accounting for Management: Current Practice and Future Trends* (Sheffield, UK: Greenleaf Publishing): 152-61.

Burritt, R.L. (1999a) 'Commonwealth Greenhouse Challenge: The Reporting and Verification Process', *Australian Journal of Environmental Management* 6.1: 44-51.

Burritt, R.L. (1999b) 'Accounting and Reporting for Sustainability: Time for a Ratings Agency?' (paper presented at the National Public Sector Accountants Conference, Australian Society of Certified Practising Accountants, Adelaide, 8 April 1999).

Burritt, R.L., and L. Cummings (1999) 'Environmental Accounting and the Disclosures of Earth Sanctuaries Ltd' (Annual AAANZ Conference, Cairns, Australia).

Burritt, R.L., and K. Gibson (1993) 'Accounting for the Environment', *Australian Accountant* 63.6: 17-21.

Burritt, R.L., and G. Lehman (1995) The Body Shop Wind Farm: An Analysis of Accountability and Ethics', *The British Accounting Review* 27.3: 167-86.

Burritt, R.L., and P.F. Luckett (1982) 'Direct Costing: Is It Allocation Free?', *Management International Review* 4.

Burtraw, D., and E. Mansur (1999) 'Environmental Effects of SO_2 Trading and Banking', *Environmental Science and Technology*, 31 August 1999.

BUS (Bundesamt für Umweltschutz) (1984) *Ökobilanzen von Packstoffen* (Bern: BUS).

Buser, H., and S. Schaltegger (1998) 'Activation of Nature by Eco-controlling?', in S. Schaltegger and A. Sturm (eds.), *Eco-efficiency by Eco-controlling* (Zürich: Verlag der Fachvereine [vdf]).

Business and the Environment (1995a) 'New Study: Survey Highlights Environmental Performance Measurement and Reporting', *Business and the Environment* 6.2 (February 1995): 10.

Business and the Environment (1995b) 'Denmark to Adopt Reporting Law', *Business and the Environment* 6.6 (June 1995): 4-5.

BUWAL (Bundesamt für Umwelt, Wald und Landschaft) (1991) *Ökobilanz von Packstoffen* (Schriftenreihe Umwelt [SRU] 132; Bern: BUWAL).

Byrd, J., and T. Zwirlein (1994) 'Environmental Protection and Forward Contracts: Sulfur Dioxide Emission Allowances', *Journal of Applied Corporate Finance*, Fall 1994: 109-10.

Cairncross, F. (1991) *Costing the Earth: What governments must do, what consumers need to know, how business can profit* (London: Great Britain Books).

Cairns, D. (1995) *A Guide to Applying International Accounting Standards* (Milton Keynes, UK: Institute of Chartered Accountants).

Camejo, P. (1992) 'The Greening of Wall Street', *The Environmental Forum*, November/December 1992.

Carlton, C., and B. Howell (1992) 'Life Cycle Analysis: A Tool for Solving Environmental Problems?', *European Environment* 2.3 (April 1992): 2-5.

CCME (Canadian Council of Ministers of the Environment) (1995) *Sources of Data for the Life-Cycle Analyses of Canadian Packaging Products* (Ottawa: CCME).

CEC (Commission of the European Communities) (1998) 'EU Eco-management and Audit Scheme', *ENDS Report* 286 (November 1998): 3.

CEC (Commission of the European Communities) (1999) 'Europe's Environment: What Directions for the Future?' (communication from the CEC, Environment Directorate-General, COM[1999]543 final; Brussels: CEC).

CEEC (Council of the European Economic Community) (1992) 'Council Regulation (EEC) No. 880/92 of 23 March 1992 on a Community Eco-label Award Scheme', *Official Journal of the European Communities* L (1 July 1992): 99.

CEEC (Council of the European Economic Community) (1994) 'Environmental Issues in Financial Reporting' (working document for the Accounting Advisory Board Forum; New York: CEEC).

CEFIC (European Chemical Industry Council) (1993) *CEFIC Guidelines on Environmental Reporting for the European Chemical Industry* (Brussels: CEFIC).

CERCLA (Comprehensive Environmental Response, Compensation and Liability Act) (1980) (USC 46N-4682; Washington, DC: US Government Printing Office).

CERES (Coalition of Environmentally Responsible Economies) (1992) *The CERES Principles* (Boston, MA: CERES).

Chaddick, B., R. Rouse and J. Surma (1993) 'Perspectives on Environmental Reporting', *The CPA Journal*, January 1993: 18-24.

Chambers, R.J. (1957) *Accounting and Action* (Sydney: The Law Book Company of Australasia Proprietary Ltd).

Chambers, R.J. (1966) *Accounting, Evaluation and Economic Behavior* (Houston, TX: Scholars Book Co.).

Chambers, R.J. (1970) 'Financial Reporting and Administrative Accounting: Harmony or Conflict?', *Canadian Chartered Accountant*, August 1970: 114-21.

Chambers, R.J. (1999) 'The Case for Simplicity in Accounting', *Abacus* 35.2: 121-37.

Cherry, C. (1961) *On Human Communication* (New York: Science Editions).

Christenson, C. (1983) 'The Methodology of Positive Accounting', *The Accounting Review* 58.1: 1-22.

Chynoweth, E. (1994) 'Environmental Reporting: Different Things for Different People', *Chemical Week* 155.1: 106.

CICA (Canadian Institute of Chartered Accountants) (1992) 'Environmental Accounting and the Role of the Accounting Profession' (Toronto: CICA).

CICA (Canadian Institute of Chartered Accountants) (1993) 'Environmental Costs and Liabilities: Accounting and Financial Reporting Issues' (research report; Toronto: CICA).

CICA (Canadian Institute of Chartered Accountants) (1994) 'Reporting on Environmental Performance' (Toronto: CICA)

CICA (Canadian Institute of Chartered Accountants) (1995) 'Accounting Recommendations: Specific Items—Research and Development Costs' (Ottawa: CICA).

CICA (Canadian Institute of Chartered Accountants) (1997) 'Full Cost Accounting from an Environmental Perspective' (Toronto: CICA).

Chemical Engineering (1993) 'Europe's Toxics: How to Keep Score', *Chemical Engineering* 100.1 (January 1993): 39.

Clark, J.M. (1923) *The Incidence of Overhead Costs* (Chicago, IL: University of Chicago Press; Melbourne: Accountants Publishing Company Ltd).

Clausen, J., H. Hallay and M. Strobel (1992) 'Umweltkennzahlen für Unternehmen' (discussion paper 20; Berlin: Institut für Wirtschaft und Ökologie [IWÖ]).

Clean Air Act (1990) (EPA 450-K-92-001; Washington, DC: US Government Printing Office).

CMR (*Chemical Marketing Reporter*) (1994a) 'TRI exemption plan drawing fire', *Chemical Marketing Reporter* 246.6 (8 August 1994): 4.

CMR (*Chemical Marketing Reporter*) (1994b) 'EPA final rule adds 286 chemicals to TRI list', *Chemical Marketing Reporter* 246.22 (28 November 1994): 3.

Cochran, P., and R. Wood (1975) 'Corporate Social Responsibility and Financial Performance', *California Management Review* 18.2.

Coenenberg, A. (1993) *Kostenrechnung und Kostenanalyse* (Landsberg am Lech, Germany: Moderne Industrie, 2nd edn).

Cohen, M. (1994) 'Lead or Look On? The Corporate Environmental Dilemma' *Insight*, Spring 1994 (Nashville, TN: Owen Graduate School of Management).

Cohen, M., S. Fenn and J. Naimon (1995) *Environmental and Financial Performance: Are they related?* (Washington, DC: Investor Responsibility Research Centre).

Colby, S., T. Kingsley and B. Whitehead (1995) 'The Real Green Issue: Debunking the Myths of Environmental Management', *The McKinsey Quarterly* 2: 132-43.

COM (Commission of the European Communities) (1992) 'Amended Proposal for a Council Regulation (EEC) Allowing Voluntary Participation by Companies in the Industrial Sector in a Community Eco-management and Audit Scheme' (COM/93 97 Final, 16 March 1992; Brussels: Council of the European Communities).

COM (Commission of the European Communities) (1993) 'Council Regulation No. 1836/93 of June 1993 Allowing Voluntary Participation by Companies in the Industrial Sector in a Community Eco-management and Audit Scheme', *Official Journal of the European Communities* L.168: 1-18.

Common, M. (1995) *Sustainability and Policy* (Cambridge, UK: Cambridge University Press).

Commonwealth of Australia (1999) 'Regulations and Guidelines under the Environment Protection and Biodiversity Conservation Act 1999' (consultation paper; Canberra: Australian Government Publishing Service): 27.

Company Law Review Act (1998) s. 299(1) (f) (Canberra: Australian Government Publishing Service).

Consoli, F. (1993) *Guidelines for Lifecycle Assessment: A Code of Practice* (Brussels: Society of Environmental Toxicology and Chemistry).

Cooper, C. (1992a) 'The Non and Nom of Accounting for (M)other Nature', *Accounting, Auditing and Accountability Journal* 5.3: 16-39.

Cooper, C. (1992b) 'M[othering] View on: "Some Feminisms and their Implications for Accounting Practice" ', *Accounting, Auditing and Accountability Journal* 5.3: 71-75.

Copeland, T., T. Koller and J. Murrin (1993) *Valuation: Measuring and Managing the Value of Companies* (New York: John Wiley).

Corrigan, A. (1998) 'Performance Measurement: Knowing the Dynamics', *Australian CPA* 68.9: 30-31.

Cowe, R. (1994) 'Greenpeace campaign targets investors over PVC flotation', *The Guardian*, 22 October 1994.

Crasselt, N., and C. Tomaszewski (1998) 'Bewertung von Realoptionen unter Berücksichtigung des Investitionsverhaltens von Wettbewerbern: Analyse am Beispiel der strategischen Unternehmensbewertung' (IUU working paper 74; Bochum, Germany: Ruhr-Universität Bochum).

Crawford, C. (1992) 'Campaign for Cleaner Corporations: America's Corporate Polluters' (research report; New York: Council on Economic Priorities).

Cuganesan, S., R. Gibson and R. Petty (1997) 'Exploring Accounting Education's Enabling Possibilities: An Analysis of a Management Accounting Text', *Accounting, Auditing and Accountability Journal* 10.3: 432-53.

Cummings, L.S., and R.L. Burritt (1999) 'Corporate Social Disclosure Characteristics and the Role of Ethical Investment Trusts', *Asian Review of Accounting* 7.1: 20-42.

Cyert, R.M., and J.G. March (1963) *A Behavioral Theory of the Firm* (Englewood Cliffs, NJ: Prentice–Hall).

Daly, H. (1968) 'On Economics as a Life Science', *Journal of Political Economy* 76 (Summer 1968): 392-406.

Daly, H. (1992) 'Allocation, Distribution and Scale: Towards an Economics that is Efficient, Just and Sustainable', *Ecological Economics* 6.3: 185-93.

Deegan, C., and M. Rankin (1999) 'The Environmental Reporting Expectations Gap: Australian Evidence', *British Accounting Review* 31.3: 313-46.

Deming, E. (1982) *Out of the Crises* (Cambridge, MA: MIT Press).

Deming, E. (1993) *The New Economics for Industry, Government, Education* (Cambridge, MA: MIT Press).

Dickson, G., and J. Wetherbe (1985) *The Management of Information Systems* (New York: McGraw–Hill).

Dierkes, M., and L. Preston (1977) 'Corporate Social Accounting and Reporting for the Physical Environment', *Accounting, Organizations and Society* 2.1: 3-22.

Dietachmair, T. (1996) 'Bedeutung und Einsatzbereiche ökologischer Kennzahlen im betrieblichen Umweltmanagement', in A. Malinsky (ed.), *Betriebliche Umweltwirtschaft* (Wiesbaden, Germany: Gabler): 259-89.

Dirks, H. (1991) 'Recognition and Measurement Issues in Environmental Clean-up Costs', *Environmental Finance*, Summer 1991: 233-36.

Ditz, D., J. Ranganathan and R.D. Banks (eds.) (1995) *Green Ledgers: Case Studies in Corporate Environmental Accounting* (Baltimore, MD: World Resources Institute).

Dixit, A., and R. Pindyck (1993) *Investment Under Uncertainty* (Princeton, NJ: Princeton University Press).

Dixit, A., and R. Pindyck (1995) 'The Options Approach to Capital Investment', *Harvard Business Review* (May/June 1995): 105-15.

Dobes, L. (1998) *Trading Greenhouse Emissions: Some Australian Perspectives* (Canberra: The Bureau of Transport Economics, Commonwealth of Australia).

Dobyns, L., and C. Crawford-Mason (1991) *Quality or Else* (New York: Houghton Mifflin).

DTTI/IISD/SustainAbility (Deloitte Touche Tohmatsu International/International Institute for Sustainable Development/SustainAbility Ltd) (1993) *Coming Clean: Corporate Environmental Reporting: Opening up for Sustainable Development* (London: DTTI).

DuPont (1993) 'Corporate Environmentalism: Progress Report' (Wilmington, DE: DuPont).

Dyllick, T. (1989) *Management der Umweltbeziehungen: Öffentliche Auseinandersetzung als Herausforderung* (Wiesbaden, Germany: Gabler).

Dyllick, T., and U. Schneidewind (1995) 'Ökologische Benchmarks: Erfolgsindikatoren für das Umweltmanagement von Unternehmen' (discussion paper 26; St Gallen, Switzerland: IWÖ)

Eckel, L., K. Fisher and G. Russel (1992) 'Environmental Performance Measurement', *CMA Magazine*, March 1992: 16-23.

Economist (1994a) 'After Valdez', *The Economist*, 18 June 1994: 20.

Economist (1994b) 'Corporate Liability: UnExxonerated', *The Economist*, 18 June 1994: 62.

Economist (1994c) 'Insurers get that sinking feeling', *The Economist*, 20 August 1994: 57-58.

Economist (1994d) 'Where there's muck . . . ', *The Economist*, December 1994: 9.

Economist (1995) 'Environmental Policy: Could Try Harder', *The Economist*, 21 October 1995: 62f.

Economist (1997a) 'Valuing Companies: A Star to Sail By?', *The Economist*, August 1997: 57-59.

Economist (1997b) 'Environmental Scares: Plenty of Gloom', *The Economist*, 20 December 1997: 21-23.

Edward, F. (ed.) (1992) *Environmental Auditing: The Challenge of the 1990s* (Calgary, Canada: University of Calgary Press).

Edwards, E.O., and P.W. Bell (1961) *The Theory and Measurement of Business Income* (Berkeley, CA: University of California Press).

EEEIW (European Eco-efficiency Indicators Workshop) (1999) 'European Eco-efficiency Indicators Workshop, Brussels, 18–19 May 1999'.

EIA (Environment Institute of Australia) (1999) 'National Pollutant Inventory Handbooks', *Newsletter* 20 (Melbourne: EIA, June 1999).

EIRIS (Ethical Investment Research Service) (1989) 'The Financial Performance of Ethical Investments' (London: EIRIS).

EITF (Emerging Issues Task Force of the US Financial Accounting Standards Board) (1993b) 'Interpretation No. 14: Reasonable Estimation of the Amount of a Loss (An Interpretation of FASB Statement No. 5)' (Norwalk, CT: FASB).

EITF (Emerging Issues Task Force of the US Financial Accounting Standards Board) (1990) 'Issue 90-8: Capitalization of Costs to Treat Environmental Contamination' (Norwalk, CT: FASB).

EIU/AIU (Economist Intelligence Unit/American International Underwriters) (1993) 'Environmental Finance: Evaluating Risk and Exposure in the 1990s' (New York: EIU).

ELI (Environmental Law Institute) (1997) 'Implementing an Emissions Cap and Allowance Trading System for Greenhouse Gases: Lessons from the Acid Rain Programme' (Washington, DC: ELI, September 1997).

Elkington, J. (1998) *Cannibals with Forks* (Oxford, UK: Capstone Publishing).

Elkington J. (1999) 'Triple Bottom-Line Reporting: Looking for Balance', *Australian CPA*, March 1999: 18-21.

Ellipson (1997) 'ISO 14001: Implementing an Environmental Management System (Basel: Ellipson Ltd).

ENDS (Environmental Data Services) (1994a) 'Carton makers fall foul of LCA trap', *ENDS Report* 230 (March 1994).

ENDS (Environmental Data Services) (1994b) 'The Elusive Consensus on Life-Cycle Assessment: Environmental Impact Analysis No. 38', *ENDS Report* 231 (April 1994): 20-25.

ENDS (Environmental Data Services) (1998a) 'EMAS uptake grows but ISO 14001 levels off', *ENDS Report* 282 (June 1998): 8.

ENDS (Environmental Data Services) (1998b) 'Meacher asks top firms to report on greenhouse gases', *ENDS Report* 285 (October 1998): 6.

ENDS (Environmental Data Services) (1999a) 'Volvo issues externally verified product profile based on LCA', *ENDS Report* 288 (January 1999): 26-28.

ENDS (Environmental Data Services) (1999b) 'BP Amoco Trading in CO_2', *ENDS Report* 294 (July 1999).

Environment Act (1995) *Pubic General Acts—Elizabeth II* (Chapter 25; London: The Stationery Office)

Environment Australia (1999) 'Cleaner Production in Confectionery Manufacturing: Cadbury Schweppes Pty Ltd' (Cleaner Production Case Studies; Canberra: Environment Australia).

Environment Today (1994) 'EPA would lift thresholds for TRI's Form R', *Environment Today*, September 1994: 6.

EPA (US Environmental Protection Agency) (1986) 'Environmental Auditing Policy Statement', *Federal Register* 51.131: 25,004-25,010.

EPA (US Environmental Protection Agency) (1987) 'Toxic Release Inventory: Public Data Release Report' (Washington, DC: Office of Pollution Prevention and Toxics, US EPA).

EPA (US Environmental Protection Agency) (1988) 'Toxic Release Inventory: Public Data Release Report' (Washington, DC: Office of Pollution Prevention and Toxics, US EPA).

EPA (US Environmental Protection Agency) (1989) 'Toxic Release Inventory: Public Data Release Report' (Washington, DC: Office of Pollution Prevention and Toxics, US EPA).

EPA (US Environmental Protection Agency) (1990) 'Toxic Release Inventory: Public Data Release Report' (Washington, DC: Office of Pollution Prevention and Toxics, US EPA).

EPA (US Environmental Protection Agency) (1991a) 'Total Cost Assessment: Accelerating Industrial Pollution Prevention through Innovation' (Washington, DC: Office of Pollution Prevention and Toxics, US EPA).

EPA (US Environmental Protection Agency) (1991b) 'Toxic Release Inventory: Public Data Release Report' (Washington, DC: Office of Pollution Prevention and Toxics, US EPA).

EPA (US Environmental Protection Agency) (1992a) 'Total Cost Assessment: Accelerating Industrial Pollution Prevention through Innovative Project Financial Analysis' (Washington, DC: US EPA).

EPA (US Environmental Protection Agency) (1992b) 'Life-Cycle Assessment: Inventory Guidelines and Principles' (Washington, DC: Franklin Associates).

EPA (US Environmental Protection Agency) (1992c) 'Life-Cycle Assessment: Inventory Guidelines and Principles' (Cincinnati, OH: Risk Reduction Engineering Laboratory, Office of Research and Development, US EPA).

EPA (US Environmental Protection Agency) (1992d) 'Toxic Release Inventory: Public Data Release Report' (Washington, DC: Office of Pollution Prevention and Toxics, US EPA).

EPA (US Environmental Protection Agency) (1993a) 'Life-Cycle Assessment: Public Data Sources for the LCA Practitioner' (final draft, report to US EPA; Washington, DC: Battelle).

EPA (US Environmental Protection Agency) (1993b) 'Life Cycle Design Manual: Environmental Requirements and the Product System' (Washington, DC: US EPA).

EPA (US Environmental Protection Agency) (1993c) 'Life Cycle Design Guidance Manual: Environmental Requirements and the Product System' (Washington, DC: Office of Research and Development, US EPA).

EPA (US Environmental Protection Agency) (1993d) 'Toxic Release Inventory: Public Data Release Report' (Washington, DC: Office of Pollution Prevention and Toxics, US EPA).

EPA (US Environmental Protection Agency) (1994a) 'Stakeholder's Action Agenda: A Report of the Workshop on Accounting and Capital Budgeting for Environmental Costs' (Washington, DC: US EPA).

EPA (US Environmental Protection Agency) (1994b) 'Toxic Release Inventory: Public Data Release Report' (Washington, DC: Office of Pollution Prevention and Toxics, US EPA).

EPA (US Environmental Protection Agency) (1995a) 'TRI-Phase 3: Expansion of the EPA Community's Right-to-know Program to Increase the Information Available to the Public on Chemical Use' (issues papers 2 and 3; Washington, DC: Office of Pollution Prevention and Toxics).

EPA (US Environmental Protection Agency) (1995b) 'Design for the Environment: EPA's Environmental Network for Managerial Accounting and Capital Budgeting' (Washington, DC: US EPA, March 1995).

EPA (US Environmental Protection Agency) (1995c) 'Introduction to Environmental Accounting' (Washington, DC: US EPA).

EPA (US Environmental Protection Agency) (1995d) 'Toxic Release Inventory: Public Data Release Report' (Washington, DC: Office of Pollution Prevention and Toxics, US EPA).

EPA (US Environmental Protection Agency) (1996a) 'Environmental Accounting Case Studies: Full Cost Accounting for Decision Making at Ontario Hydro' (Washington, DC: US EPA).

EPA (US Environmental Protection Agency) (1996b) 'Toxic Release Inventory: Public Data Release Report' (Washington, DC: Office of Pollution Prevention and Toxics, US EPA).

EPA (US Environmental Protection Agency) (1997) 'Toxic Release Inventory: Public Data Release Report' (Washington, DC: Office of Pollution Prevention and Toxics, US EPA).

EPA (US Environmental Protection Agency) (1998a) 'Full-Cost Accounting for Decision-Making at Ontario Hydro', in M. Bennett and P. James (eds.), *The Green Bottom Line. Environmental Accounting for Management: Current Practices and Future Trends* (Sheffield, UK: Greenleaf Publishing): 310-32.

EPA (US Environmental Protection Agency) (1998b) 'Toxic Release Inventory: Public Data Release Report' (Washington, DC: Office of Pollution Prevention and Toxics, US EPA).

EPA (US Environmental Protection Agency) (1999) 'Toxic Release Inventory: Public Data Release Report' (Washington, DC: Office of Pollution Prevention and Toxics, US EPA).

EPCRA (Emergency Planning and Community Right-to-Know Act) (1986) (42 USC 11001 *et seq.*; Washington, DC: US Government Printing Agency).

Epstein, M.J. (1996) *Measuring Corporate Environmental Performance: Best Practices for Costing and Managing an Effective Environmental Strategy* (Chicago: Irwin).

Epstein, M.J., and M.-J. Roy (1997) 'Strategic Learning through Corporate Environmental Management: Implementing the ISO 14001 Standard' (Center for the Management of Environmental Resources [CMER] working paper 97/61/AC; Fontainebleau, France: INSEAD Research and Development Department).

Epstein, M.J., and M.-J. Roy (1998) 'Integrating Environmental Impacts into Capital Investment Decisions', in M. Bennett and P. James (eds.), *The Green Bottom Line. Environmental Accounting for Management: Current Practice and Future Trends* (Sheffield, UK: Greenleaf Publishing): 100-14.

Epstein, L.N., S. Greetham and S. Karuba (1995) 'Ranking Refineries: What do we know about oil refinery pollution from right-to-know data?' (Washington, DC: Environmental Defense Fund).

Ernst & Young (1992) 'Lender Liability for Contaminated Sites: Issues for Lenders and Investors' (working paper 3; Ottawa: National Round Table on the Environment and the Economy).

ESU (Gruppe Energie-Stoffe-Umwelt der Eidgenössischen Technischen Hochschule, Zürich) (1994) 'Basisdaten für Energiesysteme' (Zürich: ESU).

Eurostat (1994) 'Environmental Protection Expenditure: Data Collection Methods in the Public Sector and Industry' (Luxembourg: Office for the Official Publications of the European Communities).

Ewer, S.R. (1996) 'Having it Both Ways. Clean Air via Market Incentives: An Examination of Internal Auditor Readiness', *The International Journal of Accounting and Business Society* 4.2: 1-13.

Ewer, S., J. Nance and S. Hamlin (1992) 'Accounting for Tomorrow's Pollution Control: The Problems CPAs will Face—and Suggested Solutions—When Dealing with Future Environmental Laws', *Journal of Accountancy*, July 1992: 69-74.

FASB (US Financial Accounting Standards Board) (1980) *Accounting for Preacquisition Contingencies of Purchased Enterprises* (Norwalk, CT: FASB).

FASB (US Financial Accounting Standards Board) (1993) 'Miscellaneous Accounting', *SEC Docket* 54.6.

FASB (US Financial Accounting Standards Board) (1994) *Accounting Standards: Current Text* (Norwalk, CT: FASB).

FASB (US Financial Accounting Standards Board) (1999) *The IASC–US Comparison Project: A Report on the Similarities and Differences between IASC Standards and US GAAP* (Hartford, CT: FASB, 2nd edn, October 1999).

Fava, J., R. Denison, B. Jones, M. Curran, B. Vigon, S. Selke and J. Barnum (eds.) (1991) *A Technical Framework for Life-Cycle Assessment* (Smugglers Notch, VT: Society of Environmental Toxicology and Chemistry).

Fava, J., A. Jensen, S. Pomper, B. DeSmet, J. Warren and B. Vignon (eds.) (1992) *Life-Cycle Assessment Data Quality: A Conceptual Framework* (Wintergreen Society of Environmental Toxicology and Chemistry).

Feder, B. (1993) 'Sold: $21 Million of Air Pollution', *The New York Times*, 30 March: C1.

FEE (Féderation des Expertes Comptables Européens) (1993) 'Environmental Accounting and Auditing: Survey of Current Activities and Developments' (Paris: FEE).

FEE (Fédération des Experts Comptables Européens) (1999a) 'Providing Assurance on Environmental Reports' (discussion paper; Brussels: FEE).

FEE (Fédération des Experts Comptables Européens) (1999b) 'Toward a Generally Accepted Framework for Environmental Reporting' (discussion paper; Brussels: FEE, January 1999).

Feldman, S.J., P.A. Soyka and P. Ameer (1997) 'Does Improving a Firm's Environmental Management System and Environmental Performance Result in a Higher Stock Price?', *Journal of Investing* 6.4: 87-97.

Fenn, S. (1995) 'Great Heat', *Technology Review* 98.5: 62-69.

FER (Fachkommission für Empfehlungen zur Rechnungslegung) (1994) *10 Jahresbericht* (Zürich: FER).

Fichter, K. (1995) *Die EG-Öko-Audit-Verordnung: Mit Öko-Controlling zum zertifizierten Umweltmanagementsystem* (Munich: Hanser).

Fichter, K., T. Loew and E. Seidel (1997) *Betriebliche Umweltkostenrechnung* (Berlin: Springer Verlag).

Figge, F. (1995) 'Vergleichende ökologieorientierte Bewertung von Unternehmen (Öko-Rating) Notwendigkeit, erste Ansätze, zukünftige Entwicklungen' (discussion paper 9518; Basel: Wirtschaftswissenschaftliches Zentrum [WWZ]).

Figge, F. (1997) 'Systematisierung ökonomischer Risiken durch globale Umweltprobleme', *Zeitschrift für Angewandte Umweltforschung* 2.

Fischer, H., and R. Blasius (1995) 'Umweltkostenrechnung', in Bundesministerium für Umwelt and Umweltbundesamt (eds.), *Handbuch Umweltcontolling* (Munich: Vahlen): 439-57.

Fischer, H., C. Wucherer, B. Wagner and C. Burschel (1997) *Umweltkostenmanagement: Kosten senken durch praxiserprobtes Umweltcontrolling* (Munich: Hanser).

Fischer, R. (1993) 'Ökologisch orientiertes Controlling', *Controlling* 3: 140-46.

Fleischmann, E., and H. Paudke (1977) 'Rechnungswesen: Kosten des Umweltschutzes', in J. Vogl, A. Heigl and K. Schäfer (eds.), *Handbuch des Umweltschutzes: Grundwerk* (vol. M/III; Landsberg am Lech, Germany: Moderne Industrie).

Fröschle, G. (1993) 'Die Bilanzierung von Umweltschutzmaßnahmen aus bilanztheoretischer Sicht', *Der Betrieb* 46.24 (18 June 1993): 1197-203.

Fouhy, K. (1995) 'New Payback for Environmental Commitment', *Chemical Engineering* 102.3 (March 1995): 49.

Frank, M., and E. Ruppel (1976) *Thermodynamik und Energieanalyse von Produkten* (Berlin: Technische Universität Berlin).

Freedman, J. (1995) 'Results of IMA Co-sponsored Survey Being Released at Corporate Environmental Accounting Conference', *Management Accounting* 76.10: 68.

Freeman, E. (1984) *Strategic Management: A Stakeholder Approach* (Marshfield, MA: Pitman).

Freese, E., and J. Kloock (1989) 'Internes Rechnungswesen und Organisation aus der Sicht des Umweltschutzes', *Betriebswirtschaftliche Forschung und Praxis* 41.2: 1-29.

Freidank, C. (1991) *Kostenrechnung. Einführung in die begrifflichen, theoretischen, verfahrenstechnischen sowie planung- und kontrollorientierten Grundlagen des innverbetrieblichen Rechnungswesens* (Munich: Campus, 3rd edn).

Frey, B., and G. Kirchgässner (1994) *Demokratische Wirtschaftspolitik* (Munich: Vahlen, 2nd edn).

Frey, R.L. (1993) 'Strategien und Instrumente', in R.L. Frey, H. Blöchliger and E. Staehelin-Witt (eds.), *Mit Ökonomie zur Ökologie* (Bern: Helbing & Lichtenhahn; Stuttgart: Schäffer-Poeschel): 67-110.

Frey, R.L. (1997) *Wirtschaft, Staat und Wohlfahrt* (Basel: Helbing & Lichtenhahn, 10th edn).

Frey, R.L., H. Blöchliger and E. Staehelin-Witt (eds.) (1993) *Mit Ökonomie zur Ökologie* (Basel: Helbing & Lichtenhahn, 10th edn).

Friedman, B. (1992) *All about Environmental Auditing* (New York: Harper).

Friedrichs, R. (1987) 'Rechnungslegung bei Umweltschutzmaßnahmen', *Der Betrieb* 51/52 (18 December 1987): 2580-88.

Fritsche, U., L. Rausch and K. Simon (1989) *Umweltwirkungsanalyse von Energiesystemen (GEMIS)* (Wiesbaden, Germany: Hessisches Ministerium für Wirtschaft und Technik).

Fritzler, M. (1994) 'Wer weiß schon, was ein "gedipptes" Schaf ist?', *Future-Magazin* 4: 20.

Gallhofer, S. (1992) 'M[othering] View on: "The Non and Nom of Accounting for (M)other Nature" ', *Accounting, Auditing and Accountability Journal* 5.3: 40-51.

Gallhofer, S., and J. Haslen (1997) 'The Directions of Green Accounting Policy: Critical Reflections', *Accounting, Auditing and Accountability* 10.2: 148-74.

Garber, S., and J.K. Hammitt (1998) 'Risk Premiums for Environmental Liability: Does Superfund Increase the Cost of Capital?' *Journal of Environmental Economics and Management* 36: 267-94.

Garrison, R.H., and E.W. Noreen (2000) *Managerial Accounting* (Boston, MA: Irwin, McGraw–Hill).

GEFIU (Gesellschaft für Finanzwirtschaft in der Unternehmensführung) (1993) 'Bilanzielle Fragen im Zusammenhang mit der Sanierung schadstoffverunreinigter Wirtschaftsgüter', *Der Betrieb* 46.31 (August 1993): 1529-32.

Georgescu-Roegen, N. (1971) *The Entropy Law and the Economic Process* (Cambridge, MA: Harvard University Press).

Gibson, K. (1996) 'The Problem with Reporting Pollution Allowances: Reporting is not the problem', *Critical Perspectives on Accounting* 7: 655-65.

Gibson, K. (1997) 'Courses on Environmental Accounting', *Accounting, Auditing and Accountability Journal* 10.4: 584-93.

Glasson, J., R. Therivel and A. Chadwick (1994) *Introduction to Environmental Impact Assessment* (London: UCL Press).

Goldmann, B., and J. Schellens (1995) *Betriebliche Umweltkennzahlen und ökologisches Benchmarking* (Cologne: Westdeutscher Verlag).

Goodstein, E. (1995) 'The Economic Roots of Environmental Decline: Property Rights or Path Dependence?', *Journal of Economic Issues* 29.4 (December 1995): 1029-43.

Gottschalk, E. (1994) 'Many "nice guy" funds fail to make nice profits', *Wall Street Journal*, 7 July 1994: C1, C16.

Götze, U., and J. Bloech (1993) *Investitionsrechnung: Modelle und Analysen zur Beurteilung von Investitionsvorhaben* (Berlin: Springer Verlag).

Graedel, T.E., B.R. Allenby and P.R. Comrie (1995) 'Matrix Approaches to Abridged Life-Cycle Assessment', *Environmental Science and Technology* 29.3.

Gray, R. (1990a) *The Greening of Accountancy: The Profession after Pearce* (research report 17; London: Association of Chartered Certified Accountants).

Gray, R. (1990b) 'The Accountant's Task as a Friend to the Earth', *Accountancy*, June 1990: 65-69.

Gray, R. (1992) 'Accounting and Environmentalism: An Exploration of the Challenge of Gently Accounting for Accountability, Transparency and Sustainability', *Accounting, Organizations and Society* 17.5: 399-425.

Gray, R. (with J. Bebbington and D. Walters) (1993) *Accounting for the Environment* (London: Chapman Publishing).

Gray, R. (1994) 'Environmental Accounting and Auditing: Survey of Current Activities and Developments', *Accounting and Business Research* 24.95: 285-86.

Gray, R., and R. Laughlin (eds.) (1991) 'Green Accounting' (Special Issue), *Accounting, Auditing and Accountability Journal* 4.3.

Gray, R., and D. Owen (1993) *The Developing Approaches to Environmental Disclosure: The Second Year of the Associations Award Scheme* (London: Association of Chartered Certified Accountants).

Gray, R., J. Bebbington, D. Collison, R. Kowhai, R. Lyn, C. Reid, A. Russell, and L. Stevenson (1998) *The Valuation of Assets and Liabilities: Environmental Law and the Impact of the Environmental Agenda for Business* (Edinburgh: Institute of Chartered Accountants of Scotland).

Gray, R., D. Owen and C. Adams (1996) *Accounting and Accountability: Changes and Challenges in Corporate Social and Environmental Reporting* (London: Prentice–Hall Europe).

Grayson, L., H. Woolston, and I. Tanega (1993) *Business and Environmental Accountability: An Overview and Guide to the Literature* (London: Technical Communications).

Greenberg, R., and C. Unger (1991) 'Getting Started: Introducing Total Quality Management Measures into Environmental Programs', *Corporate Quality and Environmental Management* 35-39.

Greenpeace (1994) 'Greenpeace Intervenes in ECV Flotation', *Greenpeace Business* 22 (December 1994).

GRI (Global Reporting Initiative) (1999) 'Sustainability Reporting Guidelines: Exposure Draft for Public Comment and Pilot Testing' (Boston, MA: Coalition for Environmentally Responsible Economies, March 1999).

Grimsted, B., S. Schaltegger, C. Stinson and C. Waldron (1994) 'A Multimedia Assessment Scheme to Evaluate Chemical Effects on the Environment and Human Health', *Pollution Prevention Review*, Summer 1994: 259-68.

Grittner, P. (1978) *Versuch der Begründung einer thermodynamischen Theorie des Wertes von Produkten am Beispiel von Aluminium und Kupfer* (Bamberg, Germany: Schadel).

Guinée, J., and R. Heijungs (1993) 'A Proposal for the Classification of Toxic Substances within the Framework of Life-Cycle Assessment of Products', *Chemosphere* 26.10: 1925-44.

Gunn, T. (1992) *Creating Winning Business Performance: 21st Century Manufacturing* (New York: Harper Business).

Gunningham, N., and P. Grabosky (1998) *Smart Regulation: Designing Environmental Policy* (Oxford, UK: Clarendon Press).

Günther, E. (1993) *Ökologieorientiertes Controlling: Konzeption eines Systems zur ökologieorientierten Steuerung und empirische Validierung* (Munich: Vahlen).

Günther, E., and B. Wagner (1993) 'Ökologieorientierung des Controlling', *Die Betriebswirtschaft* 53.2: 143-66.

Gupta, S., G. Van Houtuen and M. Cropper (1996) 'Paying for Performance: An Economic Analysis of EPA's Cleanup Decisions at Superfund Sites', *RAND Journal of Economics* 27.3: 563-82.

Haasis, H. (1992) 'Umweltschutzkosten in der betrieblichen Vollkostenrechnung', *Wirtschaftsstudium* 3 (March 1992): 118-22.

Hahn, R. (1984) 'Market Power and Transferable Property Rights', *Quantitative Journal of Economics* 99: 753-65.

Hahn, R., and R. Stavins (1991) 'Incentive-Based Environmental Regulation: A New Era from an Old Idea?', *Ecology Law Quarterly* 18.1: 1-41.

Hall, R., and D. Case (1992) *All about Environmental Auditing* (Washington, DC: Federal Publications).

Hallay, H. (1992) 'Öko-Controlling: Ein Führungsinstrument der Zukunft', in H. Glauber and R. Pfriem (eds.), *Ökologisch Wirtschaften: Erfahrungen, Strategien, Modelle* (Frankfurt: Fischer): 114-23.

Hallay, H., and R. Pfriem (1992) *Öko-Controlling: Umweltschutz in mittelständischen Unternehmen* (Frankfurt: Campus).

Hamilton, J. (1995) 'Pollution as News: Media and Stock Market Reactions to the Toxics Release Inventory Data', *Journal of Environmental Economics and Management* 28.1 (January 1995): 98-113.

Hansen, D.R., and M.M. Mowen (2000) *Cost Management: Accounting and Control* (Cincinnati, OH: South Western College Publishing).

Hanson, D. (1995) 'Toxic Release Inventory: Chemical industry again cuts emissions', *Chemical and Engineering News* 73.14 (3 April 1995): 4-5.

Harding, R. (1998) *Environmental Decision Making: The Roles of Scientists, Engineers and the Public* (Sydney: The Federation Press).

Hart, S.L., and G. Ahuja (1996) 'Does it pay to be green? An Empirical Examination of the Relationship between Emission Reduction and Firm Performance', *Business Strategy and the Environment* 5: 30-37.

Hautau, H., U. Lorenzen, D. Sander and M. Bertram (1987) *Monetäre Bewertungsansätze von Umweltbelastungen* (Göttingen, Germany: Vandenhoeck & Ruprecht).

Haveman, M., and T. Foecke (1998) 'Applying Environmental Accounting to Electroplating Operations: An In-Depth Analysis', in M. Bennett and P. James (eds.), *The Green Bottom Line. Environmental Accounting for Management: Current Practice and Future Trends* (Sheffield, UK: Greenleaf Publishing): 212-35.

Hawkshaw, A. (1991) 'Status Quo Vadis', *CA Magazine*, March 1991: 24-25.

Hayek, F. (1945) 'The Use of Knowledge in Society', *American Economic Review* 4 (September 1945): 519-30.

Hazardous Waste Reduction Act (1990) (70.95 RCW; Washington, DC: US Government Printing Office).

Hector, G. (1992) 'A new reason you can't get a loan', *Fortune* 126. 6 (September 1992): 107-10.

Hedley, B. (1977) 'Strategy and the Business Portfolio', *Long Range Planning* 10: 3-15.

Heigl, A. (1989) 'Ertragssteuerliche Anreize für Investitionen in den Umweltschutz', *Betriebswirtschaftliche Forschung und Praxis* 41.1/89, 66-81.

Heijungs, R., J. Guinée, G. Huppes, R. Lankreijer, H. Udo de Haes and A. Sleeswijk (1992) *Environmental Life Cycle Assessment of Products: Guide and Backgrounds* (Leiden, Netherlands: Center of Environmental Science [CML]).

Heinrich, L. (1996) *Informationsmanagement: Planung, Überwachung und Steuerung der Informationsinfrastruktur* (Munich: Oldenbourg).

Henn, C., and J. Fava (1984) *Life Cycle Analysis and Resource Management* (New York: McGraw–Hill).

Hess, G. (1994) 'The Right Direction; Industry-wide emissions are declining steadily, while the EPA looks into expansion of the Toxics Release Inventory', *Chemical Marketing Reporter* 246.7 (15 August 1994).

Hess, G. (1995) 'EPA proposal seeks to ease reporting burden in industry', *Chemical Marketing Reporter* 247.8 (20 February 1994): 24.

Heuvels, K. (1993) 'Die EG-Öko-Audit-Verordnung im Praxistest: Erfahrungen aus einem Pilot-Audit-Programm der Europäischen Gemeinschaften', *Umwelt WirtschaftsForum* 3: 41-48.

Hibbit, C. (1994) 'Green Reporting: It's time the UK 6*Accountancy* 114.1214 (October 1994): 97-98.

Hillary, R. (1993) *The Eco-Management and Audit Scheme: A Practical Guide* (London: Technical Communications).

Hillary, R. (1995) 'Environmental Reporting Requirements under the EU Eco-management and Audit Scheme (EMAS)', *The Environmentalist* 15: 293-99.

Hill, C., and G. Jones (1992) *Strategic Management: An Integrated Approach* (Boston, MA: Houghton Mifflin).

Himelstein, L., and B. Regan (1993) 'Fresh Ammo for the Eco-Cops: What Price Pollution? New methods try to calculate it to the dollar', *Business Week*, 29 November 1993: 93-94.

Hines, R. (1991) 'On Valuing Nature', *Accounting, Auditing and Accountability Journal* 4.3: 27-29.

Hirschman, A. (1970) *Exit, Voice and Loyalty: Responses to Decline in Firms, Organizations and States* (Cambridge, MA: Harvard University Press).

Hirshleifer, J. (1980) *Price Theory and Applications* (Englewood Cliffs, NJ: Prentice–Hall, 2nd edn).

Hofer, P., and D. Schendel (1978) *Strategy Formulation: Analytical Concepts* (St Paul, MN: West).

Holmark, D., P. Rikhardsson and H. Jørgensen (1995) *The Annual Environmental Report: Measuring and Reporting Environmental Performance* (Copenhagen: Price Waterhouse).

Hope, J., and R. Fraser (1997) 'Beyond Budgeting: Breaking through the Barrier to "the Third Wave" ', *Management Accounting* (December 1997).

Hopfenbeck, W., and C. Jasch (1993) *Öko-Controlling: Umdenken zahlt sich aus! Audits, Umweltberichte und Ökobilanzen als betriebliche Führungsinstrumente* (Landsberg, Germany: Verlag Moderne Industrie).

Horngren, C., and G. Foster (1987) *Cost Accounting: A Managerial Emphasis* (Englewood Cliffs, NJ: Prentice–Hall, 6th edn).

Horngren, C.T., G. Foster and S.M. Datar (2000) *Cost Accounting: A Managerial Emphasis* (Englewood Cliffs, NJ: Prentice–Hall International).

Horvath, P. (1990) *Controlling* (Munich: Vahlen, 3rd edn).

Horvath, P., and R. Mayer (1989) 'Prozeßkostenrechnung: Der neue Weg zu mehr Kostentransparenz und wirkungsvolleren Unternehmensstrategien', *Controlling* 1.4: 214-19.

Horvath, P., and R. Mayer (1993) 'Prozeßkostenrechnung: Konzeption und Entwicklungen', *Kostenrechnungspraxis* 2: 15-28.

Hosbach, H., G. Karlaganis and H. Saxer (1995) 'Schadstoff-Emissionsregister schaffen Transparenz und fördern das Umweltbewußtsein der Verursacher', *BUWAL Bulletin* 3: 31-34.

Hrauda, G., C. Jasch, V. Puchinger and V. Rubik (1993) *Ökobilanzen von Packstoffen in Theorie und Praxis: Eine Iststandserhebung* (Vienna: Österreichisches Bundesministerium für Umwelt, Jugend und Familie and Institut für Ökologische Wirtschaftsforschung).

HUI (Hamburger Umweltinstitut) (1994, 1996 [update]) *The Top 50 Ranking: Eine Untersuchung zur Umweltverträglichkeit der 50 größten Chemie- und Pharmaunternehmen weltweit* (Hamburg: HUI).

Hummel, S., and W. Männel (1993) *Kostenrechnung. II. Moderne Verfahren und Systeme* (Wiesbaden, Germany: Gabler, 3rd edn).

HDFD (Hundred Group of Finance Directors) (1992) 'Statement of Good Practice: Environmental Reporting in Annual Reports' (London: Environmental Working Party, HGFD).

Hunt, C.B., and E.R. Auster (1990) 'Proactive Environmental Management: Avoiding the Toxic Trap', *Sloan Management Review*, Winter 1990: 7-18.

Hutchings, D. (1999) 'New pollution inventory shows significant reduction in key pollutants' (document 48mayst; London: Environment Agency).

IASC (International Accounting Standards Committee) (1992) 'Property, Plant and Equipment: International Accounting Standard' (proposed statement, exposure draft 43; London: IASC, May 1992).

IASC (International Accounting Standards Committee) (1993) *International Accounting Standards 1993* (London: IASC).

IASC (International Accounting Standards Committee) (1994) 'Future Work Programme', *IASC Insight*, 12 September 1994.

IASC (International Accounting Standards Committee) (1995) *International Accounting Standards 1995* (London: IASC).

IASC (International Accounting Standards Committee) (1998a) 'International Accounting Standard 1: Presentation of Financial Statements' (London: IASC).

IASC (International Accounting Standards Committee) (1998b) 'International Accounting Standard 37: Provisions, Contingent Liabilities and Contingent Assets (London: IASC).

ICC (International Chamber of Commerce) (1991) *The Business Charter for Sustainable Development* (Paris: ICC).

IER (International Environmental Reporter) (1995) 'Danish proposal would require industry to set up separate "green" accounting system', *International Environmental Reporter*, 22 February 1995: 143-44.

IFAC (International Federation of Accountants) (1997) *The Consideration of Environmental Matters in the Audit of Financial Statements* (New York: International Auditing Practices Committee, IFAC).

IFAC (International Federation of Accountants) (1998) *Environmental Management in Organizations: The Role of Management Accounting* (study 6; New York: Financial and Management Accounting Committee, IFAC, March 1998).

IISD (International Institute for Sustainable Development) (1996) *The Bellagio Principles* (Winnipeg: IISD).

IISD (International Institute for Sustainable Development) (1998) *Beyond Regulation: Exporters and Voluntary Environmental Measures* (Winnipeg: IISD).

Ijiri, Y. (1983) 'On the Accountability-based Conceptual Framework of Accounting', *Journal of Accounting and Public Policy* 2: 75-81.

Ilinitch, A., and S. Schaltegger (1995) 'Developing a Green Business Portfolio', *Long Range Planning* 28: 2.

Ilinitch, A.Y., N.S. Soderstrom, and T.E. Thomas (1998) 'Measuring Corporate Environmental Performance', *Journal of Accounting and Public Policy* 17.4/5: 383-408.

INSEE (Institut National de la Statistique et des Etudes Economiques) (1986a) 'Les comptes satellites de l'environnement: Méthodes et resultats' (series C 130; Paris: Ministère de l'Environnement, INSEE).

INSEE (Institut National de la Statistique et des Etudes Economiques) (1986b) 'Les Comptes du Patrimoine Naturel' (series C 137-138; Paris: Ministère de l'Environnement, INSEE).

ISO (International Organization for Standardization) (1994a) 'Environmental Management Systems: Specification with Guidance for Use: Committee Draft ISO/CD 14001' (London: ISO).

ISO (International Organization for Standardization) (1994b) 'Life-Cycle Impact Assessment' (draft to be included in WG 1 document 'Life-Cycle Assessment: General Principles and Procedures'; London: ISO).

ISO (International Organization for Standardization) (1994c) 'ISO TC 207: Environmental Performance Evaluation Framework Document on Definitions, Principles and Methodology' (final draft; Toronto: Environmental Management Subcommittee 4, ISO).

ISO (International Organization for Standardization) (1999a) *Environmental Management and ISO 14000: Development Manual 10* (Geneva: ISO).

ISO (International Organization for Standardization) (1999b) *ISO 14031: Environmental Performance Evaluation* (Geneva: ISO).

James, P., and M. Bennett (1998) 'Environment under the Spotlight: Current Practice Trends in Environment-Related Performance Measures for Business' (London: Association of Chartered Certified Accountants).

Janke, G. (1995) *Öko-Auditing: Handbuch für die interne Revision des Umweltschutzes im Unternehmen* (Berlin: Schmidt).

Janzen, H. (1996) *Ökologisches Controlling im Dienste von Umwelt- und Risikomanagment* (Stuttgart: Schäffer-Poeschel).

Jasch, C. (1999) 'Ecobalancing in Austria', in M. Bennett and P. James (eds.), *Sustainable Measures: Evaluation and Reporting of Environmental and Social Performance* (Sheffield, UK: Greenleaf Publishing): 151-69.

Jauch, L., and W. Glueck (1988) *Business Policy and Strategic Management* (New York: McGraw–Hill).

JEA (Japan Environment Agency) (1998) 'Guideline of Measures to Prevent Global Warming: Measures towards 2010 to Prevent Global Warming' (Tokyo: Global Warming Prevention Headquarters, JEA, 19 June 1998).

Johanson, P. (1990) 'Valuing Environmental Damage', *Oxford Review of Economic Policy* 6.1: 34-50.

Johnson, H., and R. Kaplan (1987a) *Relevance Lost: The Rise and Fall of Management Accounting* (Boston, MA: Harvard Business School Press).

Johnson, H., and R. Kaplan (1987b) 'The Rise and Fall of Management Accounting: Management accounting information is too late, too aggregated, and too distorted to be relevant', *Management Accounting*, January 1987: 22-29.

Johnson, H.T. (1998) 'Using Performance Measurement to Improve Results: A Life-System Perspective', *International Journal of Strategic Cost Management* 1.1: 1-6.

Johnson, L. (ed.) (1991) *The FASB Cases on Recognition and Measurement* (Chicago: Irwin).

Johnson, L. (1993) 'Research on Environmental Reporting', *Accounting Horizons* 7.3: 118-23.

Jones, K. (1999) 'Study on Environmental Reporting by Companies' (Brussels: Commission of the European Communities).

Jones, M.J. (1996) 'Accounting for Biodiversity: A Pilot Study', *British Accounting Review* 28.4: 281-303.

Judge, W.Q., and T.J. Douglas (1998) 'Performance Implications of Incorporating Natural Environmental Issues into the Strategic Planning Process: An Empirical Assessment', *Journal of Management Studies* 35.2: 241-62.

Kaplan, R.S. (1984) 'The Evolution of Management Accounting', *The Accounting Review* LIX.3: 390-418.

Kaplan, R. (1992) 'The Balanced Scorecard: Measures that Drive Performance', *Harvard Business Review*, January/February 1992: 71-79.

Kaplan, R. (1995) 'Das neue Rollenverständnis für den Controller', *Controlling* 2: 60-70.

Kaplan, R., and D. Norton (1996) *The Balanced Scorecard: Translating Strategy into Action* (Boston, MA: Harvard Business School Press).

Karl, H. (1992) 'Mehr Umweltschutz durch Umwelt-Auditing? Audit-Konzeption der Europäischen Gemeinschaft', *Zeitschrift für angewandte Umweltforschung* 5.3: 297-303.

Karl, H. (1993) 'Europäische Initiative für die Einführung von Umweltschutz-Audits: Kritische Würdigung aus ökonomischer Sicht', *List Forum für Wirtschaftspolitik* 19.3: 207-20.

Karr, J. (1993) 'Protecting Ecological Integrity', *The Yale Law Journal of International Law* 18.1 (Winter 1993): 297-306.

Keeney, R. (1996) *Value-Focused Thinking: A Path to Creative Decisionmaking* (Cambridge, MA: Harvard University Press).

Keeney, R., and H. Raiffa (1976) *Decisions with Multiple Objectives: Preferences and Value Tradeoffs* (New York: John Wiley).

Keidanren (Japan Federation of Economic Organisations) (1991) *Keidanren Global Environment Charter* (Tokyo: Keidanren).

Kennedy, J., T. Mitchell and S.E. Sefcik (1998) 'Disclosure of Contingent Environmental Liabilities: Some Unintended Consequences?', *Journal of Accounting Research* 36.2: 257-77.

Khanna, M., W.R.H. Quimio and D. Bojilova (1998) 'Toxics Release Information: A Policy Tool for Environmental Protection', *Journal of Environmental Economics and Management* 36: 243-66.

Kilger, W. (1992) *Einführung in die Kostenrechnung* (Wiesbaden, Germany: Gabler, 3rd edn).

Kilger, W. (1993) *Flexible Plankostenrechnung und Deckungbeitragsrechnung* (Wiesbaden, Germany: Gabler, 10th edn).

Kircher, N. (1994) 'Im Würgegriff des Zinses. Zahlen mit Talent: Ein neues System sorgt für Zündstoff', *Schweizerische Handelszeitung* 10 (March 1994).

Klassen, R.D., and C.P. McLaughlin (1996) 'The Impact of Environmental Management on Firm Performance', *Management Science* 42.8: 1199-214.

Klich, T. (1993) 'Eignung qualitativer Planungs- und Analyseinstrumente für Zwecke des Umweltschutz-Controlling', *Zeitschrift für Betriebswirtschaft* 2: 105-17.

Kloock, J. (1990) 'Umweltkostenrechnung', in E. Scheer (ed.), *Rechnungswesen und EDV* (Heidelberg): 129-56.

Kloock, J. (1993) 'Neuere Entwicklungen betrieblicher Umweltkostenrechnungen', in G. Wagner (ed.), *Betriebswirtschaft und Umweltschutz* (Stuttgart: Vahlen): 179-206.

Kloock, J. (1995) 'Umweltkostenrechnung', in M. Junkernheinrich, P. Klemmer and G. Wagner (eds.), *Handbuch zur Umwelökonomie* (Berlin: Springer Verlag): 295-301.

Klüppel, H.-J. (1998) 'ISO 14041. Environmental Management: Life Cycle Assessment, Goal and Scope Definition, Inventory Analysis', *The International Journal of Life Cycle Assessment* 3.5: editorial.

Knapp, M. (1996) *Financial Accounting: A Focus on Decision Making* (Minneapolis, MN: West).

Knight, P. (1994) 'What Price Natural Disasters?', *Tomorrow*: 48-50.

Knörzer, A. (1995) *Ökologische Aspekte im Investment Research* (Bern: Haupt).

Koechlin, D., and K. Müller (1992) 'Environmental Management and Investment Decisions', in D. Koechlin and K. Müller (eds.), *Green Business Opportunities: The Profit Potential* (London: Financial Times/Pitman).

Konar, S., and M.A. Cohen (1995) 'Information as Regulation: The Effect of Community Right to Know Laws on Toxic Emissions' (available as at 9 January 1999 at www.vanderbilt.edu/VCEMS/papers/pubs.html; forthcoming in *Journal of Environmental Economics and Management*).

Kosiol, E. (1979) *Kosten- und Leistungsrechnung: Grundlagen, Verfahren und Anwendungen* (Berlin: Springer Verlag).

Kottmann, H., T. Loew and J. Clausen (1999) *Umweltmanagement mit Indikatoren* (Munich: Vahlen).

Kreuze, J., and G. Newell (1994) 'ABC and Life-Cycle Costing for Environmental Expenditures: The combination gives companies a more accurate snapshot', *Management Accounting US* 75.8: 38-42.

Krut, R., and H. Gleckman (1998) *ISO 14001: A Missed Opportunity for Sustainable Global Industrial Development* (London: Earthscan).

Kunert AG, Kienbaum and Institut für Management und Umwelt (IMU) (eds.) (1995) Modellprojekt Umweltkostenmanagement (Immenstadt, Germany: IMU).

Landis & Gyr (1995) 'Eco-efficiency Report' (Zug, Switzerland: Landis & Gyr).

Lascelles, D. (1993) 'Rating Environmental Risk' (London: Centre for the Study of Financial Innovation).

Laughlin, B., and L. Varangu (1991) 'Accounting for Waste or Garbage Accounting: Some Thoughts from Non-Accountants', *Accounting, Auditing and Accountability Journal* 4.3: 43-50.

Lave, L.B., E. Cobas-Flores, C.T. Henderson and F.C. McMichael (1995) 'Life-Cycle Assessment: Using Input–Output Analysis to Estimate Economy-Wide Discharges', *Environmental Science and Technology* 29.9.

Leggett, J. (1996) *Climate Change and the Financial Sector* (Munich: Gerling).

Lehman, G. (1996) 'Environmental Accounting: Pollution Permits or Selling the Environment', *Critical Perspectives on Accounting* 7: 667-76.

Lehman, G. (1999) 'Disclosing New Worlds: A Role for Social and Environmental Accounting and Auditing', *Accounting, Organizations and Society* 24.3: 217-41.

Lehmann, S., and J. Clausen (1991) 'Öko-Controlling: Informationsinstrument für ökologische Unternehmensführung', *Wechselwirkung* 51 (October 1991): 11-15.

Lehmann, S. (1990) 'Ökobilanzen und Öko-Controlling als Instrumente einer präventiven Umweltpolitik in Unternehmen', in G. Kozmiensky (ed.), *Vermeidung und Verwertung von Abfällen* (Berlin: EF-Verlag): 101-09.

Lehni, M. (1999) 'Eco-efficiency Indicators Concept: Only what's measured gets done!' (Eco-efficiency workshop, 25–26 May 1999; Perth, Australia: World Business Council for Sustainable Development).

Leibenstein, H. (1966) 'Allocative Efficiency versus X-Efficiency', *American Economic Review* 56: 392-415.

Lewis, H. (1996) 'Data Quality for Life Cycle Assessment' (address to the National Conference on Life Cycle Assessment: Shaping Australia's Environmental Future, Melbourne, Australia, 29 February–1 March 1996).

Li, Y., and B.J. McConomy (1999) 'An Empirical Examination of Factors Affecting the Timing of Environmental Accounting Standard Adoption and the Impact on Corporate Valuation', *Journal of Accounting, Auditing and Finance* 14.3: 279-319.

Li, Y., G.D. Richardson and D.B. Thornton (1997) 'Corporate Disclosure of Environmental Liability Information: Theory and Evidence', *Corporate Accounting Research* 14.7: 435-74.

Libby, R.T. (1999) *Eco-Wars: Political Campaigns and Social Movements (Power, Conflict, and Democracy)* (New York: Columbia University Press).

Liebl, F. (1996) *Strategische Frühaufklärung* (Munich: Oldenbourg).

Lifset, R. (1991) 'Raising the Ante for Life Cycle Analysis', *Biocycle: Journal of Composting and Recycling* 32.

Lindlar, A. (1995) *Umwelt-Audits: Ein Leitfaden für Unternehmen über das EG-Gemeinschaftssystem für das Umweltmanagement und die Betriebsprüfung* (Bonn: Economica).

Lintner, J. (1965) 'Security Prices, Risk, and Maximal Gains from Diversification', *The Journal of Finance* 20: 587-615.

Lobos, I. (1992) 'Boeing will pay fine over hazardous waste: EPA assesses largest charge of its kind', *The Seattle Times*, 14 January 1992: B1.

Loderer, C. (1996) 'Rethinking Project Valuation', *Finanzmarkt und Portfolio Management* 10.2: 133-47.

Loew, T. (1996) 'Transparenz durch Umweltkennzahlen', *Unternehmer Magazin* 11: 20.

Loew, T., and H. Hjálmarsdòttir (1996) 'Umweltkennzahlen für das betriebliche Umwelt-management' (discussion paper 40; Berlin: Institut für ökologische Wirtschaftsforschung).

Loew, T., and H. Kottmann (1996) 'Umweltkennzahlen im Umweltmanagement', *Ökologisches Wirtschaften* 2: 10-12.

Losee, R.M. (1997) 'A Discipline-Independent Definition of Information', *Journal of the American Society for Information Science* 48.3: 254-69.

Lutz, E., and M. Munasinghe (1991) 'Accounting for the Environment', *Finance and Development*, March 1991: 19-21.

McGuire, J., A. Sundgren and T. Schneeweis (1981) 'Corporate Social Responsibility and Firm Financial Performance', *Academy of Management Journal* 31.4: 854-72.

McKenzie D. (1998) 'Activism Shrinks but Grows', *Tomorrow* VIII.1: 29.

McKeown, J.C. (1999) 'Discussion [of] Y. Li and B.J. McConomy (1999) "An Empirical Examination of Factors Affecting the Timing of Environmental Accounting Standard Adoption and the Impact on Corporate Valuation" ', *Journal of Accounting, Auditing and Finance* 14.3: 279-319.

McMurray, S. (1992) 'Monsanto Doubles Liability Provision for Treating Toxic Waste to $245 Million', *Wall Street Journal*, 23 March 1992: A7.

Mcnaghten, P., R. Grove-White, M. Jacobs and B. Wynne (1997) 'Sustainability and Indicators', in P. McDonagh and A. Prothero (eds.), *Green Management: A Reader* (London: Dryden Press): 148-53.

McNurlin, B., and R. Sprague (1989) *Information Systems Management in Practice* (Englewood Cliffs, NJ: Prentice–Hall, 2nd edn).

McPhail, K., and A. Davy (1998) 'Integrating Social Concerns into Private Sector Decisionmaking: A Review of Corporate Practices in the Mining, Oil and Gas Sectors' (discussion paper 384; Washington, DC: World Bank).

Mansley, M. (1995) 'Long Term Financial Risks to the Carbon Fuel from the Climate Change' (London: The Delphi Industry Group).

Margenau, H. (1996) 'What is a Theory?', in S. Krupp (ed.), *The Structure of Economic Science* (New York: Prentice–Hall).

Marshall, J. (1993) 'A Nearly Useless Energy Tax', *The New York Times*, 11 April 1993: 13.

Martins, L.L., C.J. Fombrun and A.T. Marlin (1995) 'Assessing Corporate Environmental Performance', in F. Capra and G. Pauli (eds.), *Steering Business Toward Sustainability* (Tokyo/New Delhi: United Nations University Press).

Mathews, R. (1997) 'Twenty-Five Years of Social and Environmental Accounting Research: Is there a silver jubilee to celebrate?' *Accounting, Auditing and Accountability Journal* 10.4: 481-531.

Maunders, K., and R.L. Burritt (1991) 'Accounting and Ecological Crisis', *Accounting, Auditing and Accountability Journal* 4.3: 9-26.

Meadows, D., D. Meadows and J. Randers (1992) *Beyond the Limits: Confronting Global Collapse, Envisioning a Sustainable Future* (Post Mills, VT: Chelsea Green Publishers).

Meffert, H., and M. Bruhn (1996) 'Das Umweltbewußtsein von Konsumenten', *Die Betriebswirtschaft* 56.5: 631-48.

Merchant, K.A. (1998) *Modern Management Control Systems: Text and Cases* (Englewood Cliffs, NJ: Prentice–Hall).

Mishan, E. (1980) *Die Wachstumsdebatte: Wachstum zwischen Wirtschaft und Ökologie* (Stuttgart: Klett-Cotta).

Monhemius, K. (1993) *Umweltbewußtes Kaufverhalten von Konsumenten: Ein Beitrag zur Operational-isierung, Erklärung und Typologie des Verhaltens in der Kaufsituation* (Frankfurt: Gabler).

Moore, D. (1991) 'At the Drawing Board', *CA Magazine*, March 1991: 54-56.

Mooren, C., H. Müller and M. Muhr (1991) 'Umweltorientierte Fördermaßnahmen des Staates in betrieblichen Investitionskalkülen', *Zeitschrift für angewandte Umweltforschung* 4.3: 267-82.

Morrow, M. (1992) *Activity-Based Management: New Approaches to Measuring Performance and Managing Costs* (New York: Woodhead-Faulkner).

Mostowfi, M. (1997) 'Bewertung von Investitionen unter Berücksichtigung zeitlicher Flexibilität', *Betriebswirtschaftliche Forschung und Praxis* 50.5: 580-92.

MPI (Minerals Policy Institute) (1998) 'Glossy Reports, Grim Reality: A Case Study of WMC Ltd' (Sydney: MPI).

Müller, K., and A. Wittke (1998) 'The Ciba Case: The Financial Quantification of Environmental Strategies with Value-Based Environmental Management', in S. Schaltegger and A. Sturm (eds.), *Eco-Efficiency by Eco-Controlling* (Zürich: VDF).

Müller, K., J. de Frutos, K. Schüssler and H. Haarbosch (1994) 'Environmental Reporting and Disclosures: The Financial Analyst's View' (London: Working Group of Environmental Issues of the Accounting Commission of the European Federation of Financial Analysts Society).

Müller-Wenk, R. (1978) *Die ökologische Buchhaltung* (Frankfurt: Campus).

Münchner Rückversicherung (1995) *Jahresbericht* (Munich: Münchner Rückversicherung).

Myddleton, D. (1995) 'Accounting Issues: Standards: Non-Solution to a Non-Problem', *Accountancy* 9: 92.

Naimon, J. (1995) 'Corporate reporting picks up speed', *Tomorrow*, January–March 1995.

Napolitano, G. (1995) 'Company-Specific Effect of Environmental Compliance', *The Quarterly Accounting Review*, June 1995.

Nation's Business (1994) 'Voluntary EPA Programs', *Nation's Business*, September 1994: 64.

Navrud, S., and G.J. Pruckner (1997) 'Environmental Valuation: To Use or Not to Use?—A Comparative Study of the United States and Europe', *Environmental and Resource Economics* 10.1: 1-25.

NCM (Nordic Council of Ministers) (1995) 'LCA: Nordic Technical Reports' (various numbers; Copenhagen: NCM).

NEPC (National Environment Protection Council) (1997) 'National Environment Protection Measure and Impact Statement for Ambient Air Quality' (Adelaide: NEPC).

Neumann-Szyszka, J. (1994) *Kostenrechnung und umweltorientiertes Controlling: Möglichkeiten und Grenzen des Einsatzes eines traditionellen Controllinginstruments im umweltorientierten Controlling* (Wiesbaden: Deutscher Universitätsverlag).

Newell, G., J. Kreuze and S. Newell (1990) 'Accounting for Hazardous Waste: Does your firm face potential environmental liabilities?', *Management Accounting*, May 1990: 58-61.

NSW EPA (New South Wales Environmental Protection Agency) (1995) *Hunter River Salinity Trading Scheme: Guideline and Rulebook* (Environmental Economics Series, publication 95/32; Sydney: NSW EPA).

NZZ (Neue Zürcher Zeitung) (1994a) 'Exxon im Fall Valdez für fahrlässig befunden: Große Forderungen an den Erdölkonzern', *Neue Zürcher Zeitung* 137: 19.

NZZ (Neue Zürcher Zeitung) (1994b) 'Mildes Urteil gegen Exxon', *Neue Zürcher Zeitung* 187: 20.

NZZ (Neue Zürcher Zeitung) (1994c) 'Umweltschutz mit der Unterstützung des Marktes: Bilanz des Handels von Schadstoff-Zertifikaten in den USA', *Neue Zürcher Zeitung* 304: 23.

NZZ (Neue Zürcher Zeitung) (1995) 'Wachsende Bedeutung der Rechnungslegung nach IAS', *Neue Zürcher Zeitung* 60: 13.

OAGC (Office of the Auditor General of Canada) (1997) 'Report of the Commissioner of the Environment and Sustainable Development to the House of Commons, Minister of Public Works and Government Services' (Ottawa: OAGC).

ÖB *(Ökologische Briefe)* (1995) 'Saubere Umwelt durch öffentlichen Informationszugang?', *Ökologische Briefe* 26: 5-6.

Occupational Hazards (1994) 'Is 33/50 a "Sham"?', *Occupational Hazards* 56.8 (August 1994): 60-62.

Odum, H.T. (1996) *Environmental Accounting, Emergy and Decision Making* (New York: John Wiley).

OECD (Organisation for Economic Co-operation and Development) (1992) *OECD Guidelines for Multinational Enterprises* (Paris: OECD).

OECD (Organisation for Economic Co-operation and Development) (1993) *Systèmes d'Information et Indicateurs d'Environnement* (Paris: OECD).

OECD (Organisation for Economic Co-operation and Development) (1994a) *Managing the Environment: The Role of Economic Instruments* (Paris: OECD).

OECD (Organisation for Economic Co-operation and Development) (1994b) *Natural Resource Accounts: Taking Stock in OECD Countries* (environment monograph 84; Paris: OECD).

OECD (Organisation for Economic Co-operation and Development) (1995) *PRTR Guidance to Governments Document: Data Management and Reporting for a National Pollutant Release and Transfer Register* (Paris: Pollution Prevention and Control Group, OECD).

OECD (Organisation for Economic Co-operation and Development) (1996a) *Pollutant Release and Transfer Registers (PRTRs): A Tool for Environmental Policy and Sustainable Development: Guidance Manual for Governments* (document OECD/GD(96)32; Paris: OECD).

OECD (Organisation for Economic Co-operation and Development) (1996b) *The Global Environmental Goods and Services Industry* (Paris: OECD).

OECD (Organisation for Economic Co-operation and Development) (1998a) 'Recommendation of the Council on Environmental Information' (C[98] 67; Paris: OECD, April 1998).

OECD (Organisation for Economic Co-operation and Development) (1998b) *Eco-efficiency* (Paris: OECD).

OECD (Organisation for Economic Co-operation and Development) (1998c) *Extended and Shared Producer Responsibility* (document ENV/EPOC/PPC[97]19/REV2; Paris: Group on Pollution Prevention and Control, OECD).

OECD (Organisation for Economic Co-operation and Development) (1999) *Proceedings of the OECD International Conference on Pollutant Release and Transfer Registers (PRTRs): National and Global Responsibility. Part 1* (document ENV/JM/MONO[99]16/PART1; Paris: OECD).

Ojala, M. (1998) 'Gresham's Law of Information', *Database*, June 1998: 8.

Olson, M. (1965) *The Logic of Collective Action* (Cambridge, MA: Harvard University Press).

Orwat, C. (1996) *Informationsinstrumente des Umweltmanagements* (Berlin: Analytica).

OTA (Office of Technology Assessment, US Congress) (1994) *Industry, Technology and the Environment: Competitive Challenges and Business Opportunities* (Washington, DC: US Government Printing Office).

Ottoboni, A. (1991) *The Dose Makes the Poison: A Plain-Language Guide to Toxicology* (New York: Van Nostrand Reinhold).

Owen, D.L. (1994) 'The Need for Environmental Accounting Standards', *Accounting Forum* 17.4: 31-46.

Paasikivi, R. (1994) 'Towards a European Standard', *EEE Bulletin*, Winter 1994: 8-10.

Panaiotov, T. (Theodore Panayotou) (1998) *Instruments of Change: Motivating and Financing Sustainable Development* (London: Earthscan).

Panayotou, T. (1996) *Internalization of Environmental Costs* (Environmental Economics Series, Paper 23; United Nations Environment Programme, Economics, Trade and Environment Unit).

Pariser, D., and A. Neidermeyer (1991) 'Environmental due Diligence: The Internal Auditor's Role', *Journal of Bank Accounting and Auditing*, Winter 1991: 22-30.

Parker, L. (1999) Environmental Costing: An Exploratory Examination (Melbourne: Australian Society of Certified Practising Accountants, February 1999).

PCEQ (President's Commission on Environmental Quality) (1991) 'The Report of the President's Commission on Environmental Quality' (Washington, DC: PCEQ).

PCSD (President's Council on Sustainable Development) (1996) 'Eco-efficiency: Task Force Report' (Washington, DC: PCSD).

Pearce, D., and K. Turner (1994) *Economics of Natural Resources and the Environment* (New York: Harvester Wheatsheaf).

Pearce, J., and R. Robinson (1991) *Strategic Management: Formulation, Implementation, and Control* (Homewood, IL: Irwin).

Pearman, A. (1994) 'The Use of Stated Preference Methods in the Evaluation of Environmental Change', in R. Pethig (ed.), *Valuing the Environment: Methodological and Measurement Issues* (Dordrecht, Netherlands: Kluwer Academic).

Peat Marwick, Mitchell & Co. (ed.) (1987) *Bilanzrichtliniengesetz* (Munich: Beck, 2nd edn).

Peemöller, V., B. Keller and C. Schöpf (1996) 'Ansätze zur Entwicklung von Umweltmanagement-kennzahlensystemen', *Umwelt WirtschaftsForum* 2: 4-13.

Pekelney, D. (1993) 'Emissions Trading: Applications to Improve Air and Water Quality', *Pollution Prevention Review*, Spring 1993: 139-48.

Perriman, R. (1995) 'Is LCA losing its way?', *LCA News* 5.1: 4-5.

Peskin, H. (1991) 'Alternative Environmental and Resource Accounting Approaches', in R. Costanza (ed.), *Ecological Economics: The Science and Management of Sustainability* (New York: Columbia University Press): 176-93.

Pethig, R. (ed.) (1994) *Valuing the Environment: Methodological and Measurement Issues* (Dordrecht, Netherlands: Kluwer Academic).

Petrauskas, H. (1992) 'Manufacturing and the Environment: Implementing Quality Environmental Management' (speech given at the University of Michigan, 20 November 1992).

Pfriem, R. (1991) 'Öko-Controlling und Organisationsentwicklung von Unternehmen', *IÖW-Informationsdienst* 6.2/91: 1-14.

Pidgeon, S., and D. Brown (1994) 'The Role of Lifecycle Analysis in Environmental Management: A General Panacea or One of Several Useful Paradigms?', *Greener Management International* 7 (July 1994): 36-44.

Pohl, C., M. Ros, B. Waldeck and F. Dinkel (1996) 'Imprecision and Uncertainty in LCA', in S. Schaltegger (ed.), *Life Cycle Assessment (LCA): Quo Vadis?* (Basel: Birkhäuser).

Pojasek, R. (1997) 'Materials Accounting and P2', *Pollution Prevention Review*, Autumn 1997: 95-103.

Pojasek, R. (1998) 'Activity Based Costing for EHS Improvement', *Pollution Prevention Review*, Winter 1998: 111-20.

Pojasek, R., and L. Cali (1991a) 'Measuring Pollution Prevention Progress', *Pollution Prevention Review*, Spring 1991: 119-29.

Pojasek, R., and L. Cali (1991b) 'Contrasting Approaches to Pollution Prevention', *Pollution Prevention Review*, Summer 1991: 225-35.

Polimeni, R., F. Fabozzi and A. Adelberg (1986) *Cost Accounting: Concepts and Applications for Managerial Decision Making* (New York: McGraw–Hill).

Popoff, F., and D. Buzzelli (1993) 'Full-Cost Accounting', *Chemical and Engineering News (CandEN)*, 11 January 1993: 8-10.

Porter, M.E. (1980) *Competitive Advantage* (Boston, MA: Harvard University Press).

Porter, M.E. (1989) *Wettbewerbsstrategie* (Frankfurt: Campus).

Porter, M.E. (1990) 'The Competitive Advantage of Nations', *Harvard Business Review*, March/April 1990: 73-95.

Porter, M.E., and C. van der Linde (1995) 'Green and Competitive: Ending the Stalemate', *Harvard Business Review* 73 (September/October 1995): 120-33.

Power, M. (1997) *The Audit Society: Rituals of Verification* (Oxford, UK: Oxford University Press).

Price Waterhouse (1991) *Environmental Accounting: The Issues, the Developing Solutions* (New York: Price Waterhouse).

Price Waterhouse (1992) *Accounting for Environmental Compliance: Crossroad of GAAP, Engineering, and Government: A Survey of Corporate America's Accounting for Environmental Costs* (New York: Price Waterhouse).

Price Waterhouse (1993) *Environmental Costs: Accounting and Disclosure* (New York: Price Waterhouse).

Price Waterhouse (1994) *Progress on the Environmental Challenge: A Survey of Corporate America's Environmental Accounting and Management* (New York: Price Waterhouse).

Pritchard, J. (1995) 'Finally . . . someone at the IRS called the EPA: Accounting for Environmental Clean Up Costs', *The CPA Journal Online*, January 1995.

Protection of the Environment Operations [General] Regulation (1998) *NSW Consolidated Regulations* (Sydney: AustLii).

PWMI (European Center for Plastics and the Environment Plastics Waste Management Institute) (1992) 'Eco-Profiles of the European Plastics Industry' (report 1; Brussels: PWMI).

Rabinowitz, D., and N. Murphy (1992) *Environmental Disclosure. What the SEC Requires: Understanding Environmental Accounting and Disclosures Today* (New York: Executive Enterprises Publications).

Raftelis, G. (1991) 'Financial Accounting Measures as Part of Pollution Prevention Assessment', *Environmental Finance*, Summer 1991: 129-50.

Raiborn, C., J. Barfield and M. Kinney (1996) *Managerial Accounting* (Minneapolis, MN: West, 2nd edn).

Rappaport, A. (1986) *Creating Shareholder Value: The New Standards for Business Performance* (New York: Free Press).

Rappaport, A. (1998) *Creating Shareholder Value: A Guide for Managers and Investors* (New York: Simon & Schuster, rev. edn).

Ratnatunga, J. (ed.) (1999) *Strategic Management Accounting* (Glen Waverley, Australia: Quill Press).

Ream, T., and C. French (1993) *A Framework and Methods for Conducting a Life-Cycle Impact Assessment* (Research Triangle Park, NC: US Environmental Protection Agency).

Ream, T., and T. Mohin (1992) 'Life Cycle Impact Analysis. I. Issues' (Research Triangle Park, NC: Research Triangle Institute, on behalf of US Environmental Protection Agency).

Reinhardt, F.L. (1999) 'Bringing the Environment Down to Earth', *Harvard Business Review*, July/August 1999: 149-57.

Repetto, R. (1992) 'Accounting for Environmental Assets', *Scientific American*, June 1992: 64-70.

Repetto, R., R. Dower, R. Jenkins and J. Geoghegan (1992) *Green Fees: How a Tax Shift Can Work for the Environment and the Economy* (Washington, DC: World Resource Institute).

Resource Conservation and Recovery Act (1976) (42 USC S/S 6901; Washington, DC: US Government Printing Office).

Reuters (1995a) ' "Schmutzige" Industrie soll schon bald "grüne" Bilanzen vorlegen: Gesetzesentwurf sieht Veröffentlichung von umweltbelastenden Faktoren bei der Produktion vor', *Nordschleswiger*, 19 January 1995.

Reuters (1995b) 'Branche schloß pro Kemi aus', *Nordschleswiger*, 25 February 1995.

Rikhardsson, P.M. (1999a) 'Information Systems for Corporate Environmental Management Accounting and Performance Measurement', in M. Bennett and P. James (eds.), *Sustainable Measures: Evaluation and Reporting of Environmental and Social Performance* (Sheffield, UK: Greenleaf Publishing): 132-50.

Rikhardsson, P.M. (1999b) 'Statutory Environmental Reporting in Denmark: Status and Challenges', in M. Bennett and P. James (eds.), *Sustainable Measures: Evaluation and Reporting of Environmental and Social Performance* (Sheffield, UK: Greenleaf Publishing): 344-52.

Riebel, P. (1992) 'Einzelerlös, Einzelkosten- und Deckungsbeitragsrechnung als Kern einer ganzheitlichen Führungsrechnung', in W. Männel (ed.), *Handbuch Kostenrechnung* (Wiesbaden, Germany: Gabler): 247-99.

Riebel, P. (1994) *Einzelkosten- und Deckungsbeitragsrechnung: Grundfragen einer markt- und entscheidungsorientierten Unternehmensrechnung* (Wiesbaden, Germany: Gabler, 7th edn).

Rifkin, J. (1985) *Entropie* (Frankfurt: Ullstein).

Roberts, R. (1994a) 'SAB 92 and the SEC's Environmental Liability' (speech given at the 1994 Quinn, Ward and Kershaw Environmental Law Symposium, University of Maryland School of Law, Baltimore, MD, April 1994).

Roberts, R. (1994b) 'Environmental Liability Disclosure Developments' (speech given at the Corporate Environmental Management Workshop on Environmental Reporting and Accountability, Environmental Law Institute, Washington, DC, June 1994).

Roche (1995) *Safety, Health and Environment at Roche* (Basel: Hoffmann-La Roche AG).

Roberts, M. (1994c), 'UK takes step toward TRI-style reporting', *Chemical Week* 155.10 (September 1994): 20.

Roden, S. (1996) 'Anderson Top Again', *International Accounting Bulletin*, 13 December 1996: 7-10.

Rose, K. (1995) *Grundlagen der Wachstumstheorie* (Göttingen, Germany: Vandenhoeck & Ruprecht, 6th edn).

Ross, A. (1985) 'Accounting for Hazardous Waste: Cleanups may have a significant financial impact', *Journal of Accountancy*, March 1985: 72-82.

Roth, U. (1992) *Umweltkostenrechnung: Grundlagen und Konzeption aus betriebswirtschaftlicher Sicht* (Wiesbaden, Germany: Deutscher Universitätsverlag).

Roussey, R. (1991) *Environmental Liabilities in the 1990s* (New York: Arthur Andersen).

Rubenstein, D.B. (1991) 'Lessons of Love', *CA Magazine*, March 1991: 34-41.

Rubenstein, D.B. (1994) *Environmental Accounting for the Sustainable Corporation* (Westport, CT: Quorum).

Rückle, D. (1989) 'Investitionskalküle für Umweltschutzinvestitionen', *Betriebswirtschaftliche Forschung und Praxis* 41.1: 51-65.

Rufer, F., and J. Atteslander (1999) 'Die IASC-Normen bringen neue Denkansätze', *Neue Zürcher Zeitung*, 3 September 1999: 8.

Ryan, C. (1996) 'Life Cycle Analysis and Design: A Productive Relationship?' (paper presented at the First National Conference on Life Cycle Assessment, 29 February–1 March 1996, World Congress Centre, Melbourne).

Sachs, W. (ed.) (1992) *The Development Dictionary* (London: Zed Books).

Sandman, P.M. (1986) *Explaining Environmental Risk* (Washington, DC: Office of Toxic Substances, US Environmental Protection Agency).

Sandor, R., and M. Walsh (1993) 'Environmental Futures: Preliminary Thoughts on the Market for Sulfur Dioxide Emission Allowances' (discussion paper; Palo Alto, CA: Stanford University).

Saporito, B. (1993) 'The Most Dangerous in America', *Fortune*, 31 May 1993: 130-40.

Schalit, L., and K. Wolfe (1978) 'SAM/IA: A Rapid Screening Method for Environmental Assessment for Fossil Energy Process Effluents' (EPA-600/7-78-015; Washington, DC: US Environmental Protection Agency).

Schaltegger, S. (1993) 'Strategic Management and Measurement of Corporate Pollution. Ecological Accounting: A Strategic Approach for Environmental Assessment' (study 183; Minneapolis, MN: Strategic Management Research Centre, University of Minnesota).

Schaltegger, S. (1994a) 'Zeitgemässe Instrumente des betrieblichen Umweltschutzes', *Die Unternehmung* 4: 117-31.

Schaltegger, S. (1994b) *Öko-Controlling für das Eidgenössische Militärdepartement* (Bern: Eidgenössische Militärdepartement).

Schaltegger, S. (1996a) *Corporate Environmental Accounting* (with contribution from K. Müller and H. Hindrichsen; London: John Wiley).

Schaltegger, S. (ed.) (1996b) *Life Cycle Assessment (LCA): Quo Vadis?* (Basel: Birkhäuser).

Schaltegger, S. (1997a) 'Economics of Life Cycle Assessment: Inefficiency of the Present Approach', *Business Strategy and the Environment* 6.1: 1-8.

Schaltegger, S. (1997b) 'Information Costs, Quality of Information and Stakeholder Involvement: The Necessity of International Standards of Ecological Accounting', *Eco-Management and Auditing*, November 1997: 1-11.

Schaltegger, S., and F. Figge (1997) *Environmental Shareholder Value* (study 54, December; Basel: Wirtschaftswissenschaftliches Zentrum [WWZ]/Sarasin, 5th edn [1st edn August 1997]).

Schaltegger, S., and F. Figge (1999) 'Öko-Investment: Spagat zwischen Shareholder Value und Sustainable Development?', *UmweltWirtschaftsForum* 7.3: 4-8.

Schaltegger, S., and S. Kempke (1996) 'Öko-Controlling: Überblick bisheriger Ansätze', *Zeitschrift für Betriebswirtschaft* 2: 1-96.

Schaltegger, S., and R. Kubat (1995) *Glossary of LCA: Terms and Definitions* (study 45; Basel: Wirtschaftswissenschaftliches Zentrum [WWZ], 4th edn [1st edn 1994]).

Schaltegger, S., and K. Müller (1998) 'Calculating the True Profitability of Pollution Prevention', in M. Bennett and P. James (eds.), *The Green Bottom Line. Environmental Accounting for Management: Current Practice and Future Trends* (Sheffield, UK: Greenleaf Publishing): 86-99.

Schaltegger, S., and C. Stinson (1994) 'Issues and Research Opportunities in Environmental Accounting' (discussion paper 9124; Basel: Wirtschaftswissenschaftliches Zentrum [WWZ]).

Schaltegger, S., and A. Sturm (1990) 'Ökologische Rationalität: Ansatzpunkte zur Ausgestaltung von ökologieorientierten Managementinstrumenten', *Die Unternehmung* 4: 273-90.

Schaltegger, S., and A. Sturm (1992a) *Ökologieorientierte Entscheidungen in Unternehmen: Ökologisches Rechnungswesen statt Ökobilanzierung: Notwendigkeit, Kriterien, Konzepte* (Bern: Haupt, 1st edn).

Schaltegger, S., and A. Sturm (1992b) 'Öko-Controlling als Management- und Führungsinstrument', *Io-Management* 6: 71-75.

Schaltegger, S., and A. Sturm (1992c) 'Eco-controlling: An Integrated Economic–Ecological Management Tool', in D. Koechlin and K. Müller (eds.), *Green Business Opportunities: The Profit Potential* (London: Pitman/Financial Times): 229-40.

Schaltegger, S., and A. Sturm (1993) 'Ökologieorientiertes Management', in R.L. Frey, H. Blöchliger and E. Staehelin-Witt (eds.), *Mit Ökonomie zur Ökologie* (Bern: Helbing & Lichtenhahn; Stuttgart: Schäffer-Poeschel, 2nd edn): 179-201.

Schaltegger, S., and A. Sturm (1994) *Ökologieorientierte Entscheidungen in Unternehmen. Ökologisches Rechnungswesen statt Ökobilanzierung: Notwendigkeit, Kriterien, Konzepte* (Bern: Haupt, 2nd edn).

Schaltegger, S., and A. Sturm (1995) *Öko-Effizienz durch Öko-Controlling: Zur Umsetzung von EMAS und ISO 14000* (Zurich: Vdf; Stuttgart: Schäffer-Poeschel).

Schaltegger, S., and A. Sturm (1996) 'Managerial Eco-Control in Manufacturing and Process Industries', *Greener Management International* 13 (January 1996): 78-91.

Schaltegger, S., and A. Sturm (1998) *Eco-efficiency by Eco-controlling* (Zurich: Vdf).

Schaltegger, S., and T. Thomas (1994) 'PACT für einen Schadschöpfungs-Zertifikatshandel', *Zeitschrift für Umweltpolitik und Umweltrecht* 3: 357-81.

Schaltegger, S., and T. Thomas (1996) 'Pollution Added Credit Trading (PACT): New Dimensions in Emissions Trading', *Ecological Economics* 19: 35-53.

Schaltegger, S., R. Kubat, C. Hilber and S. Vaterlaus (with A. Sturm and A. Flütsch) (1996) *Innovatives Management staatlicher Umweltpolitik: New Public Environmental Management* (Basel: Birkhäuser).

Schendel, D., and C. Hofer (1978) *Strategy Formulation* (St Paul, MN: West).

Schierenbeck, H. (1994) *Bank- und Versicherungslexikon* (Munich: Oldenbourg, 2nd edn).

Schierenbeck, H. (1996) *Grundzüge der Betriebswirtschaftslehre* (Giessen, Germany: Schmidt, 12th edn).

Schierenbeck, H. (1997) 'Ertragsorientiertes Bankmanagement im Visier des Shareholder Value-Konzepts', in Basler Bankenvereinigung (ed.), *Shareholder Value-Konzepte in Banken* (Bern: Haupt): 1-20.

Schmidheiny, S. (ed.) (1992) *Changing Course: A Global Business Perspective on Development and the Environment* (Cambridge, MA: MIT Press, with the Business Council for Sustainable Development).

Schmidheiny, S., and F. Zorraquín (1996) *Financing Change* (Cambridge, MA: MIT Press, with the World Business Council for Sustainable Development).

Schmidt-Bleek, F. (1994) *Wieviel Umwelt braucht der Mensch. Mips: Das Maß für ökologisches Wirtschaften* (Basel: Birkhäuser).

Schneider, D. (1981) *Geschichte betriebswirtschaftlicher Theorie* (Munich: Gabler).

Schneidewind, U., J. Hummel and F. Belz (1997) 'Instrumente zur Umsetzung von COSY (Company Oriented Sustainability) in Unternehmen und Branchen', *UmweltWirtschaftsForum* 2: 36-44.

Schreiner, M. (1988) *Umweltmanagement in 22 Lektionen: Ein ökonomischer Weg in eine ökologische Wirtschaft* (Wiesbaden, Germany: Gabler).

Schreiner, M. (1991) 'Ökologische Herausforderungen an die Kosten- und Leistungsrechnung', in J. Freimann (ed.), *Ökologische Herausforderung der Betriebswirtschaftslehre* (Wiesbaden, Germany: Gabler).

Schroeder, G., and M. Winter (1998) 'Environmental Accounting at Sulzer Technology Corporation', in M. Bennett and P. James (eds.), *The Green Bottom Line. Environmental Accounting for Management: Current Practice and Future Trends* (Sheffield, UK: Greenleaf Publishing): 333-46.

Schulz, E., and W. Schulz (1994) *Umweltcontrolling in der Praxis* (Munich: Vahlen).

Schulz, T. (1995) *Ökologieorientierte Berichterstattung von Unternehmen: Ökologieorientierte Berichterstattung in Geschäfts- und Umweltberichten unter Berücksichtigung der Informationsbedürfnisse der Stakeholder, untersucht in der europäischen Chemieindustrie* (Bern: Haupt).

Schulz, W. (1985) *Der monetäre Wert besserer Luft* (Frankfurt: Lang).

Schulz, W. (1989) 'Betriebliche Umweltinformationssysteme', in A. Heigl (ed.), *Handbuch Umwelt und Energie* (Freiburg, Germany: Haufe): 33-98.

Schulz, W. (1991) 'Ökocontrolling', in Organisation, Führung und Weiterbildung (OFW) (ed.), *Umweltmanagement im Spannungsfeld zwischen Ökologie und Ökonomie* (Wiesbaden, Germany: Gabler): 221-42.

Schwab, N., and N. Soguel (1995) *Contingent Valuation: Transport Safety and the Value of Life* (Boston, MA: Kluwer).

Schweizer Rück (1995) *Swiss Re: Annual Report 1994* (Zurich: Schweizer Rückversicherung).

SCS (Scientific Certification Systems) (1996) Various product evaluation forms (San Francisco: SCS).

SDA (Scweizerische Depeschen Agentur) (1994a) 'Die Verseuchung einer Siedlung in den USA: Chemiefirma zahlt 120 Millionen Dollar', *Neue Zürcher Zeitung* 144 (23 June 1994): 19.

SDA (Scweizerische Depeschen Agentur) (1994b) 'Exxon muß den Fischern 286 Millionen Dollar zahlen', *Basler Zeitung*, 13 August 1994.

SEC (US Securities and Exchange Commission) (1989) Management's Discussion and Analysis of Financial Condition and Results of Operations (releases 33-6835, 34-26831, IC-16961, FR-36; Washington, DC: US SEC).

SEC (US Securities and Exchange Commission) (1993) 'SAB [Staff Accounting Bulletin] 92' (Washington, DC: US SEC).

Seidel, E. (1988) 'Ökologisches Controlling', in R. Wunderer (ed.), *Betriebswirtschaftslehre als Management- und Führungslehre* (Stuttgart: Poeschel): 367-82.

Seidel, E., J. Clausen and E. Seifert (1998) *Umweltkennzahlen* (Munich: Vahlen).

Seidel, E., B. Goldmann and F. Weber (1989) 'Umweltkennzahlen', in M. Rieck (ed.), *BJU-Umweltschutzberater: Handbuch für wirtschaftliches Umweltmanagement im Unternehmen* (Section 4.9.2.1; Cologne: Westdeutscher Verlag).

Seidel, E., B. Goldmann and F. Weber (1994) 'Umweltkennzahlen: Anwendung in der betrieblichen Praxis', in A. Heigl (ed.), *Umwelt und Energie: Handbuch für die betriebliche Praxis* (supplement 10; Freiburg, Germany: Haufe, April 1994).

SETAC (Society of Environmental Toxicology and Chemistry) (1991) A Technical Framework for Life-Cycle Assessment (Washington, DC: SETAC).

SGCI (Schweizerische Gesellschaft für Chemische Industrie) (1991) *Responsible Care* (Zurich: SGCI).

Shank, J.K., and V. Govindarajan (1992) 'Strategic Cost Analysis of Technological Investments', *Sloan Management Review*, Autumn 1992: 39-51.

Shapero, K., and A. White (1997) Pathway to Product Stewardship: Life-Cycle Design as a Business Decision-Support Tool (report to the US Environmental Protection Agency; Boston, MA: Tellus Institute, November 1997).

Sharpe, W. (1964) 'Capital Asset Prices: A Theory of Market Equilibrium under Conditions of Risk', *The Journal of Finance* 19: 425-42.

Sheldon, C. (ed.) (1996) *ISO 14001 and Beyond: Environmental Management Systems in the Real World* (Sheffield, UK: Greenleaf Publishing).

Shell (1997) *Report to Society* (London: Shell International).

Shell (1998) *Profits and Principles: Does there have to be a choice? The Shell Report 1998* (London: Shell International Ltd).

Shrivastava, P. (1993) 'Crisis Theory–Practice: Towards a Sustainable Future', *Industrial and Environmental Crises Quarterly* 7.1: 23-42.

Shrivastava, P. (1995) 'The Role of Corporations in Achieving Ecological Sustainability', *Academy of Management Review* 20.4: 936-60.

Sietz, M. (ed.) (1996) *Umweltbetriebsprüfung und Öko-Auditing: Anwendungen und Praxisbeispiele* (Berlin: Springer Verlag, 2nd edn).

Simon, B. (1991) 'Sharks in the Water', *Financial Times*, 27 November 1991: 16.

Simon, H.A. (1957) *Models of Man* (New York: John Wiley).

Skellenger, B. (1992) 'Limitation of Liability Clauses Gaining Popularity among Environmental Consultants', *Environline* 3 (Spring 1992): 4-5.

Smith, M. (1995) *Strategic Management Accounting: Issues and Cases* (Sydney: Butterworth).

Solomon, C. (1993) 'Clearing the Air: What Really Pollutes? Study of a Refinery Proves an Eye-Opener', *The Wall Street Journal*, 29 March 1993: 1.

Solomons, S. (1965) *Divisional Performance: Measurement and Control* (Homewood, IL: Irwin).

Solow, R. (1992) An Almost Practicable Step toward Sustainability (mimeograph; Washington, DC: Resources for the Future).

Speich, C. (1992) 'Zarte Knospen sprießen: Bilanz-Test Geschäftsberichte', *Bilanz* 5: 163-68.

Spicer, B. (1978) 'Investors, Corporate Social Performance and Informational Disclosure: An Empirical Study', *Accounting Review* 53: 94-111.

Spiller, A. (1996) 'Kennzahlen für Nachhaltigkeit', *Ökologisches Wirtschaften* 2: 22-24.

Spitzer, M. (1992) 'Calculating the Benefits of Pollution Prevention', *Pollution Engineering*, September 1992: 33-38.

Spitzer, M., R. Pojasek, F. Robertaccio and J. Nelson (1993) 'Accounting and Capital Budgeting for Pollution Prevention' (paper presented at the Engineering Foundation Conference San Diego, CA, January 1993).

Stade, R. (1987) 'Rechnungslegung bei Umweltschutzmaßnahmen', *Der Betrieb* 37.51/52: 2580-88.

Staehelin-Witt, E. (1993) 'Bewertung von Umweltgütern', in R.L. Frey, H. Blöchliger and E. Staehelin-Witt (eds.), *Mit Ökonomie zur Ökologie* (Basel: Helbing & Lichtenhahn; Stuttgart: Schäffer-Poeschel): 94-111.

Staehelin-Witt, E., and A. Spillmann (1992) Emissionshandel: Ein marktwirtschaftlicher Weg für die schweizerische Umweltpolitik' (study 40; Basel: Wirtschaftswissenschaftliches Zentrum [WWZ]).

Stavins, R. (1992) 'Harnessing the Marketplace: We have to do more with less', *EPA Journal*, May/June 1992: 21-25.

Steen, B., and S. Ryding (1994) 'The EPS-environ-accounting Method: An Application of Environmental Accounting Principles for Evaluation and Valuation of Environmental Impact in Product Design' (report B 1080; Stockholm: Swedish Environmental Research Institute Ltd [IVL]).

Steger, U., and M. Winter (1996) 'Strategische Früherkennung zur Antizipation ökologisch motivierter Marktveränderungen', *Die Betriebswirtschaft* 56.5: 607-29.

Sterling, R.R. (1970) 'On Theory Construction and Verification', *The Accounting Review*, July 1970: 444-57.

Stevenson, R. (1992) 'Monitoring Pollution at its Source', *The New York Times*, 8 April 1992: C1, C6.

Stigson, B. (1999) 'Business is shaping the agenda', *Tomorrow* 9.4: WBCSD News.

Stinson, C. (1993) 'Environmental Accounting: A Growth Industry', *Puget Sound Business Journal*, February 1993: 5-11.

Stockwell, J., J. Sorensen, J. Eckert and E. Carreras (1993) 'The USEPA Geographic Information System for Mapping Environmental Releases of Toxic Chemical Release Inventory (TRI) Chemicals', *Risk Analysis* 13.2: 155-64.

Stölzle, W. (1990) 'Ansätze zur Erfassung von Umweltschutzkosten in der betriebswirtschaftlichen Kostenrechnung', *Zeitschrift für Umweltpolitik und Umweltrecht* 4: 379-412.

Studer, T. (1992) 'Unternehmensbewertung im Umbruch: Cash Flow-basierte Verfahren im Vormarsch', *Der Schweizer Treuhänder* 6 (June 1992): 303-308.

Studer, T. (1996) 'Shareholder Value: Ein finanzwirtschaftliches Konzept im Brennpunkt', *Uni Nova* 77: 32-34.

Sturm, A., M. Wackernagel and K. Müller (1999) *Die Gewinner und Verlierer im globalen Wettbewerb* (Zürich: Ruegger).

Surma, J., and A. Vondra (1992) 'Accounting for Environmental Costs: A Hazardous Subject', *Journal of Accountancy*, March 1992: 51-55.

SustainAbility (1993) 'What do we mean by sustainability?', *EPE Workshop* module 1, letter 1.1.

SustainAbility, Spold and Business in the Environment (eds.) (1992) *The LCA Sourcebook* (London: Spold/ SustainAbility).

SustainAbility and UNEP (United Nations Environment Programme) (1996a) *Engaging Stakeholders. I. The Benchmark Survey: The Second International Progress Report on Company Environmental Reporting* (Paris: UNEP; London: SustainAbility).

SustainAbility and UNEP (United Nations Environment Programme) (1996b) *Engaging Stakeholders. II. The Case Studies* (London: SustainAbility/UNEP).

Suter, P., and P. Hofstetter (1989) 'Die ökologische Rückzahldauer', *Schweizer Ingenieur und Architekt* 49: 1342-46.

SWMD (Solid Waste Management Division [of Environment Canada]) (1995) 'The Life-Cycle Concept: Backgrounder', *Ecocycle* 1: 6.

Tabakoff, N. (1995) 'Top accountant fights world of standards', *Australian Financial Review* 3: 30.

Tanega, J. (1995) 'Environment and the Capital Markets' (unpublished manuscript; Kingston University Business School).

Taylor, M. (1995) 'What's wrong with the Chemical Release Inventory? The Fundamental Flaws' (Luton, UK: Friends of the Earth, October 1995).

Tellus (1992) *The Tellus Packaging Study* (Boston, MA: Tellus Institute).

Thomas, A. (1974) 'The Allocation Problem: Part Two' (Evanston, IL: American Accounting Association).

Tibor, T., and I. Feldman (1996) *ISO 14000: A Guide to the New Environmental Management Standards* (Chicago: Irwin).

Tibor, T., and I. Feldman (1997) *Implementing ISO 14000: A Practical, Comprehensive Guide to the ISO 14000 Environmental Management Standards* (New York: McGraw–Hill).

Tietenberg, T. (1980) 'Transferable Discharge Permits and the Control of Air Pollution: A Survey and Synthesis', *Zeitschrift für Umweltpolitik und Umweltrecht* 3.1: 477-508.

Tietenberg, T. (1989) 'Marketable Permits in the US: A Decade of Experience', in K. Roskamp (ed.), *Public Finance and the Performance of Enterprises* (Detroit: Wayne State University Press).

Tietenberg, T. (1992) *Environmental and Natural Resource Economics* (New York: Harper Collins).

Tilt, C.A. (1994) 'The Influence of External Pressure Groups on Corporate Social Disclosure Some Empirical Evidence', *Accounting, Auditing and Accountability Journal* 7.4: 47-72.

Tinbergen, J. (1956) *Economic Policy: Principles and Design* (Amsterdam: Rombach).

Todd, R. (1992) 'Zero-Loss Environmental Accounting Systems' (discussion paper; New York: Columbia University, Accounting Department).

Töpfer, K. (1993) 'Die Diskussion um die Ökobilanz wird nun erst richtig beginnen', *Handelsblatt*, 28 September 1993: B1.

Tribe, D. (1994) 'Company Values: Approach with Caution', *Sydney Morning Herald*, 23 November 1994: 39.

UBA (Umweltbundesamt) (1992) *Ökobilanzen—Sachstand—Perspektiven* (Berlin: UBA).

Udo de Haes, H. (ed.) (1995) 'The Methodology of Life Cycle Impact Assessment: Report of the SETAC-Europe Working Groups on Life Cycle Impact Assessment' (Leiden, Netherlands: SETAC).

UIG (Urgent Issues Group of the Australian Accounting Research Foundation) (1995) 'Disclosure of Accounting Policies for Restoration Obligations in the Extractive Industries' (abstract 4; Melbourne: UIG, AARF, August 1995).

Ullmann, A. (1976) 'The Corporate Environmental Accounting System: A Management Tool for Fighting Environmental Degradation', *Accounting, Organizations and Society* 1.1: 71-79.

Ulrich, H., W. Hill and B. Kunz (1989) *Brevier des Rechnungswesens* (Bern: Haupt).

UNCTAD (United Nations Centre for Trade and Development) (1998) 'Report of the Intergovernmental Working Group of Experts on International Standards of Accounting and Reporting on its Fifteenth Session' (TD/B/COM.2/ISAR/3; Geneva: UNCTAD, February 1998).

UNEP (United Nations Environment Programme) (1991) 'Managing Change: Discussion Paper for the Executive Director's Advisory Group on Commercial Banks and the Environment' (Geneva: UNEP).

UNEP (United Nations Environment Programme) (1994) 'Company Environmental Reporting: A Measure of Progress in Business and Industry towards Sustainable Development' (technical report 24; Geneva: UNEP).

UNEP (United Nations Environment Programme) (1995) 'Environmental Management Tools: Facts and Figures', *Industry and Environment* 18.2–3: 4-10.

UNEP (United Nations Environment Programme) (1998) 'Voluntary Industry Codes of Conduct for the Environment' (technical report 40; Paris: UNEP).

United Nations (1990) Environmental Assessment: Procedures in the UN System (Geneva,: United Nations).

United Nations (1991a) 'Accounting for Environmental Protection Measures' (New York: UN Economic and Social Council; Commission on Transnational Corporations; Intergovernmental Working Group of Experts on International Standards of Accounting and Reporting).

United Nations (1991b) 'Environmental Accounting for Sustainable Development: Note by the Secretariat' (Geneva: UN, Intergovernmental Working Group of Experts on International Standards of Accounting and Reporting).

United Nations (1991c) 'Transnational Corporations and Industrial Hazards Disclosure' (New York: United Nations).

United Nations (1991d) 'Integrated Economic–Environmental Accounting: Progress Report of the Secretary-General of the Conference' (UN Conference on Environment and Development, August–September 1991; Geneva: UN Preparatory Committee for the UN Conference on Environment and Development).

United Nations (1992a) 'Environmental Accounting: Current Issues, Abstracts and Bibliography' (New York: United Nations).

United Nations (1992b) 'Environmental Disclosures: International Survey of Corporate Reporting Practices' (New York: United Nations).

United Nations (1992c) 'International Accounting and Reporting Issues: 1991 Review' (New York: United Nations).

United Nations (1992d) 'Climate Change and Transnational Corporations: Analysis and Trends' (New York: United Nations).

United Nations (1992e) 'Agenda 21: Report of the United Nations Conference on Environment and Development (Annex II)' (A/Conf.151/26; New York: UNCED).

United Nations (1997) 'Kyoto Protocol to the United Nations Framework Convention Climate Change Framework Convention on Climate Change' (Kyoto: United Nations, December 1997).

United Nations (1999) 'Governments' Role in Promoting Environmental Managerial Accounting' (draft report of the Expert Working Group Meeting, August 1999).

Vaughan, D., and C. Mickle (1993) *Environmental Profiles of European Business* (London: Royal Institute for International Affairs).

Vaughan, S. (1994) *Greening Financial Markets* (Geneva: International Academy of the Environment [IAE]).

VDI (Verein Deutscher Ingenieure) (1979) *VDI-Richtlinie 3800: Kostenermittlung für Anlagen und Maßnahmen zur Emissionsminderung* (Düsseldorf: VDI).

Vedsø, L. (1993) *Green Management* (Copenhagen: Systime).

Vesely, E. (1990) *Strategic Data Management: The Key to Corporate Competitiveness* (Englewood Cliffs, NJ: Yourdon).

Vinten, G. (1991) 'The Greening of Audit', *Internal Auditor*, October 1991: 30-36.

Volkart, R. (1996) 'Shareholder Value Management: Kritische Überlegungen zur wertorientierten Führung', *Der Schweizer Treuhänder* 12: 1064-67.

Volksbank Siegen (1996) *Umweltbericht 1996* (Siegen, Germany: Volksbank Siegen).

Von Weizsäcker, E.U., A.B. Lovins and L.H. Lovins (1997) *Factor Four: Doubling Wealth, Halving Resource Use* (new report to the Club of Rome; Sydney: Allen & Unwin; London: Earthscan).

Wackernagel, M., and C. Rees (1996) *Our Ecological Footprint* (Gabriola Island, Canada: New Society Publishers).

Wagner, B. (1995) *Arbeitsmaterialien: Umweltmanagement, Kontaktstudium Management der Universität Augsburg* (Augsburg, Germany: Skript).

Wagner, G., and H. Janzen (1991) 'Ökologisches Controlling: Mehr als ein Schlagwort?', *Controlling* 3.3: 120-29.

Wainman, D. (1991) 'Balancing Nature's Books', *CA Magazine, Toronto*, March 1991.

Walker, B. (1995) 'BHP's Hidden $1.3 Billion Liability', *New Accountant*, 31 August 1995.

Walleck, A., J.D. O'Halloran and C. Leader (1991) 'Benchmarking Worldclass Performance', *The McKinsey Quarterly* 1: 3-24.

Walley, N., and B. Whitehead (1994) 'It's not easy being green', *Harvard Business Review*, May/June 1994: 46-52.

Walton, M. (1986) *The Deming Management Method* (New York: Perigée).

Wambsganss, J.R., and B. Sanford (1996) 'The Problem with Reporting Pollution Allowances', *Critical Perspectives on Accounting* 7: 643-52.

Watson, G. (1993) *Strategic Benchmarking* (New York: John Wiley).

Watts, R.L., and J.L. Zimmerman (1978) 'Towards a Positive Theory of the Determination of Accounting Standards', *The Accounting Review* 53.1: 112-34.

Watts, R.L., and J.L. Zimmerman (1990) 'Positive Accounting Theory: A Ten Year Perspective', *The Accounting Review* 65.1: 131-56.

WBCSD (World Business Council for Sustainable Development) (1997) 'Environmental Performance and Shareholder Value' (Geneva: WBCSD).

WBCSD (World Business Council for Sustainable Development) (1999) 'Eco-efficiency Indicators and Reporting: Report on the Status of the Project's Work in Progress and Guideline for Pilot Application' (Geneva: WBCSD, April 1999).

WCED (World Commission on Environment and Development) (1987) *Our Common Future* ('The Brundtland Report'; Oxford, UK: Oxford University Press).

Weir, D., and P. Yamin (1993) 'Toxic Ten: America's Truant Corporations', *Mother Jones* (January/February 1993): 39-42.

Welford, R., and A. Gouldson (1993) *Environmental Management and Business Strategy* (London: Pitman).

Wells, M.C. (1978) 'Accounting for Common Costs' (Illinois University, Centre for International Education and Research in Accounting).

Wheeler, D., and M. Sillanpää (1997) *The Stakeholder Corporation: A Blueprint for Maximizing Stakeholder Value* (London: Pitman).

Whelan, E.M. (1993) 'Toxic Terror: The Truth behind the Cancer Scares', in E.M. Whelan (ed.), *The Disaster of Love Canal* (Buffalo, NY: Prometheus Books).

White, A., and M. Becker (1992) 'Total Cost Assessment: Catalyzing Corporate Self Interest in Pollution Prevention', *New Solutions*, Winter 1992: 34-38.

White, A., and D. Zinkl (1997) 'Corporate Environmental Performance Indicators: A Benchmark Survey of Business Decision Makers' (Boston, MA: Tellus Institute).

White, A., and D. Zinkl (1998) *Touchstone: Issues in Sustainability Reporting. Volume 1* (Boston, MA: Coalition of Environmentally Responsible Economies, July 1998).

White, A., and D. Zinkl (1999) 'Standardisation: The Next Chapter in Corporate Environmental Performance Evaluation and Reporting', in M. Bennett and P. James (eds.), *Sustainable Measures: Evaluation and Reporting of Environmental and Social Performance* (Sheffield, UK: Greenleaf Publishing): 117-31.

White, P., B. De Smet, H. Udo de Haes and R. Heijungs (1995) 'LCA Back on Track: But is it One Track or Two?', *LCA News* 5.3: 2-4.

Whittington, G. (1992) *The Elements of Accounting: An Introduction* (Cambridge, UK: University of Cambridge Press).

WICE (World Industry Council for the Environment) (1994) *Environmental Reporting: A Manager's Guide* (Paris: WICE).

Wicke, L. (1992) *Betriebliche Umweltökonomie: Eine praxisorientierte Einführung* (Munich: Vahlen).

Wicke, L. (1998) *Umweltökonomie* (Munich: Vahlen).

Wicks, P. (1998) 'EU Emissions Register to Name Top Polluters', *Business and the Environment* 11.11.

Wiethoff, H. (1996) 'Öko-Controlling in der Instandhaltung: Schaffung einer Informationsbasis für umweltgerechtes Handeln durch Umweltkennzahlen', *Controlling* 2: 102-09.

Wilkinson, J. (1989) *Accounting Information Systems: Essential Concepts and Applications* (New York: John Wiley).

Williams, G., and T. Phillips (1994) 'Cleaning Up Our Act: Accounting for Environmental Liabilities: Current financial reporting doesn't do the job', *Management Accounting*, February 1994: 30-33.

Winter, M. (1997) *Ökologisch motiviertes Organisationslernen* (Wiesbaden, Germany: Deutscher Universitätsverlag).

Wittmann, W. (1959) *Unternehmung und unvollkommene Information: Unternehmerische Voraussicht: Ungewißheit und Planung* (Cologne: Westdeutscher Verlag).

Wittmann, W. (1982) *Betriebswirtschaftslehre* (vol. 1; Tübingen, Germany: J.C.B. Mohr).

WMC (Western Mining Corporation) (1998) 'Environment Progress Reports 1998: Site Reports' (Southbank, Australia: WMC Ltd).

Wöhe, G. (in collaboration with U. von Döring) (1990) *Einführung in die Allgemeine Betriebswirtschaftslehre* (Munich: Vahlen, 17th edn).

WSDOE (Washington State Department of Ecology) (1992a) 'Guidance Paper: Economic Analysis for Pollution Prevention' (Olympia, WA: WSDOE).

WSDOE (Washington State Department of Ecology) (1992b) *Success through Waste Reduction, Volume I* (Olympia, WA: WSDOE).

WSDOE (Washington State Department of Ecology) (1992c) *Success through Waste Reduction: Proven Techniques for Washington Businesses, Volume II* (Olympia, WA: WSDOE).

WSDOE (Washington State Department of Ecology) (1993a) *Pollution Prevention Planning in Washington State Businesses, Volumes I–III* (Olympia, WA: WSDOE).

WSDOE (Washington State Department of Ecology) (1993b) *Success through Waste Reduction: Pollution Prevention Planning in Washington State Businesses* (Olympia, WA: WSDOE).

WSDOE (Washington State Department of Ecology) (1997) 'Environmental Management System (EMS) Alternative to Pollution Prevention Planning' (publication 97-401; Olympia, WA: WSDOE, February 1997).

Würth, S. (1993) *Umwelt-Auditing: Die Revision im ökologischen Bereich als wirksames Überwachungsinstrument für die ökologiebewusste Unternehmung* (Winterthur, Switzerland: Schellenberg).

WWI (World Watch Institute) (1995) *State of the World* (New York: W.W. Norton).

WWF (World Wide Fund for Nature International) (1992) 'Methodology for the Calculation of Sustainable National Income' (Gland, Switzerland: WWF International).

WWF (World Wide Fund for Nature) (1993) 'Sustainable Use of Natural Resources: Concepts, Issues and Criteria: WWF International Position Paper' (Gland, Switzerland: WWF).

Wygal, D.E., D.E. Stout and J. Volpe (1987) 'Reporting Practices in Four Countries', *Management Accounting* 37-42.

Wynn, L., and E. Lee (1993) Life-Cycle Assessment: Guidelines for Assessing Data Quality (Research Triangle Park, NC: US Environmental Protection Agency).

Young, C.W., and P.M. Rikhardsson (1996) 'Environmental Performance Indicators for Business', *Eco-Management and Auditing* 3: 113-25.

Young, P. (ed.) (1985) *Cost Allocation: Methods, Principles, Applications* (Amsterdam: North-Holland).

Young, W., and R. Welford (1999) 'An Environmental Performance Measurement Framework for Business', in M. Bennett and P. James (eds.), *Sustainable Measures: Evaluation and Reporting of Environmental and Social Performance* (Sheffield, UK: Greenleaf Publishing): 98-116.

Zenhäusern, M., and P. Bertschinger (1993) *Konzernrechnungslegung* (Bern: Haupt).

Zimmerman, J.L. (1979) 'The Costs and Benefits of Cost Allocation', *The Accounting Review* 54: 504-21.

Zuber, G., and C. Berry (1992) 'Assessing Environmental Risk', *Journal of Accountancy*, March 1992: 43-48.

ABBREVIATIONS

AAA	American Accounting Association
AAFEU	Accounting Advisory Forum of the European Union
AARF	Australian Accounting Research Foundation
ABC	activity-based costing
ABS	Australian Bureau of Statistics
ACBE	Advisory Committee on Business and the Environment
ACCA	Association of Chartered Certified Accountants
ACN	Association Canadienne de Normalisation
ACOFB	additional cost of future benefits approach
ACTEW	Australian Capital Territory Electricity & Water Corporation
AICPA	American Institute of Certified Public Accountants
AIU	American International Underwriters
AP	Associated Press
API	American Petroleum Institute
ASB	Australian Accounting Standards Board
ASB	UK Accounting Standards Board
ASCPA	Australian Society of Certified Practising Accountants
ASRB	Accounting Standards Review Board (Australia)
ASU	Arbeitsgemeinschaft Selbständiger Unternehmer (Germany)
ASVS	Arbeitsgemeinschaft Schweizerische Vereinigung für Sonnenenergie
AT&T	American Telephone & Telegraph Co.
BAK	Konjunkturforschung Basel AG
BAZ	*Basler Zeitung* (Germany)
BCSD	Business Council for Sustainable Development (now WBCSD)
BfK	Bundesamt für Konjunkturforschung (Switzerland)
BHP	The Broken Hill Proprietary Company Ltd (Australia)
BImSchG	Bundesimmissionsschutzgesetz (Germany)
BMU	Bundesumweltministerium (Germany)
BRT	Business Roundtable (USA)
BS	British Standard (of the BSI)
BSI	British Standards Institution
BUJF	Bundesministerium für Umwelt, Jugend und Familie (Austria)
BUS	Bundesamt für Umwelt (Switzerland; now BUWAL)
BUWAL	Bundesamt für Umwelt, Wald und Landschaft (Switzerland)
CCME	Canadian Council of Ministers of the Environment
CEC	Commission of the European Communities
CEEC	Council of the European Economic Community
CEFIC	European Chemical Industry Council
CEP	Council on Economic Priorities (USA)
CERCLA	Comprehensive Environmental Response, Compensation, and Liability Act of 1980 (USA)

CERES	Coalition of Environmentally Responsible Economies
CFC	chlorofluorocarbon
CH_4	methane
CHF	Swiss Franc
CICA	Canadian Institute of Chartered Accountants
CM	contribution margin
CML	Centrum voor Milieukunde (Center of Environmental Science), University of Leiden (Netherlands)
CO_2	carbon dioxide
COM	Commission of the European Communities
CRI	Chemical Release Inventory (UK)
DIN	Deutsches Institut für Normung (Germany)
DSR	driving-force–state–response
DTTI	Deloitte Touche Tohmatsu International
EAA	European Accounting Association
EAR	ecological advantage ratio
EEEIW	European Eco-efficiency Indicators Workshop
EIA	environmental impact added
EIA	Environmental Institute of Australia
EIRIS	Ethical Investment Research Service (UK)
EITF	Emerging Issues Task Force of FASB
EIU	Economist Intelligence Unit
ELI	Environmental Law Institute (USA)
EMAS	Eco-management and Audit Scheme (EU)
EMS	environmental management system
EP	eco-efficiency path
EPA	Environmental Protection Agency
EPCRA	Emergency Planning and Community Right-to-Know Act (USA)
EPD	environmental product declaration (Sweden)
EPP	ecological payback period
ESU	Gruppe Energie, Stoffe, Umwelt der Eidgenössischen Technischen Hochschule Zürich
EU	European Union
EVA	economic value added
FAS	Financial Accounting Standard (of the FASB)
FASB	Financial Accounting Standards Board (USA)
FEE	Féderation des Expertes Comptables Européens
FER	Fachkommission für Empfehlungen zur Rechnungslegung (Switzerland)
FERC	Federal Energy Regulatory Commission (USA)
GAAP	Generally Accepted Accounting Principles (USA)
GDP	gross domestic product
GEFIU	Gesellschaft für Finanzwirtschaft in der Unternehmensführung (Switzerland)
GEMI	Global Environmental Management Initiative
GNP	gross national product
GRI	Global Reporting Initiative
HCFC	hydrochlorofluorocarbon
HDFD	Hundred Group of Finance Directors (UK)
HUI	Hamburger Umweltinstitut
IAS	International Accounting Standard (of the IASC)
IASC	International Accounting Standards Committee
ICC	International Chamber of Commerce
IER	*International Environmental Reporter*
IFAC	International Federation of Accountants
IFB	increased future benefits
IISD	International Institute for Sustainable Development

INSEE	Institut National de la Statistique et des Etudes Economiques
IÖW	Institut für ökologische Wirtschaftsforschung (Switzerland)
IPPC	Integrated Pollution Prevention and Control (EU)
IRRC	Investor Responsibility Research Center
IRS	Inland Revenue Service (USA)
ISAR	Intergovernmental Working Group of Experts on International Standards of Accounting and Reporting of the United Nations
ISO	International Organization for Standardization
JEA	Japan Environment Agency
IT	information technology
LCA	life-cycle assessment
LRQA	Lloyds Register Quality Assurance
MD&A	management discussion and analysis
MPI	Minerals Policy Institute (Australia)
MVD	Miljövarudeklarationer (Sweden)
NCM	Nordic Council of Ministers
NEPC	National Environment Protection Council (Australia)
NEPM	national environment protection measure (Australia)
NGO	non-governmental organisation
NIMBY	'not in my back yard'
NO_3	nitrogene oxide
NO_x	nitrogen oxide
NPEIA	net present environmental impact added
NPRI	Canadian National Pollutant Release Inventory
NPV	net present value
NSW EPA	New South Wales Environmental Protection Authority (Australia)
NZZ	*Neue Zürcher Zeitung*
O_3	Ozone (photochemical smog)
OAGC	Office of the Auditor General of Canada
ÖB	*Ökologische Briefe*
ODP	ozone depletion potential
ODS	ozone-depleting substance
OECD	Organisation for Economic Co-operation and Development
OTA	Office of Technology Assessment of the US Congress
PCEQ	President's Commission on Environmental Quality
PCSD	President's Council on Sustainable Development
PER	Polluting Emissions Register (UK)
PI	Pollution Inventory (UK)
PRTR	pollution release and transfer register
PVC	polyvinyl chloride
PWMI	Plastics and Waste Management Initiative (European Center for Plastics and the Environment)
R&D	research and development
RCRA	Resource Conservation and Recovery Act of 1976 (USA)
REPA	resource and environmental profile analysis
ROCE	return on capital employed
SBU	strategic business unit
SCS	Scientific Certification Systems
SDA	Schweizerische Depeschen Agentur
SEC	US Securities and Exchange Commission
SETAC	Society of Environmental Toxicology and Chemistry
SGCI	Schweizerische Gesellschaft für Chemische Industrie
SHV	shareholder value
SO_2	Sulphur dioxide
SO_4	Sulphur oxide

SOLE	Society of Logistics Engineers
SWMD	Solid Waste Management Division of Environment Canada
TOC	total organic compounds
TQEM	total quality environmental management
TQM	total quality management
TRI	Toxic Release Inventory (USA)
TSP	total suspended particulates
UBA	Umweltbundesamt (Germany)
UIG	Urgent Issues Group of the Australian Accounting Research Foundation
UNCED	United Nations Conference on Environment and Development
UNCSD	United Nations Commission for Sustainable Development
UNCTAD	United Nations Centre for Trade and Development
UNEP	United Nations Environment Programme
VA	value added
VDI	Verein Deutscher Ingenieure (Germany)
VOC	volatile organic compound
WBCSD	World Business Council for Sustainable Development (formerly BCSD)
WCED	World Council for Environment and Development
WICE	World Industry Council for the Environment
WMC	Previously known as Western Mining Corporation Ltd (Australia)
WSDOE	Washington State Department of Ecology
WRI	World Resources Institute
WWF	World Wide Fund for Nature
WWI	Worldwatch Institute

INDEX